The Morgans
November 2003
Set forth your case
conference
@ JFBC

PHILOSOPHICAL FOUNDATIONS FOR A CHRISTIAN WORLDVIEW

J. P. MORELAND
& WILLIAM LANE CRAIG

InterVarsity Press
Downers Grove, Illinois

InterVarsity Press
P.O. Box 1400, Downers Grove, IL 60515-1426
World Wide Web: www.ivpress.com
E-mail: mail@ivpress.com

InterVarsity Press® is the book-publishing division of InterVarsity Christian Fellowship/USA®, a student movement active on campus at hundreds of universities, colleges and schools of nursing in the United States of America, and a member movement of the International Fellowship of Evangelical Students. For information about local and regional activities, write Public Relations Dept., InterVarsity Christian Fellowship/USA, 6400 Schroeder Rd., P.O. Box 7895, Madison, WI 53707-7895, or visit the IVCF website at <www.ivcf.org>.

Cover image: Mel Curtis/Photonica

ISBN 0-8308-2694-7

Printed in the United States of America ∞

Library of Congress Cataloging-in-Publication Data

Moreland, James Porter, 1948-
  Philosophical foundations for a Christian worldview / J.P. Moreland
and William Lane Craig.
     p. cm.
Includes bibliographical references and indexes.
  ISBN 0-8308-2694-7 (cloth: alk. paper)
  1. Christianity—Philosophy. I. Craig, William Lane. II. Title
  BR100 .M68 2003
  261.5'1—dc21

                                                                                      2002154307

P	19	18	17	16	15	14	13	12	11	10	9	8	7	6	5	4	3	2	1
Y	17	16	15	14	13	12	11	10	09	08	07	06	05	04	03				

To Dallas Willard and Stuart Hackett

Remember those who led you,
who spoke the word of God to you;
and considering the result of their conduct,
imitate their faith. (Hebrews 13:7 NASB)

CONTENTS

PART V ETHICS

PART VI PHILOSOPHY OF RELIGION
AND PHILOSOPHICAL THEOLOGY

OUTLINE OF THE BOOK

PART VI PHILOSOPHY OF RELIGION AND PHILOSOPHICAL THEOLOGY

23 THE EXISTENCE OF GOD (I)

1 Introduction
2 The Existence of God
   2.1 The Cosmological Argument
      2.1.1 Exposition of the Arguments
      2.1.2 Evaluation of the Arguments
Chapter Summary
Checklist of Basic Terms and Concepts

24 THE EXISTENCE OF GOD (II)

1 The Teleological Argument
2 The Axiological Argument
3 The Ontological Argument
Chapter Summary
Checklist of Basic Terms and Concepts

25 THE COHERENCE OF THEISM (I)

1 Introduction
2 Necessity
3 Aseity
4 Incorporeality
5 Omnipresence
6 Eternity
Chapter Summary
Checklist of Basic Terms and Concepts

26 THE COHERENCE OF THEISM (II)

1 Omniscience
2 Simplicity
3 Immutability
4 Omnipotence
5 Goodness
Chapter Summary
Checklist of Basic Terms and Concepts

27 THE PROBLEM OF EVIL

1 Introduction
2 The Intellectual Problem of Evil
   2.1 The Internal Problem of Evil
      2.1.1 The Logical Version
      2.1.2 The Probabilistic Version
   2.2 The External Problem of Evil

AN INVITATION TO CHRISTIAN PHILOSOPHY

1 WHY PHILOSOPHY MATTERS

On a clear autumn day in 1980, twenty-five miles west of Chicago in Wheaton, Illinois, Charles Malik, a distinguished academic and statesman, rose to the podium to deliver the inaugural address at the dedication of the new Billy Graham Center on the campus of Wheaton College. His announced topic was "The Two Tasks of Evangelism." What he said must have shocked his audience.

We face two tasks in our evangelism, he told them, "saving the soul and saving the mind"—that is, converting people not only spiritually but intellectually as well—and the church, he warned, is lagging dangerously behind with respect to this second task. We should do well to ponder Malik's words:

> I must be frank with you: the greatest danger confronting American evangelical Christianity is the danger of anti-intellectualism. The mind in its greatest and deepest reaches is not cared for enough. But intellectual nurture cannot take place apart from profound immersion for a period of years in the history of thought and the spirit. People who are in a hurry to get out of the university and start earning money or serving the church or preaching the gospel have no idea of the infinite value of spending years of leisure conversing with the greatest minds and souls of the past, ripening and sharpening and enlarging their powers of thinking. The result is that the arena of creative thinking is vacated and abdicated to the enemy. Who among evangelicals can stand up to the great secular scholars on their own terms of scholarship? Who among evangelical scholars is quoted as a normative source by the greatest secular authorities on history or philosophy or psychology or sociology or politics? Does the evangelical mode of thinking have the slightest chance of becoming the dominant mode in the great universities of Europe and America that stamp our entire civilization with their spirit and ideas? For the sake of greater effectiveness in witnessing to Jesus Christ, as well as for their own sakes, evangelicals cannot afford to keep on living on the periphery of responsible intellectual existence.[1]

These words hit like a hammer. The average Christian does not realize that there is an intellectual struggle going on in the universities and scholarly journals and professional societies. Enlightenment naturalism and postmodern antirealism are arrayed in an unholy alliance against a broadly theistic and specifically Christian worldview.

Christians cannot afford to be indifferent to the outcome of this struggle.

---

[1]Charles Malik, "The Other Side of Evangelism," *Christianity Today*, November 7, 1980, p. 40. For the original address, see *The Two Tasks* (Wheaton, Ill.: Billy Graham Center, 2000).

For the single most important institution shaping Western culture is the university. It is at the university that our future political leaders, our journalists, our teachers, our business executives, our lawyers, our artists, will be trained. It is at the university that they will formulate or, more likely, simply absorb the worldview that will shape their lives. And since these are the opinion-makers and leaders who shape our culture, the worldview that they imbibe at the university will be the one that shapes our culture. If the Christian worldview can be restored to a place of prominence and respect at the university, it will have a leavening effect throughout society. If we change the university, we change our culture through those who shape culture.

Why is this important? Simply because the gospel is never heard in isolation. It is always heard against the background of the cultural milieu in which one lives. A person raised in a cultural milieu in which Christianity is still seen as an intellectually viable option will display an openness to the gospel that a person who is secularized will not. One may as well tell a secular person to believe in fairies or leprechauns as in Jesus Christ! Or, to give a more realistic illustration, it is like our being approached on the street by a devotee of the Hare Krishna movement, who invites us to believe in Krishna. Such an invitation strikes us as bizarre, freakish, perhaps even amusing. But to a person on the streets of Bombay, such an invitation would, one expects, appear quite reasonable and be serious cause for reflection. Do evangelicals appear any less weird to persons on the streets of Bonn, London or New York than do the devotees of Krishna?

One of the awesome tasks of Christian philosophers is to help turn the contemporary intellectual tide in such a way as to foster a sociocultural milieu in which Christian faith can be regarded as an intellectually credible option for thinking men and women. As the great Princeton theologian J. Gresham Machen explained,

> God usually exerts [his regenerative] power in connection with certain prior conditions of the human mind, and it should be ours to create, so far as we can, with the help of God, those favourable conditions for the reception of the gospel. False ideas are the greatest obstacles to the reception of the gospel. We may preach with all the fervour of a reformer and yet succeed only in winning a straggler here and there, if we permit the whole collective thought of the nation or of the world to be controlled by ideas which, by the resistless force of logic, prevent Christianity from being regarded as anything more than a harmless delusion.[2]

Since philosophy is foundational to every discipline of the university, philosophy is the most strategic discipline to be influenced for Christ. Malik himself realized and emphasized this:

> It will take a different spirit altogether to overcome this great danger of anti-intellectualism. For example, I say this different spirit, so far as philosophy alone—the most important domain for thought and intellect—is concerned, must see the tremendous value of spending an entire year doing nothing but poring intensely over the *Republic* or the *Sophist* of Plato, or two years over the *Metaphysics* or the *Ethics* of Aristotle, or three years over the *City of God* of Augustine.[3]

---

[2]Address delivered on September 20, 1912, at the opening of the 101st session of Princeton Theological Seminary. Reprinted in J. Gresham Machen, *What Is Christianity?* (Grand Rapids, Mich.: Eerdmans, 1951), p. 162.
[3]Malik, "Other Side of Evangelism," p. 40.

Now in one sense it is theology, not philosophy, which is most important domain for thought and intellect. As the medievals rightly saw, theology is the queen of the sciences, to be studied as the crowning discipline only after one has been trained in the other disciplines. Unfortunately, the queen is currently in exile from the Western university. But her handmaid, philosophy, still has a place at court and is thus strategically positioned so as to act on behalf of her queen. The reason that Malik could call philosophy, in the absence of the queen, the most important intellectual domain is because it is the most foundational of the disciplines, since it examines the presuppositions and ramifications of every discipline at the university—including itself! Whether it be philosophy of science, philosophy of education, philosophy of law, philosophy of mathematics, or what have you, every discipline will have an associated field of philosophy foundational to that discipline. The philosophy of these respective disciplines is not theologically neutral. Adoption of presuppositions consonant with or inimical to orthodox Christian theism will have a significant leavening effect throughout that discipline which will, in turn, dispose its practitioners for or against the Christian faith. Christian philosophers, by influencing the philosophy of these various disciplines, can thus help to shape the thinking of the entire university in such a way as to dispose our future generations of leaders to the reception of the gospel.

It is already happening. Over the last forty years a revolution has been occurring in Anglo-American philosophy. Since the late 1960s Christian philosophers have been coming out of the closet and defending the truth of the Christian worldview with philosophically sophisticated arguments in the finest scholarly journals and professional societies. And the face of Anglo-American philosophy has been transformed as a result. In a recent article lamenting "the desecularization of academia that evolved in philosophy departments since the late 1960s," one atheist philosopher observes that whereas theists in other disciplines tend to compartmentalize their theistic beliefs from their professional work, "in philosophy, it became, almost overnight, 'academically respectable' to argue for theism, making philosophy a favored field of entry for the most intelligent and talented theists entering academia today."[4] He complains, "Naturalists passively watched as realist versions of theism . . . began to sweep through the philosophical community, until today perhaps one-quarter or one-third of philosophy professors are theists, with most being orthodox Christians."[5] He concludes, "God is not 'dead' in academia; he returned to life in the late 1960s and is now alive and well in his last academic stronghold, philosophy departments."[6]

This is the testimony of a prominent atheist philosopher to the change that has transpired before his eyes in Anglo-American philosophy. He is probably exaggerating when he estimates that one-quarter to one-third of American philosophers are theists; but what his estimates do reveal is the perceived impact of Christian philosophers on this field. Like Gideon's army, a committed minority of activists can have an impact far out of proportion to their numbers. The

---

[4]Quentin Smith, "The Metaphilosophy of Naturalism," *Philo* 4, no. 2 (2001): 3.
[5]Ibid.
[6]Ibid., p. 4.

principal error he makes is calling philosophy departments God's "last strong-hold" at the university. On the contrary, philosophy departments are a beach-head, from which operations can be launched to impact other disciplines at the university for Christ, thereby helping to transform the sociocultural milieu in which we live.

But it is not just those who plan to enter the academy professionally who need to have training in philosophy. Christian philosophy is also an integral part of training for Christian ministry. A model for us here is a man like John Wesley, who was at once a Spirit-filled revivalist and an Oxford-educated scholar. In 1756 Wesley delivered "An Address to the Clergy," which we commend to all future ministers when commencing their seminary studies. In discussing what sort of abilities a minister ought to have, Wesley distin-guished between natural gifts and acquired abilities. And it is extremely in-structive to look at the abilities that Wesley thought a minister ought to acquire. One of them is a basic grasp of philosophy. He challenged his audi-ence to ask themselves,

> Am I a tolerable master of the sciences? Have I gone through the very gate of them, logic? If not, I am not likely to go much farther when I stumble at the threshold. . . . Rather, have not my stupid indolence and laziness made me very ready to believe, what the little wits and pretty gentlemen affirm, "that logic is good for nothing?" It is good for this at least, . . . to make people talk less; by showing them both what is, and what is not, to the point; and how extremely hard it is to prove any thing. Do I understand metaphysics; if not the depths of the Schoolmen, the subtleties of Scotus or Aquinas, yet the first rudiments, the general principles, of that useful science? Have I conquered so much of it, as to clear my apprehension and range my ideas under proper heads; so much as en-ables me to read with ease and pleasure, as well as profit, Dr. Henry Moore's *Works*, Malbranche's "Search after Truth," and Dr. Clarke's "Demonstration of the Being and Attributes of God?"[7]

Wesley's vision of a pastor is remarkable: a gentleman, skilled in the Scrip-tures and conversant with history, philosophy and the science of his day. How do the pastors graduating from our seminaries compare to this model?

The authors of this book can both testify personally to the immense practi-cality and even indispensability of philosophical training for Christian ministry. For many years we have each been involved, not just in scholarly work but in speaking evangelistically on university campuses with groups like InterVarsity Christian Fellowship, Campus Crusade for Christ and the Veritas Forum. Again and again, we have seen the practical value of philosophical studies in reaching students for Christ. From questions dealing with the meaning of life or the basis of moral values to the problem of suffering and evil and the challenge of reli-gious pluralism, students are asking profound philosophical questions that are much more difficult to answer than to pose. They deserve a thoughtful re-sponse rather than pat answers or appeals to mystery. The conventional wis-dom says, "You can't use arguments to bring people to Christ." This has not

---

[7]"An Address to the Clergy," delivered February 6, 1756. Reprinted in *The Works of John Wesley*, 3d ed., 7 vols. (Grand Rapids, Mich.: Baker, 1996), 6:217-31.

been our experience. The fact is that there is tremendous interest among unbelieving students in hearing a rational presentation and defense of the gospel, and some will be ready to respond with trust in Christ. To speak frankly, we do not know how one could minister effectively in a public way on our university campuses without training in philosophy.

Finally, it is not just scholars and ministers who will benefit from training in philosophy, but also laypeople who need to be intellectually engaged if our culture is to be effectively reformed. Our churches are unfortunately overly-populated with people whose minds, as Christians, are going to waste. As Malik observed, they may be spiritually regenerate, but their minds have not been converted; they still think like nonbelievers. Despite their Christian commitment, they remain largely empty selves. What is an empty self? An empty self is a person who is passive, sensate, busy and hurried, incapable of developing an interior life. Such a person is inordinately individualistic, infantile and narcissistic.

Imagine now a church filled with such people. What will be the theological understanding, the evangelistic courage, the cultural penetration of such a church? If the interior life does not really matter all that much, why should one spend the time trying to develop an intellectual, spiritually mature life? If someone is basically passive, he will just not make the effort to read, preferring instead to be entertained. If a person is sensate in orientation, then music, magazines filled with pictures, and visual media in general will be more important than mere words on a page or abstract thoughts. If one is hurried and distracted, one will have little patience for theoretical knowledge and too short an attention span to stay with an idea while it is being carefully developed. And if someone is overly individualistic, infantile and narcissistic, what *will* that person read, if he reads at all? Books about Christian celebrities, Christian romance novels imitating the worst that the world has to offer, Christian self-help books filled with slogans, simplistic moralizing, lots of stories and pictures, and inadequate diagnoses of the problems facing the reader. What will *not* be read are books that equip people to develop a well-reasoned, theological understanding of the Christian faith and to assume their role in the broader work of the kingdom of God. Such a church will become impotent to stand against the powerful forces of secularism that threaten to wash away Christian ideas in a flood of thoughtless pluralism and misguided scientism. Such a church will be tempted to measure her success largely in terms of numbers—numbers achieved by cultural accommodation to empty selves. In this way, the church will become her own grave digger; for her means of short-term "success" will turn out in the long run to be the very thing that buries her.

What makes this envisioned scenario so distressing is that we do not have to imagine such a church; rather, this *is* an apt description of far too many American evangelical churches today. It is no wonder, then, that despite its resurgence, evangelical Christianity has been thus far so limited in its cultural impact. David Wells reflects,

> The vast growth in evangelically minded people . . . should by now have revolu-
> tionized American culture. With a third of American adults now claiming to have

experienced spiritual rebirth, a powerful countercurrent of morality growing out of a powerful and alternative worldview should have been unleashed in factories, offices, and board rooms, in the media, universities, and professions, from one end of the country to the other. The results should by now be unmistakable. Secular values should be reeling, and those who are their proponents should be very troubled. But as it turns out, all of this swelling of the evangelical ranks has passed unnoticed in the culture. . . . The presence of evangelicals in American culture has barely caused a ripple.[8]

The problem, says Wells, is that while evangelicals have for the most part correct Christian beliefs, for far too many these beliefs lie largely at the periphery of their existence rather than at the center of their identity. At core they are hollow men, empty selves. If we as the church are to engender a current of reform throughout our culture, then we need laypeople who are intellectually engaged with their faith and take their Christian identity to be definitive for their self-conception.

Besides cultural reform, a revival of intellectual engagement is absolutely critical for restoring vibrant, life-transforming apprenticeship under the lordship of Jesus, the Master Teacher. No apprentice will become like his teacher if he does not respect the authority of that teacher to direct the apprentice's life and activities. However, today the authority of the Bible in general, and of Jesus Christ in particular, is widely disregarded. The general attitude, even among many of Christ's own followers, is that while Jesus Christ is holy, powerful and so forth, the worldview he taught and from which he lived is no longer credible for thinking people. As Dallas Willard observes,

> The crushing weight of the secular outlook . . . permeates or pressures every thought we have today. Sometimes it even forces those who self-identify as Christian teachers to set aside Jesus' plain statements about the reality and total relevance of the kingdom of God and replace them with philosophical speculations whose only recommendation is their consistency with a "modern" [i.e., contemporary] mindset. The powerful though vague and unsubstantiated presumption is that *something has been found out* that renders a spiritual understanding of reality in the manner of Jesus simply foolish to those who are "in the know."[9]

Willard concludes that in order to restore spiritual vitality to the church, we must recapture a view of Jesus as an intellectually competent person who knew what he was talking about.

For Willard, who is himself a philosopher, this will include revitalizing philosophical reflection in the church. Philosophical reflection is, indeed, a powerful means of kindling the life of the mind in Christian discipleship and in the church. Again, the authors of this book can testify that our worship of God is deeper precisely because of, not in spite of, our philosophical studies. As we reflect philosophically on our various areas of specialization within the field of philosophy, our appreciation of God's truth and awe of his person have become more profound. We look forward to future study because of the deeper appreciation we are sure it will bring of God's person and work. Christian faith is not

---

[8]David F. Wells, *No Place for Truth* (Grand Rapids, Mich.: Eerdmans, 1993), p. 293.
[9]Dallas Willard, *The Divine Conspiracy* (San Francisco: Harper, 1998), p. 92. Cf. pp. 75, 79, 134, 184-85.

an apathetic faith, a brain-dead faith, but a living, inquiring faith. As Anselm put it, ours is a faith that seeks understanding.

These are very exciting times in which to be alive and working in the field of philosophy, where God is doing a fresh work before our eyes. It is our hope and prayer that he will be pleased to use this book to call even more Christian thinkers to this effervescing field and to equip the church and her ministers to serve him and his kingdom even more effectively into the twenty-first century.

2 AN INVITATION TO DIALOGUE

Convinced of the benefit of philosophical training for Christian scholars, ministers and laymen, we offer *Philosophical Foundations for a Christian Worldview* as an introductory text to the field of philosophy from a Christian point of view. We do not affect, therefore, some pretended neutrality on the issues we discuss. Our text is intentionally Christian and therefore aims to offer, not just a soporific review of positions pro and con, but rather an articulation of what we take to be the most plausible stance a Christian can take on various questions. Of course, we recognize that other stances are permissible for Christian thinkers, and in some cases we ourselves might disagree on the preferred position or leave multiple options open. We welcome critique and dialogue on all the positions we defend. So when we argue for particular positions that we recognize to be matters of controversy, such as anthropological dualism, a tensed theory of time, social trinitarianism or christological monotheletism, we intend, not to close, but to open discussion on these matters. We invite our readers to engage our arguments for the positions we defend.

Philosophical Foundations is obviously a large book, covering a wide range of issues in epistemology, metaphysics, philosophy of science, ethics and philosophy of religion, as well as basic rules of reasoning. Much of it will be difficult reading for newcomers to the field, so that those who use the book as a text will find it fertile soil for discussions. We do not anticipate, therefore, that students will be expected to plow through the whole book in a single semester. Rather, the professor may choose selectively chapters to assign which mesh best with the questions he finds most interesting or important, leaving aside the rest. Of course, we hope that students' interest will be sufficiently piqued that they will eventually return to the book at some later time to read and wrestle with the unassigned material!

Each chapter includes an exposition of the most important questions raised by the issue under discussion, along with a Christian perspective on the problem, and closes with a condensed summary of the chapter and a list of key terms employed in that chapter. These key terms are printed in **boldface** type when they are first introduced and are defined in the text. Students would do well to add these words to their working vocabulary. A list of suggested further reading for each chapter is included at the back of the book.

We have tried to keep footnotes to a minimum. The suggested further reading will, we trust, adequately point the reader to the literature discussed in each respective chapter.

3 ACKNOWLEDGMENTS

We gratefully acknowledge the meticulous editorial work and patience of Jim Hoover of InterVarsity Press in bringing this large project to realization. We are indebted to Mark and Jennifer Jensen for their careful preparation of the indexes. We also wish to thank the Discovery Institute, Howard Hoffman, and Paul and Lisa Wolfe for grants that greatly helped this project come to completion. Finally, we wish to acknowledge the spiritual support and intellectual stimulation we have received from our faculty colleagues and graduate students at Talbot School of Theology, especially from those in the Talbot Department of Philosophy and Ethics.

PART I

INTRODUCTION

1

WHAT IS PHILOSOPHY?

Where am I or What?
From what causes do I derive my existence,
and to what condition shall I return?
Whose favor shall I court, and whose anger must I dread?
What beings surround me?
And on whom Have I any influence, or who have any influence on me?
I am confounded with all these questions,
and begin to fancy myself in the most deplorable condition imaginable,
inviron'd with the deepest darkness,
and utterly deprived of the use of every member and faculty.
DAVID HUME, A TREATISE OF HUMAN NATURE

Not every problem, nor every thesis, should be examined,
but only one which might puzzle one of those who need argument.
ARISTOTLE TOPICS 1.11 (105A1-5)

Ought not a Minister to have,
First, a good understanding, a clear apprehension, a sound judgment,
and a capacity of reasoningwith some closeness. . . .
Is not some acquaintance with what has been termed the second part of logic,
(metaphysics), if not so necessary as [logic itself], yet highly expedient?
Should not a Minister be acquainted with at least the
general grounds of natural philosophy?
JOHN WESLEY, ADDRESS TO THE CLERGY

1 INTRODUCTION

You are about to embark on an exciting and fascinating journey—the philosophical exploration of some of life's most important ideas, ideas about reality, God, the soul, knowledge and truth, goodness, and much, much more. Make no mistake about it. Ideas matter. The ideas one really believes largely determine the kind of person one becomes. Everyone has a philosophy of life. That is not optional. What is optional and, thus, of extreme importance is the adequacy of one's philosophy of life. Are one's views rational or irrational, true or false, carefully formed and precise or conveniently formed and fuzzy? Are they conducive to human flourishing or do they cater to one's fallen nature? Are they honoring or dishonoring to the triune God? The discipline of philosophy can be of great help in aiding someone in the search for an increasingly rich and robust philosophy of life.

For centuries, people have recognized the importance of philosophy. In particular, throughout the history of Christianity, philosophy has played an important role in the life of the church and the spread and defense of the gospel of Christ. The great theologian Augustine (354-430) summarized the views of many early church fathers when he said, "We must show our Scriptures not to be in conflict with whatever [our critics] can demonstrate about the nature of things from reliable sources."[1] Philosophy was the main tool Augustine used in this task. In 1756, John Wesley delivered an address to a group of men preparing for ministry. He exhorted them to acquire skills which today are often neglected in seminary education but which seminaries would do well to reinstate. And much of what he said is sound advice for all Christians. For Wesley, among the factors crucial for the service of Christ was a tolerable mastery of logic and philosophy in general.

Unfortunately, today things are different. Theologian R. C. Sproul has called this the most anti-intellectual period in the history of the church, and former Secretary-General of the United Nations and Christian statesman Charles Malik warns that the greatest danger facing modern evangelicalism is a lack of cultivation of the mind, especially as it relates to philosophy.

This trend within the church is coupled with two unfortunate features of Western culture: the rampant pragmatism in society with the concomitant devaluation of the humanities in university life and the nonexistence of philosophy in our precollege educational curricula. The result is that philosophy departments are endangered species in Christian colleges and seminaries, and serious philosophical reflection is virtually absent from most church fellowships. This, in turn, has contributed to intellectual shallowness and a lack of cultural discernment in the body of Christ.

But is philosophy really that important for the life, health and witness of the church? Are God's people not warned in Scripture itself to avoid philosophy and worldly wisdom? And just what is philosophy, anyway? How does it help believers form an integrated Christian worldview? How does philosophy relate to other disciplines taught at the university?

2 THE NATURE OF PHILOSOPHY

Scholars generally are agreed that there is no airtight definition that expresses a set of necessary and sufficient conditions for classifying some activity as philosophical, conditions which all and only philosophy satisfies. But this should not be troubling. In general, one does not need a definition of something before one can know features of the thing in question and recognize examples of it. One can recognize examples of historical study, love, a person, art, matter, sport and a host of other things without possessing an airtight definition. Nevertheless,

---

[1]Augustine *On the Literal Interpretation of Genesis* 1.21.

definitions are useful, and a reasonably adequate definition of philosophy can be provided.

How might someone go about formulating such a definition? Three ways suggest themselves. First one could focus on the etymology of the word **philosophy**. The word comes from two Greek words *philein*, "to love," and *sophia*, "wisdom." Thus a philosopher is a lover of wisdom. Socrates held that the unexamined life is not worth living, and the ancient Greek philosophers sought wisdom regarding truth, knowledge, beauty and goodness. In this sense, then, philosophy is the attempt to think hard about life, the world as a whole and the things that matter most in order to secure knowledge and wisdom about these matters. Accordingly, philosophy may be defined as the attempt to think rationally and critically about life's most important questions in order to obtain knowledge and wisdom about them. Philosophy can help someone form a rationally justified, true **worldview**, that is, an ordered set of propositions that one believes, especially propositions about life's most important questions.

Second, our understanding of philosophy will be enhanced if we observe that philosophy often functions as a **second-order discipline**. For example, biology is a **first-order discipline** that studies living organisms, but philosophy is a second-order discipline that studies biology. In general, it is possible have a philosophy of *x*, where *x* can be any discipline whatever; for example, law, mathematics, education, science, government, medicine, history or literature. When philosophers examine another discipline to formulate a philosophy of that field, they ask normative questions about that discipline (e.g., questions about what one ought and ought not believe in that discipline and why), analyze and criticize the assumptions underlying it, clarify the concepts within it and integrate that discipline with other fields.

Consider biology again. Philosophers ask questions like these: Is there an external world that is knowable and, if so, how does one know it? What is life, and how does it differ from nonlife? How should someone form, test and use scientific theories and laws? Is it morally permissible to experiment on living things? When biologists talk about information in DNA, how should we understand this talk? How does the biological notion of being a member of the kind *Homo sapiens* relate to the theological notion of being made in the image of God or to the metaphysical notion of being a person with legal/moral rights? These questions are all philosophical in nature, and by examining them it becomes evident that philosophers ask and seek to answer presuppositional, normative, conceptual and integrative questions about other fields of study. Thus, by its very nature philosophy is, perhaps, the most important foundational discipline in the task of integrating Christian theology with other fields of study. This claim is examined in more detail later.

One more observation is important. Because philosophy operates at a presuppositional level by clarifying and justifying the presuppositions of a discipline, philosophy is the only field of study that has no unquestioned assumptions within its own domain. In other words, philosophy is a self-referential discipline, for questions about the definition, justification and methodology of philosophy are themselves philosophical in nature. Philosophers keep the books on everyone, including themselves. The justification of the assumptions of any discipline, including philosophy, is largely a philosophical matter.

A third way to characterize philosophy is simply to list the various sub-branches of philosophy. In addition to the different second-order branches of philosophy, such as philosophy of science (see part four) or religion (see part six), a number of standard areas of study are first-order parts of philosophy. For example, **logic** (see chap. 2) investigates the principles of right reasoning and focuses on questions such as When can a conclusion legitimately be drawn from premises and why? **Epistemology** is the study of knowledge and justified belief (see part two). What is knowledge? Can we have it? How do we know things and justify our beliefs? What are the kinds of things we can know? **Metaphysics** is the study of being or reality (see part three). Here are some metaphysical questions: What does it mean for something to exist? What are the ultimate kinds of things that exist? What is a substance? What is a property? Is matter real? Is mind real? What are space, time and causation? What is linguistic meaning? **Value theory** is the study of value; for example, ethical value (see part five) and aesthetic value. What does it mean to say something is right or wrong, beautiful or ugly? How do we justify our beliefs in these areas?

These subbranches combine with the various second-order areas of investigation to constitute the subject matter of philosophy. In these areas of study, philosophy serves both a critical and a constructive function. Philosophy is critical because it examines assumptions, asks questions of justification, seeks to clarify and analyze concepts, and so on. Philosophy is constructive because it attempts to provide synoptic vision; that is, it seeks to organize all relevant facts into a rational system and speculate about the formation and justification of general worldviews. Chapter two includes an examination of the role of philosophy in forming and assessing a worldview.

We have briefly examined the different aspects of philosophy in order to get a better grasp on what the discipline is and the sorts of issues within its purview. Let us now look at the importance of philosophy for the Christian life in general and the Christian university in particular.

3 A CHRISTIAN JUSTIFICATION OF PHILOSOPHY

The history of the church reveals that philosophy has always played a crucial role in the nurture of believers and in the proclamation of a Christian worldview in general and the gospel in particular. The first universities in Europe were, of course, Christian, and the study of philosophy was considered of central importance to the health and vitality of the university and the Christian life. This is no less true today. In fact, there are at least seven reasons why philosophy is crucial to the texture, curricula and mission of the Christian university and the development of a robust Christian life.

First, philosophy is an aid in the task of **apologetics**. Apologetics is the task of giving a reasoned defense of Christian theism in light of objections raised against it and of offering positive evidence on its behalf. Scripture commands us to engage in apologetics (see 1 Pet 3:15; Jude 3). The Old Testament prophets often appealed to broad arguments from the nature of the world to justify the religion of Israel. For example, they would ridicule pagan idols for their frailty and smallness. The world is too big, they claimed, to have been made by something that small (see Is 44—45). Arguments like this assume a philosophical position on the nature of causation; for example, that an effect (the world) cannot come from something of lesser power than itself (the idol). Again, the Old Testament prophets often appealed to general principles of moral reasoning in criticizing the immorality of pagan nations (e.g., Amos 1—2). Arguments such as this utilize natural moral law and general philosophical principles of moral reasoning.

In the New Testament, the apostles used philosophical argumentation and reasoning to proclaim Christ to unbelievers (see Acts 17:2-4, 17-31; 18:4; 19:8). Their practice was consistent with that of the Old Testament prophets in this regard. Philosophy aids a person in stating arguments for God's existence. It also helps one clarify and defend a broad view of what it is for something to exist so as to include nonphysical and nonspatiotemporal entities; for example, God, angels and perhaps disembodied souls. When an objection against Christianity comes from some discipline of study, that objection almost always involves the use of philosophy. When Freud argued against religion on the grounds that our ideas of God are mere illusions, grounded in and caused by our fears and the need for a father figure, his attack, while rooted in psychology, nevertheless involved the discipline of philosophy. He was considering the basic question of how the source of our belief relates to our justification for that belief.

Second, philosophy aids the church in its task of **polemics**. Whereas apologetics involves the defense of Christian theism, polemics is the task of criticizing and refuting alternative views of the world. For example, in the field of artificial intelligence and cognitive psychology there is a tendency to view a human being in physicalist terms, that is, as a complex physical system. Despite protests to the contrary from some Christian thinkers, dualism (the view that we are composed of both a physical and a mental entity) is the view taught in Scripture (see 2 Cor 5:1-8; Phil 1:21-24). Part of the task of a believer working in the areas of artificial intelligence or cognitive psychology is to develop a critique of a purely physicalist vision of being human, and this task includes issues in the philosophy of mind (see chaps. 11-12).

Third, philosophy is a central expression of the image of God in us. It is very difficult to come up with an airtight definition of the image of God, but most theologians have agreed that it includes the ability to engage in abstract reasoning, especially in areas having to do with ethical, religious and philosophical issues. God himself is a rational being, and humans are made like him in this respect. This is one of the reasons humans are commanded to love God with all of their minds (Mt 22:37). Since philosophy, like religion, is a discipline that chiefly focuses on ultimate questions near the very heart of existence, then philosophical reflection about God's special and general revelation can be part of loving him and thinking his thoughts after him.

Fourth, philosophy permeates systematic theology and serves as its handmaid in several ways. Philosophy helps to add clarity to the concepts of systematic theology. For example, philosophers help to clarify the different attributes of God; they can show that the doctrines of the Trinity and the Incarnation are not contradictory; they can shed light on the nature of human freedom, and so on.

Further, philosophy can help to extend biblical teaching into areas where the

Bible is not explicit. For example, several areas currently under discussion in medical ethics (active/passive euthanasia, genetic screening, withholding artificial food and hydration, artificial insemination) are not explicitly mentioned in Scripture. The philosopher can, however, take the language and doctrines of the Bible and appropriately recast them in the relevant categories under discussion. In this way the philosopher can help to shed biblical light on an issue not explicitly mentioned in Scripture by providing conceptual categories and analysis that fit the situation and preserve the tenor and substance of biblical teaching.

Fifth, the discipline of philosophy can facilitate the spiritual discipline of study. Study is itself a spiritual discipline, and the very act of study can change the self. One who undergoes the discipline of study lives through certain types of experiences where certain skills are developed through habitual study: framing an issue, solving problems, learning how to weigh evidence and eliminate irrelevant factors, cultivating the ability to see important distinctions instead of blurring them, and so on. The discipline of study also aids in the development of certain virtues and values; for example, a desire for the truth, honesty with data, an openness to criticism, self-reflection and an ability to get along nondefensively with those who differ with one.

Of course, the discipline of study is not unique to philosophy. But philosophy is among the most rigorous of fields, and its approach and subject matter are so central to life, close to religion and foundational to other fields of investigation, that the discipline of philosophical study can aid someone in the pursuit of truth in any other area of life or university study.

Sixth, the discipline of philosophy can enhance the boldness and self-image of the Christian community in general. It is well known that a group, especially a minority group, will be vital and active only if it feels good about itself in comparison with outsiders. Further, there will be more tolerance of internal group differences, and thus more harmony, when a group feels comfortable toward outsiders.

In a fascinating study, John G. Gager argues that the early church faced intellectual and cultural ridicule from Romans and Greeks. This ridicule threatened internal cohesion within the church and its evangelistic boldness toward unbelievers. Gager argues that it was primarily the presence of philosophers and apologists within the church that enhanced the self-image of the Christian community because these early scholars showed that the Christian community was just as rich intellectually and culturally as was the pagan culture surrounding it. Says Gager:

> Whether or not the apologists persuaded pagan critics to revise their view of Christians as illiterate fools, they succeeded in projecting for the group as a whole a favorable image of itself as the embodiment of true wisdom and piety. . . . Whatever we may say about the expressed purpose of these apologies, their latent function was not so much to change the pagan image of Christians as to prevent that image from being internalized by Christians themselves.[2]

Gager's point could and should be applied to the value of Christian scholar-

---

[2]John G. Gager, *Kingdom and Community: The Social World of Early Christianity* (Englewood Cliffs, N.J.: Prentice-Hall, 1975), pp. 86-87.

ship in general, but the applicability of his remarks to the field of philosophy should be obvious. Historically, philosophy has been the main discipline that has aided the church in its intellectual relationship with unbelievers. Because of the very nature of philosophy itself—its areas of study and their importance for answering ultimate questions, the questions it asks and answers, its closeness to theology—the potential of this discipline for enhancing the self-respect of the believing community is enormous.

It seems clear that evangelicalism in America is having a serious self-image problem. The reasons for this are no doubt varied, but it can hardly be an accident that the average Bible college has no philosophy department, and many evangelical seminaries do not offer serious, formal training in philosophy and apologetics beyond a course here and there.

Seventh, the discipline of philosophy is absolutely essential for the task of **integration**. To integrate means to blend or form into a whole. In this sense, integration occurs when one's theological beliefs, primarily rooted in Scripture, are blended and unified with propositions judged as rational from other sources into a coherent, intellectually adequate Christian worldview. Since this will be the main topic of discussion below, little need be added at this point except to note that the need for integration occurs in at least three ways.

For one thing, the believing community needs to draw from all areas of knowledge in forming an integrated Christian worldview consistent with Scripture. Second, a person grows to maturity to the extent that he or she becomes an integrated, unfragmented self, and one of the ways to become an integrated person is to have the various aspects of one's intellectual life in harmony. If Smith believes one thing in church and another thing in the lab or office, he will to that extent be a fragmented, dichotomized individual wherein Christ can dwell only in a shrinking religious compartment of his life. Finally, when the gospel confronts a new culture, Christian theology must be related to that culture in a way that is at once sensitive to the culture and faithful to Scripture. Such a task will include questions of value, knowledge and thought forms, and these questions essentially involve philosophical clarification and comment.

These are some of the reasons why the church has always found philosophy to be necessary. C. S. Lewis once remarked that "to be ignorant and simple now—not to be able to meet the enemies on their own ground—would be to throw down our weapons, and to betray our uneducated brethren who have, under God, no defence but us against the intellectual attacks of the heathen. Good philosophy must exist, if for no other reason, because bad philosophy needs to be answered."[3]

The great social critic William Wilberforce (1759-1833) was a man of deep devotion to God and great passion for practical ministry. But Wilberforce saw the value of philosophy and apologetics even for the training of children in the church! Queried Wilberforce, "In an age in which infidelity abounds, do we observe [believers] carefully instructing their children in the principles of faith they profess? Or do they furnish their children with arguments for the defense

---

[3]C. S. Lewis, *The Weight of Glory* (Grand Rapids, Mich.: Eerdmans, 1949), p. 50.

of that faith?"[4] Sources for similar attitudes could be cited throughout the history of the church: Justin Martyr, Augustine, Anselm, Aquinas, Calvin, Jonathan Edwards, John Wesley, Francis Schaeffer, Carl Henry. Nevertheless, there is a general perception among many believers that philosophy is intrinsically hostile to the Christian faith and should not be of concern to believers. There are at least four reasons frequently cited for such an attitude.

First, the claim is made that human depravity has made the mind so darkened that the **noetic effects of sin**, that is, sin's effect on the mind, render the human intellect incapable of knowing truth. However, this claim is an exaggeration. The Fall brought about the perversion of human faculties, but it did not destroy those faculties. Human reasoning abilities are affected but not eliminated. This can be seen in the fact that the writers of Scripture often appeal to the minds of unbelievers by citing evidence on behalf of their claims, using logical inferences in building their case and speaking in the language and thought forms of those outside the faith.

Second, it is sometimes claimed that faith and reason are hostile to each other, and whatever is of reason cannot be of faith. But this represents misunderstanding of the biblical concept of **faith**. The biblical notion of faith includes three components: *notitia* (understanding the content of the Christian faith), *fiducia* (trust) and *assensus* (the assent of the intellect to the truth of some proposition). Trust is based on understanding, knowledge and the intellect's assent to truth. Belief *in* rests on belief *that*. One is called to trust in what he or she has reason to give intellectual assent (*assensus*) to. In Scripture, faith involves placing trust in what you have reason to believe is true. Faith is not a blind, irrational leap into the dark. So faith and reason cooperate on a biblical view of faith. They are not intrinsically hostile.

Third, some cite Colossians 2:8 as evidence against philosophy: "See to it that no one takes you captive through hollow and deceptive philosophy, which depends on human tradition and the basic principles of this world rather than on Christ" (NIV). However, on an investigation of the structure of the verse, it becomes clear that philosophy in general was not the focus. Rather, the Greek grammar indicates that "hollow and deceptive" go together with "philosophy," that is, vain and hostile philosophy was the subject of discussion, not philosophy per se. In the context of Colossians, Paul was warning the church not to form and base its doctrinal views according to a philosophical system hostile to orthodoxy. His remarks were a simple warning not to embrace heresy. They were not meant in context to represent the apostle's views of philosophy as a discipline of study. Those views are not relevant to the context and do not square with the grammar of the passage.

Finally, 1 Corinthians 1—2 is cited as evidence against philosophy. Here Paul argues against the wisdom of the world and reminds his readers that he did not visit them with persuasive words of wisdom. But again, this passage must be understood in context. For one thing, if it is an indictment against argumentation and philosophical reason, then it contradicts Paul's own practices in Acts and his explicit appeal to argument and evidence on behalf of the resurrection

---

[4]William Wilberforce, *Real Christianity* (Portland, Ore.: Multnomah Press, 1982; based on the 1829 edition), pp. 1-2.

in 1 Corinthians 15. It also contradicts other passages (e.g., 1 Pet 3:15) as well as the practice of Old Testament prophets and preachers.

The passage is better seen as a condemnation of the false, prideful use of reason, not of reason itself. It is *hubris* (pride) that is in view, not *nous* (mind). The passage may also be a condemnation of Greek rhetoric. Greek orators prided themselves in possessing "persuasive words of wisdom," and it was their practice to persuade a crowd of any side of an issue for the right price. They did not base their persuasion on rational considerations, but on speaking ability, thus bypassing issues of substance. Paul is most likely contrasting himself with Greek rhetoricians.

Paul could also be making the claim that the content of the gospel cannot be deduced from some set of first principles by pure reason. Thus the gospel of salvation could never have been discovered by philosophy, but had to be revealed by the biblical God who acts in history. So the passage may be showing the inadequacy of pure reason to deduce the gospel from abstract principles, not its inability to argue for the truth.

We have seen that there are good reasons why the church has historically valued the role of philosophy in her life and mission, and reasons to the contrary are inadequate. It is time now to turn to the issue of the role of philosophy in the integrative task of forming a Christian worldview.

4 THE ROLE OF PHILOSOPHY IN INTEGRATION

It may be helpful to begin this section by listing examples of issues in a field of study that naturally suggest the relevance of philosophical reflection and where someone in that field of study may, inadvertently, don a philosopher's cap.

4.1
EXAMPLES OF
THE NEED FOR
PHILOSOPHY

1. A biblical exegete becomes aware of how much her own cultural background shapes what she can see in the biblical text, and she begins to wonder whether meanings might not reside in the interpretation of a text and not in the text itself. She also wonders if certain methodologies may be inappropriate given the nature of the Bible as revelation.

2. A psychologist reads the literature regarding identical twins who are reared in separate environments. He notes that they usually exhibit similar adult behavior. He then wonders if there is really any such thing as freedom of the will, and if not, he ponders what to make of moral responsibility and punishment.

3. A political science professor reads John Rawls's A *Theory of Justice* and grapples with the idea that society's primary goods could be distributed in such a way that those on the bottom get the maximum benefit even if people on the top have to be constrained. He wonders how this compares with a meritocracy wherein individual merit is rewarded regardless of social distribution. Several questions run through his mind: What is the state? How should a Christian view the state and the church? What is justice, and what principles of social ordering ought we adopt? Should one seek a Christian state or merely a just state?

4. A neurophysiologist establishes specific correlations between certain brain functions and certain feelings of pain, and she puzzles over the question of whether or not there is a soul or mind distinct from the brain.

5. An anthropologist notes that cultures frequently differ over basic moral principles and goes on to argue that this proves that there are no objectively true moral values that transcend culture.

6. A businessman notices that the government is not adequately caring for the poor. He discusses with a friend the issue of whether or not businesses have corporate moral responsibilities or whether only individuals have moral responsibility.

7. A mathematician teaches Euclidean geometry and some of its alternatives and goes on to ask the class if mathematics is a field that really conveys true knowledge about a subject matter or if it merely offers internally consistent formal languages expressible in symbols. If the former, then what is it that mathematics describes? Do numbers exist and, if so, what are they?

8. An education major is asked to state his philosophy of education. In order to do this, he must state his views on human nature, the nature of truth, how people learn, what role values play in life, what the purpose of education ought to be and who should be entitled to an education.

9. A physicist ponders Einstein's theory about the relativity of space and time, and she believes that space and time themselves must be distinguished from the empirical, operational space and time utilized in scientific observations and tests. She agrees that the latter are relative, but she does not think that this settles the question of the real nature of actual space and time.

Each example is a case where philosophy is relevant to some other discipline of study and crucial for the task of forming a well-reasoned, integrated Christian worldview. Philosophy asks normative questions (What ought one believe and why? What ought one do and why?), it deals with foundational issues (What is real? What is truth? What can humans know? What is right and wrong? Do right and wrong exist? What are the principles of good reasoning and evidence evaluation?), and it seeks knowledge of what some phenomenon must be in all possible worlds, not what may happen to be the case in this actual world.

**4.2
DIFFERENT
MODELS OF
INTEGRATION**

In each of the cases listed above, there is a need for the person in question, if he or she is a Christian, to think hard about the issue in light of the need for developing a Christian worldview. When one addresses problems like these, there will emerge a number of different ways that Christian doctrine and theology can interact with an issue in a discipline outside theology. And philosophy can be useful both in deciding which model is the best one to use in a specific case and in helping a person do the work of integration within that chosen model. Here are some of the different ways that such interaction can take place.

1. *Propositions, theories or methodologies in theology and another discipline may involve two distinct, nonoverlapping areas of investigation.* For example, de-

bates about angels or the extent of the atonement have little to do with organic chemistry. Similarly, it is of little interest to theology whether a methane molecule has three or four hydrogen atoms in it.

2. *Propositions, theories or methodologies in theology and another discipline may involve two different, complementary, noninteracting approaches to the same reality.* Sociological aspects of church growth, certain psychological aspects of conversion may be sociological or psychological descriptions of certain phenomena that are complementary to a theological description of church growth or conversion.

3. *Propositions, theories or methodologies in theology and another discipline may directly interact in such a way that either one area of study offers rational support for the other or one area of study raises rational difficulties for the other.* For example, certain theological teachings about the existence of the soul raise rational problems for philosophical or scientific claims that deny the existence of the soul. The general theory of evolution raises various difficulties for certain ways of understanding the book of Genesis. Some have argued that the big bang theory tends to support the theological proposition that the universe had a beginning.

4. *Theology tends to support the presuppositions of another discipline and vice versa.* Some have argued that many of the presuppositions of a realist understanding of science (see chap. 16) (e.g., the existence of truth, the rational, orderly nature of reality, the adequacy of our sensory and cognitive faculties as tools suited for knowing the external world) make sense and are easy to justify given Christian theism, but are odd and without ultimate justification in a naturalistic worldview. Similarly, some have argued that philosophical critiques of epistemological skepticism and defenses of the existence of a real, theory-independent world and a correspondence theory of truth (according to which true propositions correspond with the "external" world; see chaps. 5-6) offer justification for some of the presuppositions of theology.

5. *Theology fills out and adds details to general principles in another discipline and vice versa, and theology helps one practically apply principles in another discipline and vice versa.* For example, theology teaches that fathers should not provoke their children to anger, and psychology can add important details about what this means by offering information about family systems, the nature and causes of anger, etc. Psychology can devise various tests for assessing whether one is or is not a mature person, and theology can offer a normative definition to psychology as to what a mature person is.

These are some of the ways that integration takes place. From the examples and models listed above, it should be clear that philosophy is central to the task of integration. Nevertheless, the task of forming an integrated worldview is a very difficult one, and there is no set of easy steps or principles that exhaustively describes how that task is to be conducted or what role philosophy should play in the quest for integration. With this in mind, the following is a list of principles

4.3
SOME
PHILOSOPHICAL
PRINCIPLES
USED IN
INTEGRATION

that can aid someone unfamiliar with philosophy to think more clearly about its role in integration.

1. Philosophy can make clear that an issue thought to be a part of another discipline is really a philosophical issue. It often happens that scholars, untrained in philosophy, will discuss some issue in their field and without knowing it, cross over into philosophy. When this happens, the discussion may still be about the original discipline, but it is a philosophical discussion about that discipline.

For example, attempts to put limits on a given discipline and attempts to draw a line of demarcation between one field of study and another, say between science and theology, are largely philosophical matters. This is because such attempts assume a vantage point outside of and above the discipline in question where one asks second-order questions about that discipline. Philosophy, it will be recalled, focuses on these kinds of second-order questions.

Consider the following six propositions that describe conditions under which science places a limit on theology or vice versa:

S1. Theological beliefs are reasonable only if science renders them so.

S2. Theological beliefs are unreasonable if science renders them so.

S3. Theological beliefs are reasonable only if arrived at by something closely akin to scientific methodology.

T1. Scientific beliefs are reasonable only if theology renders them so.

T2. Scientific beliefs are unreasonable if theology renders them so.

T3. Scientific beliefs are reasonable only if arrived at by theologically appropriate methods.

Contrary to initial appearances, these propositions are not examples of science or theology directly placing limits on the other, for none is a statement *of* science or theology. Rather, all are philosophical statements *about* science and theology. Principles *about* science and theology are not the same as principles *of* science and theology. These six principles are philosophical attempts to limit science and theology and show their relationship.

Consider a second example of where a discussion crosses over into philosophy almost unnoticed.

Evolutionist: The origin of life from inanimate matter is a well-established scientific fact.

Creationist: But if life arose in the oceans (abiogenesis) as you claim, then dilution factors would have kept the concentration of large, macromolecules to levels so small as to have been negligible.

Evolutionist: Well, so what? I do not think abiogenesis took place in the ocean anyway. Rather, it took place in some isolated pool that had some concentrating mechanism in place.

Creationist: But the probabilities for such a process are incredibly small, and in any case, evidence appears to be coming in that the early earth's atmosphere was a reducing atmosphere, in which case the relevant reactions could not occur.

Evolutionist: Give us more time, and we will solve these problems. The only alternative, creationism, is too fantastic to believe, and it involves religious concepts and is not science at all.

Creationist: Well, neither is evolution science. Science requires firsthand observation, and since no one was there to observe the origin of first life, any theory about that origin is not science, strictly speaking.

The discussion starts out as a scientific interaction about chemical reactions, probabilities, geological evidence and so on. But it slides over into a second-order philosophical discussion (one that represents a misunderstanding of the nature of both creationism and science; see chaps. 15-17), about what science is and how one should define it. These issues are surely relevant to the debate, but there is no guarantee that two disputants trained in some first-order scientific discipline have any expertise at all about the second-order questions of what science is and how it should be practiced. If scientists are going to interact on these issues, then philosophy will be an essential part of that interaction.

2. Philosophy undergirds other disciplines at a foundational level by providing clarity, justification for or arguments against the essential presuppositions of that discipline. Since philosophy operates as a second-order discipline that investigates other disciplines, and since philosophy examines broad, foundational, axiological, epistemological, logical and metaphysical issues in those other disciplines, then philosophy is properly suited to investigate the presuppositions of other disciplines. For example, in linguistic studies, issues are discussed regarding the existence, nature and knowability of meaning. These issues, as well as questions about whether and how language accomplishes reference to things in the world, are the main focus of the philosophy of language and epistemology.

Again, science assumes there is an external world that is orderly and knowable, that inductive inferences are legitimate, that the senses and mind are reliable, that truth exists and can be known, and so on. Orthodox theology assumes that religious language is cognitive, that knowledge is possible, that an intelligible sense can be given to the claim that something exists that is not located in space and time, that the correspondence theory of truth is the essential part of an overall theory of truth and that linguistic meaning is objective and knowable. These presuppositions, and a host of others besides, have all been challenged. The task of clarifying, defending or criticizing them is essentially a philosophical task.

3. Philosophy can aid a discipline by helping to clarify concepts, argument forms and other cognitive issues internal to a field. Sometimes the concepts in a discipline appear to be contradictory, vague, unclear or circularly defined. Philosophers who study a particular discipline can aid that discipline by bringing conceptual clarity to it. An example would be the wave-particle nature of electromagnetic radiation and the wave nature of matter. These concepts appear to be self-contradictory or vague, and attempts have been made to clarify them or to show different ways of understanding them.

Another example concerns some conceptions of the mechanisms involved in evolutionary theory. Some scientists have held that evolution promotes the survival of the fittest. But when asked what the "fittest" were, the answer is that the "fittest" were those that survived. This was a problem of circularity within evolutionary theory, and attempts have been made to redefine the notion of fitness and the goal of evolution (e.g., the selection of those organisms that are reproductively favorable) to avoid circularity. Whether or not these responses have been successful is not the point here. The point is, rather, that philosophers have raised problems for a scientific theory because of issues of conceptual clarity. In these and other examples like them, philosophy can help to clarify issues within a discipline. When philosophy is brought to bear on questions of this sort, the result may be that the theory in question is problematic because it involves an internal contradiction or is somehow self-refuting.

For example, the sociological claim that there is no difference between **intellectual history** (roughly, the attempt to trace the development of ideas through history by focusing on the rational factors involved in the ideas themselves, including their own inner logic and relationships to ideas coming after them, e.g., the development of empiricism from John Locke to George Berkeley to David Hume) and the **sociology of knowledge** (the attempt to trace the development of ideas as a result of nonrational factors in a given culture, e.g., social status, economic conditions and so on) is sometimes justified by an appeal to conceptual relativism. The claim is made that different cultures have different language games, different views of the world and so forth, and that all of one's views are determined by nonrational factors and thus are not to be trusted. Such a claim is self-refuting, for presumably this theory itself would be untrustworthy on its own terms.

4. Philosophy provides a common language or conceptual grid wherein two disciplines can be directly related to one another and integrated. Sometimes two different disciplines will use a term in a slightly different but not completely unrelated way. When this occurs, philosophy can help to clarify the relationship between the different disciplinary uses of the term in question.

For example, sometimes an **operational definition** of some notion can be related to an ordinary language definition of that notion or a definition from another field. An operational definition is, roughly, a definition of some concept totally in terms of certain laboratory or experimental operations or test scores. Thus one could operationally define a number of sociological concepts (minority group, traditional family roles, group leadership) or psychological terms (depression, intelligence) completely in terms of some operation or test score. A person could be said to be depressed if and only if that person scored between such and such a range on some standard psychological test.

Now these operational definitions may be related to our ordinary language notions of the relevant concepts in question; but they may not be clearly related, and in any case, they are certainly not identical to them. So philosophical clarity needs to be given before we can specify the relationship between *depression* as it is understood in ordinary language and *depression* as it is operationally defined in some test.

This type of philosophical elucidation is especially important when the term in question appears to be normative in nature. Thus, if one tries to give an operational, psychological definition of a "mature" or "healthy" adult, then all one can give is a descriptive definition, not a prescriptive one, for psychology as it is currently practiced is a descriptive field. Philosophy focuses on moral prescriptions and oughts; psychology focuses on factual descriptions. So philosophy becomes relevant in clarifying the relationship between a "mature" adult, psychologically defined, and a "mature" adult taken as a normative notion (i.e., as something one ought to try to achieve).

Philosophy also helps to clarify and relate the different disciplinary descriptions of the same phenomenon. For example, biologists describe a human being as a member of the classification *Homo sapiens*. Philosophy, theology, law and political science (to name a few) treat a human being as a living entity called a *human person*. It is a philosophical question as to whether the two notions are identical and, if they are not, how they relate to one another.

5. Philosophy provides **external conceptual problems** *for other disciplines to consider as part of the rational appraisal of theories in those disciplines* (and vice versa). A philosophical external conceptual problem arises for some theory in a discipline outside of philosophy when that theory conflicts with a doctrine of some philosophical theory, provided that the philosophical theory and its component doctrines are rationally well founded. For example, suppose there were a good philosophical argument against the view that history has crossed an actual infinite number of events throughout the past to reach the present moment. If this argument is a reasonable one, then it tends to count against some scientific theory (e.g., an oscillating universe) which postulates that the past was beginningless and actually infinite. If there were a good philosophical argument for the claim that space and time are absolute, then this argument would tend to count against scientific theories to the contrary.

Again, if there are good philosophical arguments for the existence of genuine freedom of the will or arguments for the existence of real moral responsibility and the necessity of full-blown freedom as a presupposition of moral responsibility, then these would tend to count against sociological, economic or psychological theories that are deterministic in nature. In cases like these, a rationally defensible position is present within philosophy, and it runs contrary to a theory surfaced in another field. The philosophical external conceptual problem may not be sufficient to require abandonment or suspension of judgment of the theory in the other discipline; it may merely tend to count against it. Even so, these kinds of conceptual problems show that philosophical considerations are relevant to the rationality of theory-assessment in other disciplines.

In sum, we have looked at five different ways that philosophy enters into the task of integration in a Christian university. It is important to realize that the Christian philosopher should adopt the attitude of faith seeking under-

standing. The Christian philosopher will try to undergird, defend and clarify
the various aspects of a worldview compatible with Scripture. This will involve working not only on broad theological themes—for example, the dignity of being human—but on defending and clarifying specific verses in
Scripture. Of course, caution must be exercised. One should not automatically assume that one's particular interpretation of a biblical text is the only
option for an evangelical, and one should not automatically assume that the
biblical text was intended to speak to the issue at hand. But when due care is
given to these warnings, it is nevertheless important that the Christian philosopher tries to forge a worldview that includes the teaching of specific biblical texts, properly interpreted.

Earlier in the chapter reference was made to a remark from Saint Augustine
to the effect that the Christian intellectual must work on behalf of the church
to show that Scripture does not conflict with any rationally justified belief from
some other discipline. Over seventy-five years ago the great evangelical Presby-
terian scholar J. Gresham Machen remarked that false ideas were the greatest
hindrance to the gospel. According to Machen, we can preach with all the fer-
vor of a reformer and even win a straggler here and there; but if we permit the
whole collective thought of the nation or world to be dominated by ideas that,
by their very logic, prevent Christianity from being regarded as anything more
than a hopeless delusion, then we do damage to our religion.

Members of the Christian family have a responsibility to promote worldwide
evangelization, the nurture of the saints and the penetration of culture with a
Christian worldview. This task is important to the very life and health of the
church, and when we engage in it, philosophy is now, as it has always been, an
essential participant in this great task.

CHAPTER SUMMARY

While there is no airtight definition for philosophy, nevertheless, three features
of philosophy help us understand what it is. The term *philosophy* means love of
wisdom, and philosophy is an attempt to think rationally and critically about
life's most important questions. Moreover, philosophy is a second-order discipline. Finally, there are several first-order areas of philosophy itself, such as
logic, metaphysics, epistemology and value theory.

From a Christian perspective, philosophy can be an aid to apologetics, polemics and systematic theology. Further, work in philosophy can be a central
expression of the image of God and can be a spiritual discipline. Finally, philosophy can help to extend biblical teaching to areas not explicitly mentioned in
Scripture, it can enhance the self-image of the believing community, and it can
aid in the task of integrating theology with other disciplines in forming a Christian worldview. Moreover, four arguments against philosophy were evaluated
and rejected.

The last section of the chapter cited examples of the need for integration
and for philosophy to be involved in that activity, various models of integration were listed, and five philosophical principles used in integration were
examined.

CHECKLIST OF BASIC TERMS AND CONCEPTS

apologetics
epistemology
external conceptual problem
faith
first-order discipline
integration
intellectual history
logic
metaphysics
noetic effects of sin
operational definition
philosophy
polemics
second-order discipline
sociology of knowledge
value theory
worldview

2

ARGUMENTATION
AND LOGIC

Come now, let us argue it out.
ISAIAH 1:18

1 INTRODUCTION

Philosophy, Alvin Plantinga has remarked, is just thinking hard about something. If that is the case, then doing good philosophy will be a matter of learning to think well. That serves to differentiate philosophy from mere emotional expressions of what we feel to be true or hopeful expressions of what we wish to be true. What, then, does it mean to think well? It will involve, among other things, the ability to formulate and assess **arguments** for various claims to truth. When we speak of arguments for a position, we do not, of course, mean quarreling about it. Rather, an argument in the philosophical sense is a set of statements which serve as **premises** leading to a **conclusion**.

Every one of us already employs the rules of argumentation whether we realize it or not. For these rules apply to all reasoning everywhere, no matter what the subject. We use these rules unconsciously every day in normal life. For example: Suppose a friend says to you, "I've got to go to the library today to check out a book." And you reply, "You can't do that today." "Why not?" he asks. "Because today is Sunday," you explain, "and the library isn't open on Sunday." In effect, you have just presented an argument to your friend. You have reasoned:

1. If today is Sunday, the library is closed.
2. Today is Sunday.
3. Therefore, the library is closed.

Sentences (1) and (2) are the premises of the argument, and sentence (3) is the conclusion. You are saying that if premises (1) and (2) are true, then the conclusion (3) is also true. It is not just your opinion that the library is closed; you have given an argument for that conclusion.

What makes for a good argument? That depends. Arguments may be either deductive or inductive. In a good **deductive argument** the premises guarantee the truth of their conclusions. In a good **inductive argument** the premises render the conclusion more probable than its competitors. What makes for a good argument depends on whether that argument is deductive or inductive.

2 DEDUCTIVE ARGUMENTS

A good deductive argument will be one which is formally and informally valid, which has true premises, and whose premises are more plausible than their contradictories. Let us say a word of explanation about each of these criteria.

First, a good argument must be **formally valid**. That is to say, the conclusion must follow from the premises in accord with the **rules of logic**. **Logic** is the study of the rules of reasoning. Although the word *logic* is often used colloquially as a synonym for something like "common sense," logic is, in fact, a highly technical subdiscipline of philosophy akin to mathematics. It is a multifaceted field, consisting of various subfields such as sentential logic, first-order predicate logic, many-valued logic, modal logic, tense logic, and so forth. Fortunately, for our purposes, we need only take a superficial look at the role logic plays in our formulating and assessing simple arguments.

An argument whose conclusion does not follow from the premises in accord with the rules of logic is said to be **invalid**, even if the conclusion happens to be true. For example,

1. If Sherrie gets an "A" in epistemology, she'll be proud of her work.
2. Sherrie is proud of her work.
3. Therefore, Sherrie got an "A" in epistemology.

All three of these statements may in fact be true. But because (3) does not follow logically from (1) and (2), this is an invalid argument. From the knowledge of (1) and (2), you cannot know that (3) is also true. The above is therefore not a good argument.

Second, a good argument will be not only formally valid but also **informally valid**. As we shall see, there is a multitude of fallacies in reasoning which, while not breaking any rule of logic, disqualify an argument from being a good one— for example, reasoning in a circle. Consider the following argument.

1. If the Bible is God's Word, then it is God's Word.
2. The Bible is God's Word.
3. Therefore, the Bible is God's Word.

This is a logically valid argument, but few people will be impressed with it. For it assumes what it sets out to prove and therefore proves nothing new. A good argument will not only follow the rules of formal logic but will also avoid informal fallacies.

Third, the premises in a good argument must be true. An argument can be formally and informally valid and yet lead to a false conclusion because one of the premises is false. For example,

1. Anything with webbed feet is a bird.
2. A platypus has webbed feet.
3. Therefore, a platypus is a bird.

This is a valid argument, but unfortunately premise (1) is false. There are animals other than birds that have webbed feet. Therefore, this is not a good argument for the truth of the conclusion. An argument that is both logically valid and has true premises is called a **sound argument**. An **unsound argument** is either invalid or else has a false premise.

Fourth, a good argument has premises that are more plausible than their contradictories or denials. For an argument to be a good one, it is not required that we have 100% certainty of the truth of the premises. Some of the premises in a good argument may strike us as only slightly more plausible than their denials; other premises may seem to us highly plausible in contrast to their denials. But so long as a statement is more plausible than its **contradictory** (that is, its negation), then one should believe it rather than its negation, and so it may serve as a premise in a good argument. Thus a good argument for God's existence need not make it *certain* that God exists. Certainty is what most people are thinking of when they say, "You can't prove that God exists!" If we equate "proof" with 100% certainty, then we may agree with them and yet insist that there are still good arguments to think that God exists. For example, one version of the axiological argument may be formulated:

1. If God did not exist, objective moral values would not exist.
2. Objective moral values do exist.
3. Therefore, God exists.

Someone may object to premise (1) of our argument by saying, "But it's possible that moral values exist as abstract objects without God." We may happily agree. That is **epistemically possible**, that is to say, the premise is not known to be true with certainty. But possibilities come cheap. The question is not whether the contradictory of a particular premise in an argument is epistemically possible (or even plausible); the question is whether the contradictory is as plausible or more plausible than the premise. If it is not, then one should believe the premise rather than its contradictory.

In summary, then, a good argument will be formally and informally valid and have true premises that are more plausible than their contradictories. In order to assist readers in formulating and assessing arguments, we shall now explain each of these features in somewhat more detail.

<table>
<tr><td>

2.1.
LOGICALLY
VALID

2.1.1
SENTENTIAL
LOGIC

2.1.1.1
NINE RULES OF
LOGIC

</td><td>

Sentential or **propositional logic** is the most basic level of logic, dealing with inferences based on sentential connectives like "if . . . , then," "or" and "and." There are only nine rules of inference which readers must learn, along with a few logical equivalences, in order to carry out the reasoning governed by this domain of logic. Equipped with the nine rules, readers will be able to assess the validity of most of the arguments they will ever encounter.

Rule #1: *modus ponens*

1. $P \rightarrow Q$
2. P

---

3. Q

</td></tr>
</table>

In **symbolic logic** one uses letters and symbols to stand for sentences and the words that connect them. In (1) the **P** and the **Q** stand for any two different sentences, and the arrow stands for the connecting words, "if . . . , then . . . ." To read premise (1) we say, "If **P**, then **Q**." Another way of reading $P \rightarrow Q$ is to say: "**P** implies **Q**." To read premise (2) we just say, "**P**." The reason letters and symbols are used is because sentences that are very different grammatically may still have the same logical form. For example, the sentences "I'll go if you go" and "If you go, then I'll go," though different grammatically, obviously have the same logical form. By using symbols and letters instead of the sentences themselves we can make the logical form of a sentence clear without being distracted by its grammatical form.

The rule *modus ponens* tells us that from the two premises $P \rightarrow Q$ and P, we may validly conclude Q. This rule of inference is one that we use unconsciously all the time, as the following examples should make clear.

Example 1:

1. If John studies hard, then he will get a good grade in logic.
2. John studies hard.

---

3. He will get a good grade in logic.

Example 2:

1. If John does not study hard, then he will not get a good grade in logic.
2. John does not study hard.

---

3. He will not get a good grade in logic.

Notice that our two examples are both valid arguments (they are both in accord with the rule *modus ponens*), but they reach opposite conclusions. So they cannot both be sound; at least one of them must have a false premise. If we wanted to figure out which one of these examples is a sound argument, we would need to look at the evidence for the premises. Based on John's past performance, for example, we discover that when he studies hard for a class, he gets a good grade. That gives good grounds for thinking that premise (1) of example 1 is true. Moreover, we observe that John is putting in long hours studying for his logic class. So we have good grounds for thinking that premise (2) of example 1 is true as well. So we have good grounds for thinking example 1 to be a valid argument with true premises. So it is a sound argument for the conclusion that John will in fact get a good grade.

What about example 2? If John were a real genius, it might be the case that he would get a good grade in logic even if he did not study hard. Maybe if he studies hard he will get a good grade, and if he does not study hard he will get a good grade. But we observe, in fact, that John is not that smart. If he does not work hard, he fails to achieve his goals. So we have good reason to believe that premise (1) of example 2 is true. But then we come to premise (2). And this premise is clearly false, for John is no slacker but studies hard for his logic class. Therefore, example 2 is not a sound argument because it has a false premise. It is valid but unsound.

Rule #2: *modus tollens*

1. $P \rightarrow Q$

2. $\neg Q$

---

3. $\neg P$

Once again the **P** and the **Q** stand for any two sentences, and the arrow stands for "if . . . , then . . ." The sign ¬ stands for "not." It is the sign of negation. So premise (1) reads, "If **P**, then **Q**." Premise (2) reads, "Not-**Q**." The rule *modus tollens* tells us that from these two premises, we may validly conclude, "Not-**P**." The following examples should make this rule clear.

Example 1:

1. If Joan has been working out, then she can run the 5 K race.
2. She cannot run the 5 K race.

---

3. Joan has not been working out.

Example 2:

1. If it is Saturday morning, then my roommate is sleeping in.
2. My roommate is not sleeping in.

---

3. It is not Saturday morning.

Modus tollens involves negating a premise. If the premise is already a negation, then we have *double negation*, which is logically the same as an affirmative sentence. Thus ¬¬**Q** is equivalent to **Q**. So from the premises

1. ¬**P** → **Q**
2. ¬**Q**

we can conclude

3. ¬¬**P**

which is logically the same as

4. **P**

In this case the initial conclusion ¬¬**P** becomes itself a premise from which to draw the further conclusion in (4). Another example of double negation in action would be

1. **P** → ¬**Q**
2. **Q**

In order to use *modus tollens* we first convert (2) to

3. ¬¬**Q**

which is the negation of ¬**Q**. That allows us to use *modus tollens* to conclude to

4. ¬**P**

Modus ponens and *modus tollens* help to bring out an important feature of conditional sentences: The antecedent "if" clause states a *sufficient condition* of the consequent "then" clause. The consequent "then" clause states a *necessary condition* of the antecedent "if" clause. For if **P** is true, then **Q** is also true. The truth of **P** is sufficient for the truth of **Q**. At the same time **P** is never true without **Q**: if **Q** is not true, then **P** is not true either. So in any sentence of the form **P** → **Q**, **P** is a sufficient condition of **Q**, and **Q** is a necessary condition of **P**.

There are other ways of expressing sufficient and necessary conditions besides the expression "if . . . , then . . ." For example, we frequently express a necessary condition by saying "only if . . ." Your professor says, "Extra credit will be permitted *only if* you have completed all the required work." He is saying that completing the required work is a necessary condition of doing extra credit work. Therefore, if we let **P** = "You may do extra credit work" and **Q** = "You have completed the required work," we can symbolize his sentence as **P → Q**. This is tricky because when the beginner sees the words "only if," he might think that we should symbolize the clause that comes after them as **P**. But that is incorrect. When he sees the words "only if," he should think immediately "necessary condition" and realize that he should symbolize what comes afterward as **Q**.

This distinction between necessary and sufficient conditions is vitally important because ignoring it can lead to great misunderstandings. For example, you might conclude from your professor's above statement that if you complete the required work, then you may do extra credit work. But that is not, in fact, what he said! He stated a *necessary* condition of your doing extra credit work, not a *sufficient* condition. He asserted **P → Q**, but he did not assert **Q → P**. There may be *other* conditions that have to be met as well before one may do extra credit work. So if you concluded on the basis of his statement that you could do extra credit work after completing the required work, you would be guilty of an invalid inference, which might prove ruinous to your grade! So in a sentence, the clause that follows a simple "if" is the antecedent clause symbolized **P**, a sufficient condition. The clause that follows "only if" is the consequent clause symbolized **Q**, the necessary condition.

We now draw attention to a very common logical fallacy: Affirming the consequent.

Example 1:
1. If George and Barbara are enjoying soft-boiled eggs, toast and coffee, then they are having breakfast.
2. George and Barbara are having breakfast.

3. They are enjoying soft-boiled eggs, toast and coffee.

Example 2:
1. If God is timeless, then he is intrinsically changeless.
2. God is intrinsically changeless.

3. He is timeless.

What is wrong with this reasoning is that in both examples (1) states only a *sufficient*, not a *necessary*, condition of (2). If George and Barbara are eating those things, then they are having breakfast. But it does not follow that if they are having breakfast, then they are eating those things! If God is timeless, then he is intrinsically unchanging. But that does not imply that if he is intrinsically unchanging, he is therefore timeless.

If **P → Q**, *modus ponens* tells us that if we affirm that the antecedent **P** is true, then the consequent is also true. *Modus tollens* tells us that if we deny that the consequent **Q** is true, then the antecedent **P** must also be denied. Thus, if **P →Q**, it is valid reasoning to either *affirm the antecedent* or *deny the consequent* and draw the appropriate conclusion. But we must not make the mistake of *affirming the consequent.* If **P → Q**, and **Q** is true, we may not validly conclude anything.

Rule #3: Hypothetical Syllogism

1. **P → Q**

2. **Q → R**

_____

3. **P → R**

The third rule, hypothetical syllogism, states that if **P** implies **Q**, and **Q** implies **R**, then **P** implies **R**. Since we do not know in this case if **P** is true, we cannot conclude that **R** is true. But at least we can know on the basis of premises (1) and (2) that if **P** is true, then **R** is true.

Example 1:

1. If it is Valentine's Day, Guillaume will invite Jeanette to dine at a fine restaurant.
2. If Guillaume will invite Jeanette to dine at a fine restaurant, then they will dine at L'Auberge St. Pierre.

_____

3. If it is Valentine's Day, then Guillaume and Jeanette will dine at L'Auberge St. Pierre.

Example 2:

1. If Jeanette orders *médallions de veau*, then Guillaume will have *saumon grillé*.
2. If Guillaume has *saumon grillé*, he will not have room for dessert.

_____

3. If Jeanette orders *médaillons de veau*, then Guillaume will not have room for dessert.

We can use our three logical rules in conjunction with one another to draw more complicated inferences. For example, we can use *modus ponens* (MP) and hypothetical syllogism (HS) to see that the following argument is valid.

1. **P → Q**
2. **Q → R**
3. **P**
4. **P → R**   (HS, 1, 2)
5. **R**   (MP, 3, 4)

The first three steps are the given premises. Steps (4) and (5) are conclusions we can draw using the logical rules we have learned. To the right we abbreviate the rule that allows us to take each step, along with the numbers of the premises we used to draw that conclusion. Notice that a conclusion validly drawn from the premises becomes itself a premise for a further conclusion.

Here is another example:

1. P → Q
2. Q → R
3. ¬R
4. P → R (HS, 1, 2)
5. ¬P (MT, 3, 4)

The more rules we learn, the more complicated the arguments we may handle.

Rule #4: Conjunction

1. P
2. Q

---

3. P & Q

Here we introduce the symbol **&,** which is the symbol for conjunction. It is read as "and." This rule is perspicuous: If **P** is true, and **Q** is true, then the conjunction "**P** and **Q**" is also true.

Example 1:

1. Charity is playing the piano.
2. Jimmy is trying to play the piano.

---

3. Charity is playing the piano, and Jimmy is trying to play the piano.

Example 2:

1. If Louise studies hard, she will master logic.
2. If Jan studies hard, she will master logic.

---

3. If Louise studies hard, she will master logic, and if Jan studies hard, she will master logic.

As example 2 illustrates, any sentences can be joined by **&.** When the premises in our arguments get complicated, it helps to introduce parentheses to keep things straight. For example, you would symbolize the conclusion (**P → Q**) **&** (**R → S**).

The symbol **&** symbolizes many more words than just *and*. It symbolizes any conjunction. Thus the logical form of sentences having the connective words *but, while, although, whereas* and many other words is the same. We symbolize them all using **&.** For example, the sentence "They ate their spinach, even though they didn't like it" would be symbolized **P & Q**. **P** symbolizes "They ate their spinach," **Q** symbolizes "they didn't like it," and **&** symbolizes the conjunction "even though."

Rule #5: Simplification

1. P & Q   1. P & Q

---   ---

2. P   2. Q

Again, one does not need to be a rocket scientist to understand this rule! In order for a conjunction like **P & Q** to be true, both **P** and **Q** must be true. So simplification allows you to conclude from **P & Q** that **P** is true and that **Q** is true.

Example 1:

1. Bill is bagging groceries, and James is stocking the shelves.

2. James is stocking the shelves.

Example 2:

1. If Susan is typing, she will not answer the phone;
   and if Gary is reading, he will not answer the phone.

2. If Gary is reading, he will not answer the phone.

The main usefulness of this rule is that if you have the premise **P & Q** and you need either **P** by itself or **Q** by itself to draw a conclusion, simplification can give it to you.

For example:

1. P & Q
2. P → R
3. P   (Simp, 1)
4. R   (MP, 2, 3)

Rule #6: Absorption

1. P → Q

2. P → (P & Q)

This is a rule which one hardly ever uses but which nonetheless states a valid way of reasoning. The basic idea is that since **P** implies itself, it implies itself along with anything else it implies.

Example 1:

1. If Allison goes shopping, she will buy a new top.

2. If Allison goes shopping, then she will go shopping and buy a new top.

Example 2:

1. If you do the assignment, then you will get an "A."

2. If you do the assignment, then you do the assignment and you will get an "A."

The main use for absorption will be in cases where you need to have **P & Q** in order to take a further step in the argument. For example:

1. P → Q
2. (P & Q) → R

3. P → (P & Q)   (Abs, 1)
4. P → R   (HS, 2, 3)

Rule #7: Addition

1. P
_____

2. P v Q

For this rule we introduce a new symbol: **v**, which is read "or." We can use it to symbolize sentences connected by the word *or*. A sentence which is composed of two sentences connected by *or* is called a disjunction.

Addition seems at first to be a strange rule of inference: It states that if **P** is true, then "**P** or **Q**" is also true. What needs to be kept in mind is this: in order for a disjunction to be true *only one part* of the disjunction has to be true. So if one knows that **P** is already true, it follows that "**P** or **Q**" is also true, no matter what **Q** is!

Example 1:

1. Mallory will carefully work on decorating their new apartment.
_____

2. Either Mallory will carefully work on decorating their new apartment, or she will allow it to degenerate into a pigsty.

Example 2:

1. Jim will make the honor roll.
_____

2. Either Jim will make the honor roll or his dad will fly to the moon.

Addition is another one of those "house-keeping" rules that are useful for tidying up an argument by helping us to get some needed part of a premise. For example:

1. P
2. (P v Q) → R
3. P v Q   (Add, 1)
4. R   (MP, 2, 3)

Rule #8: Disjunctive Syllogism

1. P v Q	1. P v Q
2. ¬P	2. ¬Q
_____	_____
3. Q	3. P

This rule tells us that if a disjunction of two sentences is true, and one of the sentences is false, then the other sentence is true.

Example 1:

1. Either Mary will grade the exams herself or she will enlist Jason's aid.
2. She will not grade the exams herself.
_____

3. She will enlist Jason's aid.

Example 2:

1. Either Amy worked in the garden or Mack spent his Saturday morning doing paperwork.
2. Mack did not spend his Saturday morning doing paperwork.

3. Amy worked in the garden.

The important thing to remember about logical disjunctions is that *both* of the sentences connected by *or* could be true. In other words, the alternatives do not have to be mutually exclusive. In example 2 both sentences in premise (1) could be true. Therefore, one cannot conclude that because one of the disjuncts is true, the other is false. Both could be true. So disjunctive syllogism allows you to conclude only that if one part of a true disjunction is *false*, then the other disjunct is true.

As mentioned, when the premises in one's arguments are complicated, it helps to introduce parentheses to keep things straight. For example, one would symbolize the sentence, "If Amy replants the bushes, she will water them or they will die" by $P \rightarrow (Q \lor R)$. This is quite different from $(P \rightarrow Q) \lor R$. The latter would symbolize the disjunction "If Amy replants the bushes, she will water them; or they will die."

In figuring out whether more complex arguments are valid, it is important to remember that one cannot use a logical rule on just *part* of a step, but only on the *whole* step. So, for example, if one has

1. $P \rightarrow (Q \lor R)$
2. $\neg Q$

one cannot conclude that

3. R

In order to get to (3) we also need the premise

4. P

Then we can conclude

5. $Q \lor R$ (MP, 1, 4)

And that allows us to arrive at

3. R (DS, 2, 5)

Finally, keep in mind that the logical form of a sentence may be quite different from its verbal form. Often we do not bother to repeat the subject or the verb of the first sentence in a disjunction; for example, "Either Sherry or Patti will go with you to the airport." This is logically a disjunction: "Either Sherry will go with you to the airport or Patti will go with you to the airport." But this latter is not the normal way we talk. So sometimes we have to figure out the logical form of a sentence.

We must be careful because not every use of *or* in a sentence indicates that the sentence is a disjunction. Suppose you come to the plate with the bases loaded and two out, and your coach says, "If you get a single or a walk, we'll win!" Is he saying, "If you get a single, we'll win, or if you get a walk, we'll win!"

$(P \rightarrow Q) \vee (R \rightarrow Q)$? Surely not! For then he could just as well have said, "If you get a single or an out, we'll win!" That whole disjunction would be true because $P \rightarrow Q$ is true even if $R \rightarrow Q$ is false. Rather, we should symbolize the coach's advice as $(P \vee R) \rightarrow Q$. He's saying that whichever you get, a single or a walk, is a sufficient condition for us to win the game.

Rule #9: Constructive Dilemma

1. $(P \rightarrow Q) \& (R \rightarrow S)$
2. $P \vee R$

───────────

3. $Q \vee S$

According to constructive dilemma, if P implies Q and R implies S, then if P or R is true, it follows that either Q or S is true.

Example 1:

1. If Jennifer buys dwarf fruit trees, she can make peach pies; and if she plants flowers, the yard will look colorful.
2. Either Jennifer buys dwarf fruit trees or she plants flowers.

───────────

3. Either Jennifer can make peach pies or the yard will look colorful.

Example 2:

1. If Yvette comes along on the trip, then Jim will be happy; and if Jim goes without Yvette, then he will be lonely.
2. Either Yvette comes along on the trip or Jim goes without her.

───────────

3. Either Jim will be happy or Jim will be lonely.

This rule is useful for deducing the consequences of either-or situations, when we know the implications of each of the alternatives.

With these nine rules one can assess the validity of a vast range of arguments and, of course, formulate valid arguments of one's own. The following exercises will help readers to apply what they have learned.

Symbolize each argument and draw the conclusion, stating the rule that justifies each step.

2.1.1.2
EXERCISES OVER
THE NINE RULES

A.

1. Either Millie will buy ten shares of Acme, Inc., or she will sell out.
2. She will not sell out.

B.

1. God is timeless only if he is immutable.
2. God is immutable only if he does not know what time it is now.
3. If God is omniscient, then he knows what time it is now.
4. God is omnipotent and omniscient.

C.

1. Only if God is temporal can he become incarnate.
2. If Jesus was God or Krishna was God, then God can become incarnate.
3. Jesus was God.

D.

1. If God is all-good, then he wants to prevent evil.
2. If God is all-powerful, then he can prevent evil.
3. God is all-good and all-powerful.
4. If God wants to prevent evil and God can prevent evil, then evil does not exist.

E.

1. Keith gets up on time.
2. If Keith gets up on time, he will wake up Ashley.
3. If Keith wakes up Ashley, she will either loaf around or vacuum the house.
4. If she loafs around, Keith will go swimming by himself.
5. Ashley will not vacuum the house.

F.

1. If the butler was the murderer, his fingerprints were on the weapon.
2. Either the maid or the gardener was the murderer if the butler was not.
3. If the gardener was the murderer, there will be blood on the garden fork.
4. If the maid was the murderer, then the master was killed with a kitchen knife.
5. The butler's fingerprints were not on the weapon.
6. There was no blood on the garden fork.

G.

1. We'll have a debate if either Parsons or Flew agrees.
2. If we have a debate, it will be videotaped.
3. If the debate will be videotaped or audiotaped, you can get a copy of what went on.
4. If you can get a copy of what went on, then you don't need to feel bad about missing the debate.
5. Parsons will agree to debate.

H.

1. If God hears prayer, then he will answer if I pray.
2. God hears prayer.
3. I'll pray.

**2.1.1.3
SOME
EQUIVALENCES**

In addition to the nine logical rules we have learned, there are a number of logical equivalences which should be mastered.

P	is equivalent to	$\neg\neg$**P**
P v P	is equivalent to	**P**
P → Q	is equivalent to	$\neg$**P v Q**
P → Q	is equivalent to	$\neg$**Q → $\neg$P**

Moreover, there is a very handy way of converting a conjunction to a disjunction and vice versa. There are three steps:

Step 1. You put ¬ in front of each letter.
Step 2. You change the **&** to **v** (or the **v** to **&**).
Step 3. You put the whole thing in parentheses and put ¬ in front.

Example 1: Change **P & Q** to a disjunction.

Step 1. ¬P & ¬Q
Step 2. ¬P v ¬Q
Step 3. ¬ (¬P v ¬Q)

Example 2: Change **P v Q** to a conjunction.

Step 1. ¬P v ¬Q
Step 2. ¬P & ¬Q
Step 3. ¬ (¬P & ¬Q)

Sometimes you have to use double negation:

Example 3: Change **¬P & Q** to a disjunction.

Step 1. ¬¬P & ¬Q
Step 2. P v ¬Q
Step 3. ¬ (P v ¬Q)

Using this procedure we can find that

¬P & ¬Q	is equivalent to	¬ (P v Q)
¬P v ¬Q	is equivalent to	¬ (P & Q)

Since equivalent statements are logically the same, you can replace a premise with its equivalent. Then you may be able to use the new premise along with other premises to draw further conclusions.

Example 1:

1. If God exists, humanism is not true.
2. If God does not exist, humanism is not true.
3. God exists or he does not exist.
4. Therefore, if God exists, humanism is not true; and if God does not exist, humanism is not true. (Conj, 1, 2)
5. Therefore, either humanism is not true or humanism is not true. (CD, 3, 4)
6. Therefore, humanism is not true. (Equiv, 5)

Example 2:

1. If God does not foreknow the future, then either he determines everything or he gambles.
2. If God determines everything, then he is the author of sin.
3. If God gambles, then he is not sovereign.
4. God is sovereign, but he is not the author of sin.
5. Therefore, God is sovereign. (Simp, 4)

6. Therefore, God is not the author of sin. (Simp, 4)
7. Therefore, God does not determine everything. (MT, 2, 6)
8. Therefore, God does not gamble. (MT, 3, 5)
9. Therefore, God does not determine everything, and God does not gamble. (Conj, 7, 8)
10. Therefore, it is not true that either God determines everything or God gambles. (Equiv, 9)
11. Therefore, God does not not foreknow the future. (MT, 1, 10)
12. Therefore, God does foreknow the future. (Equiv, 11)

2.1.1.4
CONDITIONAL
PROOF

In formulating arguments of one's own, one of the most powerful logical techniques one can use is called **conditional proof**. Many times we find ourselves in situations where we want to argue that *if* something is true, then certain conclusions follow. What we need is a way of introducing a new premise into our argument. We can do this by constructing a conditional proof.

Here is how it works. Suppose we are given the following premises:

1. P → Q
2. Q → R & S

Suppose we want to argue that if **P** is true, then **S** is also true. This cannot be done using just premises (1) and (2). So what we do is introduce **P** as a *conditional* premise. It is as though we were to say, "*Suppose* **P** is true. Then what?" In order to make it clear that **P** is just a conditional premise, we can indent it.

1. P → Q
2. Q → R & S
3.   P

Then we apply our rules of logic to draw the conclusion. Remember to keep subsequent steps indented to remind us that each inference is based on the condition that **P** is true.

1. P → Q
2. Q → R & S
3.   P
4.   Q   (MP, 1, 3)
5.   R & S   (MP, 2, 4)
6.   S   (Simp, 5)

Finally, the last step is to combine our conditional premise with the conclusion we can draw if we suppose that the conditional premise is true. In other words, we know that if premise (3) is true, then our conclusion (6) is true. So we link the conditional premise (3) with the conclusion (6) by →. This final conclusion is not indented because we know that it is true by conditional proof (CP).

1. P → Q
2. Q → R & S
3.   P
4.   Q   (MP, 1, 3)

5. **R & S**   (MP, 2, 4)
6. **S**   (Simp, 5)
7. **P → S**   (CP, 3-6)

Conditional proof is very useful in proving conditional statements.

Example:

1. If God exists and the present moment is real, then God is in time.
2. If God is in time, then he knows what is happening absolutely now.
3. If God knows what is happening absolutely now, then there is a moment that is absolutely now.
4. Either there is no moment that is absolutely now or Einstein's special theory of relativity is wrong.
5. The present moment is real.
6.   God exists.   (Conditional premise)
7.   Therefore, God exists and the present moment is real.   (Conj, 5, 6)
8.   Therefore, God is in time.   (MP, 1, 7)
9.   Therefore, he knows what is happening absolutely now.   (MP, 2, 8)
10.   Therefore, there is a moment that is absolutely now.   (MP, 3, 9)
11.   Therefore, there is not no moment that is absolutely now. (Equiv, 10)
12.   Therefore, Einstein's special theory of relativity is wrong.   (DS, 4, 11)
13. Therefore, if God exists, then Einstein's special theory of relativity is wrong.   (CP, 6-12)

A special kind of conditional proof is called **reductio ad absurdum** (reduction to absurdity). Here we show that if some premise is supposed to be true, then it implies a contradiction, which is absurd. Therefore we can conclude that the premise is not true after all. This is an especially powerful way of arguing against a view, for if we can show that a view implies a contradiction, then it cannot be true.

Usually, you will begin with premises for your argument on which you and your opponent agree. Then you add to the list of premises the conditional premise that your opponent thinks is also true, but that you think is false. Then you show how the assumption of that premise leads to a contradiction. Since you have reduced his view to absurdity by showing that it implies a contradiction, you negate the conditional premise and write RAA out to the side.

2.1.1.5
REDUCTIO AD
ABSURDUM

Example:

1. We have a moral duty to love our fellow men as ourselves.
2. If God does not exist, then our fellow men are just animals.
3. If our fellow men are just animals, we have no moral duty to love them as ourselves.
4.   God does not exist.   (Conditional Premise)
5.   Therefore, our fellow men are just animals.   (MP, 2, 4)
6.   Therefore, we have no moral duty to love our fellow men as ourselves.   (MP, 3, 5)
7.   Therefore, we have a moral duty to love our fellow men as ourselves, and we have no moral duty to love our fellow men as ourselves.   (Conj, 1, 6)

8. Therefore, if God does not exist, we have a moral duty to love
   our fellow men as ourselves, and we have no moral duty
   to love our fellow men as ourselves.   (CP, 4-7)
9. Therefore, God does not not exist.   (RAA, 8)
10. Therefore, God exists.   (Equiv, 9)

Confronted with this argument, your atheist friend may choose to give up one of
his original premises rather than give up his belief in (4). But that should not
bother you. Your argument has served to show what it will cost him to hold onto
his atheism. He will have to give up belief in (1), (2) or (3). But each of these
statements seems to be pretty clearly true—at least more clearly true than (4)!
When we present an argument using *reductio ad absurdum,* we try to make the
cost of giving up one of the other premises as high as possible, in the hope that
our opponent will give up his belief in the conditional premise instead.

2.1.2
FIRST-ORDER
PREDICATE
LOGIC

In first-order predicate logic we learn how to deal with sentences that predicate
some property of a subject. This is important because it will enable us to deal
with quantified sentences, that is to say, sentences about groups of things.
Quantification deals with statements about *all* or *none* or *some* of a group. We
often draw conclusions about such matters in everyday life. But what we have
learned so far in this chapter does not enable us to do so validly. For example,
suppose we are given the premises

1. All men are mortal.
2. Socrates is a man.

From (1) and (2) it obviously follows that
3. Socrates is mortal.

But we cannot draw such a conclusion using only the nine rules learned so far.
For this argument would be symbolized as

1. **P**
2. **Q**
   _____
3. **R**

which is clearly invalid.

Fortunately, we do not need any new rules of inference to solve this problem. We just need to learn something about the logical form of quantified statements. We present here just a snippet of quantified logic, enough to enable you
to deal with most of the arguments you will come across.

2.1.2.1
UNIVERSAL
QUANTIFICATION

Statements about *all* or *none* of a group are called **universally quantified statements**, since the statement covers every member in a group. When we analyze
the logical form of such statements, we discover that they turn out to be disguised "if . . . , then . . ." statements. For example, when we say, "All bears are
mammals," logically we are saying, "If anything is a bear, then it is a mammal."
Or if we say, "No goose is hairy," logically we are saying, "If anything is a goose,
then it is not hairy."

So we can symbolize universally quantified statements as "if . . . , then . . ." statements. In order to do so, we introduce the letter *x* as a variable that can be replaced by any individual thing. We symbolize the antecedent clause using some capital letter (usually the first letter of the main word in the antecedent to make it easy to remember). For example, we can symbolize "Anything is a bear" by **Bx**. We do the same thing with the consequent. For example, "it is a mammal" can be symbolized **Mx**. The whole sentence is then symbolized as follows:

$(x) (Bx \rightarrow Mx)$

You can read this as "For any *x*, if *x* is a bear, then *x* is a mammal."

There are many different ways in English of making such affirmative, universally quantified statements. *All, every, each, any* are just a few of the words we use to speak about all the things in a class. Sometimes we just make a generalization; for example, "Bears are four-footed" or "Bears have claws." This can be tricky because some generalizations are not really universal but are meant to be true of only some members of a class; for example, "Bears live at the North Pole." We have to try to understand what the person meant when he made the statement in order to discern whether a universal statement was being made or not.

Now we are ready to symbolize an argument involving universal quantification and derive the conclusion.

1. Every vegetable planted by Xiu Li sprouted.
2. One vegetable she planted was corn.

We symbolize (1) by letting **V** = "is a vegetable planted by Xiu Li" and **S** = "sprouted."

1. $(x) (Vx \rightarrow Sx)$

We symbolize (2) by letting *c* = "corn."

2. **Vc**

Now we replace the variable *x* in (1) with *c*.

3. $Vc \rightarrow Sc$

This has the effect of transforming (1) into a statement about one member of the class, namely, corn. It symbolizes "If corn is a vegetable planted by Xiu Li, then it sprouted." Now we simply apply our nine rules, and we get:

4. **Sc**   (MP, 2, 3)

Thus we are able to conclude validly that the corn sprouted.

Some universal statements are negative. They assert that if anything is a member of a certain group, then it does *not* have the property in question. We symbolize such a statement by negating the consequent. So, for example, we can symbolize "No goose is hairy" as

$(x) (Gx \rightarrow \neg Hx)$

This is read as "For any *x*, if *x* is a goose, then *x* is not hairy." Again, there are many ways to express a universal, negative statement in English. *No, none, noth-*

ing, no one or just negative generalizations can be used to express such statements.

Let us symbolize an argument using a universally quantified, negative premise.

1. No goose is hairy.
2. Red Goose is a goose.

We symbolize (1) and (2) as
   1. $(x) (Gx \rightarrow \neg Hx)$
   2. Gr

Then we plug in r for the variable x to get
   3. $Gr \rightarrow \neg Hr$

That allows us to infer
   4. $\neg Hr$ (MP, 2, 3)

Often we encounter arguments with more than one universally quantified premise. For example,

1. All bears have claws.
2. Anything with claws can scratch.
3. Brown Bear is a bear.

These are symbolized

   1. $(x) (Bx \rightarrow Cx)$
   2. $(x) (Cx \rightarrow Sx)$
   3. Bb

We go ahead and plug in b for the variable and then apply our rules of inference:

   4. $Bb \rightarrow Cb$
   5. $Cb \rightarrow Sb$
   6. $Bb \rightarrow Sb$ (HS, 4, 5)
   7. Sb (MP, 3, 6)

Suppose we did not have premise (3). Then we can take a shortcut and just conclude by hypothetical syllogism that $(x) (Bx \rightarrow Sx)$.

2.1.2.2
EXISTENTIAL
QUANTIFICATION Statements which are about only *some* members of a group are called **existentially quantified** statements. They tell us that there really exists at least one thing that has the property in question. For example, the statement "Some bears are white" tells us that there is at least one thing in the world that is both a bear and white. The statement "Some bears are not white" says that there is at least one thing that is a bear and is not white.

We symbolize existentially quantified statements by using the symbol ∃. It may be read as "There is at least one ___ such that . . . ." We fill in the blank with the variable x, which can be replaced by any individual thing. So if we let Bx = "x is a bear" and Wx = "x is white," we can symbolize "Some bears are white" as

   $(\exists x) (Bx \ \& \ Wx)$

This is read as "There is at least one *x* such that *x* is a bear and *x* is white." Notice that existentially quantified statements are symbolized using **&**, not **→** as universally quantified statements are. We must not confuse the two by symbolizing "Some bears are white" as

(∃x) (Bx → Wx).

We can symbolize "Some bears are not white" as

(∃x) (Bx & ¬Wx).

This is read as "There is at least one *x* such that *x* is a bear and *x* is not white."

Now immediately we see that *both* the affirmative and negative statements can be true. "Some bears are white and some bears are not white" is not a contradiction. So affirmative and negative existentially quantified statements are not contradictory. So what is the opposite of an affirmative existentially quantified statement? It would be symbolized

¬ (∃x) (Bx & Wx).

This states that there is nothing which is both a bear and white, or, in other words, that there are no white bears. So it turns out that the opposite of an affirmative existentially quantified statement is a negative universally quantified statement. So

(x) (Bx → ¬Wx) is contradictory to **(∃x) (Bx & Wx).**

Similarly, the contradictory of a negative, existentially quantified statement would symbolized

¬ (∃x) (Bx & ¬Wx).

This tells us that there is nothing which is a nonwhite bear. In other words, all bears are white. So the opposite of a negative, existentially quantified statement is an affirmative, universally quantified statement. So

(x) (Bx → Wx) is contradictory to **(∃x) (Bx & ¬Wx).**

We can construct a diagram for displaying contradictories for universally and existentially quantified statements (figure 2.1).

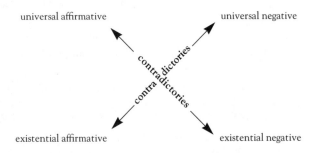

Fig. 2.1 **Contradictories for universally and existentially quantified statements**

When we symbolize an argument involving existentially quantified premises, we also plug in a letter symbolizing some individual for the variable x. But in this case we can only use a letter as a substitute for x if we have not already used that letter before to symbolize a previous premise. So if we have an argument involving both universally quantified and existentially quantified premises, we must be sure to symbolize the existentially quantified premise first, regardless of the order of the premises. (Otherwise things can get all messed up!) So, for example, suppose we have the premises

1. All bears are mammals.
2. Some bears are white.

These are symbolized as

1. $(x) (Bx \rightarrow Mx)$
2. $(\exists x) (Bx \, \& \, Wx)$.

Now to apply our rules of reasoning we plug in letters symbolizing particular individuals. First, we do the existentially quantified premise to get

3. $Ba \, \& \, Wa$.

Then we do the universally quantified premise to get

4. $Ba \rightarrow Ma$.

Now we apply our rules:

5. Ba (Simp, 3)
6. Ma (MP, 4, 5)
7. Wa (Simp, 3)
8. $Ma \, \& \, Wa$ (Conj, 6, 7)

Since at least one mammal, namely the one represented by a, is white, we can conclude that some mammals are white, or $(\exists x) (Mx \, \& \, Wx)$.

Arguments having several quantified premises can get very complicated. But realistically, with an understanding of the above rudiments of quantified logic readers will be able to handle most of the arguments they will confront without a great deal of difficulty.

2.1.3
MODAL LOGIC

One of the subdisciplines of advanced logic is **modal logic**, which deals with notions of **necessary** and **possible truth**—the modes of truth, as it were. It is evident that there are such modes of truth, since some statements just happen to be true but obviously could have been false—for example, "Garrett DeWeese teaches at Talbot School of Theology." But other statements do not just happen to be true; they must be true and could not have been false—for example, "If **P** implies **Q**, and **P** is true, then **Q** is true." Still other statements are false and could not have been true—for example, "God both exists and does not exist." Statements which could not have had a different truth value than the one they have are said to be either necessarily true or necessarily false. We can use the symbol □ to stand for the mode of necessity:

□**P** is to be read as "Necessarily, **P**" and indicates that **P** is necessarily true.

□¬**P** is to be read as "Necessarily, not-**P**" and indicates that **P** is necessarily false.

Now if **P** is necessarily false, then it could not possibly be true. Letting ◇ stand for the mode of possibility, we can see that

□¬**P** is logically equivalent to ¬◇**P**, which may be read as "Not-possibly, **P**."

This is to say that it is impossible for **P** to be true. The contradictory of ¬◇**P** is ◇**P**, or "Possibly, **P**." Now if **P** is necessarily true, it is obviously also possibly true; otherwise its truth would be impossible. So □**P** implies ◇**P**; but it precludes the truth of ◇¬**P**. Indeed, □**P** is equivalent to ¬◇¬**P**. That is to say, if **P** is necessarily true, then it is impossible that **P** be false. If, on the other hand, it is possible for **P** to be true and possible for **P** to be false, then **P** is a **contingent statement**, being either contingently true or contingently false. Thus we may construct a handy square of opposition (figure 2.2) exhibiting contradictories, contraries and subimplications.

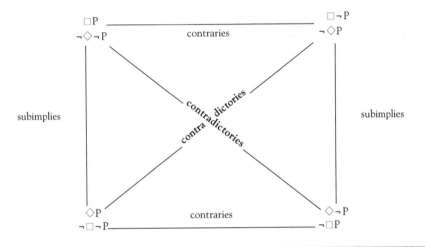

Fig. 2.2 Square of opposition for modal statements

The square shows us that "Necessarily, **P**" (symbolized either as □**P** or as ¬◇¬**P**) is contradictory to "Possibly, not-**P**" (symbolized as either ◇¬**P** or as ¬□**P**), so that if one of these statements is true, the other is false. And "Necessarily, not-**P**" (□¬**P** or ¬◇**P**) is the contradictory of "Possibly, **P**" (◇**P** or ¬□¬**P**), so that if one of these statements is true, the other is false. We also see that "Necessarily, **P**" is the contrary of "Necessarily, not-**P**," so that both these statements cannot be true, though (unlike contradictories) they could both be false (namely, if **P** is contingent and so is neither necessarily true nor necessarily false). We also see that "Possibly, **P**" and "Possibly, not-**P**" are contraries, in that they cannot both be false (for if ◇¬**P**, for example, were false, then ¬◇¬**P** would be true, which is equivalent to □**P**, which implies that ◇**P** is true, the contrary of ◇¬**P**), though they could both be true (namely, if **P** is a contingent statement). Finally, we see that if □**P** is true, then ◇**P** is also true, and if □¬**P** is true, then ◇¬**P** is true as well.

In recent years an interpretation called **possible worlds semantics** has been given to modal syntax, which vividly illustrates the key modal notions.

A **possible world** is a way the world might be. One can think of a possible world as a maximal description of reality; nothing is left out. It may be thought of as a maximal state of affairs, which includes every other state of affairs or its complement, or as an enormous conjunction composed every of statement or its contradictory. These states of affairs or statements must be compossible, that is, able to obtain together or to be true together, otherwise they would not constitute a possible world. Moreover, such a maximal state of affairs must be **actualizable** or capable of being actual. Just what that means is unclear. Some philosophers take actualizability to mean **strict logical possibility,** mere freedom from contradiction. Others demur, regarding such an understanding of actualizability as far too generous. To borrow Plantinga's example, the statement "The Prime Minister is a prime number" is strictly logically consistent, but such a state of affairs is not actualizable. Plantinga prefers to construe actualizability in terms of **broad logical possibility**, a notion that he leaves undefined but merely illustrates. The situation is further complicated by the hypothesis of theism, for if God's existence is necessary then some worlds which seem intuitively to be broadly logically possible may not be actualizable after all because God, necessarily, would not actualize them. For example, a world in which human beings all freely reject God's plan of salvation and fail to reach heaven seems to be broadly logically possible, but it may not be actualizable because God is essentially too good to actualize such a world. Such problems have led some thinkers to differentiate between broadly logical possibility and **metaphysical possibility**, or actualizability. In any case, these debates make clear that possible worlds semantics do not explain or ground our modal notions, but at best illustrate them.

In possible worlds semantics necessary truth is interpreted in terms of truth in every possible world. To say that a statement **P** is true in a possible world **W** is to say that if **W** were actual, then **P** would be true. So a *necessary truth* is one that is true regardless which possible world is actual. *Possible truth* is construed as truth in at least one possible world. *Necessary falsehood* is understood as truth in no possible world or, in other words, a statement's being false in every possible world. *Possible falsehood* is a statement's being false in at least one possible world. A statement that is true in some worlds and false in others is contingently true or false.

Care must be taken in dealing with modal statements because it is sometimes ambiguous whether the necessity at issue is *de dicto* or *de re*. **Necessity de dicto** is the necessity attributed to a statement (a *dictum*) that is true in all possible worlds. **Necessity de re** is the necessity of a thing's (a *res*) possessing a certain property, or in other words, a thing's having a property essentially. If something has a property essentially, then it has it in every possible world in which it is true that this thing exists, even if this thing does not exist in every possible world. So, for example, when it is said, "Necessarily, Socrates is a human being," it is not meant that the statement "Socrates is a human being" is true in every possible world, for Socrates does not exist in every possible world. Rather, what is meant is that Socrates is essentially human. Sometimes the ambiguity is compounded. For example, "Necessarily, God is good" could be taken to assert either that the statement "God is good" is true in every possible world or that God is essentially good (even if there are possible worlds in which he does not exist) or both.

All of the rules of inference which we learned in our section on sentential logic have their modal counterparts. For example, Modal *modus ponens* is a valid inference form:

1. $\Box(P \rightarrow Q)$
2. $\Box P$

___

3. $\Box Q$

Thus one need not learn a whole new set of rules.

The rub comes, however, in arguments having a mixture of modal and non-modal premises. Here mistakes are easy, and we wish to alert the reader to a couple of the most frequent modal fallacies to beware of. As we shall later see (chap. 26), extremely important metaphysical and theological conclusions have been drawn on the basis of these seductive fallacies. One common fallacy is the following inference:

1. $\Box(P \lor \neg P)$

___

2. $\Box P \lor \Box \neg P$

This inference pattern underlies many arguments for fatalism. For example, it is thought, "Necessarily, either I shall be killed in the bombing or I shall not be killed in the bombing. But then why take precautions, since nothing I do can make a difference?" The fatalist fallaciously assumes that his being necessarily killed or his necessarily not being killed follows from the composite necessity of his being killed or not. Medieval philosophers were aware of this fallacy and labeled it a confusion of **necessity in sensu composito** (in the composite sense) and **necessity in sensu diviso** (in the divided sense).

A similar confusion of composite (or undistributed) and divided (or distributed) necessity is involved in the fallacious inference:

1. $\Box(P \lor Q)$
2. $\neg Q$

___

3. $\Box P$

Someone might fallaciously reason as follows: "Necessarily, either God has willed that *x* will happen, or else *x* will not happen. But *x* did happen. Therefore, necessarily God has willed that *x* happen." It does not follow, however, that *necessarily* God has willed that *x* happen, but merely that God *has* willed that *x* happen. For from (1) and (2) it follows only that **P** is true, not that it is necessarily true.

Finally, a very common modal fallacy involves *modus ponens*:

1. $\Box(P \rightarrow Q)$
2. P

___

3. $\Box Q$

This fallacy is involved in reasoning such as the following: "Necessarily, if Christ predicted Judas's betrayal, then Judas would betray Jesus. Christ did, in fact, predict Judas's betrayal. Therefore, it was necessary that Judas betray Jesus—which obliterates Judas's freedom." But again, from (1) and (2) it only follows that Judas would betray Jesus, not that he would do so necessarily. Thus the necessity of Christ's predictions being accurate and his prediction of Judas's betrayal do not necessitate Judas's betrayal. Medieval philosophers also spotted this fallacy and labeled it confusing the *necessitas consequentiae* (necessity of the consequences or the inference) with the *necessitas consequentis* (necessity of the consequent). That is to say, the inference of Q from the premises $\Box(P \to Q)$ and P is necessary in accordance with *modus ponens*; but Q itself, the consequent of the conditional $\Box(P \to Q)$ is not itself necessary.

A wary eye for these modal fallacies will greatly assist the reader in thinking accurately about various philosophical problems.

2.1.4 COUNTERFACTUAL LOGIC

Counterfactuals are conditional statements in the subjunctive mood, and they have a logic of their own. Such conditionals are interestingly different from their indicative counterparts. Compare, for example,

1. If Oswald didn't shoot Kennedy, then somebody else did.
2. If Oswald hadn't shot Kennedy, then somebody else would have.

The indicative conditional (1) is evidently true in light of Kennedy's death. But the counterfactual conditional (2) is by no means true; on the contrary it seems very likely that if Oswald had not shot the president, then Kennedy's motorcade would have proceeded uneventfully. Counterfactuals are so called because the antecedent and consequent of the conditional are contrary to fact. But not all **subjunctive conditionals** are strictly counterfactual. In **deliberative conditionals**, for example, we entertain some antecedent with a view toward discerning its consequences, as a result of which we may take the course of action described in the antecedent, so that the consequent becomes true. For instance, as a result of thinking "If I were to quit smoking, then my breath would smell better," one decides to quit smoking and his breath improves. Nonetheless, the term *counterfactuals* is widely used to cover all subjunctive conditionals.

Counterfactuals come in two sorts: **"would" counterfactuals** and **"might" counterfactuals**. The former state what would happen if the antecedent were true, while the latter state what might happen if the antecedent were true. The sentential connective symbol often used for "would" counterfactuals is $\Box\!\to$. A "would" counterfactual is symbolized

$$P \Box\!\to Q,$$

where P and Q are indicative sentences, and is read "If it were the case that P, then it would be the case that Q." Similarly, a "might" counterfactual is symbolized

$$P \Diamond\!\to Q,$$

and is read, "If it were the case that **P**, then it might be the case that **Q**." "Might" counterfactuals should not be confused with subjunctive conditionals involving the word "could." "Could" is taken to express mere possibility and so is a constituent of a modal statement expressing a possible truth. The distinction is important because the fact that something could happen under certain circumstances does not imply that it might happen under those circumstances. "Might" is more restrictive than "could" and indicates a genuine, live option under the circumstances, not a bare logical possibility. In counterfactual logic $\mathbf{P} \diamond\!\!\rightarrow \mathbf{Q}$ is simply defined as the contradictory of $\mathbf{P} \square\!\!\rightarrow \neg\mathbf{Q}$, that is to say, as $\neg (\mathbf{P} \square\!\!\rightarrow \neg\mathbf{Q})$. Thus, although $\mathbf{P} \square\!\!\rightarrow \neg\mathbf{Q}$ is logically incompatible with $\mathbf{P} \diamond\!\!\rightarrow \mathbf{Q}$, it remains true that if $\mathbf{P}$ were the case it still *could* be the case that $\mathbf{Q}$. We can also construct a square of opposition for counterfactual statements (see figure 2.3).

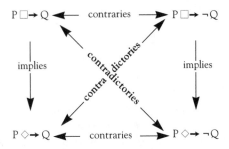

Fig. 2.3 **Square of opposition for counterfactual statements**

There is no really satisfactory semantics for counterfactual conditionals. But for want of a better alternative, most philosophers use the Stalnaker-Lewis semantics. Since counterfactuals are contingent statements (necessary counterfactuals reduce to indicative conditionals), they are true or false relative to a possible world. For convenience, we shall take the actual world as our departure point. One then ranges other possible worlds into concentric spheres of worlds centered on our world on the basis of a similarity relation to the actual world, the most similar worlds being in the nearest sphere. Now we consider the worlds in the nearest sphere in which the antecedent of our counterfactual is true. If in all of the worlds in which the antecedent is true, the consequent is also true, then a "would" counterfactual $\mathbf{P} \square\!\!\rightarrow \mathbf{Q}$ is true. If in some of the worlds in which the antecedent is true, the consequent is also true, then a "might" counterfactual $\mathbf{P} \diamond\!\!\rightarrow \mathbf{Q}$ is true.

Such a semantics is inadequate, among other reasons, because it cannot deal with counterfactuals having impossible antecedents (sometimes called **counterpossibles**). Since impossible statements are not true in any possible world, no sphere of worlds, no matter how distant, will contain worlds in which the antecedent is true. But then such counterfactuals all become trivially true because in all the worlds in the nearest sphere in which the antecedent is true the consequent is also true; that is, there is no sphere of antecedent-permitting worlds in which the consequent fails to be true. But such a result is highly counterintuitive. For consider the two conditionals

1. If God did not exist, the universe would not exist.

2. If God did not exist, the universe would still exist.

If God exists necessarily, then the antecedent of (1) and (2) is impossible. But in that case on the customary semantics both (1) and (2) are trivially true. But surely that is not correct. (1) seems to be the sober truth about the world, and (2) seems patently false. Therefore, the customary semantics is not adequate. For want of a better alternative, we may continue to employ the usual semantics, but one should take with a grain of salt philosophical objections to a metaphysical position that are based on the customary semantics for counterfactual conditionals.

Counterfactual logic is peculiar in that certain rules of inference do not apply to it that apply to sentential logic. For example, although our beloved *modus ponens* and *modus tollens* hold for counterfactual conditionals, hypothetical syllogism does not. It is invalid to argue:

1. $P \mathbin{\square\!\!\rightarrow} Q$
2. $Q \mathbin{\square\!\!\rightarrow} R$

---

3. $P \mathbin{\square\!\!\rightarrow} R$

Thus it would be fallacious to reason, "If Billy Graham had married another woman, he would be having sex with someone other than Ruth. If Billy Graham were having sex with someone other than Ruth, he would be an adulterer. Therefore, if Billy Graham had married another woman, he would be an adulterer." Both of the first two statements are true, but the conclusion clearly does not follow from them.

In sentential logic $P \rightarrow Q$ is equivalent to $\neg Q \rightarrow \neg P$. But in counterfactual logic, this equivalence fails. It is invalid to argue as follows:

1. $P \mathbin{\square\!\!\rightarrow} Q$

---

2. $\neg Q \mathbin{\square\!\!\rightarrow} \neg P$

For example, it would be fallacious to think, "If Bonds had homered, the Giants would still have lost. Therefore, if the Giants had won, then Bonds would still not have homered."

Finally, there is a fallacy in counterfactual logic called "strengthening the antecedent":

1. $P \mathbin{\square\!\!\rightarrow} Q$

---

2. $P \mathbin{\&} R \mathbin{\square\!\!\rightarrow} Q$

Thus it would be fallacious to argue as follows: "If I were to quit smoking, my breath would smell better. Therefore, if I were to quit smoking and start eating raw garlic, my breath would smell better."

On the other hand, there are some argument forms that are valid in counterfactual logic that are particularly useful in cases in which hypothetical syllogism cannot be used. For example, it is valid to argue

1. $P \mathbin{\square\!\!\rightarrow} Q$

2. P & Q □→ R

---

3. P □→ R

Plantinga has employed this argument form in dealing with a theistic version of a problem in decision theory called Newcomb's paradox.[1] You are presented with two boxes A and B and are given the choice of having the contents of either both boxes or of just A alone. Here's the catch: You know there is $1,000 in box B. If you choose only box A, then God will have foreknown your choice and put $1,000,000 in A. But if you're greedy and pick both boxes, then God will have foreknown this and so put nothing in box A. The money already is or is not in A. What should you choose? Plantinga argues that you should choose only box A on the basis of the following reasoning:

1. If you were to choose both boxes, God would have believed that you would choose both boxes.
2. If you were to choose both boxes and God believed that you would choose both boxes, then God would not have put any money in A.

---

3. Therefore, if you were to choose both boxes, God would not have put any money in A.

(A parallel argument shows that if you were to choose A alone, then God would have put the $1,000,000 in A. So the one-box choice is the winning strategy.) This reasoning has important application to the problem of divine foreknowledge and human freedom.

Another valid inference form is

1. P □→ Q
2. Q □→ P
3. Q □→ R

---

4. P □→ R

Thomas Flint has employed this inference pattern profitably in his work on divine providence.[2] He reasons as follows:

1. If Paul were to mow the lawn next Saturday, then God would have foreknown that Paul would mow the lawn next Saturday.
2. If God were to have foreknown that Paul would mow the lawn next Saturday, then Paul would mow the lawn next Saturday.
3. If God were to have foreknown that Paul would mow the lawn next Saturday, then God would prevent it from raining.

---

4. If Paul were to mow the lawn next Saturday, then God would prevent it from raining.

[1]Alvin Plantinga, "On Ockham's Way Out," *Faith and Philosophy* 3 (1986): 256.

[2]Thomas Flint, *Divine Providence*, Cornell Studies in the Philosophy of Religion (Ithaca, N.Y.: Cornell University Press, 1998), p. 236.

Such reasoning plays a vital role in a Molinist account of divine providence (chap. 28).

A final valid inference pattern of note blends counterfactual and modal premises:

1. $P \,\square\!\!\rightarrow Q$
2. $\square(Q \rightarrow R)$

___

3. $P \,\square\!\!\rightarrow R$

Again, Flint employs this argument form gainfully in his discussions of divine providence. He reasons:

1. If Paul were to mow the lawn next Saturday, then God would prevent it from raining.
2. Necessarily, if God prevents it from raining, then it will not rain next Saturday.

___

3. Therefore, if Paul were to mow the lawn next Saturday, then it would not rain next Saturday.

It should be noted, however, that philosophers who believe that there are nontrivially true counterpossibles (counterfactuals with impossible antecedents) reject this inference pattern. For if this inference pattern is valid, then one can show that $\square(P \rightarrow Q)$ implies that $P \,\square\!\!\rightarrow Q$.[3] But this implication does not always hold if there are nontrivially true counterpossibles. The key to understanding here is to realize that if P is an impossible (necessarily false) statement, then P necessarily implies anything and everything. So if P is an impossible statement, then it is true that $\square(P \rightarrow Q)$, no matter what Q represents. So, for example, it is true both that "Necessarily, if God does not exist, the universe does not exist" and "Necessarily, if God does not exist, the universe exists anyway." But if there are nontrivially true counterpossibles, it does not follow from the truth of "Necessarily, if God does not exist, the universe exists anyway" that "If God were not to exist, then the universe would exist anyway." Thus, if there are nontrivially true counterpossibles, then it is not the case that $\square(P \rightarrow Q)$ implies that $P \,\square\!\!\rightarrow Q$. But if that implication fails, then the transitive inference pattern that entails this implication also fails. Still, with ordinary counterfactuals at least, the inference pattern is unobjectionable. These three argument forms may help one to make a transitive argument without appeal to the invalid hypothetical syllogism.

We have only scratched the surface of the field of logic, but our goal has not

___

[3]We first assume the obviously true premise:

1. $P \,\square\!\!\rightarrow P$

Then, using (1), we write out the inference pattern as one premise:

2. $[(P \,\square\!\!\rightarrow P) \,\&\, \square(P \rightarrow Q)] \rightarrow (P \,\square\!\!\rightarrow Q)$

Then using conditional proof, we can reason as follows:

3. $\quad\quad \square(P \rightarrow Q)$ (Conditional Premise)
4. $\quad\quad (P \,\square\!\!\rightarrow P) \,\&\, \square(P \rightarrow Q)$ (Conj, 1, 3)
5. $\quad\quad P \,\square\!\!\rightarrow Q$ (MP, 2, 4)
6. $\square(P \rightarrow Q) \rightarrow (P \,\square\!\!\rightarrow Q)$ (CP, 3-5)

been to survey the field, even superficially, but rather to provide readers with a basic grasp of a few rules of inference to assist them in assessing arguments they encounter and in formulating good arguments of their own.

A good deductive argument, it will be recalled, must be not only formally valid but also informally valid. In practice, the primary **informal fallacy** to be on the alert for is the fallacy called *petitio principii* (begging the question). Sometimes this fallacy is also called circular reasoning. If one reasons in a circle, the conclusion of one's argument is taken as one of the premises somewhere in the argument. Although this does happen, it is very unlikely that any sophisticated thinker will beg the question in so blatant a fashion as that. Rather, question-begging usually occurs in a more subtle way. We can say that a person begs the question if his only reason for thinking a premise in an argument to be true is his belief that the conclusion is true. Consider the following argument for God's existence:

1. Either God exists or the moon is made of green cheese.
2. The moon is not made of green cheese.
3. Therefore, God exists.

This is a logically valid argument, having the inference form of disjunctive syllogism ($\mathbf{P} \vee \mathbf{Q}$; $\neg\mathbf{Q}$; therefore, $\mathbf{P}$). Moreover, theists will regard the premises as true (recall that for $\mathbf{P} \vee \mathbf{Q}$ to be true, only one disjunct needs to be true). Therefore, the above is a sound argument for God's existence. But such an argument will hardly rival one of Thomas Aquinas's five ways of proving God's existence! The reason for the argument's failure is that it is question-begging: the only reason one would have for thinking that (1) is true is that one already believes that (3) is true. Thus, far from serving as a proof that God exists, the argument will be regarded as unsound or unconvincing by any person who is not already convinced that God exists. This subtle form of question-begging does go on and needs to be exposed.

There are many other informal fallacies in argumentation; but despite their high profile in texts on critical thinking, realistically one is not apt to encounter these often in serious philosophical work. Still, a couple are worth mentioning:

Genetic Fallacy. This is the fallacy of arguing that a belief is mistaken or false because of the way that belief originated. Some sociobiologists, for example, seem to commit this fallacy when they assert that because moral beliefs are shaped by biological and social influences, therefore those beliefs are not objectively true. Or again, some atheists still try to invalidate theistic belief on the basis that it originated out of fear or ignorance. How or why a belief came to be held is simply irrelevant to the truth or falsity of the proposition that is the object of that belief.

Argument from Ignorance. This is the fallacy of arguing that a claim is false because there is not sufficient evidence that the claim is true. Our ignorance of evidence for a claim's truth does not imply the falsity of the claim.

Equivocation. This is the fallacy of using a word in such a way as to have two meanings. This fallacy is committed in the following argument: "Socrates is a Greek; Greek is a language; therefore, Socrates is a language." The danger of equivocation should motivate us to define the terms in our arguments as clearly as possible. By offering careful definitions and using words univocally, we can blunt charges that we have committed this fallacy.

Amphiboly. This is the fallacy of formulating our premises in such a way that their meaning is ambiguous. For example, the statement "If God wills *x*, then necessarily *x* will happen" is amphibolous. Do we mean "□(God wills *x* → *x* will happen)" or "God wills *x* → □(*x* will happen)"? Again, in order to avoid the errors in reasoning that will result from ambiguous formulation of premises, we need to take great care in expressing them. One of the major tasks of philosophical analysis is not only careful definition of terms, but differentiating the different meanings a premise in an argument might have and then assessing respectively their plausibility.

Composition. This is the fallacy of inferring that a whole has a certain property because all its parts have that property. Of course, sometimes wholes do have the properties of their parts, but it is fallacious to infer that a whole has a property just because its every part does. This fallacy seems to be committed by those who argue that because every part of an infinite past can be "traversed" to reach the present, therefore the whole infinite past can be traversed.

There are scores of such informal fallacies, but the above are some of the more common ones to look out for and avoid.

| 2.2 TRUE PREMISES | Little needs to be said by way of clarification of this criterion of a good deductive argument. Logical validity is a necessary condition of a cogent argument, but not a sufficient condition. In order for an argument to be sound, it must not only be valid but its premises must also be true. The main point to keep in mind here is that one must not confuse the epistemic status of the premises (their knowability) with their alethic status, or truth value. In order to be sound, an argument's premises must be true, but their truth could be not merely uncertain but utterly unknown to us. Of course, if we are utterly ignorant of the premises' truth, the argument will be of little use to us, even if it be, unknown to us, sound. But if we are warranted in believing the premises to be true, then the argument warrants us in accepting the conclusion. |

2.2 TRUE PREMISES

Little needs to be said by way of clarification of this criterion of a good deductive argument. Logical validity is a necessary condition of a cogent argument, but not a sufficient condition. In order for an argument to be sound, it must not only be valid but its premises must also be true. The main point to keep in mind here is that one must not confuse the epistemic status of the premises (their knowability) with their alethic status, or truth value. In order to be sound, an argument's premises must be true, but their truth could be not merely uncertain but utterly unknown to us. Of course, if we are utterly ignorant of the premises' truth, the argument will be of little use to us, even if it be, unknown to us, sound. But if we are warranted in believing the premises to be true, then the argument warrants us in accepting the conclusion.

2.3 PREMISES MORE PLAUSIBLE THAN THEIR DENIALS

An argument may be sound and informally valid and yet not a good argument. In order for the argument to be a good one, the premises need to have a particular epistemic status for us. But what sort of status is that? Certainty is an unrealistic and unattainable ideal. Were we to require certainty of the truth of an argument's premises, the result for us would be skepticism. Plausibility or epistemic probability might be thought to be sufficient, but plausibility seems to be neither a necessary nor a sufficient condition of a good argument. It is not necessary because in some cases both the premise and its denial (or contradictory) may strike us as implausible. One thinks of premises concerning the nature of the subatomic realm as described by quantum physics, for example. On the other hand, neither is plausibility sufficient because both the premise and its denial may have equal plausibility or the denial may have even more plausibility than a quite plausible premise. This suggests that what we are looking for is a comparative criterion: the premises in a good argument will have greater plausibility than their respective denials.

Now plausibility is to a great extent a person-dependent notion. Some people may find a premise plausible and others not. Accordingly, some people will agree that a particular argument is a good one, while others will say that it is a bad argument. Given our diverse backgrounds and biases, we should expect such disagreements. Obviously, the most persuasive arguments will be those that are based on premises which enjoy the support of widely accepted evidence or seem intuitively to be true. But in cases of disagreement we simply have to dig deeper and ask what reasons we each have for thinking a premise to be true or false. When we do so, we may discover that it is we who have made the mistake. After all, one can present bad arguments for a true conclusion! But we might find instead that our interlocutor has no good reason for rejecting our premise or that his rejection is based on misinformation, or ignorance of the evidence, or a fallacious objection. In such a case we may persuade him by giving him better information or evidence or by gently correcting his error. Or we may find that the reason he denies our premise is that he does not like the conclusion it is leading to, and so to avoid that conclusion he denies a premise which he really ought to find quite plausible. Ironically, it is thus possible, as Plantinga has observed, to move someone from knowledge to ignorance by presenting him with a valid argument based on premises he knows to be true!

3 INDUCTIVE REASONING

Up to this point we have focused only on deductive reasoning. In a sound deductive argument the conclusion follows necessarily from the premises: if the premises are true and the inference form valid, then it is impossible that the conclusion be false. It is worth observing that an argument's having a deductive form is irrelevant to the epistemic status of the premises and conclusion. The difference between a deductive and an inductive argument is not to be found in the degree to which they approach demonstrative proof of some conclusion. A good deductive argument may make a conclusion only slightly epistemically probable if its premises are themselves far from certain, whereas an inductive argument could give us overwhelming evidence for and, hence, confidence in its conclusion. This fact is especially evident when we reflect that some of the premises in a deductive argument may themselves be established on the basis of inductive evidence. Thus, contrary to the impression sometimes given, an argument's being inductive or deductive in form is not an indication of the certainty of the argument's conclusion.

An inductive argument is one for which it is possible that the premises be true and no invalid inferences be made, and yet the conclusion still be false. A good inductive argument must, like a good deductive argument, have true premises which are more plausible than their contradictories and be informally valid. But because the truth of their premises does not guarantee the truth of their conclusions, one cannot properly speak of their being formally either valid or invalid. In such reasoning the evidence and rules of inference are said to "underdetermine" the conclusion; that is to say, they render the conclusion plausible or likely, but do not guarantee its truth. Here is an example of a good inductive argument:

1. Groups A, B and C were composed of similar persons suffering from the same disease.

2. Group A was administered a certain new drug, group B was administered a placebo, and group C was not given any treatment.
3. The rate of death from the disease was subsequently lower in group A by 75% in comparison with both groups B and C.
4. Therefore, the new drug is effective in reducing the death rate from said disease.

The conclusion is quite likely true based on the evidence and rules of inductive reasoning, but it is not inevitably true; maybe the people in group A were just lucky or some unknown variable caused their improvement.

3.1
BAYES'S
THEOREM
Although inductive reasoning is part and parcel of everyday life, the description of such reasoning is a matter of controversy among philosophers. One way of understanding inductive reasoning is by means of the **probability calculus**. Probability theorists have formulated various rules for accurately calculating the probability of particular statements or events given the truth or occurrence of certain other statements or events. Such probabilities are called **conditional probabilities** and are symbolized Pr (A/B). This is to be read as the probability of A on B, or A given B, where A and B stand for particular statements or events. Probabilities range between 0 and 1, with 1 representing the highest and 0 the lowest probability. Thus a value >.5 indicates some positive probability of a statement or event and <.5 some improbability, while .5 would indicate a precise balance between the two.

Many of the typical cases of inductive reasoning involve inferences from sample cases to generalizations—for example, the probability of Jones's contracting lung cancer given that he is a smoker—and so have greater relevance to scientific than to philosophical concerns. Still a philosophical position can constitute a hypothesis, and that hypothesis can be argued to be more probable than not, or more probable than a particular competing philosophical hypothesis, given various other facts taken as one's evidence. In such cases, the philosopher may have recourse to **Bayes's theorem**, which lays down formulas for calculating the probability of a hypothesis (H) on given evidence (E).

One form of Bayes's theorem is the following:

$$\text{Pr (H/E)} = \frac{\text{Pr (H)} \times \text{Pr (E/H)}}{\text{Pr (H)} \times \text{Pr (E/H)} + \text{Pr (}\neg\text{H)} \times \text{Pr (E/}\neg\text{H)}}$$

In order to compute the probability of H/E, we plug in numerical values for the various probabilities in the numerator and denominator. In philosophical, as opposed to scientific, discussions this is usually impossible to do with precision, so we must be content with vague approximations like "highly improbable" (which is represented as <<.5) or "highly probable" (which is represented as >>.5) or "approximately even" (which is represented as ≈.5). Such vague approximations may still prove useful in arguing for one's hypothesis.

In the numerator we multiply the intrinsic probability of H by H's explanatory power (E/H). The intrinsic probability of H does not mean the probability of H taken in utter isolation, but merely in isolation from the specific evidence E. The intrinsic probability of H is the conditional probability of H relative to our general background knowledge (B), or Pr (H/B). Similarly, B is implicit in H's explanatory power (E/H & B). The formula takes B tacitly as assumed. The Pr (E/H) registers our rational expectation of E given that H is the case. If E would be surprising on H, then Pr(E/H) <.5, whereas if we are not surprised to find E, given H, then Pr (E/H) is >.5.

In the denominator of the formula, we take the product of H's intrinsic probability and explanatory power and add to it the product of the intrinsic probability and explanatory power of the denial of H. Notice that the smaller this latter product is, the better it is for one's hypothesis. For in the limit case that Pr ($\neg$H) × Pr (E/$\neg$H) is zero, then the numerator and denominator have the same number, so that the ratio is equal to 1, which means that one's hypothesis is certain given the evidence. So one will want to argue that while one's hypothesis has great intrinsic probability and explanatory power, the denial of the hypothesis has low intrinsic probability and explanatory power.

One of the difficulties in using the above form of Bayes's theorem in arguing inductively is that the negation of one's hypothesis comprises such a diversity of alternatives that it may be difficult to show that H is more probable than not. For example, if H is the theistic hypothesis that God exists, then $\neg$H is not simply naturalism, but also pantheism, polytheism, panentheism, idealism and the host of their variants. A specific body of evidence E may make theism more probable than, say, naturalism, but not more probable than polytheism. It may be not only very difficult to calculate the probability of $\neg$H, but it may also be rather beside the point. One's interest may be, not to show that H is more probable than not relative to a specific body of evidence, but that H is more probable than its chief competitor H_1.

If that is our interest, then we can employ the odds form of Bayes's theorem to calculate the comparative probability of two competing hypotheses H_1 and H_2:

$$\frac{Pr(H_1/E)}{Pr(H_2/E)} = \frac{Pr(H_1)}{Pr(H_2)} \times \frac{Pr(E/H_1)}{Pr(E/H_2)}$$

Here one's goal is to show that H_1's intrinsic probability and explanatory power exceed that of H_2, so that H_1 is the more probable hypothesis.

The drawback of all such appeals to Bayes's theorem in understanding inductive reasoning is that the probabilities can seem inscrutable and thus the conditional probability of one's hypothesis incalculable. Nonetheless, Bayesian approaches to the so-called problem of evil (see chap. 5) have been fashionable in recent years and merit consideration.

A different approach to inductive reasoning that is apt to be more useful in philosophical discussions is provided by **inference to the best explanation**. In inference to the best explanation, we are confronted with certain data to be explained. We then assemble a pool of live options consisting of various explanations for the data in question. From the pool of live options we then select the explanation that, if true, best explains the data. Just what criteria go toward making an explanation the best is disputed; but among the commonly acknowledged criteria will be properties such as the following:

1. *Explanatory scope.* The best hypothesis will explain a wider range of data than will rival hypotheses.

2. *Explanatory power.* The best hypothesis will make the observable data more epistemically probable than rival hypotheses.

3. *Plausibility.* The best hypothesis will be implied by a greater variety of accepted truths and its negation implied by fewer accepted truths than rival hypotheses.

4. *Less ad hoc.* The best hypothesis will involve fewer new suppositions not already implied by existing knowledge than rival hypotheses.

5. *Accord with accepted beliefs.* The best hypothesis, when conjoined with accepted truths, will imply fewer falsehoods than rival hypotheses.

6. *Comparative superiority:* The best hypothesis will so exceed its rivals in meeting conditions (1) through (5) that there is little chance of a rival hypothesis's exceeding it in fulfilling those conditions.

The neo-Darwinian theory of biological evolution is a good example of inference to the best explanation. Darwinists recognize that the theory represents a huge extrapolation from the data, which support micro-evolutionary change but do not provide evidence of macro-evolutionary development. They further freely admit that none of the evidence, taken in isolation, whether it be from microbiology, paleogeography, paleontology and so forth provides proof of the theory. But their point is that the theory is nonetheless the best explanation, in virtue of its explanatory power, scope and so on.

By contrast, the charge leveled by critics of the neo-Darwinian synthesis like Phillip Johnson that the theory presupposes naturalism is best understood as the claim that the explanatory superiority of the neo-Darwinian theory is a function of the pool of live options' being restricted by an unjustified methodological constraint, namely, the philosophical presupposition of naturalism. Johnson is quite happy to agree that the neo-Darwinian synthesis is the best naturalistic explanation available (in contrast to Lamarckianism, self-organization theories and so on). But he insists that the interesting and important question is not whether the neo-Darwinian theory is the best naturalistic explanation, but whether it is the best explanation, that is to say, whether it is correct. Johnson argues that once hypotheses positing Intelligent Design are allowed into the pool of live options, then the explanatory superiority of the neo-Darwinian theory is no longer apparent. On the contrary, its deficiencies, particularly in the explanatory power of its mechanisms of random mutation and natural selection, stand in stark relief. What is intriguing is that several of Johnson's detractors have openly admitted that Darwinism's explanatory superiority depends on limiting the pool of live options to naturalistic hypotheses, but they claim that such a constraint is a necessary condition of doing science—a claim which is not, as such, scientific, but is a philosophical claim about the nature of science (see chap. 17). In any case, this controversy serves as a vivid illustration of inference to the best explanation, and many misdirected criticisms are launched from both sides due to a failure to understand this pattern of inductive reasoning.

CHAPTER SUMMARY

A good deductive argument is formally and informally valid, has true premises and has premises that are more plausible than their denials. Several rules of inference of sentential logic should be kept in mind:

Rule #1: *modus ponens*

1. P → Q
2. P

_____

3. Q

Rule #2: *modus tollens*

1. P → Q
2. ¬Q

_____

3. ¬P

Rule #3: Hypothetical Syllogism

1. P → Q
2. Q → R

_____

3. P → R

Rule #4: Conjunction

1. P
2. Q

_____

3. P & Q

Rule #5: Simplification

1. P & Q	1. P & Q
2. P	2. Q

Rule #6: Absorption

1. $P \rightarrow Q$

---

2. $P \rightarrow (P \mathbin{\&} Q)$

Rule #7: Addition

1. P

---

2. $P \vee Q$

Rule #8: Disjunctive Syllogism

1. $P \vee Q$	1. $P \vee Q$
2. $\neg P$	2. $\neg Q$
---	---
3. Q	3. P

Rule #9: Constructive Dilemma

1. $(P \rightarrow Q) \mathbin{\&} (R \rightarrow S)$
2. $P \vee R$

---

3. $Q \vee S$

In addition to the nine rules of inference, there are a number of logical equivalences which should be mastered.

P	is equivalent to	$\neg\,\neg P$
$P \vee P$	is equivalent to	P
$P \rightarrow Q$	is equivalent to	$\neg P \vee Q$
$P \rightarrow Q$	is equivalent to	$\neg Q \rightarrow \neg P$

We can convert a conjunction to a disjunction and vice versa by the following procedure:

Step 1. Put $\neg$ in front of each letter.
Step 2. Change the $\&$ to $\vee$ (or the $\vee$ to $\&$).
Step 3. Put the whole thing in parentheses and put $\neg$ in front.

In predicate logic we deal with classes of things. Universally quantified statements are understood to have the logical form of conditional statements. Letting **F** and **G** stand for arbitrary predicates, we can symbolized an affirmative, universally quantified statement as $(x)\ (Fx \rightarrow Gx)$. A negative, universally quantified statement may be symbolized as $(x)\ (Fx \rightarrow \neg Gx)$. Existentially quantified statements typically have the form of conjunctions. An affirmative, existentially quantified statement can be symbolized as $(\exists x)\ (Bx \mathbin{\&} Wx)$. A negative, existentially quantified statement may be symbolized as $(\exists x)\ (Bx \mathbin{\&} \neg Wx)$. We plug in some individual for the variable x and then apply our nine rules of inference to draw deductions.

Modal logic is a branch of advanced logic dealing with possible and necessary truth. In possible worlds semantics necessary truth is interpreted as truth in all possible worlds, and possible truth as truth in some possible world. We need to keep clear the distinction between necessity *de dicto*, which is the necessity attributed to a statement that is true (or false) in all possible worlds, and necessity *de re,* which is the necessity of a thing's possessing a certain property, or a thing's having a property essentially. We must take care to avoid the following fallacies in modal reasoning:

1. $\Box(P \lor \neg P)$

---

2. $\Box P \lor \Box \neg P$

1. $\Box(P \lor Q)$
2. $\neg Q$

---

3. $\Box P$

1. $\Box(P \rightarrow Q)$
2. P

---

3. $\Box Q$

Counterfactual logic deals with inferences involving subjunctive conditionals, either of the "would" variety or of the "might" variety. In counterfactual logic, hypothetical syllogism, the equivalence known as contraposition, and strengthening the antecedent are all invalid. But several other interesting inference forms are valid, namely:

1. $P \Box\!\!\rightarrow Q$
2. $P \,\&\, Q \Box\!\!\rightarrow R$

---

3. $P \Box\!\!\rightarrow R$

1. $P \Box\!\!\rightarrow Q$
2. $Q \Box\!\!\rightarrow P$
3. $Q \Box\!\!\rightarrow R$

---

4. $P \Box\!\!\rightarrow R$

1. $P \Box\!\!\rightarrow Q$
2. $\Box(Q \rightarrow R)$

---

3. $P \Box\!\!\rightarrow R$

Some of the most common informal fallacies are begging the question (having no reason for accepting a premise other than one's belief in the argument's conclusion), genetic fallacy (arguing that a belief is mistaken or false because of the way that belief originated), argument from ignorance (arguing that a claim is false because there is not sufficient evidence that the claim is true), equivocation (using a word in such a way as to have two meanings), amphiboly (formulating our premises in such a way that their meaning is ambiguous) and composition (inferring that a whole has a certain property because all its parts have that property).

A good deductive argument must have true premises but need not have premises that are known with certainty to be true. Rather, in a good argument the premises are more plausible than their denials.

Good inductive arguments must also have true premises that are more plausible than their contradictories and be informally valid. But because the truth of their premises does not guarantee the truth of their conclusions, one cannot speak of validity with respect to them. Arguments involving probability calculations should be assessed according to Bayes's theorem, one form of which is the following:

$$Pr\,(H/E) = \frac{Pr\,(H) \times Pr\,(E/H)}{Pr\,(H) \times Pr\,(E/H) + Pr\,(\neg H) \times Pr\,(E/\neg H)}$$

The odds form of the theorem can be used to assess two rival hypotheses:

$$\frac{Pr\,(H_1/E)}{Pr\,(H_2/E)} = \frac{Pr\,(H_1)}{Pr\,(H_2)} \times \frac{Pr\,(E/H_1)}{Pr\,(E/H_2)}$$

We may also think of inductive reasoning as inference to the best explanation. In such an inference we choose from a pool of live options the explanation that, if true, would best explain the facts at hand. We assess which explanation is the best in terms of such criteria as explanatory scope, explanatory power, plausibility, degree to which it is ad hoc, accord with accepted beliefs and comparative superiority vis-à-vis its rivals.

CHECKLIST OF BASIC TERMS AND CONCEPTS
actualizable
arguments
Bayes's theorem
broad logical possibility
conclusion
conditional probability
conditional proof
contingent statement
contradictory
counterfactual

counterpossibles
deductive argument
deliberative conditional
epistemically possible
existentially quantified statement
formally valid
inductive argument
inference to the best explanation
informal fallacy
invalid
logic
metaphysical possibility
"might" counterfactual
modal logic
necessary truth
necessitas consequentiae
necessitas consequentis
necessity *de dicto*
necessity *de re*
necessity *in sensu composito*
necessity *in sensu diviso*
possible truth
possible world
possible worlds semantics
premise
probability calculus
propositional logic
quantification
reductio ad absurdum
rules of logic
sentential logic
sound argument
strict logical possibility
subjunctive conditional
symbolic logic
universally quantified statement
unsound argument
"would" counterfactual

PART II

EPISTEMOLOGY

3

KNOWLEDGE
AND RATIONALITY

All men by nature desire to know.
ARISTOTLE METAPHYSICS 1.1

1 INTRODUCTION

People's mental lives constantly teem with activity. They experience sounds, shapes and colors, they experience their own thoughts, desires and pains, and they can simply see the truth of certain obvious propositions such as $2 + 2 = 4$. People form, discard, maintain and test beliefs. There are many things people know and many things they do not know. Some beliefs are quite reasonable and some of them are unreasonable.

Epistemology is the branch of philosophy that tries to make sense out of knowledge, rationality and justified or unjustified beliefs. The term *epistemology* comes from the Greek word *epistēmē*, which means knowledge. Accordingly, epistemology is the study of knowledge and justified or warranted belief. Actually, there are four major areas of focus within the field of epistemology. First, there is the conceptual analysis of key concepts in epistemology: What is knowledge? What is rationality, justification or warrant? This first area of epistemology works hand in hand with the philosophy of language in that the focus of study is the clarification of important epistemological notions in order to be clear about what these concepts really are. The main focus of this chapter will be in this branch of epistemology. Chapter six attempts to spell out what sort of a thing truth itself is. Questions about the nature of truth, that is, questions about what truth itself is (as opposed to questions about how one knows that one has the truth) are really metaphysical and not epistemological questions, since metaphysics is the branch of study that investigates what kinds of things exist. But it is customary to look at the nature of truth in conjunction with the field of epistemology, and we will follow that custom by looking at theories of truth in the part of this book concerning epistemology, specifically, in chapter six.

Second, there is the problem of **skepticism**. Do people really have knowledge or justified belief? If people do have knowledge or justified beliefs in one area, say in mathematics, do they have it in other areas; for example, is there moral or religious knowledge? Can one know something if he is not one hundred percent certain that he is not wrong about it? The problem of skepticism is discussed in chapter four and, in a different way, in chapter six.

Third, there is the question of the sources and scope of knowledge and justified belief. If people do in fact have knowledge and justified beliefs, how is it that they have these things? What are the different kinds of knowledge? Surely one's five senses in some way are a source of perceptual knowledge about the external world. But are there other kinds of knowledge and sources for them beyond sensory perception? Is there also knowledge and justified beliefs about the past (memory), about one's own inner mental states (introspection), about the thoughts, feelings and minds of other persons, about logic, mathematics, metaphysics, morality, God? What are the sources of these different types of knowledge?

Fourth, there is the question of criteria for knowledge or justification. Suppose that Jill has some belief that is warranted or justified for her, say the belief that there is an oak tree outside her window. What is it that confers warrant or justification on that belief? How does one belief or set of beliefs provide the basis for holding to another belief? Can things besides beliefs—for instance, experiences or the way people go about forming their beliefs—provide support for a justified belief? Or are other beliefs the only things that can support a given belief? These questions are the focus of chapter five.

Before turning to the topic of knowledge, one more preliminary remark about epistemology needs to be made. Traditionally, epistemology has centered its attention on questions like these: Can *I* know anything? What is it that *I* can know? How can *I myself* assess whether or not a belief of *mine* is actually justified? These kinds of questions have been called **Socratic questions** because they all, in one way or another, are questions we ask about ourselves. In other words, epistemology is concerned first and foremost with the first-person perspective, issues involved with an individual as an experiencing, believing and knowing first-person subject. Insofar as the fields of psychology, biology, neurophysiology, etc. study humans from a third-person perspective, that is, as objects studied from the "outside" as it were, then to that extent these other fields of study leave out something essential to epistemology.

The remaining part of this chapter analyzes and clarifies two different notions: knowledge and rationality.

2 WHAT IS KNOWLEDGE?

The following three sentences reveal three different types of knowledge:

1. I know the ball in front of me.
2. I know how to play golf.
3. I know that Reagan was a Republican president.

Sentence (1) expresses what is known as **knowledge by acquaintance**. Here one knows something in that the object of knowledge is directly present to one's consciousness. Dan knows the ball in front of him in that he sees the ball, he is directly aware of it, he knows it by sensory intuition. Here, the word **intuition** does not mean a guess or irrational hunch, but rather a direct awareness of something that is directly present to consciousness. People know many things by acquaintance or intuition: their own mental states (thoughts, feelings, sensations), physical objects with which they are acquainted by the five senses, and, some would argue, basic principles of mathematics. If one asks how people know that

1. $2 + 2 = 4$

or

2. (A) If it is raining outside then it is wet outside and (B) it is raining outside, then it must be the case that (C) it is wet outside,

the answer seems to be that people can simply "see" that $2 + 2 = 4$ or that (C) must follow if (A) and (B) are accepted. What kind of seeing is this? Many believe that it involves an intuitional form of awareness or perception of abstract, immaterial objects and the relationships among them—numbers and mathematical relations or propositions and the laws of logic. Arguably, all of these examples of knowledge are cases of knowledge by acquaintance.

Sentence (2) involves what is called **know-how.** Know-how is the ability or skill to behave in a certain way and perform some task or set of behaviors. One can know how to speak Greek, play golf, ride a bicycle or perform a number of other skills. Know-how does not always involve conscious awareness of what one is doing. Someone can learn how to do something by repeated practice without being consciously aware that one is doing the activity in question or without having any idea of the theory behind the practice. For example, one can know how to adjust one's swing for a curve ball without consciously being aware that one's stride is changing or without knowing any background theory of hitting technique.

Sentence (3) expresses what Bertrand Russell called **knowledge by description** or what is more typically called by philosophers **propositional knowledge.** Here someone knows that P where P is a proposition. For present purposes, a proposition may be defined as the content of a sentence or statement. Epistemology involves all three kinds of knowledge.

Ever since the time of Plato, philosophers have tried to offer an adequate definition of propositional knowledge (hereafter, simply called knowledge). In his dialogue *Theaetetus,* Plato offered (though he did not completely endorse) what is known as the **standard definition of (propositional) knowledge.** The standard way of stating this definition is to say that knowledge is justified true belief (sometimes called the **tripartite analysis** or alluded to as simply JTB). It will be helpful to analyze this definition further. If someone knows something, then what he knows must be true. It would make no sense to say that Jones knows that milk is in the refrigerator but that, nevertheless, it is false that the milk is there. So a necessary condition of knowledge is that what is known is true. But truth is not sufficient for knowledge. There are many truths that no one has ever thought of, much less known. And there are some truths that someone may think about but not know.

Besides truth, a second part of knowledge is belief. If Jones knows something in the propositional sense, he must at least believe it. It would make no sense to say that Jones knows that milk is in the refrigerator but that, nevertheless, he does not believe that milk is in the refrigerator. So belief is a necessary condition for knowledge. But mere belief is not sufficient for knowledge. People believe many things that they do not know to be true.

True belief is a necessary condition for knowledge. But is true belief sufficient for knowledge? No, it is not. The reason is that someone can believe things that are true but have no justification or warrant at all for those beliefs. It may be that one's belief is true by simple accident. Suppose, for example, the following random thought pops into someone's mind: *It is raining right now in Moscow.*

Suppose, further, that the person believes this thought and, further, as a matter of sheer coincidence, it is actually raining in Moscow at that time. Then the person would have a true belief, but the person would not have knowledge of the proposition in question. Or suppose that the person said to himself, "I will believe the first piece of graffiti on the bathroom wall," and the first thing he sees is the sentence "It is raining right now in Moscow." Again, even if the sentence were true, the person would not have knowledge of the proposition.

What is missing in these cases? The person lacks justification or warrant for the belief in question. In chapter five, different theories of **"justification"** or **"warrant"** will be examined. It will become evident that some philosophers equate the two while others draw a distinction between them. But for now, it may simply be noted that justification (or warrant) for a belief amounts to something like this: one has sufficient evidence for the belief, one formed and maintained the belief in a reliable way (e.g., on the basis of his senses or expert testimony and not by palm reading), or one's intellectual and sensory faculties were functioning properly in a good intellectual environment when he formed the belief in question. For present purposes, the main idea is that there is a big difference between a mere true belief and a true belief that has warrant or justification. And the traditional or standard definition of propositional knowledge is the view that knowledge is justified true belief. In other words, a person S knows that P if and only if

1. S believes that P.
2. P is true.
3. The belief that P is justified for S at the time S believes it.

For a long time, the standard definition of propositional knowledge was more or less accepted as adequate by philosophers. And while there were a few counterexamples raised against the standard definition (e.g., by Alexius Meinong and by Bertrand Russell in the early 1900s) it was not until 1963 that the standard definition was subjected to severe criticism. In 1963 Edmund Gettier published a short paper that raised problems for the standard definition.[1] Gettier's paper presented two short counterexamples designed to show that while justified true belief may be necessary for knowledge it is not sufficient. Since then, a host of similar counterexamples have been raised, and they are usually called **Gettier-type counterexamples** to the standard JTB definition of knowledge.

Here is one of Gettier's original examples. Smith and Jones have applied for a certain job and Smith has strong evidence for the following proposition:

a. Jones is the man who will get the job and Jones has ten coins in his pocket.

Smith's evidence for (a) includes the fact that the company's president has assured him that Jones would be selected and that Smith himself has counted the coins in Jones's pocket ten minutes ago. On the basis of (a) Smith infers a new proposition that he now believes:

b. The man who will get the job has ten coins in his pocket.

---

[1] Edmund L. Gettier, "Is Justified True Belief Knowledge?" *Analysis* 23 (1963): 121-23.

Imagine further, says Gettier, that unknown to Smith, he himself gets the job and happens to have ten coins in his pocket. In this case, proposition (b) is true, Smith believes (b), and (b) is strongly justified for Smith. In short, he has justified true belief regarding (b), but surely, one would not want to say he *knows* (b). JTB may be necessary for knowledge but it is not sufficient.

Here is another example. Suppose Fred believes that his wife Betty is at work and the basis for this belief is the fact that he has just seen her leave for work thirty minutes ago, she always goes directly to work every day, and she had told him as she left that she was going straight to work because she had a busy day ahead. However, suppose further that, in reality, Betty was fooling Fred and, instead of driving to work, she went to a clothing store to get Fred a new suit. On arrival at the store, Betty was kidnapped by her friends and taken to work for a surprise birthday party for Betty. In this case, Fred's belief that Betty is at work would be a justified true belief, but it would not seem to be something that Fred knows.

Here is a final example. Suppose that the Dallas Cowboys are playing the Buffalo Bills in the Super Bowl for the second straight year. Suppose further that Harry is watching the Cowboys beat the Bills in the Super Bowl on television. As the game ends, he forms the belief that the Cowboys have just won the Super Bowl. However, unknown to him, the Super Bowl telecast has been stopped due to technical difficulties, and the television is showing a rerun of last year's Cowboy victory instead of this year's game. As a matter of fact, however, the Cowboys have just beaten the Bills for the second straight year, but the end of the current game has not been on television. In this case, Harry has a justified true belief that the Cowboys just won the Super Bowl, but it would not seem that he knows this to be the case.

What is going on here? In each case, the example tries to give a case in which justified true belief, while perhaps necessary, is nevertheless not sufficient for knowledge, i.e., that the tripartite analysis is too weak or broad since it counts as knowledge cases in which knowledge does not, in fact, obtain.

Several types of strategies (with different versions of each strategy) have been offered as responses to Gettier-type examples:

Strategy #1:   Retain the standard definition and show that the Gettier-type examples do not work because the people in them didn't really have justification, i.e., it is still the case that knowledge = JTB.

Strategy #2:   Accept the examples, hold that JTB is necessary but not sufficient for knowledge and look for a fourth condition, i.e., knowledge = JTB + ?.

Strategy #3:   Accept the examples, abandon the tripartite analysis of knowledge but replacing "justification" with something else to form a new tripartite definition of knowledge, i.e., knowledge = ?TB.

Before examining the different strategies, something should be said briefly about justification and a related issue—the **internalism-externalism** debate. The topic of justification will be studied more fully later in this chapter and in chapter five. But for now a few preliminary remarks should suffice to understand the different strategies offered as responses to Gettier cases.

The term *justification* is usually associated with beliefs—it is a belief (e.g., that Smith did the robbery) that either is or is not justified for some person at some time. Furthermore, justification is a normative term of epistemic appraisal. If we say a belief is justified, we usually mean that we either have a right to believe it, that we ought to believe it, or that accepting the belief is an intrinsically good, rational thing to do. Often, it is reasonable to take a belief to be true, perhaps because there is good evidence or ground for the belief (and some would add that one must either actually be aware of this good evidence or ground or that one must both be aware of the evidence or the ground and see the connection between the evidence or ground and the belief one accepts on the basis of the evidence or ground). Jill's belief that there is a tree before her may be justified on the grounds that she has certain sensory experiences (she has an appearance of a green and brown tree-shaped object). Jack's belief that Smith did the robbery may be justified on the good evidence that he was there with a motive and with the stolen goods in his hands.

Some have argued that the normativity of justification should be understood in terms of faithfully fulfilling certain epistemic duties or rules, i.e., cognitive rules that specify duties for obtaining rational, justified beliefs. Some of these rules may include "Obtain true beliefs and avoid false ones," "Obtain rational beliefs and avoid irrational ones," "If something appears red to you, then believe it is, in fact, red until you have sufficient evidence to the contrary," and so on. Finally, justification comes in degrees. A belief can grow in its justification for someone if his evidence or grounds for that belief grows. Likewise one can lose justification for a belief if he comes to believe things that defeat his belief in some way or another.

Justification is often closely related to a second issue: the internalist-externalist debate. Roughly, an internalist is one who holds that the sole factors that justify a belief are "internal" or "cognitively accessible" to the believing agent or subject. These factors are various mental states (experiences, sensations, thoughts, beliefs) to which the agent himself has direct access by simply reflecting on or being aware of his own states of consciousness. Justification is grounded in what is internal to the mind of and directly accessible to the believing subject. They are factors the subject can be aware of by simply reflecting upon himself. For example, Ashley's having a red sensation confers some justification on the belief that there is a red object in front of her and the red sensation itself is internal to her—it is a state of consciousness to which she has direct access. An externalist is one who denies internalism, that is, who affirms that among the factors that justify a belief are those to which the believing subject does not have or does not need to have cognitive access. For example, an externalist could hold that among the things that justify a belief is the causal process that caused the belief to be formed—light waves reflecting off of objects and interacting with the eyes and optic nerve in the right way—even though this causal process is entirely outside of the subject's awareness.

So far, internalism was defined as the view that the *sole* justifying factors of a belief are those internal to the subject. And this is, indeed, the standard way of defining internalism. However, it is possible to make a distinction between **strong** and **weak internalism**. In order to appreciate this distinction, it will be useful to look for a moment at two different intellectual factors that have given rise to internalism.

The first is called a **deontological view of justification**, which centers on the notion, mentioned above, of fulfilling one's epistemic duties. This view of justification pictures it as a matter of doing one's best to form one's beliefs according to certain epistemological rules; for example, "Form your beliefs objectively and carefully," "If something looks red to you and you have no reason for thinking it is not red, then you may believe that it is, in fact, red," "Proportion the strength of your beliefs to the strength of the evidence for them." Having justification for a belief is a matter of doing one's intellectual duty, of trying one's best to follow the correct epistemological rules. If someone obeys the correct rules in forming and maintaining his beliefs, then he has done his intellectual duty, his beliefs are justified for him, and he is not to be held responsible even if his beliefs are, in fact, false. Having justified beliefs is a matter of fulfilling one's intellectual duties and being intellectually responsible.

Second, if people have intellectual duties and responsibilities, if they can be guilty or innocent of carrying out those duties, then they must be free to do or not do their duties. That is, if one is to have justified beliefs, and since having justified beliefs amounts to doing one's duty here, then one must be free to obey or disobey epistemic rules. Otherwise, one could not be held responsible for his intellectual behavior. Now one is not responsible for or free with respect to what happens outside of oneself. He can only control factors internal to him as a subject.

For example, as long as one has tried one's best to pay attention to his sensations and beliefs and form justified beliefs on the basis of correct rules regarding them, then even if there is an evil demon outside him who tricks him into experiencing and believing in an external world that is not there, he can still have justified beliefs about that external world. He cannot control evil demons or other external factors, so they are not relevant to justification. Since justification is a matter of intellectual responsibility, and since responsibility requires freedom, and since internal factors are the only factors about which one is free, then an internalist view of justification is demanded. The deontological impetus to internalism leads to strong internalism—the view that the sole factors relevant to justification are internal ones, that internal factors are necessary and sufficient for justification.

A second intellectual factor also motivates internalism: the first-person perspective (see chap. 14). Here, epistemology in general, and justification in particular, are viewed as topics that essentially focus on first-person knowing and experiencing subjects. Thus epistemology is primarily a study of first-person issues, e.g., how can *I myself* obtain justified beliefs? On this view, epistemology cannot be reduced to a third-person perspective that abandons the first-person standpoint. Now the first-person perspective is essentially one that involves factors internal to knowing and experiencing subjects, namely, experiences and beliefs. This impetus toward internalism leads to weak internalism: the view that internal factors are necessary but, most likely, not sufficient for justification. Weak internalism is compatible with some forms of externalism.

As with internalism, there is also a distinction between **weak** and **strong externalism**. According to strong externalism *no* factors that contribute to a belief's justification are internal to the agent. A philosopher could be favorable to this position if she wishes to avoid mind-body dualism (see chaps. 11-12) and if, as seems reasonable, internalism implies some form of dualism. According to weak externalism, at least some factors that contribute to a belief's justification must be external to the agent.

In sum, there are different versions of internalism and externalism. Moreover, weak internalism and externalism are compatible with each other. The chapter will continue to use *internalism* and *externalism* for the strong versions of each unless otherwise indicated because this usage is more common among philosophers.

As noted above, externalism in either form implies the denial of strong internalism. According to externalists, either part or all of what justifies a belief are factors external to the agent and to which the agent need have no access at all. Sally's belief that a red object is in the room is justified for her by factors like these: the lighting was good, the object itself is what *caused* her to believe it is there, her belief was formed by reliable methods (say by her sensory organs and not by consulting a palm reader to tell her what was in the room), etc. Note that for the externalist, Sally does not have to have access to or awareness of any of these justifying factors. She does not have to be aware (or even be able to be aware) of the lighting, of what caused her belief or of what method she used to form it.

Now what exactly does the internalist-externalist debate have to do with justification? Simply this. Most philosophers have used *justification* in an internalist way. For them, *justification* means relying on internal factors. Thus, if a philosopher is a strong externalist, he or she will abandon the notion of justification altogether, replace it with something else, and form a new tripartite definition. Alternatively, a philosopher may retain justification and search for a supplementary fourth condition for knowledge. Applying this insight to the standard definition of knowledge allows the reader to understand the three types of strategies to follow. The best way to show this is to look at the strategies themselves.

2.1
STRATEGY #1:
RETAIN THE
STANDARD
DEFINITION

Advocates of this view claim that knowledge is justified true belief but that the individuals in the Gettier-type examples fail to have justification. Why? Because even though they had some evidence for their true belief, it was not enough evidence to count as justification. On this view, what the Gettier examples show is that the amount of evidence required for justification should be elevated. Accordingly, one has justification for some belief only if that justification entails the truth of the belief. In other words, one cannot have a justified false belief. There is no justification for a belief unless the belief is true. Justification is such a strong thing that the evidence that justifies a belief entails the truth of that justified belief. Since the evidence for the people in the Gettier cases did not entail the truth of the proposition they believed—that evidence could be true but the supported belief false—they did not really have justification in the first place and that is why they did not have knowledge.

Few philosophers have accepted this solution to Gettier cases and for a very good reason. It would severely limit the things that people know and would imply that people do not know most of the things they do, in fact, know. On this view there would only be two kinds of things people could know: their own immediate mental states and simple truths of logic and mathematics (called a priori truths). Arguably, the justification for Doug's belief that he is in pain is simply his being in pain, and being in pain does, in fact, entail that the belief that he is in pain is true. One's belief that $2 + 2 = 4$ is justified by one's simply being able to "see" that the proposition must be true once coming to understand what it says. Here, the evidence (one's seeing that the proposition must be true upon understanding it) does entail that the proposition is true.

But on the view under consideration, most of the things people know would not count as knowledge: their knowledge of the past based on memory, or of the external world based on sensory experience, their knowledge in science, history, of the minds of others, ethics, religion and a host of other things. In each of these cases, the factors that justify people's beliefs and give them knowledge do not entail the truth of those beliefs. These factors could be true yet the belief they justify false. Consider a belief about the external world, say that there is a red object in front of one. Suppose that the factor justifying this belief is one's sensory experience—one's being appeared to in a red type of way. Now having such a sensory experience does not entail that there is a red object before one. One could be hallucinating or, due to taking drugs or poorly functioning eyes, the object could be blue but appear red to him. So even though the factors that justify our true beliefs about the external world do not entail the truth of those beliefs (and the same point could be made about the other areas of knowledge), they still give people knowledge. For this reason, the view under consideration must be rejected.

The second strategy accepts the Gettier cases, takes the tripartite definition to be a necessary condition for knowledge, and formulates a fourth condition. There have been a number of different candidates offered as the correct fourth condition. Two of them will be examined.

2.2
STRATEGY #2:
SUPPLEMENT
THE STANDARD
DEFINITION

According to the "no relevant falsehood" view, knowledge is justified true belief plus no relevant falsehood. To understand the idea behind this position, recall the Gettier case involving Smith, Jones, and the man who gets the job with ten coins in his pocket. What is it that goes wrong in this case? Note that Smith's justified true belief (the man who will get the job has ten coins in his pocket) is true by accident, that is, its truth has nothing to do with Smith's reasons for believing it. In fact, Smith infers this belief from the false belief that Jones is the man who will get the job. In light of this, some have suggested the following addition to the tripartite definition: the belief must not receive justification from a false belief. Since Smith's belief violates this fourth condition, there is now an answer as to why he did not have knowledge.

2.2.1
NO RELEVANT
FALSEHOOD

Unfortunately, the "no relevant falsehood" view fails for at least two reasons. First, it is not a necessary condition for knowledge—one can still have knowledge and violate this principle. Suppose Gary knows that the stock market rose yesterday and his justification for this belief is four pieces of information: he heard it on the radio, read about it in the newspaper, had a friend report it to him at breakfast and had his wife tell him she heard it on television. Now suppose that his wife did not really hear it on television but only thought she did. Then his belief would be (partly) based on a false belief. On the "no relevant falsehood" view, his belief would not count as knowledge, but surely he does, in fact, know this. Attempts have been made to fix this requirement, but none has succeeded. The problem is this. People often have many pieces of evidence for a belief that they know and among their evidence is one or more false beliefs, yet they still have knowledge. How many false beliefs can one have and still have knowledge? What percentage of true versus false beliefs must one have? It is very difficult to say.

Second, the view is not sufficient for knowledge. One can have a justified true belief not justified by a relevant false belief and still fail to have knowledge. Alvin Goldman presents a case in which Henry is driving through the countryside and sees a normal looking barn a few feet away. Since his senses are working fine he has a justified true belief that there is a barn that he sees. However,

> unknown to Henry, the district he has entered is full of paper-mache facsimiles of barns. These facsimiles look from the road exactly like barns, but are really just facades, without back walls or interiors, quite incapable of being used as barns. Having just entered the district, Henry has not encountered any facsimiles; the object he sees is a genuine barn. But if the object on that site were a facsimile, Henry would mistake it for a barn.[2]

Henry has justified true belief about the barn, and his belief is not based on anything false. Yet he still doesn't have knowledge. This example has suggested to some a different view of how to solve the Gettier challenge.

2.2.2 DEFEASIBILITY

The barn example suggests a shift in the fourth condition away from there not being a relevant falsehood to there not being a relevant truth that could defeat one's knowledge. In Henry's case, there is such a relevant truth (unknown to him), namely, that there were a number of facsimiles in the countryside. Had he known that, his knowledge that he was seeing the barn would have been defeated. This suggests the following fourth condition for the standard definition: there must be no relevant truth which is such that if the person believed it, it would serve as a defeater for his justification. Knowledge must not be **defeasible** (capable of being annulled or made void) in this way.

What should one say to this condition? It obviously handles the barn case. However, the main problem with this solution is that it is not a necessary condition for knowledge because one can have knowledge and violate the condition. Suppose Beth has reasons that justify her in knowing that her children are playing at school. However, unknown to her, a neighbor called her husband this morning and invited the children to skip school and go to Disneyland. Suppose further that her husband has been saying for some time that he was going to let the children do this some day soon. Finally, suppose that her children have a

---

[2]Alvin Goldman, "Discrimination and Perceptual Knowledge," *Journal of Philosophy* 73 (1976): 771-91.

test that day at school and her husband turned down the invitation.

Does she know they are playing at school? It would seem so, yet there is, in fact, a truth that, if known to her, would defeat her justification for knowledge (that the neighbor had called to invite them to Disneyland). In this case, though, there is also a defeater for the defeater (her husband's refusal). The condition under consideration fails to take into account the fact that people often know things with true but unknown defeaters because there are defeaters for the defeaters and there may be further defeaters of those defeaters and so on. Unless one stipulates an omniscience requirement (one knows all the truths available)—which would severely limit what people know—this condition fails.

The two views just considered are examples of internalist strategies since they make reference to relevant falsehoods or truths that the person either is or can become directly aware of in his own field of consciousness and, in this way, could serve as a defeater of knowledge. The next two positions can either be offered as supplements to an internalist view of justification (knowledge is JTB + ? where "justification" is ultimately understood in terms of some state internal to the agent) or as replacements of internalism (knowledge is ?TB where the internalist notion of justification is replaced with something external to the agent). We will primarily look at them as replacements for internalism, though what shall be said about them, with minor adjustments, could apply equally to these views understood as supplements to internalism.

The **causal theory** can be understood in one of two ways: (1) knowledge is JTB + suitably caused belief or (2) knowledge is suitably caused TB. In the second case the internalist notion of justification is abandoned and replaced with the notion of being suitably caused. As mentioned above, this is the view we will examine. There are different versions of this position, but the basic idea can be stated according to an early formulation of the view by Alvin Goldman: a person knows that P if and only if his true belief that P was caused by the state of affairs consisting in P itself.

2.3
STRATEGY #3:
READJUST THE
TRIPARTITE
ANALYSIS

2.3.1
THE CAUSAL
THEORY

Returning to the Smith and Jones example, the thing that causes Smith to believe that the next man to get the job has ten coins in his pocket is not caused by the ten coins in the pocket of the person about which the belief is directed (Jones) but by the ten coins in his own pocket. Thus Smith fails to have knowledge because his true belief is not caused (and certainly not "suitably" caused) by the state of affairs involved in the belief. On the other hand, if a red object is before someone and is what causes him to truly believe that it is there and red while looking at it, then we have an account of just how it is that the person knows this fact, or so say advocates of the causal theory. Note that it is being claimed here that one can have knowledge of the fact that a red object is there without being aware of the causal processes (e.g., the light waves interacting with my retinas, etc.) producing such a belief. Indeed, people in ancient times had sensory knowledge with no knowledge of the scientific facts about light waves.

As with the other views, the causal theory has been subjected to several criticisms. First, there are cases where one can know that P without P *causing* that knowledge and, thus, the causal view is not necessary for knowledge. For example, our knowledge that $2 + 2 = 4$ is, arguably, knowledge about certain abstract objects (nonphysical objects that do not exist in space or time; see chap. 10), namely numbers and the mathematical relations that obtain among them. But it does not seem to be correct to say that these nonphysical abstract objects *cause* our knowledge of them. Again, one can know that if tree A is taller than tree B and tree B is taller than tree C, then it must be the case that tree A is taller than tree C. But what is it that causes this knowledge? It is not the trees because the knowledge itself does not depend on any specific objects in space or time but on the logic of the relation called "taller than." Another (more controversial) example is our knowledge of the future. Mike can know that his wife will shout for joy this afternoon when she comes home and sees the diamond ring he has bought her, but this fact cannot *cause* this knowledge because it does not exist yet.

Second, the causal view is not sufficient for knowledge. There are cases where the fact that P does cause one to have a true belief that P but, because it causes such a belief in an epistemically irrelevant way, no knowledge obtains. Suppose a short person is outside working on his car, and suddenly growing tired, goes inside and watches the evening news. Suppose further that, unknown to him, a certain internal disorder is what caused him to grow tired and come inside. Upon watching the news, he learns that most people who suffer this disorder are short, and since he is a hypochondriac, he concludes that he has the disorder he does, in fact, have. In this case he surely would not know he had this disorder, despite the fact that he does have it causally contributed to his true belief that he did.

2.3.2
THE
RELIABILITY
THEORY

The final view to be considered (and it has several different versions) is the position that knowledge is a true belief that is produced and sustained by a reliable belief-forming method. For example, people tend to increase their willingness to count as knowledge a belief based on someone else's testimony to the degree that they consider the person to be reliable. Hope's true belief that there is an object in front of her is knowledge if and only if it is produced by a reliable method, in this case, by her visual processes. Sue's true belief that she had breakfast this morning is knowledge if and only if it is reliably produced by her memory mechanisms and powers. One does not need to have any awareness or even possible awareness of these mechanisms or their reliability; one's beliefs must merely be formed by them. Since the beliefs in the Gettier case were not produced by reliable methods, no knowledge obtains.

Several objections have been raised against this view. First, how does one determine which processes are, in fact, reliable and just how reliable they have to be to give knowledge? Consider vision. How does one know the visual processes that contribute to the formation of perceptual beliefs are, in fact, reliable and know just how reliable they are? Their reliability varies greatly as circumstances inside and outside the knower change. If one is sick or drunk or if the lighting is poor or the object far away, the processes forming one's visual beliefs are less reliable. Some argue that the only noncircular way to answer this is to fall back on an internalist view of justification. The **reliability theories** cannot say that reliable beliefs are those produced by reliable methods and reliable methods are those that produce reliable beliefs. This would be circular. The solution to this problem seems to involve the idea that people have a notion of justification that is independent of reliability and, further, that this notion of justification is the one related to knowledge. For example, people already know a number of visual experiences are justified before they ever go on to look at visual mechanisms, and they identify the reliable ones as those that produce what they already have justification to believe. Reliability advocates could respond that in order for our true beliefs to become knowledge they simply have to be formed by a reliable method. People do not have to have any knowledge of those methods or even the possibility of such knowledge. But how can a process justify a belief, asks the internalist, if people have no idea whether or not that process is operating in a given case or whether it is fully or only partly reliable?

A second objection to the reliability theory is this: The reliability thesis is not sufficient for knowledge because one can have a true belief formed by a reliable method but still not have knowledge. Laurence BonJour presents such a case:

> Norman, under certain conditions which usually obtain, is a completely reliable clairvoyant with respect to certain kinds of subject matter. He possesses no evidence or reasons of any kind for or against the general possibility of such a cognitive power or for or against the thesis that he possesses it. One day Norman comes to believe that the President is in New York City, though he has no evidence either for or against this belief. In fact the belief is true and results from his clairvoyant power under circumstances in which it is completely reliable.[3]

Norman, it would seem, has a reliably formed true belief but no knowledge. This completes our survey of some (but far from all) of the different responses to Gettier counterexamples to the standard definition of knowledge. It is now time to state some lessons to be learned from these examples and to provide some final reflections about knowledge itself.

First, even if one cannot solve the Gettier problems precisely, it is still reasonable to say that knowledge is at least true belief plus something that confers justification, warrant or rationality on that belief. In this sense, knowledge presupposes truth. There could be truth without knowledge, but no knowledge without truth. Moreover, knowledge is a normative notion. Because it includes the notion of justification or warrant, it involves believing what one epistemically ought to believe, believing what it is right to believe, believing what it is intrinsically valuable or warranted to believe from an intellectual standpoint.

Second, when one tries to formulate a definition of knowledge or, more generally, when one investigates matters in epistemology, one does not start with a set of necessary and sufficient conditions for something to count as knowledge. Instead, one starts with paradigm cases of knowledge: central, clear cases of where knowledge does or does not obtain. In evaluating the Gettier examples, we constantly appealed to cases that did or did not count as knowledge. We then move from these clear cases to the formulation of various definitions of

2.4
FINAL
REFLECTIONS
ABOUT
KNOWLEDGE

---

[3]Laurence BonJour, *The Structure of Empirical Knowledge* (Cambridge, Mass.: Harvard University Press, 1985), p. 41.

knowledge that we then use to evaluate alleged cases of knowledge that are less than clear, i.e., borderline cases. We start with clear cases of knowledge, formulate definitions and criteria for knowledge justified by those clear cases, and extend these definitions and criteria to less clear cases. In this sense, people already have knowledge and many examples of it before they ever start doing epistemology. This will be important to keep in mind in the next chapter when skepticism is examined.

Third, does knowing something include knowing that one knows it? That is, must one know that he knows something before he can know it? It would seem not for at least two reasons. First, a farmer can know he owns a tractor without ever reflecting on whether or not he knows this, without ever asking himself what knowledge is or whether he has it. Knowing that one knows something would seem to require that someone have the concept of what knowledge is in that person's mind and recognize that his knowledge—say, that he owns a tractor—satisfies that conception of knowledge. But it is obvious that many people never reflect on knowledge itself or on their own states of knowing. Nevertheless they still have knowledge. Second, if one can know something only by first knowing that he knows it, then this would lead to a vicious infinite regress. Why? Because one could not know that he knows something unless he already knew that he knew that he knew it and so on. Thus one must be able to know without first knowing that he knows.

However, if a person (1) does know something, (2) has at least an approximate understanding of what knowledge is, and (3) asks himself if he does, in fact, know something, then he can surely know that he knows it. In this way the study of knowledge does not make knowledge possible but it does give *insight* into the intellectual status of what people know by helping them understand that they do have knowledge of the things they know.

Here is one final point about knowledge that will be developed in the next chapter. If someone knows something, it does not necessarily mean that the person has complete certainty about that thing. "Being completely certain" in this context means "is logically impossible to be mistaken about." This is a pretty high standard for knowledge. It requires it to be logically impossible for someone to be mistaken about a claim before one can know the claim in question.

On this view, a test for a knowledge claim is this: If person S knows that P, then it is a logical contradiction to say that that S merely takes himself to know that P but P is false. Descartes thought that "I think, therefore I am" passed this test, and thus one could, indeed, know that one existed because it is contradictory to say "I take it to be the case that I think, therefore I exist, but it is false that I exist." On the other hand, at least at one stage of his argument (i.e., without having established the existence of God), Descartes did not think that one could know that the external, physical world existed. Why? Because the proposition *I take it that I am seeing an external world, but there is no external world that exists* is not a contradiction. It is logically possible, even though not plausible, that one is hallucinating the external world, merely dreaming about it, or being tricked about its existence by a demon, all while the external world is unreal.

Such a requirement for knowledge—complete certainty—is too stringent and eliminates as knowledge many things that we do, in fact, know. For example, Allison can know that her light is on even though this knowledge is not completely certain: The proposition *Allison takes herself to know that the light is on, but in fact it is not* is not self-contradictory. However, Allison's knowledge that the light is on does not require that this proposition be self-contradictory. Thus one can have knowledge even though it is logically possible that one is mistaken. In fact, we sometimes contrast knowing something with knowing it *with certainty*, implying that there is a contrast between knowing with certainty and simply knowing. Thus simple knowing is still knowing even if it is not for certain.

3 REASON AND RATIONALITY

In addition to knowledge, **rationality** is a term of epistemological importance. In this section, we will look at different aspects of rationality, beginning with a list of three different notions often associated with the term.

First, there is what can be called **Aristotelian rationality**. In this sense, Aristotle called man a rational animal. Here, *rational* refers to a being with *ratio*—a Latin word referring to the ultimate capacity or power to form concepts, think, deliberate, reflect, have intentionality (mental states like thoughts, beliefs, sensations that are *of* or *about* things). Humans are rational animals in that, by nature, they have this power of reason. Two things should be kept in mind here. First, other beings besides humans—angels and, perhaps certain animals—have some rational abilities. Second, humans are rational even if through defect (e.g., being a defective newborn) they cannot exercise that power, because the power of reason is possessed simply in virtue of having a human nature. It is important to distinguish between having a power and being able to exercise or develop it.

3.1
THREE NOTIONS
OF REASON AND
RATIONALITY

A second sense of *rational* involves rationality as the **deliverances of reason**. Here, the **faculty of reason** is considered a source of certain items of knowledge and is contrasted with the **sensory faculties**. Thus, according to the traditional view known as **rationalism** (not to be confused with the view that there is no God or that belief in God is irrational), truths in logic (*modus ponens*, if P is larger than Q and Q is larger than R, then P is larger than R) and mathematics ($2 + 2 = 4$) can be known **a priori**. Roughly, a priori refers to the idea that justification for them does not appeal to sensory experiences, as would justification for an **a posteriori** claim (e.g., there is a tree in the yard). According to rationalism, some a priori truths are **self-evident**: upon simply understanding the proposition in question, one can see or feel a strong inclination to accept that the proposition is a necessary truth—it does not just happen to be true, but rather it could not possibly be false.

Finally, a third sense of *rational* is closely connected to justification or warrant. In this sense, to say that a belief (or, better, an episode of believing) is rational for some person S at some time t is to say that the belief has justification or warrant for S at t. It is this third sense of *rational* that will occupy our attention in the remainder of this section.

3.2
RATIONALITY AS
JUSTIFICATION
OR WARRANT

3.2.1
RATIONALITY
AND TRUTH

Whatever else one should say about rationality, one thing seems to be of fundamental importance: Rationality has instrumental value as a means to the end of
obtaining truth (see chap. 6 for more on the nature of truth itself). The claim
that a belief is rational means, first and foremost, that we take it to be likely that
the belief is true because it *is* rational. It is only if people think that rationality or
epistemic justification constitutes a means to truth that they have any reason
for thinking that rationality is cognitively important. Of course, one could still
value rationality and not believe in truth in that one could hold rational behavior to be a means to cultural power, happiness or something else. But if rationality is to be valuable precisely as something related to cognitive and intellectual
excellence, then the existence of truth is a necessary condition for such value.

This insight suggests that there are two fundamental tasks for people as intellectual, knowing beings. These tasks are to obtain or at least try to obtain a set of
beliefs that is such that one believes as many truths as possible and avoids believing as many falsehoods as possible, especially in regard to important truths and
falsehoods. Now each of these tasks would be easy to accomplish in the absence
of the other. One could believe as many truths as possible by just believing everything that popped into his mind, but in this case many false beliefs would be
accepted in the process. Similarly, one could avoid believing as many falsehoods
as possible by simply refusing to believe anything. But because both tasks are
central to us as intellectual beings the need for rationality becomes evident. By
learning to be rational and hold beliefs that are justified people trust that they
can increase their stock of true beliefs and decrease their number of false ones.

When one thinks of rationality as justification or warrant for a belief, it is natural to think of rationality as being intellectually or epistemically valuable. In
other words, there is a close connection between rationality and **epistemic
value**: to have a justified belief is to have something of intellectual worth. How
should one understand this connection between justification and epistemic
value? Philosophers differ over this issue.

As noted earlier in the chapter, some thinkers hold to a deontological view
of justification. The word *deontological* comes from the Greek word *deon*, which
means "binding duty." According to the deontological view of justification,
there are certain **epistemic duties** or **rules** such that if one's beliefs are formed,
maintained and based on (and structured among themselves in accordance
with) those rules and duties, then they are justified. This means that one has an
intellectual right to hold the belief—the belief is either permissible or obligatory
to hold, given certain factors and the correct set of epistemic rules. Since
epistemic rules are norms governing our reasoning, they state conditions under
which it is either rational (permissible or obligatory) to hold a belief and conditions under which it is irrational (intellectually forbidden) to hold a belief. Here
are some examples of epistemic norms: (1) If x looks F (e.g., red) to you and you
have no reason for thinking it isn't F (red), then you are permitted to believe
that it is, in fact, F (red). (2) Try to obtain reasonable beliefs and avoid unreasonable ones. (3) Proportion your beliefs to the evidence; believe something if
and only if there is good evidence to do so. (4) Other things being equal, suppose other people are like you in that they have certain mental states (e.g.,

pain) following certain stimuli (e.g., being stuck with a pin) that are similar to yours in analogous circumstances. (5) Accept beliefs that cohere well with your entire set of coherent beliefs.

Deontological understandings of rationality assume what is called **doxastic voluntarism** (*doxastic* means "having to do with beliefs" as opposed to, say, sensory experiences themselves)—the notion that people have at least some voluntary control over and choice about their beliefs, and thus they are intellectually responsible for choosing the right beliefs and avoiding a choice of unreasonable ones. Doxastic voluntarism is a controversial thesis, but it is important to keep in mind that it does not mean one has direct, immediate control over one's beliefs. If someone offered you a million dollars to believe right now that a pink elephant was in your room, you could not do it if you wanted to. People's beliefs usually just come to them. Upon looking at a red object, one simply finds himself believing it is red. Nevertheless, one could still have indirect control over a belief. Perhaps people cannot directly change their beliefs, but they may be free to do certain things (e.g., study certain evidence and avoid other evidence) to move themselves to a position to change their beliefs.

There are other, nondeontological views about rationality and justification. On these views, justification does not amount to following correct epistemic rules, but rather it involves exemplifying certain states of affairs that are intrinsically valuable (valuable in themselves). Here are some examples of such states of affairs: having beliefs formed by a reliable method or that are caused by the thing believed, holding more true than false beliefs, forming and maintaining beliefs by means of properly functioning sensory and intellectual faculties in an environment for which they were designed, having coherent beliefs, etc. Here, justification is conceived of as forming and maintaining (and structuring) beliefs in such a way that people embody one or more of these intrinsically valuable states of affairs. But these states of affairs are not to be thought of as rules specifying duties. For example, according to some, a belief is rational if and only if it is formed by a reliable method, but there is no duty to "form or try to form your beliefs according to a reliable method."

In sum, rationality in the sense of justified or warranted belief is connected to that which is valuable from an epistemological or intellectual perspective: either rules people are to follow in forming and maintaining their beliefs or states of affairs people either do or do not embody in forming and maintaining their beliefs. In chapter five we will look at an important aspect of justification: What *structure* should one's set of beliefs have such that those beliefs do, in fact, have justification for that person.

In a certain sense, truth does not come in degrees nor does it change. The fact that $2 + 2 = 4$ or that George Brett retired from baseball in 1993 are either completely true or completely false (both are true!) and their truthfulness does not change over time. By contrast, rationality comes in degrees and can change over time.

For any belief *P*, say the belief that God exists, there are three important cognitive postures we can take regarding *P*: we can believe *P* (as theists do), we can believe *not-P* (as atheists do), or we can withhold *P* (as agnostics do) and

3.2.3
DEGREES OF
RATIONALITY

neither believe *P* nor believe *not-P.* Epistemologically speaking, a person should withhold a belief about *P* if *P* is counterbalanced for that person: *P* and *not-P* are equally justified for the person; neither position is more justified than the other. If one moves from withholding to believing *P* or believing *not-P,* his degree of justification can grow and change over time. For example, in a court of law, the evidence for a guilty verdict can grow in such a way that the belief of guilt becomes more and more (or less and less) justified. Moreover, one could have extremely good reasons to hold a person guilty at one time, but given the addition of new evidence, that belief could pass from being well justified to unjustified. Thus rationality, in contrast to truth, comes in degrees and can change over time.

One factor that affects whether and to what degree a belief is justified is the presence of **defeaters** for that belief. Suppose Smith has a belief that *Q* (e.g., that a statue is blue), and suppose that *R* (e.g., the way the statue looks to him) is a reason or ground Smith has for holding to *Q.* A defeater removes or weakens justification for a belief. There are at least two kinds of defeaters. First, there are **rebutting defeaters**, which directly attack the conclusion or thing being believed. In the case above, a rebutting defeater would be a reason to believe *not-Q,* i.e., a reason to believe that the statue is not blue. An example would be a case where the museum director and a number of reliable, honest people assure you that the statue is gray. Second, there are **undercutting defeaters**. These defeaters do not directly attack the thing believed (by trying to show that it is false), but rather they attack the notion that *R* is a good reason for *Q.* Undercutting defeaters do not attack *Q* directly; they attack *R* and in some way undercut *R* as a good reason for *Q.* In the example above, an undercutting defeater would be evidence that there is blue lighting around the statue that makes everything in that room look blue to people. In the example, the undercutting defeater removes one's reason for thinking that the statue is blue and the rebutting defeater gives one reason for thinking that the statue is notblue. In different ways, defeaters can remove the justification for a belief.

In this chapter, the field of epistemology was introduced and different aspects of knowledge and rationality were examined. But do people really know or have justified beliefs about anything? This is part of the problem of skepticism and to skeptical issues we now turn.

CHAPTER SUMMARY

Epistemology is the branch of philosophy that focuses on the study of knowledge and justified belief. Four major areas of epistemology are (1) the analysis of concepts like knowledge, justification and rationality, (2) the problem of skepticism (do people have knowledge or justified beliefs?), (3) the sources and scope of knowledge or justified belief and (4) the study of criteria for knowledge or justified belief.

There are three types of knowledge: knowledge by acquaintance, know-how and propositional knowledge. Regarding the last, the standard definition of knowledge has identified it with justified true belief. Gettier-type counterexamples have been raised against the standard definition. Philosophers have responded to these examples in one of three ways: reject the examples and retain the standard definition, add a fourth condition to justified true belief or replace justification with something else (reliability, being suitably caused) to form a new tripartite definition. Whatever one says about this debate, it seems reasonable to affirm this about knowledge: It is normative; people start epistemology with particular cases of knowledge and not with necessary or sufficient conditions for a definition of knowledge; and people do not have to know they know before they can know.

Rationality is another important epistemological notion. We use the term *rational* in three senses: Aristotelian rationality, the deliverances of reason, and rationality as justification or warrant. Regarding the latter, rationality is a means to truth and it can be understood in terms of fulfilling certain epistemic duties or embodying certain states of affairs deemed intrinsically valuable from an epistemic point of view. Finally, rationality comes in degrees and can change over time, and one way this takes place is through the presence of different kinds of defeaters.

CHECKLIST OF BASIC TERMS AND CONCEPTS

a posteriori
a priori
Aristotelian rationality
causal theory
defeasible
defeater
deliverances of reason
deontological view of justification
doxastic voluntarism
epistemic duties or rules
epistemic value
epistemology
externalism
faculty of reason
Gettier-type counterexamples
internalism
intuition
justification
know-how
knowledge by acquaintance
knowledge by description
propositional knowledge
rationalism
rationality
rebutting defeater
reliability theory
self-evident
sensory faculties

skepticism
Socratic questions
standard definition of knowledge
strong externalism
strong internalism
tripartite analysis
undercutting defeaters
warrant
weak externalism
weak internalism

4

THE PROBLEM
OF SKEPTICISM

The Skeptics . . . were constantly engaged in overthrowing
the dogmas of all schools, but enunciated none themselves;
and though they would go so far as to
bring forward and expound the dogmas of the others,
they themselves laid down nothing definitely,
not even the laying down of nothing.
DIOGENES LAERTIUS LIVES OF EMINENT PHILOSOPHERS

Prove to me that I do not know them,
you who do not deny that such matters
pertain to philosophy and who maintain that
none of these things can be known.
AUGUSTINE AGAINST THE ACADEMICIANS

[S]ince reason already convinces me that I should abstain
from the belief in things which are not entirely
certain and indubitable . . . it will be enough to make me
reject them all if I can find in each some ground for doubt.
RENÉ DESCARTES MEDITATIONS ON FIRST PHILOSOPHY 1

1 INTRODUCTION

Common sense assures us that we all know and have justified beliefs about many things: the external world, God, morality, the past, mathematics, our own mental life and the existence of other minds. And while Scripture places an important emphasis on faith, it places an equally important emphasis on things we can, should and do know. Thus Scripture unites with common sense to affirm that there are many examples of knowledge and justified belief for human beings. However, we have all met skeptics who, in one way or another, reject this or that item of knowledge or justified belief. And some skeptics claim to reject knowledge or justified belief altogether. This chapter examines skepticism and provides important insights relevant throughout one's intellectual life.

Skepticism has had a long and varied history. During the Hellenistic period of ancient Greek philosophy, two schools of skepticism arose. The first, known as **Academic skepticism**, flourished in the third and second centuries B.C. It was founded by Arcesilaus (315-240 B.C.), a philosopher in Plato's Academy, and was propagated by Carneades in the second century B.C. There is some controversy over what the Academic skeptics actually affirmed, but the traditional view is that they asserted two things: (1) The skeptical thesis: All things are inapprehensible, no one has any knowledge. (2) Regarding the skeptical thesis itself, we can dogmatically affirm that we *know* that no one has any knowledge.

It should be clear that, as stated above, Academic skepticism was a difficult position to maintain. For one thing, statement two is self-refuting because it asserts that people know that there is nothing they can know. However, it may be that in asserting the skeptical thesis itself (statement one), the Academic skeptics did not really say that there is no knowledge at all, but rather that there is only one thing that people know: namely, that they cannot know anything else. But this affirmation, while not self-refuting, is still hard to maintain. Is it really possible to know only one thing? Would not a person claiming to know this statement also be implicitly claiming to know that he himself existed, that he knew what the statement meant, that he knew that the statement was true, and thus that there was such a thing as truth? Further, if someone can simply assert that there is one exception to the skeptical thesis (namely, the thesis itself), what would keep others from simply asserting other exceptions to the thesis, say, that they know red is a color? For these and other reasons, a second school of ancient skepticism was more prominent.

The second school was called **Pyrrhonian skepticism** after its founder Pyrrho of Ellis (360-270 B.C.). It flourished in Alexandria, Egypt, and reached its zenith in the last great Pyrrhonian, Sextus Empiricus, who lived during the last half of the second and the first quarter of the third century A.D. This form of skepticism is rooted in the view that philosophy seeks wisdom and wisdom includes knowledge of truths relevant for living a good, skilled life. The main human problem is unhappiness and this comes, primarily, from a disparity between one's desires and what he believes to be true in the world. So the key to dealing with unhappiness is to give up on the search for wisdom, suspend judgment about all of one's beliefs and be free.

The Pyrrhonian skeptics rejected dogmatism and proceeded in three stages: (1) **antithesis** (both sides of an issue are placed in opposition to each other and skeptical arguments called "tropes" or "modes" are used for each side); (2) **epoche** (the suspension of judgment); (3) **ataraxia** (the ultimate, desired state of tranquility). In contrast to the Academic skeptics, the Pyrrhonians suspended judgment about all things, including the skeptical thesis itself.

With the spread of Christianity and writings critical of skepticism such as Augustine's *Against the Skeptics*, skepticism did not flourish until the time of René Descartes (A.D. 1596-1650) when it began to flower again. Descartes set out to refute skepticism and set knowledge on a sure foundation. Especially important in this regard is Descartes's *Meditations on First Philosophy* first published in 1641. Descartes began his quest for knowledge by adopting **methodological doubt**. This amounted to the idea that knowledge requires absolute certainty (sometimes called **Cartesian certainty**) and that if it were logically possible to be mistaken about something, then one could not know the thing in question. Armed with methodological doubt, Descartes first argued against knowledge of the external world on the grounds that people's senses sometimes deceive them. Second, he pointed out that people sometimes think there is an external world before them but they are only dreaming and that it is logically possible that one is now dreaming and no external world is there. Finally, Descartes opined that a malevolent demon could be tricking people with sensory experiences of an external world when no such world is really "out there." The logical possibility of such a malevolent demon meant for Descartes that people cannot know the laws of logic or mathematics, since the demon may be tricking people into accepting these laws even though they are false. But there is one thing about which the demon could not trick someone—one's own existence, for before one can doubt one's existence he must exist. This insight was expressed in Descartes's famous maxim (which had been stated in a different form by Augustine) *Cogito ergo sum* ("I think, therefore, I am"). This was one secure item of knowledge that could not possibly be doubted.

Descartes went on from the *cogito* to reaffirm knowledge of God, logic and mathematics, and the external world. The details of his procedure are not of importance here. But one thing about Descartes is crucial—he accepted a **burden of proof** over against the skeptic (one does not know something unless he can prove he does against the skeptic) and knowledge requires complete certainty to qualify as such.

Until now, the purpose has been to illustrate some key episodes in the history of skepticism to give the reader a feel for what skepticism is. In the remainder of the chapter, four items are discussed: the varieties of skepticism, some of the main skeptical arguments for skepticism, different critiques of skepticism and a brief word about skepticism and naturalistic versions of evolutionary theory.

2 VARIETIES OF SKEPTICISM

Skepticism is a family of viewpoints and not one simple position. For the purposes of this chapter, three forms of skepticism require only a brief mention: iterative, metaepistemological, and heuristic or methodological skepticism. **Iterative skepticism** occurs when the skeptic refuses to offer an argument for his view but, instead, simply responds to every assertion with the question, how do you know? When this question is answered, the iterative skeptic merely repeats the question, and so on, indefinitely. This form of skepticism is not a genuine philosophical position, since its advocates are not willing to advance arguments against knowledge or accept arguments for knowledge. Iterative skepticism is merely a verbal game and should be treated as such.

Second, **metaepistemological skepticism** has been advanced by philosophers like W. V. O. Quine and Richard Rorty. Advocates of this view are skeptical about and reject philosophy (and especially epistemology) as traditionally conceived (e.g., epistemology is a normative search for a theory of justification and knowledge), and claim that philosophy is on a continuum with or merely a part of natural science. Metaepistemological skeptics hold to an extreme form of what is called **naturalized epistemology**. In its stronger versions, this viewpoint implies that epistemology should be naturalized in the sense that it should be reduced to and treated as a branch of psychology and neurophysiology. Instead of focusing on the normative question of what justifies our beliefs, naturalized epistemology simply describes how people do, in fact, form their beliefs. The task of naturalized epistemology is to describe causal factors and processes in scientific, natural terms as to how people's beliefs are normally—in the statistical sense of typically or usually—formed.

Most philosophers reject this extreme form of naturalized epistemology and the metaepistemological skepticism it entails. For one thing, it leaves out what is crucial to epistemology—the normative element. Traditional epistemology provides an account of justification and knowledge, of epistemic virtues and duties and of how one decides what one ought and ought not believe. Purely psychological or neurophysiological descriptions of causal, belief-forming processes are merely descriptive and not normative or prescriptive. Thus they leave out the crucial normative element in traditional epistemology. Second, it will become evident in chapters fifteen through seventeen that science has certain philosophical presuppositions (e.g., that there is truth, that people do, in fact, have knowledge and justified beliefs about the external world). Because of this, the epistemic authority of science rests on that of philosophy (including epistemology), not the other way around. Third, while not all philosophers are in agreement about this, some have argued that the statements asserting naturalized epistemology and metaepistemological skepticism are self-refuting because they are themselves normative philosophical statements (not scientific ones) that stand in need of justification.

A third form of skepticism is **heuristic** or **methodological skepticism**. Here, knowledge and justified belief are acknowledged, and skepticism—especially the question "How does one know that X?" and the use of doubt—is taken as a guiding principle to aid people in their search for a better understanding of epistemological issues. In this sense, skepticism is not a position to be refuted or rebutted, but a guiding method to help people understand knowledge. This form of skepticism is, indeed, very helpful, since doubting and questioning knowledge claims can lead one to deeper understanding. But one must be careful here to distinguish between doubt as a method and doubt as a habitual character trait. The former employs the use of doubt to develop knowledge. The latter is rooted in a skeptical character or heart and is not completely desirable from a Christian perspective because, as Christians, we are to cultivate faith and knowledge while at the same time not being gullible or naive. If doubt, understood as a character trait, helps one avoid naivete, then it is an intellectual virtue. If it produces cynicism and a loss of faith, then it is an intellectual vice. Wisdom requires a balanced perspective.

We turn, now, to further versions of skepticism, traditionally conceived, versions that express more deeply what skepticism is when viewed as a substantive philosophical thesis. First, there is a distinction between knowledge skepticism and justificational skepticism. **Knowledge skepticism** is a thesis to the effect that the conditions for knowledge do not obtain and people do not have knowledge. **Justificational skepticism** is the same thesis directed, not at knowledge, but at justification and justified beliefs. One could be a knowledge skeptic and not a justificational skeptic. For example, one could deny knowledge on the grounds that there is no such thing as truth (and since knowledge includes justified *true* belief, there is no knowledge) or on the grounds that the standards for knowledge are so high (e.g., knowledge requires absolute certainty) that they are never met. But one could go on to accept the claim that people often have justification for their beliefs. Alternatively, one could accept the fact that there is knowledge but be skeptical about the existence of justified beliefs if that person held that justification is not part of knowledge.

Both knowledge and justificational skeptics can direct their skepticism at either the generation, transmission or sources of belief. That is, the skeptic can direct his arguments against (1) the origination of knowledge or justified beliefs in the first place (e.g., the belief that one is experiencing a red sensation generated by the fact that one is, indeed, having that sensation), (2) the fact that some justified or known beliefs (e.g., that one is experiencing a red sensation) transfer justification to other beliefs (e.g., that there is, in fact, a red object before one) or (3) entire epistemic faculties that serve as sources of knowledge and justification (e.g., against memory, sensory faculties, reason, introspection).

In this chapter we will focus on knowledge skepticism, not justificational skepticism, for two reasons. First, much of what is said about knowledge skepticism could be applied to justificational skepticism. Second, part of the task of considering justificational skepticism is the analysis of different theories of justification and this will be done in chapter five.

Skeptics also differ in regard to the depth of their skepticism. We have already seen this in regard to the affirmation of the skeptical thesis itself, academic skeptics being dogmatic and certain about skepticism itself and Pyrrhonic skeptics being less deep and more tentative about skepticism. But apart from the skeptical thesis itself, skeptics differ in regard to the depth of their position about knowledge in general. **Unmitigated skepticism** holds its skepticism with greater assurance and certainty than does **mitigated skepticism**, which is more tentative about knowledge claims. For any item of alleged knowledge, the unmitigated skeptic asserts that it is not a case of knowledge, but a mitigated skeptic is more inclined to withhold judgment about this assertion.

Within the category of unmitigated skeptics, there are three grades of strength with which unmitigated skepticism is affirmed. Going from stronger to weaker forms of unmitigated skepticism, these grades are as follows: (1) No proposition is knowable, that is, it is not possible for any proposition to be known. (2) While it may be possible for a proposition to be known, as a matter of fact, no proposition *is* known. (3) While there may be some propositions that are known in some weak sense of that word, nevertheless, no propositions are known with complete certainty.

Skeptics also differ in regard to the width or breadth of their skepticism. **Global skepticism** is the view that there is no knowledge (or justified belief) in any area of human thought. By contrast, **local skepticism** allows for knowledge in some areas (e.g., in science or in our sensory knowledge of the external world), but local skeptics deny knowledge in this or that specific area (e.g., in theology, ethics, mathematics). More specifically, local skeptics can direct their skepticism at certain alleged objects, faculties or subject matters of knowledge.

If objects are in view, then the skeptic denies that people have knowledge of certain objects or kinds of objects (e.g., of other minds, God, causal connections, matter). If faculties are in view, then the skeptic denies that knowledge can be gained by the utilization of some faculty or set of capacities people are supposed to possess (e.g., the senses, reason, other forms of intuition). If a certain subject matter is involved, then the skeptic denies that knowledge obtains in that subject matter (e.g., history, theology, science, ethics).

We will not look at local skepticism in the remainder of this chapter for three reasons. First, global skepticism is more interesting from a philosophical point of view and it is more central because if it is acceptable, then local skepticism follows. Second, it is hard to sustain local skepticism because the considerations that drive it in some specific domain are hard to limit solely to that domain. Skeptical considerations have a tendency to spill out into other areas, or to change the metaphor, once the camel's nose is in the tent, it is hard limit the camel's movement throughout the tent. Third, in later chapters (e.g., chaps. 19-20, 23-24), we will examine skepticism about morality and religion, respectively, so we may safely postpone further reflection about local skepticism until then.

Finally, there is a distinction between first-order and second-order skepticism. **First-order skepticism** is the more typical version and it involves skepticism directed at people's everyday beliefs, that is, beliefs about the external world (there is a tree in the yard) or about an ethical proposition (*Mercy as such is a virtue*). **Second-order skepticism** is directed at people's beliefs about these other beliefs. Here the skeptic does not directly question whether people have knowledge of this or that particular item. Rather, he challenges the idea that people know that they have this knowledge. It is normally the case that a first-order skeptic will also be a second-order skeptic because if people do not have knowledge of this or that, then they cannot have knowledge that they do have knowledge of this or that. On the other hand, one could be a second-order skeptic and not a first-order skeptic. One could hold that people know that a tree is in the yard but that they cannot know that they have this knowledge because such second-order knowledge requires, first, that they have an understanding of what knowledge itself is and, in light of Gettier counterexamples (see chap. 3), that understanding is not available.

We will not look at all of these different versions of skepticism. Such a task is important but too detailed for present purposes. But the considerations to follow will often apply, sometimes with minor adjustments, to several different skeptical positions. We will focus our attention on global, unmitigated, first-order knowledge skepticism. Further, we will focus on our sensory knowledge of the external world unless otherwise indicated. However, before we look at arguments for and against such skepticism, we need to get clear on an important purpose for this inquiry. Our goal here, and a major goal of epistemology in general, is to improve our epistemic situation. Part of such an improvement is to gain more knowledge and justified beliefs (and increase the strength of justification for our beliefs that are already justified to some degree) and to remove unjustified or false beliefs from the things we accept. In light of this, a distinction should be drawn between refuting the skeptic and rebutting the skeptic. **Refut-**

ing the skeptic involves proving that skepticism is false, perhaps even proving this to the skeptic himself. This strategy involves accepting a burden of proof on part of the **cognitivist**—the one who accepts the fact that people do have knowledge. By contrast, **rebutting the skeptic** involves showing that skeptical arguments do not establish the fact that people do not have knowledge. Our primary concern here is not with refuting, but with rebutting the skeptic. Such a stance involves placing the burden of proof on the skeptic and it expresses at least initial confidence in our noetic equipment (e.g., sensory and cognitive faculties). Such an expression of confidence is quite at home in a Christian theistic worldview, because God is a good, trustworthy, rational being who created and designed humans to have knowledge about him and his world. Whether such confidence is justified within an evolutionary naturalistic framework is something we will consider at the end of the chapter. But for now, let us press on in earnest and look at some of the arguments skeptics have offered in defense of their thesis.

3 ARGUMENTS FOR SKEPTICISM
Several arguments have been offered on behalf of skepticism, among which are the following.

We can all cite cases where we have been wrong in the past; we have mistakenly thought we had knowledge when we did not or when our senses deceived us. An oar looks bent in the water; railroad tracks appear to touch in the distance; ice will feel hot in certain circumstances; we see someone in the dark, take him to be a friend, and later find out we were wrong. The skeptic cites this problem, labeled the **argument from error**, and generalizes it in this way. In each case of past error we confused appearance with reality and mistakenly thought we had knowledge. How do we know that this is not happening right now? How do we know that this is not universally the case in our sensory awareness of the world? Since we have been mistaken in the past, for all we know we could always be mistaken in our beliefs. If this is so, how can we claim to have knowledge? How do I know I am not mistaken right now?

3.1
THE ARGUMENT
FROM ERROR
AND FALLIBILITY

Perhaps skeptics do not need to argue from the fact that we *have* been mistaken on occasions. Instead, skeptics may offer various **brain-in-the-vat arguments**; they simply need to point out that it is merely possible, logically speaking, that we are mistaken in our knowledge claims. And from the mere logical possibility of error (the fact that a skeptical thesis about any putative knowledge claim is not a logical contradiction), it follows that we cannot have knowledge. It is logically possible that an evil demon is tricking us by giving us sensory experiences of an external world when, in fact, no such world exists. Perhaps some scientist has put our brains in a vat in a laboratory and is stimulating them in such a way that we have a full range of sensory experiences of an external world when no such world is really appearing to us. Since it is logically possible that these things are happening to me and since there would be nothing in my experience that could indicate this to me one way or another (the brain-in-the-vat and the gen-

3.2
EVIL DEMONS,
BRAIN-IN-
THE-VAT
ARGUMENTS
AND THE
POSSIBILITY OF
ERROR

uine sensory knowledge of the external world scenarios are empirically equivalent), then I cannot have knowledge since the skeptical arguments are logically
possible. How do I know that these skeptical scenarios are not happening to me
right now?

3.3
TRANSFER OF
JUSTIFICATION
ARGUMENTS

Some skeptics are willing to grant, for the sake of argument, that we do have
sensory knowledge that we are presently aware of at this very moment (e.g.,
that there is a green tree before me right now or that I am having a green sensation now). But we all claim to know many things that go beyond our present
sensory experiences. These claims raise **transfer of justification arguments**,
that is, arguments about the transfer of justification to knowledge claims beyond our present experience. For example, cognitivists claim that one can
know what is in one's study even when one is not there, that the sun will rise
tomorrow, that since all previously experienced emeralds have been green,
then it is likely that all emeralds whatever are green, that the tree before one
now was here ten minutes ago. The problem with all these knowledge claims,
says the skeptic, is that they are not entailed by one's present knowledge.
That is, one's current belief that there is a green tree before one right now
could be true and the belief that the tree was there ten minutes ago could be
false. Similarly, one's study may be burned down, the sun may not rise tomorrow, some emerald somewhere may be blue. These are all cases of inductive
knowledge, cases where the truth of the premises do not guarantee, but
merely lend support to the truth of the conclusions. In the transfer of justification from premises to conclusion, something is lost and error or loss of justification is possible. The skeptic asks, how do I know in each of these cases
that I have not lost my justification for the conclusion even if it is granted
that I know the premise?

4 A CRITIQUE OF SKEPTICISM

4.1
SKEPTICISM AND
THE PROBLEM OF
THE CRITERION

A good way to begin an evaluation of skepticism is to focus on what is called the
problem of the criterion. We can distinguish two different questions in epistemology. First, we can ask, what is it that we know? This is a question about the
specific items of knowledge we possess and about the *extent* of our knowledge.
Second, we can ask, how do we decide in any given case whether or not we have
knowledge in that case? What are the criteria for knowledge? This is a question
about our *criteria* for knowledge.

Now suppose that people wish to sort all of their beliefs into two groups—
the true or justified ones and the false or unjustified ones—in order to retain
the former and dispose of the latter in their entire set of beliefs. Such a sorting would allow them to improve their epistemic situation and grow in knowledge and justification. But now a problem arises regarding how one is able to
proceed in this sorting activity. It would seem that one would need an answer
to one of the two questions above in order to proceed. But before one can
have an answer to the first question about the extent of knowledge, one
would seem to need an answer to the second question about criteria for
knowledge. But before one can have an answer to the second question, it

seems that one needs an answer to the first question. This is the problem of the criterion.[1]

There are three main solutions to the problem. First, there is skepticism. The skeptic claims, among other things, that no cognitivist solution to the problem exists and thus there is no knowledge. The next two solutions are advocated by cognitivists who claim that people do have knowledge. **Methodism** is the name of the second solution and it has been advocated by philosophers such as John Locke, René Descartes, logical positivists and others. According to methodism, one starts the enterprise of knowing with a criterion for what does and does not count as knowledge, in other words, one starts with an answer to question two and not question one. Methodists claim that before one can know some specific proposition P (e.g., *There is a tree in the yard*), one must first know some general criterion Q and, further, one must know that P is a good example of or measures up to Q. For example, Q might be "If you can test some item of belief with the five senses, then it can be an item of knowledge," or perhaps, "If something appears to your senses in a certain way, then in the absence of defeaters, you know that the thing is as it appears to you."

Unfortunately, methodism is not a good epistemic strategy because it leads to a **vicious infinite regress**. To see this, note that in general, methodism implies that before one can know anything, P, one must know two other things: Q (one's criterion for knowledge) and R (the fact that P satisfies Q). But now the skeptic can ask how it is that one knows Q and R, and the methodist will have to offer a new criterion Q' that specifies how he knows Q, and R' that tells how he knows that Q satisfies Q'. Obviously, the same problem will arise for Q' and R', and a vicious regress is set up. Another way to see this is to note that there have been major debates about what are and are not good criteria for knowledge. Locke offered something akin to the notion that an item of knowledge about the external world must pass the criterion that the item of knowledge must be derived from simple sensory ideas or impressions (roughly, testing it with the senses). By contrast, Descartes offered a radically different criterion: the item of knowledge must be clear (precise, not fuzzy) and distinct (not confused with other ideas) when brought before the mind. If one is a methodist, how is one to settle disputes about criteria for knowledge? The answer will be that one will have to offer criteria for one's criteria, and so on. It would seem, then, that methodism is in trouble.

There is a third solution to the problem, known as **particularism**, advocated by philosophers such as Thomas Reid, Roderick Chisholm and G. E. Moore. According to particularists, people start by knowing specific, clear items of knowledge: that one had eggs for breakfast this morning, that there is a tree before one or, perhaps, that one seems to see a tree, that $7 + 5 = 12$, that mercy is a virtue and so on. One can know some things directly and simply without having to have criteria for how one knows them and without having to know how or even that one knows them. People know many things without being able to prove that they do or without fully understanding the things they know.

---

[1]See Roderick Chisholm, *The Problem of the Criterion* (Milwaukee, Wis.: Marquette University Press, 1973); Robert P. Amico, *The Problem of the Criterion* (Lanham, Md.: Rowman & Littlefield, 1993).

People simply identify clear instances of knowing without applying any criteria for knowledge or justification. One may reflect on these instances and go on to develop criteria for knowledge consistent with them, and then use these criteria to make judgments in borderline cases of knowledge. But the criteria are justified by their congruence with specific instances of knowledge, not the other way around.

For example, one may start with moral knowledge (murder is wrong) and legal knowledge (taxes are to be paid by April 15) and go on to formulate criteria for when something is moral or legal. One could then use these criteria for judging borderline cases (intentionally driving on the wrong side of the street). In general, we start with clear instances of knowledge, formulate criteria based on those clear instances, and extend our knowledge by using those criteria to resolve borderline, unclear cases.

The skeptic can raise two basic objections against the particularist. First, particularism allegedly begs the question against the skeptic by simply assuming the point at issue—whether people have knowledge. How does the particularist know that people have this? Is it not possible in the cases cited above that the particularist is wrong and he only thinks he has knowledge?

Particularists respond to this objection in at least four ways. First, regarding begging the question, if the skeptic is an iterative skeptic, his question can be ignored because it is not a substantive position or argument. If, on the other hand, his skeptical question is the result of an argument, then this argument must be reasonable before it can be held as a serious objection against knowledge. However, if one did not know some things one could not *reasonably* doubt anything (e.g., the reason for doubting one's senses now is one's knowledge that they have misled him in the past). Global, unmitigated skepticism is not a rationally defensible position, and the skeptical question cannot be rationally asserted and defended without presupposing knowledge.

Second, the skeptic tries to force the particularist to be a methodist by asking the "How do you know?" question since the skeptic is implying that before one can know, one must have criteria for knowledge. And the skeptic knows he can refute the methodist. But the particularist will resist the slide into methodism by reaffirming that he can know some specific item without having to say how he knows it.

Third, the particularist argues that just because it is logically possible that he is mistaken in a specific case of knowledge, that does not mean he is mistaken or that he has any good reason to think he is wrong. And until the skeptic can give him good reason for thinking his instances of knowledge fail, the mere logical possibility that he is wrong will not suffice.

The particularist and skeptic have very different approaches to knowledge. For the skeptic, the burden of proof is on the cognitivist. If it is logically possible that one might be mistaken, then knowledge is not present because knowledge requires certainty. Of the two main tasks of epistemology (obtaining true or justified beliefs and avoiding false or unjustified beliefs), the skeptic elevates the latter and requires that his position be refuted before knowledge can be justified. Moreover, if one asks what it means to have "a **right to be sure**" that one has knowledge, two different senses of this phrase are involved: (1) one can dogmatically assert that one has knowledge and refuse to look at further evidence or (2) one can have the right to rely on the truth of the belief in explaining things and in forming other beliefs while remaining open to further evidence in the future. The skeptic claims that the particularist assertion of knowledge is an example of the former sense of the right to be sure, not the latter.

By contrast, the cognitivist places the burden of proof on the skeptic. Just because it is logically possible to be mistaken in a given case, it does not follow that one might be mistaken in an epistemic sense. There is a distinction between a **logical "might"** and an **epistemic "might"** in "you *might* be mistaken." The former means that there is no logical contradiction in asserting that a knowledge claim is in error. The latter means that there are good reasons for thinking that one actually is mistaken in a knowledge claim. The particularist claims that all the skeptic provides is the logical possibility of error in certain clear cases of knowledge, but not the epistemic possibility of error (good reasons for thinking one actually is in error), and it is the latter that is required to defeat a knowledge claim. The particularist holds that (1) knowledge does not require certainty; (2) the burden of proof is on the skeptic, that all the particularist needs to do is rebut, not refute the skeptic; (3) of the two main tasks of epistemology, having true or justified beliefs takes precedent over avoiding false, unjustified beliefs; and (4) the appropriate notion of the "right to be sure" is the second one.

These different perspectives are summarizes as follows:

Issue	The Skeptic	The Particularist
burden of proof	on the particularist	on the skeptic
knowledge	requires certainty	does not require certainty
"you might be wrong"	uses a logical "might"	uses an epistemic "might"
dealing with the skeptic	skeptic must be refuted	skeptic must be rebutted
two tasks of epistemology	emphasizes avoidance of false or unjustified beliefs	emphasizes obtaining true or justified beliefs
the particularist's use of "the right to be sure"	dogmatically asserted in a closed-minded way	the right to use our knowledge while remaining open

There is one final point the particularist makes in his defense. The particularist claims that his view has advantages over the other two positions. Regarding methodism, the particularist avoids a vicious infinite regress. Regarding skepticism, particularism accords and skepticism does not accord with the fact that, after all, people do know many things.

We are now in a position to understand the dialectic between skeptic and particularist about a second major skeptical objection to particularism. Simply put, the objection is that particularism might easily be abused. One could just go around and assert that he or she knows all kinds of things and sanction this intellectual irresponsibility by claiming to be a particularist.

In light of what we have seen above, the particularist response should be clear. Just because it is logically possible to abuse particularism, it does not follow in a particular case that one is actually abusing it. Instead of focusing on generalities and mere logical possibilities, one should look at specific cases of knowledge claims and require that the skeptic give good reasons for thinking that particularism is being abused in that very case. The mere possibility that such an abuse is going on is not sufficient to prove the skeptic's case, and the particularist does not need a criterion for telling when particularism itself is and is not being abused before he can adopt a particularist standpoint in a specific instance of knowledge.

4.2
BRIEF
RESPONSES TO
THE MAIN
SKEPTICAL
ARGUMENTS

1. The argument from error. From the fact that one has been mistaken in the past, it does not follow that there are good reasons for thinking that one's senses are currently deceiving him right now. Until such reasons are given as **defeaters**, one has a right to be sure that one's current sensory beliefs are examples of knowledge. One's current sensory beliefs are **prima facie justified**, that is, innocent until "proven" guilty. If something appears red to someone right now, and he forms his belief that "Something before me is red right now" on that basis, then *in the absence of defeaters (factors that refute or undercut one's justification), or perhaps in the absence of being aware of reasons for thinking that there are defeaters,* one has a right to be sure of one's sensory belief. Moreover, if people do have knowledge about human fallibility and past deceptions, then, obviously, they know certain things.

2. Evil demons and the mere possibility of error. Just because it is logically possible that one's current beliefs are mistaken, it does not follow that it is epistemically possible that one is mistaken, i.e., that one has any grounds for doubting one's current beliefs. Someone does not need to refute the skeptic before he can know things, and the burden of proof is on the skeptic. The mere suggestion that it is logically possible that one might be mistaken does not meet that burden of proof. Knowledge does not require total certainty. Of course if the skeptic says that we have *grounds* for doubting our beliefs, then we must be given those grounds. And we cannot be given grounds for doubting without knowing something that puts us in a position to take the grounds for doubting to be justified.

3. The transfer of justification. Just because a set of grounds or premises do not guarantee a conclusion it does not follow that people do not know that conclusion. Knowledge does not require absolute certainty. Moreover, people can have inductive knowledge without first having a theory as to how the premises for or grounds of such knowledge transfer justification to the item they know.

Our responses here have been brief because they really represent applications of the issues discussed in the analysis of the problem of the criterion. From our discussion of that problem, it should be evident that the skeptic and the particularist have different attitudes of confidence in the human ability to obtain knowledge and in the trustworthiness of human noetic equipment (e.g., sensory and cognitive faculties). But is it really sensible to have confidence in that equipment?

Interestingly, one's worldview will have an affect on how this question should be answered. More specifically, from the time of Darwin to the present, many thinkers have expressed the thought that if naturalistic evolutionary theory is true, we would have little reason to trust our noetic equipment, but if Christian theism is true, we would have good worldview considerations that help to justify such confidence. We will close this chapter with a brief examination of this issue.

5 EVOLUTIONARY NATURALISM AND OUR NOETIC EQUIPMENT

Several thinkers, C. S. Lewis, Richard Taylor and Alvin Plantinga among them, have argued in one way or another that naturalism in general, and evolutionary naturalism in particular, lead to skepticism.[2] This idea is not new. In fact, the same problem troubled Darwin himself: "With me the horrid doubt always arises whether the convictions of man's mind, which has been developed from the mind of lower animals, are of any value or at all trustworthy. Would any one trust in the convictions of a monkey's mind, if there are any convictions in such a mind?"[3] In what follows, we will give a simple overview of the way Alvin Plantinga develops this argument.

According to Plantinga, knowledge is warranted true belief, and a belief has **warrant** for some person just in case ("just in case" means "if and only if") that belief was formed by cognitive faculties that are functioning properly and in accordance with a good design plan in a cognitive environment appropriate for the way those faculties were designed and when the design plan for our faculties is aimed at obtaining truth. The important point here is that, according to Plantinga, warrant is a normative notion, and an essential part of warrant is that our faculties are functioning properly, that is, functioning the way they *ought* to function. Since **proper function** is normative (understood in terms of the way our faculties *ought* to function), "proper function" cannot be understood as a mere description of the statistically usual or normal way that human faculties do, in fact, function. These two notions (normative functioning versus statistically usual functioning) are not the same thing. Someone could have sensory and intellectual faculties that functioned the way they ought to and be the only person to function that way if everyone else had defectively functioning faculties. Similarly, one could have faculties that functioned in the statistically usual way without having faculties that operated the way they ought to if most people's faculties were defective.

Now the notion of proper function, understood as functioning the way something ought to function, makes clear sense for artifacts that are designed by an intelligence. Why? Because the claim that something functions the way it

---

[2]C. S. Lewis, *Miracles* (New York: Macmillan, 1947), chaps. 1-4, 13; Richard Taylor, *Metaphysics* (Englewood Cliffs, N.J.: Prentice-Hall, 1963), pp. 112-19; Alvin Plantinga, *Warrant and Proper Function* (New York: Oxford University Press, 1993), chaps. 11-12.

[3]This is from Darwin's letter to William Graham Down, dated July 3, 1881, in *The Life and Letters of Charles Darwin Including an Autobiographical Chapter*, ed. Francis Darwin, 2 vols. (London: John Murray, Albermarle Street, 1887), 1:315-16.

ought to is easily understood in terms of functioning the way it was designed to function. An engine functions properly in that it functions the way it was designed to function. Now if knowledge presupposes warranted belief, and if warrant beliefs presuppose that those beliefs were produced by properly functioning faculties, and if the notion of properly functioning faculties presupposes the notion of being designed to function in a certain way, then knowledge presupposes a designer.

The naturalist owes us an account of what it would mean for humans to have properly functioning cognitive and sensory faculties that can avoid the idea of a designer and, says Plantinga, those accounts have not been successful. In one way or another, they all define "proper functioning" in terms of functioning in a statistically normal, usual way (e.g., a heart functions normally if it functions the way most hearts do) or in a way that enhances the survival value of the organisms that have the organ or faculty in question. But these do not give us a normative notion of proper functioning faculties, and in any case one cannot define proper functioning in terms of evolutionary theory and survival value because even if evolution is true, it is a contingent truth (evolution could have been false; indeed it most likely is false) and there could have been proper functioning faculties even if evolution had been false. So the truth of evolution cannot be required to make sense of proper functioning faculties. Whatever account we give of properly functioning faculties should apply in possible worlds where evolution is true and in worlds where it is flase. A definition that captures the real essence of something, in this case "properly functioning faculties," cannot contingently apply to the thing being defined depending on whether or not some other factor (evolution) is true.

Plantinga's case is more detailed than we can present here. But if his argument is correct, then metaphysical naturalism, including evolutionary naturalism, is false. The issue is this: if knowledge exists and if properly functioning faculties are necessary conditions for knowledge, then if the notion of proper function requires the existence of a designer of those faculties and cannot be adequately understood in strictly naturalistic terms, we can conclude that metaphysical naturalism is false.

Next, Plantinga develops arguments that try to show not that evolutionary naturalism is false, but that even if it is true, it is still irrational to believe it. He begins by pointing out that, according to naturalistic evolutionary theory, human beings, their parts and cognitive faculties, arose by a blind, mindless, purposeless process such that these things were selected for solely in virtue of survival value and reproductive advantage. If our cognitive faculties arose this way, then their ultimate purpose (assuming they have one; see above) is to guarantee that we *behave* in certain ways, i.e., that we *move* appropriately in getting nourishment, avoiding danger, fighting and reproducing such that our chances of survival are enhanced. From this perspective, beliefs, and certainly beliefs that are true, take a hindmost role if they play any role at all. Thus naturalistic evolutionary theory gives us reason to doubt that our cognitive systems have the production of true beliefs as a purpose or that they do, in fact, furnish us with mostly true beliefs.

But could not someone object to this in the following way? Surely an organism with trustworthy sensory and cognitive faculties would be more likely to survive than those without those faculties, and thus the processes of evolution would select trustworthy faculties and make their existence likely. According to Plantinga, this is not so. That is, the probability that our faculties would be reliable, given the truth of evolutionary naturalism and the existence of the faculties we possess, is either (1) very low indeed or (2) something about which we should remain agnostic. Why does Plantinga think this? Evolution is likely to select behavior that is adaptive, but we cannot say the same for faculties that produce true beliefs because, given evolutionary naturalism, at least five different scenarios regarding our beliefs (or those of a hypothetical creature or, say, a monkey) and our noetic faculties are possible and cannot be ruled out.

First, evolutionary processes could produce beliefs that have no causal relationship whatever to behavior and thus no purpose or function. In this case, evolution would select adaptive behavior but beliefs would be mere epiphenomena, entities that "float on top" of physical states in an organism with no purpose or function. Beliefs would not cause or be caused by behaviors and thus would be invisible to evolution. We can add a further point to Plantinga's argument here.

In chapters eleven and twelve, we will see that naturalistic evolutionary theory seems to imply a physicalist view of living organisms, that is, that they are merely complex physical objects. Why? Because on this view, living organisms are solely the result of physical evolutionary processes operating on solely physical materials, and thus the products of evolution (living organisms) would be solely physical. Now, at least two things seem to be mental entities and not physical ones: beliefs and our relationship to them. Our beliefs (e.g., that red is a color) seem to be states of the mind with certain mental contents (the meaning or propositional content of the belief) being essential to them. Moreover, as cognitive beings, we sustain certain relations to our beliefs that are mental and not physical in nature: We grasp, attend to, affirm, hold and ponder our beliefs. Thus, if beliefs and our relationship to them are mental in nature, evolutionary naturalism would seem to imply that there would be no beliefs or mental relations. If beliefs do not exist, they can hardly be said to cause or be caused by behavior.

Second, evolution could produce beliefs that are effects but not causes of behavior (in option one, beliefs were neither). In this case, beliefs would be like a decoration and would not be a part of a causal chain leading to action. Waking beliefs would be much like dreams are to us now.

Third, evolution could produce beliefs that do have causal efficacy (they are caused by and, in turn, cause behaviors), but not in virtue of what they essentially are as beliefs, that is, not in virtue of their semantics or mental contents, but in virtue of the physical characteristics or syntax that are associated with (or part of) them. Plantinga illustrates this with a person who reads a poem so loudly that it breaks a glass but this causal effect is not produced by the meanings or contents of the poem (they, like beliefs in this third option, are causally irrelevant), but by the sound waves coming from the reader's mouth.

Fourth, evolution could produce beliefs that are, in fact, causally efficacious syntactically and semantically (in virtue of their content), but such beliefs and belief systems could be maladaptive in at least two ways (in general maladaptive features such as being an albino can be fixed in a species and passed on to off-spring; similarly, the presence of a certain belief system or the propensity to form beliefs could be maladaptive and still be fixed in a species and passed on to offspring). First, beliefs could be energy expensive distractions causing creatures to engage in survival enhancing behavior but in a way less efficient and economical than if the causal connections producing that behavior bypassed belief altogether. In support of Plantinga's point, some scientists have argued that the possession of rational abilities (e.g., belief processing systems) can be a disadvantage because such systems require increased information-processing capacities associated with the nervous system and this is a reproductive liability prenatally (such a system requires a longer and more vulnerable gestation period) and postnatally (it takes longer to raise and teach the young). Second, beliefs could directly produce maladaptive behavior but the organism could survive anyway, perhaps due to other, overriding factors.

Finally, evolution could produce beliefs that are causally efficacious in virtue of their contents and that are adaptive. However, in this case we can still ask: What would be the likelihood that the noetic faculties producing such beliefs would be reliable guides to having *true* beliefs? Not very high, says Plantinga, and to see why, we need to note that beliefs don't produce behaviors directly; rather, entire sets of beliefs, desires and other factors (e.g., sensations, acts of will, or persons themselves) are among the things that produce behavior. Plantinga invites us to consider Paul, a prehistoric hominid whose survival requires that he display various types of tiger-avoidance behavior (e.g., fleeing, hiding). Call these behaviors B. Now B could be caused by Paul's desire to avoid being eaten plus the true belief that B will increase his chances of avoiding such a fate.

However, indefinitely many other belief-desire systems could easily produce B as well, even if they contain false beliefs (and wrong desires or inaccurate sensory experiences). For example, perhaps Paul likes the idea of being eaten but always runs away from tigers, looking for a better prospect because he thinks it unlikely that the tiger before him will eat him. Or perhaps he thinks a tiger is a large, friendly pussycat and wants to pet the tiger before him, but also believes the best way to pet it is to run away from it. Or perhaps he confuses running toward it with running away from it. All of these belief-desire sets would get Paul's body in the right place so far as survival is concerned, but most of them will not need to contain true beliefs to do this. To elaborate on Plantinga's point, from an evolutionary perspective, organisms are black boxes insofar as their beliefs, desires, sensations and willings are concerned. Organisms that move the right way (for survival purposes) given the right circumstances, need not have true beliefs about or accurate sensations of the world around them. Thus the possession of trustworthy faculties that regularly produce true beliefs is not required by the demands of survival. This is especially true when it comes to the ability to have true beliefs about abstract issues or to engage in intellectual theorizing, e.g., philosophical reflection, scientific theorizing and so forth, including the ability to argue for or against evolutionary theory itself. These abilities go far beyond what would be required within the constraints of reproductive advantage and survival.

Now each of these five scenarios is possible. And given no further evidence either way about the reliability of our cognitive equipment, the likelihood that those faculties would be reliable, given evolutionary naturalism and the faculties that we have, would either be very low or something we would simply have to be agnostic about. Thus evolutionary naturalism serves as an undercutting defeater that removes our grounds for trusting in the reliability of our noetic equipment. Plantinga likens this to a case in which a person enters a factory, sees an assembly line carrying apparently red widgets, and is then told that these widgets are being irradiated by various red lights that make everything look red. A given widget before the person could still be red, but the person would have no grounds for believing this. She has an undercutting defeater for such a belief.

Someone might object and claim that we do have grounds independent of evolutionary theory for trusting our noetic equipment, namely, the fact that we engage in reasoning to true beliefs all the time. But, says Plantinga, such a claim is **pragmatically circular** in that it alleges to give a reason for trusting our noetic equipment, but the reason is itself trustworthy only if those faculties are indeed trustworthy. If I have come to doubt my noetic equipment, I cannot give an *argument* using that equipment for I will rely on the very equipment in doubt.

An evolutionary naturalist could respond to this charge of pragmatic circularity in this way: He claims to start with evolutionary naturalism, comes to see Plantinga's argument and thus to distrust his noetic equipment, but at the same time realizes that his distrust also removes any reason he has for trusting Plantinga's argument itself, and thus comes in the end no longer to have reason to distrust his noetic equipment. Plantinga's response to this is to show that, in fact, the evolutionary naturalist is caught in a paralyzing **dialectical loop** like the one noted long ago by David Hume:

> This [skeptical] argument is not just; because the skeptical reasonings, were it possible for them to exist, and were they not destroy'd by their subtility, wou'd be successively both strong and weak, according to the successive dispositions of the mind. Reason first appears in possession of the throne, prescribing laws, and imposing maxims, with an absolute sway and authority. Her enemy, therefore, is oblig'd to take shelter under her protection, and by making use of rational arguments to prove the fallaciousness and imbecility of reason, produces, in a manner, a patent under her hand and seal. This patent has at first an authority, proposition'd to the present and immediate authority of reason, from which it is deriv'd. But as it is suppos'd to be contradictory to reason, it gradually diminishes the force of that governing power, and its own at the same time; till at last they both vanish away into nothing, by a regular and just diminution.[4]

Hume's argument against skepticism can be rephrased in this way. We start by trusting our reason. But, later, we encounter skeptical arguments against

---

[4]David Hume, *A Treatise of Human Nature*, analytical index by L. A. Selby-Bigge, 2d ed. with text revised and notes by P. H. Nidditch (Oxford: Clarendon, 1978; first ed., 1888), book 1, part 4, section 1, pp. 186-87.

that trust and so we stop trusting reason. But once we do this, we no longer have any reason to accept the skeptical arguments themselves and continue our mistrust of reason. At this point, I begin to trust reason again, but then, the skeptical arguments reassert themselves and so forth. We have entered a vicious dialectical loop that, eventually, will reach a sort of intellectual paralysis. According to Plantinga, evolutionary naturalists are caught in this same sort of loop. This shows that evolutionary naturalism is an ultimately undefeated defeater of our grounds for trusting the reliability of our noetic equipment. Put another way, evolutionary naturalism is self-defeating because it provides for itself a defeater (grounds for not trusting our noetic equipment) that is ultimately undefeated (cannot be removed by more basic considerations). Given that evolutionary naturalism and traditional theism are our options, this provides an argument for traditional theism which, among other things, teaches that a rational, good God designed our noetic equipment and placed us in a conducive cognitive environment so we could have knowledge of many things about him and his world.

We cannot undertake an evaluation of arguments against Plantinga's line of thought or of responses to those arguments. But one thing should be mentioned. The trustworthiness of our cognitive faculties is closely related to broad worldview considerations relating to the nature, function and origin of those faculties. Thus the problem of skepticism should be analyzed, at least in part, in light of the resources that different worldviews bring to bear on that problem.

CHAPTER SUMMARY

Skepticism has had a long history from the ancient Academic and Pyrrhonian skeptics up to the present. There are several forms of skepticism. Iterative skeptics merely repeat the question, how do you know?; metaepistemological skeptics are skeptical about philosophy and epistemology themselves; and heuristic skepticism is merely a guiding approach to developing epistemological insights. Knowledge skepticism and justificational skepticism are directed at knowledge and justification, respectively, and utilize arguments against the origination, transfer or sources of knowledge or justification. Unmitigated skeptics are more certain of skepticism, and mitigated skeptics are more tentative. Global skeptics claim that there is no knowledge in any area of human thought, and local skeptics limit skepticism to a specific object (or kind of object), faculty or subject matter. First-order skepticism focuses on ordinary beliefs, and second-order skepticism centers on knowing that we know. There is a key difference between refuting and rebutting the skeptic.

Three main skeptical arguments were stated: the argument from error, the argument from the possibility of error and arguments about the transfer of knowledge. In responding to skepticism, we saw that the central area of focus was the problem of the criterion and its application to the debate among skeptics, methodists and particularists. Part of the debate about skepticism involves confidence in our noetic equipment, and this confidence is, in part, a function of one's overall worldview. In particular, naturalist evolutionary theory fails to have the resources for justifying confidence in the trustworthiness of our noetic equipment.

CHECKLIST OF BASIC TERMS AND CONCEPTS

Academic skepticism
antithesis
argument from error
ataraxia
brain-in-the-vat arguments
burden of proof
Cartesian certainty
cognitivist
defeaters
dialectical loop
epistemic "might"
epoche
first-order skepticism
global skepticism
heuristic or methodological skepticism
iterative skepticism
justificational skepticism
knowledge skepticism
local skepticism
logical "might"
metaepistemological skepticism
methodism
methodological doubt
mitigated skepticism
naturalized epistemology
particularism
pragmatically circular
prima facie justified
problem of the criterion
proper function
Pyrrhonian skepticism
rebutting the skeptic
refuting the skeptic
right to be sure
second-order skepticism
transfer of justification arguments
unmitigated skepticism
vicious infinite regress
warrant

5

THE STRUCTURE OF JUSTIFICATION

Now a truth can come into the mind in two ways,
namely, as known in itself, and as known through another.
THOMAS AQUINAS SUMMA THEOLOGIAE IA. Q.84, A.2

[W]hen really pressed, we never anywhere
or at any time use any test [for truth] but one.
Coherence is our sole criterion of truth.
BRAND BLANSHARD, THE NATURE OF THOUGHT

Constructing a coherence theory of justification
without making use of basic apprehensions
is not unlike recording your new song by taping other recordings
without ever having given a live performance.
RODERICK CHISHOLM, THEORY OF KNOWLEDGE, 3D ED.

1 INTRODUCTION

In the previous three chapters, we have looked at the nature of knowledge and rationality, at various skeptical challenges to knowledge and justified belief and at the different sources and views about the scope of knowledge and justified belief. In all three chapters we had occasion to mention the epistemic notions of justification and justified beliefs, and we have seen at least two things about them. First, people do, in fact, have justified beliefs in many areas of cognitive activity. Second, justification is a normative concept, a concept that has to do with positive epistemic appraisal. If we say that a belief has justification, then we say something positive about it from an epistemological point of view. And most likely, justification is a necessary condition for knowledge. In this chapter, we shall look more deeply at the structure of justification and justified beliefs by focusing on the debate between foundationalist and coherentist theories of justification. After a few introductory remarks, we will clarify and evaluate foundationalism and coherentism in that order.

The term **noetic structure** stands for the entire set of propositions that some person, S, believes, together with the various epistemological relations that obtain among those beliefs themselves (e.g., some beliefs—that apples are red—entail other beliefs—that apples are colored), plus the relations among S himself and those beliefs (e.g., S accepts some beliefs on the basis of other beliefs). **Foundationalism** and **coherentism** are normative theories about how a noetic structure *ought* to be structured such that the beliefs in that structure are justified for the person possessing that structure.

We all accept some beliefs on the basis of accepting other beliefs. Sarah hears a rustling sound outside due to the movement of leaves on her tree. She realizes that a wind is blowing. Her belief that there is a wind blowing is based on and justified by her belief that the leaves are rustling. This second belief is indirect, i.e., it is justified mediately through or by means of the first belief. Now we may ask, what is it that justifies the belief that a wind is blowing? Is it another belief? Or is it a sensory experience—the hearing of a sound?

In general, suppose P, Q, and R are three beliefs accepted by some person and suppose P is justified on the basis of Q, and Q on the basis of R. We call a chain of beliefs like P, Q, and R where P is justified on the basis of Q, and Q on the basis of R an **epistemic chain**. Now what should we say about R and its justification? Four major options suggest themselves.

First, R could be justified by S, S by T, and so on. Most philosophers do not accept this option because it seems to exhibit a vicious infinite regress. Second, a person could simply stop the chain of justification with R and say that R is merely an unjustified, brute faith assumption. Again, most philosophers have looked unfavorably at this alternative. Why? The justification for P and Q ultimately rests on the justification for R. How can R justify P and Q if R itself has no justification and is merely a brute posit? It cannot. Third, one could stop with R and say that, somehow, R itself is justified but not on the basis of some other belief. Perhaps R is self-evident or produced in a reliable way or grounded in a sensory experience but not in a perceptual belief. This is the strategy adopted by foundationalists. Fourth, one could form a circle of justification by asserting that R is justified by P, or form a web of justification by claiming that P, Q, and R all justify each other in a mutually supporting pattern of interaction. This is the coherentist perspective.

Foundationalists and coherentists differ on these questions and hold competing views about the nature of noetic structures that exhibit justified beliefs. For the foundationalist, epistemic chains of justification stop with beliefs that are not justified on the basis of other beliefs. For the coherentist, the only thing that justifies a belief is other beliefs, specifically, the fact that the belief in question "coheres with" other beliefs in the right way.

Before we look more deeply at these two schools of thought, we need to make a distinction between a **sensation** and a **belief**. Not all philosophers agree here, but according to one traditional account, a sensation is a nonpropositional experience possessed by an experiencing subject. If a person has a red sensation, then the person is appeared to in a red-type way. The person has a certain sensory property within his consciousness, namely, being-an-appearing-of-red. Sensations do not contain beliefs or, put somewhat differently, **simple seeing** does not require **seeing as** or **seeing that**. If one sees a red apple, then one has a sensation-of-red, i.e., is appeared to in a red-type way. If one sees the object *as* red, then one possesses the concept "being red" and applies it to the object of perception. Finally, if one sees *that* this is a red apple, then one accepts the proposition that (and thus has the perceptual belief that) this object is a red apple. In order to have a sensory experience of something, one need not have concepts or propositions in one's mind. By contrast, a belief includes the acceptance of a proposition and is the way something seems to a subject when he thinks about the belief in question. According to a traditional view, sensations are not propositional; beliefs are.

2 FOUNDATIONALISM

In one form or another, foundationalism has been the dominant theory of epistemic justification throughout most of the history of Western philosophy. Current advocates of some form or another of foundationalism include Roderick Chisholm, Robert Audi and Alvin Plantinga. Foundationalist theories are distinguished by the notion that all knowledge rests on **foundations**. More specifically, the foundationalist notes a fundamental division between those beliefs we justifiably accept on the evidential basis of other beliefs (e.g., the belief that the wind is blowing is evidentially based on the belief that the leaves are rustling) versus those we justifiably accept in a basic way, that is, not entirely on the basis of the support that they receive from other beliefs.

2.1
EXPOSITION OF
FOUNDATION-
ALISM

For the foundationalist, all beliefs are either **basic** or **nonbasic**. Basic beliefs are, somehow, immediately justified. All nonbasic beliefs are mediately justified in some way by the relationship they sustain to the basic beliefs. For example, the belief that $13 \times 12 = 156$ is nonbasic and justified by other beliefs (e.g., $2 \times 3 = 6$) that are basic and immediately justified. The metaphor of a pyramid has sometimes been used to picture foundationalism. Just as upper regions of a pyramid are supported by lower regions and, ultimately, by the foundation, which is not supported by other parts of the pyramid, so nonbasic beliefs are related to basic, foundational ones. With this brief sketch of foundationalism in mind, let us look more carefully at some of the details of foundationalism.

2.1.1
PROPER
BASICALITY
AND THE
FOUNDATIONS

To begin with, according to foundationalism, there are beliefs that are called **properly basic beliefs**. Such beliefs are basic in the sense that they are not justified by or based on other beliefs. If we use the term **evidence** to mean "propositional evidence," then *evidence* refers to cases in which a person S believes a proposition and this serves as the basis for believing another proposition. A properly basic belief is basic in the sense that it is not believed on the basis of evidence, that is, it is not based on belief in another proposition. Moreover, a belief is *properly* if and only if it is (1) basic and (2) meets some other condition that specifies why it is proper to take the belief in question as basic. We will look at some of these alleged conditions below, but for now the point is that not just any old belief should be taken as basic but only those for which it is proper to do so.

Second, there is a difference among foundationalists as to which beliefs ought to be placed in the foundations. According to **classical foundationalism**, only sensory beliefs or beliefs about the truths of reason should be allowed in the foundations. Other foundationalists claim that additional beliefs should be in the foundations as well; for example, certain moral beliefs (e.g., *Mercy is a virtue*) and theological beliefs (e.g., *God exists*). Roughly, a truth of reason is one that can be known independent of sense experience, that is, without requiring a sense experience or sensory belief for its justification. Examples are certain truths of mathematics (*Necessarily, 2 + 2 = 4*), logic (*Necessarily, either P or Q, not P, therefore Q*), or metaphysics (*Necessarily, red is a color*). Concerning the last example, one may need to have a sensory experience of redness before one can form the concept of being red required to understand the proposition that necessarily, red is a color. But one does not appeal to a sensory experience to justify the proposition. According to one tradition, foundational truths of reason are justified by rational intuition, roughly, the internal awareness of or insight into the facts that make these propositions true. In these cases, one can simply "see," i.e., rationally intuit, the truth in question.

Moreover, limiting the discussion to sensory beliefs about the external world for a moment, one can draw a distinction between **ancient** and **modern classical foundationalism**. Ancient classical foundationalism, embraced by Aristotle and Aquinas, is the view that certain sensory beliefs are evident to the senses and should be taken as foundational, e g., beliefs like "There is a tree before me" or "A red object is there on the table." Note that these beliefs are about objects that exist in the external world outside the consciousness of the believing subject. Modern classical foundationalism, embraced by thinkers from René Descartes to Roderick Chisholm in the present century, hold beliefs like the following to be in the foundation: (1) I *seem* to see a tree. (2) I am being appeared to redly. Here, the beliefs are not about external objects, but instead, are about **self-presenting properties**, i.e., psychological attributes (such as sensory states or thinking states) or modes of consciousness within the experiencing subject himself. (1) and (2) are about the way something seems or appears to one from the first-person perspective.

Third, foundationalists differ about how strong the justification is for foundational beliefs. Strong foundationalism is the view that foundational beliefs are infallible, certain, indubitable or incorrigible. These terms are all attempts to get at the same thing, but they differ somewhat in their meaning. A belief is **infallible** if it is impossible in some sense for a person to hold to the belief and be mistaken about it. Sometimes the term **incorrigible** is used in the same way. On other occasions, a belief is incorrigible just in case the person holding the belief could never be in a position to correct it. The notion of **certainty** has two different senses. Sometimes it refers to a certain depth of psychological conviction with which a belief is held. On the other hand, a belief is sometimes called *certain* in the sense that at least this must be true of it: accepting that belief is at least as justified as accepting any other belief whatever. Finally, **indubitability** refers to a feature a belief has when no one could have grounds for doubting the belief in question.

For the strong foundationalist, the point of this family of terms is that for a belief to qualify as foundational it must be as strongly justified as is it could possibly be, and it must exhibit certain "epistemic immunities." It must be immune to correction, incapable of being doubted reasonably, incapable of being mistakenly believed and so forth. **Weak foundationalists** deny that foundational beliefs must have such a strong epistemic status. For them, foundational beliefs must be merely **prima facie justified**. Very roughly, a belief is prima facie justified for some person just in case that person holds the belief in question and has no good reason to think that he is not justified in doing so, in other words, he has no reason to think that there are defeaters of the belief sufficient on balance to remove his justification for the belief.

Fourth, foundationalists differ regarding the conditions necessary for a basic belief to be counted as *properly* basic. A foundationalist denies that properly basic beliefs can be based on *evidence* from other beliefs. But the foundationalist still holds that properly basic beliefs must have some kind of **ground**, that is, have some basis other than another belief. If a properly basic belief is grounded in some way, then the belief receives positive epistemic support or justification even though there is no evidence for it (no other proposition that serves as the basis for it).

Some foundationalists are internalists; **internalism** claims that the conditions that ground properly basic beliefs are internal to the knower, e.g., the belief is "self-evident" or grounded in a sensory or intellectual experience of some sort. For example, the belief that there is a wind blowing gets evidential support from the belief that the leaves are rustling, but this latter belief is properly basic. It receives no support from other beliefs, but is grounded in a sensory experience, a way of "being appeared to" (in this case, hearing the sound of rustling). The belief that 13 x 12 = 156 received evidential support from the belief that 2 x 3 = 6, but this latter belief is "self-evident": once one understands the meaning of the proposition, one can simply "see" that it must be true. What is it that one "sees" or experiences in this case? Perhaps it is a certain luster or luminosity, or a certain obviousness that is experienced. Or perhaps it is the felt, irresistible inclination to believe the proposition to be true. In any case, the properly basic beliefs are grounded in something (an experience) within the knowing subject. Other foundationalists are externalists, and **externalism** claims that the factors grounding the justification of a properly basic belief are not those to which the subject must have internal access: perhaps the belief is caused or reliably produced in a certain way.

2.1.2
THE
RELATIONSHIP
BETWEEN
BASIC AND
NONBASIC
BELIEFS

Three important issues are involved in clarifying foundationalist perspectives about the relationship between basic and nonbasic beliefs. Let us call this relationship the **basing relation** (sometimes called the "believed-on-the-basis-of" relation); for example, the belief that the leaves are rustling stands in the basing relation to the belief that there is a wind blowing. First, this relation is irreflexive and asymmetrical. A relation is **irreflexive** if something cannot stand in that relation to itself. For example, "larger than" is irreflexive since nothing is larger than itself. Applied to beliefs, this means that no belief is based on itself. A self-evident belief is not based on itself, even though it is justified immediately; rather, it is grounded in its experienced luster or obviousness, in the felt, unavoidable inclination to believe it, or in some other way.

A relation is **asymmetrical** in that, given two things A and B, if A stands in that relation to B, then B does not stand in that relation to A. "Larger than" is asymmetrical. If A is larger than B, B cannot be larger than A. By contrast, "the same size as" is symmetrical since if A is the same size as B, B is the same size as A. Applied to beliefs, this means that if A is the basis for B, then B cannot be the basis for A.

The second issue has to do with the strength of the basing relation, an issue on which foundationalists differ. Historically, some foundationalists claimed that the relationship between a basic and nonbasic belief is one of deductive certainty—the basic beliefs entail the truth of the nonbasic beliefs. However, most foundationalists deny this today and for good reason. Many properly basic beliefs support nonbasic ones without entailing or guaranteeing the truth of those nonbasic beliefs. The belief that the leaves are rustling does not entail the belief that the wind is blowing—the former could be true and the latter false. For this reason, most foundationalists allow for some sort of inductive relation between basic and nonbasic beliefs. Foundationalists have had some difficulty clarifying this relationship precisely.

Third, foundationalists allow the notion of coherence to play a role in justification. Later when we examine coherentism, we will look more carefully at just what coherence is supposed to be, but for now, we note that two roles have been assigned to coherence in foundationalist accounts of the support that nonbasic beliefs get from basic ones. First, coherence plays a negative function. If one's set of beliefs are incoherent, say they contain a logical contradiction, then that counts against that set of beliefs. For example, if one forms ten perceptual beliefs as one walks around the kitchen table with a red apple on it, and if the first nine express the idea that one seems to see a red object but the tenth expresses the idea that one does not seem to see a red, but a blue object, then this tenth belief does not cohere well with the other nine and that counts against that set of basic beliefs (and more strongly, against the tenth belief itself) serving as a basis for the belief that there is, indeed, a red object on the table.

Second, each member of a set of beliefs can confer some basis on a nonbasic belief, but if an entire set of basic beliefs cohere well with each other, this increases the positive support that those beliefs give to the nonbasic one. For example, each perceptual belief (e.g., one seems to see a red object now), expressed in the example above gives some support to the belief that there is, indeed, a red object on the table. But if all ten express the same notion (and none of the beliefs is that one seems to see a blue object), then the coherence of all ten beliefs increases one's basis for believing that there really is a red object on the table. Thus foundationalists allow for coherence to play a role in their overall theory of epistemic justification.

Regarding our sensory beliefs about the external world, some foundationalists argue that if we pay careful attention to the way our consciousness actually works and to the way we actually justify many of our beliefs, then it becomes evident that sensory experiences and perceptual beliefs at the periphery of a body of beliefs (those beliefs more closely related to what we experience in sensation) have a privileged epistemic status. Setting aside the issue of whether or not our beliefs about our own sensations are incorrigible, our sensory experiences and perceptual beliefs just seem to be immediately justified (or grounded) and to justify less basic beliefs. One's sensory experience of a sound and one's perceptual belief that he hears a rustling justify the belief that the wind is blowing in a way depicted by foundationalism. Coherentism allows no room for experience itself to contribute to the justification of our beliefs (since coherentists

2.2
ARGUMENTS
FOR FOUNDA-
TIONALISM

2.2.1
THE ROLE OF
EXPERIENCE
AND
PERCEPTUAL
BELIEFS IN
JUSTIFICATION

claim that beliefs and beliefs alone are what confer justification), and coherent-ism cannot account for the special role perceptual beliefs (the belief that one hears a rustling) or sensory experiences play in justification.

Coherentists respond to this point in at least three ways. First, most coher-entists deny the **myth of the given**, i.e., the idea that facts are directly present or "given" to consciousness in a preconceptual, prejudgmental way. Put differ-ently, they claim that all perception is theory laden and that there is no seeing without seeing as or seeing that. However, in spite of this claim, it does seem that we can see things directly. One can be aware of a bird flying overhead and not notice it due to being preoccupied with exam preparation, but later recall the experience to memory and the awareness of the bird can serve as justifica-tion for the belief that one saw the bird earlier. Or so it would seem. In any case, the theory-ladenness of perception is a point of debate between some foundationalists and coherentists.

Second, coherentists claim that whatever is taken to immediately justify a belief (e.g., a sensory experience or perceptual belief) can do so only if a person has an argument justifying the idea that the alleged immediate factor has what it takes to function as an immediate justifier. Thus, since the justification of the alleged immediate factor requires this higher or meta-level justification, the original factor is not immediately justified but mediately justified by some sort of meta-level argument. For example, before the experience of a sound or the perceptual belief that one hears a rustling can be justified and the justifier of the further belief that the wind is blowing, one must have an argument that the former are, in fact, functioning in this way. Foundationalists respond that there is no sufficient reason to think that this meta-level justification is required to justify what appears to be an immediate justifier of a belief. A sensory experi-ence or perceptual belief can justify a nonbasic belief (e.g., that the wind is blowing) without the person having to stop first and construct an argument for the fact that this is what is occurring.

Third, some coherentists claim that as a matter of psychological fact, sensory experiences are possible without having beliefs, otherwise infants or various kinds of animals (or adults in certain circumstances, as in the bird case above) could not have sensory experiences without first having beliefs, and this seems absurd. The beings just mentioned do not clearly have beliefs at all but surely seem to have sensory experiences. Nevertheless, say some coherentists, the ex-istence of sensory experiences without perceptual beliefs is only a psychological fact and not an epistemological one. That is, psychologically speaking, experi-ences may exist temporally prior to beliefs, but epistemologically speaking, ex-periences do not serve to ground or confer justification on beliefs.

Foundationalists respond to this third coherentist claim in two ways. First, foundationalism seems to be a theory of justification that is more congruent with the way our sensory and belief-forming processes actually work than is co-herentism, and surely this counts against coherentism. Since sensations can oc-cur temporally and psychologically prior to perceptual or less basic beliefs, then if a theory of justification—in this case, foundationalism—appropriates this fact in its theory of justification, all things being equal, this counts in favor of that theory. The psychological priority of sensory experience to perceptual beliefs is ad hoc in a coherence theory of justification, foundationalists argue, but it fits naturally in a foundationalist view. Second, foundationalists argue that a major reason coherentists are forced to admit the existence of sensory experiences without beliefs is the fact that such an admission is a better reflection of the way our subjective lives present themselves to us. But a careful description of our subjective lives will contain something else too: the fact that those sensory experiences often serve to ground our perceptual beliefs. The coherentist arbitrarily stops taking account of our subjective lives when it is convenient for him to do so.

Foundationalists also argue that certain types of a priori knowledge, specifically, our knowledge of self-evident truths of reason, fit well into foundationalism and not coherentism. Examples include our knowledge that necessarily $2 + 2 = 4$ or that necessarily if A is taller than B and B is taller than C, then A is taller than C. In cases like these, people are justified in believing them without that justification coming from some other things they believe. These truths are "self-evident" and the justification for them is immediate. People can simply "see" that they are necessary truths once they understand them, perhaps by being aware of a certain obviousness or of their strong, felt inclination to believe them. This argument has been especially difficult to answer for coherentists. As a result, a popular coherentist response is to adjust his or her coherentism by limiting it to sensory knowledge and by not including knowledge of certain truths of reason.

2.2.2
TRUTHS OF
REASON

To understand the **regress argument**, recall the epistemic chain mentioned earlier in the chapter where the belief that P is based on the belief that Q, which, in turn, is based on the belief that R. There are only four options available for understanding such a chain, and the first two are clearly inadequate: the vicious regress option (where R is based on S, S on T, and so on to infinity) and the brute posit option (where the regress is stopped with R, taken as an unjustified brute posit accepted by blind faith). This leaves only two alternatives: foundationalism (where R is taken as basic—justified, but not on the basis of a further *belief*) and coherentism (where R is based on P or on mutual coherence relations among P, Q, and R). But, argue foundationalists, coherentist treatments of epistemic chains turn out to be viciously circular, and thus the only reasonable way to construe such chains is the foundationalist way.

2.2.3
THE REGRESS
ARGUMENT

But why should one think that coherentism is viciously circular? To understand the foundationalist argument here, it may be helpful to focus our attention on cases where A causes the existence of B. Let us refer to this as a case in which A stands in a causal relation to B. Now such a causal relation is irreflexive. A cannot cause itself because this would require A to exist prior to its own existence in order to cause its existence, and that is absurd. It is also asymmetrical. If A causes B, then B cannot cause A because B cannot cause A to exist unless B already exists. But B cannot exist without A causing it to do so; thus A would be causing B to cause A or, in short, A would cause itself to exist, and that is absurd. Now if the causal relation is irreflexive and asymmetrical, then it must be noncircular, that is, if A (one's hand moving) causes B (the moving of the broom) and B causes C (the moving of the dirt), then C

cannot cause *A* because this would really amount to the claim that *A* had some role in causing itself.

Now the epistemic relation called "the basic relation" (*P* is believed on the basis of or justified by the belief that *Q*) is irreflexive and asymmetrical as well. Thus at least some coherentist versions of justification are viciously circular because in asserting that *P* is based on *Q* and *Q* on *R*, and *R* on *P*, the coherentist implicitly asserts that each belief is at least partly based on itself. In this way, we see that the foundationalist notion of a basic perceptual belief or sensory experience is a sort of epistemological "unmoved mover": it confers justification on other beliefs without needing justification to be conferred on it by something else. Later in the chapter we will examine coherentism in more detail and we will look at coherentist attempts to circumvent this argument.

2.3 **ARGUMENTS** **AGAINST** **FOUNDATION-** **ALISM**

The main objection to classical foundationalism is the claim that there simply are no incorrigible (or infallible, certain, indubitable) beliefs. Critics of strong foundationalism cite ways that alleged incorrigible beliefs could turn out to be corrigible or fallible and use these counterexamples to argue against the existence of incorrigible beliefs.

2.3.1
INCORRIGIBILITY
OF THE
FOUNDATIONS

Foundationalists respond to this strategy in two different ways. First, some foundationalists accept the criticism and adopt weak foundationalism, which takes basic beliefs to be prima facie justified and not incorrigible. The essence of foundationalism is the existence of properly basic beliefs and the asymmetry between basic and nonbasic beliefs, not the degree of strength possessed by properly basic beliefs. Thus the debate between foundationalism and coherentism is not primarily a debate about the existence of incorrigible beliefs.

Second, other foundationalists attempt to respond to the arguments and reassert the existence of incorrigible beliefs. In order to understand this dialogue, suppose one has a red sensation, that is, one is appeared to redly. Now, if the person reflects on his own sensory experience and believes that he is being appeared to redly, then if such a belief is incorrigible, he *is* being appeared to redly. In general, if being *R* is a self-presenting property (e.g., being appeared to redly), if person *S* is *R* (e.g., *S* is appeared to redly), and if on that ground *S* believes himself or herself to be *R*, then it is incorrigible for *S* that he is *R*.

Recall that a self-presenting property is a psychological attribute, a mode of consciousness, a property of a first-person mental state. Sensory properties are self-presenting. In the statement above, *R* could be a red sensory experience or, more precisely, the property of having-a-red-image or, preferably, being-appeared-to-redly. Thus, if person *P* is being appeared to redly, and if, grounded in this sensory state, *P* believes himself to be appeared to redly (e.g., he reflects on his own sensation and forms this belief), then it is incorrigible (infallible, etc.) for *S* that he is, in fact, being appeared to redly.

The idea here is that one can know one's sensory states incorrigibly. But this idea needs to be qualified, for there do seem to be certain sources of error here. For example, one can have a false belief about a present sensation if one's memory is poor and he groups it with past sensations in the wrong way. Thus one may mistakenly compare his present red sensation with past orange sensations, and mistakenly believe (due to poor memory) that this is a sensation like those (orange) sensations. In this and other ways, one could use the wrong word (*orange*) to report the present sensation to others.

Second, one could have a sensation in his visual field and, due to preoccupation and inattention, fail to notice it and later deny having had the sensation. In this case, one has a vague awareness of a sensation, perhaps, a clear sensation. Third, one can have a clear awareness of a vague sensation that serves as a source of error. Thus one could be aware of a person at 150 yards and mistakenly believe that his sensation is of his friend Bill due to the fact that the person and his face appear vague and undefined to the perceiver. Fourth, one can have a very complex sensation, taken as a whole, that can be a source of error because some of one's beliefs about the whole sensation require the use of memory. Thus one can be aware of 24 dots on a wall, but report that his sensation is one by means of which only 22 dots appear to him. In this case, he must count the dots in his visual field, so he is actually having a number of different sensations as he counts each dot and he is holding past sensations of counted dots in his memory to finish the count. An error could occur due to a mistake in memory.

Now the strong foundationalist can admit all of this but still ask, if we limit ourselves to whole sensations that are simple enough to be present before the mind in their entirety in one simple act of noticing (such as a state of being appeared to redly taken by itself), can one be mistaken about this if one believes oneself to be appeared to redly and one's belief is grounded in that appearance? Perhaps, but it is hard to see how. Critics offer certain counterexamples that purport to show that one can be mistaken in these cases. For example, some argue that before one's belief that one is being appeared to redly can have any content to it, one or both of two things must be true. First, one must have a general conception of what it is for something to be a red sensation derived from comparing one's current sensation with similar ones in the past, and then go on to judge that the present sensation fits the class of red sensations accurately. Second, before one's belief that one is being appeared to redly can have any content, one must have mastered language (e.g., one knows how to use the terms "being appeared to," "red" and so forth) because people can think only in language. And surely, the critic continues, one cannot report to others what one's sensation is unless one uses language. Either way, there are sources of error because one can always use language in a mistaken way.

Both of these arguments seem to be mistaken. First, before one can be aware of what a current sensation is or have a belief about it, that person does not first have to compare it with other sensations for two reasons. For one thing, this idea (that before one can have a justified belief about one thing, e.g., one's current sensation, one must have justified beliefs about two other things, e.g., other sensations similar to this one and the judgment that this present sensation falls into a certain class of sensations) leads to a vicious infinite regress of justification and fails to allow for what many people would be an obvious fact: That one can be directly and simply aware of some things and form beliefs about them without making comparative judgments at all. For another thing, this idea has the correct order backwards. Before one can form classes of sensation based on memory and similarity judgments (e.g., the class of all red sensations), one must first be able to be aware of and form beliefs about individual sensations.

Regarding the second argument about language, it mistakenly assumes that people must think in language. But this does not seem to be the case. People often experience themselves to be thinking rapidly without any sensory signs flying through their minds, and infants and other creatures seem to be able to think without having acquired a language. Moreover, if people could not think without a language, how could someone ever enter into a language to learn it in the first place? Finally, we must distinguish between having a true belief about my present sensation (which, arguably, can be incorrigible) versus using language to tell someone else about the sensation (which, through mis-reporting or other sources of error listed above, can be mistaken). The two are different things.

Another **counterexample** to incorrigibility is this: Suppose a brain physiol-ogist located that part of the brain associated with a person's being appeared to redly and could use a reliable machine to monitor that part of the brain. Now suppose the person believed that he was being appeared to redly but the brain monitor indicated otherwise. In this case, couldn't the person be mis-taken and thus have a corrigible belief about his current sensation? In re-sponse, it could be pointed out that this argument begs the question. If such a belief is incorrigible, the brain physiologist should not continue to insist that the person was not having a red sensation. After all, his monitor was devel-oped by correlating brain readings with first-person reports as to what sensa-tions a subject was having while his brain was doing such and such. Thus the reliability of the monitor is based on the justification of first-person reports in the first place. If it is used to undercut the authority of first-person reports, this, in turn, undercuts its own reliability.

In sum, the arguments against incorrigibility are not conclusive, but phi-losophers are divided about this issue. But even if there are no incorrigible beliefs, all that follows is that strong, as opposed to weak foundationalism is in trouble.

2.3.2
ALL PERCEPTION
IS THEORY
LADEN

This argument amounts to the claim that all perception is theory laden, that there is no seeing without *seeing as* or *seeing that*, and thus there are no basic sensory experiences, no uninterpreted data, nothing merely "given" to con-sciousness. Further, all perceptual beliefs and, indeed, all beliefs whatever, in-volve a theoretical interpretation of some sort. From this, two things follow. First, no perceptual beliefs are immune from error since theories can be changed and interpretations corrected, at least in principle. Second, theories are, among other things, coherent webs or networks of interrelated beliefs. Since perceptual beliefs are really part of theoretical networks, they get their support from their coherence with other beliefs in a theory. This means that such beliefs are not basic, as the foundationalist supposes.

We have already looked at the issue of the theory-ladenness of perception in this chapter. The important thing to note here is that the issue is closely related to the foundationalist-coherentist debate, the former denying and the latter af-firming the theory-ladenness of all perception.

Finally, coherentists claim that foundationalists have not clarified the relation-ship between basic and nonbasic beliefs in a way that explains how the former transfer justification to the latter. Moreover, the actual beliefs in the founda-tions are too slim in number and content to serve as a sufficient floor for con-structing the edifice of all the things we are justified in believing. For these reasons, foundationalism must be rejected.

Regarding the first objection, foundationalists have, indeed, had some diffi-culty clarifying the relation between basic beliefs (e.g., a number of beliefs of the following sort formed while walking around a table: I am being appeared to redly now) and nonbasic ones (e.g., There is a red apple on the table). The rela-tion is not deductive (the former could be true and the latter false) nor are non-basic beliefs reached by enumerative induction. For example, one does not take an inductive sample of, say, a thousand cases of having a red sensation where there was actually a red object before one and go on to claim that, probably, there is a red apple now before one on the basis of (1) one's current red sensa-tion and (2) the frequency with which such sensations are, indeed, correlated with external objects of perception. And while foundationalists continue to work on this problem, the best thing they can say at present is that coherentists fare no better on this score due to various ambiguities in trying to clarify the notion of "coherence." We will look at this shortly.

Regarding the second objection (that the actual beliefs in the foundation are too slim in number or content to serve as an adequate basis for justification), it is beyond the scope of this chapter to deal with this problem. But foundational-ists must work out detailed theories of justification in which it becomes plausi-ble to suggest that the foundational beliefs are, in fact, sufficient as a ground on which to build the edifice of justification. And some foundationalists, such as Robert Audi and Roderick Chisholm, believe they have already done so.

3 COHERENTISM

Our treatment of coherentism can be briefer than our discussion of foundation-alism because many of the issues have already been surfaced. There are several versions of coherentism that differ from one another in one way or another, but the essence of coherentism lies in the fact that there are no asymmetries between basic and nonbasic beliefs. All beliefs are on a par with each other and the main, or more likely, sole source of the justification of a belief is the fact that the belief appropriately "coheres" with the other beliefs in one's noetic structure. Important coherentists have been F. H. Bradley, Brand Blanshard and, more recently, Keith Lehrer and Nicholas Rescher.

As we have stated it, coherentism is a theory about *epistemic justification*. But there are two other types of coherentism that are often, though not always, associated with **coherence theories of justification**. First, there are **coherence theories of *belief* or *meaning***. These are theories that claim, in one way or an-other, that the content of a belief, the thing that makes a belief what it is, is the role the belief plays in an entire system of beliefs. This position is sometimes called the holist theory of meaning. Second, there are **coherence theories of truth**, roughly, the notion that a proposition is true if and only if it is part of a coherent set of propositions. This theory of truth contrasts with the **correspondence theory of truth**, roughly, the notion that the truth of a proposition is a function of its correspondence with the "external" world. Theories of truth will be mentioned later in this chapter and in chapter six, but for now it should be pointed out that one could consistently hold to a coherence theory of justification and a correspondence theory of truth. Our concern at the moment is with the former, and we need to characterize it in more detail.

<table>
<tr><td>

3.1.1
COHERENTISM
AND THE
DOXASTIC
ASSUMPTION

</td><td>

The **doxastic assumption** (from the Greek *doxa*, "belief") refers to the view that the sole factor that justifies a belief for a person is the other beliefs that the person holds. So understood, coherentists (at least strong coherentists; see below) accept the doxastic assumption. Sensory experiences (e.g., being appeared to redly) themselves serve no role in grounding beliefs, even perceptual beliefs, and, in general, a belief acquires no justification whatever from its relationship to experience. Nor do externalist factors like the proper functioning of one's sensory faculties play a role in justification. Only a belief or set of beliefs can confer justification on another belief. This means, among other things, that all versions of coherentism are internalist theories, whereas foundationalist theories can be either internalist or externalist in orientation.

</td></tr>
<tr><td>

3.1.2
NO
ASYMMETRIES
BETWEEN BASIC
AND NONBASIC
BELIEFS

</td><td>

For the coherentist, there is no basic, privileged class of beliefs (e.g., those expressing perceptual beliefs such as *I am being appeared to redly now*) that serve as a foundation *for* justifying other beliefs but which need no justification *from* other beliefs. Our noetic structure does not (or should not) have such asymmetries in it. If the pyramid is a good metaphor for a foundationalist picture of a good noetic structure, many think that a raft is a good one for a coherentist picture. Moreover, all sensory experiences are theory laden and thus turn out to be perceptual judgments, not nonpropositional ways of being appeared to. In one's overall set of beliefs, there may be those closer to the periphery of experience than others, but this is just a matter of degree, not of difference in kind.

</td></tr>
<tr><td>

3.1.3
THE NATURE
OF COHERENCE
ITSELF

</td><td>

The basic idea here is that what justifies a belief is the way it "coheres" with other beliefs in one's noetic structure. A better way to put this is to say that a belief is justified for a person just in case the belief is a member of a coherent set of beliefs for that person. Justification is primarily a feature of individual beliefs; coherence is a feature, not of individual beliefs, but of an entire set of beliefs taken as a whole. For example, if a person wonders how he knows that the wind is blowing, he could say that the leaves are rustling. If asked how he knows that, he could respond that he knows that he hears the leaves rustling, and further, he knows that he hears leaves rustling because the wind is, in fact blowing. Here, each belief is justified by being a part of a coherent set of beliefs.

</td></tr>
</table>

Coherentists have been divided about their views as to just what coherence itself amounts to. In this way, they are like foundationalists who have been divided about the best account of the justification relation between basic and nonbasic beliefs. Almost all coherentists agree that coherence must at least mean **logical consistency**, that is, a set of beliefs cannot explicitly or implicitly contain contradictory propositions, P and $\neg P$. But this alone is not enough. A person could believe that he was Napoleon, that everyone else denied he was Napoleon, but that they all were conspiring to lie. This would be a logically consistent set, but hardly one that confers justification on the members of the set.

Different coherentists have added further conditions on what coherence must include. One candidate has been **entailment coherence**: a set of beliefs is coherent only if each member of the set is entailed by all the other members of the set. Another, more popular candidate is called **explanatory coherence**: each member of a set of beliefs helps to explain and is explained by the other members of the set. As a set of beliefs grows in size, the coherence of the set (and thus the justification of each member of the set) increases as the mutual explanatory power among the beliefs in the set grows in quality and strength. Still another candidate is called **probability coherence**: a set of beliefs is coherent only if it does not include the belief that P and the belief that P is improbable.

Finally, a taxonomy of coherence theories will include different versions of coherentism. First, there is **positive** and **negative coherentism**. According to the former, if a belief coheres with a set of beliefs, then that provides positive justification for the belief. Here, positive reasons are required before a belief can be justified, and coherence provides that justification. According to negative coherentism, if a belief fails to cohere with a set of beliefs, then the belief is unjustified. Here, beliefs are innocent until proven guilty, that is, they are justified to some degree unless they fail to pass the test of coherence.

Second, there is **weak** and **strong coherentism**. Weak coherence theories imply that coherence is but one determinant of justification, and thus weak coherentism is compatible with versions of foundationalism that allow coherence to play a role in justification. Strong coherence theories assert that coherence is the sole determinant of justification and this version of coherentism will be evaluated shortly.

Finally, there is a difference between **linear** and **holistic coherentism**. According to linear coherentism, beliefs are justified by other individual beliefs (or small sets of belief) in a linear, circular chain. Thus P justifies Q, Q justifies R, and so on in a single, inferential line until a loop is completed. If the loop is rich and large enough, it confers justification on its members. Holistic coherentism affirms that in order for some person S to be justified in believing P, P must be in a coherent relation with the set of *all* of that person's beliefs. It is the entire pattern of interlocking, mutual coherence that provides justification.

We have already encountered most of the main arguments for coherentism in our evaluation of foundationalism. In fact, much of the support for coherentism lies in the alleged failure of foundationalism, coupled with the view that coherentism is the only viable alternative: the denial of basic beliefs and of the asymmetry between basic and nonbasic beliefs, the inadequacy of the foundations to support all that people are justified in believing, the weaknesses in foundationalist accounts of the relationship between basic and nonbasic beliefs, the theory-ladenness of all perception, etc. In addition to this essentially negative argument for coherentism, coherentists are convinced about the correctness of their account of how it is that people actually go about justifying their beliefs. Coherentists claim that if we pay careful attention to the way beliefs are, in fact, justified, the correctness of coherentism becomes manifest.

In spite of this claim, a number of serious criticisms have been raised against strong coherence theories of justification. These criticisms tend to cluster around three main issues. First, there is an objection that focuses on the vicious circularity and implausibility of coherence views of the transfer of justification from one belief to another. Consider linear positive coherentism. On this view, the transfer of justification proceeds in a linear circle: P justifies Q, Q justifies R, etc. until the loop is closed with Z justifying P. The problem here is that the loop is viciously circular and implausible.

Regarding vicious circularity, recall what was said earlier in the chapter in this context. The basis relation is like the causal relation: both are irreflexive (A cannot cause or be the basis of itself) and asymmetrical (if A causes or is the basis of B, then B cannot cause or be the basis of A). But this means that no belief can be the basis of itself in whole or in part and this is what linear positive coherentism requires. P justifies a chain (R, S, . . . , Z) and that chain in turn justifies P. But the chain cannot justify P if it is not justified. Thus R through Z justify P because P justifies them and, in this sense, P helps to justify itself. And the same will be true of other members of the chain.

Moreover, such a circle of justification is not only viciously circular, but also implausible in its treatment of perceptual beliefs. Suppose Frank sees that a red apple is on the table and believes this to be so. The foundationalist could justify this by referring to Frank's belief that he is being appeared to redly, which, in turn, is grounded in the fact that he is, indeed, having the perceptual experience in question. But the coherentist must justify Frank's belief about the apple by looping back up to higher-order beliefs (those further away from Frank's immediate experience); for example, ordinary physical object beliefs (that a table has been in the room for a long time, that a friend placed an apple on the desk an hour ago, that the lighting in the room is normal, that no one else has come into the room since then, etc.) which are, in turn, based on other ordinary physical object beliefs (tables don't disappear randomly, no one usually takes one's furniture, when a friend brings an apple, he doesn't come back later and take it home). Or the coherentist can justify Frank's belief about the apple by reference to a second-order belief that he believes the red apple is there.

Now the problem with these strategies is that they are implausible as accounts of how the belief is actually justified, namely, by reference to Frank's present experience of the apple being on the table. Coherentists respond to this charge by denying that experiences themselves can ground a belief because all sensations are theory laden and only beliefs can justify other beliefs. But the point of the objection here is to show that this notion of justification simply seems implausible in light of what people actually find to be the justifying factors in their ordinary perceptual beliefs.

What about the problem of vicious circularity? Coherentists respond to this problem in at least two ways. First, some claim that if a circle of justification is small, then circularity is, indeed, vicious. But if the circle is large and contains a lot of members in the loop, then circular justification is not problematic. However, this assertion fails as an argument. It may be a psychological fact about us that if a circle of justification is large enough, people will not be bothered by it because they will not become aware of the circularity and its inadequacy. But the problem of viciousness, rooted in the irreflexive, asymmetrical nature of the relation by which justification is transferred, is present in small or large loops.

A second response is to abandon linear positive coherentism and adopt holistic coherentism. On this account, coherentism is a view, not about the *transfer* of justification, but about its *source*. That is, the essence of coherentism is the idea that the mutual, holistic coherence among the beliefs in a web of beliefs is the source that confers justification on those beliefs. Coherentism is not primarily a view about how that justification, once is it present due to coherence, is transferred from one belief to another. However, even if holistic coherentism avoids the problem of circularity, it still suffers from implausibility due to an important factor: It does not allow for sensory experience or reason (in the case of knowledge of truths of reason as in logic and mathematics) to contribute to the justification of our beliefs. The fact that one is appeared to redly or that one can simply see that $2 + 2 = 4$ does seem to play a crucial role in justification, in spite of what coherentism implies. In short, there are sources of justification besides coherence.

This leads us to a second major objection to coherentism: the **isolation problem**. There are several closely related difficulties that are usually associated with this problem. For one thing, some have argued that coherence theories cut justification off from the external world and the way that world really is. Justification is solely a function of the internal relations among beliefs in one's noetic structure (their coherence), and thus justification has nothing to do with anything outside one's set of beliefs (as does one's sensory experiences), such as the external world or truth, which is a relationship between our beliefs and that external world. Since the objective of justification is to give us knowledge of that external world, then if coherence theories leave us cut off from that world, they must be inadequate theories of justification.

Coherentists have responded to this problem in one of three ways. First, some have abandoned a correspondence theory of truth and have added a coherence theory of truth to a coherence theory of justification. Here, truth is not a correspondence relation between a proposition and the external world. Instead, to say that a proposition is true is to say that it is a member of a set of coherent propositions. And just as coherence can be a matter of degree (a set of beliefs can be more or less coherent), so truth is a matter of degree. The reason that justification gives us truth is that both are to be understood in terms of coherence. As our beliefs become more and more justified, due to their being members of increasingly more coherent sets of beliefs, we come closer to true beliefs because the truth of a belief is a matter of its being a member of a coherent set of beliefs. We cannot evaluate this response here. Theories of truth will be discussed in chapter six. But if truth itself does not come in degrees and if the correspondence theory of truth is superior to the coherence theory, then this response is inadequate.

A second response by some coherentists claims that the notion of a theory-independent world or of there being something called "*the* way the world is," available from a God's eye perspective, is incoherent. Our only notion of an "external" world or of "the way the world is" is one that reduces to the idea of "the way the world is in a given theory or set of beliefs." There is no single way the world is; there are only different worlds in different theories. Thus the theory-world distinction ultimately breaks down. This response denies a realist view that there is, in fact, a world independent of theory (mind, language). We will consider this issue more fully in chapter eight.

Finally, some coherentists respond that the external world does, in their view, influence our beliefs about that world in that our beliefs are caused by "inputs" from the external world, e.g., wavelengths impinging on our sensory organs. Thus the external world does not play a role in justifying our beliefs, but it does play a causal role in producing and influencing the beliefs we actually have. The problem with this response is that it leaves no room for the external world—for example our direct awareness of that world—to play a *rational* role in justifying our beliefs, and it is this role that is of relevance to epistemology.

This last remark leads to a second difficulty related to the isolation problem: Coherentism leaves no room for experience or other factors (e.g., the trustworthiness of our sensory and cognitive equipment) to play a role in justification since beliefs and beliefs alone are relevant to justification. For the coherentist, the justification of a belief is solely a function of the coherence that the belief holds to other beliefs. If one holds the same set of beliefs in two different circumstances, then any belief he holds will have the same degree of justification even if sensory experiences or factors outside the believing subject change drastically. This means, among other things, that coherentists cannot supply the criteria needed to distinguish between coherent illusions that do not have justification (e.g., coherent fairy tales, dreams, or dysfunctional, hallucinatory sets of beliefs) and equally coherent sets of beliefs that do have justification. Thus coherence is not sufficient for justification.

Here are two examples cited by Alvin Plantinga that show the insufficiency of coherence theories of justification:

> Oliver Sacks recounts the case of the Lost Mariner, who suffered from Korsakov's syndrome, a profound and permanent devastation of memory caused by alcoholic destruction of the mammillary bodies in the brain. He completely forgot a thirty-year stretch of his life, believing that he was 19 years old when in fact he was 49; he believed it was 1945 when in fact it was 1975. His beliefs (we may stipulate) were coherent; but many of them, due to this devastating pathology, had little or no warrant. . . .
>
> Finally, consider the Case of the Epistemically Inflexible Climber. Ric is climbing Guide's Wall, on Storm Point in the Grand Tetons; having just led the difficult next to last pitch, he is seated on a comfortable ledge, bringing his partner up. He believes that Cascade Canyon is down to his left, that the cliffs of Mount Owen are directly in front of him, that there is a hawk gliding in lazy circles 200 feet below him, that he is wearing his new *Fire* rock shoes, and so on. His beliefs, we may stipulate, are coherent. Now add that Ric is struck by a wayward burst of hi-energy radiation. This induces a cognitive malfunction; his beliefs become fixed, no longer responsive to changes in experience. No matter what his experience, his beliefs remain the same. At the cost of considerable effort his partner gets him down and, in a desperate last-ditch attempt at therapy, takes him to the

opera in nearby Jackson, where the New York Metropolitan Opera on tour is performing *La Traviata.* Ric is appeared to in the same way as everyone else there; he is inundated by wave after wave of golden sound. Sadly enough, the effort at therapy fails; Ric's beliefs remain fixed and wholly unresponsive to his experience; he still believes that he is on the belay ledge at the top of the next to last pitch of Guide's Wall, that Cascade Canyon is down to his left, . . . and so on. Furthermore, since he believes the very same things he believed when seated on the ledge, his beliefs are coherent. But surely they have little or no warrant for him. The reason is cognitive malfunction; his beliefs are not appropriately responsive to his experience.[1]

There is a third difficulty related to the isolation problem called the **plurality objection.** There could be two or more equally coherent sets of beliefs that could, nevertheless, be logically incompatible with each other. A schizophrenic person who thinks he is John the Baptist could have a set of beliefs equally coherent with those of his therapist. In this case, the coherentist would have to say that the beliefs in each set are equally justified, but surely this is not the case. Only one set of beliefs is true and it would seem that only one set contains justified beliefs, namely, those of the therapist.

Besides vicious circularity and the isolation problem, some have raised difficulties against the notion of coherence itself, claiming that it is either inadequate or too unclear to be satisfactory. Space does not allow for an analysis of these problems and, in any case, the same claim has been made against foundationalist treatments of the relationship between basic and nonbasic beliefs. In our view, foundationalism is a better view of epistemic justification than is coherentism, but the reader will have to reach his or her own conclusions about this issue.

CHAPTER SUMMARY

The debate between foundationalism and coherentism is primarily focused on different normative views about a noetic structure. Foundationalists distinguish between basic and nonbasic beliefs. Properly basic beliefs are those basic beliefs not justified by other beliefs, even though they can be grounded in some other way. There is an asymmetry between basic and nonbasic beliefs, and the basing relation is irreflexive and asymmetrical. Different versions of foundationalism include strong and weak foundationalism. Foundationalists offer at least three main arguments for their view: the role of experience and perceptual beliefs in justification, the basic nature of certain truths of reason, and the regress argument. Coherentists attack the incorrigibility of the foundations, a thesis central to strong foundationalism; many coherentists claim that all perception is theory laden, and they criticize foundationalist views of the transfer of justification.

Coherence theories of justification accept the doxastic assumption—the view that the sole factor that justifies a belief for a person is other beliefs. Moreover, coherentists deny the asymmetry between basic and nonbasic beliefs. Third, coherentists differ over the nature of coherence itself, with logical con-

---

[1]Alvin Plantinga, *Warrant: The Current Debate* (Oxford: Oxford University Press, 1993), pp. 81-82.

sistency, entailment, explanatory power and probability being among the most popular views. Finally, there are different versions of coherentism, including linear and holistic coherentism. Much of the support for coherentism lies in the alleged inadequacies of foundationalism and the superiority of coherence views of how our beliefs are actually justified. Foundationalists claim that coherence theories, at least positive linear ones, are viciously circular, that all coherence theories are implausible accounts of how at least perceptual beliefs are justified, and they claim that coherence theories leave no room for sensory experiences to play a positive epistemological role in justification. Finally, foundationalists cite the isolation problem and the plurality objection as difficulties for coherence theories.

CHECKLIST OF BASIC TERMS AND CONCEPTS
ancient classical foundationalism
asymmetrical
basic belief
basing relation
belief
certain
classical foundationalism
coherence theories of belief (meaning)
coherence theories of justification
coherence theories of truth
coherentism
correspondence theory of truth
doxastic assumption
entailment coherence
epistemic chain
evidence
explanatory coherence
externalism
foundationalism
foundations
ground
holistic coherentism
incorrigible
indubitable
infallible
internalism
irreflexive
isolation problem
linear coherentism
logical consistency
modern classical foundationalism
myth of the given
negative coherentism

noetic structure
nonbasic belief
plurality objection
positive coherentism
prima facie justified
probability coherence
properly basic beliefs
regress argument
seeing as
seeing that
self-presenting property
sensation
simple seeing
strong coherentism
strong foundationalism
weak coherentism
weak foundationalism

6

THEORIES OF TRUTH
AND POSTMODERNISM

To say of what is that it is, or of what is not that it is not, is true.
ARISTOTLE METAPHYSICS 1077^B26

If a prophet speaks in the name of the LORD
but if the thing does not take place or prove true,
it is a word that the LORD has not spoken.
DEUTERONOMY 18:22

Pilate asked, "So you are a king?"
Jesus answered, "You say that I am a king.
For this I was born, and for this I came
into the world, to testify to the truth.
Everyone who belongs to the truth listens to my voice."
Pilate asked him, "What is truth?"
JOHN 18:37-38

1 INTRODUCTION

Down through the ages, people have asked Pilate's question. Is there such a thing as truth and, if so, what exactly is it? The Christian religion, as well as its rivals, essentially contains claims about reality, which are either true or false. Moreover, competing truth claims, especially those at the core of competing worldviews, often have very different consequences for life. As C. S. Lewis put it, "We are now getting to the point at which different beliefs about the universe lead to different behavior. Religion involves a series of statements about facts, which must be either true or false. If they are true, one set of conclusions will follow about the right sailing of the human fleet; if they are false, quite a different set."[1]

The notion of truth employed in Lewis's statement is called the **correspondence theory of truth**, roughly, the idea that truth is a matter of a proposition (belief, thought, statement, representation) corresponding to reality; truth obtains when reality is the way a proposition represents it to be. The correspondence theory of truth may properly be called the classical theory of truth

---

[1]C. S. Lewis, *Mere Christianity* (New York: Macmillan, 1960), p. 58.

because, with very little exception, it was held by virtually everyone until the nineteenth century. However, since then, the correspondence theory has come under criticism, and alternative theories of truth have been formulated. Moreover, according to many of its advocates, an important contemporary ideology—**postmodernism**—rejects the existence of truth, especially if it is construed according to some version of the correspondence theory.

In order to get at these issues, this chapter is divided into two sections: theories of truth and postmodernism. In the first section, after looking at some preliminary issues, a correspondence theory of truth will be analyzed and evaluated, followed by a discussion of alternative theories of truth. In the second section, different aspects of postmodernism will be presented and assessed.

2 THEORIES OF TRUTH

Is there a biblical view of truth? The answer seems to be no and yes, depending on what one means. No, there is no peculiarly Christian theory of truth, one that is used only in the Bible and not elsewhere. If there were a peculiarly Christian view of truth, two disastrous implications would follow: claims that certain Christian doctrines are true would be equivocal compared to ordinary, everyday assertions of truth, and Christianity's claim to be true would be circular or system-dependent and, therefore, trivial. Further, the Bible does not use technical philosophical vocabulary to proffer a precise theory of truth nor is advocation of a specific theory of truth the primary intent of scriptural teaching.

However, none of this means that biblical teaching does not presuppose or make the most sense in light of a particular theory of truth. The Old and New Testament terms for truth are, respectively, *'emet* and *alētheia*. The meaning of these terms and, more generally, a biblical conception of truth are broad and multifaceted: fidelity, moral rectitude, being real, being genuine, faithfulness, having veracity, being complete. Two aspects of the biblical conception of truth appear to be primary: faithfulness and conformity to fact. The latter appears to involve a correspondence theory of truth. Arguably, the former may presuppose a correspondence theory. Thus faithfulness may be understood as a person's actions' corresponding to the person's assertions or promises, and a similar point could be made about genuineness, moral rectitude and so forth.

Whether or not this first aspect of a biblical conception of truth presupposes a correspondence theory, there are numerous passages in the second group, "conformity to fact," that do. Two interesting sorts of texts, with numerous examples of each, fall within this second group. First, hundreds of passages explicitly ascribe truth to propositions (assertions and so forth) in a correspondence sense. Thus God says, "I the LORD speak the truth, I declare what is right" (Is 45:19). Proverbs 8:7 says, "For my mouth will utter truth," and Proverbs 14:25 proclaims, "A truthful witness saves lives, but one who utters lies is a betrayer." According to Jeremiah 9:5, "They all deceive their neighbors, and no one speaks the truth." In John 8:44-45, Jesus says that the devil is a liar and deceiver who cannot stand the truth but that he, Jesus, speaks the truth. In John 17:17,

Jesus affirms that the word of God is truth, and in John 10:35 he assures us that it cannot be broken (i.e., assert a falsehood).

Second, numerous passages explicitly contrast true propositions with falsehoods. Thus in Romans 1:25 we are told that "they exchanged the truth about God for a lie." Repeatedly, the Old Testament warns against false prophets whose words do not correspond to reality, and the ninth commandment warns against bearing false testimony, that is, testimony that fails to correspond to what actually happened (Ex 20:16).

It would seem, then, that Scripture regularly presupposes some form of correspondence theory of truth and, indeed, this is both the commonsense view and the classic position embraced by virtually all philosophers until the nineteenth century. However, prior to our analysis of the correspondence theory and its two chief rivals, two more preliminary issues should be mentioned. Admittedly, these two issues cannot be fully treated without some clarity about truth itself, and this sought-after clarity comes from analyzing theories of truth. So the discussion appears to be caught in a cul-de-sac. Fortunately, there is a way out. For at least two reasons, it is appropriate to ponder these two issues before analyzing the theories of truth. For one thing, while these preliminary issues cannot be adequately discussed without looking at theories of truth, the converse is also true. Since one has to start somewhere, these two issues are as good a place as any for launching the discussion. More importantly, before one comes to philosophy, one already has a commonsense notion of what truth is. As noted above, some form of correspondence theory appears to capture both commonsense intuitions and biblical teaching. Even if further analysis justifies rejection of the correspondence theory, its preanalytic justification gives one something with which to start.

The first issue is the distinction between absolutist and relativist depictions of truth claims. According to **relativism**, a claim is true relative to the beliefs or valuations of an individual or group that accepts it. According to relativism, a claim is made true for those who accept it by that very act. A moral analogy may help to make this clear. There is no absolute moral obligation to drive on the right side of the road. That obligation is genuine relative to America but not to England. Similarly, *The earth is flat* was true for the ancients but is false for moderns.

Those who claim that truth does not vary from person to person, group to group, accept **absolute truth**, also called **objective truth**. On this view, people discover truth, they do not create it, and a claim is made true or false in some way or another by reality itself, totally independent of whether the claim is accepted by anyone. Moreover, an absolute truth conforms to the three fundamental laws of logic, which are themselves absolute truths. Consider some declarative proposition, P, say, *Two is an even number*. The **law of identity** says that P is identical to itself and different from other things, say, Q, *Grass is green*. The **law of noncontradiction** says that P cannot be both true and false in the same sense at the same time. The **law of excluded middle** says that P is either true or false or, put somewhat differently, either P is true or its negation, *not-P*, is true. Note carefully, that these three laws say nothing about one's ability to verify the truth of P. For example, a colorblind person may not know whether

Q above is true or false. The law of excluded middle says that *Q* is one or the other; it says nothing about people's ability to discover which is correct.

Who is correct, the absolutists or relativists? For at least two reasons, the absolutists are right about the nature of truth. These two responses will be discussed more fully throughout the analysis below of the three theories of truth, but they may be briefly stated here. First, relativism itself is either true or false in the absolutist sense. If the former, relativism is self-refuting, since it amounts to the objective truth that there are no objective truths. If the latter, it amounts to a mere expression of preference or custom by a group or individual without objective, universal validity. Thus it cannot be recommended to others as something they should believe because it is the objective truth of the matter and this is a serious difficulty for those who "advocate" relativism.

Second, the reasons for relativism are confused in at least three ways. For one thing, consider the relativist claim "The earth was flat for the ancients and is not flat for us moderns." This claim suffers from an ambiguity that makes the assertion somewhat plausible. The ambiguity rests in phrases such at "*P* is true for them (him), false for us (me)." Shortening the phrase to enhance ease of exposition, ontologically (that is, with regard to being or existence), the phrase should be construed as "*P* is true-for-me" and, epistemologically (that is, with regard to knowing), it should be read as "*P* is true for me." The ontological sense is, indeed, an expression of relativism and it implies that something is made true by the act of believing it. However, the epistemological sense expresses an opinion that *P* is true in the objective sense: "I take *P* to be objectively true, but I'm not sure of that and, in fact, I lack confidence in my ability to defend *P*. So I'll hedge my bets and say simply that the truth of *P* is just an opinion I hold." So understood, the epistemological sense requires absolute truth. When most people claim that *P* is true (or false) to them and false (or true) to others, they are speaking epistemologically, not ontologically, and relativists are wrong if they think otherwise.

The second confusion among those who argue for relativism is the confusion of truth conditions and criteria for truth. A **truth condition** is a description of what constitutes the truth of a claim. So understood, a truth condition is ontological and it is associated with what the truth itself *is*. For example, the truth conditions for *S* "Unicorns live in Kansas City" would be the obtaining of a real state of affairs, namely, unicorns actually living in Kansas City. **Criteria for truth** consist in epistemological tests for deciding or justifying which claims are true and false. Criteria for *S* would be things like eyewitness reports of unicorn sightings, the discovery of unicorn tracks and so on. Now in a certain sense, the epistemological justification for a claim is relative to individuals or groups in that some may be aware of evidence unknown to others. In light of the available evidence, the ancients may have been justified in believing that the earth was flat. In light of new evidence, this belief is no longer justified. So in this benign sense, a claim's satisfaction of criteria for truth is relative to the possession or lack of relevant evidence. But it does not follow that the truth conditions are relative. "The earth was flat" is objectively true or false, quite independent of our evidence.

Finally, sometimes relativists are confused about the three fundamental laws of logic associated with the absolutist position. Some claim that they are expressions of Aristotelian logic and, as such, are merely Western constructions or Western logic, which are not applicable crossculturally. This "argument" confuses the logical status of a proposition or argument with the linguistic style used to express the proposition or the social processes used to reach a conclusion.

In his *Summa theologiae*, Thomas used a literary style in which his prose explicitly follows strict logical form and syllogistic presentation. By contrast, an isolated culture in the mountains of Brazil may use a poetic form of oral tradition, their sentences may not follow an explicit, tidy subject-predicate form, and they may reach tribal conclusions in ways quite foreign to Western culture. But none of this has anything to do with the deep logical structure that underlies their claims or with the conformance of their individual assertions to the three laws of logic, and it is simply a mistake to think otherwise. We invite the reader to present any declarative utterance in any culture, including the assertion that "Western logic" is culturally relative, that does not conform to Aristotle's three laws of logic. Any such assertion, to the degree that it is meaningful or asserted as true or false, will conform to the three laws of logic. Any alleged counterexample will either be self-refuting or meaningless. After all, Aristotle did not invent these laws any more than Columbus invented the New World. Aristotle may have been a Western thinker and he may have discovered these laws, but that does not imply that the laws themselves are Western constructions.

The second preliminary issue involves **deflationary theories of truth**. The three theories of truth examined below all take truth to be a real and important feature of the items that exhibit truth. But a recent view, the deflationary theory of truth, implies that there is no such property or relation as truth, and thus it is wrongheaded to develop a theory that clarifies the nature of truth itself. A major version of the deflationary theory of truth is the **redundancy theory of truth**, according to which the word *true* has no unique or special function within language and can be eliminated without limiting what can be expressed in language. Sentences that appeal to truth—for example, *T*: "It is true that Lincoln is dead"—have exactly the same content as others that contain no such appeal—for example, *U*: "Lincoln is dead." Some advocates of the redundancy theory draw the conclusion that the role of assertions of truth is, at best, a way of expressing agreement with what is being asserted ("I agree that Lincoln is dead") and, at worst, redundant.

A proper evaluation of deflationary theories lies beyond the scope of an introductory text. But two brief replies are in order. First, as we shall see in the treatment of the correspondence theory, it is arguably the case that people actually experience truth itself, that is, they are aware of truth itself. If this is correct, then truth exists. Second, it does not seem to be the case that *T* and *U* express the same thing. *U* is a statement about a state of affairs in the world; namely, Lincoln's being dead. *T* is not directly about Lincoln. Rather, *T* is a statement about an assertion—*U* itself—and says of *U* that it has truth. Moreover, *U* and *T* play different functions in one's life. One may be interested in *U* because one wants to know if Lincoln actually lived and, if so, whether he is still alive. By contrast, one who is interested in *T* may be concerned with inventorying his set of beliefs in an attempt to discern how many of them are true. Thus *T* functions to describe one of his beliefs, but *U* does not.

It is time to look at three important theories of truth, beginning with the correspondence theory.

In its simplest form, the correspondence theory of truth says that a proposition (sentence, belief) is true just in case it corresponds to reality, when what it asserts to be the case is the case. Many correspondence theorists would hold that, more abstractly, truth obtains when a truth-bearer stands in an appropriate correspondence relation to a truth-maker. Thus a proper analysis of truth involves analyzing the truth-bearer, the correspondence relation, and the truth-maker.

2.2
THE
CORRESPONDENCE
THEORY OF
TRUTH

Different versions of the correspondence theory analyze these three constituents differently. In fact, one of the main criticisms of the correspondence theory is that its advocates either cannot agree about the details of this analysis or provide mysterious, queer entities in their analysis. Setting these criticisms aside for the moment, let us look at some issues and alternatives in analyzing these three constituents.

First, what is the **truth-bearer**? Three main types of candidates have been offered. To begin with, two linguistic candidates are sentences and statements. Second, two mental states, thoughts and beliefs, have been proffered. Finally, propositions have been named as the basic truth-bearer. Let us probe these in the order just presented, beginning with the linguistic options. A **sentence** is a linguistic type or token consisting in a sense-perceptible string of markings formed according to a culturally arbitrary set of syntactical rules. A **statement** is a sequence of sounds or body movements employed by a speaker to assert a sentence on a specific occasion. So understood, neither sentences nor statements are good candidates for the basic truth-bearer. For one thing, a truth-bearer cannot be true unless it has meaning, and there are meaningful and meaningless sentences/statements. Further, some sentences/statements ask questions, express emotions ("Ouch!"), or perform actions (uttering "I do!" at the right moment during a wedding). These sentences/statements are neither true nor false. In response to these problems, one could claim that it is the content of a declarative sentence/statement—what is being asserted—that is the relevant truth-bearer. Unfortunately, while this response seems correct, it also seems to move away from linguistic truth-bearers to propositions.

Second, certain mental states, namely thoughts and beliefs, have been identified as the appropriate truth-bearer. Compared to linguistic entities, these candidates seem to be a step forward for two reasons. First, it would appear to be only those sentences/statements that express thoughts or beliefs that can be true or false, so the latter are more fundamental to truth than the former. Second, while language helps people develop their thoughts and beliefs, people—for example, young children—can have true or false thoughts/beliefs without thinking in language or without yet having acquired language.

On the other hand, there is a problem with identifying thoughts or beliefs as the basic truth-bearer. To see this, consider a person having the thought that grass is green. Considered from one angle, this thought is merely an individual mental event, a dated conscious episode. So understood, it may occur to a person at noon, last five seconds, and pass away. Considered solely as individual mental events, thoughts or beliefs do not appear to have meaning nor are they true or false. However, viewed from a different angle, a thought does seem to possess these features. It is the content of the thought that is true or false. An individual thinking event seems to exemplify a mental content—for example, that grass is green—and this is what is true or false.

So far, our study of truth-bearers has led to this conclusion: In the basic sense, it is the content of declarative sentences/statements and thoughts/beliefs that is true or false. Such a content is called a **proposition** and it represents the third candidate for the truth-bearer. What are propositions? Philosophers who accept their existence are not in agreement on the answer to this question. However, here are some things relevant to answering it: A proposition (1) is not located in space or time; (2) is not identical to the linguistic entities that may be used to express it; (3) is not sense-perceptible; (4) is such that the same proposition may be in more then one mind at once; (5) need not be grasped by any (at least finite) person to exist and be what it is; (6) may itself be an object of thought when, for example, one is thinking about the content of one's own thought processes; (7) is in no sense a physical entity. Though assessing the debate about the precise nature of propositions is beyond the scope of the present study, we shall return to propositions shortly.

What about **truth-makers**? What is it that makes a proposition true and how does it do so? The most popular answer to the first question is **facts** or **states of affairs**. Some distinguish facts from states of affairs, but they seem to be identical and the present discussion will treat them as such. What, exactly, is a state of affairs? Providing an adequate definition is more difficult than citing examples. A state of affairs is any actually existing whole that is ordered by the relation of predication or exemplification (see chap. 10). For example, two's being even, the apple's being red, middle C's being higher than middle A are all states of affairs.

How does a state of affairs make a proposition true, and given a specific proposition, which state of affairs is the relevant one? To answer these questions, consider the proposition *Grass is green*. This proposition is true just in case a specific state of affairs, viz., grass's being green, actually obtains. The important thing to note is that propositions have **intentionality**—ofness, aboutness, directedness towards an object. In fact, it is because an individual thought exemplifies the proposition *Grass is green* that the thought is about grass and not, say, about the state of Missouri. The intentionality of a proposition is a natural affinity or intrinsic directedness towards its intentional object, i.e., the specific state of affairs it picks out. Thus truth-makers make truth-bearers true, not in the sense that the former stand in an efficient causal relation with the latter and cause them to be true. Rather, the truth-bearer, the proposition, picks out a specific state of affairs due to the proposition's intrinsic intentionality, and that specific state of affairs "makes" the proposition true just in case it actually is the way the proposition represents it to be.

Certain counterexamples have been offered that purport to show that propositions can be true without having a truth-maker. If successful, these counter-examples may undermine the correspondence theory of truth by showing that truth-makers are superfluous.

Some advocates of the correspondence theory respond to critics by rejecting what is called truth-maker maximalism, roughly, the view that there must be a truth-maker for each true proposition. These thinkers hold that in the vast majority of cases in which there is a true proposition, there is a truth-maker just as the correspondence theory specifies. But in certain troublesome cases—cases in which it is not clear what the truth-maker is—there is still a sense in which the propositions are true without the relevant truth-maker. Other advocates of the correspondence theory resist adjusting the theory in this way and seek to provide an appropriate truth-maker for the problematic cases. Is there a plausible truth-maker for these cases? Advocates of the correspondence theory are divided on this question, and the reader will have to make up his own mind about the matter. To facilitate reflection on the issue, consider the following examples:

1. Baal does not exist.
2. Dinosaurs are extinct today.
3. All ravens are black.
4. Loving a child is morally right.
5. The U.S. president in 2070 will be a woman.
6. If Jones were rich, he would buy a Lexus.

Are these examples of true propositions that fail to have truth-makers? It is at least plausible to think that a relevant truth-maker may be found for each proposition.

Consider (1). The truth-maker for (1) is simply the fact that all the states of affairs that obtain in the actual world lack the state of affairs of "Baal's existing." This is a real lack, a real privation that genuinely characterizes reality. Consequently, we have a truth-maker for (1).

Proposition (2) actually makes two claims: First, it asserts that at some time prior to today there were such things as dinosaurs (thus distinguishing (2) from such propositions as *Unicorns do not exist today*), and second, dinosaurs fail to exist today. Thus there must be two truth-makers for (2). The first is that at some time prior to today the state of affairs of "there being dinosaurs" was real, while the second is that there is a real lack of "there being dinosaurs" in all the states of affairs that obtain in the actual world today.

(3) is a universally quantified statement. As such, it applies to all ravens whatever, both actual and possible, and not just to those that just happen to exist. So the truth-maker cannot be "actually existing ravens' being black." What then is the truth-maker for (3)? The truth-maker is the conditionally obtaining state of affairs "if something is a raven, then it is black," that is, on the condition that there is something that is a raven, then it will have the property of blackness. (There is a further metaphysical ground for this conditional being true, namely, there is a lawlike relation between the property of being a raven and the property of being black.)

(4) is a proposition of morality that implies neither that children exist, nor that any that do exist are actually being loved. What then is the truth-maker for

(4)? We suggest the following. There is a type of action, namely, *loving a child*, that has the moral property of being right. This type of act actually has the property of moral rightness in all possible worlds, including those worlds without children, or without creatures capable of love. In worlds where there are individual examples of children being loved, each of those examples would have the property of moral rightness. Thus the truth-maker for (4) would be the state of affairs of *the type of act loving a child having the property moral rightness*.

As a future tense statement, (5) poses distinct problems. Let us grant for the sake of argument that the U.S. president in 2070 will be a woman. The problem with (5) is that in some sense it appears to be true now, even though the election of a female to the presidency has not yet occurred. How then should we handle (5)? Two strategies seem to be possible.[2] First, sentence (5) may be translated as (5'): "It is (tenselessly) true that the U.S. president in 2070 is a woman." On this strategy, the state of affairs "the U.S. president's being a woman in 2070" tenselessly obtains, and is the truth-maker for (5). The second strategy does not translate (5) to eliminate tense, but posits a tensed state of affairs as its truth-maker. That is, the state of affairs "the U.S. president's being a woman" has the property of obtaining in the future, specifically, in 2070. The fact that the state of affairs "the U.S. president's being a woman" currently has this future tense property is what grounds the truth of (5) on the second strategy.

(6) expresses a true counterfactual of creaturely freedom, namely, what poor Jones would purchase if only he were rich. In examining (5), we learned that there may well be tensed facts about the future, facts that now exist even though the objects or events they are about do not. Similarly, we claim that there are "counterfacts" (counterfactual states of affairs) that actually exist, even though the objects or events they are about do not. Thus what serves as the truth-maker for (6) is the counterfactual state of affairs "if Jones were rich, he would buy a Lexus."[3]

It would seem then that there are plausible ways of handling these putative counterexamples that do not require abandoning the truth-maker requirement, but again, the reader will have to decide whether these responses are plausible. In any case, our investigation of these alleged counterexamples has reminded us of two things. First, truth-makers do not *cause* propositions to be true; rather, they are the intentional objects in virtue of which propositions that correspond to them are true. Second, a truth-maker does not need to be a concrete object; in many cases it is some type of abstract state of affairs.

Our study of truth-bearers has already taken us into the topic of the **correspondence relation**. What, exactly, is this relation? Note first, that correspondence is not a monadic property of a proposition like redness is with respect to

---

[2]The difference between these two strategies depends on two different theories of time, the dynamic and the static theories, called A-theory and B-theory, respectively. Discussion of the difference is beyond the scope of this chapter. See, for example, discussion in Gregory E. Ganssle, ed., *God and Time: Four Views* (Downers Grove, Ill.: InterVarsity Press, 2001).

[3]Just what makes counterfactuals of creaturely freedom true is a problem that is attracting much attention in contemporary philosophy and philosophy of religion. Giving a satisfactory answer is important generally in answering the claims of "open theism" that God cannot know future contingent propositions, and in defending a middle knowledge approach to divine foreknowledge in particular. For extended discussion, see Thomas P. Flint, *Divine Providence: A Molinist Account* (Ithaca, N.Y.: Cornell University Press, 1998), chap. 5; William Lane Craig, "Middle Knowledge, Truth-Makers, and the 'Grounding Objection,'" *Faith and Philosophy* (forthcoming).

an apple. A monadic property is an attribute that requires only one thing to possess it. Rather, correspondence is a two-placed relation between a proposition and the state of affairs that is its **intentional object**. A two-placed relation, such as "larger than," is one that requires two entities to be instantiated. Thus truth is grounded in intentionality. The intrinsic ofness of a proposition is directed toward a state of affairs, and the truth relation is exemplified just in case that intentional object matches, conforms to, corresponds with the proposition.

Second, the correspondence relation seems to be unique among relations. As will be noted below, the correspondence relation itself can be directly experienced and made an object of thought, and it does not seem to be reducible to something else. It is not a causal relation, it is not physical nor is it sense-perceptible. Neither is it a picturing relation. Propositions do not picture or mirror the states of affairs that correspond to them. This seems clear for states of affairs that are not themselves sense-perceptible; for example, two's being even, mercifulness's being a virtue, Gabriel's being an angel. But it is also true for sense-perceptible states of affairs. The proposition *Grass is green* does not picture the state of affairs, grass's being green. The proposition can be instantiated in a mind but is not itself green or sense-perceptible at all, while the corresponding state of affairs is, indeed, green. Thus the former is not a picture of the latter.

When we look at criticisms of the correspondence theory, we will see that some object to it on the grounds that the correspondence relation is too mysterious to admit into one's ontology (one's view of reality). For this reason, some advocates have sought to state the correspondence theory without employing the correspondence relation. For example, some claim that a true proposition is one such that what it asserts to be the case is, in fact, the case. Note that the claim does not explicitly mention correspondence. It may be that this expresses an adequate correspondence theory without mentioning the correspondence relation. However, it is more likely that this claim makes implicit use of the correspondence relation without mentioning it. When we ask what it is for something to actually be what an assertion claims to be the case, an answer seems to be possible: it is for the former (what is the case) to correspond to the latter (what is asserted to be the case).

Two main arguments have been advanced for the correspondence theory, one phenomenological and one dialectical. Edmund Husserl (1859-1938) stated the **phenomenological argument** most powerfully. The phenomenological argument focuses on a careful description and presentation of specific cases to see what can be learned from them about truth. As an example, consider the case of Joe and Frank. While in his office, Joe receives a call from the university bookstore that a specific book he had ordered—Richard Swinburne's *The Evolution of the Soul*—has arrived and is waiting for him. At this point, a new mental state occurs in Joe's mind—the thought that Swinburne's *The Evolution of the Soul* is in the bookstore. Now Joe, being aware of the content of the thought, becomes aware of two things closely related to it: the nature of the thought's intentional object (Swinburne's book being in the bookstore) and certain verification steps that would help him to determine the truth of the thought. For example, he knows that it would be irrelevant for verifying the thought to go swimming in the Pacific Ocean. Rather, he knows that he must take a series of steps that will bring him to a specific building and look in certain places for Swinburne's book in the university bookstore. So Joe starts out for the bookstore, all the while being guided by the proposition *Swinburne's "The Evolution of the Soul" is in the bookstore.* Along the way, his friend Frank joins him, though Joe does not tell Frank where he is going or why. They arrive at the store and both see Swinburne's book there. At that moment, Joe and Frank simultaneously have a certain sensory experience of seeing Swinburne's book *The Evolution of the Soul.* But Joe has a second experience not possessed by Frank. Joe experiences that his thought matches, corresponds with an actual state of affairs. He is able to compare his thought with its intentional object and "see," be directly aware that the thought is true. In this case, Joe actually experiences the correspondence relation itself and truth itself becomes an object of his awareness.

The example just cited presents a case of experiencing truth in which the relevant intentional object is a sense-perceptible one, a specific book being in the bookstore. But this need not be the case. A student, upon being taught *modus ponens,* can bring this thought to specific cases of logical inferences and "see" the truth of *modus ponens.* Similarly, a person can form the thought that he is practicing denial regarding his anger towards his father, and through introspection, he can discover whether or not this thought corresponds with his own internal mental states.

Some may reject the phenomenological argument on the grounds that it is overly simplistic. But it is not clear that this is so. The argument is simple but not simplistic because more sophisticated cases of the same sort can be supplied in which scientists, mathematicians or other scholars experience truth. Moreover, it is a virtue of a theory of truth that it accords with (corresponds with!) what we all experience each day before we ever come to philosophy.

The **dialectical argument** asserts that those who advance alternative theories of truth or who simply reject the correspondence theory actually presuppose it in their own assertions, especially when they present arguments for their views or defend them against defeaters. Sometimes this argument is stated in the form of a dilemma: Those who reject the correspondence theory either take their own utterances to be true in the correspondence sense or they do not. If the former, then those utterances are self-defeating. If the latter, there is no reason to accept them, because one cannot take their utterances to be true.

A critic could respond that the second horn of this dilemma begs the question. The critic could claim either that his own assertions are not being offered as true or else they are offered as true in accordance with the coherence or pragmatic theory of truth (see below). The defender of the correspondence theory could reply as follows to each alternative: First, as we will see in more detail later in the discussion of postmodernism, a person may say that he does not take his own utterances to be true, but when one actually reads that person's writings or listens carefully to his statements, one usually gets the distinct impression that the person really does, in fact, take his own claims to be true in spite of protests to the contrary. Second, it would, indeed, be consistent to reject the correspondence theory and take that rejection itself to be true according to a different theory of truth. However, when one looks carefully at the writings of those who defend alternative theories of truth, if often seems that they take their own points to be true because they correspond to reality. As a simple example, defenders of a coherence theory of truth sometimes argue for their position on the grounds that people cannot escape their web of beliefs and get to reality itself, or on the grounds that people actually justify their beliefs and take them to be true because they cohere well with their other beliefs. The most natural way to take these assertions is along the lines of the correspondence theory: the proposition that people cannot escape their web of beliefs actually corresponds to the way people and their beliefs really are, and similarly with the point about how people relate coherence to their beliefs.

Three main objections have been raised against the correspondence theory. First, some argue that since there is no clear, widely accepted theory about the three entities that constitute the correspondence theory, it should be rejected. Two things may be said in response. For one thing, even if it is granted for the sake of argument that no widely accepted account of the three entities is available, it only follows that more work needs to be done to develop the theory, not that it is false or unjustified. After all, we often know many things, that God knows the future, that electrons attract protons, even if there is no single, widely accepted theory for fleshing out the details of what we know. Second, we believe the analysis given above, though briefly presented, is along the right lines and can be given a more sophisticated defense. The correspondence theory also seems to accord well with clear cases such as the one involving Joe and Frank, and this fact may well provide enough justification to override the strength of this criticism if it is granted that it has some dialectical force.

Second, it has been argued that by distinguishing truth from the evidence one has for truth, that is, by claiming that truth transcends and is not identical to evidence, the correspondence theory leaves us vulnerable to skepticism. Why? Because if the correspondence theory is correct, then one could have all the evidence in the world for a belief and the belief could still be false. Two things can be said in response. First, even if the point is granted, it only follows that we cannot attain truth; it does not follow that the correspondence theory is false. Second, while evidence is truth-conducive, it is actually the case that evidence is not the same thing as truth itself. So it is, indeed, logically possible, even if implausible, to say that one could possess all the evidence one could possibly get and still be wrong. Thus the argument actually surfaces a virtue of the correspondence theory, not a vice. Moreover, in chapter four, a detailed argument was presented for the claim that the logical possibility of error does not render one vulnerable to skepticism.

Finally, some argue that the correspondence theory involves mysterious, queer entities—propositions, irreducible intentionality and the correspondence relation—and thus should be rejected. It is hard to see much force in this argument as it stands. That an entity is "mysterious" is not sufficient reason to reject it. Moreover, it is a virtue of the phenomenological argument for the correspondence theory that these three entities all seem to be ordinary and commonsensical, not mysterious or queer. Everyday people experience the propositional content of their thoughts/beliefs, the intentionality of those thoughts/beliefs and the associated intentional objects, and the correspondence relation itself.

Critics who raise this argument usually mean something more specific by it. They approach metaphysics with a prior commitment to philosophical naturalism, including some requirement that a knowledge claim must be in some way or another "be connected to" what is sense-perceptible. As a result, they hold that reality must fit into a naturalistic worldview, and this often means that some form of physicalism is required. The argument is that if naturalism is true, then entities such as propositions, irreducible intentionality and the correspondence relation do not exist. It is open to a defender of the correspondence theory to adopt the *modus tollens* form of the argument: Since these three kinds of entities exist, naturalism is false. Truth has always been a hard thing to countenance within the confines of an empiricist epistemology or a naturalist worldview. The reader should be in a position to see why this is the case.

2.3
THE
COHERENCE
THEORY OF
TRUTH

Since the discussion of the correspondence theory has already taken us into some of the key arguments and counterarguments regarding truth, it is permissible to treat the next two theories much more briefly.

According to the coherence theory, a belief (statement, proposition, etc.) is true if and only if it coheres well with the entire set of one's beliefs, assuming that the set is itself a strongly coherent one. Thus the truth or falsity of a belief is not a matter of its match with a real, external world. Rather, it is a function of the belief's relationship with other beliefs within one's web of beliefs. Key advocates have been Spinoza (1632-1677), Hegel (1770-1831) and Brand Blanshard (1892-1987).

It is important to distinguish a **coherence theory of truth** from a **coherence theory of justification** (see chap. 5). The latter offers coherence as a test for truth and it is consistent with a correspondence theory of truth, since one could hold that when a belief coheres well with one's other beliefs, it is likely to correspond to reality.

One of the major problems for the coherence theory of truth is the lack of an adequate notion of **coherence** and, in fact, it has never been precisely defined, at least not in a way that is plausible. The trick is to define it in a way that is neither too strong nor too weak. It would be too strong to define coherence as entailment such that a belief is true just in case it entails other beliefs. One's sensory belief that one seems to see a table could be true but this does not entail that there is a table there even though both propositions (that one seems to see a table and that there is a table there) could be true and even though both "cohere well" with each other. It would be too weak to define coherence as mere logical consistency (two or more beliefs do not contradict each other). A person could have a bizarre set of logically consistent beliefs that would not be true. For example, if Tom Crisp believed that he was an eggplant, that eggplants are conscious, and that all attempts by others to change his mind were lies, Crisp would have a logically consistent but false belief about himself. In response to this problem, some coherentists define *coherence* as mutual explanatory power, hanging together, fitting together, or being in agreement with one's set of beliefs.

Apart from alleged difficulties with the correspondence theory, the main argument for the coherence theory of truth derives from a commitment to a coherence theory of justification along with a desire to avoid skepticism. Recall that on the correspondence theory, one could have highly justified false beliefs since a justified belief could fail to correspond to external reality. It is this gap between justification and truth that provides ammunition to the skeptic who can argue that knowledge is impossible since justification does not guarantee truth. (Issues regarding justification and skepticism were taken up in chapters four and five, and they will not be rehearsed here.) The coherence theory of truth, however, defeats the skeptic because there is no longer a gap between adequate justified beliefs and true beliefs. Since truth just is an adequate coherence of a belief with an appropriate set of beliefs, when a belief is justified by way of a coherence account, it is automatically true. Truth is a matter of a belief's internal relations with one's other beliefs, not its external relations with reality outside the system of beliefs itself.

This argument for a coherence theory of truth provides a fitting occasion to turn to objections to the theory. First, according to the coherence theory, there is no such thing as an appropriately justified false belief since "appropriate justification" and truth are the same thing. Indeed, this is claimed as a virtue of the theory. But, in fact, it is a vice because it is entirely possible and, indeed, actually the case that one has an appropriately justified belief that is false. The only way to avoid this problem is to define "appropriate justification" as the same thing as truth, but this begs the question. Further, the coherence theory is cut off from the world since, on this view, truth is entirely a function of a belief's relations within one's system of other beliefs with no reference whatsoever to a reality outside the system. This is a serious problem. In response, most coherentists simply deny the existence of a mind-independent reality (independent of language or belief). In other words, they accept antirealism regarding reality. However, this move will be a further sign of the theory's inadequacy for those who believe or actually know that there is an external world.

Third, the coherence theory allows for the possibility of completely different, contradictory beliefs to be true as long as they cohere well with alternative systems of beliefs. Consider the Tom Crisp case again. If *P* is *Tom Crisp is an eggplant*, then *P* is true since it coheres well with Crisp's overall set of beliefs, and it is false since it fails to cohere well with one of Crisp's critic's beliefs. Since the coherence theory allows that *P* is both true and false, the coherence theory must be rejected.

A coherence advocate could respond by claiming that coherentism is a form of relativism regarding truth, and thus it avoids treating *P* as both true and false in the same sense. On this view, *P* is true relative to Crisp's system and false relative to his critic's. Earlier, criticisms were raised against truth relativism, and those criticisms, along with problems regarding relativism in general, apply equally to this coherence move.

Finally, the coherence theory fails in light of the phenomenological argument for the correspondence theory, as we saw in the case of Joe and Frank. That case, and countless examples of real human experience, teach us that we often bring individual propositions (*Swinburne's "Evolution of the Soul" is in the bookstore*) and not entire systems of belief to reality to judge their truth value. We are often able to be directly aware of reality itself due to the intentionality of our mental states, and we are often able to step outside of our thoughts/beliefs, so to speak, and compare them with their intentional objects in the external world. When this happens, we experience the truth or falsity of our beliefs. The correspondence theory makes sense of all of this, but the coherence theory fails on this score and, accordingly, should be rejected

2.4
THE PRAGMATIC
THEORY OF
TRUTH

In one form or another, the **pragmatic theory of truth** has been advanced by William James (1842-1910), John Dewey (1859-1952) and contemporary philosophers Hilary Putnam and Richard Rorty. In general terms, the pragmatic theory implies that a belief P is true if and only if P works or is useful to have. P is true just in case P exhibits certain values for those who accept it. Pragmatism is widely taken to be an expression of antirealism regarding external reality.

Pragmatists differ about how to interpret *works* or *useful to have*, and accordingly, there is a distinction between nonepistemic and epistemic versions of pragmatism. According to **nonepistemic pragmatism**, a belief is true just in case accepting it is useful, where "useful" is spelled out in terms that make no reference to epistemic values. For example, P is true if and only if "behavior based on accepting P leads in the long run to beneficial results for the believer" or "accepting P provokes actions with desirable results." These "beneficial results" or "desirable results" may, in turn, be identified with things such as the maximization of happiness, of the net balance of pleasure over pain, of technology and control over nature, and so on.

More frequently, *works* or *useful to have* is depicted in epistemic terms, according to **epistemic pragmatism**. For example, P is true if and only if P is (1) what one's colleagues will allow one to assert rationally or (2) what one is ideally justified in asserting or (3) what an ideally rational scientific community with all the relevant evidence would accept or (4) such that P exhibits simplicity, explanatory power, empirical adequacy, the tendency to lead to successful predictions and so forth. In one way or another, epistemic versions of pragmatism identify the truth of a proposition with its epistemic success.

Advocates of pragmatism claim that problems with the other two theories, our inability to transcend our theories (language, beliefs) and get to the external world (if there is such a thing; most pragmatists are antirealists) all favor pragmatism. Critics claim that it is self-refuting, that in their defense of the view, its advocates do not recommend pragmatism because the theory is itself "useful" but because it corresponds to certain facts about language, scientific theory testing and so forth, that it is a form of relativism, and that it fails the phenomenological argument for the correspondence theory. Since these arguments have already been presented, we leave to the reader the task of developing in more detail an assessment of pragmatism.

3 POSTMODERNISM

In the contemporary setting, a discussion of truth would be incomplete without an analysis of **postmodernism**. Unfortunately, for two reasons, such an analysis is extremely difficult to do in a brief, introductory way. For one thing, postmodernism is a loose coalition of diverse thinkers from several different academic disciplines, and it would be difficult to characterize postmodernism in a way that would be fair to this diversity. Further, part of the nature of postmodernism is a rejection of certain things—for example, truth, objective rationality, authorial meaning in texts along with the existence of stable verbal meanings and universally valid linguistic definitions—that make accurate definitions possible. Still, it is possible to provide a fairly accurate characterization of postmodernism in general, since its friends and foes understand it well enough to discuss the view. But the reader should keep in mind that an advocate of postmodernism should be allowed to speak for himself or herself, and it would be wrong to attribute to an individual thinker every aspect of the characterization to follow unless such an attribution is justified.

Postmodernism is both a historical, chronological notion and a philosophical ideology. Understood historically, postmodernism refers to a period of thought that follows, and is a reaction to the period called **modernity**. Modernity is the period of European thought that developed out of the Renaissance (14th-17th centuries) and flourished in the Enlightenment (17th-19th centuries) in the ideas of people like Descartes, Locke, Berkeley, Hume, Leibniz and Kant. In the chronological sense, postmodernism is sometimes called "post modernism." So understood, it is fair to say that postmodernism is often guilty of a simplistic characterization of modernity, because the thinkers in that time period were far from monolithic. Indeed, Descartes, Hume and Kant have elements in their thought that are more at home in postmodernism than they are in the so-called modern era. Nevertheless, setting historical accuracy aside, the chronological notion of postmodernism depicts it as an era that began and, in some sense, replaces modernity.

> 3.1
> GENERAL
> CHARACTER-
> IZATION OF
> POSTMODERNISM

As a philosophical standpoint, postmodernism is primarily a reinterpretation of what knowledge is and what counts as knowledge. More broadly, it represents a form of cultural relativism about such things as reality, truth, reason, value, linguistic meaning, the self and other notions. Important postmodern thinkers are Friedrich Nietzsche, Ludwig Wittgenstein, Jacques Derrida, Thomas Kuhn, Michel Foucault, Martin Heidegger and Jean-François Lyotard. To grasp postmodernism more adequately, it will be helpful to break it down into seven different aspects.

Philosophically, metaphysical realism includes a commitment to (1) the existence of a theory-independent or language-independent reality, (2) the notion that there is one way the world really is and (3) the notion that the basic laws of logic (identity, noncontradiction, excluded middle) apply to reality. Postmodernism involves an antirealist rejection of these realist commitments. According to postmodernism, "reality" is a **social construction**. Language creates reality, and what is real for one linguistic group may be unreal for another. Thus God exists relative to Christians but does not exist relative to atheists. Further, the basic laws of logic are Western constructions, and in no way are they to be taken as universally valid laws of reality itself.

Some postmodernists, who may be called neo-Kantian postmodernists, agree that there is in some sense a thing-in-itself, an external reality. But they also hold

> 3.1.1
> POSTMODERNISM
> AND
> METAPHYSICAL
> REALISM

that we have no way to get to reality and, since we know nothing about it, reality itself is a useless notion and, for all practical purposes, it can simply be ignored.

3.1.2 **REJECTION** **OF THE** **CORRESPOND-** **ENCE THEORY** **OF TRUTH**	Postmodernists reject the correspondence theory of truth. Some eschew any talk of truth at all, while others advance a coherentist or, more frequently, pragmatist notion of truth. The important thing is that truth is relative to a linguistic community that shares the same narrative (see below). There is no objective truth, no God's eye view of things. Rather, all thought is historically and socially conditioned. Moreover, postmodernists reject **dichotomous thinking**. Dichotomous thinking occurs when someone divides a range of phenomena into two groups and goes on to claim that one is better than the other. Here are some dichotomies: real/unreal, true/false, rational/irrational, right/wrong, virtue/vice, good/bad and beautiful/ugly. Each pair represents a dichotomy in which the first member is to be preferred to the second one. By contrast, postmodernists claim that assertions that employ these terms are relative to a widely diverse range of groups constituted by a shared language, narrative, culture. Thus there are as many ways of dividing these pairs, as there are groups that divide them because all such divisions are social constructions.
3.1.3 **RATIONALITY** **AND** **KNOWLEDGE**	Postmodernists reject the idea that there are universal, transcultural standards, such as the laws of logic or principles of inductive inference, for determining whether a belief is true or false, rational or irrational, good or bad. There is no predefined rationality. Postmodernists also reject the notion that rationality is objective on the grounds that no one approaches life in a totally objective way without bias. Thus objectivity is impossible, and observations, beliefs and entire narratives are theory laden. There is no neutral standpoint from which to approach the world, and thus observations, beliefs and so forth are perspectival constructions that reflect the viewpoint implicit in one's own web of beliefs. Regarding knowledge, postmodernists believe that there is no point of view from which one can define knowledge itself without begging the question in favor of one's own view. "Knowledge" is a construction of one's social, linguistic structures, not a justified, truthful representation of reality by one's mental states. For example, knowledge amounts to what is deemed to be appropriate according to the professional certification practices of various professional associations. As such, knowledge is a construction that expresses the social, linguistic structures of those associations, nothing more, nothing less.
3.1.4 **ANTIFOUN-** **DATIONALISM**	Postmodernists reject foundationalism as a theory of epistemic justification (see chap. 5). Some of the reasons for this rejection are covered in the previous chapter in the discussion of criticisms of and alternatives to foundationalism; for example, the rejection of simple seeing. However, there is an additional reason for the postmodernist rejection of foundationalism that one finds peppered throughout postmodern literature: Foundationalism represents a quest for epistemic certainty, and it is this desire to have certainty that provides the intellectual impetus for foundationalism. This desire, the so-called **Cartesian anxiety**, is the root of foundationalist theories of epistemic justification. But there is no such certainty, and the quest for it is an impossible one. Further,

that quest is misguided because people do not need certainty to live their lives well. Sometimes Christian postmodernists support this claim by asserting that the quest for certainty is at odds with biblical teaching about faith, the sinfulness of our intellectual and sensory faculties and the impossibility of grasping an infinite God.

Postmodernists deny the existence of universals (see chap. 10). A universal is an entity that can be in more than one place at the same time or in the same place at different, interrupted time intervals. Redness, justice, being even, humanness are examples of universals. If redness is a universal, then if one sees (the same shade of) redness on Monday and again on Tuesday, the redness seen on Tuesday is identical to, is the very same thing as the redness seen on Monday. Postmodernists deny such identities and claim that nothing is repeatable, nothing is literally the same from one moment to the next, nothing can be present at one time or place and literally be present at another time or place. Thus postmodernists hold to some form of **nominalism**, that is, rather than terms such as *redness* representing real universals, they consider such terms to be only names for groups of things.

**3.1.5
ANTIESSENTIAL-
ISM AND
NOMINALISM**

Postmodernists also reject **essentialism**. According to essentialism, some things have essential and accidental properties. A thing's essential properties are those such that if the thing in question loses them, it ceases to exist. A thing's essential properties answer the most fundamental question, what sort of thing is this? For example, being even is an essential property of the number two, being human is essential to Socrates, being omnipotent is essential to God, being H_2O is essential to water. An accidental property is one such that a thing can lose it and still exist. For example, being five feet tall is accidental to Socrates. According to postmodernists, there is no distinction in reality between essential and accidental properties. Rather, this division is relative to our interests, values and classificatory purposes and, as such, the division is itself a social construction that will not be uniform throughout social groups. For example, if a group's definition of birds includes having a beak, then, assuming for the purpose of illustration that everything that has a beak has feathers, having a feather is an essential property of birds. If the group defines birds so as to include bats, having a feather is an accidental property. Thus what is essential to birds is not a reflection of reality; it is a construction relative to a group's linguistic practices.

According to postmodernism, an item of language, such as a literary text, does not have an authorial meaning, at least one that is accessible to interpreters. Thus the author is in no privileged position to interpret his own work. In fact, the meaning of a text is created by and resides in the community of readers who share an interpretation of the text. Thus there is not such thing as a book of Romans. Rather, there is a Lutheran, Catholic and Marxist book of Romans.

**3.1.6
LANGUAGE,
MEANING AND
THOUGHT**

Further, there is no such thing as thinking without language and, in fact, thinking is simply linguistic behavior in which people exhibit the correct public know-how in their use of words according to the linguistic practices of one's social group.

Third, postmodernists adopt a linguistic version of René Descartes's idea theory of perception. To understand the idea theory, and the postmodern adaptation of it, a good place to start is with a common sense, **critical realist theory of perception**. According to critical realism, when a subject is looking at a red object such as an apple, the object itself is the direct object of the sensory state. What one sees directly is the apple itself. True, one must have a sensation of red to apprehend the apple, but on the critical realist view, the sensation of red is to be understood as a case of being appeared to redly and analyzed as a **self-presenting property**. What is a self-presenting property? If some property F is a self-presenting one, then it is by means of F that a relevant external object is presented directly to a person, and F presents itself directly to the person as well. Thus F presents its object mediately though directly, and itself immediately.

This is not as hard to understand as it first may appear. Sensations, such as being-appeared-to-redly, are an important class of self-presenting properties. If Jones is having a sensation of red while looking at an apple, then having the property of being-appeared-to-redly as part of his consciousness modifies his substantial self. When Jones has this sensation, it is a tool that presents the red apple mediately to him and the sensation also presents itself to Jones. What does it mean to say that the sensation presents the apple to him mediately? Simply this: it is in virtue of or by means of the sensation that Jones sees the apple.

Moreover, by having the sensation of red, Jones is directly aware of both the apple and his own awareness of the apple. For the critical realist, the sensation of red may, indeed, be a tool or means that Jones uses to become aware of the apple, but he is thereby directly aware of the apple. His awareness of the apple is direct in that nothing stands between Jones and the apple, not even his sensation of the apple. That sensation presents the apple directly, though as a tool, Jones must have the sensation as a necessary condition for seeing the apple.

For Descartes's **idea theory of perception**, on the other hand, one's ideas, in this case, sensations, stand between the subject and the object of perception. Jones is directly aware of his own sensation of the apple and indirectly aware of the apple in the sense that it is what causes the sensation to happen. On the idea theory, a perceiving subject is trapped behind his own sensations and cannot get outside them to the external world in order to compare his sensations to their objects in order to see if those sensations are accurate.

Now, in a certain sense, postmodernists believe that people are trapped behind something in the attempt to get to the external world. However, for them the wall between people and reality is not composed of sensations as it was for Descartes; rather, it is constituted by one's linguistic categories and practices. One's language serves as a sort of distorting and, indeed, creative filter. One cannot get outside one's language to see if one's talk about the world is the way the world is. In fact, it is superfluous to even talk about an external world, and for this reason, postmodernists claim that the "external world" is just a construction. In fact, the self itself is a construction of language. There is no unified, substantial ego. The "self" is a bundle of social roles, such as being a wife, a mother, a graduate student, an insurance salesperson, and these roles are created by the linguistic practices associated with them. For the postmodernist, consciousness and the self are social, not individual.

Finally, postmodernists reject what is called the **referential use of language**. Consider the sentence "The dog is in the yard." According to the referential use of language, the term *dog* functions, among other things, to refer to an entity—a specific dog—in the language-independent world. On this view, people use language to refer to reality all the time. Postmodernists disagree and claim that linguistic units such as words actually refer to other words or, more accurately, gain their use in a community by their relationship to other words. Thus *dog* is not a term that refers to a real object; rather, it is a term that is socially related to other terms such as "man's best friend," "the pet that guards our house" and so forth.

According to postmodernists, there are no **metanarratives**. The notion of a metanarrative has two senses. Sometimes it refers to a procedure for determining which among competing conceptual schemes or worldviews is true or rational. More often, it refers to broad, general worldviews that have come to be accepted by large groups of people, such as Buddhism, atheism, Christianity and so forth. In claiming that there are no metanarratives, postmodernists mean that there is no way to decide which among competing worldviews is true, and more importantly, there is not single worldview true for everyone. There are no metanarratives, only local ones.

3.1.7
NO
METANARRATIVES

In some ways, this entire book is a critique of and alternative to postmodernism, so there is little need to develop a detailed critique here. In chapter two, basic principles of logic and reasoning were stated and defended for their universal validity. In chapters three and four, the nature of knowledge was clarified and defended against various forms of skepticism. In chapter five, foundationalism was discussed and defended, and it was seen that the main arguments for foundationalism have little or nothing to do with the quest for Cartesian certainty. Foundationalism just seems to be the way that people actually and appropriately go about justifying their beliefs. In chapter nine the nature of existence will be discussed and it should become obvious that people must enter that debate by starting with the real existence of particular things they are trying to explain. In chapter ten the existence of universals will be defended against different versions of nominalism, and chapters eleven and twelve include a defense of the claim that consciousness and the self are real and individual, not merely social constructions. In chapters twenty-three through twenty-eight, topics will be included that justify the claim that Christianity is a metanarrative, a worldview true for everyone. To be sure, the items treated in the chapters just mentioned do far more than defend the theses in question, but they do include such a defense and, as such, they provide grounds for rejecting postmodernism. Earlier in this chapter, the correspondence theory of truth was defended, as was the claim that one does not need to think in language. And the phenomenological argument for the correspondence theory of truth also supports the referential use of language and a critical realist theory of perception.

3.2
ASSESSMENT OF
POSTMODERNISM

While a detailed critique of postmodernism is not necessary in light of all this, two objections to postmodernism should be raised as this chapter comes to a close. The first has to do with the postmodern rejection of objective rationality on the grounds that no one achieves it because everyone is biased in some way or another. As a first step towards a response to this claim, we need to draw a distinction between psychological and rational objectivity. Psychological objectivity is the absence of bias, a lack of commitment either way on a topic.

Do people ever have psychological objectivity? Yes, they do, typically, in areas in which they have no interest or about which they have not thought deeply. Note carefully two things about psychological objectivity. For one thing, it is not necessarily a virtue. It is if one has not thought deeply about an issue and has no convictions regarding it. But as one develops thoughtful, intelligent convictions about a topic, it would be wrong to remain unbiased, that is, uncommitted regarding it. Otherwise, what role would study and evidence play in the development of a one's approach to life? Should one remain unbiased that cancer is a disease, that rape is wrong, that the New Testament was written in the first century, that there is design in the universe, if one has discovered good reasons for each belief? No, one should not.

For another thing, while it is possible to be psychologically objective in some cases, most people are not psychologically objective regarding the vast majority of the things they believe. In these cases, it is crucial to observe that a lack of psychological objectivity does not matter, nor does it cut one off from presenting and arguing for one's convictions. Why? *Because a lack of psychological objectivity does not imply a lack of rational objectivity, and it is the latter than matters most, not the former.*

To understand this, we need to get clear on the notion of rational objectivity. One has rational objectivity just in case one can discern the difference between genuinely good and bad reasons for a belief and one holds to the belief for genuinely good reasons. The important thing here is that bias does not eliminate a person's ability to assess the reasons for something. Bias may make it more difficult, but not impossible. If bias made rational objectivity impossible, then no teacher—atheist, Christian or whatever—could responsibly teach any view the teacher believed on any subject! Nor could the teacher teach opposing viewpoints, because he or she would be biased against them!

By way of application, a Christian can lack psychological objectivity regarding the existence of God, the resurrection of Jesus and so forth, and still have and present good reasons for the empty tomb, the reality of God and the like. Rational objectivity is possible even if psychological objectivity is not present, and this is what makes civil debate, rational dialogue and the development of thoughtful convictions possible. When a Christian, Sharon, for instance, tries to present objectively good reasons for a position and is greeted with a claim of disqualification on the grounds of bias, the proper response is this: Tell the other person that she has changed the subject from the issue to the messenger, that while the Christian appreciates the attention and focus on her inner drives and motives, she thinks that the dialogue should get refocused on the strength of the case just presented. Perhaps at another time they could talk about each other's personal motivations and drives, but for now, a case, a set of arguments has been presented and a response to those arguments is required.

Here is the second objection. Put simply, postmodernism is self-refuting.

Postmodernists appear to claim that their own assertions about the modern era, about how language and consciousness work and so forth are true and rational, they write literary texts and protest when people misinterpret the authorial intent in their own writings, they purport to give us the real essence of what language is and how it works, and they employ the dichotomy between modernism and postmodernism while claiming superiority for the latter. In these and other ways postmodernism seems to be self-refuting.

Postmodernists do have a response to this argument. For one thing, they can claim that critics misrepresent postmodernism and defeat a strawman. For example, some postmodernists defend their rejection of the objectivity of truth in the following way: To say that truth is not objectively "out there" in the real world is to say merely that where there are no sentences there is no truth, that sentences are elements of human language, and that human languages are social constructions. Unfortunately, this defense is not only false, but, understood in a certain way, it also fails to avoid the problem of self-defeat. The defense is false because it assumes that the proper truth-bearer is language. But as we saw earlier, a more adequate candidate is propositions. Moreover, there are numerous truths, such as mathematical truths, that have never been and may never be uttered in language, but they are surely "out there." The defense may not avoid self-defeat because if the argument assumes a relativist notion of truth, then if the argument itself is presented as an objective truth in the nonrelativist sense, it is self-refuting. If it merely amounts to the claim that people are not able to express a truth unless they do so by way of language, then the point can be granted but it is irrelevant in the debate over the adequacy of postmodernism as a philosophical standpoint.

Sometimes postmodernists respond by denying that they take their own assertions and writing to be true, rational, constituted by their own authorial intent and so forth. If these claims are correct, then they would, indeed, save postmodernism from self-refutation. But for two reasons, this response must be rejected. First, when one actually reads carefully postmodernist writings, it is very hard to avoid the impression that they do, indeed, present their assertions as true, rational and so forth. In this sense, when on the defensive a postmodernist may deny that his or her writings exhibit these features, but an examination of those writings seems to undermine those denials. Second, postmodernists would need to offer postmodernist alternatives to truth, rationality and so forth that make sense of their own claims while avoiding these undesired notions. It would seem that such alternatives have not yet been convincingly presented. But suppose they are forthcoming. What should we then make of postmodernism? Since postmodernism would not in this case be offering itself as true, rational and capable of being understood by way of careful interpretation of postmodernist writings, it would not be self-refuting. But neither would there be any reason at all for accepting it, since it would not be claiming to be true, rational or even understandable in a determinate way. It would be hard to know how a postmodernist could recommend his or her views to others or what the point would be in uttering them in public.

Does all this mean that there are no advantages to be gained from postmodernism? No, postmodernists are right to warn us of the dangers of using language to gain power over others, to recommend the importance of story and narrative, and to warn against the historical excesses of scientism and reductionism that grew out of an abuse of modernist ideas. But this admission does not mean that Christians should adopt a neutral or even favorable standpoint towards postmodernism, rejecting its problems and embracing its advantages.

To see this, consider Nazi ideology. Surely, some aspects of Nazi thought, say a commitment to a strong national defense and to solid education for youth, are correct and appropriate. But for two reasons, it would be wrong to say that one was neutral or even favorable towards Nazi thought, rejecting its problems and embracing its advantages. First, Nazi thought is so horrible and its overall impact so harmful, that its bad features far outweigh whatever relatively trivial advantages it offers. Thus such an attitude would be inappropriate towards Nazi thought. Second, none of the advantages just cited (strong national defense and solid education) requires Nazi ideology for its justification.

The same points apply to postmodernism. Its harm to the cause of Christ and human flourishing far outweigh any advantages that may accrue to it, and whatever those advantages are, they do not require postmodernism for their justification. After all, the importance of narrative and story and the need to be aware of the inappropriate use of power have been understood long before postmodernism came on the scene. Moreover, the way to avoid scientism and reductionism is to argue against them by using the very things postmodernists deny. The only alternative to argument is the use of mere rhetoric or sheer politically correct public power to marginalize scientism and reductionism, and this use of power is the very thing postmodernists rightly abhor.

CHAPTER SUMMARY

The chapter began by supporting the claim that the correspondence theory of truth seems to be an important part of a biblical understanding of truth. Next, an absolutist or objectivist notion of truth was defended over against a relativist notion, and deflationary theories of truth were rejected.

The correspondence theory of truth was defined and an analysis was given of the three key entities relevant to it: the truth-bearer, the truth-maker and the correspondence relation. A phenomenological and a dialectical argument were offered on behalf of the correspondence theory of truth, and three objections to the theory were examined.

The coherence theory of truth was analyzed and arguments for and against the theory were presented. The phenomenological argument was offered as a serious difficulty for the coherence theory. Next, a pragmatic theory of truth was described, a distinction was made between epistemic and nonepistemic versions of pragmatism, and the strengths and weaknesses of the view were briefly described.

The chapter closed with an examination of postmodernism. Seven important aspects of postmodernism were clarified, and difficulties with postmodernism were examined.

CHECKLIST OF BASIC TERMS AND CONCEPTS

absolute truth
Cartesian anxiety
coherence
coherence theory of justification
coherence theory of truth
correspondence relation
correspondence theory of truth
criteria for truth
critical realist theory of perception
deflationary theories of truth
dialectical argument
dichotomous thinking
epistemic pragmatism
essentialism
fact
idea theory of perception
intentional object
intentionality
law of excluded middle
law of identity
law of noncontradiction
metanarrative
modernity
nominalism
nonepistemic pragmatism
objective truth
phenomenological argument
postmodernism
pragmatic theory of truth
proposition
redundancy theory of truth
referential use of language
relativism
self-presenting property
sentence
social construction
state of affairs
statement
truth conditions
truth-bearer
truth-maker

7

RELIGIOUS
EPISTEMOLOGY

Enlightenment critiques of the reasonableness of religious belief
point to defects not so much in religious belief as in the
conceptions of knowledge uncritically adopted as the basis of these critiques.
Maybe religious knowledge looks dubious because we have the wrong idea
about what it is to know something and how we know what we know.
C. STEPHEN EVANS AND MEROLD WESTPHAL,
CHRISTIAN PERSPECTIVES ON RELIGIOUS KNOWLEDGE

1 INTRODUCTION

When we come to religious epistemology we encounter the intersection of traditional epistemology with the newly burgeoning field of philosophy of religion. One of the most rapidly developing areas of philosophy of religion has been the exploration of the epistemic status of religious truth claims, their rationality and warrant.

2 POSITIVISM AND THE PRESUMPTION OF ATHEISM

We may gain an appreciation of how religious epistemology has changed in recent years by casting a backward glance at questions facing the previous generation of philosophers. As mid-twentieth-century philosophers of religion struggled under the pall of **logical positivism**, they were forced to defend the very meaningfulness of their claims against the attacks of positivists and their philosophical ilk. Positivists championed a **verification principle** of meaning, according to which an informative sentence, in order to be meaningful, must be capable in principle of being empirically verified. Since religious statements like "God exists" or "God loves the world" were, in their opinion, incapable of being empirically verified, positivistic philosophers held them to be literally meaningless, as if one had asserted, " 'twas brillig, and the slythey toves did gyre and gimble in the wabe." Under criticism, the verification principle underwent a number of changes, including its permutation into the **falsification principle**, which held that a meaningful sentence must be capable in principle of being empirically falsified. The fate of religious language was thought to be no brighter under falsificationism than under verificationism, as became evident at a famous Oxford University symposium on "Theology and Falsification" held in 1948.

At the symposium Antony Flew borrowed a story told several years earlier by John Wisdom concerning two explorers who came upon a patch of flowers in a jungle clearing. One explorer was convinced that the flowers were tended by a gardener. In the ensuing days, however, despite the explorers' every effort to find him, no gardener was ever detected. To save his hypothesis, the one explorer was progressively forced to qualify his original hypothesis to the point that the hypothesized gardener must be invisible, intangible and undetectable. To which his exasperated companion finally replied, "Just how does what you call an invisible, intangible, eternally elusive gardener differ . . . from no gardener at all?"[1] The gardener in the story is obviously a symbol of God, the putatively invisible, intangible, eternally elusive Creator of the world.

Now we would all agree with Flew that the explorer's original gardener hypothesis had suffered death by a thousand qualifications. But why? The evident answer is that the hypothesis—like the aether hypothesis of nineteenth-century physics—had become increasingly ad hoc, or contrived to fit the data, which counts against its being the best explanation of the facts. But Flew maintained that the problem lay in the fact that anything that would count against an assertion must be part of the *meaning* of that assertion. Since nothing is allowed to count against the gardener- or God-hypothesis, that hypothesis therefore asserts nothing. On Flew's view, the God-hypothesis is not false but simply meaningless.

Flew's theory of meaning was clearly mistaken. The very fact that the two explorers in the story could disagree about the merits of the undetectable gardener-hypothesis (or that Flew's colleagues on the panel understood the story's ending!) shows that the explorer's statement was meaningful. The extraordinary ad hoc-ness of the hypothesis counted against its truth, not its meaningfulness.

In general, verificationist analyses of meaning ran into two insuperable problems: (1) The verification/falsification principle was too restrictive. It was quickly realized that on such theories of meaning vast tracts of obviously meaningful discourse would have to be declared meaningless, including even scientific statements, which the principle had aimed to preserve. (2) The principle was self-refuting. The statement "In order to be meaningful, an informative sentence must be capable in principle of being empirically verified/falsified" is itself incapable of being verified or falsified. Therefore, it is by its own lights a meaningless statement—or, at best, an arbitrary definition, which we are free to reject. The inadequacies of the positivistic theory of meaning led to the complete collapse of logical positivism during the second half of the twentieth century, helping to spark a revival of interest not only in metaphysics but in philosophy of religion as well. Today Flew's sort of challenge, which loomed so large in mid-century discussions, is scarcely a blip on the philosophical radar screen.

Similarly, another philosophical relic is the much-vaunted **presumption of atheism**. At face value, this is the claim that in the absence of evidence for the existence of God, we should presume that God does not exist. Atheism is a sort of default position, and the theist bears a special burden of proof with regard to his belief that God exists.

So understood, such an alleged presumption seems to conflate atheism with

---

[1]Antony Flew, R. M. Hare and Basil Mitchell, "Theology and Falsification," in *New Essays in Philosophical Theology*, ed. Antony Flew and Alasdair McIntyre (New York: Macmillan, 1955), p. 96.

agnosticism. The assertion "God does not exist" is just as much a claim to knowledge as the assertion "God exists," and therefore the former requires justification just as the latter does. It is the agnostic who makes no knowledge claim at all with respect to God's existence, confessing that he does not know whether God exists or does not exist, and so who requires no justification. (We speak here only of a "soft" agnosticism, which is really just a confession of ignorance, rather than of a "hard" agnosticism, which claims that it cannot be known whether or not God exists; such a positive assertion would, indeed, require justification.) If anything, then, one should speak at most of a presumption of agnosticism.

In fact, when one looks more closely at how protagonists of the presumption of atheism use the term *atheist*, one discovers they are sometimes defining the word in a nonstandard way, synonymous with *nontheist*, which would encompass agnostics and traditional atheists, along with those who think the question meaningless. As Flew confesses,

> the word "atheist" has in the present context to be construed in an unusual way. Nowadays it is normally taken to mean someone who explicitly denies the existence . . . of God. . . . But here it has to be understood not positively but negatively, with the originally Greek prefix "a-" being read in this same way in "atheist" as it customarily is in . . . words as "amoral.". . . In this interpretation an atheist becomes not someone who positively asserts the non-existence of God, but someone who is simply not a theist.[2]

Such a redefinition of the word *atheist* trivializes the claim of the presumption of atheism, for on this definition, atheism ceases to be a view, and even babies, who hold no views at all on the matter, count as atheists! One would still require justification in order to know either that God exists or that he does not exist.

Other advocates of the presumption of atheism continued to use the word in the standard way and so recognized their need of justification for their claim that atheism is true, but they insisted that it was precisely the absence of evidence for theism that justified their claim that God does not exist. Thus, in the absence of evidence for God, one is justified in the presumption of atheism.

The problem with such a position is captured neatly by the aphorism "Absence of evidence is not evidence of absence." For example, in theoretical physics entities are frequently postulated for which there is (as yet) no evidence, but that absence of evidence in no way justifies one in thinking that such entities do not exist. To give an illustration, it has become commonplace in astrophysical cosmology to postulate an early inflationary era in the expansion of the universe in order to explain such features of the universe as its flat space-time curvature and large scale isotropy. Unfortunately, by the very nature of the case, any evidence of such an era will have been pushed by the inflationary expansion out beyond our event horizon, so that it is unobservable. But woe be to the cosmologist who asserts that this absence of evidence is proof that inflation did not take place! At the most we are left with agnosticism.

Now clearly there are cases in which the absence of evidence does constitute

[2]Antony Flew, "The Presumption of Atheism," in *Companion to Philosophy of Religion*, ed. Philip Quinn and Charles Taliaferro (Oxford: Blackwell, 1997).

evidence of absence. If someone were to assert that there is an elephant on the quad, then the failure to observe an elephant there would be good reason to think that there is no elephant there. But if someone were to assert that there is a flea on the quad, then one's failure to observe it there would not constitute good evidence that there is no flea on the quad. The salient difference between these two cases is that in the one, but not the other, we should expect to see some evidence of the entity if in fact it existed. Thus the absence of evidence is evidence of absence only in cases in which, were the postulated entity to exist, we should expect to have some evidence of its existence. Moreover, the justification conferred in such cases will be proportional to the ratio between the amount of evidence that we do have and the amount of evidence that we should expect to have if the entity existed. If the ratio is small, then little justification is conferred on the belief that the entity does not exist.

Again, the advocates of the presumption of atheism recognized this. Michael Scriven, for example, maintained that in the absence of evidence rendering the existence of some entity probable, we are justified in believing that it does not exist, provided that (1) it is not something that might leave no traces and (2) we have comprehensively surveyed the area where the evidence would be found if the entity existed. But if this is correct, then our justification for atheism depends on (1) the probability that God would leave more evidence of his existence than what we have and (2) the probability that we have comprehensively surveyed the field for evidence of his existence. That puts a different face on the matter! Suddenly the presumer of atheism, who sought to shirk his share of the burden of proof, finds himself saddled with the very considerable burden of proving (1) and (2) to be the case.

The debate among contemporary philosophers has therefore moved beyond the facile presumption of atheism to a discussion of the so-called **hiddenness of God**—in effect, a discussion of the probability or expectation that God, if he existed, would leave more evidence of his existence than what we have. One's perspective on this issue cannot but be influenced by one's assessment of the project of natural theology (see chaps. 27-28). For if one is convinced that God has left pretty convincing evidence of his existence, then one is apt to be skeptical that we should expect to see much more evidence of his existence than that which we have. Scriven, in the end, held that we are justified in rejecting the existence of some entity only if the claim that it exists is *wholly unsupported*, that is to say, there is no particular evidence for it and not even general considerations in its favor. By this criterion, Scriven advocated that we remain merely agnostic, rather than disbelieving, even about such entities as the Loch Ness monster and the Abominable Snowman! But surely any unprejudiced observer will discern as much evidence for God as for the Loch Ness monster.

Unsatisfied with the evidence we have, some atheists have argued that God, if he existed, would have prevented the world's unbelief by making his existence starkly apparent (say, by inscribing the label "made by God" on every atom or planting a neon cross in the heavens with the message "Jesus saves"). But why should God want to do such a thing? As Paul Moser has emphasized, on the Christian view it is actually a matter of relative indifference to God whether people believe that he exists or not. For what God is interested in is building a love relationship with us, not just getting us to believe that he exists. Even the demons believe that God exists—and tremble, for they have no saving relationship with him (Jas 2:19). Of course, in order to believe *in* God, we must believe *that* God exists. But there is no reason at all to think that if God were to make his existence more manifest, more people would come into a saving relationship with him. Mere showmanship will not bring about a change of heart (Lk 16:30-31). It is interesting that, as the Bible describes the history of God's dealings with mankind, there has been a progressive interiorization of this interaction with an increasing emphasis on the Spirit's witness to our inner selves (Rom 8:16-17). In the Old Testament God is described as revealing himself to his people in manifest wonders: the plagues upon Egypt, the pillar of fire and smoke, the parting of the Red Sea. But did such wonders produce lasting heart-change in the people? No, Israel fell into apostasy with tiresome repetitiveness. If God were to inscribe his name on every atom or place a neon cross in the sky, people might believe that he exists; but what confidence could we have that after time they would not begin to chafe under the brazen advertisements of their Creator and even come to resent such effrontery? In fact, we have no way of knowing that in a world of free creatures in which God's existence is as obvious as the nose on your face that more people would come to love him and know his salvation than in the actual world. But then the claim that if God existed he would make his existence more evident has little or no warrant, thereby undermining the claim that the absence of such evidence is itself positive evidence that God does not exist.

3 RELIGIOUS BELIEF WITHOUT WARRANT

One of the presuppositions underlying the original discussions of the presumption of atheism was **theological rationalism** or, as it has come to be known, **evidentialism**. According to this view, religious belief, if it is to be justified, must have supporting evidence. Thus Scriven asserts that if someone claims that "theism is a kind of belief that does not need justification by evidence," then there must be "some other way of checking that it is correct besides looking at the evidence for it," but that cannot be right because "any method of showing that belief is likely to be true is, by definition, a justification of that belief, i.e., an appeal to reason."[3] Here Scriven equates holding a belief justifiably with being able to show that belief to be true, and he assumes that an appeal to reason in order to justify a belief involves providing evidence for that belief. Both of these assumptions have been vigorously challenged by contemporary epistemologists.

A number of thinkers have argued that one can have **pragmatic justification** for holding a belief, wholly apart from that belief's being epistemically justified, or its being knowledge, for the person holding it. Following Alvin Plantinga, let us refer to epistemic justification as **warrant**, that property which serves to transform mere true belief into knowledge. Proponents of pragmatic arguments aim to show that we are sometimes within our rights in holding beliefs for which we have no warrant. A **pragmatic argument** seeks to provide grounds for holding a particular belief because of the benefits gained from holding that belief. Jeff

[3]Michael Scriven, *Primary Philosophy* (New York: McGraw-Hill, 1966), p. 99.

Jordan has helpfully distinguished two types of pragmatic arguments: truth-dependent and truth-independent arguments. A **truth-dependent argument** recommends holding a belief because of the great benefits to be gained from holding that belief if it should turn out to be true. A **truth-independent argument** recommends holding a belief because of the great benefits to be gained from holding that belief whether or not it turns out to be true.

The most celebrated and oft-discussed, truth-dependent, pragmatic argument is **Pascal's wager**, the brainchild of the French mathematical genius Blaise Pascal. Pascal argued, in effect, that belief in God is pragmatically justified because we have nothing to lose and everything to gain from holding that belief. Although Pascal's wager can be formulated in a number of ways, one way to understand it is by constructing a payoff matrix (table 7.1) exhibiting the expected utility of one's choices relative to the truth of the belief that God exists:

Table 7.1 Payoff matrix for belief in God

	I. God exists	II. God does not exist
i. I believe	A. Infinite gain minus finite loss	B. Finite loss
ii. I do not believe	C. Finite gain minus infinite loss	D. Finite gain

Pascal reasons that if I believe God exists and it turns out that he does, then I have gained heaven at the small sacrifice of foregoing the pleasures of sin for a season. If I believe and it turns out that God does not exist, then I gain nothing and have suffered the finite loss of the pleasures of sin I have foregone. On the other hand, if I do not believe and it turns out that God does, in fact, exist, then I have gained the pleasures of sin for a season at the expense of losing eternal life. If I do not believe and it turns out that there is no God, then I have the finite gain of the pleasures afforded by my libertine lifestyle.

Now according to a principle of decision theory called the **expected utility principle**, in order to maximize the utility or benefit of my choices, I should multiply each of the mutually exclusive outcomes by the probability of each of the two states' obtaining, add these products together, then make that choice having the highest expected utility. In Pascal's wager the odds of states (I) and (II) are assumed to be even (the evidence for and against God's existence is of exactly the same weight). So, letting $\aleph_0$ stand for infinity and n for any natural number, we may calculate the utility of choices (i) and (ii) as follows:

i. $(A \times .5) + (B \times .5) = (\aleph_0 \times .5) + (-n \times .5) = \aleph_0$
ii. $(C \times .5) + (D \times .5) = (-\aleph_0 \times .5) + (n \times .5) = -\aleph_0$

In other words, choice (i) has infinite gain and choice (ii) infinite loss. Thus it is clear that belief in God has greater expected utility than unbelief. Therefore, even in the absence of preponderant evidence for theism, we should believe in the existence of God.

Two principal objections have been raised against the wager argument. First, in standard decision theory infinite utilities cannot be handled. In particular, since division of infinite quantities is prohibited in transfinite arithmetic, it makes no sense to speak of $\aleph_0 \times .5$. But this problem is easily resolved: simply substitute for $\aleph_0$ any arbitrarily high finite quantity, and it will still swamp the lower quantity n representing our finite loss or gain.

However, the truly serious objection to Pascal's wager is the so-called many gods objection. A Muslim could set up a similar payoff matrix for belief in Allah. A Mormon could do the same thing for his god. In other words, state (II) *God does not exist* is actually an indefinitely complex disjunction of various deities who might exist if the Christian God does not. Thus the choice is not so simple, for if I believe that the Christian God exists and it turns out that Allah exists instead, then I shall suffer infinite loss in hell for my sin of associating something (Christ) with God.

There are two possible responses to this objection. First, in a decision-theoretic context we are justified in ignoring states which have remotely small probability of obtaining. Thus I need not concern myself with the possibility that, say, Zeus or Odin might exist. Second, we could try to limit the live options to the two at hand or to a tractable number of alternatives. This may have been Pascal's own strategy. The wager is a fragment of a larger, unfinished *Apology* for Christian theism cut short by Pascal's untimely death. As we look at other fragments of this work, we find that although Pascal disdained philosophical arguments for God's existence, he embraced enthusiastically Christian evidences, such as the evidence for Christ's resurrection. It may be that he thought on the basis of such evidence that the live options could be narrowed down to Christian theism or naturalism. If the alternatives can be narrowed down in this way, then Pascal's wager goes through successfully.

A good example of a truth-independent, pragmatic argument for theistic belief may be found in William James's classic essay "The Will to Believe." Written in response to W. K. Clifford's ringing pronouncement that it is wrong, always, everywhere and for anyone to believe anything on insufficient evidence, James wants to show that we are sometimes pragmatically justified in willing to believe something in the absence of evidence of its truth. In cases in which we have no preponderant evidence in favor of a belief, we may resort to pragmatic considerations, James insists, if and only if the belief is for us a genuine option, that is to say, a choice which is living, momentous and forced. A living choice is one which presents to me a belief to which I can give genuine assent. A choice is momentous if a great deal hangs on it, it presents to me a rare opportunity, and its consequences are irreversible. Finally, a choice is forced if there is no option of remaining indifferent, if to not choose to believe is, in effect, to choose to not believe. James held that religious belief meets these criteria. Moreover, he was convinced that religious belief is beneficial in this life, regardless of its promises for the next. His studies had convinced him that religious believers are more balanced, happier and more virtuous people than unbelievers. Regardless of religion's truth, then, religious belief is beneficial and, in view of such benefits, pragmatically justified.

4 WARRANT WITHOUT EVIDENCE

The evidentialist might insist that while pragmatic arguments show that holding certain beliefs, including religious beliefs, is beneficial and therefore prudent, nevertheless that does not show that holding such beliefs is epistemically permissible, that one has not violated some epistemic duty in believing without evidence. One of the most significant developments in contemporary religious epistemology has been so-called Reformed epistemology, spearheaded and developed by Alvin Plantinga, which directly assaults the evidentialist construal of rationality. Plantinga's epistemology developed gradually over the course of three decades, but he has articulated it fully in a monumental three-volume series *Warrant: The Current Debate* (1993), *Warrant and Proper Function* (1993) and *Warranted Christian Belief* (2000). Here we can sketch only the broad outlines of his theory.

Plantinga distinguishes between what he calls de facto and de jure objections to Christian belief. A **de facto objection** is one aimed at the truth of the Christian faith; it attempts to show that Christian truth claims are false. By contrast a **de jure objection** attempts to undermine Christian belief even if Christianity is, in fact, true. Plantinga identifies three versions of the de jure objection: that Christian belief is *unjustified,* that it is *irrational,* and that it is *unwarranted.* Plantinga's aim is to show that all such de jure objections to Christian belief are unsuccessful, or, in other words, that Christian belief can be shown to be unjustified, irrational or unwarranted only if it is shown that Christian beliefs are false. There is thus no de jure objection to Christian belief independent of a de facto objection.

Plantinga endeavors to show this by developing a model or theory of warranted Christian belief, that is to say, an account of how it is that we know the truth of various Christian truth claims. On behalf of his model Plantinga claims, not that it is true, but (a) that it is epistemically possible, that is to say, for all we know, it may be true; (b) that if Christianity is true, there are no philosophical objections to the model; and (c) that if Christianity is true, then something like the model is very likely to be true. So Plantinga sets for himself two projects, one public and one Christian: (1) to show that there is no reason to think that Christian belief lacks justification, rationality or warrant (apart from presupposing the falsehood of Christian belief) and (2) to provide from a Christian perspective an epistemological account of warranted Christian belief.

Consider, then, the de jure objection to religious belief, for instance, to the belief that God exists. According to the evidentialist, even if it is true that God exists, one is unjustified or irrational in believing that God exists unless one has evidence supporting that belief. For according to the evidentialist, one is rationally justified in believing a proposition to be true only if that proposition is either foundational to knowledge or is established by evidence that is ultimately based on such a foundation. According to this viewpoint, since the proposition *God exists* is not foundational, it would be irrational to believe this proposition apart from rational evidence for its truth. But, Plantinga asks, why cannot the proposition *God exists* be itself part of the foundation, so that no rational evidence is necessary? The evidentialist replies that only propositions that are **properly basic** can be part of the foundation of knowledge. What, then, are the criteria that determine whether or not a proposition is properly basic? Typically, the evidentialist asserts that only propositions that are self-evident or incorrigible are properly basic (see chap. 5). For example, the proposition *The sum of the* *squares of the sides of a right triangle is equal to the square of the hypotenuse* is self-evidently true. Similarly, the proposition expressed by the sentence "I feel pain" is incorrigibly true, since even if I am only imagining my injury, it is still true that I feel pain. Since the proposition *God exists* is neither self-evident nor incorrigible, then according to the evidentialist it is not properly basic and therefore requires evidence if it is to be believed. To believe this proposition without evidence is therefore irrational.

Now Plantinga does not deny that self-evident and incorrigible propositions are properly basic, but he does demand, how do we know that these are the only properly basic propositions or beliefs? He presents two considerations to prove that such a restriction is untenable: (1) If only self-evident and incorrigible propositions are properly basic, then we are all irrational, since we commonly accept numerous beliefs that are not based on evidence and that are neither self-evident nor incorrigible. For example, take the belief that the world was not created five minutes ago with built-in memory traces, food in our stomachs from the breakfasts we never really ate, and other appearances of age. Surely it is rational to believe that the world has existed longer than five minutes, even though there is no way to prove this. The evidentialist's criteria for properly basicality must be flawed. (2) In fact, what about the status of those criteria? Is the proposition *Only propositions that are self-evident or incorrigible are properly basic* itself properly basic? Apparently not, for it is certainly not self-evident nor incorrigible. Therefore, if we are to believe this proposition, we must have evidence that it is true. But there is no such evidence. The proposition appears to be just an arbitrary definition—and not a very plausible one at that! Hence, the evidentialist cannot exclude the possibility that belief in God is also a properly basic belief.

In fact, Plantinga thinks that belief in God is properly basic, not only with respect to justification but also with respect to warrant. For Plantinga, **justification** involves obedience to one's epistemic duties or possession of a sound noetic structure of beliefs, whereas **warrant** is that property that converts mere true belief into knowledge when possessed in sufficient degree. Plantinga thinks that the theist is not only within his epistemic rights in believing in God without evidence, but that he actually knows apart from evidence that God exists. In order to show that such a view is tenable, Plantinga introduces his epistemological model of religious belief. Quoting John Calvin's teaching "There is within the human mind, and indeed by natural instinct, an awareness of divinity. . . . a sense of divinity which can never be effaced is engraved upon men's minds" (*Institutes* 1.3.1, 3), Plantinga proposes that "there is a kind of faculty or cognitive mechanism, what Calvin calls a *sensus divinitatis* or sense of divinity, which in a wide variety of circumstances produces in us beliefs about God."[4] Plantinga also speaks of the ***sensus divinitatis*** as "a disposition or set of dispositions to form theistic beliefs in various circumstances or stimuli that trigger the working of this sense of divinity."[5] Just as perceptual beliefs like "There is a tree" are not based on arguments from more basic beliefs but arise sponta-

---

[4]Alvin Plantinga, *Warranted Christian Belief* (Oxford: Oxford University Press, 2000), p. 172.
[5]Ibid., p. 173.

neously in me when I am in the circumstances of a tree's appearing to be there, so the belief "God exists" arises spontaneously in me when I am in appropriate circumstances, such as moments of guilt, gratitude or awe at nature's grandeur, as a result of the working of the *sensus divinitatis*. Plantinga emphasizes that God's existence is not inferred from such circumstances—such an argument would be manifestly inadequate—rather, the circumstances form the context in which the *sensus divinitatis* operates to produce a basic belief in God. Thus belief in God is not arbitrary; it is grounded by the appropriate circumstances and so is properly basic. Hence, if such a model of theistic belief is true, the theist whose belief is produced in the described way violates no epistemic duty in believing and so is justified in believing that God exists.

But does he *know* that God exists? We often are justified in holding beliefs that turn out to be false (for example, the object I thought was a tree turns out to be a papier-mâché simulation). Is our belief that God exists not merely justified, but warranted, and therefore knowledge? That all depends on what warrant is. In the first volume of his warrant trilogy, Plantinga surveys and criticizes all major theories of warrant that are offered by epistemologists today, such as deontologism, reliablism, coherentism and so forth. Fundamentally, Plantinga's method of exposing the inadequacy of such theories is to construct thought experiments or scenarios in which all the conditions for warrant stipulated by a theory are met and yet in which it is obvious that the person in question does not have knowledge of the proposition that he believes because his cognitive faculties are malfunctioning in forming the belief. This common failing suggests that rational warrant inherently involves the notion of the proper functioning of one's cognitive faculties. But this raises the troublesome question, what does it mean for one's cognitive faculties to be "functioning properly"? Here Plantinga drops a bomb into mainstream epistemology by proposing a peculiarly theistic account of rational warrant and proper functioning, namely, that one's cognitive faculties are functioning properly only if they are functioning as God designed them to. He summarizes the conditions for warrant as follows:

> This view can be stated to a first approximation as follows: S knows p if (1) the belief that p is produced in S by cognitive faculties that are functioning properly (working as they ought to work, suffering from no dysfunction), (2) the cognitive environment in which p is produced is appropriate for those faculties, (3) the purpose of the module of the epistemic faculties producing the belief in question is to produce true beliefs (alternatively, the module of the design plan governing the production of p is aimed at the production of true beliefs), and (4) the objective probability of a belief's being true, given that it is produced under those conditions, is high.[6]

Although he adds various subtle qualifications, the basic idea of Plantinga's account is that a belief is warranted for a person just in the case that his cognitive faculties are, in forming that belief, functioning in an appropriate environment as God designed them to. The more firmly such a person holds the belief in question, the more warrant it has for him, and if he believes it firmly enough,

---

[6]Alvin Plantinga, "A Defense of Religious Exclusivism," in *Philosophy of Religion*, 3d ed., ed. Louis Pojman (Belmont, Calif.: Wadsworth, 1998), p. 529.

it has sufficient warrant to constitute knowledge. With respect to the belief that God exists, Plantinga holds that God has so constituted us that we naturally form this belief under certain circumstances; since the belief is thus formed by properly functioning cognitive faculties in an appropriate environment, it is warranted for us, and, insofar as our faculties are not disrupted by the noetic effects of sin, we shall believe this proposition deeply and firmly, so that we can be said, in virtue of the great warrant accruing to this belief for us, to know that God exists.

So, Plantinga maintains, if his model is true, theistic belief is both justified and warranted. So is theistic belief warranted? That all depends on whether or not God exists. If he does not, then theistic belief is probably not warranted. If he does, then Plantinga thinks that it is. For if God exists, then he has created us in his image, he loves us, and he desires that we know and love him.

> And if that is so, the natural thing to think is that he created us in such a way that we would come to hold such true beliefs as that there is such a person as God. . . . And if *that* is so, then the natural thing to think is that the cognitive processes that *do* produce belief in God are aimed by their designer at producing that belief. But then the belief in question will be produced by cognitive faculties functioning properly according to a design plan successfully aimed at truth: it will therefore have warrant.[7]

The bottom line is that the question of whether belief in God is warranted is at root not epistemological, but rather metaphysical or theological. The question "can't be settled just by attending to epistemological considerations; it is at bottom not merely an epistemological dispute, but an ontological or theological dispute."[8] It follows that there is no de jure objection to theistic belief independent of the de facto question of whether theism is true.

But if there is no de jure objection to theistic belief, what about specifically Christian beliefs? How can one be justified and warranted in holding to Christian theism? In order to answer this question, Plantinga extends his model to include not just the *sensus divinitatis* but also the inner witness or instigation of the Holy Spirit.

The extended model postulates that our fall into sin has had disastrous cognitive and affective consequences. The *sensus divinitatis* has been damaged and deformed, its deliverances muted. Moreover, our affections have been skewed, so that we resist what deliverances of the *sensus divinitatis* remain, being self-centered rather than God-centered. Here the **inner witness** or **instigation of the Holy Spirit** comes into play. God in his grace needed to find a way to inform us of the plan of salvation that he has made available, and he has chosen to do so by means of (1) the Scriptures, inspired by him and laying out the great truths of the gospel, (2) the presence and action of the Holy Spirit in repairing the cognitive and affective damage of sin, thereby enabling us to grasp and believe the great truths of the gospel, and (3) faith, which is the principal work of the Holy Spirit produced in believers' hearts. When a person is informed of the great truths of the gospel, the Holy Spirit produces in him, if he is willing, assent

[7]Plantinga, *Warranted Christian Belief*, pp. 188-89.
[8]Ibid., p. 190.

to these truths. The internal instigation of the Holy Spirit is therefore "a source of belief, a cognitive process that produces in us belief in the main lines of the Christian story."[9]

In Plantinga's view the internal instigation of the Holy Spirit is the close analogue of a cognitive faculty in that it, too, is a belief-forming "mechanism." As such the beliefs formed by this process meet the conditions for warrant: (1) they are produced by cognitive processes functioning properly, (2) the environment in which we find ourselves, including the cognitive contamination wrought by sin, is the cognitive environment in which this process was designed to function, (3) the process is designed to produce true beliefs, and (4) the beliefs produced by it, namely, the great truths of the gospel, are in fact true, so that the process is successfully aimed at producing true beliefs. Therefore, one can be said to know the great truths of the gospel through the instigation of the Holy Spirit.

Because we know the great truths of the gospel through the Holy Spirit's work, we have no need of evidence for them. Rather, they are properly basic for us, both with respect to justification and warrant. Plantinga therefore affirms that "according to the model, the central truths of the gospel are self-authenticating,"[10] that is to say, "they do not get their evidence or warrant by way of being believed on the evidential basis of other propositions."[11]

Once again, then, Plantinga concludes that if Christianity is true, then it probably has warrant in a way similar to the way described in the model. For if Christian belief is true, then we have fallen into sin and are in need of salvation.

> Furthermore, the typical way of appropriating this restoral is by way of faith, which, of course involves belief . . . in the great things of the gospel. If so, however, God would intend that we be able to be aware of these truths. And if *that* is so, the natural thing to think is that the cognitive processes that do indeed produce belief in the central elements of the Christian faith are aimed by their designer at producing that belief.[12]

A great deal more could be said about Plantinga's religious epistemology, such as his claim that it constitutes a sort of theistic argument, since no naturalistic account of warrant and, in particular, proper functioning is forthcoming, or his claim that naturalism cannot be rationally affirmed, since the naturalist can have no confidence that his cognitive faculties produce true beliefs as opposed to beliefs merely conducive to survival; but what has been said provides a general picture of his epistemology.

5 ASSESSMENT OF PLANTINGA'S RELIGIOUS EPISTEMOLOGY

What might be said by way of assessment of Plantinga's religious epistemology? It will be recalled that Plantinga embarked on two projects, a public one and a private, Christian one. His public project was to show that there is no reason to

---

[9]Ibid., p. 206.
[10]Ibid., p. 261.
[11]Ibid., p. 262.
[12]Ibid., p. 285.

think that Christian belief lacks justification, rationality or warrant, apart from presupposing Christianity's falsehood. The most common objection lodged against the success of this public project is that it leads to a radical relativism. If belief in God or Christianity can be properly basic, then just any belief, it is alleged, such as Linus's belief in the Great Pumpkin, can also be properly basic. Now with respect to justification, this allegation is, in fact, true. We can imagine someone placed in circumstances in which belief in the Great Pumpkin would be justified for him in a properly basic way. For example, perhaps Linus's parents assured him of the existence of the Great Pumpkin, just as some normally trustworthy parents assure their children of the reality of Santa Claus. Since beliefs grounded in testimony are on Plantinga's analysis properly basic, it follows that Linus's belief in the Great Pumpkin is in such circumstances properly basic with respect to justification. But this admission is for Plantinga inconsequential. It does not imply that bizarre beliefs like belief in the Great Pumpkin are properly basic for normally situated adults. In order to be properly basic with respect to justification, a belief must be appropriately grounded in the circumstances, and for most people belief in the Great Pumpkin is not. More importantly, belief in the Great Pumpkin is not, in any case, implied by Plantinga's epistemology to be properly basic with respect to warrant. Just because certain beliefs are properly basic in respect to warrant in no way implies that any arbitrarily selected belief is also warranted in this way. In Linus's case the cognitive environment is not appropriate because he is being lied to, and therefore his belief is unwarranted. Thus, even if on Plantinga's theory Linus is within his rational rights in believing in the Great Pumpkin, it does not follow that he knows that the Great Pumpkin exists.

But, it has been objected, if Christian epistemologists can legitimately claim that their beliefs are properly basic, then any community of epistemologists—for example, voodoo epistemologists—can also legitimately claim that their beliefs are properly basic, no matter how bizarre they might be. Plantinga calls this objection the "Son of Great Pumpkin" objection. Again, he freely admits that the allegation is correct with respect to justification. We can easily imagine circumstances under which voodoo epistemologists could legitimately claim that their beliefs in voodoo are justified in a basic way. The important question is whether they could legitimately claim that voodoo beliefs are properly basic with respect to warrant. The answer to that question, says Plantinga, will depend on what we mean by *legitimately*. If we mean merely *justifiably*, then once again Plantinga freely admits that they could; but he sees no relativistic consequences flowing from this admission. Being justified is just too easy a state to attain to be of much significance. Voodoo epistemologists under the influence of a native narcotic might well be within their rational rights in thinking that voodoo beliefs are properly basic with respect to warrant. But no relativistic conclusion follows from that. Do we mean by *legitimately*, then, *warrantedly*? If so, then nothing in Plantinga's model implies that the voodoo epistemologists are warranted in their claim. On the contrary, insofar as voodoo beliefs are incompatible with the innate *sensus divinitatis*, Plantinga's model implies that voodoo epistemologists cannot be warranted in claiming that their beliefs are properly basic with respect to warrant. Thus Plantinga's model does not lead to relativism.

Interestingly, Plantinga does concede that practitioners of other theistic religions could, like the Christian, argue with equal cogency that, say, a Muslim version of Plantinga's model is epistemically possible, philosophically unobjectionable given the truth of Islam, and probably warranted in a way similar to that described in the model if Islam is true. But such a conclusion does not support relativism. It merely shows that there is no de jure objection to other theistic faiths independent of de facto objections to them. Perhaps even more significantly, it is not the case that such a concession holds for any belief set; in particular it does not hold, in Plantinga's view, for naturalism. For if naturalism is true, then it is not likely that our belief-forming mechanisms are reliable, since they are not aimed at truth but are merely selected for survival. Thus, although adherents of other theistic religions could cogently argue on behalf of their religions what Plantinga argues on behalf of Christian belief, the same cannot be said for what, in the Western academic world, is the main alternative to Christian belief today.

What, then, of Plantinga's private project? How well has he fared in providing an epistemological account of Christian belief from a Christian perspective? Here reservations need to be expressed. The aim of this project is to show that if Christianity is true, then Plantinga's extended epistemological model or something like it is very probably true. Oddly, Plantinga's argument in support of this contention is surprisingly thin. All of the intricate machinery concerning proper functioning, cognitive environment, design plan and so forth, along with the nuanced descriptions of the *sensus divinitatis* and internal instigation of the Holy Spirit, play no role in this argument. In fact, all we get is about a paragraph or two, quoted above, that if God existed, then he would want us to know him and so would provide a means to do so. Thus, if Christianity is true, it is likely to be warranted. But with this conclusion the Christian evidentialist would enthusiastically concur, adding, "Therefore, it is very likely that God has provided evidence of his existence such that all culpable persons can draw a warranted inference that God exists." At most, then, Plantinga's argument shows that

1. If (Christian) theistic belief is true, then it is warranted.

This statement is neutral with regard to an evidentialist or Plantingian model. Now Plantinga also asserts that it is probably true that

2. If (Christian) theistic belief is true, the model or something similar is correct.

But Plantinga seems to provide no argument in support of this assertion. Reflecting on (1) and (2), one wonders if Plantinga intends to infer (2) from (1) with the help of the assumed premise:

3. If (Christian) theistic belief is warranted, the model or something similar is correct.

By hypothetical syllogism, (2) follows validly from (1) and (3). Now Plantinga argues at length against a proposition deceptively similar to (3), namely,

4. If (Christian) theistic belief is warranted, then belief in the model or something similar is warranted.

Plantinga is quite clear that our Christian theistic belief can be warranted, but that we might not be warranted in believing the model. Indeed, for most Christians (who have never read Plantinga), their Christian theistic belief is warranted, and yet they have no warrant for believing in Plantinga's model, of which they have not even heard. But while Plantinga rejects (4), it seems that he should find (3) unobjectionable. Indeed, (3) would seem to be the crucial premise differentiating Plantinga's view from those of evidentialists, authoritarians and so on. But so far as we can tell, Plantinga provides no argument at all in support of (3).

In the absence of any philosophical argument for (3), the Christian, in assessing the worth of Plantinga's model as an account of how believers are warranted in their Christian belief, will turn to Scripture and Christian experience in order to size up the model by its approximation to their deliverances. When we do so, however, the model would seem to be in need of important modifications.

Take, first, Plantinga's postulation of a *sensus divinitatis*. It is worth noting that Plantinga seriously misinterprets Calvin on this score. When the French Reformer spoke of an innate sense of divinity, he meant an *awareness* of God, just as we speak of a sense of fear, or a sense of foreboding, or a sense of being watched. But Plantinga takes him to mean a cognitive *faculty* akin to our sense of sight, or sense of hearing, or sense of touch. Nothing in Calvin supports the idea that we have a special inborn cognitive mechanism that produces belief in God. Now, as Plantinga reminds us, the model is Plantinga's, not Calvin's. But when we turn to Scripture, neither do we find there any such suggestion of a special faculty of the soul that is designed to produce belief in God. In fact, we do not find in Scripture even any unambiguous support for Calvin's weaker notion of an innate awareness of divinity (Jn 1:9 would be an exegetical stretch). What about the appeal to Christian experience? The difficulty here is that it is impossible to distinguish experientially between an inborn *sensus divinitatis* and the *testimonium Spiritu Sancti internum* (inner witness of the Holy Spirit). The Scripture does teach that the Holy Spirit works in people's hearts to bring conviction of Christian truth claims, both in the case of the unbeliever (Jn 16:7-11) and the believer (Rom 8:15-16; 1 Jn 2:20, 26-27; 3:24; 4:13; 5:6-10), and any awareness one might experience of God can be as plausibly ascribed to the Spirit's work as to an inborn sense of divinity. Thus scriptural teaching inclines against the postulation of a *sensus divinitatis*, and Christian experience does not require it.

What shall we say about Plantinga's doctrine of the internal instigation of the Holy Spirit? Certainly, Scripture teaches that there is such a witness. But nothing in Scripture supports Plantinga's surprising claim that the witness of the Spirit is given only in response to human sin and fallenness. Given that sin quenches the work of the Holy Spirit, it would be surprising if Adam, had he not fallen into sin, would not have enjoyed the fullness and fellowship of the Holy Spirit. In fact, we have compelling grounds for rejecting Plantinga's view in light of the life of our Lord, who, though sinless, was nonetheless led and inspired by the Holy Spirit in his ministry, just as the Old Testament judges and prophets had been in theirs.[13] Plantinga's construal of the witness of the Holy

---

[13]See the extended treatment by James D. G. Dunn, *Jesus and the Spirit* (London: SCM Press, 1975).

Spirit results from his doctrine of the *sensus divinitatis* as a cognitive faculty functioning properly prior to the Fall but then damaged by the noetic effects of the Fall—a doctrine that finds no support in Scripture.[14]

Moreover, Plantinga's understanding of the instigation of the Holy Spirit as a belief-forming process analogous to a cognitive faculty is surely suspicious. It is as though there were a faculty outside myself which forms beliefs in me. But since this faculty or process is not mine, not being part of my cognitive equipment, then it cannot literally be true that "*I* have believed in God," which contradicts both Scripture and experience. Certainly, the belief is formed in me, but I am not the one who formed it, and, therefore, I have not truly believed. For this reason, it seems preferable to construe the *testimonium Spiritu Sancti internum* either literally as a form of testimony and thus its deliverances as properly basic, or else as part of the circumstances that serve to ground belief in God and the great truths of the gospel and thus again the beliefs formed in the context of the Spirit's witness as properly basic. In either case, it is we, employing the soul's ordinary, God-given capacities, who, in response to the Spirit's testimony or in the circumstances of experiencing his prevenient convicting and drawing, come to believe in God and the great things of the gospel.

Such a modified model seems better suited than Plantinga's original model to serve Christians as an account of how Christian belief is warranted. Nonetheless, it is still so close to Plantinga's approach that he seems correct that if Christian belief is true, his model or something very similar is likely to be correct.

CHAPTER SUMMARY

Great advances in religious epistemology have been made in the last generation. Positivistic challenges to the cognitive significance of religious belief are now passé, having been shown to be based on a criterion of meaning that was overly restrictive and self-refuting.

Similarly, claims that atheists and theists have differential burdens of proof, so that in the absence of preponderant evidence for theism, the presumption is that atheism is true, are obsolete. The absence of evidence counts against an existence claim only if it were to be expected that the entity, were it to exist, would leave evidence of its existence in excess of that which we have. This debate has moved on to the question of the hiddenness of God. The difficulty of the atheist is to show why the Christian God should not, as the Bible declares, hide himself from certain unbelievers.

Pragmatic arguments for theism may be either truth-dependent, as in the case of Pascal's wager, or truth-independent, as in the case of James's Will to Believe. Such arguments, if successful, show that theistic belief may be prudent.

Reformed epistemology, whose foremost exponent is Alvin Plantinga, directly attacks evidentialism. Plantinga provides an epistemological model in order to show that there is no de jure objection to Christian belief and to provide an account of warranted Christian belief. He claims that his model is epistemi-

---

[14]Plantinga inconsistently portrays the *sensus divinitatis* as both operative today and as part of the narrow image of God, which was destroyed, not merely damaged, in the Fall (Plantinga, *Warranted Christian Belief*, pp. 204-5).

cally possible, philosophically unobjectionable given Christianity's truth and probably true if Christianity is true—claims that could also be cogently argued by adherents of certain non-Christian theistic religions, but not by naturalists. The model appeals to a cognitive faculty, the *sensus divinitatis*, to explain how belief in God is properly basic with respect to both justification and warrant, the latter being analyzed in terms of the proper functioning of our cognitive faculties. In order to explain how fundamental Christian belief is similarly properly basic, the model appeals to the witness of the Holy Spirit to the truths enunciated in Scripture and his internal instigation of faith in the believer.

CHECKLIST OF BASIC TERMS AND CONCEPTS
de facto objection
de jure objection
evidentialism
expected utility principle
falsification principle
hiddenness of God
inner witness (or instigation) of the Holy Spirit
justification
logical positivism
Pascal's wager
pragmatic argument
pragmatic justification
presumption of atheism
properly basic
sensus divinitatis
theological rationalism
truth-dependent argument
truth-independent argument
verification principle
warrant

PART III

METAPHYSICS

8
WHAT IS METAPHYSICS?

Since we are seeking this knowledge,
we must inquire of what kind are the causes and the principles,
the knowledge of which is Wisdom.
ARISTOTLE METAPHYSICS 982^5

What can be seen is temporary, but what cannot be seen is eternal.
2 CORINTHIANS 4:18

That all depends upon what the meaning of "is" is.
WILLIAM JEFFERSON CLINTON

1 INTRODUCTION

Metaphysics has a public relations problem. When some people hear the word they are likely to think of a certain area of the bookstore at the mall where you get books on the New Age movement, astral projection and eastern herbal cooking! Others are likely to think of metaphysics as pure intellectual speculation about a subject when science cannot give us an answer to our questions about that subject. However popular, neither of these opinions is accurate. Metaphysics has a long, distinguished history boasting of some of the greatest thinkers of all time: Plato, Aristotle, Augustine, Boethius, Aquinas, Descartes, Leibniz, Locke and many others. Along with logic and epistemology, metaphysics is the most basic part of philosophy. And metaphysics has been the long-standing friend of theology. The early creeds of Christendom are filled with metaphysical terms—person, essence, substance, subsistence—and they give testimony to the help that metaphysics can give to the development of systematic theology.

The term *metaphysics* was first used as a title for a group of works by Aristotle (384-322 B.C.). One set of his writings was about "the things of nature" and came to be called the *Physics*. Another set of works (which Aristotle himself never named) was called "the books after the *Physics*" (*ta meta ta physica*) by some ancient editors that collected and edited his writings in the first century B.C. Thus *metaphysics* originally meant "after the *Physics*" and, while metaphysical reflection existed before Aristotle, the title was first used in the way just mentioned, and it has continued to refer to a certain branch of philosophy ever since.

It is difficult, if not impossible to come up with an adequate definition of metaphysics. Usually, it is characterized as the philosophical study of the nature of being or reality and the ultimate categories or kinds of things that are real.

This definition is adequate to capture much of what is done in metaphysics. Typical metaphysical questions are these: What is the difference between existing and not-existing? Is reality one or many? Are there abstract objects that exist but are not spatial and temporal? Are there substances and, if so, what are they? Are we free or determined? Is matter real and, if so, what is it? Do humans have minds as well as bodies? Is the property of being red real and, if so, what is it? Where is it?

A metaphysical problem is usually a puzzle about some ultimate kind of issue expressed in a question like one of the following:

1. How could there be x's, given that certain things are the case?
2. How could there fail to be x's, given that certain things are the case?

Examples of (1) include, how could there be living things, given that everything in the universe is matter? How could values exist, given that everything that exists must exist at some point in space and time? Examples of (2) include, how could there fail to be abstract objects called numbers, given that statements of arithmetic $(2 + 4 = 6)$ are necessarily true? How could there fail to be a soul, given the existence of freedom of the will?

These questions should give the reader a feel for the kinds of problems that metaphysicians address. In the remainder of this chapter, we will look at the main branches of metaphysics and survey some general guidelines often used in metaphysical investigation. The final pages of the chapter will look briefly at a major debate in metaphysics in order to illustrate a type of metaphysical dispute that has been around since at least the time of Plato: the debate between naturalists and ontologists about the existence of **abstract entities** (e.g., properties, numbers, propositions, sets, relations).

2 MAIN BRANCHES OF METAPHYSICS

Metaphysics is the philosophical study of **being** or reality. To help clarify this issue, consider the following sentences:

1. Socrates is real.
2. Socrates is the teacher of Plato.
3. Socrates is human.
4. Socrates is white.
5. Socrates is skin and bone.

Each of these sentences uses a different sense of the word *is*. Part of metaphysical investigation is the task of distinguishing these different senses and saying something helpful about each one of them. Sentence (1) uses an *is* of being or existence. It asserts that Socrates exists. This sense of "to be" raises the question, what is it to exist or not exist? What is it about something that accounts for its existence? Sentence (2) uses an *is* of **identity**. It says that Socrates is identical to, is the very same thing as, the teacher of Plato. This raises another question: What does it mean for some thing x and some thing y to be the same thing? What is it for something to be identical to itself and different from everything else?

Sentence (3) employs an *is* of **essential predication**. It says that being human is the very **essence** of Socrates. This raises the question, what does it mean to say that something (being human) is the essence of something else (Socrates)? Do things really have essences and, if so, what are they? Sentence (4) contains an *is* of **accidental predication**. It says that Socrates has a property, being white, that is "present in" him. This raises the question of whether properties exist and, if so, what are they? Is there a distinction between essential and accidental properties? Does humanness relate to Socrates in a way different from the way whiteness relates to Socrates? Finally, sentence (5) uses an *is* of **constitution**, sometimes called a **part-whole** *is*. It says that Socrates is a whole with skin and bones as parts. Socrates is constituted by these parts. This raises the question of whether parts are different than properties. Can something lose parts and still be the same thing?

These five sentences and the questions they surface form the most basic area of metaphysical investigation. Philosophers have reflected on them for some time, and their reflections have led to some widely accepted subbranches of metaphysics. The main two divisions of metaphysics are general ontology (sometimes simply called ontology) and special metaphysics. Let us look at these in order.

General ontology is the most basic aspect of metaphysics, and there are three main tasks that make up this branch of metaphysical study. First, general ontology focuses on the nature of existence itself. What is it to be or exist? Is existence a property that something has? Does nothingness itself exist in some sense? Is there a sense of being such that fictional objects like the unicorn Pegasus have being even though they do not exist? The nature of existence will be part of the focus of chapter nine.

2.1
GENERAL
ONTOLOGY

Second, in general ontology we study general principles of being, general features that are true of all things whatsoever. Medieval philosophers used the term **transcendentals** to stand for all those features that characterize all the different kinds of entities that exist. The notions of existence, unity, truth and goodness have been taken by some to be examples of a transcendental. Everything that is, say a carbon atom, a person, a number or the property of being green, is such that it exists, is a unity (i.e., is one entity in some sense), and is true and good. In chapter nine, we will investigate one such feature of reality—the nature of identity. Everything whatever is identical to itself and different from everything else. The study of the nature of identity can be classified as part of general ontology in that identity is a transcendental feature of all entities that exist.

Third, general ontology includes what is called **categorial analysis**. It is possible to classify or group things that exist in various ways ranging from very specific to very broad types of classification. For example, consider a light brown dog, Spot, standing to the left of a desk. The dog itself can be classified in broader and broader ways according to the following scheme: an individual dog, a mammal, an animal, a living thing, a substance. The color of the dog can be classified in this way: light brown, brown, a visible property, a property. The relationship between Spot and the desk can be grouped as follows: to the left of, a spatial relation, a relation.

In the example just mentioned, the ultimate **categories** used are those of substance, property and relation. A set of categories is a collection of the ultimate, broadest classifications of all existent entities whatsoever such that (1) each entity will fit into a specific category and (2) the categories taken as a group will allow us to classify all entities. A set of categories is a set of mutually exclusive and exhaustive classifications of all entities. A set of categories is mutually exclusive in that a given category will have a distinguishing feature that sets entities in that category off and makes them distinct from the entities in the other categories. A set of categories is exhaustive in that all entities (except the transcendentals) will fit into one of the categories.

Note that the example of Spot includes higher and higher groupings that are more and more inclusive. For example, as one goes from light brown to brown to visible property to property, one goes from a less inclusive classification to a broader, more inclusive or more general classification. Sometimes the relationship between a higher, broader and a lower, more specific classification is called a **genus-species relationship**. Here are some examples of genus-species relationships: being a visible property or being brown; being a shape or being a square; being a sound or being the note C; being a spatial relation or being on-top-of.

In each case, the genus is broader than the species. In fact, a traditional way of viewing the genus-species distinction (going back to Aristotle) takes the species as a way that the genus can exist. There can be an example of a genus without a particular species (e.g., some entity can be a visible property without being brown, say, by being the property green) but there cannot be a case of a particular species without the genus above it being present as well (e.g., if Spot has the property of being brown, Spot also has the property of being a visible property).

One of the tasks of general ontology is to formulate a categorial classification of reality and study the features of each ultimate category that makes it unique. In general ontology, we also study the various genera and species that form the hierarchy of classification within each ultimate category. A set of categories of being can be very useful in clarifying and helping to solve various philosophical problems.

For example, many philosophers have noted that a distinguishing mark of the mind is **intentionality**. Roughly, intentionality is the ofness or aboutness of the mind. For every mental state (e.g., a state of hoping, thinking, believing, fearing, wishing), that state is always a state of or about something beyond it (and this is true even if the object of the mental state does not exist, say, when someone has a fear of Zeus). An interesting and very important question we can ask about intentionality is this: Is intentionality a property or a relation? This question focuses attention on how we should understand and classify intentionality itself. In chapter ten, we will look at two important categories of being: substance and property.

In the history of philosophy, there have been various opinions about the nature of categories, that is, about what a set of categories amounts to. However, two main schools of thought about categories are represented by Aristotle and Immanuel Kant. According to Aristotle, there are ten basic categories of reality: substance, quantity, quality, relation, place, time, posture, state, action and passivity. These ten categories for Aristotle can, in turn, be understood as taking the category of substance as fundamental or basic and the other nine categories as different ways that a substance can be modified or qualified. For example, the substance, Spot, can be 25 pounds, brown and so forth.

What is most crucial for Aristotle's view of the categories, however, is not the precise nature or number of his classifications. Rather, the thing of central importance in Aristotle's approach to the categories is that he took them to give us real divisions in the actual world itself as it exists "out there," i.e., as it is in itself independent of human thought or language. For him, the categories are the broadest, real divisions of being.

For Kant, the categories (he lists twelve of them in *The Critique of Pure Reason*) are not divisions of the world as it is in itself (he called this the **noumenal world**), but rather they express the divisions of the world as it appears to us as knowing subjects (he called this the **phenomenal world**). Thus Kant's categories express the different ways that knowing subjects organize and classify the world of their sensory experience. A Kantian category is a broadest division of the phenomenal world, the sensory world as it is experienced by us. Thus, according to Kant, a study of the categories does not tell us about real divisions in the world as it is in itself. Rather, it gives us insight about how we as sensing and knowing subjects must divide the world of sensory experience to make it knowable to us.

We cannot enter into the debate here as to which view of the categories is correct. Part of this debate involves issues in epistemology, especially skepticism, the nature of perception and the adequacy of postmodernism and various forms of deconstructionism. Some of these issues are taken up in part two of this text. Suffice it to say here that we think that the best philosophical arguments, as well as the most reasonable way to understand Christian theology, imply that Kant was wrong about the categories. Whether or not we are right in this understanding, we will, nevertheless, approach our study of some categories in the next few chapters in a way that sides with the spirit of Aristotle's views: we will take the categories to be discussed to be real categories of the external world as it is in itself.

In addition to the debate about how to understand what the categories themselves are, there has been a division of opinion about the exact identity and number of the ultimate categories of being. Aristotle thought there were ten ultimate categories, with the category of substance being most basic. Others—for example, **process philosophers**—hold to a different set of categories, with the category "event" being most basic. Still other philosophers have listed various other categories as necessary to make sense of reality. As already mentioned, we will look at only two categories: substance and property. But one should remember that some philosophers reject these categories while others accept but add additional categories to them.

Besides general ontology, a second area of study in metaphysics is called special metaphysics. In **special metaphysics**, two different types of concerns are in view. First, there is the study of specific topics of special interest: Is there a soul or mind? Are humans free or determined? Is there such a thing as personal iden-

2.2
SPECIAL
METAPHYSICS

tity, i.e., do persons remain the same through change or are persons best viewed as a series of events called person stages? Is there such a thing as causation?

Second, there is the second-order metaphysical clarification and investigation of other fields of study, e.g., sociology, biology, physics and psychology. Here, the metaphysician asks questions like, are there electrons and, if so, what are they? Do social groups exist as wholes that are "more than" the sum of their parts? And so on. It should be clear that there is an order between general ontology and special metaphysics. The problems of special metaphysics should be tackled after work has been done in general ontology. In light of the positions one adopts in general ontology, one will have more conceptual tools to employ in working on the topics in special metaphysics. For example, if someone says that a carbon atom is a substance, the insights of general ontology will help to clarify how this should or should not be understood. In chapters eleven through fourteen, we will investigate certain issues in special metaphysics after we have looked at problems in general ontology in chapters nine through ten.

3 METHODS OF APPROACH IN METAPHYSICS

When we do metaphysical investigation, how should we proceed? What methodology should we employ? Unfortunately, there is no general agreement among philosophers about how to answer these questions, and in fact, one's view about methodology in metaphysics will be dependent, at least in part, on one's positions about general solutions to philosophical questions.

For example, some philosophers are philosophical **naturalists** who hold that reality is exhausted by the spatiotemporal world of physical objects embraced by our best scientific theories. In their view, science is the main approach to investigating the world, not philosophy. Many who embrace this sort of naturalism see the role of metaphysics to be that of clarifying our use of language, especially our use of scientific language. The methodology of the metaphysician is to take scientific theories, analyze and clarify the use of metaphysical terms within those theories, and formulate a worldview built upon those theories. Metaphysics is not the study of reality—science is—but rather of our talk, especially scientific talk of reality. On this view, **linguistic analysis** is the main tool of the philosopher engaged in metaphysics. He or she will analyze and clarify the scientist's use of the terms *substance* and *property* in sentences like "carbon is a substance with such and such properties."

Unfortunately, this approach is wrong-headed. It *is* a part of metaphysics to analyze and clarify our use of language, including scientific language. However, there is no good reason to limit metaphysical investigation in this way, especially when we realize that science presupposes philosophical and metaphysical doctrines (see chaps. 15-18). Thus metaphysics is conceptually prior to science, not vice versa. Science may offer help to metaphysics in various ways, but science cannot dictate to the metaphysician what he or she ought to believe about reality or about the methods to be used in metaphysics. Moreover, language (including scientific language) itself exists. Therefore, metaphysics cannot be reduced to language because language itself is part of metaphysical study.

In spite of the fact that there are no generally accepted methods of approach in metaphysics, it is still possible to state some general guidelines that should be followed in metaphysics unless there is good reason to set them aside. Here are some of them:

1. Metaphysical study should begin with and take into account the things we already know or have reason to believe are true before we begin doing metaphysics. Metaphysics is rooted in wonder and puzzlement about what we know or have reason to believe, and it is an attempt to analyze, clarify and account for those items of knowledge and rational belief. There are at least four sources of these beliefs. First, metaphysics focuses on what we know from the critical use of common sense. By this we mean that our commonsense beliefs, when we are "critical" of them in the sense of being aware of them, reflecting carefully about them, seeing if they make sense and stand up to scrutiny, provide material for metaphysical study. For example, it would seem to be an item of critical common sense that, say, an apple is both red and sweet. The redness of the apple is real, is different from the sweetness of the apple, and is the color of the apple's surface. Metaphysics tries to account for this item of common sense. Critical common sense can, of course, be wrong, but it should be trusted unless there is good reason to abandon it. The burden of proof works on behalf of critical common sense, not against it for at least three reasons. For one thing, we simply do, in fact, know many of the things critical common sense offers us. Moreover, much of the point of metaphysics is rooted in wonder and puzzlement over the things we have reason to believe in critical common sense. Finally, Christian theism implies that, generally, we can trust our various faculties to give us true, rational beliefs, and these beliefs are part of the core of common sense. To the degree that some idea of common sense can be shown to be a result of cultural indoctrination, to that degree it is suspect (though, of course, it could still be true). But many of the beliefs of common sense that generate metaphysical speculation (like the apple example above) are not like this.

Second, we should use our knowledge from Christianity to help us do metaphysics in at least three ways. First, certain truths in theology require metaphysical study to help clarify them. The doctrine of the Trinity illustrates this. Second, truths from Christianity can be used as background knowledge to guide us in rejecting certain metaphysical positions and in seeking further, independent reasons for that rejection. If we take physicalism to be the view that a human being is simply a material object, nothing more and nothing less, then the Old and New Testament teaching about the soul, understood in the most natural way exegetically and in keeping with the history of the church, will lead us to reject physicalism as false and unreasonable, and we will do metaphysics to find further, independent reasons for our understanding of the Christian view. This can, of course, be abused. So we need to be careful that we have understood Christian teaching on the issue carefully and with a sense of integrity regarding genuine options within orthodox theology. But theology is still an important source of propositions for doing metaphysics.

Finally, Christian theology can remove certain intellectual barriers that force some thinkers to adopt positions in metaphysics in a one-sided way. In these cases, the Christian philosopher can be more open than his or her secular counterpart to seeing both sides of a dispute. For example, philosophers who hold to physicalism as a metaphysical worldview cannot embrace the existence of abstract objects (nonphysical entities that do not exist in space or time) such as numbers because they are not material. The Christian philosopher can be open to embracing the existence of numbers as abstract objects or to rejecting them since he or she is not forced to do metaphysics in light of physicalism. On the other hand, Christian teaching can introduce metaphysical problems of its own. For example, if abstract objects like numbers exist, then since they are neither in time nor space, they did not come into being at a moment of time. This means that they were not created in the same way that trees and rivers were created, so the Christian philosopher who embraces abstract entities must harmonize their existence with the doctrine of God as creator of everything.

In addition to critical common sense and Christian teaching, our knowledge of our own self is a third important source of information for metaphysics. A careful description of our awareness of our own selves, for instance, that we seem to be continuing, enduring beings who are distinct from the rest of the world (one's desk is not part of oneself), that we are conscious, make decisions, have beliefs and sensory experiences, could (at least) possibly survive the death of our bodies and so forth, can give us insights into metaphysics. Any broad metaphysical system must take into account what we have reason to believe about our own selves.

A final source of beliefs for metaphysical reflection is reliable information from other fields of study. If a business professor claims that corporations have moral responsibility, does this mean that corporations exist? If the self can "split" in brain operations or in cases of multiple personality, can we still make sense of the soul as a unified entity? If living organisms evolved, can we still believe that they have natures? In cases like these, other disciplines provide material for metaphysical study. Keep in mind, however, that questions like these are primarily metaphysical questions, not primarily questions of neurophysiology and so forth. Attempts to answer them will require careful treatment from philosophers trained in metaphysics who try to give genuine attention to the real facts present in other fields of study. Metaphysics *is* concerned with the facts. But more importantly, it is the distinctive concern of metaphysics that we correctly interpret those facts in a philosophical way.

2. State the metaphysical problem you are trying to solve and what gives rise to the problem. For example, two roses seem to have the very same smell. The problem becomes this: How can each rose have the same smell? Does that mean that the specific smell is in both roses at the same time? How can something be in more than one thing at once? On the other hand, if each rose has its own smell, how are we to account for the fact that the smell seems to be the same in both roses? If we say that the smell of one rose exactly resembles the smell of the other, doesn't this just mean that the roses resemble each other in that they have the same smell (since they do not resemble each other, say, in color or shape)?

After the problem is stated, list the different metaphysical alternatives to the problem, along with the assumptions made by each alternative, draw the implications of each alternative, and see which is most reasonable. In the example about the roses, two alternatives would be that the roses have the same smell or that each has its own smell exactly resembling the smell of the other. The assumption of the first alternative is that properties like a specific rosy smell can be in more than one thing at once and the second alternative denies this. In any metaphysical study, it is important to state the implications that follow from either accepting or denying that something is real. In Plato's dialogue *Parmenides* 136a, Plato reminds us through the lips of Parmenides, "If you want to be thoroughly exercised, you must not merely make the supposition that such and such a thing *is* and then consider the consequences; you must also take the supposition that the same thing *is not*." If we deny that properties, truth, God, freedom, the soul or other entities are real, what follows from this denial? What follows from embracing their reality?

3. *Use* **thought experiments** *as sources for counterexamples to metaphysical arguments.* In metaphysics, we are primarily interested in what something must be, not in what it merely happens to be by accident. For example, the number two must be even but it happens to be Uncle Larry's favorite number. Again, all individual human beings necessarily have the property of being human, but they also all happen to have the property of being born on earth. In each case (being even and being human), the former information is more central to metaphysics than the latter. Metaphysical study seeks to uncover what numbers, causation, minds, values, properties and so forth *must* be. What is their very nature and essence?

This aspect about metaphysics leads to an insight about the role of thought experiments as sources of counterexamples for assessing metaphysical claims. To understand this insight, we need to introduce the notion of something called a possible world. When some philosophers talk about the existence of various possible worlds, they mean to describe alternative parallel universes that are all equally real. This is not what we mean by a possible world. Our use of the notion of a possible world can be clarified as follows. The **actual world**, the real world of all and only entities that exist, can be described by a conjunction of all and only true propositions. For example, the proposition *There are goats in Virginia* is a proposition truly describing the actual world, but *There are unicorns in Nebraska* does not. The actual world is the world God really created (it also includes God himself). An **impossible world** is a world that cannot exist; the conjunction of propositions describing it includes a logically impossible proposition. Such a world is one that God could not make. No conceivable set of circumstances could exist to make such a world a reality. For example, a world with square circles in Missouri is an impossible world. A **possible world** is a world whose description does not include a logically impossible proposition. A possible world is a world that God could create, it is a world that could have existed even though it may not. For example, a world with unicorns in California is not the actual world (we hope!), but it is a possible world.

Now, in metaphysics, a philosopher will often argue that some entity P is really nothing but Q. For example, heat is really nothing but the motion of molecules, the mind is really nothing but the brain, the color red is really nothing but the word *red* being used of an object or, perhaps, red is just a certain wavelength of light. At other times, a philosopher will argue that C is the very essence of D, i.e., that D could not exist without C existing and being the very nature of what D is. For example, some have claimed that the very essence of the number two is to be the smallest even number greater than one, the nature of squareness is to be a shape, the essence of being a person is to be a material object, and the essence of existing is to be located at a place in space and time.

In each of the examples cited, we can test the proposal it illustrates by using a thought experiment to suggest a **counterexample** that runs contrary to the proposal in question. These thought experiments can be seen as attempts to state a possible world where one can have P but not Q or Q but not P. For example, if there is a possible world where there are minds without brains (say in a disembodied form of existence) or brains without minds (a zombie world), then the proposal that minds are nothing but brains is false. Furthermore, if C is offered as the very nature of D, then every world where D exists, C must exist also. If we can state a possible world where D exists without C, then C cannot be taken to be the essence of D. If C is "Uncle Larry's favorite number" and D is the number two, then there could be a world where D (the number two) exists but C does not (in worlds where Uncle Larry is dead or hates the number two). This possible world is a **counterexample** to the proposal in question.

4. In metaphysics, as with other forms in knowledge generally, we are not constrained to operate within the bounds of sense experience. Advocates of strong forms of empiricism claim that all knowledge is limited to what can be directly or indirectly tested by sensory experiences from the five senses. Advocates of strong forms of empiricism have never been fond of metaphysics and for good reason. There is almost no issue of interest in metaphysics whose solution can be stated or substantiated solely within the confines of strong empiricism. The conclusion to draw from this is not that metaphysics is an illusion or mere speculation, but rather that strong empiricism is an inadequate epistemology for accounting for what we can know in general, especially for metaphysical knowledge.

Not only is it unduly confining to limit what we can know in metaphysics or elsewhere to the bounds of sensory experience, it is also a hindrance to the development of faith. In *The Screwtape Letters*, C. S. Lewis has the demon Screwtape remind his "junior tempter" Wormwood about how to keep his human "patient" from becoming a Christian. Screwtape warns Wormwood not to argue with the patient because reasoning moves the discussion onto territory where the Enemy (God) can operate too. Says Screwtape,

> By the very act of arguing, you awaken the patient's reason; and once it is awake, who can foresee the result? Even if a particular train of thought can be twisted so as to end in our favour, you will find that you have been strengthening in your patient the fatal habit of attending to universal issues and withdrawing his attention from the stream of immediate sense experiences. Your business is to fix his attention on the stream. Teach him to call it "real life" and don't let him ask what he means by "real."[1]

Lewis's remarks here provide an occasion to point out that metaphysical

---

[1]C. S. Lewis, *The Screwtape Letters* (New York: Macmillan, 1961), p. 8.

study—which includes "the fatal habit of attending to universal issues"—can be a real aid to Christian growth for a number of reasons, not the least of which is that it helps the intellect form habits that free it from grasping only issues and truths within the boundary of sensation.

In this chapter, we have looked at the main branches of metaphysics and surveyed some guidelines useful for metaphysical study. We can gain a further sense of what metaphysics is by briefly looking at a major metaphysical controversy that has been around since the time of Plato (428-348 B.C.).

4 THE DISPUTE BETWEEN NATURALISTS AND ONTOLOGISTS

In one of Plato's last dialogues, he describes a metaphysical debate that was raging during his own day. In *Sophist* 246a-c we read:

Stranger: What we shall see is something like a battle of gods and giants going on between them over their quarrel about reality.

Theaetetus: How so?

Stranger: One party is trying to drag everything down to earth out of heaven and the unseen, literally grasping rocks and trees in their hands, for they lay hold upon every stock and stone and strenuously affirm that real existence belongs only to that which can be handled and offers resistance to the touch. They define reality as the same thing as body, and as soon as one of the opposite party asserts that anything without a body is real, they are utterly contemptuous and will not listen to another word.

Theaetetus: The people you describe are certainly a formidable crew. I have met quite a number of them before now.

Stranger: Yes, and accordingly their adversaries are very wary in defending their position somewhere in the heights of the unseen, maintaining with all their force that true reality consists in certain intelligible and bodiless forms. In the clash of argument they shatter and pulverize those bodies which their opponents wield, and what those others allege to be true reality they call, not real being but a sort of moving process of becoming. On this issue an interminable battle is always going on between two camps.

In this text, Plato makes reference to a metaphysical dispute which, to put it in contemporary terms, centers over the existence of abstract entities. We cannot investigate the details of this debate here—some aspects of the dialogue will be covered in chapter ten. For now, it will help to clarify the nature of metaphysical issues and positions if we state what this debate is about and what the major options have been regarding it. Let us define the **universe** as the total spatiotemporal system of matter and (impersonal) energy, that is, as the sum total of material objects, in some way accessible to the senses and to scientific investigation. The universe consists of individual things, events and processes that exist within space and time, e.g., atoms, rocks, rivers, osmosis and flashes of lightning. For any entity in the universe, it is appropriate to ask where and when it is.

In addition to the universe, many philosophers have, like Plato, believed in another realm of entities that are called abstract objects. Abstract objects are immaterial (i.e., nonphysical) entities that do not exist inside space and time; instead, they are timeless and spaceless. It makes no sense to ask where or when they exist.

There have been many examples of abstract entities: properties, relations, sets, numbers and propositions. On this view, **properties** are entities that can be exemplified by many things at the same time (e.g., redness, goodness, triangularity, humanness) and **relations** are entities that can relate two or more things and can be in more than one group of things at the same time (e.g., brighter than, father of, larger than). Properties and relations are called **universals** because, as was mentioned, they can be in more than one thing at once or can relate more than one group at once. Several apples can have the same color of red and several groups of people can enter into the "father of" relation.

A **set** is a group or collection of things called the members of the set. The set of all numbers from one to ten is an example of a set. **Numbers** are the things that enter into certain mathematical relationships, e.g., addition, subtraction. **Propositions** are the contents expressed in declarative sentences and contained in people's minds when they are thinking. Propositions are also the things that are either true or false and that can be related to each other by means of the laws of logic (e.g., "if, then," "if and only if").

Let us call the **world** the sum total of everything whatever that exists including nonspatiotemporal abstract entities as well as the spatiotemporal universe of physical entities. The metaphysical debate alluded to by Plato can now be put as follows: Do abstract entities exist? Or put another way: Does the world exist or is there only a universe? **Ontologists** are those philosophers who, like Plato, believe in the world and abstract entities.[2] The term **naturalism** has many different meanings, but a standard use of the term defines it as the view that the universe alone exists. Since most current forms of naturalism are physicalist in flavor, naturalism has come to mean that reality is exhausted by the spatiotemporal world of physical objects accessible in some way to the senses and embraced by our best scientific theories. The naturalist has three tasks before he or she can defend naturalism as a broad metaphysical view:

1. The naturalist must show that mental entities are not real (a) by denying their existence outright (e.g., since beliefs, if they exist, must be mental, then we should treat beliefs like a flat earth and deny that there are such things) or (b) by reducing them to physical entities in space and time (e.g., beliefs exist, but they are really nothing but states of the brain) or (c) by trying to show that in some way or another they depend on the physical world for their existence.

2. The naturalist must deny that properties and relations are abstract entities by either (a) denying that they exist (**extreme nominalism**) or (b) accepting the existence of properties and relations but treating them as material realities that are wholly inside of space and time (**nominalism** and **impure realism**).

---

[2]See Reinhardt Grossmann, *The Existence of the World: An Introduction to Ontology* (London: Routledge, 1992), pp. 1-45.

3. *The naturalist must show that abstract entities are not real* by either (a) denying their existence outright (e.g., propositions, like witches, do not exist at all) or (b) reducing them to physical entities in space and time (e.g., propositions exist but they are really nothing but physical scratchings called sentences).

The debate between ontologists and naturalists is a clear example of a metaphysical dispute. We mention it here only as an illustration of metaphysics and not as an occasion to journey into the nuances of the dispute. However, proposition (1) will be discussed in chapters eleven and twelve and to a lesser degree in chapters thirteen and fourteen. Propositions (2) and (3) (especially 2) will be a major center of focus in chapter ten. However, before we can look at these issues, a more fundamental set of metaphysical notions should be clarified (see chap. 9): the nature of existence, identity and reductionism. To these issues we now turn.

CHAPTER SUMMARY

The term *metaphysics* was first used as a title for a group of works by Aristotle. Roughly, it is the philosophical study of the nature of being or reality and the ultimate categories or kinds of things that are real. The two main divisions of metaphysics are general ontology (sometimes called ontology) and special metaphysics. There are three main tasks in general ontology: (1) to understand the nature of existence itself and the difference between existing and not existing; (2) to study general principles of being (transcendentals) true of all things whatsoever; (3) to give a set of exhaustive, mutually exclusive categories that are the ultimate, broadest classification of all entities whatever. Aristotle took categories to be real divisions of the external world; Kant took them to be divisions of how we as knowing subjects organize the phenomenal world. Special metaphysics focuses on (1) specific topics of special interest (e.g., are we free or determined?) and (2) the metaphysical clarification of other fields of study.

There is no agreed upon method for doing metaphysics. However, the following principles are helpful guidelines for metaphysical investigation: (1) Metaphysics must take into account what we already know or have reason to believe prior to doing metaphysics. (2) The metaphysician should state a problem clearly, along with alternative solutions and the facts and assumptions used in each one, draw the implications of each solution and see which is most reasonable. (3) In metaphysics we can use possible worlds to state thought experiments that serve as counterexamples to metaphysical claims. (4) In metaphysics, we need not operate within the bounds of crude empiricism.

The debate between naturalists and ontologists over the existence of the world and abstract entities is a good example of a metaphysical dispute.

CHECKLIST OF BASIC TERMS AND CONCEPTS

abstract entities
accidental predication

actual world
being
categorial analysis
categories
constitution
essence
essential predication
extreme nominalism
general ontology
genus-species relationship
identity
impossible world
impure realism
intentionality
linguistic analysis
naturalism
naturalists
nominalism
noumenal world
numbers
ontologists
ontology
part-whole
phenomenal world
possible world
process philosophers
properties
propositions
relations
sets
special metaphysics
thought experiments
transcendentals
universals
universe
world

9

GENERAL ONTOLOGY
Existence, Identity
and Reductionism

What "Lions are real" means is that
some particular property . . . the property of being a lion . . .
does in fact belong to something.
G. E. MOORE

Each thing is what it is
and not another thing.
JOSEPH BUTLER

1 INTRODUCTION

In chapter eight, we saw that two main tasks of general ontology are to explain what existence itself is and to describe general features that are true of all entities whatsoever. In this chapter, we will engage in these tasks by first looking at issues in the theory of being or existence. What is it to exist versus not exist? Second, we will investigate one feature that is true of all entities, namely, the fact that everything is identical to itself and different from all other entities. What is identity and what role does an understanding of it play in philosophy? Finally, we will examine some aspects of an area of metaphysics closely related to existence and identity: replacement and reductionism. What does it mean to reduce one thing to another; for example, to reduce color to wavelengths, heat to the movement of molecules, minds to brains?

2 THE NATURE OF EXISTENCE

Suppose we have before us a real, live horse named Fury. Now think about something that is not real, say the unicorn Pegasus. There are many things true of Fury: he is black, a horse and so on. But the most fundamental thing true of Fury is that Fury exists. If we compare Fury with Pegasus, clearly there is something different between them: Fury exists and Pegasus does not. This difference is as real as the difference in color between a brown and blue billiard ball. How are we to account for the difference between Fury and Pegasus? This and related questions are what a theory of existence tries to answer. However, before we look more deeply at theories of existence, we need to glance at a prior question: Is being a genus?

If being is a **genus**—that is, a univocal notion that applies in the sames way to all things that have being—then this means that whatever existence itself turns out to be, everything that exists will have existence or being in the same sense. Being is a univocal notion that means the same thing for all entities whatsoever. On the other hand, if being is not a genus, then what it is for one thing to exist, say the number two, may be entirely different from what it is for a carbon atom to exist. It is most natural to take being as a genus, that is, to hold that a general theory of existence will give us a univocal notion of being that is equally true of all things that do, in fact, exist. When we contemplate all the things that do and do not exist, we seem to have a uniform notion we are using that characterizes the former group but not the latter.

However, not all philosophers agree that being is a genus. To understand their main argument against such a view, consider a heap of sand. Each grain of sand exists. So does the heap itself taken as a whole with the grains as parts. Those who deny that being is a genus would say that existence itself, possessed by the grains and the whole heap, is very different in the two cases. The grains have independent existence (they could exist outside the heap), but the heap itself has dependent existence.

But should we explain the difference between the heap and the grains as a difference in two distinct kinds of existence? Probably not. To see this we need to make a distinction between what it is to exist (i.e., existence in and of itself), on the one hand, and the different kinds of things that have existence, on the other. We need not explain the heap and sand example by saying that there are two different kinds of existence involved (when existence is considered in and of itself). Rather, we can say that the heap and the grains both exist in the same sense (and we will look at different views about what existence itself is shortly), even though they are two different kinds of things that *have* existence: The heap is a dependent thing that has existence and the grains are independent things that have existence. In short, the grains and the heap do not have different kinds of existence; instead, they are different kinds of things that have existence.

Given that being is a genus, we are in a position to try to find out what existence or being is, in other words, to formulate a general theory of existence applicable to all entities whatever. In this section, we will look at theories of existence in two steps: (1) general characteristics a theory of existence ought to have; (2) different accounts of what existence is.

2.2.1
FIVE
CHARACTERISTICS
OF AN
ADEQUATE
THEORY OF
EXISTENCE

There are five different traits that a good theory of existence ought to have. For one thing, it needs to be consistent with and explain what actually does and does not exist. Second, it needs to be consistent with and explain what could have existed but either does not exist or is not believed to exist (perhaps falsely) by the person advocating a given view of existence. For example, even though unicorns do not, in fact, exist, they could have existed. God could have made a world where Pegasus exists in the same sense that Fury exists. Physicalists do not believe the soul is real, but even if they are right (see chaps. 11-12), surely existence is such that souls *could have* existed.

Third, a theory of existence must allow for the fact that existence itself exists. To put the point differently, it must not be self-refuting. For example, if someone claims that to exist is the same thing as being inside space and time (existence itself is being spatiotemporally located), then, on at least some views, space and time would not themselves exist since they are not inside space and time. Whatever existence amounts to, one thing is clear: it makes a real difference in the world and it must itself exist in order to make such a difference. If existence itself does not exist, then nothing else could exist in virtue of having existence.

Fourth, a theory of existence must not violate the fundamental laws of logic: the laws of identity (*P* is identical to *P*), noncontradiction (*P* cannot be both true and false at the same time in the same sense) and excluded middle (*P* must be either true or false). Contradictory states of affairs, e.g., a square circle or its simultaneously raining in Grandview and not raining in Grandview, do not exist. Moreover, something must either exist or not exist, and nothing can exist and not exist at the same time.

Fifth, a theory of existence must allow for the existence of acts of knowing. Since a theory of existence is a theory, it will depend for its rational acceptability on knowledge that people have. Now an act of knowing something is, among other things, a conscious act of a person. Thus any theory of existence that denies the existence of conscious persons who know things is false. It has been said, not unfairly, that some versions of physicalism suffer from this problem (see chaps. 11-12).

Someone might think that Christian theology has a fairly straightforward answer to the question "What is existence?": to exist is to be created by God or to be God. Now it is certainly true that everything other than God has been created. But this answer will still not do. Why? Because it is circular. Suppose we want to know what it means to say "X exists," and we answer, "X is created by God." If we now ask what this statement means, we will answer, "For God to give x existence." Thus "X exists" will amount to "X is given existence by God," and we have made no progress. We want to know exactly what God does when he creates something. To answer this, we need a theory of existence.

2.2.2
DIFFERENT
THEORIES OF
WHAT
EXISTENCE
ITSELF IS

Several theories of existence have been offered. Here are some that are inadequate. To exist is to (a) be located in space and time; (b) be physical; (c) be causally efficacious, i.e., to be capable of being an efficient cause (that by means of which an effect is produced) or of being acted on by an efficient cause; (d) be an event or a bundle of events; (e) be perceived or be a perceiver; (f) be a property; (g) be a property of properties (e.g., to be a second-order property of first-order properties).

We will not apply each of the five features of a theory of existence to each view of existence, but it would be a good exercise to do. However, a few remarks should give you a feel for how to use the five features listed above to evaluate different views of existence. Feature three (existence itself exists) would seem to rule out (a) and (c). Space and time are not themselves located in space and time; when an efficient cause produces an effect, the cause and effect enter into a causal relation and that relation itself is not causally efficacious, yet it exists.

Feature two (what could have but does not exist or is not believed to exist) counts against (e) (which was held by George Berkeley [1685-1753]). Surely, mountains and dinosaurs could exist even though no one is looking at them; and even though God constantly looks at mountains even if humans do not, it is not God's gaze that gives mountains being, but his creative act of speaking them into existence and continually holding them in being. Moreover, one could be "seeing" a mountain in a hallucination, and it would not follow that a real, extra-mental mountain existed. Feature two also counts against (b) (as well as others on the list) because disembodied existence is surely possible, even if it is not real, and (b) rules out the very *possibility* of disembodied existence since it would not be physical existence. It also makes God's existence metaphysically impossible, and this is quite a strong claim.

Feature one (what actually does and does not exist) eliminates (b) and (d) if minds, God, values and abstract objects exist, since they are neither events, groups of events nor physical entities. It also rules out (g). If (g) is true, then existence is a second-order property of properties. That is, existence is something that truly applies only to properties; for example, to being red, hardness, triangularity, humanness. But we all know that, in addition to properties, various individuals exist as well, such as a specific red ball. If existence is a feature only of properties, then individuals could not have existence; since they do, in fact, have existence, (g) must be false.

The point here is to illustrate ways that features of a theory of existence can be used to evaluate alternative proposals for existence itself. So far, nothing has been said about (f): existence is a property. Throughout the history of philosophy, many thinkers (e.g., Plato and Descartes) have held that existence is a property in the same sense that redness or being square is a property. For a ball to be red is for it to have the property of redness; for it to exist is for it to have the property of existence. Now at first glance, something seems right about this proposal. We do say, quite appropriately, that the ball *has* redness and that it *has* reality as well. In some sense, then, things can be said to have or not have existence.

However, something seems wrong with this proposal too. Existence is simply not a normal property like redness. This point was made by Immanuel Kant (1724-1804) in *Critique of Pure Reason* (A 600/B 628):

> By whatever and by however many predicates [properties] we may think a thing—even if we completely determine it—we do not make the least addition to the thing when we further declare the thing *is*. Otherwise, it would not be exactly the same thing that exists, but something more than we had thought in the concept; and we could not, therefore, say that the exact object of my concept exists.

Kant's point can be understood in this way. When you think of a ball, it adds to your conception of the thing to be told that it is red. But it does not add to your conception of the ball to be told that it exists. Put differently, saying that a ball is red tells us something about the character of the ball. But saying that it is real says that the ball, with all of its properties, does in fact exist. Thus existence does not relate to the ball like being red does.

Kant seems right here; nevertheless, saying that the ball is real does add something because there is, in fact, a real difference between existence and nonexistence. Can we shed more light on what this difference is? Perhaps so. Consider the statement "Tigers exist." This would appear to assert the following: (1) The property of being a tiger (2) belongs to something (an individual tiger, say Tony). In chapter ten we will look at this "belonging" relation, but for now, it should be noted that it has gone by several names: **exemplification, predication** and **instancing.** The claim that tigers exist is the claim that the **essence** of being a tiger (the *what* of being a tiger) is actually exemplified by or belongs to something (the *that* or *fact* of an individual tiger existing).

Note that when "Tigers exist" is broken down into the two aspects above, (1) refers to the essence or nature of being a tiger and (2) expresses reality or existence. From this we learn two things. First, there is a difference between a thing's essence and its existence. Knowledge of what a tiger is does not tell us that tigers exist. There is a fundamental difference between essence (whatness) and existence (thatness).

Second, existence is not a property that belongs, but is the belonging of a property. **Existence** is the entering into the predication or exemplification relation and, in general, the following characterization of existence seems to fit the five features of a theory of existence: *existence is either the belonging of some property or the being belonged to by a property or, more simply, the entering into the nexus of exemplification.* In the case of Tony the tiger, the fact that the property of being a tiger belongs to something and that something has this property belonging to it is what confers existence. Existence is the entering into the predication or exemplification relation.

How does this view square with the five features of a theory of existence? It would seem to account for everything that does or could exist and that does not or could not exist. Things that exist have properties. When something such as Zeus fails to exist, there is no object Zeus that actually has properties. Since unicorns could have existed, this means that the property of being a unicorn could have belonged to something. It would also account for existence itself existing because the belonging-to (exemplification, predication) relation is itself exemplified (a nonfictional, real tiger named Tony and the property of being a tiger both enter into this belonging relation) and the belonging-to relation exemplifies other features (e.g., it has the property of being a relation that belongs to it). Finally, this view of existence does not violate the fundamental laws of logic nor does it rule out the existence of acts of knowing.

In sum, we have learned three things from our brief discussion of existence: (A) There is a genuine difference between existing and not existing. (B) This difference is not a normal property like the property of being red. (C) Existence is not part of the essence or "whatness" of ordinary entities, that is, for ordinary entities there is a difference between essence and existence.

There are three further remarks to be made about existence. First, our characterization of existence allows us to specify some other notions: **coming-to-be** and **perishing.** Since we already have an idea of what existence itself is, and since coming-to-be and perishing involve gaining and losing existence, then these latter notions can be understood in terms of our general theory of existence itself. The symbol = Df may be read as "is defined as."

2.2.3
FINAL
OBSERVATIONS
ABOUT
EXISTENCE

E comes into being = Df There is at least one property which is such that E has that property and there is no property which is such that E had that property.

E perishes = Df There was at least one property which was such that E had it and there is no longer any property which is such that E has it.

When something comes into existence, there must be at least one property that belongs to that thing. For example, when a human being comes-to-be, then the property of being human belongs to that individual at that moment. When something ceases-to-be, it no longer has any properties whatever. Coming-to-be and perishing should be kept distinct from what philosophers call **alteration**. An example of an alteration is an apple's going from sweet to sour. Alterations are types of **change**. Before change is possible, two things must be true: (1) the thing that is changing must exist and (2) the thing that changes must exist at the beginning, during the process and at the end of change. In the example above, the apple exists and continues to exist while it is sweet, during the time it changes to being sour and while it is sour. An alteration is a case in which a thing changes in the properties it has; it is not a case in which something changes with respect to existence itself. Alterations presuppose and, therefore, cannot be the same thing as a change in existence itself.

A second remark about existence is this: **Nothingness** is just that—nothing. Nothingness has no properties whatever. Things that do not exist have no properties. For example, the flying horse Pegasus has no properties and that is what his nonexistence amounts to. You may think that he has the property of being a winged horse. But that is not true. Our *concept* of Pegasus (which is in our minds when we are thinking of Pegasus) is a concept *of* something that would have the property of being a winged horse if it existed. But Pegasus does not exist and he, along with all other cases of nothing, have no properties. It should also be said, however, that one's concept of Pegasus exists, it is in the mind of the person knowing the concept, and the concept itself does not have the property of being a winged horse.

Many philosophers also hold that **negative properties** do not exist either. For example, an apple may positively possess the property of being red, sweet and round, but, if negative properties exist, then the apple would also have the properties of not-being-green, not-being-square, and indeed, the apple would have an infinite amount of negative properties (e.g., of not-being an elephant). However, it is more natural to say that the apple *fails* to have the property of being green, instead of claiming that it *has* the property of being not-green. In general, when it is not the case that x is F (the apple is not green), we can explain this as a case where x fails to have F, rather than asserting the positive existence of negative properties, e.g., as a case where x has *not-F*.

Finally, something should be said about a position in the history of philosophy called the **modes of being** view. According to this view, being is a general category and existence is just one kind or mode of being (see figure 9.1).

Things that actually exist (e.g., lions) have existence. **Fictional objects** like Pegasus do not have existence, nor do they not exist. Rather, they have being and thus are real in a lesser way than those entities that actually exist. Existence is just one kind of being, and nonexistent fictional objects have being even though they do not exist. On this view, there are degrees of reality and the type of being that Pegasus has is halfway between existing and not-existing.

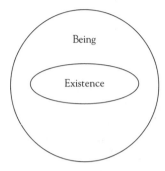

Fig. 9.1 Existence as a mode of being

In our view, this is an extravagant position. There is no good reason to believe it, and it violates the fundamental laws of logic applied to the being of things. Something either does or does not have being and everything either has or does not have being. On the modes of being view, Pegasus does and does not have being.

Moreover, the modes of being view has an inadequate treatment of coming-to-be and perishing. Coming-to-be and perishing are all or nothing affairs. They are not like walking into a library where you start outside, move to 10% inside, then 50%, and finally, you get all the way in. Coming-to-be and perishing are not gradual processes like that. Why? Existing or not existing is a matter of having or not having at least one property and, for any property, something either does or does not have that property. When something comes-to-be, it does not get a partial foothold in existence, and slide into being until it is fully real. In situations where something grows or diminishes in intensity (e.g., a sound gets louder or softer), these are cases of alteration, not cases of gradual coming-to-be and perishing. It would seem, then, that the modes of being view is inadequate.

3 THE NATURE OF IDENTITY

Existence is a fundamental metaphysical issue. So is the nature of **identity**. When philosophers talk about the problem of identity, usually one of these four issues is in mind:

1. When x and y are contemporaneous, what is it for x to be identical to (be the same entity as) y? In general, what is it for anything to be identical to itself?

2. When x and y are noncontemporaneous, what is it for x to be identical to (be the same entity as) y? Are there continuants? Do things remain the same through change, and if so, how are we to understand what accounts for this?

3. What kind of evidence or criteria are there that enable us to know that a given x and y are identical?

4. What are the different kinds of identity statements? How are we to understand sentences that contain two or more linguistic expressions that refer to the same thing?

Questions 1 and 2 are basic, metaphysical questions. Question 2 focuses on sameness through change, and we will study it when we look at the metaphysics of substance (chap. 10) and personal identity (chap. 14). Question 1 is the most basic metaphysical question about identity, and it will be the subject of investigation shortly. Question 3 is basically an epistemological question, not a metaphysical one. Often, question 3 is confused with questions 1 and 2, as we will see in our treatment of personal identity in chapter fourteen. Finally, question 4 is a matter of the philosophy of language. Its main concern is not identity itself, but identity *statements*—linguistic expressions that assert identity. We will look at this question later in the chapter. Let us begin our study of identity by looking at the issue surfaced in question 1.

3.1
THE GENERAL
NATURE OF
IDENTITY ITSELF

Suppose you wanted to know whether J. P. Moreland is identical to (is the same thing as) Eileen Spiek's youngest son. If "they" are identical, then, in reality, there is only one person: J. P. Moreland, who *is* (identical to) Eileen Spiek's youngest son. If they are not identical, then there are two people, not one. There is a general law of identity known as **Leibniz's law of the indiscernibility of identicals**:

$$(x)(y)[(x = y) \rightarrow (P)(Px \leftrightarrow Py)]$$

This principle states that for any x (e.g., that person who is J. P. Moreland) and for any y (that person who happens to be Eileen Spiek's youngest son), if "they" are identical to each other ("they" are, in reality, the very same entity), then for any property P (being 5'8", being human), P will be true of x (J. P. Moreland) if and only if (represented by $\leftrightarrow$) P is true of y (Eileen Spiek's youngest son). In general, everything is what it is and not something else. Everything is identical to itself and thus shares all properties in common with itself. This implies a test for nonidentity or **difference**: if we can find one thing true of x that is not true of y or vice versa, then x is not identical to y.

We can gain further insights about identity if we think about how it applies to events. Let us assume what is called the **property exemplification view of events**: An **event** is the coming, continued possession or going of a property by a substance at or through a time. A leaf losing greenness at noon would be an example of an event in which a substance (the leaf) loses a property (greenness) at a time (noon). If E, S, P, and t refer to an event, a substance, a property and a time, respectively, then Leibniz's law of the indiscernibility of identicals, applied to events, becomes this:

$$(E_1 = E_2) \rightarrow [(S_1 = S_2) \& (P_1 = P_2) \& (t_1 = t_2)]$$

If E_1 and E_2 are identical, then the substances, properties and times constituting "those" events will be identical as well. If the latter are not identical, then the events are different. For example, a case where S_1 is different from S_2 would be where two apples become red simultaneously; a case where P_1 is different from P_2 would be where a specific apple became red and sweet at the same time; a case where t_1 and t_2 are different would be when an apple became sweet at noon, turned sour overnight, and became sweet again the next day.

There is another law of identity that is most likely a false principle: **Leibniz's law of the identity of indiscernibles:**

$$(x)(y)[(P)(Px \leftrightarrow Py) \rightarrow (x = y)]$$

In ordinary, nonsymbolic language, this says that, for all x and y, if x and y have all and only the same properties, then they are identical to each other. This principle is false because there is more to a thing than its properties. For example, we could have two red and round disks that had the very same color, shape, size and so forth. They could share all and only the same properties but still be two disks and not one because an individual thing like a disk is not exhausted by its properties. We will say more about this in chapter ten, but for now, you should remember that "two" things that are identical will share all "their" properties, because "they" are the same thing. But two things can share all their properties and not be the same thing if the two things have more to them than properties.

The correct principle—Leibniz's law of the indiscernibility of identicals—implies another insight about identity:

$$(x)(y)[(x = y) \rightarrow \Box(x = y)]$$

In ordinary language, this says that for all x and y, if x is identical to y, then necessarily, x is identical to y. There is no possible world where that thing which is x is not identical to that thing which is y. For example, a cat may happen to be yellow and twenty pounds, but it does not just happen to be identical to itself. It is necessarily identical to itself. The fact that something is identical to itself is a necessary feature of everything. Suppose that person who is J. P. Moreland and that person who is Eileen Spiek's youngest son are different but both are 5'8". Then, in the actual world, they do not differ in height. However, if it is just possible for them to differ in height—if there is a possible world where one is 5'8" and the other is 6', then they are not identical.

Again, if disembodied existence is metaphysically possible—if there is a possible world with disembodied existence—then a person cannot be identical to his or her body because there is no possible world where the person's body exists and is disembodied. Since it is possible for a person to exist disembodied, but it is not possible for a body to exist disembodied, then a person is not identical to his or her body. Why? Because something is true of the person (the possibility of disembodied existence) not true of his or her body.

The identity relation is a relation that everything has to itself and to nothing else. This relation should be kept distinct from three other notions with which it is sometimes confused: cause-effect, coextensionality, and inseparability. With regard to **cause-effect**, if A causes B, then A is not identical to B. Smoke causes fire as its effect, but smoke is not identical to fire. Further, two things can be coextensional; **coextensionality** means one obtains if and only if the other obtains. For example, the property of being triangular is coextensive with the property of being trilateral. One obtains if and only if the other obtains; no object has one without the other. If the two properties were identical, then whatever is true of being triangular would be true of being trilateral, and conversely. But the two properties are not identical because the property of triangularity has something true of it, namely, having angles, not true of the property of being trilateral.

Finally, identity differs from **inseparability**. Two entities can be parts of some whole and be inseparable either from each other or that whole, yet still not be identical. For example, the individual white instance of color in a sugar cube cannot be separated from the individual square instance of shape in that cube and still exist, like the leg and back of a chair can be separated from each other or from the chair taken as a whole. But the instance of whiteness in the cube is an instance of color and its instance of shape is not; thus they are not identical. Again, a person's emotions cannot be separated from the person or from the person's beliefs and placed in different locations of the room like the hand and leg of his body can. But one's various emotions and beliefs are all distinct and not identical to other emotions or beliefs.

In sum, the identity-difference distinction is not the same as the cause-effect, the coextensionality, or the inseparable-separable distinctions. Before we look at identity statements, we should ponder some points made by the great medieval philosopher Francisco Suárez (1548-1617) in his work entitled *On the Various Kinds of Distinctions*. Suárez discussed certain distinctions that shed light on identity and identity statements. First, he described **real distinction**. Two entities differ by means of a real distinction just in case they can be separated and still exist. For example, the different legs of a chair bear a real distinction to each other. Independence of existence is the key here.

Second, there is what Suárez called the **distinction of reason**. If "two" things differ by means of a distinction of reason, then "they" are identical. For Suárez, there are two kinds of distinctions of reason. One is the **distinction of reasoning reason**, and it arises solely because we use the same word twice in sentences like "Peter is Peter." Here, there is no distinction that exists in reality and it is merely the process of thought or language that gives rise to a distinction in which the same, identical thing is named (or thought of) twice.

Another distinction of reason is the **distinction of reasoned reason**. An example would be, "The red object is the sweet object," said of a red, sweet apple or "The Evening Star is the Morning Star," where each description refers to the planet Venus. When the distinction of reasoned reason is present, the "objects" referred to are identical (the apple or Venus), but the concepts or terms used to refer to the object (the red versus the sweet object, the Evening versus the Morning Star) do not exhaust the object in question and they express different nonidentical aspects of the same, identical object.

A third type of distinction for Suárez was called the **modal distinction**. If A is modally distinct from B, then (1) one of them is a constituent of the other and (2) one of them, say A, could exist without the other, B, but not vice versa. If A and B are the independent and dependent entities, respectively, then B is a mode of A; B is an inseparable aspect of A; B is dependent on A. For example, consider the property of redness. When redness is exemplified by or had by an apple, then at least these three entities are involved: the property of redness, the apple and the-having-of-redness-by-the-apple. This latter entity is an instance of redness and is modally distinct from redness. Redness is modified by its being exemplified by the apple. Redness could exist without its being possessed by this apple, but the-exemplification-of-redness-by-the-apple, i.e., this specific instance of redness in this specific apple could not exist without redness. Redness is not identical to but is modally distinct from this instance of redness.

The identity relation itself is independent of language users. The sun would be identical to itself if no language user would have existed. Nevertheless, we *use* **identity statements** to express claims of identity (e.g., "Color is identical to a wavelength of light"), so it is important to mention identity statements to see if we can learn something about them and about identity itself.

3.2
IDENTITY
STATEMENTS

The ancients noticed that there was a brightest star in the evening sky and they called this star the Evening Star or Hesperus. They also noticed that there was a brightest star in the morning sky and they called this star the Morning Star or Phosphorus. However, the empirical discovery was made that the "two" stars were identical and were, in fact, the planet Venus. This discovery was contingent, i.e., dependent on what the facts turned out to be. It could have turned out that the Evening Star and the Morning Star, understood as whatever turns out to be the brightest star in the evening and morning, respectively, were two different heavenly bodies. Now consider the following two statements:

1. Hesperus is identical to Hesperus.
2. Hesperus is identical to Phosphorus.

There are a number of ways to understand identity statements like these, but two accounts are very prominent in philosophy. The first is called the **traditional** or **objectual account of identity statements**. On this view, an identity statement asserts that the thing referred to by the first term has a certain characteristic true of it, namely, it is identical to itself.

Now, this certainly does account for much of what we say when we use identity statements. However, the philosopher Gottlob Frege (1848-1925) raised a problem with the traditional account and offered a different understanding of identity statements. Frege argued that on the traditional view, statements (1) and (2) assert the same thing—the thing referred to by the first term (i.e., the planet Venus) is identical to itself. But this cannot be right because (1) and (2) do *not* assert the same thing. How do we know this? Statement (1) is not very informative. It tells us very little and seems to be necessarily true by definition. We know (1) is true before we make any empirical study of the heavens. However, (2) is very informative; the truth of (2) was an empirical discovery, and thus while an object's identity to itself is necessary, (2) seems to be a contingent truth (it could have been false and its truth depends on the discovery of certain empirical facts). It is not true by definition. Given that a thing's identity to itself runs throughout all possible worlds in which it exists, how is one to distinguish (1) from (2), and more generally, how can there be contingent identity statements if identity is necessary?

Frege sought to answer these questions and, in the process, offered a different view of identity statements called the **metalinguistic account** (*meta* here means "about," and *metalinguistic* means "about language"). On this view, an identity statement like (1) or (2) does not merely say something about the entity Venus referred to by using the words *Hesperus* and *Phosphorus*; more importantly, it mentions the words themselves, that is, it says something about the words *Hesperus* and *Phosphorus*. Identity statements are statements about language, and they assert that a certain relation holds between the two referring expressions used in the statement, namely, they are coreferring expressions, i.e., they each name the same thing.

Each account has something to be said for it, and it is beyond our purpose to weigh the strengths and weaknesses of each. However, one thing carries real importance. The identity relation itself is fairly straightforward and clear, but identity statements themselves are more ambiguous, and whenever you are looking at an identity statement itself, you should try to understand just exactly what the person using that statement is trying to say. For example, when someone says "Thank God that Beckwith is himself today," we shouldn't take this to mean that he literally was not identical to himself yesterday; rather, someone is claiming that he was acting out of character.

We have looked at two different theories of identity statements. Here are three different kinds of identity statements:

Meaning identity statements: These occur when the two referring expressions are synonyms. "A bachelor is an unmarried male" and "A motor car is an automobile" are examples. These can be found in dictionaries.

Referential or **name identity statements:** These occur when two proper names (names of individuals like "Tom Jones") or two natural kind terms (terms that name naturally occurring kinds of things like "H_2O" or "the lion") each function merely to tag or refer to its object of reference in every circumstance in which it could exist. "Mt. Everest is Chomolungma" and "Water is H_2O" are examples. "Water is H_2O" amounts to the statement, "The stuff out there that is actually water is identical to the stuff out there that is actually H_2O." These statements are not found in dictionaries. Instead, they express necessary truths about the world.

Contingent identity statements: While an entity's identity to itself is necessary, some identity statements are contingent, that is, they are true in some possible worlds and false in others. One context in which contingent identity statements occur is when two descriptions of something happen to be fulfilled by the same thing but could have been fulfilled by different things. Suppose Aunt Sally's favorite color is blue. Then "The color of the sky is Aunt Sally's favorite color" expresses an identity. But this identity statement, though true, is contingent. God could have made the sky green and Aunt Sally could still favor blue, or the sky could be blue but Aunt Sally could have preferred pink. Either way, "The color of the sky is Aunt Sally's favorite color" would be false. These kinds of identity statements can be understood as saying this: "Whatever turns out to be the color of the sky is identical to whatever turns out to be Aunt Sally's favorite color." Identity statements can be contingent, but the fact that something is identical to itself is necessary.

The nature of identity and identity statements will be of crucial importance for looking at the mind-body problems in chapters eleven and twelve. In the final section of this chapter, the notions of existence and of identity will be applied to an important metaphysical topic: replacement and reductionism.

4 REPLACEMENT AND REDUCTIONISM

As human beings, we are interested in what is real and what is not. Important intellectual debates rage about the existence of God, the soul, values and life after death, just to mention a few. Philosophically speaking, there are two important ways to deny the existence of some entity X: eliminate X and replace belief in it with belief in something else Y, or continue to believe in X but reduce X to Y.

To understand this, consider for a moment the history of science; scientific theories do not always last forever. Theory change happens in science, and theories come and go in two central ways: replacement and reductionism. Sometimes a change from one theory S to a new theory T involves an abandonment of S altogether and an elimination of the entities postulated to exist by S. An example of this kind of change, called **replacement**, was the change from phlogiston to oxygen chemistry. When a metal is heated in the atmosphere it weighs more after heating than before. In the eighteenth century, scientists explained this by saying that heating drives out an impurity in the metal known as phlogiston, which has negative weight.

In the late 1700s, A. L. Lavoisier's oxygen theory replaced phlogiston. Oxygen was seen as an entity, different from phlogiston, with positive weight and which attached to a metal when it was heated in the air. The shift from phlogiston to oxygen theory was a theory change of replacement. Lavoisier's model of oxygen was not seen as a better picture of phlogiston than that of rival scientists. Phlogiston was eliminated and replaced altogether; people no longer believed that phlogiston existed.

On the other hand, sometimes a theory change involves reduction, that is, the continued belief in some entity X, but X is no longer thought to be what theory S said it was; rather, it is now "reduced to" being Y, which the new theory claims it is. For example, scientists used to believe that when a body grows hot this is because it receives heat, understood as a subtle, weightless, invisible fluid known as caloric. Today, scientists believe that there is no such thing as caloric; instead, heat has been "reduced to" the vibration of molecules, e.g., the average kinetic energy of a gas. Heat was not eliminated and replaced in this theory change. Scientists still believe in the existence of heat. Instead, heat was first thought to be X (caloric) but now it has been "reduced to" being Y (the vibration of molecules).

The idea of replacement is fairly clear. But what does it mean to reduce one thing to another? What is reductionism? Unfortunately, the notion of reduction in philosophy has a wide variety of meanings and no common usage is employed. However, here are some of the different senses of reductionism:

1. Linguistic Reduction. This occurs when language that uses one vocabulary or set of terms is replaced with language that uses another vocabulary or set of terms. For example:

a. The average family has 2.5 children.

a'. Add the children and divide that number by the number of families and you get 2.5.

In this case, sentence (a) uses the term "the average family," and this is replaced by sentence (a') where the term is replaced by a formula for calculating (with the terms *add, divide* and *number*). Sentence (a) is the **reduced sentence** and (a') is the **reducing sentence**. In some cases of linguistic reduction, the term in the reduced sentence (e.g., "the average family") is no longer taken to designate a real entity in the world because it is left out of the reducing sentence. Sentence (a) could lead someone to think that there was a family somewhere—the average family—that actually has 2.5 children. But through linguistic reduction we see there is no such entity. However, in other cases of linguistic reduction, the mere fact that truths said in one vocabulary can be said in another vocabulary does not, by itself, mean that the entities designated in the reduced sentence do not exist. For example:

b. There are three *triangular* things in the room.

b'. There are three *trilateral* things in the room.

c. A solid body floats on a liquid if its *specific gravity* is less than that of the liquid.

c'. A solid body floats on a liquid if *the quotient of its weight and volume is less than the corresponding quotient* for the liquid.

d. *Red* is a *color.*

d'. *Red things* are *colored things.*

In the example of (b) and (b'), just because the truth value of (b) and (b') are the same (i.e., *b* is true if and only if *b'* is true), it does not follow that the thing expressed by the term *triangular* (the property of being triangular) can be reduced to (made identical to) the thing expressed by the term *trilateral* (the property of being trilateral).

In (c) and (c'), if we think of specific gravity as a real entity in the world, then we would think of it as a disposition or tendency to sink, a sort of heaviness possessed by a body. This is expressed in (c). Statement (c') treats (c) in the same way statement (a') treated (a). But just because we can replace (c) with (c') and therefore eliminate the term *specific gravity*, it does not follow that specific gravity itself, understood realistically as a tendency to sink or a heaviness, does not exist.

Finally, in (d) and (d'), even if (d) could be linguistically reduced to (d') (and in chap. 10 we will see that it cannot), it does not follow that the properties of redness and coloredness do not exist. Statement (d') eliminates the terms *red* and *color* that seem to refer to these properties and uses only terms that refer to individual particulars (individual red things and colored things, like red balls and flags). In sum, linguistic reduction may or may not mean that the entity referred to in the reduced sentence does not exist.

2. Strong Ontological Reduction. This occurs when some entity x is reduced to (i.e., identified with) some entity y. In this case, x exists and is nothing but y; in other words, x is identical to y. Some have said (erroneously in our view) that statements such as the following express strong ontological reductions: "Redness is a wavelength," "Heat is the vibration of molecules," "Pain is a certain brain state." In each case one entity (redness, heat, pain) is reduced to another entity (a wavelength, a vibration, a brain state) in that the former entity exists and is nothing more nor less than the latter entity.

3. *Weak Ontological Reduction.* Here entity x is reduced to entity y in that x is caused by or explained by or dependent on y. Y is a sufficient condition for x. For example, wetness is reduced to the molecular structure of a group of water molecules in that this structure is what causes and explains wetness. In a strong ontological reduction, the wetness would be treated as being identical to the molecular structure. In a weak ontological reduction, the wetness is supervenient or emergent upon that molecular structure. The molecular structure of a group of water molecules is different from and not identical to the wetness of that water. In this example, **emergence** means that the structure is a sufficient condition for that wetness to emerge. **Supervenience** means that, given the structure, the wetness will supervene on (be caused or explained by or dependent on) that structure.

In sum, debates about the reality of some entity or other include attempts to replace that entity with another one or to reduce that entity to another one in different ways. It should be clear that such replacement and reduction attempts must be evaluated on a case-by-case basis. And when such evaluations are made, a broad philosophical understanding of the nature of existence itself, identity and identity statements will be relevant to such assessments.

There is one more lesson to be learned from this chapter. If we define naturalism (see chap. 10) as the view that everything that exists is in space and time, and if physicalism is taken to be a version of naturalism that says that the only entities that exist are merely physical entities that are in some way accessible to the senses and to scientific investigation used in chemistry and physics, then physicalism is false.

So understood, physicalism implies that everything that exists can be, at least in principle, exhaustively described using the language of chemistry and physics. This is so because the only entities that exist are completely physical (chemical and physical) entities. However, there are two things about all entities whatsoever, including so-called physical entities like chairs, rocks and protons, that are not physical: what it is that accounts for the entity's existence (the having of properties by the entity in question) and the entity's being identical to itself. These are metaphysical facts about all existents, including all physical existents.

Thus, while there may be entities that are at least physical in that they can be partially described in the language of physics and chemistry, there are no entities that are only physical, i.e., that can be exhaustively described using only chemistry and physics. There will always be more to a physical object than its chemical and physical aspects. These will be the more fundamental aspects of existing and self-identity. In this way we see that science is only a type of knowledge of even physical things like electrons. Metaphysics gives us a more fundamental knowledge of the metaphysical, nonmaterial aspects of those physical things.

CHAPTER SUMMARY

Being is a genus and, therefore, there is a general notion of existing applicable
to all entities. A good theory of existence should account for what does/does
not and could/could not exist, it should imply that existence itself exists, it
should not violate the fundamental laws of logic, and it should imply that acts
of knowing exist. Several theories of existence fail to pass these tests. However,
one view seems to succeed. Existence is either the belonging of some property
or the being belonged to by a property. This understanding of existence was
then used to define coming-to-be and perishing, which are distinct from alteration. Nothingness has no properties and, therefore, does not exist. Negative
properties do not exist either; rather, things can fail to have a property. Finally,
the modes of being view says that fictional objects have being but not existence.
This position was rejected.

Leibniz's law of the indiscernibility of identicals is a true law expressing the
identity relation, but the identity of indiscernibles is false. The identity relation
should not be confused with any other relation, e.g., cause-effect, coextensionality or inseparability. Suárez's three distinctions are helpful in understanding
identity and identity statements. The debate between the objectual and metalinguistic accounts of identity statements illustrates how ambiguous those statements can be. Three main types of identity statements are meaning, referential
and contingent identity statements.

Debates about the existence of some entity often involve replacement or reductionism. Three main types of reduction are linguistic, strong ontological and
weak ontological reduction. Physical entities like a carbon atom are at least but
not only physical because the having of properties (existence) and the identity
relation are not physical entities.

CHECKLIST OF BASIC TERMS AND CONCEPTS

alteration
cause-effect
change
coextensionality
coming-to-be
contingent identity statement
difference
distinction of reason
distinction of reasoned reason
distinction of reasoning reason
emergence
essence
events
exemplification
existence
fictional objects
genus
identity

identity statements
inseparability
instancing
Leibniz's law of the identity of indiscernibles
Leibniz's law of the indiscernibility of identicals
linguistic reduction
meaning identity statements
metalinguistic account of identity statements
modal distinction
modes of being
negative properties
nothingness
traditional (or objectual) account of identity statements
perishing
predication
property exemplification view of events
real distinction
reduced sentence
reducing sentence
referential (or name) identity statements
replacement
strong ontological reduction
supervenience
weak ontological reduction

10

GENERAL ONTOLOGY

Two Categories—
Property and Substance

He, then, who believes in beautiful things,
but neither believes in beauty itself nor is able to follow
when someone tries to guide him to the knowledge of it—
do you think that his life is a dream or a waking?
Just consider. Is not the dream state,
whether the man is asleep or waking, just this—
the mistaking of resemblance for identity?
I should certainly call that dreaming, he said.
PLATO REPUBLIC 476C

Nothing is permanent in a substance except the law itself
which determines the continuous succession of its states.
LEIBNIZ, GERHARDT 2

1 INTRODUCTION

If a person reflects on the world around him, it will become evident that there
is a distinction between individual things like dogs and cars and their properties.
Moreover, there is a clear distinction as well between the properties within an
individual and the relations which that individual sustains to other things. A
specific dog is an individual thing called a substance, it has the property of being
brown in it, and it stands in the relation of *larger than* to its food dish. In the
history of philosophy, a number of thinkers have held that three of the categories of being are those of property, relation, and substance. In this chapter, we
will investigate philosophical issues involved in the study of properties and substances in that order.

2 PROPERTIES

2.1
THREE VIEWS OF
PROPERTIES

Suppose we have before us two red, round spots named Socrates and Plato. Socrates and Plato are exactly alike in all their qualities (i.e., properties). Since they
have the same size, shape, color and so on, Socrates and Plato are a case of what
is called **quality agreement**. Socrates and Plato are **concrete particulars**, i.e.,
particular individual things that seem to have properties (in this case, spots that

seem to have the property of being red). Other examples of concrete particulars are individual dogs, tables or gold atoms. How are we to account for quality agreement? Three broad answers to this question have been offered.

First, there is **extreme nominalism**, defended by philosophers such as W. V. O. Quine and Wilfred Sellars. In this view, properties do not exist at all and concrete particulars and groups of concrete particulars are the only things that are real. An extreme nominalist would explain the "quality agreement" between Socrates and Plato as follows:

a has the property *F* if and only if *Q*

For example, Socrates has the "property" redness if and only if *Q*. What is *Q*? *Q* may be "The word *red* is true of Socrates" or it may be "Socrates is a member of the set of red, concrete particulars." These two strategies can be pictured as in figures 10.1 and 10.2.

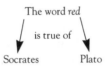

Fig. 10.1 **Extreme nominalist strategy #1**

The set of red concrete particulars:

$$\left\{ \begin{array}{c} \text{Socrates, Plato, an apple} \\ \text{a fire engine, a brick} \end{array} \right\}$$

Fig. 10.2 **Extreme nominalist strategy #2**

For the extreme nominalist, properties (e.g., redness) do not exist at all. Instead the only things that exist are concrete particulars (individual red things) and the "property words" (e.g., the word *red*) that are true of them.

A second view of quality agreement is called **nominalism**, defended by philosophers such as D. C. Williams and Keith Campbell. Nominalists accept the existence of properties but hold that they are particular, individualized qualities called **abstract particulars** that cannot be possessed by more than one concrete particular. Here the term *abstract* is not used in its standard, metaphysical sense, namely, as something that exists outside space and time. Rather, *abstract* is used by nominalists in an epistemological sense, namely, as something that is brought before the mind by disregarding other things in its environment. For example, if one disregards the shape, smell or size of a tomato and focuses only on its surface color, the tomato's redness is abstract in the epistemological sense. Returning to Socrates, it has its own, particular redness and Plato has its own, particular redness, which we can call red_1 and red_2, respectively. Redness in general is a set of individual, abstract particulars, i.e., red_1, red_2, . . . , red_n, that are in all the concrete particulars (individual apples, spots, cars). Socrates is a whole composed of all its abstract particulars (red_1, $round_1$, etc.) as parts. This can be pictured by figure 10.3.

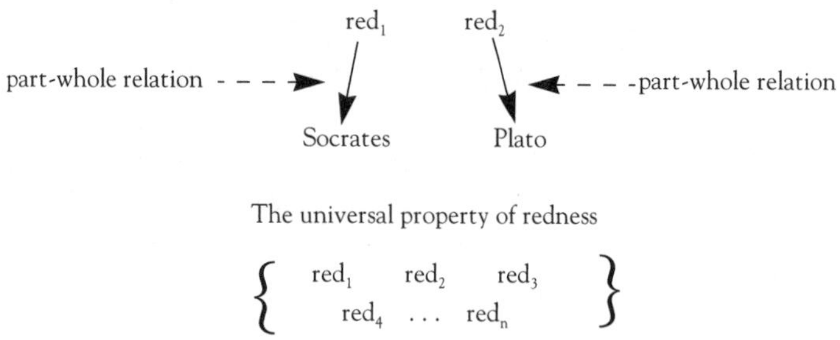

red₁   red₂

part-whole relation - - - ➤   ◀ - - - part-whole relation

Socrates   Plato

The universal property of redness

$$\left\{ \begin{array}{ccc} red_1 & red_2 & red_3 \\ red_4 & \ldots & red_n \end{array} \right\}$$

Fig. 10.3 Socrates and Plato as wholes composed of abstract particulars

A third school of thought is **realism**, advanced by thinkers like D. M. Armstrong and Reinhardt Grossmann. On this view, Socrates and Plato have the very same property, redness, in each of them. Properties are ones-in-many; they can be possessed by many concrete particulars at the same time. The relationship between a property like redness and concrete particulars like Socrates and Plato is called exemplification, predication or the **instancing** relation (one is an instance of the other). Properties are called universals, that is, multiply exemplifiable entities that can be had by many things at the same time. The redness exemplified by Socrates is identical to the redness exemplified by Plato. Realists picture quality agreement as in figure 10.4.

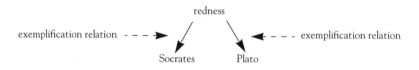

redness

exemplification relation - - - ➤   ◀ - - - exemplification relation

Socrates   Plato

Fig. 10.4 Realists' picture of quality agreement

In sum, extreme nominalism, nominalism and realism are different positions about the ontological status of properties. Extreme nominalists accept only the existence of concrete particulars (and sets of such particulars along with words true of them), nominalists embrace concrete and abstract particulars (along with sets of abstract particulars), and realists assert the reality of concrete particulars and properties understood as universals, that is, as entities that can be exemplified by many concrete particulars at once. Figure 10.5 charts these three positions.

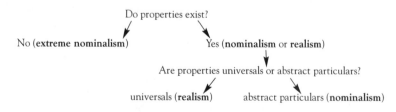

Do properties exist?

No (**extreme nominalism**)   Yes (**nominalism** or **realism**)

Are properties universals or abstract particulars?

universals (**realism**)   abstract particulars (**nominalism**)

Fig. 10.5 Chart of ontological status of properties

The debate about properties can be related to the debate about naturalism and abstract entities mentioned at the end of chapter eight. The **universe** may be defined as the total spatiotemporal system of matter and (impersonal) energy, that is, as the sum total of material objects, in some way accessible to the senses and to scientific investigation. The **world** may be defined as the sum total of everything that exists including nonspatiotemporal abstract entities. In the metaphysical sense, an **abstract entity** is a real entity that is not in space or time. Something is in space (or time) if it has spatial (or temporal) duration (we can ask, how big or how long is it?) and location (we can ask, where or when is it?). Abstract entities, in contrast, have neither spatial (or temporal) location nor duration. Naturalists believe only in the universe; philosophers who are sometimes called ontologists believe in the world. For the naturalist, therefore, nothing exists that does not have spatial (or temporal) location and/or duration (as depicted in figure 10.6).

2.2
PROPERTIES AND
THE DEBATE
ABOUT
NATURALISM

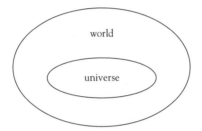

Fig. 10.6 The relation between naturalists' and ontologists' views

How does the debate about naturalism and the world relate to the debate about properties? First of all, extreme nominalists and nominalists are most often naturalists. Advocates of these views believe only in the existence of spatiotemporal concrete or abstract particulars. They deny that properties are universals. Second, all realists agree that properties can be exemplified by many things at once; the very same redness, for example, can be predicated of many red things at the same time. Does this mean that all realists believe that properties are abstract entities, that is, entities that are not inside of space and time? The answer is no, and to see why, we need to focus on the relation between a property (e.g., redness) and the things that have that property (e.g., Socrates and Plato), i.e., on the **exemplification** relation.

There are three main ways that realists have understood this relationship. The first realist view of exemplification is the **model-copy view**. According to this position, properties like redness are abstract entities that exist outside of space and time. Moreover, properties do not enter into the particulars that supposedly have them. Instead, each particular has a copy of that property. For example, Socrates and Plato do not have the property of redness in them, but rather each has its own copy of redness. To say that redness can be exemplified by many red things is to say that each red thing can have its own copy of redness. Redness itself stays entirely outside of space and time and outside of the things that possess copies of it.

The model-copy view is not widely held because of the difficulties that have been raised against it. One such difficulty has been called the **third man argu-**

ment. This argument points out that the model-copy view of properties and exemplification makes two assumptions that, taken together, lead to a vicious infinite regress. Here are these two assumptions:

The **nonidentity assumption:**   F things are F in virtue of some other
                                     thing, F-ness, which makes them F.

The **self-predication assumption:**   F-ness is itself F.

The nonidentity assumption asserts that, for example, several red things (Socrates, Plato, a brick) are red in virtue of some other entity, redness itself, which is copied in each red thing. The self-predication assumption implies that not only are individual red things red, but redness itself is red.

Many realists accept the second assumption but reject the first one. They argue that the nonidentity assumption only applies to particulars and not universals, for instance, it is true that all red *particulars* are red in virtue of some other entity (redness), but redness itself is red and not in virtue of something else. But the main point here is that the model-copy view implies both of these assumptions and, taken together, they lead to a vicious infinite regress which can be seen as follows: If we ask about a set of several red things (Socrates, Plato, a brick) what it is that accounts for their being red, the nonidentity assumption tells us that this is due to some other entity besides the red things, redness itself, that makes them red by being copied in them. So set 1 composed of three things (Socrates, Plato, a brick) is a set of red things because of redness.

But now the self-predication assumption assures us that not only are Socrates, Plato and a brick red, but redness itself is red. This means that we can now puzzle over what it is that accounts for the redness of all the items in a new set 2 composed of Socrates, Plato, a brick and redness itself. The nonidentity assumption demands that our answer must appeal to some *other* entity, call it redness$_2$, possessed by all the members of set 2. But now we can form a new set 3 composed of Socrates, Plato, a brick, redness and redness$_2$, and ask what it is that accounts for the fact that all members of this new set are red. The answer will appeal to redness$_3$, copied by all members in set 3. This procedure generates a vicious infinite regress, and thus the model-copy view should be rejected.

There are two more realist views of exemplification, which are advocated by impure realists and pure realists. These two schools of thought differ over a principle known as the **axiom of localization:** No entity whatsoever can exist at different spatial locations at once or at interrupted time intervals.

Let us focus our attention on spatial location. Concrete particulars like Socrates are at only one spatial location at one time. They cannot be in more than one place at the same time. The axiom of localization says that nothing can be in more than one place at the same time. An **impure realist**, such as D. M. Armstrong, denies the axiom of localization; properties are spatially contained inside of the things that have them. Redness is at the very place Socrates is and redness is also at the very place Plato is. This means that redness violates the axiom of localization and can be at more than one place at the same time. Impure realists are naturalists at heart. Why? Because they accept the fact that properties are universals, i.e., as entities that can be exemplified by more than one thing at once. But they do not want to deny naturalism and believe in abstract entities that are outside of space and time altogether. Thus impure realists hold that all entities are indeed inside space and time. But they embrace two different kinds of spatial entities: concrete particulars (Socrates) that are in only one place at a time, and universals (properties like redness) that are at different spatial locations at the very same time. For the impure realist, the exemplification relation is a **spatial container** relation. Socrates exemplifies redness in that redness is spatially contained inside of and at the same place as Socrates.

Pure realists, such as Reinhardt Grossmann, hold to a **nonspatial** (and atemporal) **view of exemplification**. Redness is "in" Socrates in the sense that Socrates *has* or *exemplifies* redness within its very being. But neither redness nor the exemplification relation itself is spatial. But doesn't it make sense to say that redness is at the place where Socrates is? No, says the pure realist. The way to understand this relation is to say that Socrates, the red dot, is indeed spatially located on a page, and redness is surely "in" Socrates, but this "in" is not a spatial relationship (e.g., to say redness is on a page is to say that redness is "in" a spot and the spot is on a page). Properties are not in the concrete particulars that have them in the same way sand is in a bucket. The predication or exemplification relation is not a spatial container type of relationship.

Thus the impure realist accepts properties as universals but rejects them as abstract objects. The pure realist claims that the best way of understanding what it means to say that properties are universals is to view them as abstract objects (in the metaphysical sense). Nominalists are pure naturalists because they accept the axiom of localization; impure realists are impure naturalists because they reject the axiom of localization but accept the idea that everything is in space and time in some sense; and pure realists reject naturalism altogether and embrace abstract objects.

Our discussion about extreme nominalism, nominalism and different forms of realism can be summarized as in table 10.1.

Table 10.1 Differentiating various forms of nominalism and realism

Question	Yes	No
Do properties exist?	nominalists all forms of realism	extreme nominalists
Are properties universals (multiply exemplifiable)?	all forms of realism	extreme nominalists (they do not exist) nominalists (they do exist but are abstract particulars in the epistemological sense)
Are properties abstract entities (not in space and time)?	pure realists model-copy realists	extreme nominalists nominalists impure realists
Are properties "in" the concrete particulars that have them?	pure realists (the "in" is not a spatial relation) nominalists (accept the axiom of localization and the "in" is a normal spatial relation) impure realists (reject the axiom of localization and the "in" is an abnormal spatial relation)	extreme nominalists (there are no properties) model-copy realists (copies of properties are in their particulars, not properties themselves)

Let us set aside the intramural debate among realists about the nature of exemplification and concentrate now on the debate about the reality of properties among extreme nominalists, nominalists and realists in general. Three main types of evidence have been center stage in this dispute: predication, exact resemblance, and the fact that properties themselves have properties (e.g., redness is a color). Let us briefly look at these in order, beginning with **predication**, that is, affirming something of another thing, ascribing some property to it, assigning a thing to a class or designating a feature that belongs to something. Consider these sentences:

1. Socrates is red.
2. Plato is red.

The realist has a powerful, straightforward way of explaining the truth of these sentences: (1) and (2) express the fact that Socrates and Plato exemplify the same property, redness. Thus redness is a universal predicated of each. This predication can be made explicit in this way:

1'. Socrates has redness.
2'. Plato has redness.

In general, cases of predication are examples of what is called **the one and the many**. There are many red things, yet there is one unified class of red things that includes Socrates and Plato but would exclude, say, a third round spot just like them (call it Aristotle) which is blue and not red. The realist has a clear way of explaining predication and accounting for the one and the many, i.e., for the unity of classes like the class of red things. This class is unified by the fact that all members of the class have the very same property (redness) predicated of them, and members excluded from that class (Aristotle) fail to exemplify that property. The realist challenges the extreme nominalist and the nominalist to offer a better account of predication.

How would an extreme nominalist treat (1)? He or she would offer a linguistic reduction of (1) (see chap. 9). That is, he or she would claim that (1) really asserts the same thing as (and can be replaced by) (1"): Socrates is a red thing. (1") says that Socrates is a red, concrete particular. There are different versions of extreme nominalism, and it is beyond the scope of this chapter to discuss them. But on at least one popular version, the extreme nominalist would go on to claim that the word *red* is true of Socrates and that Socrates is a member of the set of red things. Note that (1") avoids any reference to properties.

There are two main problems with the extreme nominalist view of predication. First, the extreme nominalist simply asserts that Socrates is a member of the class of red things. But the realist wants to know what accounts for the fact that Socrates and Plato are members of the set of red things while Aristotle (the round, blue spot) is not. The realist has an answer: Socrates and Plato have the property of redness and Aristotle does not. The unity of this class is grounded in a property shared by all members of the class. However, the extreme nominalist cannot make this move because of his denial of properties. Thus he can give no answer as to what grounds the unity of the class of red things and what excludes Aristotle from that class.

Second, the problem of the one and the many (how natural classes can be unified while still having many different members) does not occur only at the level of redness and red things. It also occurs regarding words themselves. For example, we may ask how many words are in this sequence: *red, red, blue.* The answer is two or three depending on what you mean by a word. There are two word types (the type *red* and the type *blue*) and three word tokens. Word **types** are universals that can be in more than one place at once; word **tokens** are particular instances of their types. Now when the extreme nominalist tries to solve the problem of how red things can be red by saying that *the* word *red* is true of each red thing, this seems to imply that it is the very same word (*red* in this case) that is used of each red thing, and this treats the word *red* as a type (a universal). In this regard, consider the following statement of extreme nominalism made by David Hume:

> When we have found a resemblance among several objects [e.g., white objects], that often occur to us, we apply *the same name* ["white"] to all of them. . . . After we have acquired a custom of this *kind*, the hearing of *that name* revives *the idea* of one of those objects and makes the imagination conceive *it* with all *its* particular circumstances and proportions.[1]

All the italicized words in Hume's statement seem to refer to universals. Hume got rid of the universal property "whiteness" itself by reducing it to the word *white* being true of all white things. But he only replaced one universal (whiteness itself) with another one (the word type "white"). The extreme nominalist can avoid this problem by saying that the word type "white" is just a class of individual word tokens of "white." But this leads to a vicious infinite regress because we can now ask what it is that accounts for the unity of the class of word tokens of "white," and either the extreme nominalist will not answer this question or else he will postulate a new word used of all the words in the class of tokens, and so on to infinity. Either way, extreme nominalism is an inadequate view of predication.

How might a nominalist solve the problem of predication? In this way:

$1'''$. Socrates has red_1, and red_1 is a member of the class of red abstract particulars.

Plato would have red_2, and Aristotle would have $blue_1$. Remember, the class mentioned in $(1''')$ is not the class of red concrete particulars, but of red abstract particulars.

Unfortunately, the nominalist view of predication suffers from the same problem that was raised against extreme nominalism. What grounds the class of red abstract particulars such that red_1 and red_2 are members of that class but $blue_1$ is not? Again, the realist would say that red_1 and red_2 have the same property (redness) in them, and $blue_1$ does not. But the nominalist cannot answer this question without involving himself in the same type of vicious regress we saw in the case of extreme nominalism.

In sum, the phenomenon of predication is a problem for extreme nominalism and nominalism because these views do not have an adequate account of what it

---

[1]David Hume, *A Treatise of Human Nature*, 2d ed., ed. P. H. Nidditsh (Oxford: Clarendon, 1976), p. 20, italics added.

is that places something in its class, that unifies the class, and that excludes other things from class membership. The realist can explain this, however, by appealing to the possession of the same property or the failure to possess that property.

The second piece of evidence used in the debate about the reality of properties is **exact resemblance**. Things in the world resemble or fail to resemble each other in various ways. Socrates, Plato and Aristotle are exactly alike in being round, but Socrates and Plato resemble each other in respect to being red and Aristotle does not. In general, when two things, a and b, are exactly alike, there will be a respect F in which they resemble each other. This respect will be the property F-ness, possessed by a and b. For the realist, therefore, the exact similarity of color between Socrates and Plato is explained by the fact that each exemplifies the very same property, redness, which constitutes the respect in which they are alike. The realist challenges the extreme nominalist and nominalist to come up with an adequate account of exact similarity.

The extreme nominalist will respond to this challenge by claiming that all red things simply stand in an exact similarity relation with each other and that this is just a basic fact that cannot be explained. As a matter of simple, brute fact, Socrates and Plato resemble each other and not a yellow dog. However, there are two problems with this approach. First, there does, in fact, seem to be a respect of resemblance between Socrates and Plato, namely, they resemble each other in being red. Socrates, Plato and Aristotle all resemble each other in a different respect—being round. In spite of what the extreme nominalist claims, these different respects of resemblance are not brute facts, but rather metaphysical phenomena that can be explained by citing a property held in common among the resembling entities that constitutes their respect of resemblance.

Second, the extreme nominalist view of resemblance either collapses into realism or it involves a vicious infinite regress. To see this, note that when Socrates, Plato and a red brick all resemble each other, the extreme nominalist will explain this by saying that they all stand in *the* relation of exact similarity. But if this is so, then the relation of exact similarity will itself become a relational universal that is repeated in every case where two things exactly resemble each other. Socrates will stand in the same exact similarity relationship to Plato that Plato stands in to the red brick. But this solution collapses into realism by treating the exact similarity relation as a universal.

To avoid this problem the extreme nominalist will have to say that each pair of red things stands in its own, individual exact similarity relation. This can be pictured as in figure 10.7 (ES stands for an exact similarity relation between two things).

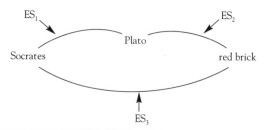

Fig. 10.7 Individual exact similarity relations

Here, Socrates and Plato stand in their own exact similarity relation to each other (ES$_1$), and so on, with Plato and the red brick and Socrates and the red brick. But now a problem arises. Each of these exact similarity relations themselves will exactly resemble each of the other exact similarity relations. How is this to be explained? The extreme nominalist will have to postulate higher exact similarity relations between each pair of lower exact similarity relations as depicted in figure 10.8.

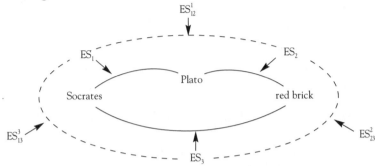

Fig. 10.8 Higher-order exact similarity relations

This extreme nominalist strategy can be repeated to infinity, and it generates a vicious regress. The nominalist has the very same problem. The only difference between the nominalist and the extreme nominalist is that the nominalist will replace Socrates, Plato and the red brick in the diagram above with red$_1$, red$_2$ and red$_3$ (the abstract particular in the brick). In sum, if the extreme nominalist and nominalist leave the exact resemblance among concrete or abstract particulars as basic, unexplainable phenomena, then this seems to be false because there will be respects of resemblance that can be specified by citing the property held in common by the resembling entities. Moreover, the exact similarity relation itself will either be a repeatable, relational universal or else there will be a vicious infinite regress of such relations. The exact resemblance among things, therefore, would seem to count in favor of realism.

A third piece of evidence in the debate is the fact that properties themselves have properties:

3. Red is a color.

This statement says that the first-order property, being red, has a second-order property, being a color. First-order properties are those directly predicated of individuals like Socrates or Plato. Second-order properties are properties of first-order properties. For example, redness and blueness have the property of being a color, but sweetness does not have that second-order property. Properties come in hierarchies. The realist has a straightforward way of explaining sentences like (3):

3′. Redness has coloredness.

The realist challenges the extreme nominalist and nominalist to explain sentences like (3). The extreme nominalist will give a linguistic reduction of (3) by claiming that it says the very same thing as and therefore can be replaced by (3″):

3″. Red things are colored things.

Note that (3″) only refers to concrete particulars and makes no reference to properties. But does (3″) really say the same things as (3), and in general, do reductions of this sort really work? If we can find an example of this type of strategy that fails, the extreme nominalist view will be refuted. Is there such an example? Yes:

4. Red things are spatially extended things.
4′. Red is an extension.

The extreme nominalist would be committed to this reductive pattern, because, in his view, (4) and (4′) say the same thing, (4) makes mention of properties, and therefore, it should be replaced by (4′), which does not mention properties. (4) is true since red things like bricks are extended throughout a region of space. However, (4′) is clearly false. Red is a color not an extension. Being six inches long is an example of the property of extension. Thus the extreme nominalist reduction strategy leads to falsehoods and, therefore, it fails.

The same things can be said of the nominalist reduction strategy. He will handle (3) as follows:

3‴. Reds are colors.

Here the reference is not to concrete but to abstract particulars. However, every red abstract particular is also extended in space (e.g., the red$_1$ of Socrates is extended throughout Socrates' surface). Thus the following sentence will be true:

5. Reds are extensions.

The nominalist reductive strategy will then enable us to derive (5′) from (5):

5′. Redness is extendedness.

But (5′) is clearly false; redness is a color, not an extendedness. It would seem, then, that sentences like (3), in which properties are possessed by other properties, cannot be adequately handled by extreme nominalism or nominalism, but they can be explained by the realist.

We have investigated different views about the existence and nature of properties, and we have looked at three pieces of evidence involved in disputes in this area of metaphysics. It would seem that properties do, in fact, exist and that they are genuine universals. However, reality involves a lot more than properties; there are also individual things like dogs and cats that have properties. Philosophers call such individuals substances, and it is to the study of the nature of substance that we now turn.

3 SUBSTANCES

The English term *substance* has many different meanings associated with it. Likewise, there have been different uses of the term in the history of philosophy. However, the most central idea of *substance* in the history of metaphysics is one which takes living organisms—individual human beings, butterflies, dogs, oak trees—as the **paradigm cases** (i.e., the standard, clearest examples) of substances. In our study of substance, we will (1) examine the traditional notion of substance, (2) compare a substance with a property-thing, (3) consider the major rival to the traditional notion of substance and (4) draw some implications from the traditional position. In order to understand what follows, let us consider an individual brown, adult dog, Fido. A doctrine of substance should explain what appear to be things we know about Fido, and the traditional notion of substance does just that.

The traditional view of substance is the one held by Aristotle and Thomas Aquinas. There are certain differences between them in this area of their thought, and not all philosophers are agreed as to the precise interpretation of every facet of these thinkers' overall positions about the metaphysics of substance. Nevertheless, Aristotle and Aquinas are sufficiently clear and agreed on their views to label their positions as the traditional view. A considerable number of philosophers up to the present have embraced the traditional view. Individual substances like Fido present certain facts to the philosopher that the metaphysics of substance tries to explain. There are seven things apparently true of Fido, and these seven features form the core of the traditional position.

**3.1
THE
TRADITIONAL
VIEW OF
SUBSTANCE**

Properties do not show up in the world all by themselves. One does not, for example, find brownness sitting on a bookshelf all by itself. Properties have owners, and a substance is the owner of properties. Substances have properties that are "in" them; properties are had by the substances that possess them. Fido has brownness, a certain shape, the property of weighing twenty-five pounds and so on. These properties are present in Fido. In this sense, substances are more basic than properties. It makes sense to ask about a property, what has that property? But it does not make sense to ask about a substance—for example, Fido—what has that substance? Properties are "in" substances, but substances are basic in that they are not "in" or had by things more basic than them. Substances do the having; properties are had. The etymology of the word *substance* (*sub* means "under," *stance* means "stand"; thus *substance* means "to stand under") brings out this aspect of substance as that which stands under properties as their owner.

**3.1.1
OWNERSHIP OF
PROPERTIES**

A substance like Fido is a whole and, as such, is a deep unity of properties, parts and capacities. First, a substance is a deep unity of properties. Properties come together in groups, not individually; for example, brownness, being twenty-five pounds, having a certain shape, are three different properties that form a unity in Fido. Moreover, the brownness is united to the shape of Fido in a way that the redness of a nearby apple is not united to Fido's shape. This would be true even if the apple was inside Fido's mouth, and thus the redness of the apple was spatially closer to parts of Fido—say, his nose—than the brownness of his tail. Finally, Fido is a deeper unity of properties than, say, a heap of salt. Such a heap would be a unity of whiteness and the heap's shape. But such a whole, though a true unity of these properties, is not as deep a unity as is Fido. Fido's properties are much more intimately related to each other than are the properties in lesser unities like heaps of parts. These facts about the unity of properties are called

**3.1.2
UNITY AND
WHOLENESS AT
A TIME**

the **adherence** of properties. Properties adhere together in substances, i.e., they are united together. What explains this fact? The traditional view says that adherence is explained by **inherence**: All of Fido's properties are united because they all are owned by (or inhere in) the same substance that stands under them.

A substance is also a unity of parts. Fido's nose, eyes, heart and legs are parts that form a unified whole. The difference between a property and a part is this: A property is a universal that would still exist even if a substance having it were extinguished from being. A different dog could have brownness even if Fido ceased to be. A **part** is a particular that would not survive if a substance having it were extinguished. If Fido were to "pop out of existence," all of his parts (e.g., his nose) would cease to be. The parts of a substance are united in such a way that the whole is prior to its parts in this sense: the parts of a substance are what they are in virtue of the role they play in the substance as a whole. Thus the identity of a substance's parts presupposes the substance as a whole. The chamber of a heart is what it is in virtue of the role it plays in the heart as a whole; a heart is what it its in virtue of the role it plays in the circulatory system; the circulatory system is what it is in virtue of the role it plays in the organism as a whole. Moreover, when the parts of a substance are removed, they change. As Aristotle said, a severed human hand is no longer human because it is no longer a part of the substance that gave it its identity. The severed hand is merely a heap of atoms and other parts, which will become evident in a few weeks. It has lost its unity.

Finally, a substance is a unity of capacities (potentialities, dispositions, tendencies). In philosophy we distinguish between some x that is F but can be G from some x that is F but cannot be G. For example, salt is solid but can be dissolved in water, and a diamond is solid but cannot be dissolved in water. Counterfactual statements are true of substances. A **counterfactual statement** is a claim that says what would be the case if, contrary to fact, such and such were to happen. For example, if an acorn were to be put in the soil (even though it is in a jar), then it would sprout a root. Such counterfactuals are explained by saying that a substance has a set of **capacities** that are true of it even though they are not actualized. The salt has the capacity of solubility while in the salt shaker; the acorn has the capacity to sprout a root in a jar. A substance is a deep unity of its capacities. Fido has the capacity to bark while silent, to run, to wag its tail and so on, and he is a deep unity of his capacities.

Capacities come in natural groupings and in hierarchies. For example, a human has various capacities to believe and think certain things, various capacities to feel certain things, and various capacities to choose certain things. These different capacities form natural groupings in an individual substance (e.g., a particular human being) that can be called intellectual, emotional and volitional capacities. Psychologists, doctors, biologists and others study the groupings and interconnections among the capacities of various types of substances such as birds, plants and so forth.

Capacities also come in hierarchies. There are first-order capacities, second-order capacities to have these first-order capacities, and so on, until ultimate capacities are reached. For example, if Jill can speak English but not Russian, then she has the first-order capacity for English as well as the second-order capacity to have this first-order capacity (which she has already developed). She also has the second-order capacity to have the capacity to speak Russian, but she may lack the first-order capacity to do so.

A higher-order capacity is realized by the development of lower-order capacities under it. An acorn has the ultimate capacity to draw nourishment from the soil, but this can be actualized and unfolded only by developing the lower capacity to have a root system, then developing the still lower capacities *of the* root system, and so on. When a substance has a defect (e.g., a child is colorblind), it does not lose its ultimate capacities. Rather, it lacks some lower-order capacity it needs for the ultimate capacity to be developed.

A substance's capacities culminate in a set of its ultimate capacities that are possessed by it solely in virtue of the substance belonging to its natural kind, e.g., Smith's ultimate capacities are his because he belongs to the **natural kind** "being human." A substance's **inner nature** includes its ordered structural unity of ultimate capacities. A substance cannot change in its ultimate capacities; that is, it cannot lose its ultimate nature and continue to exist. Smith may replace his skin color from exposure to the sun and still exist, but if he loses his humanness, his inner nature of ultimate capacities that constitutes being human, then Smith ceases to exist.

In sum, a substance is a deep unity of properties, parts and capacities. Moreover, the type of unity in a substance is to be understood by depicting the substance as a whole that is metaphysically prior to its parts in that they get their identity by the role they play in the substance as a whole.

A substance is a **continuant** that remains the same through change. This point will be more fully developed in chapter fourteen when we look at personal identity. Change presupposes sameness. If some *x* (a dog) goes from being F (being brown) to being G (being yellow) then the very same *x* (the dog itself) must be present at the beginning, during and at the end of the change. *It* changes. In fact a **change** can be understood as the coming or going of a property by a substance at or throughout a period of time. A substance regularly loses old parts, properties and lower-order capacities and gains new ones. But the substance itself underlies this change and remains the same through it.

3.1.3
IDENTITY AND
ABSOLUTE
SAMENESS
THROUGH
CHANGE

A long event like a baseball game has temporal parts and, in fact, is the sum of its temporal parts. A baseball game is a sum or totality of nine innings, and each inning is a temporal part of the game. By contrast, substances do not have temporal parts. Substances move *through* their histories; for example, Fido is fully present at every moment of his life. Fido is not a sum of individual "dog stages" like a baseball game is a sum of "game stages" (innings).

As a substance like an acorn grows, it changes through time. These changes are lawlike. That is, each new stage of development and growth comes to be and replaces older stages in repeatable, nonrandom, lawlike ways. These **lawlike changes** are grounded in a substance's inner nature, which, in this context, can be understood as a dynamic principle of activity or change immanent within the individual substance. The acorn changes in specific ways because of the dynamic inherent tendencies latent within its nature as an oak. Each natural kind

3.1.4
LAW AND
LAWLIKE
CHANGE

of thing will have its own type of lawlike changes that are normal for members of that kind, and these changes are grounded in the nature of the substances of that kind.

Moreover, this inner nature sets limits to change. If a substance breaks these limits, the substance no longer exists. For example, as a caterpillar changes into an adult butterfly, the organism's inner nature specifies the precise sequence of stages the organism can undergo in the process of growth. If the organism goes beyond the boundaries of such a change, say if the caterpillar turned into a fish, we would not say that the caterpillar still exists as a fish; rather, we would say that the caterpillar ceased to be and a fish came to be. Thus the lawlike changes that make up a substance's nature (1) specify the ordered sequence of change that will occur in the process of maturation and (2) set limits to the kind of change a thing can undergo and still exist and be counted as an example of its kind.

| 3.1.5 |
| THE UNITY OF |
| THE NATURAL |
| KIND ITSELF |

You may recall from the first half of the chapter that the unity of a natural class of things, say the class of red objects, can be explained by the realist by saying that each member of the class has the very same property in it—in this case, redness. This property explains the unity of the class, why certain objects (a fire truck) belong in the class, and why other objects (a banana) do not.

The same point can be made regarding substances. Substances fall into natural classes called natural kinds, e.g., the class of dogs, humans and so forth. This can be explained by saying that each member of a natural kind has the very same essence in it. All humans have humanness and that explains the unity of the class of humans, why certain things (Smith) belong in that class, and why other things (Fido) do not. In this sense, a thing's natural kind (essence, nature, "whatness"; Aristotle called an individual substance a primary substance and a primary substance's essence a secondary substance) is the set of properties the thing possesses such that it must have this set to be a member of the kind and if it loses any of its essential properties it ceases to exist.

| 3.1.6 |
| FINAL |
| CAUSALITY |

The traditional doctrine of substance contrasts efficient, material, formal and final causes. An **efficient cause** is that by means of which an effect takes place. The efficient cause brings about the effect. For example, when one ball hits and moves another, the first ball is an efficient cause. A **material cause** is the matter or "stuff" of which something is made. A **formal cause** is the essence or "whatness" of a thing (the humanness of Smith). A **final cause** is that for the sake of which an effect or change is produced. Many advocates of the traditional view hold that an individual substance has, within its nature (formal cause), an innate, immanent tendency (final cause) to realize fully the potentialities within its nature. An acorn changes "in order to" realize a mature oak nature; a fetus grows with the end in view of actualizing its potentialities grounded in human nature. Today, the doctrine of final causality is viewed by many to be outdated and unscientific. Instead, it is often thought that the efficient and material cause is all that is needed to explain a substance's change, that explaining an acorn's growth, for example, only requires citing the chemical parts and processes in the acorn. We cannot evaluate this claim here, but it should be pointed out that the notions of formal and final causes are (1) primarily philosophical, and arguments for and against them are beyond the scope of science; (2) compatible with and complementary to the notion of efficient and material causes.

There is a final issue regarding substances called the problem of **individuation**: Given that two things have exactly the same properties, how is it that the two are not the same thing? What differentiates them and makes them two individuals? Consider the two spots Plato and Socrates at the beginning of this chapter. They share all their properties in common. If properties are universals (both spots have the very same properties), what then is it that makes them two spots instead of just one? One may be tempted to say that the spots are different because of their different spatial locations on a sheet of paper. But clearly, this will not do. Why? Because two spots cannot be *at* different locations if, metaphysically speaking, they are not already different spots. Difference of spatial location presupposes difference and individuation and thus cannot constitute individuation.

The same problem of individuation arises with individual substances. If Smith and Jones have the very same human nature, then how are they different? What makes them two humans instead of one? Several answers have been offered to this question and we cannot survey them here. Suffice it to say that there must be something in an individual substance besides its nature that individuates it. Whatever that something is, it can be called a substance's "thisness." Thus an individual substance like Smith is sometimes called a **this-such**. By claiming that Smith is a "such," a philosopher means that Smith possesses a universal nature, shared by all members of Smith's natural kind "being human," and this nature answers the deep question, what kind of thing must Smith be to exist at all? By claiming that Smith is a "this," a philosopher means that Smith is also an individual different from other members of his kind. Thus an individual substance is a this-such; it is a combination of two metaphysical entities: a universal nature and an individuating component.

Currently, there is a debate as to whether or not living organisms are, in some sense, "reducible to" physical entities. A closely related issue is whether or not biology is "reducible to" chemistry and physics. These questions involve a number of complicated issues that require treatment beyond the scope of an introductory text in philosophy. However, a central part of this debate can be clarified by looking at different kinds of parts and wholes; specifically, at the difference between a substance, understood in the traditional sense, and a property-thing.

The world around us contains a number of different kinds of wholes with parts. Different types of wholes manifest different kinds and degrees of unity. Here are three examples that go from lesser to greater unity: a heap of salt, a car, a living organism. A **heap** is a weak kind of unity. It contains parts that are merely united in that those parts are spatially close to each other. A heap can have either homogeneous or heterogeneous parts. A pile of salt is a heap with **homogeneous parts** (all the parts, e.g., the grains of salt, are the same as each other); a pile of junk could be a heap with **heterogeneous parts**.

An artifact is a classic example of a deeper type of unity found in wholes called **property-things**, **ordered aggregates** or **structured stuff**. For example, the parts of a car are not merely united by spatial proximity; they also have a mechanical unity in the way they function together according to a design in the mind of the designer of the car. While property-things have a deeper type of unity than a mere heap, property-things have different, lesser kinds of unities than true substances. Table 10.2 brings out the difference between property-things and substances.

Table 10.2 Differences between property-things and substances

Property-thing	Substance
Requires two categories to classify it (e.g., a table is structured wood, a car is shaped metal).	Requires one category to classify it (Fido is a dog, Jim is a human).
Derives its unity from (1) an external principle in the mind of a designer artificially imposed from the outside on a set of parts to form the object or (2) contingently entering into a set of external relations to form a whole.	Derives its unity from its own internal essence or nature which serves as a principle of unity from within the substance.
Parts are metaphysically prior to the whole. The existence and nature of the whole depends on the parts.	Whole is prior to its parts. The parts are what they are in virtue of their function in the whole that informs and employs them.
Parts are related to each other by external relations. Parts are the same inside or outside of the whole and thus are indifferent to those wholes.	Parts are related to each other by internal relations. Parts lose identity when severed from the whole and thus are dependent on those wholes.
Wholes have no new properties not in parts except new utility for human purpose and new shape, dimension and spatial order.	Wholes have new kinds of properties not in parts grounded in the essence of the substance as a whole unit.
No absolute sameness and strict identity through change (e.g., through loss of old parts and gain of new ones).	Maintains absolute sameness and strict identity through change (e.g., through loss of old parts and gain of new ones).

Examples of substances include individual living organisms, e.g., a dog, an oak tree, a human being. Examples of property-things include individual artifacts, e.g., a clock, a table, a car. In order to understand the main differences between a substance and a property-thing, a few comments should be made on the points contained in table 10.3 as they apply to examples of each category.

First, consider row one. Property-things require two metaphysical categories to classify them. For example, a table is structured wood. Wood is included in the category of "stuff" and is a kind of material. The structure of the table is a set of ordering relations, in this case spatial relations of shape, size and volume. Thus the category of relation and the category of stuff is required to classify a property-thing. By contrast, a substance is a true, deep unity and only requires one category—that of substance—to classify it. Dogs, humans and oak trees are all substances.

Next, consider row two. Property-things are not deep unities, but rather accidental (i.e., nonessential) combinations of an ordering relational property (e.g., the structure of the table) artificially and externally imposed on preexistent materials (e.g., the wood). The unity of a property-thing does not spring from or reside within its own being; instead, at least for human artifacts, it resides in the plan contained in the mind of the designer of the property-thing. Here, a designer assembles an arrangement of parts and uses a principle of unity in his mind to impose externally a structural order from the outside onto a set of parts to form the object in question. The unity of a watch does not spring from within the parts of the watch or from within the watch taken as a whole; it resides in the designer's mind. Similarly, the unity of a naturally occurring property-thing, such as a mountain, derives from a set of parts (e.g., boulders, pieces of dirt) contingently entering into external relations with other parts and being held together to form the mountain By contrast, the unity of a substance springs from and resides within the substance and is due to the internal essence or **nature** of the substance that serves as its principle of unification. The unity of the parts and properties of a dog or human are due to the essence within it.

The points in row three follow naturally from the items listed in row two. For a property-thing, the parts exist prior to the whole, not only temporally (i.e., the clock's parts were on the desk before the clock was assembled), but metaphysically. The parts of a clock exist and are what they are independent of their incorporation into the clock as a whole. A table leg, watch spring and automobile tire are what they are prior to their incorporation into their wholes. These parts are identified by the stuff that composes them—structured wood for a table leg, wound iron for a clock spring. In fact, the wholes depend on those parts for their overall structure.

For substances, however, the order is reversed. The substance as a whole is prior to its parts in this sense: Its parts are gathered and formed by the direction of the substance and its essence taken as a whole, and those parts receive their identity by virtue of their incorporation into the substance as a whole. For example, a specific chamber of the heart is what it is, not by virtue of the stuff that composes it (as with parts of a property-thing), but due to the role the chamber plays in the heart taken as a whole (e.g., a chamber is that which functions to open and close in a precise way due to the nature of the heart as a whole). And a heart is what it is in virtue of the functional role it plays in the circulation system taken as a whole. Finally, the circulation system (and other systems) gains its identity by the role it plays in the organism as a whole. Thus the whole organism is prior to its parts in that the whole has a principle of unity within it that gives identity to its parts.

Row four emphasizes the fact that the parts of a property-thing are related to each other by means of **external relations**. This means that the relations do not enter into the very nature of those parts and they are indifferent to the relations. For example, the spring and gears of a clock are related to each other by various mechanical and spatial relations. But these relations do not make the parts what they are. In fact, the spring is "indifferent" to the other parts of the clock or to the clock taken as a whole. That is, the spring is the same as itself inside or outside the clock. Again, a table leg can change its relations with other parts of a table by being removed and placed in another room, but this does not affect the identity of the leg.

By contrast, the parts of a substance are related to each other by means of **internal relations**. To understand the nature of internal relations, suppose we have two entities, *a* and *b*, that are standing to each other in some relation *R*. There are two things true of internal relations as they are usually construed. First, if the *R* of *a* to *b* is internal to *a*, then anything that does not stand in *R* to *b* is not identical to *a*. If the relation "brighter than" between yellow and purple is internal to yellow, then any thing that is not brighter than purple cannot be the color yellow. Second, if one entity, *a*, is internally related to another entity, *b*, *b* may or may not be internally related to *a*. Yellow is internally related to purple and vice versa. However, on a view of animals as traditional substances, while an animal's heart is internally related to the animal as a whole, the opposite is not true. On the traditional view, the organs of an animal are what they are because of the role they play in the organism taken as a whole. Assuming this view solely for the purpose of illustration, the traditional view depicts an animal's organs as internally related to the animal such that if that organ, say a hand, is severed from the animal, it ceases to exist as an organ. But the animal as a whole is not internally related to any particular organ. If an animal loses a hand, it is still identical to the very same animal that existed with the hand.

By way of application, the parts of a substance are what they are by virtue of the relations they sustain to other parts and to the substance as a whole. If the parts drop out of those relations, the parts lose their identity. If a heart or a hand is severed from an individual human, it ceases to be a heart or a hand, it loses its principle of unity (which will become evident over time as it decays!), and it becomes a property-thing. The parts of a substance are not indifferent to their incorporation in a substance. They gain their identity from the substance of which they are parts and they lose their identity when outside those substances.

Row six emphasizes the fact that property-things have no new kinds of properties not already resident in their parts. A property-thing merely provides a structure through which an already existing natural agency can channel energy to produce an effect that can be interpreted in a new way. For example, a clock has no new *kinds* of properties not resident in its parts. It does have a different *set* of spatial properties—a new shape and dimension—but these are not new kinds of properties not already in the parts of the clock. Instead, they are different spatial properties due to a new arrangement of the spatial properties already resident within the clock's parts prior to assembly. Further, the wound spring of the clock serves as a natural agency, a natural source of energy that the structure of the clock (its gears, etc.) can channel in a new way not possible if the spring did not have the clock's structure to serve as a medium for directing that energy. This allows an effect to be produced—the moving of the clock's hands—that is new. But the newness of this effect is not due to the clock's possessing a new kind of property not present in the parts of the clock prior to assembly. Rather, this new effect can be understood as (1) a new geometrical motion (e.g., circular motion of the hands), which is the same kind of property possible for a wound spring without being in a clock (i.e., it could produce a different noncircular geometrical motion, but the motion would still be geometrical); (2) an effect that can be externally interpreted in a new way according to an artificial convention (e.g., we interpret this circular motion as "telling time," but this is not really a property of the clock's hands, but a conventional way of viewing the motion of the hands from a system outside the clock).

This feature of property-things is very controversial, and not all philosophers accept it. Some believe that property-things may have emergent properties, roughly, genuinely new kinds of properties exemplified by property-things as wholes not characteristic of their parts.

According to the traditional view, a substance—in contrast to a property-thing—has new properties true of it as a whole not true of its parts prior to their incorporation into their substances. These new properties are founded in the nature of the substance (humanness for Jim, doghood for Fido). For living organisms, these new properties include things like specific kinds of reproduction, assimilation, growth and so forth. These new properties cannot be accounted for solely by the laws of chemistry and physics and are due, in part, to the new nature governing the substance taken as a whole.

Finally, row seven mentions a topic that will be covered more fully in chapter fourteen. Here we can only assert, without much defense or detail, that when a property-thing undergoes a change by losing old parts and gaining new ones, it does not really remain the same entity. If the parts of a clock were gradually replaced by a new set of parts, the clock would literally be a different clock. However, a substance can maintain absolute identity and genuine sameness through accidental change because the substance is a whole that is prior to and underlies its parts and accidental properties.

Our purpose here is to clarify the difference between a property-thing and a substance. In the process of doing this, we have mentioned that living organisms appear to be genuine substances and not property-things. It is beyond the scope of this chapter to look further at that debate. But you should now be in a position to think about this issue for yourself. In the remaining pages of this chapter, we will look at the major rival to the traditional view of substance: the bundle theory.

According to the traditional view, a substance is not just a collection of properties. It is a thing that owns or underlies properties. For various reasons such as a rejection of the traditional view on empiricist grounds because one cannot have a sense impression of the substance that, say, underlies a dog's visible properties, some philosophers have formulated a rival view of substance called the **bundle theory**. On this view, a substance is not an individuated essence that has properties embedded in it; rather, a substance is just a collection or bundle of properties themselves, nothing more, nothing less. To clarify this, consider the dog Fido. Fido is brown, has a certain weight, shape, smell, texture and so forth. Let us call the various properties of this sort P_i—P_n.

The traditional view of substance would analyze Fido in this way:

Fido = {P_i—P_n, the individuated essence of Fido}

Fido has a essential nature, doghood, that is exemplified by an individuator (to account for the individuality of Fido compared to Spot). Further, just as pins are stuck into a pin cushion, so Fido's **accidental properties**—those he could lose and still exist—namely, P_i—P_n, are owned by and embedded in the

3.3
THE BUNDLE THEORY OF SUBSTANCE

3.3.1
A STATEMENT OF THE VIEW

substance (the individuated essence) that is Fido.

By contrast, the bundle theory of substance would analyze Fido as follows:

Fido $= \{P_i—P_n$, a bundling relation R$\}$

On the bundle theory, there is no owner of a thing's properties. They do not relate to the substance that has them as a property being possessed by a substance. Rather, the relationship between properties and a substance is very much like a part-whole relation. If you strip away all of Fido's properties, nothing is left. Fido is nothing more than a "combination," "bundle," "cluster," "collection" of properties. Now there is an obvious difference between Fido and a situation where the brownness, shape and so forth of Fido were unconnected and scattered throughout the room. Thus Fido is not just a certain list of properties; Fido is a set of certain properties bundled directly together. Thus $P_i—P_n$, together with the bundling relation R that ties these properties into the same collection exhaust a metaphysical analysis of Fido. This, then, is the difference between the traditional and the bundle theory of substance.

3.3.2 AN EVALUATION OF THE VIEW

An obvious advantage of the bundle theory is that it does not involve commitment to an entity (an individuated dog nature) that is not empirically observable. And if one believes that metaphysics should be done within the boundaries of sense impressions, then bundle theory will be attractive, since one can observe $P_i—P_n$ in Fido, as well as the fact that these properties form a single cluster. On the other hand, those who do not feel constrained to do metaphysics within the confines of sensation will not take this to be a major point.

On the negative side, two major objections have been raised against the bundle theory. First, it cannot account for the contingency of substances. Individual substances like Fido are not necessary beings. They are **contingent**—they exist in space and time, come to be and perish and, in general, they could have not existed at all. But if properties are universals, and if universals are what realists take them to be—timeless, spaceless, necessary beings (necessary in that, while they owe their existence to God, there is no possible world in which properties do not exist)—then the bundle theory turns substances into necessary beings. Why? Because the bundle theory holds that a substance like Fido is exhausted by its properties and all its properties are universals. Thus, since Fido is merely a collection of universals, Fido himself must be a necessary being.

A bundle theorist could respond that Fido is more than a collection of universal properties. He is collection of properties in a bundling relation. But this will not solve the problem because the bundling relation, R, is itself a universal that will be present in every bundle of properties. Given that properties are universals, and given that substances are merely a list of properties and a bundling relation, no account of the individuality and contingency of a substance like Fido is readily available. It will not do simply to claim that Fido is a specific, individual occurrence of certain properties being bundled together. This response begs the question and merely asserts the individuality and contingency of Fido. The issue is not whether Fido is a contingent individual. Indeed, he is. The issue is whether the bundle theory can *account* for this fact. Merely asserting what is obvious does not answer the problem.

Second, the bundle theory cannot maintain that substances are literally the same things through change. The reason is obvious. Since a substance is just a bundled cluster of certain properties, if one of those properties leaves, you have a new, different cluster. If Fido goes from brown to yellow, we have an old cluster (containing brown) ceasing to be and a new cluster (containing yellow) coming to be. On this view, Fido is not a continuant that is literally the same through change. In fact, change is an illusion. Fido is really just a succession of dog stages. At each moment of Fido's life, there is a specific bundle of properties that exist at that moment. In chapter fourteen we will investigate sameness through change. But for now, it should be pointed out that if real sameness through change of living organisms is true and reasonable to believe, then the bundle theory is in trouble.

4 A FINAL POINT TO PONDER

In this chapter we have investigated some metaphysical issues involved in two categories of being—property and substance. We have also found reason to accept a realist view of properties and a traditional notion of substances, though we readily admit that a short chapter in an introductory text in philosophy cannot hope to treat all the issues necessary to justify adequately these positions. Suffice it to say that most Christian thinkers, though by no means all of them, and many non-Christian thinkers have held to a realist doctrine of properties and a traditional notion of substance, and they have done so for good reasons. If we assume the truth of these two positions, then two things follow. First, crude, sensate forms of empiricism (knowledge and justified belief can operate only within the bounds of the five senses) are false because at least many properties (that of being triangular or of being even) are not knowable within those boundaries. Second, physicalist forms of naturalism are false as well because neither properties, nor the individuated essences that constitute substances are material beings. These conclusions, if correct, are by no means unimportant for the life of the church and the texture of modern culture.

CHAPTER SUMMARY

Properties and relations are two main categories of reality. There are three views of properties: extreme nominalism (properties do not exist), nominalism (properties are abstract particulars) and realism (properties are universals). Extreme nominalists and nominalists accept the axiom of localization and are naturalists. Impure realists deny the axiom and hold a weakened form of naturalism. Pure realists are not naturalists. Most realists reject the model-copy view of exemplification.

Three main issues are involved in the debate among extreme nominalists, nominalists and realists: predication (Socrates is red), exact resemblance (Socrates and Plato exactly resemble each other in being red) and the fact that properties themselves have properties (red is a color). These issues provide evidence for the superiority of realism.

The traditional view of substance explains several metaphysical phenomena:

the ownership of properties, unity and wholeness at a time, sameness through change, the fact of lawlike change, the unity of the natural kind itself, final causality and the problem of individuation. There are several important differences between true substances and property-things, and these differences shed light on the claim that living organisms are true substances. The bundle theory of substance is a major rival to the traditional view. However, it suffers from two main difficulties: (1) given that properties are universals, the bundle theory turns substances into necessary beings; (2) it cannot embrace real sameness through change for substances.

CHECKLIST OF BASIC TERMS AND CONCEPTS

abstract entity
abstract particular
accidental property
adherence
axiom of localization
bundle theory
capacity (potentiality, disposition, tendency)
change
concrete particular
contingent
continuant
counterfactual statement
efficient cause
exact resemblance
exemplification
external relation
extreme nominalism
final cause
formal cause
heap
heterogeneous parts
homogeneous parts
impure realist
individuation
inherence
inner nature
instancing
internal relation
lawlike change
material cause
model-copy view
natural kind
nature
nominalism
nonidentity assumption

nonspatial (and atemporal) view of exemplification
paradigm case
part
predication
property
property-thing (ordered aggregate or structured stuff)
pure realist
quality agreement
realism
relation
self-predication assumption
spatial container view of exemplification
substance
the one and the many
third man argument
this-such
tokens
types
universals
world

11

THE MIND-BODY PROBLEM
Dualism

But the soul is present as a whole not only in the entire mass of a body,
but also in every least part of the body at the same time.
AUGUSTINE ON THE IMMORTALITY OF THE SOUL 26.25

[W]e now proceed to treat of man,
who is composed of a spiritual and corporeal substance.
THOMAS AQUINAS SUMMA THEOLOGIAE PART I, Q.75

The immortality of the soul is something of such vital importance to us,
affecting us so deeply, that one must have lost all feeling
not to care about knowing the facts of the matter.
PASCAL, PENSÉES, LAFUMA EDITION, 427

I think we ought to hold not only that man has a soul,
but that it is important that he should know that he has a soul.
J. GRESHAM MACHEN, THE CHRISTIAN VIEW OF MAN

1 INTRODUCTION

It is virtually self-evident to most people that they are different from their bodies. Almost all societies throughout history (unless they are taught to think otherwise) have believed in some form of life after death, and this belief arises naturally when a human being reflects on his or her own constitution. Moreover, throughout church history, the vast majority of Christian thinkers have correctly understood the Scriptures to teach the following: (1) Human beings exhibit a holistic functional unity. (2) While a functional unity, humans are nevertheless a duality of immaterial soul/spirit and material body, both of which are intrinsically good. Setting aside the question as to whether the soul and spirit are the same or different, and acknowledging that the biblical terms for soul (*nephesh, psyche*) and spirit (*ruach, pneuma*) have a wide variety of different meanings, it is still clear that the Scriptures teach that the soul/spirit is an immaterial component different from the body (Eccles 12:7; Mt 10:28), that death involves the soul's leaving the body (Gen 35:18; 1 Kings 17:21, 22) and that after death, the soul continues to exist in a disembodied intermediate state while awaiting the resurrection of the body (Heb 12:23; Lk 23:46; 2 Cor 5:1-10;

Phil 1:21-24). (3) Since animals are living creatures, they have souls as well, they are different from human souls, and animals are not likely to survive death (Gen 1:30; Rev 8:9).

This biblical teaching must be integrated with an area of philosophy known as philosophy of mind. A main part of the philosophy of mind is something called the mind-body problem, which will occupy our attention in this and the next chapter. In this chapter, we will look at the following: preliminary issues, arguments for substance and property dualism (defined below), arguments for substance dualism alone and arguments against dualism.

2 PRELIMINARY ISSUES

In some contexts, it is possible and important to make a distinction among the mind, the soul, the spirit, the ego or the self. But for our purposes, we will use these interchangeably. Our main concern here is to focus on the **mind-body problem**, which, in turn, involves two main issues. First, is a human made of only one component, say matter, or is a human made of two components, matter and mind? Second, if the answer is two components, do mind and matter interact, and if so, how does that interaction take place?

2.1
THE MIND-
BODY PROBLEM

In this chapter, we will primarily look at the first question. The problem of the interaction between mind and matter will be discussed briefly when we consider criticisms of dualism. Currently, there are two main positions taken on the mind-body problem, as depicted in figure 11.1.

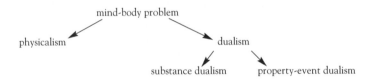

Fig. 11.1 Positions take on the mind-body problem

The two main views are physicalism and dualism. **Physicalism** claims that a human being is completely physical, and **dualism** claims that a human being is both physical and mental. Dualism, in turn, comes is two major varieties: substance dualism and property-event dualism. Physicalism comes in different varieties as well, which will be examined in the next chapter. Our present purpose is to get clear on the different views listed in the chart above.

What exactly is physicalism? It is hard to say precisely because several different views go by that name. Sometimes *physicalism* refers to whatever version of it is currently fashionable. However, we can be more precise in our usage than this. Note first of all that, historically speaking, **materialism** was the view that the only substances that exist are material substances, but (1) some of these substances (living organisms) may possess a duality of material and immaterial properties and (2) immaterial abstract objects (e.g., sets, universals) may also exist (see chap. 10 for discussion of substance, i.e., a whole that is a deep unity of properties, parts

2.2
CLARIFYING
THE OPTIONS
REGARDING
THE MIND-BODY
PROBLEM

and capacities). Today, physicalism often means something more restrictive than materialism so defined: Physicalism can be understood as the view that all entities whatsoever are merely physical entities. There are no abstract objects, and all substances, properties and events are merely physical entities. Some physicalists hold that while there are only physical substances, there are genuinely mental properties that emerge from and are dependent on their physical bases. This view seems to be a version of property dualism, and we will treat it as such.

What is meant by a physical entity? Three different things can be meant here. First, *physical* can mean whatever can be described using the language of physics and chemistry. Second, *physical* can include the sense just given and be extended to include whatever can be described in any physical science, especially including biology. Third, *physical* can be extended beyond the first two senses to include any commonsense notion of physical. This is often, though not always, taken to include the primary qualities (shape, mass, size, motion) and to exclude the secondary qualities (those experienced through only one sense organ such as color, smell, texture, sound, taste). The restricted sense of physicalism, therefore, implies that all entities whatever are merely physical in one of these three senses.

We will use *physicalism* in this more restricted sense and understand *physical* to mean whatever can be described using the language of physics and chemistry. What exists are various configurations and hierarchies of elementary particles. This sense of *physical* is widely used by physicalists in stating and defending their views, and it captures what is, for many, the driving force behind physicalism: the unity of science. The **unity of science** means, among other things, that a completely developed physics and chemistry could give a complete, unified description and explanation of all phenomena because the world is one physical system.

According to physicalism, a human being is merely a physical entity. The only things that exist are physical substances, properties and events. When it comes to humans, the physical substance is the body or brain and central nervous system. The physical substance called the brain has physical properties, such as a certain weight, volume, size, electrical activity, chemical composition and so forth.

There are also physical events that occur in the brain. For example, the brain contains a number of elongated cells that carry various impulses. These cells are called neurons. Various neurons make contact with other neurons through connections or points of contact called synapses. C-fibers are certain types of neurons that innervate the skin (i.e., supply the skin with nerves) and carry pain impulses. According to physicalism, when someone has an occasion of pain or an occurrence of a thought, these are merely physical events, namely, events where such and such C-fibers are firing or certain electrical and chemical events are happening in the brain and central nervous system. Thus physicalists believe that we are merely a physical substance (a brain and central nervous system plus a body) that has physical properties and in which occur physical events.

What is matter? There is no clear definition of matter, and the fact of the matter is that we know precious little about what matter actually is. But examples of matter are not hard to come by. Material objects are things like computers, carbon atoms and billiard balls.

Physical properties are the properties that are possessed only by physical objects. They are the properties that one finds listed in chemistry or physics books, e.g., hardness; occupying and moving through space; having a certain shape; possessing certain chemical, electrical, magnetic and gravitational properties; having density and weight; and being breakable, malleable and elastic. A physical event is the continued possession, coming or going of one or more of these properties by a physical substance (or among physical substances) at a time.

There is one very crucial observation to make about material substances, properties and events. *No material thing presupposes or requires reference to consciousness for it to exist or be characterized.* You will search in vain through a physics or chemistry textbook to find consciousness included in any description of matter. A completely physical description of the world would not include any terms that make reference to or characterize consciousness.

Dualists disagree with physicalists. According to them, mental entities are real and the mind and its contents are radically nonphysical. As with matter, it is hard to give a definition of mental entities. Some have defined a **mental entity** as something such that it would not exist if there were no sentient creatures. Others define a mental entity as something about which the subject is in a better position to know than is anyone else, or something to which a subject has private, first-person access. Mental entities belong to the private world of inner experience.

Regardless of how we define a mental entity, examples of them are easy to supply. First, there are various kinds of **sensations**: experiences of colors, sounds, smells, tastes, textures, pains, itches, etc. Sensations are individual events that occur at particular times. One can have a sensation of red after looking in a certain direction or by closing one's eyes and daydreaming. An experience of pain will arise at a certain time, say, after one is stuck with a pin.

Further, sensations are natural kinds of things that have, as their very essence, the felt quality or sensory property that makes them what they are. Part of the very essence of a pain is the felt quality it has; part of the very essence of a red sensation is the presentation of a particular shade of color to one's consciousness. Sensations are not identical to things outside a person's body, e.g., a feeling of pain is not the same thing as being stuck with a pin and shouting "ouch!" Sensations are essentially characterized by a certain conscious feel, and thus they presuppose consciousness for their existence and description. If there were no conscious beings, there would be no sensations.

Second, there are things called **propositional attitudes**: having a certain mental attitude toward a state of affairs by means of a proposition that can be expressed by a that-clause. For example, one can hope, desire, fear, dread, wish, think, believe that *P*, where *P* may be the proposition *The Royals are a great baseball team*. Here one has a certain attitude (of hoping, desiring, etc.) toward an extramental state of affairs—the Royals being a great baseball team—and this attitude is directed towards this state of affairs by means of the mental proposition expressed as follows: *The Royals are a great baseball team*.

As the example shows, propositional attitudes include at least three components. First, there is the state of affairs toward which the attitude is directed. Unless one is reflecting on a mental state itself, this state of affairs will be external to the thinking subject. Second, there is the attitude itself. Hopes, fears, dreads, wishes, thoughts, etc. are all different states of consciousness, and they are all different from each other based on their conscious feel. A hope is a different form of consciousness than an episode of fear. Third, they all have a content or a meaning embedded in the propositional attitude, namely, the propositional content of one's consciousness while one is having the propositional attitude. Dan's hope that P differs from his hope that Q because P and Q are different propositions or meanings in Dan's consciousness. Arguably, if there were no conscious selves, there would be no propositional attitudes since the last two components of such attitudes (the attitude and the propositional content) are aspects of consciousness.

Third, there are acts of will or **purposings**. What is a purposing? An example may help to answer this question. If, unknown to Judy, her arm is tied down and she still tries to raise it, then the purposing is the "trying to bring about" the event of raising her arm. Intentional actions are episodes of volition by conscious selves wherein and whereby they do various actions. They are acts of will. Such acts are episodes done by conscious selves. In sum, all of the above are cited by dualists as examples of mental entities.

In addition to the differences between physicalists and dualists, there is also an intramural debate between property dualists and substance dualists. According to **property dualism** (also called property-event dualism), there are some physical substances that have only physical properties. A billiard ball is hard and round. Further, there are no mental substances. But there is one material substance that has both physical *and* mental properties—the brain. When one experiences a pain, there is a certain physical property possessed by the brain (a C-fiber stimulation with chemical and electrical properties) and there is a certain mental property possessed by the brain (the pain itself with its felt quality).

The brain is the possessor of all mental properties. A human is not a mental self that *has* thoughts and experiences. Rather, a human is a brain and a series or bundle of successive experiences themselves.

Substance dualism, on the other hand, holds that the brain is a physical object that has physical properties and the mind or soul is a mental substance that has mental properties. When one is in pain, the brain has certain physical (e.g., electrical, chemical) properties, and the soul or self has certain mental properties (the conscious awareness of the pain). The soul is the possessor of its experiences. It stands behind, over and above them and remains the same throughout one's life. The soul and the brain can interact with each other, but they are different things with different properties. Since the soul is not to be identified with any part of the brain or with any particular mental experience, then the soul may be able to survive the destruction of the body.

2.3
DUALIST
STRATEGIES
REGARDING THE
MIND-BODY
PROBLEM

Our discussion of identity in chapter nine stated that if two entities x and y are identical, then whatever is true of x will be true of y and vice versa, because x is the very same entity as y. Physicalists are committed to the claim that alleged mental entities either do not exist at all or if they do, they are really identical to physical entities, e.g., brain states, properties of the brain, overt bodily behavior or dispositions to behave (e.g., pain is just the tendency to shout "ouch!" when stuck by a pin instead of pain being a certain mental feel). If physicalism is true and if mental entities exist but are really nothing but physical entities, then everything true of the brain (and its properties, states and dispositions) is true of the mind (and its properties, states and dispositions) and vice versa. If we can find one thing true, or even possibly true of the mind (or its states) and not the brain (or its states), or vice versa, then some form of dualism is established. The mind is not the brain.

In the next section, we will present a number of dualist arguments that try to show that something is true of the mind or its states and not the brain or its states, or vice versa, and thus the mind or its states cannot be identical to the brain or its states. But if they are not identical, physicalism is false and, taking dualism to be the only other option, dualism would be true.

Keep in mind that the relation of identity is different from any other relation—for example, causation or constant connection. It may be that brain events cause mental events or vice versa (e.g., having certain electrical activity in the brain may cause one to experience a pain, and having an intention to raise one's arm may cause bodily events). It may be that for every mental activity a neurophysiologist can find a physical activity in the brain with which it is correlated. But just because A causes B (or vice versa), or just because A and B are constantly correlated with each other, that does not mean that A is *identical to* B. Something is trilateral if and only if it is triangular. But trilaterality (the property of having three sides) is not identical to triangularity (the property of having three angles), even though they are constantly conjoined.

To establish physicalism, it is not enough that mental states and brain states are causally related or constantly conjoined with each other in an embodied person. *Physicalism needs identity to make its case, and if something is true, or possibly true of a mental substance, property or event that is not true, or possibly true of a physical substance, property or event, physicalism is false.*

3 ARGUMENTS SUPPORTING PROPERTY AND SUBSTANCE DUALISM

3.1
THE
DISTINCTIVENESS
OF MENTAL
AND PHYSICAL
PROPERTIES AND
STATES

Mental events include episodes of thoughts, feelings of pain and episodes of having a sensory experience. Physical events are happenings in the brain and central nervous system that can be described exhaustively using terms from chemistry and physics. However, physical events and properties do not have the same features that hold for mental events and properties. One's thoughts, feelings of pain or sensory experiences do not have any weight, are not located anywhere in space (one's thought of lunch cannot be closer to one's right ear than one's left one), are not composed of chemicals, and do not have electrical properties. However, the brain events associated with one's thoughts, etc., indeed, material events in general, *do* have these features.

If a doctor touches part of one's brain with an electrode, it may cause a certain mental experience, say a memory, to occur. But all that proves is that the mind is causally connected to the brain, not that they are identical. A sound is not stored in the groves of a record, but rather is causally connected with those groves (one can cause a sound by doing something to the grooves). Likewise, memories are neither parts of nor stored in the brain, but are stored in the mind, yet causally connected with the brain (one can cause a memory by doing something to the brain).

A simple thought experiment may further illustrate the point. Try to picture a pink elephant in your mind, or if you do not have a vivid imagination, look at a colored object, close your eyes, and you will continue to have an awareness of that object called an after-image. Now, if you imagine a pink elephant or have, say, a blue after-image, there will be an awareness of pink or blue (a sense datum or a sensory way of experiencing) in your mind of which you are aware. There will be no pink elephant outside of you, but there will be a pink mental image or an awareness of pink in your mind. Now at that time there will be no pink or blue entity in your brain nor any awareness of pink or blue; no neurophysiologist could open your brain and see a pink or blue entity or an awareness of such an entity while you are having the sensory experience. But, then, the sensory event has a property—being pink or blue or being an awareness of pink or blue—that no brain event has. Therefore, they cannot be identical. The sense image is a mental entity.

Some physicalists respond to this argument by simply denying it. They claim that since thoughts, memories, etc. are states of the brain, then they are, in fact, spatially located in certain regions of the brain. Likewise, they claim, memories are stored in the brain and a memory event is a brain event, perhaps one that plays a certain functional role in one's behavior, not a truly mental event causally connected with a brain event.

**3.2
SELF-
PRESENTING
PROPERTIES**

Consider the following argument:

1. No physical properties are self-presenting.

2. At least some mental properties are self-presenting.

---

3. Therefore, at least some mental properties are not physical properties.

Mental properties, like feeling sad, experiencing red, having a thought that three is an odd number, are **self-presenting properties**, that is, they present themselves directly to the subject, they are psychological attributes, they are directly present to a subject because that subject simply has them immediately in his field of consciousness. There are two pieces of evidence for the claim that mental properties are self-presenting, while physical properties are not: One can have private access to one's mental properties and not one's physical properties, and one can know at least some of one's mental properties incorrigibly, but this is not true of one's knowledge of his physical properties.

First, let us look at the issue of **private access**. A person has private access to his own mental life. A woman is in a privileged position to know about what she is thinking and sensing compared to anyone else. Whatever ways one has for finding out if someone else is presently sensing a red after-image (by analyzing the other's brain states or by looking at her behavior, say, her shouting "red" after looking at the flag), those ways are available to the other person in her attempt to know about her own sensation.

But there is a way of knowing that one is having a red after-image not available to anyone else—one's own immediate awareness of one's own mental life.

A person is in a position to know his or her own mental life in a way not available to anyone else. But that is not the case for any physical property, including one's brain and its various states. Physical objects, including one's brain, are public objects, and no one is in a privileged position regarding them. A neurophysiologist can know more about one's brain than the person himself does, but the scientist cannot know more about one's mental life than the person himself. In fact, a scientist's knowledge of one's mental states will, ultimately, depend on the first-person reports of the persons having them, but a scientist's knowledge of any physical state whatsoever will not depend on a first-person report. People have private, privileged access to their mental life because it contains self-presenting properties. Physical properties are not self-presenting.

Some physicalists respond to this by claiming that we may reach the time when a scientist will know more about a patient's current mental states than the patient does, and such scientific knowledge will not depend essentially on first-person reports. However, it is hard to see how such progress in scientific knowledge would be possible without the subject having to report verbally or by behavior his own mental states to the outside observer because he alone has private access to them.

Some physicalists also claim that when a mental state like feeling pain is self-presenting (directly given) to a mental subject, then what the subject is actually aware of is a complex property of the brain at that moment. The problem with this suggestion is this: When one is directly aware of a pain, that pain presents itself to him in such a way that he is aware of the fact that it has, necessarily, a specific kind of painful feeling as part of its very essence, and it has no physical property (described in the language of chemistry and physics) as part of its very essence. So by direct introspective awareness of a pain, one can simply "see" that it is not a physical state.

Not only do people have private access to their own mental states, but also, people can know them incorrigibly. If something is **incorrigible** to a knowing subject, then that subject is incapable of being mistaken about that thing.

Suppose Sally is experiencing what she takes to be a green rug. It is possible that the rug is not there or that the light is poor and the rug is really gray. Sally could be mistaken about the rug itself. But it does not seem to be possible for her to be mistaken that she is seeming to see something green, that she is having a sensation of green. The former claim is about a physical object (the rug); the latter claim is about a mental state within her—her seeming to see something green.

Again, one can be wrong if one thinks that a chair is in the next room. But one cannot be wrong about the fact that one at least *thinks* that the chair is there, i.e., that a certain, specific thought is occurring to one. The former claim is about a physical object (the chair); the latter is about a mental state within a person—a thought that one is currently having. In general, claims about physical states, including claims about one's brain and its properties/states, can be mistaken. But if one is being attentive, one can know one's sensory states (the ways that one is being appeared to, the current sensory experiences one is having) and one's episodes of thought (that one is having such and such thought right now).

Physicalists deny that people know their own mental states incorrigibly. For example, one may be experiencing an itch and mistakenly classify or report it to others as a pain. Dualists respond that in cases like these, people are still incorrigibly aware of the felt texture of the experience itself, even though they may not have the correct word to report it to others or even if they don't remember past experiences of different kinds of itches well enough to know how to classify the present itch in light of their past, poorly remembered experiences.

In sum, physical states/properties are not self-presenting, but at least some mental states/properties are, as evidenced by the twin phenomena of private access and incorrigibility. Thus physical states/properties are not identical to at least some mental states/properties.

3.3
THE SUBJECTIVE
NATURE OF
EXPERIENCE

The subjective character of experience is hard to capture in physicalist terms. The simple fact of consciousness, constituted by the subjective feel or texture of experience itself, is a serious difficulty for physicalists. To see this, consider the following example of what has been called the **knowledge argument**. Suppose a deaf scientist became the world's leading expert on the neurology of hearing. It would be possible for him to know and describe everything involved in the physical aspects of hearing. In this example, no knowledge of what is physical is left out of the description. However, something different *would still* be left out of what the scientist knows—the experience of what it is like to be a human who hears. As Howard Robinson puts it:

> The notion of *having something as an object of experience* is not, *prima facie*, a physical notion; it does not figure in any physical science. *Having something as an object of experience* is the same as the subjective feel or the *what it is like* of experience.[1]

Subjective states of experience are real—people experience sounds, tastes, colors, thoughts, pains—and they are essentially characterized by their subjective nature. But this does not appear to be true of anything physical.

3.4
THE EXISTENCE
OF SECONDARY
QUALITIES

Secondary qualities are qualities such as colors, tastes, sounds, smells and textures. **Primary qualities** are qualities thought to be among the properties that characterize matter—weight, shape, size, solidity, motion. According to some, physicalism seems to imply that secondary qualities do not exist in the external world. For example, some claim that color is really nothing but a wavelength of light. So in general, physicalism reduces the properties of matter to being nothing but primary qualities. We are left with a picture of matter bereft of secondary qualities.

But the world of our commonsense experience is replete with secondary qualities. Thus such qualities must exist, but if they do not exist in the external world as properties of matter, they must exist as mental entities in the conscious minds of experiencers themselves. Frank Jackson has put the point this way:

> It is a commonplace that there is an apparent clash between the picture Science gives of the world around us and the picture our senses give us. We *sense* the world as made up of coloured, materially continuous, macroscopic, stable objects;

---

[1]Howard Robinson, *Matter and Sense* (Cambridge: Cambridge University Press, 1982), p. 7.

> Science and, in particular, Physics, tells us that the material world is constituted of clouds of minute, colourless, highly-mobile particles. . . . Science forces us to acknowledge that physical or material things are not coloured. . . . This will enable us to conclude that sense-data are all mental, for they are coloured.[2]

In other words, science does away with secondary qualities in the external world, but since we know they do exist—we see them—they must exist in our minds as mental entities because they are not aspects of matter.

Not all dualists or physicalists agree with this argument, and assessing it requires, among other things, looking at various theories of perception. Unfortunately, this is beyond the scope of the present discussion. Dualists and advocates of some versions of physicalism can hold that secondary qualities exist and are genuine properties of material objects. However, the existence of secondary qualities does present a problem for physicalism for this reason: If we accept the unity of science and take physics and chemistry to be the basic sciences, then we are committed to the view that all entities can be reduced to or explained by physics and chemistry. Now there is a clear tendency in physics to claim that color is just a wavelength of light, and thus, when we say that an apple is red, this just means that the apple has certain physical dispositions to absorb certain wavelengths of light and reflect others and so forth. We do not need to postulate that the apple actually has a shade of red on its surface to explain all the scientific cause-and-effect relationships that occur between the apple, light waves and the bodies of observers. Now this same strategy is what many physicalists want to use in reducing mental states to physical states. For those physicalists who do not apply this strategy to secondary qualities, it would seem to be more consistent for them not to apply that strategy to mental states.

Some have argued that the mark of the mental is something called **intentionality**. Intentionality is the mind's "ofness" or "aboutness." Mental states have a directedness that is intrinsic to them. They point beyond themselves to other things. Every mental state one has, or at least many of them, is of or about something—a hope that Smith will come, a sensation of the apple, a thought that the painting is beautiful. Mental states can even be about things that do not exist, e.g., a fear of a goblin or a love for Zeus. The ofness or aboutness of our mental states is an intrinsic, nondispositional, irreducible feature of those states. For example, the fact that Joe's thought that the painting is beautiful is *about* the painting cannot be reduced to any physical fact about Joe's brain and central nervous system. Nor can this fact be identified with Joe's disposition or tendency to do certain things; for example, to smile and say, "How lovely that is!" after viewing the painting. If one's thinking is nothing more than his being disposed to behave in certain ways, then one would have no idea what it was that one was thinking about until that behavior was manifested!

Now intentionality is not a property or relation of anything physical because the notion of "ofness" or "aboutness" is not something that is part of the language of physics and chemistry. Physical objects can stand in various

3.5
INTENTIONALITY

---

[2]Frank Jackson, *Perception* (Cambridge: Cambridge University Press, 1977), p. 121.

physical relations with other physical objects. One physical thing can be to the left of, larger than, harder than, the same shape as, or the thing causing the motion of another physical object. But one physical thing is not *of* or *about* another one.

When one is near a podium, one can relate to it in many ways: One can be two feet from it, taller than it, and one's body can bump into it. These are all examples of physical relations one sustains to the podium. But in addition to these, one can be a conscious subject that has the podium as an object of various states of consciousness one directs toward it; one can have a thought about it, a desire for it, one can experience a sensation of it and so forth. These are all mental states and they have intentionality (ofness, aboutness) in common. In sum, at least many mental states possess intentionality; physical states do not. Thus at least many mental states are not physical states.

We will look at physicalist strategies for dealing with intentionality in the next chapter. But many of them model the intentionality of the mind along the lines of a computer. To say that a computer can think *about* arithmetic is merely to say that if the right causal inputs are fed into the computer (e.g., "2," "+," "2" "=" "enter"), then the computer will give the right output on a screen ("4"), and be ready for new input, and that is all there is to intentionality. This strategy will be assessed in chapter twelve.

4 ARGUMENTS SUPPORTING SUBSTANCE DUALISM

The arguments listed above provide grounds for preferring dualism over physicalism. They all present evidence that something is true of mental states not true of brain states and vice versa, and thus the two cannot be identical. Now it can be argued that these points count equally in favor of substance and property dualism. We will not dispute that claim. Instead, we will offer a series of arguments that, if successful, lend support to substance dualism and count against both physicalism and mere property dualism. These arguments have the following form: Some feature or ability of humans is real, and the best way to make sense of how it could be real is if substance dualism is true.

4.1
OUR BASIC
AWARENESS OF
THE SELF

When we pay attention to our own consciousness, we can become aware of a very basic fact presented to us: We are aware of our own self as being distinct from our bodies and from any particular mental experience we have. We simply have a basic, direct awareness of the fact that we are not identical to our bodies or our mental events; rather, we are the selves that *have* a body and a conscious mental life.

This point can be expanded by noting that through introspection a person is directly aware of the fact that (1) he is an immaterial center of consciousness and volition that uses his body as an instrument to interact with the material world; (2) he is the owner of his experiences and he is not identical to a bundle of mental experiences; and (3) he is an enduring self who exists as the same possessor of all his experiences through time. This direct awareness shows that a person is not identical to his or her body in whole or in part or to one's experiences, but rather is the thing that has them. In short, one is a mental substance. Physicalists and property dualists could, of course, simply deny that people are aware of these things. They would also owe us an account of why people are tricked into thinking that they are, in fact, aware of them. More will be said about this argument from awareness of the self in chapter fourteen.

The **first-person perspective** is the vantage point that one uses to describe the world from one's own point of view. Expressions of a first-person point of view utilize what are called **indexicals**—words like *I, here, now, there* and *then*. *Here* and *now* are where and when I am; *there* and *then* are where and when I am not. Indexicals refer to one's own self. *I* (and, most likely, *now*) is the most basic indexical, and it refers to one's self, which one knows by acquaintance with one's own ego in acts of self-awareness. That is, one is immediately aware of one's own self, and one knows who *I* refers to when one uses it—it refers to that very person as the owner of his or her body and mental states.

4.2
FIRST-PERSON
NOT REDUCIBLE
TO THIRD-
PERSON

According to physicalism, there are no irreducible, privileged, first-person perspectives. Everything can be exhaustively described in an object language from a **third-person perspective**. A physicalist description of Tom would say that there exists a body at a certain location that is five feet, eight inches tall, weighs 160 pounds, etc. The property dualist would add a description of the properties possessed by that body, e.g., the body is feeling pain, thinking about lunch and can remember being in Grandview, Missouri, in 1965.

But no amount of third-person descriptions capture Tom's own subjective, first-person acquaintance of his own self in acts of self-awareness. In fact, for any third-person description of Tom, it would always be an open question as to whether the person described in third-person terms was the same person as Tom is. The reason Tom knows his self is not because he knows some third-person description of a set of mental and physical properties and also knows that a certain person satisfies that description. Rather, Tom knows himself as a self immediately through being acquainted with his own self in an act of self-awareness. He can express that self-awareness by using the term *I*. Arguably, *I* refers to one's own substantial soul. It does not refer to any mental property or bundle of mental properties one is having, nor does it refer to any body described from a third-person perspective. This argument will be developed more fully in chapter fourteen.

It would seem that a person can maintain absolute sameness through change, that is, **personal identity**. More specifically, even though one's body constantly gains new parts and loses old ones, and even though one's mental states come and go in rapid succession, nevertheless, the person himself remains the same because he is a mental self that is other than his body parts and mental states. If one were merely a body or a body with mental properties, then when one's body parts or mental life changed, one would not literally be the same. As with the previous two arguments, this one will be developed more fully in chapter fourteen. All three points (our basic awareness of our self, the first- and third-person perspective and personal identity through change) focus on the relationship between dualism and personal identity.

4.3
PERSONAL
IDENTITY
THROUGH
CHANGE

4.4
FREE WILL,
MORALITY,
RESPONSIBILITY
AND
PUNISHMENT

For our purposes, when we use the term "free will" we mean what is called **libertarian freedom**: Given choices A and B, one can literally choose to do either one, no circumstances exist that are sufficient to determine one's choice; a person's choice is up to him, and if he does one of them, he could have done otherwise, or at least he could have refrained from acting at all. One acts as an agent who is the ultimate originator of one's own actions and, in this sense, is in control of one's action.

If physicalism is true, then, arguably, determinism is true as well, at least for normal-sized objects like brains or bodies. If one is just a physical system, there is nothing in him that has the capacity to choose freely to do something. Material systems, at least large-scale ones, change over time in deterministic fashion according to the initial conditions of the system and the laws of chemistry and physics. A pot of water will reach a certain temperature at a given time in a way fixed by the amount of water, the input of heat and the laws of heat transfer.

Now, when it comes to morality, if determinism is true, some argue that it is hard to make sense of moral obligation and responsibility. They seem to presuppose libertarian freedom of the will. If one "ought" to do something, it seems to be necessary to suppose that one *can* do it in the libertarian sense. No one would say that one ought to jump to the top of a fifty-floor building and save a baby, or that one ought to stop the civil war in 2002, because one does not have the ability to do either. If physicalism is true, one does not have any genuine ability to choose one's actions. It is safe to say that physicalism requires a radical revision of many people's commonsense notions of freedom, moral obligation, responsibility and punishment. On the other hand, if these commonsense notions are true, physicalism is false.

The same problem besets property dualism. There are two ways for property dualists to handle human actions. First, some property dualists are epiphenomenalists. According to **epiphenomenalism**, when matter reaches a certain organizational complexity and structure, as is the case with the human brain, then matter "produces" mental states like fire produces smoke, or the structure of hydrogen and oxygen in water "produces" wetness. The mind is to the body as smoke is to fire. Smoke is different from fire (to keep the analogy going, some physicalists would identify the smoke with the fire or the functioning of the fire), but fire causes smoke, not vice versa. Mental states are byproducts of the brain, but they are causally impotent. Mental states merely "ride" on top of the events in the brain. It should be obvious that epiphenomenalism denies free will, since it denies that mental states cause anything.

A second way that property dualists handle human action is through a notion called **event-event causation** (also called state-state causation). To understand event-event causation, consider a brick that breaks a glass. The cause in this case is not the brick itself (which is a substance), but the brick's being in a certain state, namely, a state of motion. The effect is the glass being in a certain state, namely the breaking of the glass. Thus one state or event—the moving of a brick—causes another event to occur—the breaking of the glass. When one billiard ball causes another one to move, it is the moving of the first ball that causes the moving of the second ball. In general, then, event-event causation involves a state of one thing existing as an efficient cause that is prior to an effect, which is the production of a state in another thing. Moreover, in event-event causation, when one event causes another event, there is some law of nature that connects the two events such that given the causal event and the law of nature, the effect inevitably follows.

In contrast, **agent causation** is required for many versions of libertarian freedom of the will, and it is the view of causation embraced by a number of substance dualists. An example of agent causation is a typical case of a human action—one's raising of his arm. When one raises his arm, the agent, as a substance, simply acts by spontaneously exercising his active causal powers. The agent raises his arm; he freely and spontaneously exercises the powers within his substantial soul and simply acts. No set of conditions exist within the agent that are sufficient to determine or fix the chances that the agent raises his arm.

In agent causation, substances are the cause; in event-event causation, a state within a substance is the cause. According to event-event causation, when one raises one's arm, there is some state within one that causally necessitates or determines that the arm goes up; for example, a state of desiring that one's arm go up or a state of willing that one's arm go up.

Unfortunately for property dualists, event-event causation is inconsistent with agent causation. Why? For one thing, there is no room for an agent, an ego, an *I* to intervene and contribute to his actions. The agent does not produce the action of raising his arm; rather, a state of desiring to raise the arm is sufficient to produce this effect. There is no room for one's own self, as opposed to the mental states within one, to act.

For another thing, all the mental states within a person (his states of desiring, willing, hoping) are states caused by temporally prior mental and physical states according to laws of nature. As far as action is concerned, the "I" becomes a stream of states/events in a causal chain, a passive theater through which chains of events run on their way to bodily movements as outputs. Each member of the chain causes the next member to occur. Further, each mental state emerges on and is determined by the brain states that produce it. In either case—temporal sequences of events related by natural laws and bottom-up deterministic emergence—agent causation seems to be ruled out.

In sum, property dualism denies agent causal forms of libertarian freedom because it adopts either epiphenomenalism or event-event causation. Thus property dualism, no less than physicalism, is false, given the truth of agent causation and commonsense notions of moral ability, moral responsibility and punishment. The strength of this argument depends, among other things, on whether or not we are morally responsible in the ordinary sense and on whether or not agent causation is necessary to account for such responsibility. Human freedom will be analyzed in more detail in chapter thirteen.

A number of philosophers have argued that physicalism and property dualism must be false because they imply determinism and determinism is self-refuting. For example, H. P. Owen states that

> determinism is self-stultifying. If my mental processes are totally determined, I am totally determined either to accept or to reject determinism. But if the sole reason for my believing or not believing X is that I am causally determined to believe it I have no ground for holding that my judgment is true or false.[3]

4.5 PHYSICALISM AND PROPERTY DUALISM ARE SELF-REFUTING

---

[3]H. P. Owen, *Christian Theism* (Edinburgh: T & T Clark, 1984), p. 118.

Why are physicalism and property dualism thought by many philosophers to be self-refuting? The simple answer is that they undercut the necessary preconditions for rationality itself to be possible. In other words, they make rationality itself impossible. If someone claims to know that physicalism or property dualism are true, or to embrace them for good reasons, if one claims that they choose to believe in them because of good reasons, then these claims are self-refuting. At least three factors must be assumed if there are to be genuine rational agents who exhibit rationality. All three are ruled out by strict physicalism; only the last two are inconsistent with property dualism.

First, humans must have certain mental features true of them. They must have genuine *intentionality*, they must be capable of having *thoughts* and *propositions* in their minds, they must be capable of having *awarenesses of* the things they claim to know as well as of the contents of their own minds. But intentionality, thoughts and propositions, and awarenesses are mental notions, not physical ones. Physicalists respond to this problem in various ways and we will look at some of them in the next chapter.

Second, in order to rationally think through a chain of reasoning such that one sees the inferential connections in the chain, one would have to be the same self present at the beginning of the thought process as the one present at the end. As Immanuel Kant argued long ago, the process of thought requires a genuine enduring "I." If there is one self who reflects on premise (1), namely, "If P, then Q," a second self who reflects on premise (2), namely, P, and a third self who reflects on the concluding statement (3), namely, Q, then there is literally no enduring self who thinks *through* the argument and *draws* the conclusion. As H. D. Lewis noted, "one things seems certain, namely that there must be someone or something at the centre of such experience to hold the terms and relations together in one stream of consciousness."[4] Moreover, this "I" must be (at least) an essentially thinking and reasoning and conscious, that is, a mental "I." But we have already seen that at least most versions of physicalism and property dualism deny a literal, enduring "I," and substitute for it a series of selves. Thus they are at odds with this necessary condition for rationality.

Finally, rationality seems to presuppose an agent view of the self and genuine libertarian freedom of the will. There are rational "oughts." That is, given certain evidence, one "ought" to believe certain things. One is intellectually responsible for drawing certain conclusions, given certain pieces of evidence. If one does not draw that conclusion, one is irrational. But *ought* implies *can*. If one ought to believe something, then one must have the ability to choose to believe it or not to believe it. If one is to be rational, one must be free to choose his beliefs for the sake of certain reasons.

In a certain sense, we are not free to choose our beliefs. Right now you are not free to choose to believe that fifty pink elephants are in your living room even if you wanted to believe it, say because someone offered you a large sum of money to embrace that belief. However, you are free to do certain things, for instance, to choose to investigate certain pieces of evidence, to think about certain things, and in a number of cases you will find yourself believing certain

---

[4]H. D. Lewis, *The Self and Immortality* (New York: Seabury, 1973), p. 34.

conclusions because you freely thought about certain kinds of evidence that lead to that belief. Often, one deliberates about what one is going to believe or one deliberates about the evidence for something. But such deliberations make sense only if one assumes that at some point, what one is going to do or believe is up to that person, that one is free to choose and thus responsible for irrationality if one chooses inappropriately.

But we have already seen that physicalism and property dualism seem not to be at home with an agent causal view of libertarian freedom. In sum, physicalism and property dualism seem to rule out the possibility of rationality. It is self-refuting to *argue* that one *ought* to *choose* physicalism or property dualism on the *basis* of the fact that one *should see* that the *evidence* is *good* for physicalism or property dualism. None of the words just emphasized appears to express physical notions.

5 ARGUMENTS AGAINST DUALISM

A number of arguments have been raised against dualism. We will list three of them and offer brief responses.

1. Objection: Physicalists claim that on a dualist construal of a human being, mind and body are so different that it seems impossible to explain how and where the two different entities interact. How could a soul, totally lacking in any physical properties, cause things to happen to the body or vice versa? How can the soul move the arm? How can a pin-stick in the finger cause pain in the soul?

5.1
THE PROBLEM
OF INTERACTION

2. Response: This objection assumes that if we do not know *how* A causes B, then it is not reasonable to believe *that* A causes B, especially if A and B are different. But this assumption is not a good one. We often know that one thing causes another without having any idea of how causation takes place, even when the two items are different. Even if one is not a theist, it is not inconceivable to believe it possible for God, if he exists, to create the world or to act in that world, even though God and the material universe are very different. A magnetic field can move a tack, gravity can act on a planet millions of miles away, protons exert a repulsive force on each other and so forth. In these examples, we know *that* one thing can causally interact with another thing, even though we may have no idea *how* such interaction takes place. Further, in each case the cause would seem to have a different nature from the effect—forces and fields versus solid, spatially located, particle-like entities.

In the case of mind and body, we are constantly aware of causation between them. Episodes in the body or brain (being stuck with a pin, having a head injury) can cause things in the soul (a feeling of pain, loss of memory), and the soul can cause things to happen in the body (worry can cause ulcers, one can freely and intentionally raise his arm). We have such overwhelming evidence *that* causal interaction takes place, that there is no sufficient reason to doubt it.

Furthermore, it may even be that a "how" question regarding the interaction between mind and body cannot even arise. A question about how A causally interacts with *B* is a request for an intervening mechanism between *A* and *B* that can be described. One can ask how turning the key starts a car because there is an intermediate electrical system between the key and the car's running engine that is the means by which turning the key causes the engine to start. The "how" question is a request to describe that intermediate mechanism. But the interaction between mind and body may, and most likely is, direct and immediate. There *is* no intervening mechanism, and thus a "how" question describing that mechanism does not even arise.

5.2
DUALISM IS
INCONSISTENT
WITH
NATURALISTIC
EVOLUTIONARY
THEORY

1. Objection: It is well known that one of the driving forces behind physicalism is evolutionary theory. Evolutionist Paul Churchland makes this claim:

> The important point about the standard evolutionary story is that the human species and all of its features are the wholly physical outcome of a purely physical process. . . . If this is the correct account of our origins, then there seems neither need, nor room, to fit any nonphysical substances or properties into our theoretical account of ourselves. We are creatures of matter. And we should learn to live with that fact.[5]

In other words, this objection claims the following: Since humans are merely the result of an entirely physical process (the processes of evolutionary theory) working on wholly physical materials, then humans are wholly physical beings.

2. Response: Dualists could point out that this objection is clearly question-begging. To see this, note that the objection can be put into the logical form known as *modus ponens* (see chap. 2): If humans are merely the result of naturalistic, evolutionary processes, then physicalism is true. Humans are merely the result of naturalistic, evolutionary processes. Therefore, physicalism is true.

However, the dualist could adopt the *modus tollens* form of the argument: If humans are merely the result of naturalistic, evolutionary processes, then physicalism is true. But physicalism is not true. Therefore, it is not the case that humans are merely the result of naturalistic, evolutionary processes. In other words, the evolutionary argument begs the question against the dualist. If the evidence for dualism is good, then the *modus tollens* form of the argument should be embraced, not the *modus ponens* form.

5.3
DUALISM IS
RULED OUT BY
OCKHAM'S
RAZOR

1. Objection: **Ockham's razor** states that people should not multiply entities beyond what is needed to explain something. Given two explanations of the same thing, people should prefer the one that is simpler, that is, the one that uses the fewest number of entities or kinds of entities to explain the thing in question. Now physicalism is simpler than dualism because it postulates only one type of entity (matter) to explain a human being instead of two (matter and mind). Thus in keeping with the requirements of Ockham's razor, physicalism is preferred to dualism.

2. Response: There are two main problems with the application of Ockham's razor to the mind-body problem. First, if Ockham's razor is understood to be the

---

[5]Paul Churchland, *Matter and Consciousness* (Cambridge, Mass.: MIT Press, 1984), p. 21.

fairly obvious, commonsense principle that an explanation of a phenomenon should include only elements within it necessary to explain that phenomenon, then the principle is uncontroversial. But it becomes question-begging when applied to the debate about dualism. Why? Because the dualist cites several phenomena for which physicalism as a theory is inadequate.

Dualists can agree that one should not postulate dualism needlessly, but they insist that dualism is, in fact, needed to explain honestly and fairly, important, uneliminable features of human beings. The real debate, then, is not about Ockham's razor, but about the relative merits of dualism versus physicalism. Furthermore, if Ockham's razor is used to place a burden of proof on the dualist, the following can be pointed out. In light of both first-person awareness of one's own self and the self-presenting nature of my mental states—one's knowledge of them is often incorrigible and one has private access to them, neither of which is true for physical states—one is more certain that one has a soul than that one has a body. So the burden of proof may very well be on the physicalist.

We have looked at the mind-body problem and surveyed arguments for substance and property dualism versus physicalism and for substance dualism versus property dualism and physicalism. In the next chapter we will state and assess different versions of physicalism.

CHAPTER SUMMARY

The mind-body problem involves two main issues: Is a human being composed of one or at least two different components? If two, how do mind and matter interact? We saw that physicalism and dualism are two main rivals and that substance and property dualism are two different versions of a dualist solution to the mind-body problem. We also clarified what a physical entity is and what a mental entity is (e.g., sensations, propositional attitudes and purposings).

Next, the chapter surveyed several arguments that seek to show that some form of dualism is superior to physicalism: the distinctiveness of mental and physical properties and states, the nature of self-presenting properties and their relationship to private access and incorrigibility, the subjective nature of experience and the knowledge argument, the existence of secondary qualities and the fact of intentionality. These different arguments fit a pattern of showing that something is true of mental entities not true of physical ones or vice versa, and thus they are not identical.

In the third section, arguments were offered to support substance dualism versus physicalism and property dualism. These arguments sought to show that there is some feature or ability that humans have that seems to presuppose substance dualism: our basic awareness of the self, the fact that the first-person perspective cannot be reduced to the third-person perspective, personal identity and absolute sameness of persons through change, libertarian freedom, moral responsibility and punishment, and the self-refuting nature of physicalism and property dualism.

Finally, we looked at three objections frequently raised against dualism: the problem of interaction between mind and body, the difficulty in harmonizing dualism with naturalistic evolutionary theory, and Ockham's razor.

CHECKLIST OF BASIC TERMS AND CONCEPTS

agent causation
dualism
epiphenomenalism
event-event (or state-state) causation
first-person perspective
incorrigible
intentionality
knowledge argument
libertarian freedom
materialism
mental entity
mind-body problem
Ockham's razor
personal identity
physicalism
physical property
primary quality
private access
property (or property-event) dualism
propositional attitude
purposing
secondary quality
self-presenting property
sensation
substance dualism
third-person perspective
unity of science

12

THE MIND-BODY PROBLEM
Alternatives to Dualism

*The growth in influence and the popularisation of
physical science has made the problem [of the mind] more urgent.
The idea that science captures everything,
except the centre of everyone's universe,
his own consciousness, makes a laughing-stock of its claim
to present a plausible world view. . . .
If science cannot encompass the subjective
then subjectivity becomes a door through which mystical,
irrational and religious notions can enter and reassert themselves
against the modern metaphysic of scientific realism.*
HOWARD ROBINSON, *MATTER AND SENSE*

*Seen from the perspective of the last fifty years,
the philosophy of mind, as well as cognitive science and certain
branches of psychology, present a curious spectacle.
The most striking feature is how much of mainstream philosophy
of mind of the past fifty years seems obviously false.*
JOHN SEARLE, *THE REDISCOVERY OF THE MIND*

1 INTRODUCTION

In the last chapter, we began our investigation of the mind-body problem by examining the position known as dualism. In this chapter, we will look at the major rival to dualism—physicalism. At the beginning of chapter eleven we defined physicalism as the view that all entities whatsoever are merely physical entities. Here a "physical entity" means one that can be completely described using the language of the hard sciences, especially chemistry and physics. In the last section of this chapter, we will look at why this understanding of *physical* is the most reasonable one for modern physicalists to take. Until then, this sense of the term will be utilized without further comment.

Applied to the mind-body problem, a physicalist believes that a human being is merely a physical entity. But not all physicalists are agreed as to how physicalism should be spelled out. Figure 12.1 depicts the major contemporary forms of physicalism.

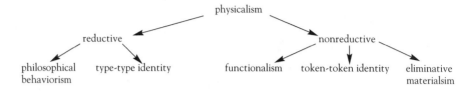

Fig. 12.1 Varieties of reductive and nonreductive physicalism

The chart shows two main physicalist strategies with different varieties of each: reductive and nonreductive physicalism. (The last section of chapter thirteen discusses the nature of reductionism and it would be a good idea to read that section before proceeding.) In the context of the mind-body problem, reductive and nonreductive physicalism mean something fairly specific. To understand these approaches to philosophy of mind, consider any type of mental state—a pain type state, an awareness of red, a thought that $2 + 2 = 4$. Each of these mental states is a repeatable type of state. One person can be in that very same type of state on different occasions and many people can be in the same type of state at the same time. Now according to **reductive physicalism**, it is possible to provide general, reductive, nonmentalistic necessary and sufficient conditions for any mental type of state. For example, it would be possible to state a set of necessary and sufficient conditions in physical terms for any and all instances of being in a painful type of state. Philosophical behaviorism and type-type identity theory are different ways of spelling out what these conditions are.

By contrast, **nonreductive physicalism** does not believe that such a general set of necessary and sufficient conditions exist or are necessary in order to provide physicalist treatments of mental entities. Nonreductive physicalists agree that everything about a human being—all of his or her parts, properties and states, are merely physical. But they do not believe that it is possible or necessary to state general conditions for ascribing a mental state to a human being. Thus nonreductive physicalists would not offer general conditions in physical terms for ascribing a pain type state to a human being. Token-token identity theory, functionalism and eliminative materialism are the three main versions of nonreductive materialism.

Functionalism was just characterized as a form of nonreductive physicalism. But this claim is not entirely accurate, and philosophers disagree about whether functionalism is a version of nonreductive physicalism. The disagreement turns on different understandings of reduction. As we have used the term, reduction requires that one provide a set of necessary and sufficient conditions for every mental type (e.g., being a pain) in terms of a uniform set of physical conditions. As we shall see later, this has proven impossible because of the problem of multiple realization. Roughly, this problem turns on the fact that creatures with radically different brain and physical types of states—humans, Vulcans, dogs, turtles—can all be in the same type of mental state, say, being in pain. Thus there is no uniform set of necessary and sufficient physical conditions to which a pain type state could be reduced.

However, there is a different sort of reduction to which physicalist versions of functionalism subscribe. This reduction is accomplished in two steps. Step 1: Functionalize the mental property. For example, the mental property of being in pain is identified with a property of having some physical property or other that plays the right role in the organism—for example, by being that physical property that is caused by pin pricks, toothaches, etc.—and which causes the organism to grimace and desire relief. Step 2: Identify the property that plays the correct role mentioned in step 1 with a physical property. Step 2 requires that the only properties that realize functional roles are physical properties. This is similar to requiring that only some sort of physical hardware can be the realizer of functional roles specified in computer software. In this way, the functionalist requires that each time a human, Vulcan, dog or turtle is in pain, that particular pain event must be taken as identical to a physical event in the brain and nervous system. Thus pain is reduced to/identified with some physical event or other, even though it remains impossible to state necessary and sufficient conditions for the type of brain event to which the type of mental state is reduced. Moreover, what makes the individual physical event a pain event is not the physical event's intrinsic features. Rather, it is a pain event because it plays the right role in the organism.

Several reasons have been offered for physicalism. Some of these are philosophical in nature. In fact, chapter eleven included two of them: the problem of interaction in a dualist view of a human being and the application of Ockham's razor to the mind-body problem to support the claim that physicalism is the preferred, simpler view. However, it is safe to say that the primary, most important set of arguments for physicalism in the current debate derive from science. John Searle, one of the leading philosophers of mind in the twentieth century, has made the following observation:

> Acceptance of the current [physicalist] views is motivated not so much by an independent conviction of their truth as by a terror of what are apparently the only alternatives. That is, the choice we are tacitly presented with is between a "scientific" approach, as represented by one or another of the current versions of "materialism," and an "unscientific" approach, as represented by Cartesianism or some other traditional religious conception of the mind.[1]

In other words, the main intellectual drive that underlies physicalism is not primarily philosophical arguments against dualism and in favor of physicalism, but what are taken to be the implications of a scientific, naturalistic worldview. Given that this is the case, for many physicalists, the main place that philosophy enters into the picture is in stating and defending plausible versions of physicalism. With this in mind, our primary concern in this chapter will be to state and evaluate these different versions of physicalism. This will be done in the section to follow. The chapter will conclude with a survey of some of the main arguments for physicalism and some final remarks about the primary intellectual impetus behind physicalism.

---

[1]John Searle, *Rediscovering the Mind* (Cambridge, Mass.: MIT Press, 1992), pp. 3-4.

2 DIFFERENT FORMS OF PHYSICALISM

Behaviorism is a term usually associated with the psychologists J. B. Watson and B. F. Skinner. Currently, there are two main forms of behaviorism: methodological behaviorism and philosophical behaviorism. **Methodological behaviorism** is the view that in doing psychology from an empirical standpoint, one should describe, report and explain mental states in terms of publicly observable behaviors and not in terms of private, first-person, inner conscious states. As a research strategy in psychology, methodological behaviorism implies that psychologists should limit their focus to the stimulus inputs and behavioral outputs of organisms and make no reference to introspective private mental states. Methodological behaviorism makes no commitment either way about the existence of the mental.

Philosophical behaviorism does make such a commitment: Mental states are identified with overt bodily behavior or tendencies to certain behaviors, given certain stimulus inputs. Actually, philosophical behaviorism places greater emphasis on the nature of mental *terms* than on the corresponding mental states themselves. Mental terms are given **operational definitions** (definitions of something solely in terms of what can be empirically tested or measured by certain tests or operations) such that mental terms *mean* public behavior or dispositions to such behavior. On this view, when we say that salt is soluble, we do not attribute some occult, unobservable entity, solubility, to salt. Rather, we simply mean that if salt is put in water it will dissolve, and this statement refers only to publicly observable behaviors of salt. Similarly, to say that Jones is in pain is simply to say that, given certain inputs (e.g., being stuck with a pin), Jones has the tendency to wince and shout "Ouch!" To say that Jones wants to go to Europe is to say merely that Jones is disposed to browse brochures about Europe, to talk about European cathedrals, to call a travel agent about European airfares and so on.

Today, philosophical behaviorism has fallen on hard times because of the strength of the objections that have been raised against it. First, a mental state like being in pain cannot be identical to certain bodily behaviors or tendencies to behave because one can be in pain without wincing, shouting or engaging in any bodily behavior, and one can exemplify such behavior and fake being in pain even though such a mental state is not present. Since you can have pain without pain behavior or tendencies to behave and vice versa, the two cannot be identical.

A closely related objection is this. By identifying pain, for example, with pain behavior, philosophical behaviorists leave out the fact that pain is what *causes* such behavior and thus cannot be identical to that behavior. Third, pain is essentially characterized by a certain type of hurtful feeling that can be directly known by acquaintance with our own inner, private, first-person subjective states of sentience, but bodily behaviors do not have this feature, so they cannot be the same thing. In short, pains hurt, but pain behavior doesn't.

Fourth, definitions of mental states in terms of a set of conditionals become unruly and indefinitely long such that they could never be learned. For example, according to philosophical behaviorism "Jones wants to go to Europe" means that "If Jones gets travel brochures, he will get European ones, if Jones gets the money, he will buy an airplane ticket to Europe and not a new horse and so on." It should be obvious that there is a potentially infinite set of further conditionals that could be added to this list.

Moreover, the conditionals that make up the behaviorist definition make sense only if we fill them out by adding terms that make reference to inner mental states. For example, Jones will get a travel brochure only if he *believes* that such a brochure will inform him about Europe. He will buy a ticket and not a horse only if he *thinks* that he cannot buy both and he *desires* to travel more than to have a horse. Thus behaviorist definitions of mental terms are circular since, in order to be complete, they must implicitly utilize other mental terms.

Sixth, if one's thinking something merely consists in being disposed to behave in certain ways given certain sensory inputs, then one would have no idea what it was he was thinking about until the behavioral disposition was manifested through his body. But surely one knows what she is thinking about before she acts and she knows her own thoughts, not by observing her own bodily actions, but through direct introspective awareness of her own states of consciousness.

Finally, two further criticisms have been raised against philosophical behaviorism. Since many philosophers believe that these criticisms apply equally to all forms of physicalism, they will be mentioned here and not repeated in detail later. But you should remember that, if successful, they apply to the other forms of physicalism listed below. For one thing, philosophical behaviorism seems to imply some form of determinism and a denial of libertarian freedom of the will. We will probe questions of freedom and determinism in the next chapter, but for those who think that libertarian freedom is true and determinism is false, this will count against philosophical behaviorism.

Secondly, philosophical behaviorism (along with other versions of physicalism) seems to imply a denial of a unified self at a point in time and an enduring self that remains literally the same through change. This point will be developed more fully in chapter fourteen, but for now it should be noted that if physicalism does, in fact, imply a denial of a unified and enduring self and if there is good reason to believe in such a self, then this raises a difficulty for physicalism in any form. These last two points illustrate the fact that many philosophers have seen an intimate connection between philosophy of mind and the dualist-physicalist debate, on the one hand, and issues in freedom and determinism and in personal identity, on the other.

In order to understand the **type-type identity theory,** it is important to be clear about the difference between a type and a token (see chap. 10). A **type** is a general kind of thing that can be in more than one place at the same time or at the same place at different, interrupted times. When pain is considered as a type, it is being viewed as a general kind of state that can be in different organisms at the same time or the same organism at different times. By contrast, a **token** is an individual, particular instance of a type. A pain token is a specific instance of the general kind of state known as a pain type state.

Advocates of the type-type identity theory claim that each type of mental state (e.g., a pain type state or a type of state in which one is thinking that $2 + 2 = 4$) is identical to (the very same thing as) a certain brain type state, say

2.2
TYPE-TYPE
IDENTITY
THEORY
(HARDWARE
VIEW #1)

a certain pattern of neurons firing. This position is therefore called a **hardware view** because types of mental states are identical to types of physical stuff or "hardware" in the brain and central nervous system.

Second, advocates of this view claim that the identity between a type of mental and physical state is a contingent identity (see chap. 9). In philosophical behaviorism, the term *pain* is identical to some term expressing a tendency to engage in some overt behavior, and the identity is analytic or true in virtue of the meaning of the terms used in the identity statement. By contrast, a contingent identity statement is one that uses two terms with different meanings but which, nevertheless, refer to the same thing as a contingent fact. For example, in the statement "The Evening Star is identical to the Morning Star" or "Heat is identical to the motion of molecules," the terms in the statements do not mean the same thing but they do (allegedly) refer to the same thing. The Evening Star could have turned out to have been a different planet than the Morning Star, but as a contingent matter of fact, an empirical discovery showed that the two terms "the Evening Star" and "the Morning Star" refer to the same thing: Venus.

In the same way, terms referring to mental states do not mean the same thing as terms referring to brain states, but as a contingent matter of fact, scientific discoveries (allegedly) have shown that both terms refer to the same thing: a neurophysiological state in the brain and central nervous system. The term *pain* refers to whatever it is in an organism that causes pain behavior and as a matter of empirical contingent fact, we now know that it is a brain state that *pain* refers to according to this position. U. T. Place, Herbert Feigl and J. J. C. Smart are philosophers who have been advocates of the type-type identity thesis.

As with philosophical behaviorism, a number of severe criticisms have been raised against the type-type identity theory. First, types of brain states and types of mental states seem to have very different properties, and therefore, they cannot be identical to each other. In this regard, Roderick Chisholm has made the following observation:

> Let us consider some particular psychophysical identity statement—the statement, say, that thinking about unicorns is the same thing as to have Q fibres that vibrate in manner N. One cannot *understand* such a statement, of course, unless one can grasp or conceive the property or properties that are referred to. . . . To the extent that we can understand the statement in question, we can *see* that the two properties referred to are not the same property—just as we can see that the property of believing that all men are mortal is different from that of wondering whether there is life in outer space. It has been held, not implausibly, that to deny the validity of such rational insights is to undermine the possibility of every type of reasoning.[2]

In chapter eleven we looked at some of the differences between mental states and physical states. Mental states are essentially characterized by their first-person, private, inner, subjective qualities (e.g., a pain is essentially characterized by its felt quality, an awareness of red by its being a subjective mode of

---

[2]Roderick Chisholm, "Mind," in *Handbook of Metaphysics and Ontology*, ed. Hans Burkhardt and Barry Smith (Munich: Philosophia Verlag, 1991), 2:556.

experience, a thought by its internal content that can stand in logical relations to other thoughts), by intentionality and so forth. By contrast, brain states do not have such characteristics, but rather possess various physical and chemical properties. Thus they cannot be identical.

As a further elaboration of this point, Saul Kripke has pointed out that pains, for example, do not merely happen to be characterized by their subjective, conscious felt quality, but they have this felt quality as part of their very essence. In every possible world, something will count as a pain if and only if it possesses this very type of felt quality. But no brain state or bodily behavior has this felt quality as part of its very essence. Moreover, even if life after death is false, surely it is possible. In fact, it is possible for a disembodied person to exist and to think, have certain feelings, beliefs, desires and so forth. But it hardly makes sense to speak of a brain state that could exist in a disembodied, immaterial mode of existence. Thus mental states and brain states cannot be the same thing.

A second criticism is sometimes called the problem of **multiple realization**. Take an alleged mental state like a pain type state and call this type of state MS_1. According to the type-type identity theory, this type of state is identical to a certain type of brain and central nervous state, BS_1, in the human body. But now a problem arises. Presumably dogs, Martians and a host of other creatures can be in pain, that is, can be in the type of state we have called MS_1. But these creatures cannot be in BS_1 because they have different hardware states composed of different patterns of physical stuff. Suppose a Martian was not composed of carbon-based chemicals but rather other physical components. Then the Martian could be in certain kinds of brain states, say BS_2, but not BS_1, which makes reference to materials constituting humans when they are in pain but which are not part of the Martian constitution. But since a pain type state, MS_1, is identical to (is nothing more or less than) BS_1, and since Martians cannot be in BS_1, then it becomes impossible for Martians (or dogs and other creatures) to be in pain.

Something has gone wrong here and the dualist has a solution to the problem. For the dualist, Martians can be in pain like humans even though they each have different types of brain states, because pains are not identical to brain states but to states essentially characterized by their conscious felt quality. Functionalism and the token-token identity theory are two physicalist responses to this problem, which we will look at below.

A third problem with the type-type identity thesis is this: Science cannot demonstrate that we should prefer the view that types of brain states are identical to types of mental states as opposed to the view that the two states are merely correlated with each other or enter into cause-effect relations with each other even though the two types of states are nonidentical. These two views—mental and brain type states are identical versus mental and brain type states are different yet correlated—are empirically equivalent. Each view is consistent with the same set of scientific observations. In light of the problems with the type-type identity view, the correlation option should be preferred. Moreover, in order to establish such correlations, the scientist must rely on first-person reports as to what is going on in the private, first-person inner conscious life of the person being studied, but the scientist does not have to rely on such reports to know something about the brain or, indeed, about any physical state whatsoever.

2.3
TOKEN-TOKEN
IDENTITY
THEORY
(HARDWARE
VIEW #2)

In order to understand the **token-token identity theory,** recall the problem of multiple realization. Martians, for example, could be in pain even though they could not be in a type of brain state possible for humans. The dualist solution to this problem was noted above. But advocates of the identity thesis have a response to it as well: rather than abandon the identity thesis per se, one should modify the type-type identity thesis and embrace the token-token identity thesis.

According to the token-token identity theory, there is no set of general conditions that can be given for identifying a *general kind* of mental state with a *general kind* of brain state. Since we have taken reductive physicalism to require that general conditions be stated for identifying mental states with physical states, then the token-token view is not reductive in this sense. But in another sense, the view *is* reductive. While advocates of the view reject the identification of mental state types and physical state types, they nevertheless accept the fact that for any specific instance of a mental state, that very state will, in fact, be identical to (and in this sense reducible to) some specific instance of a physical state. Individual mental state tokens are always identical to individual physical state tokens even if no general conditions can be stated for identifying mental state types with physical state types.

For example, even though the general mental state called a pain type state cannot be identified with a general brain state type—Martians, humans and dogs can all be in that mental state type while being in very different brain state types—it is still true that for any specific pain a human (Martian, dog) undergoes, that individual pain will be identical to a specific, individual brain state. Every token of a mental state is identical to a token of a brain state even though no identity can be stated between types of mental and brain states. A contemporary advocate of token-token identity theory is Cynthia Macdonald.

The token-token identity theory does appear to solve at least part of the problem surfaced in the example of Martian pain. A general type of mental state known as being in pain is not identical to a general brain type state, say BS_1 present in humans. Thus Martians, dogs and humans could all be in different types of brain states and still be in the type of state we would call a pain type state. This could be true even though each individual instance of pain is identical to a specific brain state token in the Martian, human or dog.

In spite of this, however, the token-token identity theory has been subjected to several criticisms. Apart from the problem of multiple realization, all the criticisms raised against the type-type identity thesis apply to the token-token identity thesis: (1) For any specific pain, that very pain has properties not true of any brain state, including the one instanced alongside the pain token. (2) It is possible that the very mental state in question (a specific pain, thought, etc.) could have obtained in a disembodied state, but the same is not true of any individual physical state. (3) There is the problem of justifying the preference of identity over correlation.

However, there is a further problem with the token-token thesis that is unique to it: What is it that gives unity to the class of all individual pains? What is it about all pain tokens that places them in the class of pains and not in, say, the class of smells, feelings of love or some other class? The dualist would say that all pain tokens are members of the type known as pain because each individual pain possesses something in common that is the essence of each pain: a specific type of conscious feeling. But obviously, this move is not available to the token-token identity theorist.

If two people are in the same kind of mental state (e.g., each is in pain) but are in different neurophysiological states, then what is it about those different neurophysiological states that makes them each a token of the same mental state? We have seen that it cannot be the possession of the same felt quality. Neither can it be the possession of the same neurophysiological features because these are different in the case we are considering.

Some advocates of token identity physicalism combine this view of individual mental events with a functionalist view of kinds of mental events. Functionalism will be described shortly. But for now, the idea is, roughly, that a mental kind, such as a pain type event, is a type of function characterized by certain inputs (e.g., being stuck with a pin) and certain outputs (e.g., shouting "Ouch!" and feeling self-pity). The only events that are allowed to play the functional role are individual brain events.

Unfortunately, this move does not solve adequately the problem of the unity of mental kinds. Why? Because the essence of an individual state must be constituted by the features intrinsic to it (its internal felt quality or its internal physical features) and not by the external relations it sustains to other things (its being caused by a pin prick and its causing certain behavior). Something (like a pain) cannot be related to something else (behavior) unless it first exists and has certain characteristics internal to it (the felt quality that makes up its inner nature). Moreover, the connection between an internal mental state and bodily inputs and outputs is contingent. Surely God could have created Martians such that after they are stuck with a pin and before they grimace and say "Ouch!" they experience not pain but a mental state of pleasure. The problem of the unity of mental state tokens within a mental state type is a serious problem for the token-token identity thesis. Thus it is more reasonable to hold that all pain events are members of the kind "being a pain" due to a feature intrinsic to each event—its hurtfulness—rather than being due to features such as functional roles that are extrinsic to each event in the kind.

Our final remarks about the token-token identity thesis provides a good transition into a very popular modern version of physicalism known as **functionalism**. There are different forms of functionalism, but they all have in common the fact that they model mental states along these lines: mental states are functional states of organisms. A popular version of functionalism is an expression of what is called **strong artificial intelligence** models of the mental: The mind is fundamentally a computer program. We can describe computers according to their hardware or software. When we describe hardware, we make reference to the physical stuff or components that make up a computer. This is similar to what advocates of both forms of the identity thesis do when describing mental states. We can also use an analogy to a computer with a **software view** by mak-

2.4
FUNCTIONALISM
(THE SOFTWARE
VIEW)

ing reference to the different inputs, outputs and other features of the program that the computer uses to operate. This is analogous to what some advocates of functionalism do with mental states.

For the functionalist, a mental state can be exhaustively described in terms of sensory inputs, behavioral outputs and other "internal" states. The essential feature of any type of mental state is the set of causal relations it bears to environmental inputs on the body, other types of "mental" states related to the state in question, and outputs understood as bodily behaviors. For example, the mental state of being in pain could be defined as that state which plays the following functional role which we can call causal role R: The state is caused by certain tissue damage as a result of a pin prick or some other input and that, in turn, causes the person to feel self-pity, to desire help and empathy, and to shout "Ouch!" while grimacing and seeking help. An organism is in pain if and only if it is in a state characterized by causal role R according to functionalism. Strictly speaking, functionalism is consistent with dualism because it could be claimed that the state which fulfills causal role R (e.g., the state that is caused by a pin prick, that causes feelings of self-pity and a desire for help, and that causes one to shout "Ouch!") is an irreducibly mental state internally characterized by the conscious feel essential to a pain. But most functionalists are physicalists and they claim that the states that happen to fulfill causal role R are neurophysiological states of the brain.

Note carefully that the defining traits of a mental state—pains, thoughts or otherwise—are not the internal, private, conscious qualities of the states themselves known through first-person introspective awareness. Rather, the defining traits of a mental state are the causal relations that obtain among certain bodily inputs, certain bodily outputs and other "mental" states. It should be clear why one way to spell out functionalism is an artificial intelligence approach to the mental. For a computer to be able to "read mathematics and be able to add," the computer must be able to receive certain input ("2," "+," "2," "="), produce certain outputs ("4" is printed on a screen), and advance to certain other internal states (it is ready to print "8" if you input the command to multiply the new total by 2). Functionalism is very similar to philosophical behaviorism, but whereas the behaviorist sought to define a mental state solely in terms of publicly observable inputs and bodily outputs, the functionalist makes reference to whatever it is within the organism that is caused by the inputs and causes the outputs, and the functionalist also makes reference to other "mental" states that are causally connected to the state in question (e.g., a pain state is one that causes, among other things, a feeling of self-pity and a desire for help).

For the functionalist, mental terms like *pain* get their meaning primarily from the role the term *pain* plays in a third-person theory used to describe and explain the behavior of others. Thus we use the term *pain* as part of our theory of why others shout "Ouch!" after they are stuck with a pin. We attribute certain states to others to explain their behavior, among other things. David Lewis and Hilary Putnam are two prominent functionalists.

As with the other physicalist theories, a number of substantive criticisms have been raised against functionalism. The first objection centers on the fact that functionalists make the defining characteristics of a mental state the causal relations of input and output to the organism and not the internal traits of the state itself known directly through introspective awareness.

A standard way to illustrate this first objection is through what is called the problem of **inverted qualia** (*qualia* is plural for *quale*, which means a specific experiential quality—for example, what it is like to experience redness or blueness). Consider two people, Jones and Smith, who both come into a room, scan it with their eyes, sort the red objects from all the rest, and point to the red objects and say, "The red ones are over here." According to functionalism, Jones and Smith are both in the very same mental state, namely, the state of being aware of redness.

However, it is metaphysically possible that Smith is color normal but Jones has an inverted color awareness: Jones has an awareness of blue every time Smith and everyone else senses red and vice versa. In this case, Smith would be sorting red objects from all the rest based on his mental state of sensing redness, but Jones would do so based on his mental state of sensing blueness. Functionalists claim that Jones and Smith are in the same mental state because they both are in that state caused by certain inputs (scanning the room) and that produces certain outputs (sorting the red objects from the others plus the belief that the word *red* applies to these objects). But Jones and Smith are *not* in the same mental state if mental states are characterized by their inner nature: Jones is aware of blueness; Smith is aware of redness. Jones and Smith function the same way based on very different mental states. Since two different mental states are consistent with the same functional states, the latter cannot be identified with the former.

A second, related objection to functionalism is called the problem of **absent qualia**. According to functionalism, if unconscious machines like computers or robots are able to imitate consciousness by embodying the right functional state, then they are, in fact, in that mental state. But this seems wrong. Even if a robot could be set up to grimace, shout "Ouch!" and so forth after being stuck with a pin, the robot would still not be in the state of being in pain because the specific conscious property of painfulness would be absent.

Another famous example of this problem has been used to show that functionalist accounts of mental states like thoughts and understanding meanings do not succeed because they treat such states as being nothing more nor less than functional states like those in a computer. The example comes from John Searle and is known as the **Chinese room**:

> Imagine that you are locked in a room, and in this room are several baskets full of Chinese symbols. Imagine that you (like me) do not understand a word of Chinese, but that you are given a rule book in English for manipulating the Chinese symbols. The rules specify the manipulations of symbols purely formally, in terms of their syntax, not their semantics. So the rule might say: "Take a squiggle-squiggle out of basket number one and put it next to a squoggle-squoggle sign from basket number two." Now suppose that some other Chinese symbols are passed into the room, and that you are given further rules for passing back Chinese symbols out of the room. Suppose that unknown to you the symbols passed into the room are called "questions" by the people outside the room, and the symbols you pass back out of the room are called "answers to the questions." Suppose, furthermore, that the programmers are so good at designing the programs and that you

are so good at manipulating the symbols, that very soon your answers are indistinguishable from those of a native Chinese speaker. There you are locked in your room shuffling your Chinese symbols and passing out Chinese symbols in response to incoming Chinese symbols. . . . Now the point of the story is simply this: by virtue of implementing a formal computer program from the point of view of an outside observer, you behave exactly as if you understood Chinese, but all the same you don't understand a word of Chinese.[3]

The Chinese room with the person inside would simulate a computer to an outside person and represents a functionalist account of mental states like thinking and understanding meaning. For a person outside, the room receives input and gives output in a way that makes it appear that the room understands Chinese. But of course, all the room does is imitate mental understanding, it does not possesses it. Computers are just like the Chinese room. They imitate mental operations, but they do not really exemplify them.

Third, functionalists have difficulty accounting for the unity of a class of mental states. We surfaced this type of objection in connection with token-token identity theory. Consider the class of all pains of a specific type. The unity of that class, the thing that makes all pains members of that class seems to be something internal to each member: the fact that they all have the same inner nature, the same qualitative subjective feel. It does not seem that each pain was caused by the same type of input (e.g., a pin prick), that each pain caused the same type of output (e.g., "Ouch!") and other "mental" states (e.g., a desire for pity). These causal relations are related externally to the pains themselves. They are contingently connected with pains—there could be pains without these causal connections. And the causal relations could be interconnected with other mental states like sensations of pleasure. God could have made us such that we experience pleasure after being stuck with a pin and before grimacing and shouting "Ouch!" Thus these causal connections do not constitute the essence of pains. In general, the essence of a mental state is its inner, mental nature, not the external causal relations that the state sustains to bodily inputs, outputs and other "mental" states.

2.5 ELIMINATIVE MATERIALISM

The last form of physicalism to be considered is, perhaps, the most radical and is called **eliminative materialism**. To understand it, we should first remember a point made in chapter nine about theory replacement in the history of science. Sometimes a new theory replaces another theory as oxygen theory replaced phlogiston theory. In cases like these, the replaced theory is abandoned and the entities postulated as real in the theory are no longer believed to exist. Several entities once thought to exist are no longer taken as real: the aether, phlogiston and caloric. These entities have been eliminated in favor of new entities postulated by advocates of the theories replacing the old ones.

Now advocates of eliminative materialism believe that terms that appear to refer to mental states—*pain*, "a belief that *P*"—are like the terms *phlogiston* and *aether*. They were part of an inadequate theory that should be abandoned

---

[3]John Searle, *Minds, Brains and Science* (Cambridge, Mass.: Harvard University Press, 1984), pp. 32-33. Cf. John Searle, "Minds, Brains and Programs," *The Behavioral and Brain Sciences* 3 (1980): 417-24.

in favor of a better theory. The inadequate theory is sometimes called **folk psychology**, and the better theory is one that comes from neurophysiology. On this view, folk psychology is a theory that uses terms referring to mental states to offer commonsense explanations for the behavior of people (and certain animals). Here are some commonsense generalizations of folk psychology that use such mental terms: People in pain tend to grimace. People who feel thirst tend to want to drink fluids. Consider the first sentence. This sentence is part of a theory that explains the behavior of people. If we ask why Mary has just grimaced, we can explain this by saying that all people who feel pain tend to grimace, Mary is in a mental state known as an experience of pain, and, therefore, Mary is grimacing.

Unfortunately, argue eliminative materialists, we now know that the states causing Mary to grimace and, indeed, all the alleged mental states postulated in folk psychology, do not exist. Instead, what causes Mary to grimace is that such and such C-fibers are vibrating in a certain manner in Mary. In general, folk psychology is false, and its conception of the mental should be abandoned and replaced by a better theory that uses only terms that refer to physical states. Eliminative materialists do not believe that mental states should be reduced to brain states any more than scientists believed that phlogiston should be reduced to oxygen. There are no mental states at all—no one has ever been in a mental state of pain, of having a thought or belief, or sensing something. Richard Rorty and Paul Churchland are two contemporary advocates of eliminative materialism.

The main criticism of eliminative materialism centers on the fact that it is simply obvious through introspective awareness of our own conscious lives that mental states like thoughts, pains and desires exist and have the natures they present themselves to us as having in such introspective acts. Eliminative materialism denies this fact and is, therefore, to be rejected. In fact, eliminative materialism has the wrong picture of the mental life and the terms we use to describe it. For one thing, the main focus of the mind-body problem is mental states themselves (e.g., pains), not the mental terms (e.g., *pain*) we use to talk about them. Thus even if we grant that our use of the term *pain* derives from folk psychology, pain itself does not. Pain itself is not part of a theory, but rather is a mental event with a certain characteristic feel made available to us in acts of self-awareness. It is hard to see how any advance in scientific knowledge could be the least bit relevant to the question of whether or not we are directly aware of pains, desires and so forth.

Furthermore, it could be argued that mental terms like the term *pain* are not primarily terms that play a role in a third-person theory (folk psychology) that attempts to explain the behavior of others first and, by extension, one's own behavior. Rather, *pain* is primarily a term we use to report to others an experience we are having, and *pain* is ostensibly defined by our own acquaintance with pain itself. Since "pain" is primarily a term used to report something and not to explain anything, it is hard to see how any explanatory theory at all (e.g., neurophysiological theory) could replace it, since basic mental terms are not primarily or simply terms used in explanation. And when we do, in fact, use *pain* to explain the behavior of others, we attribute to them an internal mental state analogous to the one we feel when we are in pain. Strictly speaking, this use of *pain* to explain the behavior of others is complementary to neurophysiological explanations of that behavior since the two could both be true descriptions of different aspects of what happens when someone is in pain. In such cases a mental pain state is exemplified in the person's soul and a certain brain state is exemplified in the person's body.

We close this survey of physicalist strategies with a statement by John Searle:

> Earlier materialists argued that there aren't any such things as separate mental phenomena, because mental phenomena *are identical* with brain states. More recent materialists argue that there aren't any such things as separate mental phenomena because they *are not identical* with brain states. I find this pattern very revealing, and what it reveals is an urge to get rid of mental phenomena at any cost.[4]

3 THE MAIN INTELLECTUAL DRIVE BEHIND PHYSICALISM

What is behind this urge to get rid of mental phenomena? This issue has already been touched on in the introduction to the chapter, but we will conclude this chapter with a few more remarks about this question. Three broad kinds of reasons are offered for physicalism over against dualism. First, it is argued that when the details of the positions themselves are examined, some version of physicalism is simply more plausible than versions of dualism. For example, dualist treatments of pain are just not as reasonable as some version of physicalism, given what we actually know about pain. Since the main thrust of this and the previous chapter was to present these different positions, we leave it to the readers to examine them again and judge for themselves as to which one is more reasonable given what it is reasonable to believe about pains, thoughts, etc.

Second, there are general philosophical arguments given either against dualism or in favor of physicalism. Two of these were briefly mentioned in chapter eleven—the problem for dualism of how and where interaction between mind and body takes place and the use of Ockham's razor to raise simplicity considerations in favor of physicalism—so we will not repeat our discussion of them here. There are two other major philosophical arguments against dualism: the problem of many minds and the problem of other minds. Let us look at these in order.

The **problem of many minds** is this: If dualism is true and the mind and body are different, then why would we expect that there would be just one mind attached to one body? When we meet a person, how could we ever know that the body before us had only one mind in it instead of seventeen minds? Since dualism cannot rule out the possibility of many minds, dualism leads to skepticism about our knowledge of how many minds others have, and thus it is to be rejected.

Four responses can be given to this problem. First, since dualism allows for the possibility of many minds in one body, and since such a state actually occurs in cases of demon possession, then the dualist allowance of this possibility is a virtue, not a vice. Second, as we saw in chapter four, from the mere fact that a position makes skepticism logically possible, it does not follow that skepticism is reasonable or that we do not have knowledge in the area in question. While we

---

[4]Searle, *Rediscovery of the Mind*, pp. 48-49.

cannot rule out the many minds possibility in an a priori fashion, nevertheless, based on inductive experience with our own consciousness and the lives of others, we are entitled to claim that someone else has only one mind attached to one body unless there is evidence (e.g., in demon possession cases) to the contrary. Third, if some version of substance dualism in the tradition of Aristotle or Aquinas is correct, then the soul (perhaps by using DNA molecules) is what makes the body and gives the body its nature (e.g., your body is human because it is informed by a human soul). The soul provides the form or essence of the body; the body is dependent on the soul for its coming into being and not vice versa. This intimate connection between one soul and one body gives us a model that justifies the expectation that there will only be one soul that is the owner of one body. In demon possession cases, the demon does not provide the essence of the body but merely inhabits it. Finally, physicalists have their own problems accounting for the unity of consciousness at a point in time and the unity of consciousness through change. This is why physicalists concentrate their efforts on mental *events* and usually bypass issues about the metaphysics of substance. This point will be developed more fully in chapter fourteen.

The **problem of other minds** is this: If dualism is true, we can never know that other people have mental states because those states are private mental entities to which we have no direct access. In this regard, dualism implies skepticism in two ways: It leaves us skeptical as to whether or not other minds exist in the first place, and even if they do, it leaves us skeptical as to what other persons' mental states are like. Perhaps they have inverted qualia compared to me—they sense redness and joy when I sense blueness and pain and vice versa. If dualism is true we could never know.

The dualist problem of other minds has been greatly exaggerated. Our response to this problem is similar to what was said in regard to the problem of many minds. First, dualism does, in fact, imply the following: From what we know about a person's brain, nervous system and behavior, we cannot logically deduce his or her mental states. But, again, far from being a vice, this implication seems to be the way things really are. Even young children occasionally wonder if they may sense colors in a way different from others. In general, it *is* in fact logically possible for one person to be in one kind of mental state and another person to be in a different kind of mental state even though their physical states are the same.

Second, the logical possibility just mentioned does not imply skepticism about other minds. We do not know something only if it is logically impossible that we are wrong about it. There are many dualist views as to how we have knowledge of other minds—for example, we postulate that others are in pain when we observe them stuck with a pin and grimacing as a simple inference to the best explanation of these facts or based on an analogy with what we know we would be experiencing in a similar situation. But regardless of how we explain our knowledge of other minds, we do, in fact, have such knowledge, and the mere logical possibility that we are wrong about the mental states of another is not sufficient to justify skepticism.

In our view, the real intellectual driving force behind modern physicalism is not the philosophical case for it and against dualism, but a cultural commitment to naturalism and to scientism. As Lynne Rudder Baker points out, "Physicalism is the product of a claim about science together with a particular conception of science. The claim is that science is the exclusive arbiter of reality. . . . On this view, scientific knowledge is exhaustive."[5]

If the space-time physical world of objects studied by science is all there is, and if science is our best or, perhaps, only rational way of gathering beliefs about the world around us, then, according to most physicalists, dualism must be false. Why? Because the existence of mental states or immaterial souls threatens the unity of science, especially the adequacy of chemistry and physics, to explain all of reality. Thus naturalism and scientism would be false.

Several alleged scientific objections have been raised against dualism. Actually, these objections do not come from science per se, but from what some philosophers tell us science must say. First, some have argued that mental entities are simply metaphysically queer and extravagant. But queer to whom? The soul is very much at home in a theistic worldview because such a perspective regards mind as more fundamental than matter. The soul is bizarre only if you already presuppose naturalism and scientism.

Second, others have argued that if mental states exist and can cause things to happen in the world, then this violates the fact that the physical universe is "causally closed," that is, any event that happens is solely the product of other physical factors that are sufficient to cause it. There are no causal influences on physical events besides other physical events. Sometimes this problem is put in terms of the first law of thermodynamics, also called the conservation of energy principle. This principle states that the amount of energy in a closed system remains constant. But if there is causal interaction between the mental and the physical, then certain physical effects are not solely the product of other physical factors and energy is introduced into the system by mental causality, violating this principle.

Dualists have offered a number of responses to this objection. First, this objection, if correct, eliminates libertarian freedom of the will, and if such freedom exists, then the objection fails (see chap. 13). Second, this objection, if correct, would rule out direct, miraculous interventions of God into the world, and if there is reason to believe in such interventions, the objection fails.

Third, the first law is formulated only for "closed systems," that is, those without outside interference. Moreover, the first law is formulated only for systems that are wholly material in nature. The dualist points out that, strictly speaking, the first law only applies to totally material, closed systems and not to systems which involve mental causal influence. When a person acts, new energy may be created, but this is a fact that is outside the scope of the first law and not a violation of it.

Still, one could argue that there have been no empirical observations of the creation of new energy in human acts, so this dualist assertion seems dubious. Two responses may be given to this counterargument. First, one may agree that while the creation of energy resulting from agent causation should be easily measurable, and thus libertarianism may be falsifiable in principle, but in actual

---

[5]Lynne Rudder Baker, *Saving Belief: A Critique of Physicalism* (Princeton, N.J.: Princeton University Press, 1987), p. 4.

practice, no one has tried to do the relevant investigation, and it is not entirely clear exactly how such a thing should be measured.

Second, it may be that an exercise of free active power involves a very little, virtually undetectable amount of energy, especially as compared to the energy involved in the entire act of, say, raising one's hand to vote. When an engineer throws a switch to release the water behind Hoover Dam, the vast amount of potential energy unleashed by the moving water is overwhelmingly greater than that involved in the engineer throwing the switch. It may be the same with libertarian acts. Perhaps the energy released in the exercise of free active power is miniscule compared to the potential energy released in the body as part of the relevant causal pathway. If this were so, then it may be very difficult, if not impossible to measure the energy created by exercises of free active power.

There is a third and final scientific objection often raised against dualism. Given the standard scientific account of how the world, in its present form, got here from the big bang through evolutionary processes, there is neither need nor room to fit into this picture the appearance of mental properties or substances. Living organisms, including humans, are solely the result of physical processes operating on physical materials, and thus the product of such mechanisms will be solely physical.

It is well known that one of the driving forces behind Darwin's exposition of evolution was materialism regarding the mind-body problem. As Howard Gruber explains:

> The idea of either a Planful or an Intervening Providence taking part in the day-to-day operations of the universe was in effect a competing theory [to Darwin's version of evolution]. If one believed that there was a God who had originally designed the world exactly as it has come to be, the theory of evolution through natural selection could be seen as superfluous. Likewise, if one believed in a God who intervened from time to time to create some of the organisms, organs, or functions found in the living world, Darwin's theory could be seen as superfluous. Any introduction of intelligent planning or decision-making reduces natural selection from the position of a necessary and universal principle to a mere possibility.[6]

Daniel Dennett notes that "Darwin saw from the outset that his theory had to include an entirely naturalistic account of the origins of 'mind,'. . . for if Man were to be the golden exception to Darwin's rule, the whole theory would be dismissible."[7] The most reasonable way to do this is to advance some version of strict physicalism because if something like mental states or substances exist, there would be one thing about living organisms beyond the explanatory scope of evolutionary theory, and this would threaten to make that theory less plausible. The mere claim that mind simply emerges from matter in the evolutionary process is an unfalsifiable assertion at best, and not one that fits naturally into a Darwinian understanding of our origins.

---

[6]Howard E. Gruber, *Darwin on Man: A Psychological Study of Scientific Creativity* (Chicago: University of Chicago Press, 1974), p. 211.

[7]Daniel Dennett, review of *Darwin and the Emergence of Evolutionary Theories of Mind and Behavior* by Robert J. Richards, *Philosophy of Science* 56 (1989): 541.

This same point has been made from Darwin's time to the present. Here are some recent examples. Paul Churchland makes this claim:

> The important point about the standard evolutionary story is that the human species and all of its features are the wholly physical outcome of a purely physical process. . . . If this is the correct account of our origins, then there seems neither need, nor room, to fit any nonphysical substances or properties into our theoretical account of ourselves. We are creatures of matter. And we should learn to live with that fact.[8]

D. M. Armstrong asserts the following:

> It is not a particularly difficult notion that, when the nervous system reaches a certain level of complexity, it should develop new properties. Nor would there be anything particularly difficult in the notion that when the nervous system reaches a certain level of complexity it should affect something that was already in existence in a new way. But it is a quite different matter to hold that the nervous system should have the power to create something else, of a quite different nature from itself, and create it out of no materials.[9]

Arthur Peacocke agrees:

> I find it very hard to see why that functional property [consciousness] coded in a certain complex physical structure requires a new entity to be invoked, of an entirely different kind, to appear on the scene to ensure its emergence. How could something substantial, some substance or some other entity different in kind from that which has been evolved so far, suddenly come in to the evolutionary, temporal sequence?[10]

Since things do not come into existence out of nothing, if naturalism is correct, then the chemical and physical properties that describe matter should be all there is because such properties are all that was there begin with. The emergence of different kinds of entities, especially, as noted by Armstrong above, those so different as to be characterized as mental, would either involve the emergence of these new kinds of entities from nothing or from latent mental potentialities in matter.

The first option violates the principle that things do not come into existence out of nothing. The second violates the nature of naturalism since it implies that mental properties are ultimate in the universe as potential properties of matter that emerge when matter is organized in certain ways. This is a major reason for embracing physicalism in the first place and it is also why the most consistent form of physicalism will define *physical* in terms of what can be described solely in the language of chemistry and physics. If we need to use descriptions of "emergent" properties that go beyond what the naturalist believes existed shortly after the big bang, the metaphysical status of such properties is a problem.

Some philosophers, like Richard Swinburne, have argued that the existence and nature of consciousness cannot be explained by science and that the best explanation for the existence of finite mental states or souls is the existence of

---

[8]Paul Churchland, *Matter and Consciousness* (Cambridge, Mass.: MIT Press, 1984), p. 21.

[9]D. M. Armstrong, *A Materialist Theory of Mind* (London: Routledge & Kegan Paul, 1968), p. 30.

[10]Arthur Peacocke and Grant Gillett, eds., *Persons & Personality* (Oxford: Basil Blackwell, 1987), p. 55.

a Grand Soul who created them. This does seem to be a reasonable argument, though we cannot develop it here and not all philosophers have agreed with it. But the fact that there may well be a clear, defensible connection between dualism and theism, and that the existence and nature of mind is best explained by theism and is hard to square with physicalist versions of naturalism, gives us a broader perspective in which to understand much of the intellectual drive toward physicalism. Dualism is a test case between a naturalistic and a theistic worldview. The existence of mental entities is not equally at home in these two worldviews. Often there is more at stake in the dualist-physicalist debate than meets the eye. In light of this, we close this chapter with a statement from Howard Robinson:

> [William] James called materialism a tough-minded theory. We began this essay by wondering why, if this is so, materialists are so often on the defensive in philosophy. The explanation seems to be that though the materialist makes a show of being tough-minded he is in fact a dogmatist, obedient not to the authority of reason, but to a certain picture of the world. That picture is hypnotising but terrifying: the world as a machine of which we are all insignificant parts. Many people share Nagel's fear of this world view, but, like Nagel, are cowed into believing that it must be true. . . . But reason joins with every other constructive human instinct in telling us that it is false and that only a parochial and servile attitude towards physical science can mislead anyone into believing it. To opt for materialism is to choose to believe something obnoxious, against the guidance of reason. This is not tough-mindedness, but a willful preference for a certain form of soulless, false and destructive modernism.[11]

CHAPTER SUMMARY

Currently, physicalism is the major rival to dualism. There are two main physicalist strategies: reductive and nonreductive physicalism. In the former, an attempt is made to give general, reductive, necessary and sufficient conditions for any type of mental state in physical terms. In the latter, no such attempt is made. There are two main versions of reductive physicalism: philosophical behaviorism and type-type identity theory. There are three main versions of nonreductive physicalism: functionalism, token-token identity theory and eliminative materialism.

Each version of physicalism was defined and evaluated. Two problems present themselves to all versions of physicalism. First, physicalism denies fullblown, libertarian freedom of the will. Second, physicalism has difficulty allowing for the unity of the self at a given time and the sameness of the self through change. Philosophical behaviorism is the view that mental terms are to be operationally defined in terms of stimulus inputs and publicly observable bodily behavior or tendencies to such behavior. Type-type identity theory identifies types of mental states with types of "hardware" or brain and central nervous states. Functionalism defines types of mental states in terms of the causal connections that obtain among sensory inputs, behavioral outputs and other "internal" states of the organism. Token-token identity theory denies the

---

[11]Howard Robinson, *Matter and Sense* (Cambridge: Cambridge University Press, 1982), p. 125.

existence of general identity conditions between types of mental and physical states but advocates the identity of individual mental and physical state tokens. Eliminative materialism denies the reality of the mental altogether by treating the mental terms in what they call folk psychology like *phlogiston* or other terms in a discarded scientific theory. Objections were raised against each view.

The chapter concluded with a survey of the three broad kinds of reasons offered for physicalism: the general superiority of some version of physicalism compared to dualism, philosophical difficulties with dualism (causal interaction, Ockham's razor, the many minds objection and the problem of other minds) and arguments from science (the queerness of the mental, dualist violations of the first law of thermodynamics, and the difficulty of accounting for the origin and nature of mind given a naturalistic account of our origins). Arguments from scientism and naturalism are the primary driving force behind modern physicalism, which illustrates that the mind-body problem is a lightning rod for a broader worldview clash.

CHECKLIST OF BASIC TERMS AND CONCEPTS

absent qualia
Chinese room
eliminative materialism
folk psychology
functionalism
hardware view
inverted qualia
methodological behaviorism
multiple realization
nonreductive physicalism
operational definition
philosophical behaviorism
problem of many minds
problem of other minds
reductive physicalism
software view
strong artificial intelligence
token
token-token identity theory
type
type-type identity theory

13

FREE WILL
AND DETERMINISM

In an ordered series of movers and things moved,
it is necessarily the fact that, when the first mover is removed
or ceases to move, no other mover will move [another] or be [itself] moved.
For the first mover is the cause of motion for all the others.
THOMAS AQUINAS SUMMA CONTRA GENTILES 1.13

Nothing happens at random; whatever comes about is by rational necessity.
LEUCIPPUS FRAGMENT (2)

The problem of natural agency is an ontological problem—
a problem about whether the existence of actions
can be admitted within a natural scientific ontology. . . .
Naturalism does not essentially employ the concept of a causal
relation whose first member is in the category of person or agent
(or even, for that matter, in the broader category of continuant or "substance").
All natural causal relations have first members
in the category of event or state of affairs.
JOHN BISHOP, NATURAL AGENCY

1 INTRODUCTION

Whether we admit it or not, we all take an ethical perspective about what is right and wrong, virtuous or villainous, worthy of praise or blame. And an ethical perspective on life depicts human beings in general as intellectually and morally responsible creatures. However, such responsibility seems to require some sort of freedom of the will as a necessary condition. But are we really free? If so, what sort of freedom do we have? Is determinism true and is it compatible with freedom?

The existence and nature of free will is a matter of practical importance for how we will employ an ethical perspective in our individual and social dealings with others. It is also a troublesome theoretical matter in light of various worldviews that people embrace. For example, some argue that if naturalism is true it is hard to see how human action could exist because naturalism seems to depict humans as passive machines that are part of a larger physical causal network. In such a view, all events are either purely uncaused and random or else determined by prior events. Either way, free actions are ruled out. For Christian theism, certain doctrines have raised problems for certain views about the existence and nature of free will: the existence and origin of evil, the sovereignty of God, predestination and election, the justice of hell, and God's foreknowledge of contingent, free acts by human beings.

In this chapter, we will look at philosophical issues involved in clarifying the nature of freedom and in defending or criticizing its reality. But what do we mean by *freedom*? Part of our purpose in this chapter will be to address this question, but for now three different senses of freedom can be distinguished. First, there is the **freedom of permission**—the social/political notion of freedom involved in discussions of rights, the authority of the state, and law. This sense of freedom will not be our concern in this chapter.

Second, there is **freedom of personal integrity**—the ability of fully developed, ideally functioning persons to act as unified selves in a responsible, mature way. This sense of freedom contrasts with the slavery and bondage that comes from being an immature, divided, undeveloped self. So understood, the freedom of personal integrity is in large measure a developmental concept largely employed in studies of psychological and spiritual formation, though it does have philosophical aspects to it.

Finally, there is **freedom of moral and rational responsibility**—that freedom, whatever it turns out to be, that is part of **human action** and **agency**, in which the human being acts as an agent who is in some sense the originator of one's own actions and, in this sense, is in control of one's action. This type of freedom serves as a necessary condition for moral and, some would say, intellectual responsibility. This third sense of freedom will be the major usage in view in this chapter, and when we talk about *freedom* or **free will**, this is what will be meant unless otherwise indicated.

All Christians are agreed that we have free will, but there are major differences among them—and among philosophers in general—about what free will is. We can define **determinism** as the view that for every event that happens, there are conditions such that, given them, nothing else could have happened. For every event that happens, its happening was caused or necessitated by prior factors such that given these prior factors, the event in question had to occur. One form of determinism defines it as the view that every event is caused by antecedent causal events and the relevant laws sufficient for the production of that event. At any time *t*, there is only one physically possible future world that can obtain. Every event is the inexorable outcome of a chain of events leading to and sufficient for that event. Hard determinists agree with libertarians in holding that determinism is incompatible with free will. **Hard determinism** denies the existence of free will (as understood by libertarians) and libertarianism accepts free will and denies determinism with respect to human freedom. **Soft determinism**, also called compatibilism, holds that freedom and determinism are compatible with each other, and thus the truth of determinism does not eliminate freedom. As we will see, compatibilists have a different understanding of free will from the one embraced by libertarians and hard determinists.

The main purpose of this chapter is to define and compare libertarianism and compatibilism and to present some of the strengths and weaknesses of each. Part of the task of being able to evaluate compatibilist and libertarian views of freedom is clarifying what the two positions are. In fact, exposition of these standpoints is a main part of the case for which view to accept, since one's decision in this regard will often come down to which theory is more congruent with one's considered intuitions about a number of issues that arise in discussing human action. With this in mind, the main section of the chapter will begin by giving a general overview of compatibilism and libertarianism followed by a comparison of the two regarding five issues of crucial importance for an adequate theory of freedom: the ability condition, the control condition, rationality, causation and the person. It will close with an examination of two final problem areas: fatalism and theological issues. In the process of exposition, comparison and contrast, arguments for and against each view will be mentioned.

2 COMPATIBILIST AND LIBERTARIAN FREEDOM

1. Compatibilism. The central idea behind **compatibilism** is this: If determinism is true, then every human action (e.g., raising one's hand to vote) is causally necessitated by events that obtained prior to the action, including events that existed before the person acting was born. That is, human actions are mere **happenings**—they are parts of causal chains of events that lead up to them in a deterministic fashion. Moreover, determinism is true. But freedom properly understood is compatible with determinism; both determinism and freedom are true.

Concerning the compatibility between determinism and freedom, a distinction needs to be made between hard compatibilists and soft compatibilists. For **hard compatibilists**, free choice is inconceivable or impossible without determinism; a free choice is one that must be determined. Why? Because, argue hard compatibilists, the only choices that are free are those caused by one's character, beliefs and desires. If a choice, say to raise one's hand to vote, is not caused by a prior event, then it is completely uncaused and utterly random or fortuitous. How can a completely random event (the raising of one's hand) over which one has no control be a "free" choice? **Soft compatibilists** argue that it is possible though not likely that libertarianism is true, and thus free choice does not require determinism. But free choice is at least compatible (i.e., consistent) with determinism, and thus the truth of determinism cannot be used as an argument against freedom.

There is another distinction among compatibilists that helps to clarify contemporary compatibilist versions of freedom: classical versus contemporary or hierarchical compatibilism. To understand this distinction, we must first recognize that, while some actions are mental only and do not require the body to move (e.g., changing what one is thinking about from one topic to another), typically, human actions require the body to move (as in raising a hand to vote). Now **classical compatibilists** like John Locke and David Hume primarily applied the notion of freedom to bodily action. For them, one was free if and only if one could act according to one's own desires and preferences in the absence of external constraint. Julie is free to leave the room if she desires to do so and no one is holding her down or keeping the door locked, even if her desire to leave is causally determined.

According to **contemporary** or **hierarchical compatibilism**, the problem with classical compatibilism is that freedom to act bodily seems to be neither necessary nor sufficient for having the type of freedom necessary to be a responsible agent. Kleptomaniacs and people with serious addictions or phobias are not free even though they can act according to their desires in the absence of external constraint. The problem with such people, say hierarchical compatibilists, is not that their choices are determined (since determinism is consistent with freedom), but rather those choices are determined in the wrong sort of way by enslaving addictions. The agent has no control over his or her choices or the desires that cause them. So the classical freedom of action is not sufficient for real freedom.

Neither is it necessary. To see this, consider a case where a person could not have done other than what he did, but still acted freely. Suppose a scientist has placed an electrode in Jones's brain so that he can read what Jones is going to do on any occasion and can cause him to do whatever the scientist desires. Now suppose the scientist wants Jones to kill Smith, and Jones himself, in the absence of any influence from the scientist, is deliberating about the murder. If Jones decides not to kill Smith, the scientist will activate the electrode and cause the killing, but he does not need to do so because Jones carries out the act on his own. Here Jones was free but could not have acted otherwise.

What this example shows is that freedom of the will is more central to the notion of freedom necessary for responsibility than is freedom of bodily action—the will is more central to the person than is mere bodily movement. Thus hierarchical compatibilists place their emphasis on freedom of the will, not freedom of action per se. Major compatibilists in the history of philosophy have been Locke, Hume and Thomas Hobbes. Contemporary advocates are Daniel Dennett and Gary Watson.

2. Libertarianism. **Libertarianism** claims that the freedom necessary for responsible action is not compatible with determinism. Real freedom requires a type of control over one's action—and, more importantly, over one's will—such that, given a choice to do A (raise one's hand and vote) or B (leave the room), nothing determines that either choice is made. Rather, the agent himself must simply exercise his own **causal powers** and will to do one alternative, say A (or have the power to refrain from willing to do something). When this happens, the agent either could have refrained from willing to do A or he could have willed to do B without anything else being different inside or outside of his being. He is the absolute originator of his own actions. As Aristotle said in *Physics* 256a, "A staff moves a stone, and is moved by a hand, which is moved by a man." The event of the staff moving is caused by the event of the hand moving which is caused by the substance known as the man himself. When an agent acts freely, he is a **first** or **unmoved mover**; no event or efficient cause causes him to act. His desires or beliefs may influence his choice or play an important role in his deliberations, but free acts are not determined or caused by prior events or states in the agent; rather, they are spontaneously done by the agent himself acting as a first mover. Thus libertarian freedom is both a position about freedom itself and a theory about the nature of agents and agency.

Suppose some person *P* freely does some act *e*, say *P* changed his thoughts or raised his arm. A more precise, initial characterization of libertarian freedom and agency can be given as follows:

1. *P* is a substance (see chap. 10) that had the power to bring about *e*.
2. *P* exerted its power as a first mover (an uncaused performer of action) to bring about *e*.
3. *P* had the ability to refrain from exerting its power to bring about *e*.
4. *P* had some reason *R* that was the end or final cause for the sake of which he did *e*.

Historically, well-known libertarians have been Thomas Aquinas and Thomas Reid. Currently, Timothy O'Connor, Peter van Inwagen and William Rowe are among the advocates of libertarian freedom. We can delve more deeply into compatibilist and libertarian accounts of freedom by looking at five areas central to an adequate theory of free will.

Most philosophers agree about the **ability condition**: that in order to have the freedom necessary for responsible agency, one must have the ability to choose or act differently from the way the agent actually does. A free choice, then, is one where a person *can* act, or at least will to do otherwise. Most compatibilists and libertarians agree about this. However, they differ about what this notion of *can* is precisely when we say, "A free act is one in which a person can act other than how he or she does act." How do we spell out this ability?

According to compatibilists, the ability necessary for freedom should be expressed as a **hypothetical ability**, also called a conditional sense of *can*. Roughly, this means that the agent would have done otherwise had some other condition obtained; for example, had the agent desired to do so. If, given a choice to do A or B, Smith freely wills to do A, then he did this, say compatibilists, because he desired to do A. But Smith could have done B on the hypothetical condition that he had desired to do B. We are free to will whatever we desire even though our desires are themselves determined. Freedom is willing to act on your strongest preference.

Libertarians claim that this notion of ability is really a sleight of hand and not adequate to give the freedom we need to be responsible agents. For libertarians, the real issue is not whether we are free to do what we want, but whether we are free to want in the first place. In other words, a free act is one in which the agent is ultimately the originating source of the act itself. Freedom requires that we have the **categorical ability** to act, or at least, to will to act. This means that if Smith freely does (or wills to do) A, he could have refrained from doing (or willing to do) A or he could have done (or willed to have done) B without any conditions whatever being different. No description of Smith's desires, beliefs, character or other things in his make-up and no description of the universe prior to and at the moment of his choice to do A is sufficient to entail that he did A. It was not necessary that anything be different for Smith to refrain from doing A or to do B instead. His ability is not conditioned on any hypothetical difference in his desires (or beliefs, etc.) at the moment of choice; it is categorical.

2.2
FIVE AREAS OF
COMPARISON
BETWEEN
COMPATIBILISM
AND
LIBERTARIANISM

2.2.1
THE ABILITY
CONDITION

Many libertarians claim that the libertarian notion of categorical ability is that of a **dual ability** (or control): If one has the ability to exert his power to do (or will to do) A, one also has the ability to refrain from exerting his power to do (or will to do) A. By contrast, the compatibilist notion of hypothetical ability is not a dual ability. Given a description of a person's circumstances and internal states at time t, only one choice could obtain and the ability to refrain is not there; its presence depends on the hypothetical condition that the person had a desire (namely, to refrain from acting) that was not actually present.

Among compatibilist objections to the categorical notion of ability, one should be mentioned at this point. This objection points out that we often find that many of our choices seem determined and the alternative act is simply impossible, given our character. For example, some people have such a developed moral sense at the present moment t, that it would simply be psychologically impossible for them to murder their next door neighbor, given their current character, desires and beliefs. If this were not the case, our actions would seem random, completely unrelated to our character, and unpredictable.

Libertarians have responded to this charge in one of two ways. First, some claim that in cases like the one just mentioned, the choice to refrain is a straightforward libertarian choice, even if it is highly improbable, because character, desires, beliefs can strongly influence our choices without necessitating them. The crucial dimension of this response is to clarify a notion of "influence" that does not beg the question against the compatibilist and that allows character to have some sort of impact on action that stops short of being sufficient for the action to take place.

Second, other libertarians make a distinction between first-order and higher-order abilities in the self. An illustration may help clarify what is meant here. A person can have the **first-order power** to speak English and not Russian, but he may have the **second-order power** to develop the ability to speak Russian. Thus, due to habit, character formation and so forth, a person at some time t may not have the categorical ability to act—for example, to murder one's neighbor—but the act of refraining can still be one that is morally responsible and free in the sense that at some time in the past the person had the categorical ability either to develop his character in the way he did or to refrain from such practices. Therefore, an act can be determined at time t, but still be a morally responsible one if a libertarian choice to exercise or refrain from exercising a higher-order power relevant to the act was made at some time prior to t.

We have seen that compatibilists and libertarians have different understandings of the sense of ability relevant to responsible agency. And our discussion of this difference suggests that a closely related issue is of importance to the free will debate: the centrality of the agent being in control of his or her actions.

2.2.2
THE CONTROL
CONDITION

Suppose Jones raises his hand to vote. Compatibilists and libertarians agree that a necessary condition of this act being a free one is that Jones must be in control of the act itself—the **control condition**. But they differ radically as to what control is.

In order to understand compatibilist views of the control condition, recall that compatibilists agree that determinism is true and that cause and effect is to be depicted as a series of events making up causal chains with earlier events together with the laws of nature causing later events. The universe is what it is at the present moment because of the state of the universe at the moment before the present together with the correct causal laws describing the universe. A crude example of such a causal chain would be a series of 100 dominos falling in sequence from the first domino on until domino 100 falls. Suppose all the dominos are black except numbers 40-50, which are green. Here we have a causal chain of events that progresses from domino one to one hundred and that "runs through" the green dominos. On the other hand, suppose that dominos 1-39 fall in order, but when domino 39 is reached, the causal chain runs through an alternative series of dominos, bypassing the green ones and returning to dominos 51-100. In this case, the causal chain that leads up to domino 100 does not run through the green dominos. It bypasses them altogether.

Now, according to compatibilism, an act is free only if it is under the agent's own control. And it is under the agent's own control only if the causal chain of events—which extends back in time to events realized before the agent was even born—that caused the act (Jones's hand being raised) "runs through" the agent himself in the correct way. Consider a situation in which a scientist places an electrode in Jones's brain and hits a button at the right time (when a person asks for those voting for the bill to raise their hands), causing Jones's hand to go up. This is not a free act for Jones because he was not in control of his hand going up. Why? The answer is not because his hand going up was an event deterministically caused by a chain of events leading up to it. For the compatibilist, the control necessary for freedom is a **one-way ability** (or control), not a dual control to act or refrain from acting, all things being the same up to the act itself. Jones does not have the control necessary to raise his hand or to refrain from raising it without further changes inside him. Rather, the reason Jones's act was not a free act is because the causal chain did not run through Jones in the correct way, but instead bypassed Jones and ran through the scientist and his machinery.

But what does it mean to say that the causal chain "runs through the agent in the correct way"? Here compatibilists differ from each other, but basically, the idea is that an agent is in control of an act just in case the act is caused in the right way by prior states of the agent himself—by the agent's own character, beliefs, desires and values.

For example, suppose a person has a conflict between two **first-order desires** (that is, a lower-order desire involving specific states or events): to smoke and to engage in healthy activity. According to Harry Frankfurt, the notion of control necessary for moral responsibility is **free action**, that is, the freedom to do what one wants, to act on one's first-order desires. Frankfurt also claims that freedom of will is necessary for a person to have the freedom of personal integrity, the freedom that consists in a mature caring about which of one's first-order desires he will act on. The notion of control necessary for free will is that one's act be the result of a **second-order desire** to have a first-order desire be effective, that is, the act must be what one wills on the matter. In the case just mentioned, if the person has a second-order desire that his first-order desire to act in a healthy manner be the desire that wins out, then this second-order desire causes the first-order desire to be effective, and the first-order desire causes an event of refraining from smoking. Such an act is free because it passes through the agent in the right way for him to be in control.

Gary Watson has a different view. According to him, we must distinguish those acts we desire without valuing them (e.g., smoking) from those we desire and which are expressions of one's **valuational system** (roughly, one's set of considered value judgments about what is the right, most reasonable thing to do in a given situation). An act is under my control if it is caused in the right way by my value system—if it is caused by and consistent with my own values.

Other compatibilists add that the act cannot be coerced, it must be done in an informed way, and so on. The basic idea here is that the chain of events leading up to the act must run through the agent in the correct way, and this means that it must be appropriately caused by the agent's own prior states of character, desire, belief and value. This is sometimes called a **causal theory of action**: An act is free if and only if it is under the agent's own control, and it is under his own control if and only if the act was appropriately caused by the right mental states existing in the agent prior to the act.

The causal theory of action has been subjected to a good deal of criticism. In order to understand the main problem with the view, consider a case in which a spy has agreed to send a signal to his compatriots if the enemy is going to attack tomorrow. He knows his friends will be using a telescope to look through the window of a meeting he will be having with the enemy that afternoon. If the attack will come, he will signal this by knocking over his cup of coffee. The meeting occurs, the attack is planned for the following day, and the spy intends to signal his countrymen in the agreed upon way. However, his desire to signal them combined with his belief that by knocking over his cup he can send the signal causes him to be so nervous that he accidentally knocks over the cup and the event is observed by those viewing through the telescope.

Now if the causal theory of action says that a free act that is under the agent's control is one that is caused by the agent's own prior mental states (in this case a belief and desire on the part of the spy), then the spy's deed would count as a free, intentional act. But obviously it is not. It was not even an act at all, but rather an accidental, jerky body movement. Thus the example shows that satisfying the causal theory is not sufficient for a free, intentional act because the spy satisfies the conditions of the theory but fails to so act. Cases like this are called examples of **causal deviance**: cases where the appropriate mental states (e.g., beliefs and desires) do in fact cause an event to take place but in an accidental way such that the event does not count as a real action.

Advocates of the causal theory of action have responded to cases of causal deviance by patching up the theory to include the idea that the act must be caused by the right mental states *in the appropriate way*. Since the spy's mental states did not cause the act in the appropriate way, it doesn't really satisfy the correct formulation of the causal theory of action. The problem with this response is that advocates of the causal theory of action have had a hard time defining "in the appropriate way."

Libertarians reject the causal theory of action and the compatibilist notion of control and instead claim that a different sense of control is needed for free-

dom to exist. To understand their view, we need to return to Aristotle's example cited above of a staff moving a stone but being itself moved by a hand that is
moved by a man. In *Summa contra Gentiles* 1.8, Thomas Aquinas states a principle about causal chains that is relevant to this example and, more generally, the
type of control necessary for freedom according to libertarians:

> In an ordered series of movers and things moved [to move is to change in some
> way], it is necessarily the fact that, when the first mover is removed or ceases to
> move, no other mover will move [another] or be [itself] moved. For the first
> mover is the cause of motion for all the others. But, if there are movers and
> things moved following an order to infinity, there will be no first mover, but all
> would be as **intermediate movers**. . . . [Now] that which moves [another] as an
> instrumental cause cannot [so] move unless there be a principal moving cause [a
> first cause, an unmoved mover].

Suppose we have nine stationary cars lined up bumper to bumper and a
tenth car runs into the first car causing each to move the next vehicle until car
nine on the end is moved. Suppose further that all the cars are black except
cars five through eight, which are green. Now, what caused the ninth car to
move? According to Aquinas, cars one through eight are not the real cause of
motion for car nine. Why? Because they are only **instrumental causes**; each of
these cars passively receives motion and transfers that motion to the next car
in the series. The first car (called the tenth car in our example) is the real cause
since in our example it is the first mover of the series. It is the source of motion
for all the others. In general, only first movers are the sources of action, not instrumental movers that merely receive motion passively and pass that on to the
next member in a causal chain.

In Aristotle's example, neither the staff nor the hand is the controlling cause
of the stone's motion since each is an intermediate cause. Rather, the man himself is the first, unmoved mover and as such is the absolute source of action. For
libertarians, it is only if agents are first causes, unmoved movers, that they have
the control necessary for freedom. An agent must be the absolute, originating
source of his own actions to be in control. If, as compatibilists picture it, an
agent is just a theater through which a chain of instrumental causes passes,
then there is no real control. Further, the control that an unmoved mover exercises in free action is a dual control—it is the power to exercise his own ability
to act or to refrain from exercising his own ability to act.

Philosophers do not agree about who is right in this debate. Libertarians
point out that the compatibilist notion of control is not genuine. The compatibilist is like the person who says that the group of green cars above (cars five
through eight) were in control of and, therefore, responsible for the damage to
car nine because the causal chain passed through the green cars in the right
way. But this is wrong because cars one through nine in the chain (including
the green ones) are passive, intermediate links in the chain and only the first
mover is responsible. Likewise, when compatibilists say that an event of raising
one's hand is not free if it is caused by a scientist's electrode but it is free if
caused by earlier character, belief, desire states in the agent, they are mistaken.
This is because in both cases, the earlier events causing the hand to go up (the
electrode being triggered versus a state of desiring to vote and believing that

raising one's hand will satisfy this desire being triggered) are the passive results of earlier events in a causal chain and no control is genuinely present. Agents are just a series of passive events in a causal chain that ultimately reaches outside the agent and extends into the past before the agent's birth. Where is there room for real control?

By contrast, compatibilists point out that the notion of an unmoved mover is mysterious and hard to understand. If an agent's character, beliefs and desires do not cause our actions, then what role *do* they play, and how is it that a person's behavior is so predictable in light of his or her character and so forth? The actions of an unmoved mover appear to be random events without any control whatever. This point leads us naturally to consider the next feature of freedom—the rationality condition.

2.2.3 THE RATIONALITY CONDITION	The **rationality condition** requires that an agent have a personal reason for acting before the act counts as a free one. Now some libertarians allow for the existence of free acts that are not done for any reason at all, such as freely moving my hand back and forth or looking at one thing and then another (where

these acts are not caused by, say, a nervous twitch or a sudden noise). Spontaneity is the name for nonrational, bare exercises of free will. But these libertarians agree with the fact that a crucial class of human actions are those done for certain reasons, so there is still an important area of debate between libertarians and compatibilists about the role of reason in free choices. Liberty is the name for this class of cases of free will.

Consider again the case of Jones raising his hand to vote. In order to understand the difference between the two schools about how to handle this case in light of the rationality condition, we need to draw a distinction between an efficient and a final cause. An **efficient cause** is that by means of which an effect is produced. One ball moving another is an example of efficient causality. By contrast, a **final cause** is that for the sake of which an effect is produced. Final causes are teleological goals, ends, purposes for which an event is done; the event is a means to the end that is the final cause.

Now a compatibilist will explain Jones's voting in terms of efficient and not final causes. According to this view, Jones had a desire to vote and a belief that raising his hand would satisfy this desire and this state of affairs in him (the **belief/desire set** composed of the two items just mentioned) caused the state of affairs of his hand going up. In general, whenever some person S does A (raises his hand) in order to B (vote), we can restate this as S does A (raises his hand) because he desired to B (vote) and believed that by A-ing (raising his hand), he would satisfy desire B. On this view, a reason for acting turns out to be a certain type of state in the agent, a belief-desire state, that is the real efficient cause of the action taking place. Persons as substances do not act; rather, states within persons cause latter states to occur. The compatibilist, in possession of a clear way to explain cases where S does A in order to B, challenges the libertarian to come up with an alternative explanation.

Many libertarians respond by saying that our reasons for acting are final causes, not efficient causes. Jones raises his hand in order to vote, or perhaps, in order to satisfy his desire to vote. In general, when person S does A in order to

B, B states the reason (e.g., a desire or a value) that is the teleological end or purpose for the sake of which S freely does A. Here the person acts as an unmoved mover by simply exercising his powers in raising his arm spontaneously. His beliefs and desires do not cause the arm to go up; he himself does. But B serves as a final cause or purpose for the sake of which he does A. Thus compatibilists embrace a belief/desire psychology (states of beliefs and desires in the agent cause the action to take place), while at least many libertarians reject it and see a different role for beliefs and desires in free acts.

There is a second difference between these two schools regarding the nature of reasons. For many libertarians, the process of reasoning known as **deliberation**, considering various reasons for and against certain actions, presupposes that the agent has libertarian freedom—one's future is genuinely open in that one has the categorical ability to do more than one thing; one is in control in the sense that the choice is up to him as a first mover; and in this sense, rationality presupposes freedom. Sometimes libertarians express this by being committed to **doxastic voluntarism**, the view that one is free to choose what one will believe. Now **direct doxastic voluntarism** is clearly false, namely, the idea that at any moment one can directly choose to believe or not to believe a given item. In general, this is not possible. One could not really choose to believe right now that a large pink elephant was sitting on this page even if offered a million dollars to do so. But many libertarians say **indirect doxastic voluntarism** may well be true: the idea that one's beliefs result from processes of deliberation in which one exercises freedom at various points along the way, in what one will or will not consider, how one will look at the issue, etc. Libertarians claim that we hold people responsible for what they believe (and the New Testament would seem to command people to believe certain things and hold them accountable for their choice to believe or not to believe), and this requires some form of doxastic voluntarism to be true.

By contrast, compatibilists reject doxastic voluntarism if by it one means that people have libertarian freedom indirectly to choose their beliefs. For the compatibilist, a process of deliberation is simply a certain type of causal chain in which a series of mental events (reasonings, desirings, ponderings, believings, etc.) causes a conclusion to be reached and a course of action to be taken. Here, freedom presupposes rationality, not the other way around. That is, if an action is not caused by some personal belief/desire set constituting the person's reason for acting, then the act is utterly random, fortuitous, and is not the sort of thing for which a person could be responsible. Christian compatibilists treat New Testament commands to believe as either expressing a form of doxastic voluntarism that utilizes a notion of freedom compatible with determinism or else they take these passages as not real commands to believe, but rather as statements that function to make clear what is already present in the listener's heart.

There is a third area of debate about reason between compatibilists and libertarians. If we take the notion of "having a reason" for acting to include motives, feelings and desires, and not just conceptual or more intellectual factors like beliefs, then this third area of debate is over the existence of **akrasia**—weakness of will. According to libertarians, weakness of will is a real phenomenon to be understood as an occasion where a person fails to act in keeping with his own personal preferences (his values, desires, beliefs, etc.) or acts against them.

For the compatibilist, people never act against their actual preferences, so if akrasia is defined in this way there is no akrasia. Actions are always caused by the strongest preferential state in the agent. People do have conflicting preferences (see the smoking case above) and sometimes one set of preferences is stronger and wins out over another set. If by akrasia we mean that one set of preferences we desire to act on to some degree is sometimes overridden by a stronger, sometimes immoral set of preferences, then there is such a thing as akrasia. In sum, libertarians and compatibilists differ over whether or not there is such a thing as akrasia and/or over how we are to define it.

2.2.4
CAUSATION

From what has already been said, we can already anticipate a difference between libertarians and compatibilists about causation. To clarify this difference, let us assume that **causation** is a relation between two things, namely, the cause and the effect. For the compatibilist, the only type of causation is called **event-event** (also called **state-state**) **causation**. The only kind of entities that can be put into the causal relation are events. Suppose a brick breaks a glass. In general, event-event causation can be defined in this way: An event of kind K (the moving of the brick and its touching of the surface of the glass) in circumstances of kind C (the glass being in a solid and not liquid state) occurring to an entity of kind E (the glass object itself) causes an event of kind Q (the breaking of the glass) to occur. If we say that the wind caused the brick to break the glass, strictly speaking, this is not correct. Rather, we should say that the moving of the wind caused a moving of the brick which, in turn, caused a breaking of the glass. Here, all causes and effects in the chain are events. Similarly, if we say that a desire to vote caused Jones to raise his arm, we are wrong. Strictly speaking, a desiring to vote caused a raising of the arm inside of Jones.

Libertarians agree that event-event causation is the correct way to account for normal events in the natural world like bricks breaking glasses. But when it comes to the free acts of persons, the person himself as a substance and as an agent occupies the first term in the causal relation (the cause) and the act is the second term (the effect). Persons are agents and, as such, in free acts they either cause their acts for the sake of reasons (called **agent causation**) or their acts are simply uncaused events they spontaneously do by exercising their powers for the sake of reasons (called a **noncausal theory of agency**). Either way, persons are seen as first causes or unmoved movers who simply have the power, as free agents, to exercise the ability to act as the ultimate originators of their actions. It is the I, the self that acts; not a state in the self that causes a moving of some kind. Libertarians claim that their view makes sense of the difference between actions (expressed by the active voice, e.g., Jones raised his hand to vote) and mere happenings (expressed by the passive voice, e.g., a raising of the hand was caused by a desiring to vote, which was caused by $x, \ldots$).

At this point it may be helpful to consider the relevance of **quantum physics** to the free will debate. According to some, certain quantum events (e.g., the precise location of an electron hitting a plate after being shot through a slit, the exact time a specific atom of uranium will decay into lead) are completely uncaused events and, as such, are indeterminate, random happenings. Thus, it is argued, a quantum view of reality abandons determinism and it makes room for **indeterminism** and for libertarian freedom.

Unfortunately, quantum physics has little relevance to the free will debate. For one thing, many scientists believe that the quantum world is just as determined as the regular world of macro-objects like baseballs and cars. We just do not (perhaps cannot) know the causes for some events and we cannot predict exactly the precise behavior of quantum entities. For another thing, even if we grant that in the quantum world determinism really is false, it could still be argued that determinism reigns in the macro world.

Third, and most important, for the libertarian, a necessary condition of free will is a view of the person as a substance that acts as an agent, that is, as a first cause or an unmoved mover. Thus determinism is sufficient for a denial of libertarian freedom, since it says that all events are caused by prior events and there are no substantial agents that act as unmoved movers. But even if determinism is false, this alone does not establish libertarian freedom, because completely uncaused events that randomly occur without reason, as in the quantum world, do not give the type of agency needed for libertarian freedom, namely, the freedom by which the agent as a substance is in control of his actions. The main debate between compatibilists and libertarians is one about the nature of agency and not determinism per se, although the truth of determinism is sufficient for the denial of libertarianism, as was already mentioned.

With this in mind, we are in a position to modify the understanding of modern compatibilism that we have used up to this point. Compatibilism is basically the thesis that freedom and determinism are compatible with each other, that they both *can* be true. But some, indeed, most compatibilists go on to accept the truth of determinism, while others do not make a commitment to accepting determinism. However, both groups of compatibilists reject libertarian agency. So while we will continue to focus on the majority of compatibilists who, in fact, accept determinism, we need to remember that the nature of agency, and not determinism per se, is the main bone of contention between compatibilists and libertarians.

Our discussion of causation has already moved into a description of the person in compatibilist and libertarian models of action, which differ over how they understand the **person as agent**. For the compatibilist, the person, insofar as he or she is an agent, is simply a series of events through which a causal chain passes on its way to producing an effect, say, one's hand going up. As long as this effect is caused by the right things in the right way (e.g., the character states in the agent) the act counts as free. Now the compatibilist could in fact hold that persons are genuine substances that sustain absolute personal identity though change. But the reasons for doing so would have to come from other philosophical considerations. As far as agency is concerned, it is consistent with compatibilism that a personal agent be a property-thing (see chap. 10) that reduces to a series of events through time and that does not sustain absolute personal identity through change (see chap. 14).

By contrast, a necessary condition for libertarian freedom is that the agent

2.2.5
THE PERSON AS
AGENT

be a genuine substance in the tradition of Aristotle and Aquinas. In chapters ten through twelve, we already saw that scientific naturalism denies that living organisms like human persons are to be understood as substances in the traditional sense. We are now in a position to understand why most naturalists deny libertarian freedom. This is not to say that all compatibilists are naturalists. Many Christians embrace compatibilism for a number of reasons, including certain views of election and predestination. But to the degree that a naturalist accepts some view of freedom, then the naturalist will most likely be a compatibilist, because as most naturalists acknowledge, naturalism denies a substance view of the agent and the reality of active power in favor of a property-thing view of the agent and event-event causation involving only passive liabilities.

We have looked at a general comparison between compatibilism and libertarianism and probed five different areas of contrast relevant to the debate about freedom: the ability condition, the control condition, the rationality condition, the nature of causation and the nature of the person as agent. We now turn to a final comparison of compatibilism and libertarianism in two problem areas: fatalism and theological reflection.

| 2.3 | Because compatibilists claim that freedom is consistent with the truth of de- |
| TWO FINAL ISSUES | terminism, some have argued that a problem arises for the compatibilist: De- |

2.3
TWO FINAL
ISSUES

2.3.1
THE PROBLEM
OF FATALISM

Because compatibilists claim that freedom is consistent with the truth of determinism, some have argued that a problem arises for the compatibilist: Determinism implies fatalism, fatalism is false, and so determinism (along with compatibilism) must be rejected. Very roughly, **fatalism** is the view that everything that happens does so necessarily and, therefore, we cannot do anything other that what we shall do. If determinism is true, all our acts are the inevitable results of events in the past that are beyond our control. Another way to state the problem is to say that determinism implies **actualism**—only what actually happens is possible. What a person actually *does* do coincides with what a person possibly *could* do. This view is sometimes called **global fatalism**. It is a controversial thesis and is to be distinguished from the relatively uncontroversial view called local fatalism. **Local fatalism** is the view that there are genuine, isolated instances in our lives where our outcome is fated irrespective of our deliberations or choices. For example, if a person jumps off a building, no amount of deliberation, no act of will can alter the person's fated trajectory! Global fatalism says that this is the case for the universe in general. According to some philosophers, global fatalism is false and it leads to passivity as a form of life.

Compatibilists and others have responded to the problem of fatalism by claiming that it is false and that determinism does not imply fatalism. It is true, given that determinism is the case, that only one future course of events can happen. But it does not follow that this future course of events will occur irrespective of our deliberations and choices. For example, it makes no sense to say of some single man named Harry that he is fated either to get married or not get married, and while we do not currently know which outcome is fated, one of them is and it will occur irrespective of Harry's choices and deliberations. These choices and deliberations play a crucial role in the causal chain leading up to the outcome. In general, the future will unfold by running through the chain of events constituting our deliberations and choices, and thus these play a crucial role in causally contributing to what the future is going to be.

Other philosophers point out that this response misses the real point of the argument from fatalism. That point is that, given determinism, our choices and deliberations are themselves determined. They are events in causal chains that extend into the past and over which we have no control. Thus, in light of determinism, there are only passive happenings in the world, not real actions; there is no categorical ability or no real possibility for alternative outcomes to be realized; there are no first movers, no agent control over our choices. Causal chains simply "run through" the person. Thus the argument from fatalism is actually an attempt to give a general picture of the world and of human action that seems to follow from determinism. So understood, it is another way to surface problems in the compatibilist treatment of ability, control, agency and causation. Whether the argument has force, then, will depend on one's view of the debate about these issues.

There are a number of important theological issues that intersect with the debate about the nature and reality of free will, three of which will be mentioned briefly. First, there is the issue of God's sovereignty, election, predestination, the nature of saving faith and related concepts. The details of this area of study are too numerous and intricate to mention here. Arminians, named after the Dutch theologian Jacobus Arminius (1560-1609), side with the libertarians and hold that (1) God's sovereignty is limited by and consistent with the libertarian choices of his creatures, (2) election and predestination are based on God's knowledge of those who would freely choose to repent and believe in Christ (or they are based on God's love but are consistent with such foreknowledge) and (3) the nature of saving faith is such that, while the unregenerate sinner may not be able to exercise saving faith without God's grace, nevertheless, once that grace is given, it is possible for the sinner to exercise or refrain from exercising saving faith. Calvinists, named after the Protestant Reformer John Calvin (1509-1564), have generally sided with the compatibilists and hold that (1) God's sovereignty determines whatsoever will come to pass in a way consistent with compatibilist freedom, (2) God's election and predestination are not based on foreknowledge, but rather his own sovereign will (**supralapsarianism** is the view that God's determination of each person's eternal destiny is logically prior to his decree to create mankind and permit the Fall; **infralapsarianism** is the view that God's determination is logically subsequent to his decrees to create and to permit the Fall) and (3) saving faith is such that once God's grace is given to a sinner, it is not possible for that person not to believe.

Second, there is the problem of reconciling God's foreknowledge of **future contingent events** (future free acts of God's creatures) with the fact that they are genuinely free. If God foreknows what that Sally will eat at McDonald's instead of Burger King on Tuesday, November 5, 2007, then how can Sally be free with regard to this choice? If she chose to eat at Burger King, she would falsify one of God's beliefs, and this cannot be the case. The issue is not a problem for compatibilists because they can claim that Sally is both de-

2.3.2
THEOLOGICAL
ISSUES

termined to eat at McDonald's and that her choice is free. But libertarians have a difficulty here. A number of responses have been offered to this problem: Some have argued that just as God cannot make a square circle and that is no limit to his power, so he cannot have foreknowledge of future free events because there is nothing for him to know until the choice is made. This solution is hard to square with a classical understanding of God's foreknowledge and with biblical passages that teach that God knows everything whatever, including the future acts of his creatures. Others claim that, strictly speaking, God is timeless, and thus he does not literally have *fore*-knowledge. When we understand that God timelessly knows the things he knows, and that his knowledge of something does not cause that thing to happen, then we have the resources for developing a response to the problem. Still others utilize a notion called **middle knowledge**, roughly, God's knowledge of what every free creature he could create would do in every possible circumstance in which they could be placed. God's middle knowledge of future free acts does not determine, but rather rests on what those choices will be. This approach is quite promising, but in order for it to be completely satisfying, its advocates must explain just how it is that God could possess such knowledge in the first place (see chap. 27).

A final theological issue is the problem of evil. This is more of a difficulty for the compatibilist. The libertarian claims that the origination of evil, and thus the responsible cause of its reality, is the libertarian free choices of angels and humans. True, God was responsible for creating such creatures in the first place. But if a case can be made that it was worth having such creatures even if God permitted evil to obtain from them, then it can be argued that the efficient cause of evil is not God but free creaturely choices. Compatibilists have a more difficult time with the existence of evil because, on their view, God determines everything that happens, including the sinful acts of his creatures. Most compatibilists agree that there is a mystery here, but nevertheless, we must continue to affirm God's goodness and human responsibility because such responsibility is consistent with determinism.

CHAPTER SUMMARY

Determinism is the view that for every event that happens, there are conditions such that, given them, nothing else could have happened. Hard determinists agree with libertarians that determinism and freedom are incompatible, the former accepting and the latter rejecting freedom. Compatibilists hold that determinism and freedom are compatible with each other. Thus a major area of difference between compatibilists and libertarians is over their understanding of freedom.

There are different notions of freedom, but the main one we have analyzed is the freedom of moral and rational responsibility—that freedom necessary for responsible agency. We have looked at both the compatibilist and libertarian perspectives on freedom and, along the way, we have seen some arguments for and against each view. Table 13.1 depicts five main areas of comparison between libertarians and compatibilists.

Table 13.1 Comparison between libertarians and compatibilists

	compatibilism	libertarianism
ability condition	hypothetical, one-way ability	categorical, two-way ability
control condition	causal theory of action	first or unmoved mover
rationality condition	reasons are efficient causes	reasons are final causes
causation	event-event causation	agent causation or noncausal agency
person as agent	consistent with but does not require person to be a substance	person must be a substance

Finally, the chapter looked at two further areas of comparison between compatibilists and libertarians: fatalism and theological issues. All Christians are agreed that human beings in general have the freedom necessary for responsible agency, but they differ as to what account of freedom is correct. The issues are complicated, but one's position will depend on biblical study, theological reflection, and philosophical judgments regarding which account is most plausible.

CHECKLIST OF BASIC TERMS AND CONCEPTS
ability condition
actualism
agency
agent causation
akrasia
belief/desire set
categorical ability
causal deviance
causal power
causal theory of action
causation
compatibilism (hard and soft, classical versus contemporary or hierarchical)
control condition
deliberation
determinism (hard and soft)
doxastic voluntarism (direct and indirect)
dual ability/control
efficient cause
event-event (or state-state) causation
fatalism (global versus local)
final cause
first or unmoved mover
first-order and second-order desires
first-order and second-order powers
free action

free will
freedom of moral and rational responsibility
freedom of permission
freedom of personal integrity
future contingent event
happening
human action
hypothetical ability
indeterminism
infralapsarianism
instrumental cause
intermediate mover
libertarianism
middle knowledge
noncausal theory of agency
one-way ability (or control)
person as agent
quantum physics
rationality condition
supralapsarianism
valuational system

14

PERSONAL IDENTITY
AND LIFE AFTER DEATH

My personal identity, therefore, implies the
continued existence of that indivisible thing which I call myself.
Whatever this self may be, it is something which thinks,
and deliberates, and resolves, and acts, and suffers.
I am not thought, I am not action, I am not feeling;
I am something that thinks, and acts, and suffers.
My thoughts, and actions, and feelings, change every moment—
they have no continued, but a successive existence;
but that self or I, to which they belong, is permanent,
and has the same relation to all the succeeding
thoughts, actions, and feelings, which I call mine.
THOMAS REID, "OF IDENTITY"

When I turn my reflection on myself,
I never can perceive this self without some one or more perceptions;
nor can I ever perceive any thing but the perceptions.
Tis the composition of these, therefore, which forms the self.
DAVID HUME, *A TREATISE OF HUMAN NATURE*

1 INTRODUCTION

Death is a dramatic, disruptive event. Nevertheless, a central truth of Christianity holds that personal immortality, in which I myself will survive death and live on in an afterlife, is real. There have been a number of different models for depicting life after death as taught in Scripture, but three of them are among the most popular. First, there is the **traditional position on immortality**, held by most in the history of the church. In this view, God alone possesses immortality in himself (cf. 1 Tim 6:16). Still, though human beings are properly and normally to be construed as a unity of material human bodies and immaterial substantial souls, at the time of death a person enters into a temporary disembodied state that is less than complete and then receives a new resurrected body at the general resurrection. The person who survives death is "I myself" in an absolute, literal sense.

A second view may be called the **immediate resurrection position on im-**

mortality. In this view, when one dies, he or she is immediately given some sort of temporal body while waiting for a final resurrected body, or his or her pre-death body is taken away by God at death and replaced with a corpse that is buried. This view has the virtue of allowing for continued personal existence in an intermediate state, but it suffers from the fact that certain biblical texts seem to describe the intermediate state as a disembodied one (cf. Ps 49:15; Mt 27:50; 2 Cor 5:1-8; Heb 12:23; Rev 6:9-11).

A third, more recent view is called the **re-creation position on immortality**: When one dies he becomes extinct—there is no disembodied person in an intermediate state—but at the resurrection of the dead God recreates that person all over again out of nothing. Apart from exegetical difficulties with this view, it is not clear that this position has the resources for holding that the person that is recreated is literally the same person who died years earlier. We will return to this question and to the issue of life after death toward the end of the chapter. However, it should be clear that the intelligibility of personal survival of death (and of any version of such survival) will partly be a matter of one's general view of personal identity through change. The issue of personal identity is of great interest for its own sake, but it also relates to belief in an afterlife.

Questions about personal identity through change are aspects of the broader issue of sameness and change in general. In chapter nine it was pointed out that before change is possible, the thing that changes must exist at the beginning, during the process and at the end of the change. If an apple goes from yellow to red, it must be the same apple throughout the change. In general, change presupposes literal, absolute sameness through change. If there is no such sameness, then there is only succession and no real change. There would be a yellow-apple-at-time x that ceased to be and a red-apple-at-time y that succeeded it. In chapter ten we saw that the traditional doctrine of substance is a metaphysical view that seeks, among other things, to account for sameness through change.

However, our purpose in this chapter is not to focus on sameness and change in general, but on the nature of personal identity in particular. What is a human person and does such a person remain the same through change? If so, how are we to understand this? Traditional Christian theology, common sense and various philosophical arguments unite to affirm that persons sustain absolute, real sameness through various kinds of change. This position is called the absolute view of personal identity, and it is most often, though not always, associated with substance dualism (see chap. 11).

However, certain contemporary ideologies such as scientism, physicalism and sensate forms of crude empiricism render absolute sameness through change impossible. For these and other reasons, various empiricist views of personal identity have been offered as alternatives to the absolute view. In this chapter, we will first look at the identity of physical artifacts through change; second, spell out the absolute view and two empiricist views of personal identity (the body position and the memory view); third, assess the arguments for and against these three positions.

Before we press on, a few preliminary distinctions should be made. First, we must distinguish an **absolute, strict sense of identity** from a loose, popular sense of identity. If an entity x at time t_1 maintains absolute, strict identity with entity y at time t_2 (say x is Smith at twelve years old and y is Smith at forty-three years old), then x and y stand in the identity relation to each other such that Leibniz's law of the indiscernibility of identicals (see chap. 9) holds for x and y (something is true of x if and only if it is true of y). Everything true of Smith at twelve is true of Smith at forty-three because the very same person who was twelve is now forty-three. In absolute sameness, a person moves through time and exists fully at each moment of his life. Persons have no temporal parts or stages; thus tenses and dates are not parts of persons. Smith at twelve was five feet tall and was to be six feet tall at forty-three. Smith at forty-three is six feet tall but was five feet tall.

We will look more closely at the **loose, popular sense of identity** when we look at the identity of physical objects. But for now, we should point out that if something sustains loose, popular identity through change, our judgment of sameness is to some extent arbitrary and not to be understood in a strict way. For example, the Kansas City Royals baseball team could change all of its players, managers, owners and even its stadium and uniforms and still be judged the same team in a loose and popular sense, even if, strictly speaking, the team is different. One issue we will look at is whether or not persons sustain strict, absolute sameness through change or merely loose, popular "sameness."

Second, the metaphysical aspects of personal identity must be kept distinct from the epistemological ones. The former focuses on what *constitutes* personal identity—What *is* personal identity and what makes it *real*? What is it to say that person x at time t_1 is the same person as y at t_2? The epistemological aspects focus on *criteria* for personal identity: How it is possible to know or justifiably believe that a person at time t_2 is the same person as someone at t_1? The epistemological problem can be broken down into two subissues that are very different: the first-person issue of how I myself know I am the same person through change versus the third-person issue of how one can know that some other person is the same person through change. Moreover, the epistemological problem includes the question of how we would know (in a first- or third-person way) that personal identity obtains in an embodied state before death versus in a disembodied intermediate state after death. In this chapter, our main focus will be on the metaphysical aspect of personal identity, though epistemological questions will be treated as part of our discussion. We cannot cover all the important views on this topic in the space of one short chapter. Rather, this chapter will focus on three main views of personal identity that have played an important role in the history of the debate regarding personal identity.

2 THE IDENTITY THROUGH CHANGE OF PHYSICAL ARTIFACTS

The world contains living entities like humans and dogs and physical artifacts like tables and ships. However, the world also contains entities called processes (e.g., the boiling of water) and events (e.g., a birthday party or a baseball game). Consider an event that takes some time such as a baseball game. An event of this sort is extended through time and thus is composed of temporal parts; a baseball game is a sum of nine temporal parts called innings.

Next, consider an artifact like a ship. Such an entity is extended throughout space and thus has spatial parts (e.g., the sides, deck, sails of the ship). Do such physical artifacts maintain strict sameness through change? Do they have temporal parts in addition to physical parts? Such questions have been part of philosophy since its inception, and they have often focused on the ship of Theseus, an ancient Greek sailor and warrior who was a king of Athens. Here is Plutarch's reference to the ship of Theseus:

> The ship wherein Theseus and the youth of Athens returned had thirty oars, and was preserved by the Athenians down even to the time of Demetrius Phalereus, for they took away the old planks as they decayed, putting in new and stronger timber in their place, insomuch that this ship became a standing example among the philosophers, for the logical question of things that grow; one side holding that the ship remained the same, and the other contending that it was not the same.[1]

Over the years the ship of Theseus had all its parts replaced plank by plank, nail by nail, and so on, so that the ship that continued to sail had all new parts and none of its original parts. Was this ship replaced or repaired? Was it literally the same ship as the original ship of Theseus or a new ship that merely resembled the original one and continued to function as a vessel of war?

To embellish the story, suppose that each time an original wooden part of the ship was replaced, a plank of frozen green Jell-O and not wood was used. Suppose further, that all the original parts that were removed piece by piece over the years were saved in a warehouse and, years later were reassembled into a ship composed of all and only the original ship's parts in the very same structural arrangement. Now, assuming for the sake of argument that the answer is one or the other, which ship would be identical to the original ship of Theseus, the frozen green Jell-O ship or the one with all and only the original parts in the very same structure? Commonsense intuitions and many philosophers have agreed that the original ship is the one with the same parts and structure and not the frozen green Jell-O one.

Let us assume what seems reasonable, namely, that this answer is the correct one. According to many philosophers, four lessons can be drawn from the ship of Theseus and our conclusion to the puzzle. First, physical artifacts do not maintain absolute, strict identity through change. An artifact cannot gain new parts and lose old ones (or have the parts structurally rearranged) and still be the very same ship. Physical artifacts are merely structured parts (property-things) and when the parts or the structure changes, the ship loses its identity. For physical artifacts, strict sameness through change is a fiction. This view is a version of what is called **mereological essentialism**, from the Greek word *meros*, which means "part." Mereological essentialism means that the parts of a thing are essential to it as a whole. If the object gains or loses parts, it is a different object. Many, though not all, philosophers adopt mereological essentialism as the most adequate account of physical objects such as the ship of Theseus.

Second, the best we can hope for is loose, popular identity for artifacts. Some philosophers would advance the idea that such objects become a series of spa-

---

[1]Plutarch, "The Life of Theseus," in *The Lives of the Noble Grecians and Romans*, trans. John Dryden, rev. Arthur H. Clough (New York: Random House, n.d.), p. 14.

tiotemporal parts, sometimes called **space-time worms** or paths, as depicted in figure 14.1.

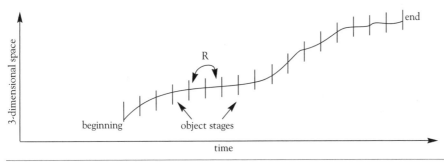

Fig. 14.1 Space-time worm or path

If we claim that a ship is the "same" over time, we mean that the ship is a sum of its spatial and temporal parts. The temporal parts are called object stages or time slices of the object. Several implications follow from this idea. First, the ship does not exist at each moment from its beginning to its destruction; rather, a ship stage exists at each moment. The ship does not exist *through* time; it is like a baseball game. The whole ship is a sum of each temporal (and spatial) part (ship stage).

Second, if we ask what it is that unites all the various stages of the ship of Theseus into the "same" ship (the same space-time path), the answer will be that all the ship stages stand to each other in some relationship R and no other ship stages (say the various time slices of a second ship owned by Ulysses) stand in that relation R to any of the stages of the ship of Theseus. Various accounts have been given for what R must be: Earlier stages must cause the existence of later stages, each stage must be continuous in space and time with its neighboring stages (no Star Trek beam up here!), each stage must closely resemble its neighbors in appearance, or the entire ship cannot lose some arbitrary amount of parts (e.g., not over fifty percent) and part replacement must be slow and gradual. Whatever R turns out to be, it is something that relates the various successive stages of the ship into "one" ship, and R is a weaker relation than identity. Sometimes this relation is called **genidentity**.

Third, identity is somewhat arbitrary and comes in degrees. For example, we can count the ship with replaced frozen Jell-O parts as the same as the original ship of Theseus until it reaches some arbitrary limit we choose: loss of fifty-one percent of original parts, loss of one part unless we color the Jell-O brown and so forth. Sameness is a matter of convention here, and the replaced ship becomes less and less "identical" with the original ship the more parts it loses or the more it fails to resemble the original ship in color, shape and so forth. We can choose any arbitrary limit for sameness we wish and after that point is reached, we can count the ship that is present a different ship and not the "same" one.

Finally, since temporal (and spatial) parts are essential to physical artifacts, now viewed as space-time paths, it follows that a specific artifact could not have had a different temporal origin and still be the same object (nor could it have lasted longer or traced a different path through space and still have been the same object). If the ship of Theseus had been made a week later from the day it was, in fact, made, it would have a different set of temporal parts, and thus it would be a different ship. As we will see later, it is not clear that the same could be said of persons.

It is time, now, to turn to a clarification of the different views of the identity of persons through time. The absolute view of personal identity holds that persons maintain strict sameness through change. Two different types of empiricist views deny this claim and treat persons like physical artifacts.

3 THREE VIEWS OF PERSONAL IDENTITY

3.1
STATEMENT OF
THE VIEWS

First, there is the commonsense view, advocated by philosophers such as Bishop Joseph Butler (1692-1752) and Thomas Reid (1710-1796), known as the **absolute view of personal identity**. According to this position, persons differ from physical artifacts in that persons maintain strict, absolute sameness through change. Leibniz's law of the indiscernibility of identicals holds between all the moments a person exists except for tenses because persons do not have temporal parts. A six-foot-tall adult is strictly identical to the three-foot-tall person who was he as a child. The child *was to have* the property of being six feet tall and the adult *currently has* that property; the adult *used to have* the property of being three feet tall that the child had, say, twenty years ago.

Personal identity is absolute; it is not a matter to be settled by convention; it does not come in degrees; and it is not partial. If we ask of a person at time t_2 if he is the same person as one existing at t_1 earlier than t_2, the question will have a yes or no answer. Contrast this with material objects. Suppose half of a table is taken away and replaced with new table parts. Is the new table the same as the old one? Strictly speaking, the answer is no. But we could say that the new table is partially the same as the old one (fifty percent in this case) and we may arbitrarily choose to draw a line at fifty percent and say that the table is still the "same" if it loses fifty percent of its original parts or less and not the same if it loses more than fifty percent. But we could draw the line at any point that suits our purposes. If we valued table legs, we might wish to say that the table was the "same" if it still had three original legs even if it had lost more than fifty percent of its original parts. Personal identity is not like that. It is an all or nothing affair, not a matter of convention, on the absolutist view.

Next, the absolutist holds that personal identity is unanalyzable and primitive. It cannot be broken down into something else more basic that could be taken to constitute personal identity. The identity of a table can be so analyzed. We can say that the "sameness" through change of a table is to be broken down into a position about the stability of the parts of the table. But personal identity cannot be defined in terms of something more basic that it. Sometimes this is put by saying that the first-person point of view, the "I," is illusive and cannot be reduced to a third-person point of view. The "I" is ultimate and serves as the unifier of persons in two senses: First, a person is a **unity at a given time**. Right now, you may be having several different but simultaneous experiences: an itch in your foot, a thought about personal identity, an awareness of music in the background, a desire for coffee, and a feeling of the chair on which you sit. These different experiences are united as experiences of the same person, namely you, because they are all owned or had by the very same center of consciousness, the same "I." Second, a person is a **unity through time**. Over the years your body parts come and go, and your various mental states—memories, personality traits, etc.—come and go. But they are all aspects of the same person because they all belong to the same enduring "I" according to the absolutist view. Thus, upon analysis, the first-person point of view turns out to be grounded in a specific sort of thing that can have a "first-person point of view," namely, an ego, an "I," a substantial center of consciousness. Because the first-person point of view is rooted in a substantial center of consciousness that has this first-person point of view, the phrase "first-person point of view," actually refers to a certain kind of point (thing, unified center, substance)--a viewing, sentient sort of point properly called an "I."

Finally, most, though not all, advocates of the absolutist view hold that substance dualism is the best way to understand the "I" or the ego that accounts for personal identity. I am essentially my soul—same soul, same person; different soul, different person—and it is because my soul exists, owns my mental life, diffuses my body and endures through change, that personal identity has a foundation. Personal identity is grounded in the soul for many advocates of the absolutist view. Thus, upon analysis, the first-person point of view turns out to be grounded in a first-person viewing kind of point—a substantially self-conscious ego.

Two radically different positions about personal identity are called empiricist views. The two main **empiricist views of personal identity** are the body view and the memory view. Before we look at each, there are three things they share in common, which center around the rejection of the absolutist position. First, empiricist positions start with a view of identity through change derived from physical artifacts and extend this to the identity of persons. This means that personal identity through change, just like that of nations and tables, comes in degrees, is partial, and is to some extent a matter of convention.

Second, personal identity is not unanalyzable. It should be defined in terms of something else. For the body view, "sameness" of person is constituted by "sameness" of body. For the memory view it will be the continuity of various psychological factors—memories, personality traits, interests and goals and, perhaps, continuity of the brain as the necessary "carrier" of those psychological factors—that constitutes personal identity. Either way, a person is like a process—a person is a series of person stages that are related to each other in an appropriate relationship. The main point of a theory of personal identity is to spell out what the relationship or connection is between various person stages that makes them all stages of the "same" person. This means that the first-person perspective, expressed with the word *I* can be exhaustively replaced without loss of any information by a third-person description of the person in question.

Finally, there is no substantive soul or ego. According to empiricist advocates, such an entity is a prescientific, unobservable, useless postulate. A person is a bundle of physical and mental states at a time (and most physicalist versions of empiricist views go on to reduce mental states to physical states as well, according to various strategies mentioned in chap. 12) and a series of physical and mental states through time.

The **body view of empiricism** holds that the connection between various person stages that unites them as stages of the "same" person is that all the mental states of the person are connected to the "same" body. The reason that you are the same as the person who read the first sentence of this paragraph is that the experience of reading this sentence is tied to a specific body, the experience of reading the first sentence was connected to a specific body, and the body is the "same" in both cases. Since sameness of person is analyzed in terms of sameness of body, advocates of this view must tell us what it means for the body to be the same, in a loose, nonabsolute sense, through change. Various answers have been given to this: new body stages must have a certain percentage of parts in common with neighboring stages just before and after it, new stages must be spatiotemporally continuous with neighboring stages, new body stages must resemble neighboring stages in appearance. In each case, the body view often allows for significant replacement of parts, change in spatial/temporal location and alteration in appearance by later body stages compared to earlier ones. But, generally speaking, such changes must be gradual and continuous and not drastic and abrupt.

The **memory view of empiricism** holds that it is continuity of psychological characteristics that constitutes personal identity. The internal connections between experiences themselves are all that is needed to make sense of the idea of a series of experiences through time being experiences of the "same" person. Chief among these psychological traits is memory. The reason that you are the "same" person as the person who got up this morning is that you currently have most of the "same" memories as the person who got up (except, of course, you now have memories of the day not possessed by your prior stage upon waking). Note that memories are not seen as epistemological criteria for determining sameness of person; memories constitute sameness of person.

Often the memory criterion is supplemented with the continuity of other psychological factors: continuity of likes and dislikes, goals and interests, character traits, feelings of warmth and ownership of earlier person stages. Some add that since the brain is what carries and contains these psychological traits, then continuity of brain is a necessary condition for continuity of psychological traits and thus for personal identity. Property and event dualists (see chap. 11) like A. J. Ayer hold that psychological states are irreducibly mental and the self is just a bundle at a time and a series through time of discrete, otherwise ownerless mental stages (feelings of pain, thoughts of lunch, desires for love). Physicalist advocates of the memory view hold that psychological states are not irreducibly mental, but rather can be reduced to brain states or treated in some other way consistent with physicalist views of a person (see chap. 12).

3.2
ASSESSMENT OF THE VIEWS

3.2.1
ARGUMENTS FOR THE ABSOLUTIST VIEW

a. Basic experience of the self. Suppose you are approaching a brown table and in three different moments of introspection you attend to your own awarenesses. At time t_1 you are five feet from the table and you experience a slight pain in your foot (P_1), a certain light brown table sensation from a specific place in the room (S_1) and a specific thought that the table seems old (T_1). A moment later at t_2 when you are three feet from the table you experience a feeling of warmth (F_1) from a heater, a different table sensation (S_2) with a different shape and slightly different shade of brown than that of S_1, and a new thought that the table reminds you of your childhood desk (T_2). Finally, a few seconds later, t_3, you feel a desire to have the table (D_1), a new table sensation from one foot away (S_3) and a new thought that you could buy it for less than twenty-five dollars (T_3).

In this series of experiences, you are aware of different things at different moments. However, at each moment of time, you are also aware that there is a self at that time that is having those experiences and that unites them into one field of consciousness. Moreover, you are also aware that the very same self had the experiences at t_1, t_2 and t_3. Finally, you are aware that the self that had all the experiences is none other than you yourself. This can be pictured as in figure 14.2.

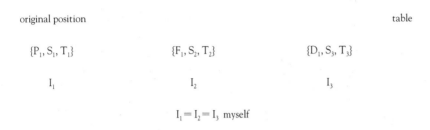

original position   table

$\{P_1, S_1, T_1\}$ $\{F_1, S_2, T_2\}$ $\{D_1, S_3, T_3\}$

I_1 I_2 I_3

$I_1 = I_2 = I_3$ myself

Fig. 14.2 **Basic experience of the self**

Through introspection, you are simply aware that you are not your body or a group of experiences. Rather, you are aware that you are the self that owns and unifies your experiences at each moment of time and that you are the same self that endures through time. In short, you are aware of being a mental subject that is in your body, that owns and unites your experience and that maintains sameness through change.

It can be argued that such awarenesses are either misleading or nonexistent. For example, David Hume claimed never to have an awareness of his own "I" but only of this or that experience or group of experiences. However, two things seem wrong with this claim. First, how did Hume know which stream of consciousness to focus on in order to look for his own "I"? Wasn't he already aware in some sense of his own self *before* he could identify which experiences were his? We will return to this point below.

Second, it may be true that we never have an experience of our own "I" if we allow only sensations (e.g., of color, taste, smell, sound, texture, pain, pleasure) to count as experiences. But it can be argued that the "I" itself is not the sort of thing that *could* be sensed in that way, and the conclusion to draw from this is not that we are not aware of our own selves, but that there are other kinds of awarenesses besides sensory awarenesses and that our awareness of our own self is by means of a different kind of awareness. It is hard to conceive of something we could be aware of with more certainty than this: While I listen to a song, I am the one having my experiences and that continues to endure during the whole performance.

b. First-person irreducible to third-person. No account of the world in terms of third-person descriptions will be able to capture without remainder my own

first-person perspective (the vantage point one uses to describe the world from one's own point of view). Nor will it be able to tell me which object in that world is I myself. No description of my body or my psychological traits will entail that the entity being described is I. A complete physicalist description of the entire material world, including all the bodies in it, could be given in the **third-person perspective** (the point of view of an observer, e.g., there is an object at location x that is six feet tall, white, etc.). This would suffice to identify all the physical objects in space and time. But no such description will tell me which body is mine or which entity I myself am.

If we add to this physicalist description an exhaustive description of all the mental states present in all the bodies (e.g., object at location x has memories of being at the 1979 Super Bowl and that object has such and such character traits, desires and so forth), the problem is still present: Such an account will not tell which entity so described is I myself. The "I" and the first-person standpoint cannot be eliminated or reduced to a third-person point of view. My own "I," my own first-person point of view, my knowledge of myself by direct acquaintance would be left out of such third-person descriptions.

Certain words are called **indexicals**: *I, here, there, now, then.* These words are **token reflexive**, that is, they systematically change their referents in a context-dependent way. For example, if Smith uses the indexical *tomorrow* to correctly say "I will arrive tomorrow," then on arrival the next day, he cannot say "I have arrived tomorrow," since the referent *tomorrow* has changed from the day before. Rather, Smith would have to say "I have arrived today."

The most basic indexical word is *I* (and, most likely, *now*). *Here* and *now* refer to where and when I am. *There* and *then* refer to where and when I am not. A complete third-person account of the world will not capture the information expressed by indexicals. This fact can be explained if I am a first-person center of consciousness, a mental substance different from my body and mental states. If my identity consisted in simply being my body or being a certain bundle of mental states, a third-person account of the world would be exhaustive and would clearly identify which object I am. Thus the irreducibility of the first-person point of view supports the absolutist position.

These basic intuitions about the unity and singularity of one's self and the first-person point of view can be illustrated with a thought experiment. Suppose it becomes possible someday to perform a brain operation on a person in such a way that exactly half of his brain along with half of his body is transplanted and joined to two different half bodies without brains awaiting the transplanted parts. Figure 14.3 diagrams the situation where half of P_1 is transplanted to P_2 and P_3.

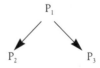

Fig. 14.3 P_1 transplanted into P_2 and P_3

Suppose further that upon recovery each of the two persons, P_2 and P_3, manifest the same character traits and have the same memories as did P_1. Note first that the transplant would have created two new persons, but P_1 cannot be identical to both P_2 and P_3 for the very simple reason that one thing cannot be the same as two things. On the memory view, sameness of person obtains if and only if sameness of character traits and memories obtain. Thus the memory view would imply that P_1 is identical to P_2 and P_3, which is absurd if taken literally. However, advocates of the memory view hold that P_2 and P_3 are each P_1 in that they both exactly resemble P_1 in psychological traits. We will return to this option later.

Since P_1 cannot literally be both P_2 and P_3, what are our other options? It may be that P_1 ceased to exist and P_2 and P_3 are two totally new people, or it may be that P_1 survived and is identical to P_2 (or P_3) and that one new person, P_3 (or P_2) came into being as a result of the operation.

Either way, we learn two things from the example. First, a person is not identical to his body or his memories and character traits (remember: persons *have* these things, they are not *identical* to them or to a collection of them). Why? Because P_2 and P_3 each have P_1's memories and character traits and an equal share of P_1's brain and body, but they cannot both *be* P_1. Therefore, the fact that P_1 is a person must amount to more than just being a brain with memories and character traits or to just being a body.

The second lesson shows us that persons are not capable of partial identity and survival as are physical objects. If you break a table in half and use each half to build two new tables, then it makes sense to say that the original table partially survives and is partly present in each of the new tables. But as we have seen in our brain operation example, the following four options are possible ways to understand what happened:[2] (1) P_1 ceases to be, and two new persons, P_2 and P_3, come to be; (2) P_1 survives and is identical to P_2, and a new person, P_3, comes to be; (3) P_1 survives and is identical to P_3, and a new person, P_2, comes to be; (4) P_1 partially survives in P_2 and P_3. Option (4) may make sense of physical objects like tables, but it is not a reasonable option with regard to persons.

To see why option (4) is not a good one, consider a second thought experiment. Suppose a mad surgeon captures you and announces that he is going to transplant your left hemisphere and body half into one half body and the right hemisphere and body half into another half body. After surgery, he is going to torture one of the resultant persons and reward the other one with a gift of a million dollars. You can choose which of the two persons, A or B, will be tortured and which will be rewarded. It is clear that whichever way you choose, your choice would be a risk. Perhaps you will cease to exist and be neither A nor B. But it is also possible that you will be either A or B. However, one thing does not seem possible—your being partially A and partially B. For in that case you would have reason to approach the surgery with both a feeling of joyous expectation and horrified dread! But it is hard to make sense of such a mixed anticipation because there will be no person after the surgery who will experience

[2]Cf. Thomas Nagel, "Brain Bisection and the Unity of Consciousness," in *Mortal Questions* (Cambridge: Cambridge University Press, 1979), pp. 147-64, esp. 154-55.

such a mixed fate. Partial survival, at least when it comes to persons, does not seem to make sense. Persons are unities, not collections or combinations of things that permit partial survival as do physical objects. The first-person point of view, the "I," captures this fact.

c. Fear of future pain and punishment for the past. Fear of some painful event in the future or blame and punishment for some deed in the past appear to make sense only if we implicitly assume that it is literally I myself that will experience the pain or that was the doer of the past deed. Future pain or past deeds are not mine by convention, and if real identity is a fiction, it is hard to make sense of these cases of fear and punishment. We would not have such fear or merit such punishment if the person in the future or past merely resembled my current self in having similar memories, psychological traits or a body spatiotemporally continuous with mine or that had many of the same parts as my current body.

Empiricist theorists have responded to this argument in different ways. Regarding future pain, some have pointed out that empiricist views give a way of grounding altruism, that in future pain we are really concerned for someone else and that is good. Others claim that fear of future pain rests solely on the continuity of "our" desires, goals and memories. If a person twenty-five years from now were to face pain but had no memories or other psychological traits in common with me now, I simply would not worry about him.

Regarding past deeds, some philosophers grant that retribution is hard to justify on an empiricist view of personal identity. But they go on to point out that other aspects of punishment can be justified (deterrence of others, rehabilitation, protection of society due to incarceration), and those aspects are all that matter in justifying punishing a present person stage for a past deed.

d. Rationality and thought processes. Some have argued that to realize the truth of any proposition or even entertain it as meaningful, the very same self must be aware of its different parts (e.g., those expressed by the associated sentence's subject, verb, predicate). If one person stage contemplated the subject, another stage the verb, and still another the predicate, literally no self would persist to think through and grasp the proposition as a whole.

The same point applies to thinking through the premises of an argument and drawing a conclusion. The same self must be present to unite and compare the premises, see whether they entail a conclusion and draw that conclusion. If nothing can occupy our attention for a while since we do not endure through time, then we could have only momentary contents and these processes would be impossible. To attend to a proposition or argument, we must continue to be. If this argument is sound, then it means that empiricist views are self-refuting if they are asserted as rational by using supporting arguments, because such theories render this type of rationality impossible.

A major response to this argument is that as each person stage emerges or ceases to be in a series of thinkings, that stage passes on to the next one its content and a feeling of ownership ("this thought was mine"). Thus, at the time a conclusion of an argument is thought, there are simultaneously a thought of the conclusion and a thought from memory of the premises of the argument.

You will have to decide for yourself whether a momentary person stage could simultaneously combine all these different thoughts at once and if, in fact, this is what is going on when we think.

e. Switch cases. Certain "switching" situations seem to be logically possible: for example, it is possible that one could wake up in an entirely different body or with a totally different set of memories and psychological traits. If he so desired, God could put person A in person B's body and vice versa, and he could give B memories exactly like A's and vice versa. In short, alternative biographies are possible: the same person could have had a different body and memories. If this is possible, then this shows that "sameness" of body or memories is not a necessary condition for personal identity. One can continue to exist without psychological or bodily continuity.

Similarly, one's current body could come to be occupied by a new person in a switch or, in cases of demon possession, one's body could be occupied by more than one person. In the same way, God could create a double of person A and give that person the very "same" memories and psychological traits as A while A himself retained qualitatively identical memories and traits. In short, distinct but qualitatively identical biographies are possible: the same body or set of memories could be possessed by different persons. If this is possible, then this shows that sameness of body or memories is not a sufficient condition for personal identity.

Advocates of empiricist views can simply deny that such cases are, in fact, logically possible. Or they can grant that they are possible or not possible depending on one's conception of personal identity and that all this shows is how arbitrary and conventional our concept of persons is.

f. Specific problems in empiricist positions. Finally, absolutists point out certain problems that plague empiricist views but, they claim, not absolutist positions of personal identity. Consider first the body view. For one thing, one can wake up in the morning and know who one is without opening up his eyes. In fact, though it may sound strange, at the moment one awakens he could simultaneously know who he is and that he is an enduring self and doubt that he even has a body (suppose he has been reading Hal Lindsey and thinks for a moment that the rapture happened during the night). The body view has difficulty accounting for this possibility.

Second, as already pointed out, surely demon possession is logically possible and, in fact, there is good evidence that it actually occurs. But in this case, the bodily principle (same body, then same person) is false because two persons "occupy" the same body. Finally, one's knowledge of oneself is incorrigible, that is, one cannot be mistaken about which self one is. It does not seem to make sense that one could misidentify one's self at the present moment. But, if self-knowledge requires one first to know facts about a certain body and then ascribe that body to oneself, then two problems arise: (1) Such self-knowledge presupposes direct acquaintance with one's own "I" before one can ascribe a given body to himself. Knowledge of one's body presupposes and cannot, therefore, constitute self-knowledge. (2) One could always make a mistake in ascribing some body to oneself. Since first-person identification is incorrigible, and since it could not be incorrigible if self-knowledge is acquired according to the picture given us by the body view, then that view must be false.

Regarding the memory view, the problem of circularity arises just as it does for the body view. From the time of Butler and Reid, it has been argued that memories presuppose and, therefore, cannot constitute personal identity. The thing that now makes me the same person as an individual in the past cannot be that I now have that past person's memories. In order for me to have those memories, I would already have to be that person. In other words, the thing that distinguishes real past memories of an event (where I was the one who did that past event) from qualitatively indistinguishable but only apparent memories, is that in the real case I was there but in the apparent case I was not. Thus memory is only an epistemological test for personal identity but does not give us the nature of such identity.

Second, consider the brain operation thought experiment mentioned earlier in the chapter. It is surely possible that a person could undergo a transplant and two persons come to have all and only the very same set of memories and psychological traits as the original person before the transplant. Some memory advocates claim that in this situation we should simply claim that the original person is the "same" as both new persons. Now it is obvious that they cannot mean by "same" here literal identity because one thing, in this case a person, cannot be literally identical to two persons. What they mean is that sameness is just resemblance. In other words, both new persons are exactly similar in traits to the preoperation person, so it is arbitrary which to count as that person.

But does this really make sense? Can one's own identity really be so arbitrary? From a first-person perspective, it is easy to imagine waking up after the operation in one body and looking at the person next to one with one's exact traits and memories. It would not be an arbitrary matter from one's first-person perspective as to which person he was, though from a third-person point of view someone else may not be able to tell which new person is the preoperation self.

Some memory advocates respond to a case like this by adding a condition to the memory criterion. Person y at time t_2 is the "same" as person x at an earlier time t_1 if and only if (1) there is continuity of memory and other psychological traits and (2) there is no other person z at time t_2 that resembles x as much as does y. The problem with this view is that the case above is simply easy to imagine: an operation could be performed, I could survive as one of the two psychologically indistinguishable people, I could know from my own point of view that I myself am the preoperation person, and all of this is quite independent of whether or not that other new person exists. How can a person's identity or nonidentity with a person at an earlier time depend on the existence or nonexistence of another person?

A final problem seems to plague both empiricist views. Since they depict persons as series of stages with temporal parts, then if parts are essential to their wholes (different parts, different wholes), then no person could have been born at a time different from his or her actual birth. However, if such a thing is possible, as would seem to be the case, then empiricist views may be inadequate.

Among the arguments raised against the absolute view, three stand out. First, David Hume and a number of others claim that we are never aware of our "I"; we are only aware of our bodies and, through introspection, of our current mental states (e.g., our current sensations of pain and color, thoughts, willings). Thus the "I" is a fiction.

Absolutists have responded in two ways. They point out that we are, in fact, aware of our own self, but such acts of awareness are not like sensations of pain and color. The empiricist limits the types of awareness we can have to the latter, but we do, in fact, have the former in cases where we are aware of ourselves as the enduring owners and unifiers of our mental life and bodies. Further, if we were not already aware of ourselves, how would we know which stream of consciousness or which body to investigate in order to confirm or rule out an awareness of my "I"? Introspection and knowledge of one's body and mental life presupposes awareness of the "I."

Second, empiricists claim that if the "I" is some immaterial entity, say a soul, that is in the body and underlies our mental states, then we could never know who someone else is because we only have their bodies, memories and character traits to go on. We have no direct acquaintance with their bare self. This is a version of the problem of other minds, which states that the absolutist view leads to skepticism about our knowledge of other selves.

Some absolutists respond in this way: They admit that it is always logically possible that, when confronted with a body or set of memories, a different person than we normally know is present. But skepticism need not be refuted by showing that skepticism is logically impossible and there is no chance whatever for error or doubt in some area of belief (see chap. 4). This same problem of skepticism is present about the existence of the external world (it is logically possible we are having sensations of a world when no world exists). To rebut the skeptic it is enough to point out that in one's own first-person case, one knows who one is and that one is an enduring self by direct introspective awareness, and that one also can correlate one's own enduring self with the continuity of one's body and psychological traits. One learns from this that a good inductive correlation exists between these, and one can then use this correlation to justify the use of bodily continuity and memory as evidence of personal identity in the case of others, even though such continuity does not constitute personal identity and it is logically possible that such judgments are wrong. Empiricists respond to this by saying that such an inductive generalization is extremely weak because it is only built on one case of correlation between an enduring self and continuity of memories and body, i.e., your own case.

Finally, some empiricists have argued that postulating an enduring soul to ground an enduring self solves nothing. How do we know that an immaterial soul is not just a collection or bundle of experiences at a time and a series of discrete souls through time? Moreover, how would one know which soul was his? The same problem of identification regarding bodies and psychological traits occurs regarding immaterial souls.

Absolutists respond by claiming that, in the first-person case, one does not "postulate" that he is an immaterial substance that owns his experiences and

body and that endures through time. One is directly aware of it and simply reports it to others. There is a major tradition in philosophy that claims that our
knowledge of our own selves is among the very best knowledge we have; the
clearest and most obvious case of a substance is in our own self-acquaintance.
And in acts of introspection we are simply aware of ourselves as enduring, immaterial centers of feelings, thoughts, beliefs, desires and willings. As a matter
of ultimate fact, one's own self simply is such an enduring entity and one's
awareness of this is basic and fundamental.

3.2.3
A FINAL
WORD ABOUT
THOUGHT
EXPERIMENTS
AND
IMAGINATION

Throughout this chapter, many arguments for or against a certain view of personal identity have relied on intuitions about what is possible or impossible.
Could body or memory switches be possible or not? Could I survive a transplant
as both of the new persons or not? The absolutist view is supported by fairly
commonsense intuitions, and it places great emphasis on the first-person perspective and our own introspective awareness. The empiricist views place emphasis on the third-person point of view and, frequently, on modern science.
That is, many philosophers believe that a modern scientific outlook rules out dualism and absolutist views of personal identity. In this view, persons are just natural, physical objects like everything else and we should assimilate our views of
personal identity to those of the identity of natural objects like chairs or rocks.

One's views about personal identity and the related mind-body problem will
depend, to a significant degree, on one's attitude about the proper order between science on the one hand and philosophy and common sense on the
other. In our view, three things stand out in this regard. First, as Christians, the
absolutist view would seem to be the most natural way to understand scriptural
teaching about the self, the reality of a disembodied intermediate state, the final resurrection, rewards and punishments and so on.

Second, philosophy is more fundamental and basic than science. In fact, scientific knowledge presupposes and is founded on presuppositions that require
philosophical formulation and defense (see chaps. 15-18). When this order is reversed and science becomes the benchmark for formulating a philosophical position on some matter, highly counterintuitive results often follow, as is the case
with empiricist positions on personal identity.

Third, strictly speaking, the absolutist (and dualist) position is quite consistent with at least certain areas of science, but not with versions of weak scientism in which the findings of science are used to argue for positions about which,
strictly speaking, science is silent. Just because computers can imitate intelligence, or because we continue to learn more about the brain and its interactions with the soul, it does not follow that there is no soul and no enduring
unified self. Empiricist views of the self are not the direct result of science, but
rather the result of science plus the philosophical position that science is the
best or perhaps only way to answer philosophical questions outside the bounds
of science properly understood. Thus one's views about personal identity will
depend not on weighing intuitions from commonsense and philosophical argument against those from science, but against those from certain philosophical
extensions of science into areas not properly part of science. It is important to
keep in mind, then, that the role of science in matters of the mind-body prob-

lem or personal identity is not as straightforward as many physicalists or empiricists about identity would have us believe.

4 FINAL REMARKS

In the introduction to this chapter, we pointed out that one's view of life after death would be influenced by one's position on personal identity and vice versa. We saw that three main competitors regarding the afterlife are being advocated by contemporary Christians: the traditional view with a disembodied intermediate state, the immediate resurrection view and the re-creation view. The traditional view is consistent with the absolutist and memory views of personal identity, but the absolutist view is the best one to hold, given the arguments of this chapter, and in fact, is the view embraced by most throughout the history of the church. The re-creation position would seem to make most sense in light of one of the empiricist views and most, though not all, of its advocates accept some empiricist view of personal identity. If that is true, and if empiricist versions of personal identity are less adequate than the absolutist position, then issues in personal identity can be raised against the re-creation position.

Throughout the chapter, we have also noted that while substance dualism is most frequently offered by Christian theists as the best way to ground the absolute view, it is not the only way to do so. A different view of human persons, which is currently gaining momentum among Christian thinkers, is called the material-constitution view (MC). Advocates of this position include Peter van Inwagen, Trenton Merricks and Kevin Corcoran. Some MC advocates (e.g., van Inwagen) accept some form of the immediate resurrection position, while others (e.g., Merricks) accept a re-creation view. Proponents of MC believe that the material-constitution position has the resources to allow for an absolute view of personal identity without having to embrace substance dualism. Advocates of an MC view of human persons are by no means in agreement about all details of their views, but a fair summary of many MC proponents may be offered as follows:

1. The *is* of composition is not the *is* of identity. Suppose we have a vase composed of bits of clay. These bits of clay are, in turn, composed of smaller separable parts. Now suppose we reach a set of all and only non-overlapping ultimate, simple, separable physical parts that compose the vase. Taken collectively, we may call these parts "the p's." When we say "The vase is the p's," we do not mean that the vase is identical to the p's. Why? Because if we destroy the vase and scatter its parts, the vase ceases to exist but the p's still exist. In this case, something is true of the vase not true of the p's, so they cannot be identical. When we say "The vase is the p's," we mean that the vase is composed of or constituted by the p's. Moreover, if we consider the p's, taken collectively, to be an object, and if we recall that the p's compose and are not identical to the vase, then it follows that we have two different objects—the p's and the vase—that occupy the same place at the same time.

2. The main concern for a Christian view of human persons according to

MC is to make intelligible the resurrection of the dead such that the human person who dies is numerically identical to the human person raised on the last day.

3. We can make sense out of the resurrection of the dead while avoiding substance dualism if we adopt a form of nonreductive physicalism regarding human persons. On this view, mental states involve the exemplification of genuinely mental properties by the human person and the human person is identical to his body taken as a physical organism. Now the body (and thus the human person identical to the body) is an enduring mereological compound (a whole composed of its ultimate physical simples). That is, it is composed of the p's (its ultimate, nonoverlapping, simple, separable parts) in such a way that it can gain new p's and lose old ones and still be the very same body. This is one of the differences, if not the most important difference between MC and the property-thing depiction of human persons (see chap. 10). The former treats human persons (bodies) as enduring mereological compounds, the latter as perduring ones. Thus advocates of MC reject mereological essentialism.

4. Just as a watch goes out of existence when dissembled but the very same watch comes back into existence when reassembled, so a human person, i.e., a body, can cease to exist at death and come back into existence at the future resurrection. Some advocates of MC adopt an extinction-re-creation view of life after death; others believe that the person survives in the intermediate state and is identical to some physical object, say, a specific body or proper part of a body.

While currently in the minority, the MC position is united with substance dualism in affirming an absolute view of personal identity. Thus proponents of these two positions agree in rejecting empiricist views such as those discussed in this chapter, but they are not united as to the grounds of absolute personal identity.

CHAPTER SUMMARY

Absolutist and empiricist views disagree about the nature of personal identity. Empiricist positions assimilate persons to physical artifacts and deny absolute, strict identity through change for persons. Instead, persons are space-time worms with temporal parts; identity is arbitrary and/or comes in degrees. The body version of empiricist views holds that continuity of body is what constitutes personal identity; memory versions reject this and claim that continuity of memory and other psychological traits are what constitute personal identity. Absolutists hold that persons maintain strict, literal sameness through change, that personal identity is unanalyzable and different from artifact identity, and that the first-person "I" is a unity at a given time and through time, which is most reasonably grounded in a substantial soul.

A number of arguments were given for the absolutist view: our basic experience of the self, the fact that the first-person cannot be reduced to the third-person, our fear of future pain and punishment for past wrong, the need for an enduring self to ground our reasoning processes, switch cases that show that body or memory criteria are neither necessary nor sufficient for personal identity, and a set of specific problems that seem to plague empiricist views.

Next, three arguments against the absolutist view were examined: we are never aware of the "I," an immaterial "I" makes knowledge of other persons impossible, and an immaterial soul does not solve problems of the unity of the self because it could be a collection of experiences at a time and a series of souls through time. Finally, we looked at the role of commonsense intuitions, philosophical arguments, science and scientism as they figure into thought experiments regarding what is and is not possible. The chapter concluded with an observation about the role of personal identity in the debate between traditional and re-creationist positions regarding life after death.

CHECKLIST OF BASIC TERMS AND CONCEPTS
absolute, strict sense of identity
absolute view of personal identity
body view of empiricism
empiricist views of personal identity
first-person perspective
genidentity
immediate resurrection position on immortality
indexical
loose, popular sense of identity
memory view of empiricism
mereological essentialism
re-creation position on immortality
space-time worm
third-person perspective
token reflexive
traditional position on immortality
unity at a time
unity through time

PART IV

PHILOSOPHY
OF
SCIENCE

15

SCIENTIFIC METHODOLOGY

At the outset it should be stated that there is no "scientific method,"
no formula with five easy steps guaranteed to lead to discoveries.
There are many methods, used at different stages of inquiry,
in widely varying circumstances.

IAN BARBOUR, *ISSUES IN SCIENCE AND RELIGION*

1 INTRODUCTION

Undoubtedly the most important influence shaping the modern world is science. People who lived during the American Civil War had more in common with Abraham than with us. From space travel and nuclear power, anesthesia and organ transplants, to DNA research and lasers, ours is a world of modern science.

If Christians are going to speak to the modern world and interact with it responsibly, they must interact with science. And if believers are going to explore God's world by means of science and integrate their theological beliefs with the results of that exploration, they need a deeper understanding of science itself. What is science? Is there such a thing as the scientific method, and if so, what is it? Are good scientific theories at least approximately true or are they merely useful fictions? How should theology and science interact? Is creation or theistic science a science or a religion? Queries of this sort are philosophical, and the next three chapters take us on a philosophical journey that explores science. This chapter begins that journey by focusing on scientific methodology. First, we will investigate the nature of philosophy of science and its relationship to science itself; second, we will examine key issues involved in clarifying scientific methodology.

2 SCIENCE AND THE PHILOSOPHY OF SCIENCE

Philosophy is, in part, a second-order discipline that studies the assumptions, concepts and argument forms of other disciplines including science. By contrast, science is a set of first-order disciplines. In philosophy of science, we investigate questions *of* philosophy *about* science. Philosophers and historians of science, and not scientists themselves, are authorities trained to deal with these types of questions. In science, we investigate questions *of* science *about* a specific realm of scientific study. Here, scientists are the authorities.

Here are some of the types of **first-order questions** scientists formulate: What is a covalent bond and how does it work? What is the structure of a methane molecule? What makes an ecosystem stable? How does the holding relationship between mother and young infant affect later childhood development? Where will the moon be on November 1, 2062? By contrast, here are some **second-order questions**—philosophical questions—about science: What is science and are there clear necessary and sufficient conditions that some intellectual activity must have for it to count as science? Is there such a thing as the scientific method and, if so, what is it? How do scientific theories explain things? How do observational data confirm a theory? If a scientific theory is a good one (e.g., makes accurate predictions, harmonizes with what we observe), does that mean that the theory is at least approximately true and that the unseen, theoretical entities (e.g., electrons) postulated by that theory really exist?

Some questions are more complicated. Formulating and answering these questions defy simple characterization and are best seen as a joint venture between science and philosophy. For example, the question of whether or not electrons exist is, first of all, a philosophical question. As we will see in chapter sixteen, many scientists and philosophers today and in the past have embraced some form of antirealism. Some antirealists deny the proposition that the theoretical entities postulated in good scientific theories are real; other antirealists merely claim that the success of a scientific theory does not provide us with sufficient justification for thinking that the theoretical entities in that theory are real, even though they may actually exist. The notion of an electron, they claim, may merely be a pragmatically useful fiction, allowing us to make predictions or develop technology. On the other hand, if scientific realism is adopted, then we should believe in the existence of the entities postulated in good theories. If this is our view, then we should believe in electrons if electron theory is judged by scientists to be a good theory. And this largely will be a scientific matter.

In sum, great care must be given to distinguish issues in the philosophy of science from those in science. And for issues that directly involve both disciplines, we should try to clarify the scientific and philosophical aspects of those issues.

There are two very different and competing approaches to the philosophy of science. The first is called an **external philosophy of science** (EPS). In this view, science itself is the object of study, and one applies a general philosophical understanding of reality (metaphysics), knowing (epistemology) and logical structure to episodes of science, evaluating the episodes as good or bad science. Philosophy is seen as a normative discipline that justifies the presuppositions of science and evaluates certain scientific claims in light of what we already have reason to believe from metaphysics and epistemology. For example, advocates of EPS deny that epistemology can be naturalized (e.g., reduced to descriptive studies in psychology) by claiming that there is a difference between asking what the psychological processes are that we go through to form our beliefs and asking the normative question about what justifies a particular belief as being rational. This is the traditional approach to the philosophy of science, and it recognizes that (1) claims about reality and knowledge within science already presuppose that there is knowledge and reality in the first place, (2) scientific assertions that some proposition is true or rational must conform to and not conflict with general features we already know about rationality and reality from philosophy and (3) philosophy is primarily a normative discipline and science is primarily a descriptive discipline.

By contrast, a recent view in the philosophy of science, developed by thinkers like W. V. O. Quine and Wilfred Sellars, is called an **internal philosophy of science** (IPS). In this view, philosophy is a branch of science. There is no difference in kind between philosophical and scientific questions but only one of degree—usually, philosophical questions (e.g., What is reality in general?) are broader than scientific ones (e.g., What is matter?). For example, epistemology is a branch of psychology, evolutionary biology and neurophysiology. Moreover, science is its own justification and does not need evaluation from some alleged higher viewpoint. In short, science is the measure of all things. The task of philosophy of science is to describe carefully just how scientists do their job and to clarify scientific language and activity. Philosophy of science is primarily linguistic and descriptive.

The inadequacies of IPS have kept most philosophers from accepting it. IPS assumes that we can already recognize the difference between good and bad science in our attempt to describe science, but such a recognition will involve distinctively philosophical assessment. Moreover, IPS begs the question against skeptics that ask why are we justified in accepting the cognitive authority of science in the first place. IPS merely asserts the epistemological authority of science and this is question begging. Finally, IPS breaks down the distinction between normative and descriptive issues. Descriptive scientific questions about how we do, in fact, form our beliefs are very different from and presuppose answers to normative philosophical questions about how we are justified in trusting beliefs in general.

In addition to the differences between science and philosophy of science, as well as the debate between external and internal philosophies of science, there are three main areas within philosophy of science as a branch of study. First, there is the **epistemology of science**, which investigates the process of discovering scientific laws and theories, how we use those laws and theories to explain things, and how laws and theories receive confirmation from various sources like successful predictions. Second, there is the **ontology of science**, which focuses on the realism-antirealism debate. Should good scientific theories be interpreted as true or approximately true descriptions of the theory-independent world and/or should we believe in the existence of the theoretical entities postulated in those theories? Or should we interpret the success of good scientific theories in ways that do not require commitment to the existence of the theoretical entities in those theories? Finally, there is the **philosophy of nature**: Given that we accept scientific realism, how should our scientific beliefs about what is real factor into our broad worldview about reality in general? The first of these areas occupies the remainder of this chapter; the second will be covered in chapter sixteen; the third was part of the topics surveyed in chapter two, the section on metaphysics, and will also be among the concerns in chapter eighteen.

3 THE EPISTEMOLOGY OF SCIENCE: SCIENTIFIC METHODOLOGY

There is a fairly widespread belief that there is something called *the* scientific method that can be characterized in a clear manner and that separates science from other disciplines. For example, the following statement, taken from a widely used high school biology text, is typical: "Scientists use the scientific method in attempting to explain nature. The *scientific method* is a means of gathering information and testing ideas. . . . The scientific method separates science from other fields of study."[1]

In this section, our exploration of scientific methodology will lead us to two discoveries: First, there is no such thing as *the* scientific method, but rather there is a cluster of practices and issues that are used in a variety of contexts and can be loosely called scientific methodologies. Second, various aspects of scientific methodologies are used in disciplines outside science. These discoveries become apparent when we take a philosophical look at scientific practice. We will begin by examining and rejecting a view of scientific methodology called inductivism. Then we will look at different aspects of a more adequate, eclectic view of scientific methodology.

3.1 INDUCTIVISM

Inductivism is a view of the scientific method made popular in the nineteenth century and usually associated with the ideas of Francis Bacon (1561-1591), J. F. W. Herschel (1792-1866) and John Stuart Mill (1806-1873), though the actual description of scientific methodology by these three figures is much more complicated than the sort of inductivism to be described in this section. Inductivism is an entire view about scientific methodology and should not be confused with **induction** itself, which is a form of inference wherein the truth of the premises does not guarantee but only supports the truth of the conclusion to one degree or another. As it came to be understood by the middle of the twentieth century, inductivism is a view of scientific method wherein scientists are seen as starting with unbiased observations of facts, progressively piling up more and more facts by means of those observations, generalizing them by enumerative induction into laws, combining these generalizations into broader and broader generalizations by piling up more facts and, finally, arriving at various levels of scientific laws whose contents are nothing but the facts in general form. Inductivism pictures the scientific method as in figure 15.1.

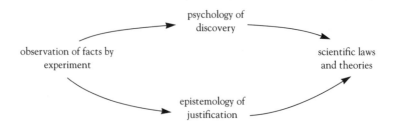

Fig. 15.1 The inductivist view of scientific method

[1]Peter Alexander et al., *Biology: Teacher's Edition* (Morristown, N.J.: Silver Burdett, 1986), p. 4.

As figure 15.1 shows, an inductivist view of the scientific method has two main components: the psychology of discovery and the epistemology of justification. The **psychology of discovery** refers to a description of the temporal, psychological process that an individual scientist or community of scientists goes through in a step-by-step fashion to form laws and theories. This is how scientists should do their work if they are to follow the scientific method according to inductivism. The scientist starts with observations and experiments and proceeds to the formation of laws and theories by **enumerative induction**, that is, by inductively deriving generalizations from past observations.

The **epistemology of justification** refers to the normative, logical structure by which a scientist or community of scientists justifies scientific laws and theories. Inductivism implies that a scientific law or theory is justified only if the evidence in favor of that law or theory fits the inductive scheme already mentioned. Scientists form and test laws and theories by (1) starting with observations without any bias or prior guesswork as to what is important or unimportant to be observed, (2) observing and analyzing the facts gathered in step 1 so as to classify them in different ways, (3) inductively deriving generalizations from this classification of facts, (4) testing these generalizations by further observations and experiments and forming higher-order generalizations. Scientific knowledge is a conjunction of well-attested facts that grows by the addition of new facts that usually leaves previous facts unaltered. One's belief in the plausibility of a law grows in proportion to the number of observed positive instances of the phenomenon described in it.

An alleged example of inductivism is the work of Gregor Mendel (1822-1884), the scientist-priest who studied the laws of inheritance by focusing on peas. Mendel studied different traits of pea plants that appeared in two different forms: seed texture (smooth/wrinkled), seed color (yellow/green) and stem length (long/short). He and his assistants grew pea plants, crossbred them, and counted the number having certain characteristics in each generation. Some of Mendel's results appear in table 15.1.

Table 15.1 Some of Mendel's results

Parental Characters	F_1*	F_2*	F_2 Ratio
Smooth × Wrinkled seeds	all smooth	5474Sx:1850W	2.96:1
Yellow × Green seeds	all yellow	6022Y:2001G	3.01:1
Long × Short stems	all long	787L:277S	2.84:1

*F_1 and F_2 are the first and second generations, respectively.

On the basis of these and other observations, Mendel allegedly derived, by pure induction, the following law: In the second generation, the ratio of the most frequent to the less frequent of two traits that correlate with each other is 3:1. How would Mendel or any other scientist derive and justify this law according to inductivism? First, one would simply start with a sample of peas, call it sample X, grow and crossbreed them, and observe the results with no prior guess as to what to observe or not to observe. After recording the results of observing sample X, one would do the same for samples Y, Z and so on. Next, one would observe the results of X, Y, Z and other samples and make a generalization for the type of peas used in these specific samples. Third, one would repeat this procedure for peas of another type, and then for other types of vegetables, and finally, for other types of living organisms, until one reached the broadest generalization possible covering all living organisms and all cases of two observable traits that correlate together into the 3:1 ratio.

Although inductivism continues to persist in the popular conception of science and even in the minds of many scientists, very few, if any, philosophers of science accept it. It fails to grasp the variegated texture of science, and the objections against it are severe.

First, one cannot merely start with observations without some guiding hypothesis or background assumptions, however tentatively they are held, to guide in deciding what is and is not relevant to observe. Pure, presuppositionless observations are a fable in science, and scientists almost never start with observations. Usually, they start with a problem to be solved and a set of assumptions and hypotheses about what is and is not relevant to observe. In the Mendel case above, Mendel and his associates did not observe and record the position of the moon, the weather in Boston or the color of shoes they wore as they did their experiments. These and a vast host of other factors were not observed because the experimenters had enough of an idea about pea breading to know that these factors were irrelevant but others (the color and texture of seeds, the length of stem) were relevant. These judgments were brought to the task of observing; they were not simply derived from observations.

Moreover, this same point can be make about classifying and arranging observations of different samples of peas and other living organisms. Without some framework about what is going on, there is no way to decide what factors should serve as the basis on which to classify particular facts.

Third, scientific laws are not formed, accumulated or justified by the progressive accumulation of brute, uninterpreted observational data. Rather, these processes involve an interpenetrating mixture of observation and theory in ways that defy simple characterization. In fact, sometimes a shift in theory can turn seeming facts into falsehoods, as Rom Harré has pointed out:

> For instance, consider the history of the determination of the atomic weights. What *were* the facts? Under the influence of Prout's hypothesis some chemists considered that the discrepancies between integral values for the atomic weights of the elements [e.g., chlorine is approximately 35.5] were errors, since Prout had maintained that all elemental atoms were combinations of whole numbers of complete hydrogen atoms, and hence their atomic weights had to be integral numbers by comparison with hydrogen. Those who did not accept or had abandoned Prout's hypothesis were inclined rather to suppose that the non-integral weights were the facts, that is a genuine measure of a natural phenomenon. What the facts were depended in part on whether one held or did not hold to a particular theory.[2]

In the case just cited, what counted as a fact depended on the prior acceptance of a theory, and this type of fact-theory interaction is not allowed by in-

---

[2]Rom Harré, *The Philosophies of Science* (Oxford: Oxford University Press, 1972), p. 43.

ductivism. But since reasoning of this type has been an appropriate part of science during its history, inductivism must be judged inadequate as a total account of scientific methodology.

Fourth, from a finite set of observational data, there will always be a potentially infinite number of general laws consistent with those data. Theories are underdetermined by observational data. The **underdetermination of theories by data** refers to the fact that those data, considered by themselves, do not unambiguously select one and only one law. But if we must operate within the confines of inductivism, how is one to choose among these alternative laws? One way to do so is to pick the most simple generalization consistent with the data. But this strategy is not part of inductivism (simplicity is not derived from observations but brought to them as a background assumption). Moreover, there are different, rival understandings of what simplicity means; resolving this debate is part of spelling out scientific methodology, and these issues go beyond the picture of science contained in inductivism.

Several other problems have been raised against inductivism: the problem of induction (what justifies the inference from "All observed A's are B" to "All A's whatsoever are B"); the difficulty of deciding between accidental generalizations about a phenomenon that merely happen to be true (e.g., plants grow from the sun's warmth) and lawlike generalizations that express real necessities in nature based on a background theory of the true nature of the phenomenon in question (e.g., plants grow from the sun's light by photosynthesis); and the fact that scientists do not try merely to describe phenomena by generalizations, but also to explain them with theories about underlying mechanisms, often unobserved or even unobservable, that account for observational generalizations.

In sum, inductivism is one view about the scientific method, but it turns out to be inadequate. A better way of picturing scientific reasoning is called the **hypothetico-deductive method**, advocated by Carl Hempel, among others. Roughly, this view sees scientists as, in one way or another, forming and putting forth a hypothesis, deriving test implications from it (along with what are called boundary conditions), then seeing if observations corroborate with the hypothesis. For example, if we accept the ideal gas equation ($PV = nRT$, where P is pressure, V is volume, T is temperature, n is the amount of gas in terms of the number of moles of gas, and R is a constant), and if we have as boundary conditions (particular values for P and V that may be plugged into the equation) P_1 and V_1 for a specific amount of a gas n_1, then we derive that T_1 ought to be its temperature. We can then make observations to see of this is supported by the data we gather. But as we shall see, even the hypothetico-deductive method does not capture everything that a scientist does. In order to probe more deeply into scientific methodology, let us turn to an examination of a more eclectic model of scientific practice.

There are seven aspects of the proposed eclectic model to explore: (1) the formation of scientific ideas, (2) the nature of scientific questions and problems, (3) the use of scientific ideas and scientific explanation, (4) the nature of scientific experiments, (5) the testing of scientific ideas (scientific confirmation), (6) the nature of scientific ideas (laws and theories) and (7) the aims and goals of scientific ideas.

3.2
AN ECLECTIC
MODEL OF
SCIENTIFIC
METHODOLOGY

Before we look at each of the seven areas, an initial observation should be made. If we are going to state a view of scientific methodology in a detailed and comprehensive way, then we will need to describe positions regarding various areas of debate within these seven aspects. As we will see, there are different ways scientific ideas are formed, different problems scientists try to solve, different ways scientific ideas are used to explain things and so forth.

Further, major debates exist within each of these seven areas. For example, not everyone agrees about how scientists should use their laws and theories to explain things. This means that several different views of scientific methodology are possible, if those views are thorough enough to offer positions in these seven areas of discussion. While some views we will look at are not as plausible as others, nevertheless, each is logically consistent with the practice of science, and this supports an **eclectic model of scientific methodology**; it shows that scientific methodology is a cluster of different methodologies and not one single method worthy of the title "*the* scientific method." In order to get a feel for the variegated texture of scientific methodology, we will examine each of these seven aspects of an eclectic model of scientific methodology in order.

1. The formation of scientific ideas. Area one is sometimes called the psychology of discovery and refers to the process by which individual scientists or communities of scientists discover and form their ideas. It is generally agreed that there is no formalized method, no step-by-step procedure that characterizes the process of scientific discovery. Sometimes scientists discover things by accident. On other occasions they generate their ideas in more bizarre ways. It is well known, for example, that F. A. Kekule (1829-1896) came up with the hexagon formula for the benzene ring by having a trancelike vision of a snake attempting to chase its own tail and thus curving into such a ring!

More frequently, however, scientists form their ideas in one of two ways. First, scientists generate ideas by a creative process of educated guesswork known as **adduction** or **abduction**. Adduction refers to the process of inventing a theory to explain observed facts. Science is a craft, and after a scientist has worked in an area for a while, this personal involvement allows the scientist to develop savvy about that area, a sense of tacit know-how. Part of this know-how is the ability to see things in a certain way, to intuit patterns of phenomena and, by the use of creative imagination, to adduce a conceptual web to explain those patterns. Often a scientist cannot say how it was that he or she came up with a theory. This same sort of tacit knowledge is used by auto mechanics, judges, biblical exegetes and others who use their knowledge of a field to weigh things and adduce a solution to a problem.

There is one difficulty with this way of generating a scientific idea. Sometimes, after working in an area for a long time, a scientist is indoctrinated so heavily into a prevailing way of seeing a realm of data that he or she can distort data by reading things into them and cannot see things in another way. That is why Thomas Kuhn pointed out that, often, discoveries in science are made by newcomers or by people working in another branch of science or another field altogether, because they have the cognitive distance from the prevailing paradigm necessary to see things differently.

Adduction is a method of discovery, as it were, "from below," that is, from a sense of savvy with data in a certain realm. There is a second way scientists have frequently discovered their ideas: a method "from above." Here, scientists are guided in their search for a theory from a broad picture of how the world is or how certain data should turn out. This broad picture can come from metaphysics, mathematics, theology or other domains. For example, some scientific discoveries have been made in light of the scientist's prior commitment to the idea that correct equations should be mathematically beautiful or elegant. Again, Copernicus was uncomfortable with Ptolemy's model of planetary motion because it departed from the Platonic ideal of uniform circular motion around a center. As a Platonist, Copernicus was guided "from above" by the geometrical idea that motion that is circular is more perfect and thus the planets seek to move in circular motion. The point is not that he was correct, but merely that he was guided in the process of discovery in this way.

Sometimes metaphysical views guide a scientist. Some scientists have had a metaphysical commitment against action at a distance and this has guided them in a search to find some intervening mechanism (e.g., an exchange of gravitons) between two bodies that allowed gravity to act on contact and not at a distance. Sometimes theological beliefs guide research and help generate scientific ideas. Leibniz (1646-1716) derived Snel's law (a ray of light traveling obliquely, i.e., neither parallel nor perpendicular, from one optical medium into another is refracted at the surface in such a way that the ratio of the sines of the angles of incidence and of refraction is a constant for any media pair: $n_1 \sin \theta_1 = n_2 \sin \theta_2$) from his metaphysical principle that nature always selects the easiest, most direct course of action given a set of alternatives. And he derived this principle from his theological conviction that God created the world such that maximum simplicity and perfection should be realized. Linnaeus and other early taxonomists were guided in their taxonomic work by the theological idea that God created organisms in distinct, classifiable types. James Clerk Maxwell derived his field picture of light, in part, from his theological convictions about the Trinity and the Incarnation. Thus fields like mathematics, philosophy and theology can enter into the very fabric of scientific methodology by providing criteria for guiding the psychology of discovery from above.

2. The nature of scientific questions and problems. Often, scientists try to solve problems by answering at least three types of questions. First there are **"what" questions**: What does the fossil record look like? What is the half-life of uranium? Here scientists try to establish facts even if they cannot, even in principle, explain those facts. For example, scientists could try to establish what the rest mass is of some alleged ultimate particle, even if they do not believe there is a further explanation for why the rest mass is some specific value because the particle is taken as ultimate. Second, scientists answer **"why" questions**: Why do metals expand when heated? Here the focus is on stating the cause for some phenomenon (e.g., the efficient or final cause). Third, scientists answer **"how" questions**: How does light dislodge an electron from the surface of a metal?

"How" questions are requests for a description of how it is that some cause accomplishes an effect.

Two things should be noted about these questions. First, disciplines outside of science ask and answer very similar types of questions. Second, scientific methodology is not exhausted by a search for answers to "how" questions. They also answer "what" and "why" questions.

Scientists ask questions and try to solve problems. Generally speaking, these problems come in two broad types: empirical problems and conceptual problems. Scientific theories contain two types of terms: observational terms, which refer to what is directly observational (e.g., "is red," "floats," "is longer than"), and theoretical terms, which express theoretical concepts (e.g., "gene," "electron," "kinetic energy"). Empirical problems focus on observational difficulties with a theory; conceptual problems focus on theoretical, conceptual difficulties with a theory.

In general, an **empirical problem** is anything about the world of observations that strikes us as odd and in need of explanation. Why do the tides move as they do? Why are there gaps in the fossil record? These are examples of empirical problems. Suppose we have two rival theories that are competing for our allegiance. Such a situation gives rise to three types of empirical problems: **unsolved problems** (those not adequately solved by any rival theory), **solved problems** (those that are solved by all rivals, perhaps in different ways) and **anomalous problems** (those solved by one rival but not another). Of the three, anomalous problems carry the most epistemological weight. However, though important, anomalies are not necessarily decisive against a theory. The strength of anomalous problems is a function of several things: How many of them are there and how important or central are they for the theory in question? How well does the rival solve them? How strong are the various rival theories in light of factors other than their ability to solve these anomalies? It is worth noting that the epistemological impact of anomalies for scientific theories is parallel to the impact of anomalies in areas outside science. For example, just exactly when is it no longer reasonable to believe in biblical inerrancy in light of anomalous data outside Scripture or problem passages? Answering this question is no easier in theology than in science.

Scientists also try to solve conceptual problems. In general, these are difficulties with the conceptual aspects of a theory, and they come in two types. First, there are **internal conceptual problems**. These arise when the concepts within a theory appear to be vague, ambiguous, circularly defined or contradictory. For example, some have argued that the wave-particle nature of electromagnetic radiation is contradictory, that the evolutionary pathway from reptile scales to bird feathers through a series of slightly changed intermediaries is unclear and vague, that the use of imaginary time by cosmologists such as Stephen Hawking is unintelligible and that "survival of the fittest" is circularly defined. The point is not that these objections have been decisive, but rather that they are examples of internal conceptual problems.

Second, there are **external conceptual problems**. An external conceptual problem arises for some scientific theory T, when T conflicts with some proposition of another theory T', when T' is rationally well founded, regardless of what discipline T' is associated with. T may be logically inconsistent with T' or they may conflict in a lesser way by being jointly implausible and not mutually reinforcing, though still logically consistent. For example, if T is an oscillating model of the universe that implies an infinite past for the universe and T' is a philosophical argument implying that the past must be finite, then T' is an external conceptual problem for T that advocates of T must solve. Again, if naturalistic evolutionary theory implies that living organisms are merely physical (because they are wholly the result of a physical process operating on physical materials), then if philosophical arguments exist for some form of mind-body dualism, these constitute external conceptual problems for naturalistic evolutionary theory. If theologians have rationally justified theological arguments against, say, views of human origins that claim that humans originated in China, then these arguments would be an external conceptual problem for that scientific theory.

Science has never exhausted the rational, and science has directly interacted with other disciplines, in epistemologically positive or negative ways, throughout the history of science. External conceptual problems provide examples of the fact that science is not merely complementary to fields like philosophy and theology, because in such problems the former directly interact with the latter. More will be said in chapter seventeen about what it means to say that science is merely complementary to philosophy and theology. But for now, we may understand such a claim to mean that a scientific description of some phenomenon (say, the formation of water from hydrogen and oxygen) and a philosophical or theological description of that phenomenon (God creates water from hydrogen and oxygen) are two different, noninteraction approaches to the same phenomenon. Such a claim may be quite proper in certain cases (the water example), but the presence of external conceptual problems is one of several factors about scientific methodology that show the inadequacy of a complementarian approach to the integration of science with theology and philosophy if that approach is understood as the final word on the subject.

3. The use of scientific ideas and scientific explanation. Scientists use laws and theories to explain things. Some philosophers like Thomas Kuhn have argued that there is no basic type of scientific explanation, but rather as many different models of scientific explanation as there are branches of science. So, very little in general can be said about scientific explanation. Others disagree and have argued that the vast majority, perhaps all of what we would count as scientific explanation, fits into one or both of two different options. First, there is the **covering-law** or **inferential model of explanation** made popular by Carl G. Hempel and Ernest Nagel. According to this view, two factors make an explanation a scientific one: the logical form of the explanation and the nature of the explanation's premises. The terms *explanans* and *explanandum* mean, respectively, "that which does the explaining" and "that which is to be explained." Regarding logical form, scientific explanations explain some phenomenon by giving a correct deductive or inductive argument for that phenomenon in one of the following three ways:

The deductive-nomological version of the covering-law model:

L_1: All metal conducts electricity.

C_1: This wire is a metal.   Explanans

E: This metal wire conducts electricity.   Explanandum

The deductive-statistical version of the covering-law model:

L_1: 50% of radioactive substance x will decay in time t.

C_1: This is z grams of substance x.   Explanans

E: 50% of z will decay in time t.   Explanandum

The inductive-statistical version of the covering-law model:

L_1: 90% of people who get penicillin recover.

C_1: Jones got penicillin.   Explanans

===

E: Jones recovered.   Explanandum

In each case, the thing to be explained (the explanandum) is explained or "covered" by inferring it from premises (the explanans), the first of which is a general law and the second of which is a statement of initial conditions. In the **deductive-nomological version**, the explanans contains only universal generalizations and the argument is deductive. In the deductive-statistical version, the explanation is a deductive argument that contains at least one statistical generalization in the explanans. In the **inductive-statistical version**, the explanation is an inductive argument (signified by the double line below C_1) that includes at least one statistical generalization in the explanans. In each case, a good scientific explanation of some explanandum E will embody one of the three logical forms above.

A second feature of the covering-law model of scientific explanation focuses, not on logical form, but on the nature of the premises. The explanans of scientific explanation must be scientifically testable in some way—for example, by observation and experiment—and some would add, they must be true, lawlike generalizations.

Most agree that the covering-law model captures at least part of the nature of scientific explanation. Nevertheless, it has had its detractors. Some have claimed that the model has certain conceptual problems (e.g., What does it mean to test something by observation and experiment? Don't fields outside science do this as well? Do scientific generalizations have to be true or only thought to be true and well-confirmed? Surely, false scientific explanations are still scientific explanations? What is a lawlike generalization and how does one differ from an accidental generalization?).

Others have pointed out that the model leaves out important aspects of scientific explanation. For example, it is hard to see how the covering-law model is explanatory in itself. The statement "This x has F because all x's have F and this is an x" merely postpones explanation by inviting the question "Why do *any* x's have F in the first place?" An explanation of this latter question will use new concepts embedded in models of what x is like (e.g., metals conduct electricity because little entities called electrons are free in metals). So the covering-law model is not sufficient for an explanation. Covering-law explanations are really just generalized descriptions of what happen, but they are not actually explanations of why things happen.

These problems have led some to embrace a second model: the **realist, causal model of explanation**. Advocates of this view point out that, according to the covering-law model, the essence of scientific explanation is describing general correlations among observational phenomena that allow us to deduce some result. An example of this would be the ideal gas equation, $PV = nRT$ (where P is pressure, V is volume, T is temperature, n the number of moles of gas present, and R is the ideal gas constant). The ideal gas equation describes the regular correlations of observational phenomena (P, V, T) in gases and allows us to deduce, say, the temperature of a gas from knowledge of its pressure and volume. But this so-called explanation is just a description of how phenomena are related, not an explanation of why they behave as they do. An explanation of why the temperature of the gas is what it is, however, will use a model that pictures unobserved entities and processes postulated as being causally responsible for observational correlations. On this view, the behavior of a gas is explained by picturing gases as groups of molecules analogous to tiny billiard balls that engage in elastic collisions, travel through space, bounce off container walls and travel in a velocity proportional to the temperature of the gas.

On the causal, realist model, scientific explanation goes beyond what can be observed by building models of theoretical entities and processes that are causally responsible for observational phenomena. It is interesting to note that philosophers like Bas C. van Fraasen and Stanley Jaki have shown that this type of scientific explanation represents a very close parallel to arguments for God's existence used in natural theology. For example, one form of the design argument starts with various types of design as observational phenomena to be explained and postulates the existence of a personal designer who is causally responsible for these phenomena.

Critics of the realist, causal model are often empiricists of one sort or another who claim that commitment to a scientific theory only involves commitment to the fact that a theory will make observationally accurate predictions. Such a commitment does not include believing in unobservable, theoretical entities which, they claim, are merely excess, metaphysical baggage for a scientific theory. This criticism will be part of our focus in the next chapter.

We have seen that there are different views about how scientific explanations should work. There are also different kinds of explanation used in science. There are **compositional** or **structural explanations**: the properties of an object are explained in terms of the properties or structural relations of its parts. There are **historical explanations**, which explain the properties and existence of an object in terms of the temporal development and history of the object and its ancestors. With **functional explanations** the capacities of an object are explained in terms of the function they play in some system— the function of x (the heart) is to do y (pump blood). **Transitional explanations** explain a change of state in some object in terms of some disturbance in the object and the state of the object at the time of the disturbance. Finally, there are **intentional explanations**, which explain the behavior of an organism or the existence of some state of affairs in terms of the beliefs, desires, fears and intentions of that organism.

Before we move to the next area of scientific methodology, one more issue should be mentioned. It is sometimes claimed that the notion of God as a creator or designer who "intervenes" in nature cannot serve as part of a scientific explanation. This claim is usually defended by some sort of covering-law model of explanation, coupled with the idea that science must explain things by using natural laws and, obviously, a miraculous act of God is not part of a natural law.

But this claim is simply false. Scientists do not merely explain by using natural laws. They also explain by citing causal entities, processes, events and actions, as we have seen. For example, cosmologists explain certain aspects of the universe, say its rate of expansion, not only by using natural laws, but also by citing the big bang as a single causal event. Now scientists in some branches of science, e.g., the search for extraterrestrial intelligence, archaeology, forensic science, psychology and sociology use personal agency and various internal states of agents (desires, willings, beliefs, intentions) as part of their description of the causal entities and processes cited in their explanations. There is no reason that can be derived from the nature of scientific explanation for why the same type of argument could not be used to explain some sort of phenomenon in biology or a related field, say in explaining the origin of life. Whether or not the explanation would be a good one would, of course, largely be a scientific question.

In this context, many scientists and philosophers make a distinction between empirical science and historical science. These broad categories of science differ in the kinds of questions asked and the explanations and methods used to answer them. In general, **empirical science** (also called "inductive," "nomological" or "operation" science) focuses on how the natural world operates in a repeatable and regular way. The study of acid-base chemical reactions is an example. **Historical science** (sometimes called "origin" science) focuses on single, past events (e.g., the death of the dinosaurs, the origin of first life) and attempts to explain how things came to be or why some event happened. This distinction relates to our present discussion about the notion of an act of God in science as follows: It can be argued that an appeal to an intelligent intervention of God is not appropriate in empirical science (unless God does, in fact, regularly "intervene" to do some repeatable action, e.g., as he does in regeneration) but it can be appropriate in historical science to explain the origin of life and so forth.

4. The nature of scientific experiments. Scientists make observations and perform experiments. An observation occurs when an observer stands outside the course of events being observed and does not manipulate them. An experiment occurs when the experimenter intervenes in the course of events by altering nature in some way to allow the experiment to take place. When scientists make observations and perform experiments, they often use instruments of at least three different types. First, there are instruments used in making measurements. Some of these are self-measurers, that is, they are examples of the thing being measured (e.g., a meter stick). Some are non-self-measurers that use the effects of some phenomenon to measure the cause (e.g., thermometers directly measure expansion and infer temperature). Second, there are instruments that extend our senses such as microscopes, telescopes, amplifiers. Third, there are instruments that isolate phenomena to allow them to be studied independently from their environment.

In using these instruments, scientists make various assumptions. Many of these assumptions are quite reasonable and some may not be. But in any case, the use of an instrument to "observe" or measure something illustrates that when a scientist claims to observe something, he or she is often interpreting data in light of a large number of theoretical background assumptions about the thing being observed and the instruments used to observe it.

5. The testing of scientific ideas: scientific confirmation. The fifth aspect of scientific methodology includes issues of testing and justifying scientific laws and theories. Two questions are of central importance in understanding this aspect of scientific methodology: (1) How do positive test results from observation and experiment lend support to a scientific law or theory? (2) What factors are involved in the claim that a scientific law or theory is rational? Let us look at these questions in order.

If a scientific theory predicts or in some other way implies that certain things should be observed, and if those things *are* observed, how does this help to confirm the theory in question? There is no universal agreement among philosophers about how to answer this question. In fact, many philosophers believe that assessing a scientific theory is so multifaceted and complicated that they believe no conclusions whatever about the truth or falsity of a theory follow from positive test results. Others disagree and claim that positive test results do, in fact, lend support to a theory or at least show that the theory has not yet been falsified. For those who hold to the value of positive text results, two major schools of thought exist: falsificationism and justificationism.

The main advocate of **falsificationism** has been Karl Popper (1902-1994), for whom positive test results only show a theory to be possibly true. Those results do not make the truth of a theory any more probable. Consider the generalization "All ravens are black." No amount of confirming instances of black ravens shows that the generalization is true because we could always find a white raven in the future. The discovery of just one white raven would show the generalization to be false. Therefore, Popper concludes, scientific theories should be bold, risky conjectures that we try to falsify. Positive test results show that the theory has not been falsified yet, and if we test a theory frequently and if it passes all our tests, then the theory is corroborated. This does not mean that we have positive evidence for the theory, but only that we have repeatedly tried to falsify the theory, we have so far failed, and thus the theory is possibly true.

Justificationists like Rudolf Carnap (1891-1970) and Carl Hempel (1905-1997) disagree. There are different forms of **justificationism**, but advocates agree that positive test results increase the degree of probability that a theory is true. The more positive test results and the less negative test results we have, the greater the degree of confirmation our theory possesses.

In sum, falsificationism is the view that positive test results only show that the theory has so far not been falsified and that it is possibly true. Justificationism is the view that in one way or another, positive test results increase the probability that the theory is true and give it positive support.

What about our second question: What factors are involved in the claim that a scientific theory is rational? To begin with, we need to distinguish between the rationality of pursuit and the rationality of acceptance. The **rationality of pursuit** refers to a case where a theory is relatively new, undeveloped and untested, but nevertheless, it appears to hold promise. In this case, one may not have enough justification to think the theory is true, but it could still be reasonable to do research in light of the theory. The **rationality of acceptance**, on the other hand, refers to a theory that has been around long enough to be accepted or rejected and for some reason or other, accepting the theory is rationally justified.

Regarding the rationality of acceptance, what is it that makes a theory rationally justified? There is no simple answer to this question and a number of factors are relevant to answering it. One factor is whether or not there is a viable rival theory. If not, then even if our theory has serious problems, it is all we have. If there are one or more rivals, then we must assess our theory by comparing its adequacy vis-à-vis those rivals.

Another factor is whether and to what extent a given theory possesses various epistemic virtues. An **epistemic virtue** is a normative property that, if possessed by a theory, confers some degree of rational justification on that theory. An epistemic virtue increases the justification for believing a theory. Examples of epistemic virtues are these: theories should be simple, empirically accurate, predictively successful, fruitful for guiding new research, capable of solving internal and external conceptual problems, and should use certain types of explanations and not others (e.g., avoid action at a distance, appeal to efficient and not final causes).

The importance of epistemic virtues complicates the assessment of a theory's rationality for at least two reasons. First, each of the epistemic virtues can be interpreted in more than one way. For example, what does it mean for a theory to be simple? Does it mean that a theory should have the lowest number of different kinds of entities, the lowest power of ten for the variables in its equations, or something else? One rival theory may utilize one interpretation of a specific epistemic virtue like simplicity and another rival may use a different interpretation.

Second, two rivals may have different rankings of the relative importance of the virtues on the list above. For example, one rival may value simplicity over empirical accuracy and the other rival may reverse this. Moreover, one rival may be successful regarding two or three virtues and its rival may be successful regarding a set of different virtues. How are we to compare rivals in these cases? Only a case by case study can, at least in principle, answer this question.

In any case, the role of epistemic virtues in assessing the rationality of a scientific theory shows that a crucial-experiment model of theory assessment is naive. On this model, one rival predicts some phenomenon P and the other rival predicts *not-P*. You do a crucial experiment to see if P or *not-P* obtains and you verify one rival and falsify the other. Unfortunately, things are not that simple when it comes to theory assessment in science—or in theology and other disciplines for that matter. This does not mean that we can never tell when a scientific theory is rational to believe, it just means that making such a judgment is not as straightforward as we are sometimes led to believe.

6. *The nature of scientific ideas: laws and theories.* So far we have been using the terms *law* and *theory* without defining them. Unfortunately, there is no universally accepted definition of either term. However, two remarks about scientific laws and theories can shed light on important distinctions used in this area of investigation. For one thing, there are three basic ways to distinguish a **law** from a **theory**. One way is to hold that a theory is roughly a hypothesis and, if it becomes well confirmed, can graduate to the status of a law. On this view, the only difference between the two is that a theory should be held tentatively and a law should be held firmly; that is, the differences lie in their relative degree of epistemological strength. While this way of speaking is fairly popular, it is the least helpful for understanding the nature of scientific methodology and thus is not widely used among philosophers of science.

A second way to distinguish a law from a theory focuses on their relative degrees of generality—a theory is broader in scope than is a law. For example Kepler's laws of planetary motion or Galileo's law of free fall ($s = 16t^2$ where s is distance and t is time) only hold for planetary motion (Kepler) or motion near the earth (Galileo). However, Newton's laws of motion hold not only in these cases but more broadly in that they apply to the motion of other heavenly bodies and other forms of motion as well. Thus, on this way of distinguishing laws and theories, Kepler's and Galileo's statements about motion would be laws and Newton's would be theories.

A third way to distinguish theories from laws is embraced especially by those who hold to some form of scientific realism (see chap. 16) and who hold to the realist, causal model of scientific explanation discussed earlier in this chapter. On this view, laws merely *describe* the lawlike regularities that are observed in nature, and theories *explain* those regularities by offering a model for the theoretical entities, structures and processes thought to be causally responsible for those regularities. The ideal gas equation, $PV = nRT$, is a law, and the kinetic gas theory (gases are swarms of tiny particles that engage in elastic collisions and so forth) is a theory.

A second remark about scientific laws and theories involves the different ways that scientific laws can be classified. First, *law* can refer to a linguistic or conceptual entity. In this sense a law is something that a scientist can discover at a point in time; he can write it on a sheet of paper or have it in his mind. On the other hand, law can refer to a real disposition (e.g., hydrogen atoms will become positively charged if they lose an electron) or real relationship (e.g., an increase in the temperature of a gas will increase its pressure at constant volume) that obtains in the theory-independent world. In the former sense of *law*, it is appropriate to say that a law does not cause anything to happen, since it is a linguistic or conceptual entity. In the latter sense, however, laws do cause things to happen in the world by being among the factors that direct the way nature behaves. So whether a law can be said to cause something depends on how one is using the word *law*.

In addition, laws can be statistical ("The probability of an atom of U^{238} decaying during this time period is 50%") or nonstatistical ("All copper expands when heated"). Further, good scientific laws are not always true. For example, the ideal gas law doesn't hold for any gas in the real world, but it is still a helpful approximation, even though, strictly speaking, it is false.

7. The aims and goals of scientific ideas. Scientists and philosophers have surfaced several different aims or goals that are explicit or implicit ends scientists intend to reach when they formulate theories. Two different types exist: **extrinsic** and **intrinsic goals of science.** Extrinsic goals are the motives or reasons that scientists do science—for example, to glorify God, to exert power over nature, to protect the environment, etc. More important for assessing the truthfulness or epistemic strength of a scientific theory are intrinsic goals. These goals are the epistemic virtues that scientists seek: simple theories, empirically accurate theories and so forth. Further, part of understanding intrinsic scientific goals is how we should interpret a scientific law or theory that embodies various epistemic virtues and is, therefore, a "good" theory. Do scientists seek virtuous theories because they seek true theories that accurately describe the real world or do they seek virtuous theories because such theories work and are useful fictions? Scientific realists adopt the former view of intrinsic scientific goals, and scientific antirealists adopt the latter. This debate will be the focus of the next chapter.

CHAPTER SUMMARY

Philosophy of science is a second-order discipline of philosophy about science. Science is a first-order discipline about a specific realm of scientific study. There are two competing approaches to the philosophy of science. An external philosophy of science is a normative approach that applies general philosophical issues to the study and justification of science. An internal philosophy of science starts with good examples of science itself, is descriptive in nature and sees philosophy as a branch of science. The three main areas of philosophy of science are the epistemology of science, the ontology of science, and the philosophy of nature. The remainder of the chapter focused on the epistemology of science.

There is no such thing as *the* scientific method. Rather, there is a cluster of practices and issues that are used as part of scientific methodology and in disciplines outside of science as well. Moreover, many who claim that there is something called "the scientific method" identify that method by the name inductivism. But inductivism is an inadequate approach to scientific methodology. A more eclectic model of scientific methodology includes various issues and debates in seven areas: the formation of scientific ideas, scientific questions and problems, the use of scientific ideas and scientific explanation, scientific experiments, testing scientific ideas and scientific confirmation, the nature of scientific laws and theories, the aims and goals of scientific ideas. Finally, our investigation of these seven areas of scientific methodology revealed several ways that theological and philosophical issues can enter into the very fabric of scientific methodology.

CHECKLIST OF BASIC TERMS AND CONCEPTS

adduction (or abduction)
anomalous problems
compositional or structural explanations
covering-law or inferential model of explanation
deductive-nomological
deductive-statistical
eclectic model of scientific methodology
empirical problems (solved, unsolved, anomalous)
empirical science
enumerative induction
epistemic virtue
epistemology of justification
epistemology of science
external conceptual problem
external philosophy of science (EPS)
extrinsic and intrinsic goals for science
falsificationism
first-order and second-order questions
historical explanations
historical science
hypothetico-deductive method
induction
inductive-statistical
inductivism
intentional explanations
internal conceptual problem
internal philosophy of science (IPS)
justificationism
laws versus theories
ontology of science
philosophy of nature
psychology of discovery
rationality of acceptance
rationality of pursuit
realist, causal model of explanation
transitional explanations
underdetermination of theories by data
"what," "why" and "how" questions

16

THE
REALISM-ANTIREALISM
DEBATE

If one wants a slogan:
realism is the truth and temperate rationalism the way.
W. H. NEWTON-SMITH, *THE RATIONALITY OF SCIENCE*

There is, I think, no theory-independent way
to reconstruct phrases like "really there";
the notion of a match between the ontology of a theory and its
"real" counterpart in nature now seems to me illusive in principle.
Besides, as a historian, I am impressed with the implausibility of the view.
THOMAS KUHN, *THE STRUCTURE OF SCIENTIFIC REVOLUTIONS*

1 INTRODUCTION

Our scientific discourse, as well as our everyday language, is permeated with terms for theoretical entities in science: quarks, quantum vacuums, electrons, DNA molecules, continental plates and a host of others. Moreover, most people today are inclined to think that our current theories about these entities—for example, our current views about DNA molecules—are reasonably accurate, approximately true depictions of the real, theory-independent world. However, in spite of these widely held opinions, it is still legitimate, and it is part of the business of philosophy, to question these views by raising this question: Given that a scientific theory is "successful" in some sense of that term (e.g., it explains facts, makes good predictions), are we then entitled to believe in the reality of the theoretical entities postulated by that theory and in the approximate truth of our descriptions of those entities?

Ever since the ancient Greeks began to investigate nature, there has been a debate about this and related questions. What is the purpose of scientific theories? What does it mean to say a scientific theory is successful? Are successful scientific theories merely useful fictions that explain empirical observations and generate accurate predictions, or do their theoretical terms actually refer to real entities, and does a successful theory provide fairly accurate descriptions of those entities? This debate is called the realist-antirealist debate, and it is still being hotly contested among scientists and philosophers. Very roughly, **scientific realism** is the view that science progressively secures true, or approximately true, theories about the real, theory-independent world "out there" and does so in a rationally justifiable way. In contrast, **antirealism**, which comes in a number of different forms, denies realist interpretations of science in favor of alternative interpretations. Thus it is important to keep in mind that a defense of the existence of the theoretical entities of science is not ultimately a question of whether or not some scientific theory is "successful." More fundamentally, it is a question about which kind of philosophy of science—scientific realism or some form of antirealism—should be preferred as a characterization of the success of scientific theories.

Why should Christians be concerned with this issue? Apart from the intellectual value of the debate, considered in and of itself, another aspect of this discussion is of interest to Christians: One's views of the realism-antirealism controversy should be factored into one's understanding of the integration of science and theology. If scientific realism is accepted as the correct view of a scientific theory—for example, the idea that by employing the notion of imaginary time as something real, one can avoid postulating that the universe had a beginning—then if that theory seems to run counter to some theological affirmation, say, that the universe had a beginning, then Christians will either have to refute that scientific theory, adjust their understanding of the theological affirmation or adopt a different strategy. Thus much depends on what it means for a theory to be well established or successful. This, in turn, is related to the debate about realism and antirealism.

However, if antirealism is adopted for and limited to scientific theories, then one would not take a well-established scientific theory to be true or approximately true—perhaps the theory is just a useful fiction—and there will be no pressure to adjust the truth of the theological affirmation. For example, if a theologian believes that all physical events have causes, and if quantum physics seems to deny this, then if quantum theory is taken in an antirealist way, there would be no need to adjust one's view of causation. On the other hand, there may be dangers in adopting antirealism for scientific theories because, once this move is made, it may be difficult to limit antirealism to scientific theories alone. For example, if one's antirealism affects one's theological assertions, then claims about God, life after death and so forth could be interpreted in ways that cash out those claims without taking them to be referring to actual entities (God, the afterlife) in the real world. Figure 16.1 depicts some of the major options in the realist-antirealist dialogue.

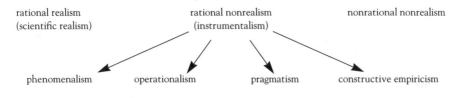

rational realism
(scientific realism)

rational nonrealism
(instrumentalism)

nonrational nonrealism

phenomenalism   operationalism   pragmatism   constructive empiricism

Fig. 16.1 Options in the realist-antirealist dialogue

In what follows, we will state and evaluate scientific realism, look at some of its antirealist rivals and offer some final thoughts about this debate relevant to the task of integrating science and theology.

2 SCIENTIFIC REALISM

Scientific realism was a minority view in the first half of the twentieth century, at least among the more vocal philosophers, but is now the majority position among current philosophers of science. Prominent scientific realists are Ernan McMullin, Richard Boyd, W. H. Newton-Smith, Karl Popper and Rom Harré. There are several different varieties of scientific realism, but its core tenets are these:

SR1: Scientific theories (in mature, developed sciences) are true or approximately true.

SR2: The central observational and theoretical terms of a mature scientific theory genuinely refer to entities in the world. These terms make existence claims.

SR3: Given two rival theories, it is in principle possible to have good reasons for thinking which is more likely to be true or approximately true. Rationality is an objective notion and conceptual relativism (what is rational for one person or group should not necessarily be so for another person or group since rationality itself is relative to a person, scientific community or theory) is false.

SR4: A scientific theory will embody certain **epistemic virtues** (simplicity, clarity, an absence of internal and external conceptual problems, predictive success, empirical accuracy, scope of relevance, fruitfulness in guiding new research, utilization of appropriate ways of explaining things—e.g., prefer efficient to final causes, etc.) if and only if it is true or approximately true.

SR5: The aim of science is a literally true conception of the theory-independent external world. Scientific progress is a fact, and science tends to converge on truer and truer conceptions of the world, with later theories usually refining and preserving the best parts of earlier theories and coming closer to the truth than earlier theories in the same domain of discourse (i.e., where the earlier and later theories are talking about the same things and are thus comparable to each other).

SR1 states that science involves some form of the correspondence theory of truth (see chap. 6): A theory is true if and only if what it says about the world is in fact the way the world is. The theory-independent world is what makes a theory true. SR1 also assumes that the notion of approximate truth is a coherent one. Some theories can better approximate the truth than others. Finally, SR1 contains the notion of a "mature, developed science," which, in turn, has two different aspects to it. For one thing, an immature area of science can become mature if it has time to develop, test and "vindicate" one of its major theories. The idea here is that a mature, developed science is one that has been around long enough to have proven itself.

There is another aspect to the notion of a mature, developed science: some sciences are considered mature in the sense of being the ideal, archetypal sciences. In this sense, physics and, perhaps, chemistry are considered mature in that they are the ideal sciences. Other areas of science are mature to the degree that they are reducible to or approximate the methods, theoretical concepts and explanatory devices used in physics and chemistry. There is an implicit **reductionism** in this notion of a mature science: there is a unity to all sciences and, in some sense, other sciences are reducible to or replaceable by physics and chemistry. For example, some reductionists believe that the laws and theories of biology will someday be reduced to the laws and theories of chemistry and physics.

SR1 expresses what is sometimes called **alethic realism** or **truth realism**, according to which the theoretical entities postulated in mature, developd sciences (e.g., electrons) are real and our descriptions of them (e.g., electrons have negative charge and a rest mass of such and such) are at least approximately true. By contrast, **entity realism** holds that ordinary observable entities (e.g., Mars), the microentities that could be observed if we were small enough (e.g., electrons) and entities that are in principle unobservable (e.g., quarks, magnetic fields) are real, but our descriptions of these entities are neither true nor approximately true. Entity realism is currently a minority postion among realists, and it will be set aside for the purposes of this and the next chapter.

SR2 is a semantic thesis, that is, a thesis about the nature of language, about how terms in language succeed in referring to things in the world and about the nature of linguistic meaning. Scientific theories include **observational terms** and **theoretical terms**. There is a debate about whether the distinction between these two types of terms is absolute (i.e., a term functions one way or the other, but not both ways at the same time in the same theory) or whether the distinction is best viewed as a continuum with observational terms being colored by theory and theoretical terms always having at least some observational content. Either way, the distinction is an important one for understanding scientific realism. Table 16.1 gives some examples of the two types of terms.

Table 16.1 Theoretical versus observational terms

Theoretical Term		Observational Term	
electron	mass	red	floats
electric field	kinetic energy	longer than	wood
atom	temperature	left of	water
molecule	gene	hard	weight
virus	charge	volume	iron

The important thing about SR2 is the claim that theoretical terms are referring terms. To understand what this means, consider the following two sentences:

1. Fido is brown.
2. The average family has 2.5 children.

In sentence (1), the term *Fido* is a referring term. It refers to the dog Fido, an "extralinguistic entity" in the world, and says of him that he has the property of brownness. If sentence (1) is true, then because *Fido* is a referring term, sentence (1) has implications for reality: the entity referred to by the term *Fido* actually exists.

Now consider sentence (2). It contains a definite description, a phrase that begins with *the* and a description of the item that satisfies that description and, therefore, to which the description refers. (2) is grammatically similar to (1) in that the definite description "the average family" appears to function as a referring term like the proper name *Fido*. Both terms occupy the subject position in what appear to be subject-predicate sentences. However, on closer inspection, we realize that "the average family" is not a referring term at all. No one would try to locate the average family and count its children to see if, in fact, it has 2.5 children. Rather, "the average family" is a shorthand term for a set of mathematical operations. This can be made clear by replacing (2) with (2'):

2'. Add the number of children and divide by the number of families and you get 2.5.

(2') may have some existence implications (there are families and children) but, basically, it is a recipe for a mathematical operation, and "the average family" does not designate an entity in a straightforward manner as does *Fido* in sentence (1).

Now consider this sentence:

3. Protons have positive charge.

SR2 says that the theoretical term *proton* is a referring term, that is, it functions like *Fido* and not like "the average family." In general, the theoretical terms in our well-established scientific theories actually refer to entities, most of them unobservable in practice or in principle (e.g., magnetic fields), but that genuinely exist.

What does it mean to say that an observational or theoretical term is central to a theory? Suppose we were trying to identify some substance, X, that we think is copper. Given our current theories about metals in general, and copper in particular, a number of theoretical properties or observational consequences are relevant for classifying X as copper: being reddish, having the melting point of 1083° C, and having the atomic number 29. Some of these are more relevant and, therefore, more conclusive than others. With respect to two theoretical or observational properties (and the terms that refer to them), one is more central to classifying X than another if and only if the possession (or lack) of that property tends to count more in favor of (or against) classifying X as copper than does the possession (or lack) of the other property.

With regard to copper, having the atomic number 29 is more important and central than the melting point, which in turn is more important than being reddish. The more central a property is, the more weight it has in settling a dispute about classification. The intuitive idea here is that scientific theories have several theoretical and observational terms in them, some of them are more important than others, and those judged more important are the ones that are more central for the purposes of classification. The more central a term is to a well-established theory, the more a scientific realist is committed to the existence claims that the term implies.

SR3 asserts that science is an objectively rational discipline, not in the sense that scientists have no biases, but in the sense that one can, at least in principle, have objective reasons or warrant for accepting or rejecting a given scientific theory. Rationality is a normative, objective notion, not a relative one. Moreover, when two rival theories are being judged, there are, in principle, considerations that can be used to decide in favor of one rival and against the other. Rival theories are **commensurable**: they can be compared vis-à-vis each other against some common ground—the data, the various epistemic virtues each embodies and so forth.

SR4 claims that if a scientific theory has certain epistemic virtues, then it is objectively rational to believe that it is true or approximately true *because* it has these virtues. If T_1 is simpler or explains more data than T_2, gives more accurate predictions, and so on, then one has more reason to believe that T_1 is true or more approximately true than T_2. Furthermore, if a theory is true and its rivals are false, or if a theory is truer than its rivals, then one should expect it to be better eventually at predicting data, containing more clarified terms or embodying other epistemic virtues. SR4 implies that rationality is connected to truth. As a theory grows in its rationality (as measured by the presence of epistemic virtues), our confidence in the truth or approximate truth of the theory grows as well.

Finally, SR5 is a thesis about the history and aims of science. It states that the aim of science is to give us not just theories that work (e.g., that help us control nature, predict phenomena, harmonize with our observations), but also theories that are true. Science tries to tell us the way the world really is, especially the way the unobserved theoretical entities and processes of the world really are.

Moreover, more recent scientific theories are more accurate pictures of the world than are their predecessors. Science progresses over time toward a true picture of the world. Scientific progress is to be understood as progress toward truth. There are two kinds of theory changes in science: replacement and refinement. In **replacement**, a latter theory replaces a former one and the earlier theory is abandoned altogether. On a realist view, the abandoned theory is judged to be false. The change from phlogiston to oxygen chemistry is an example. In **refinement**, when a latter theory refines a former one, the supposed truth-preserving components of the earlier theory are preserved in the later theory and made more precise and accurate. According to some, the change from Newtonian to Einsteinian views of space, time and mass is an example of theory refinement. SR5 implies that the history of science, while surely containing examples of theory replacement, includes as well a number of cases of theory refinement. Either way, in theory replacement or refinement, newer theories get closer to the truth than older ones.

2.3 EVALUATION OF SCIENTIFIC REALISM

This, then, is a statement of scientific realism as a philosophy of science. How should we evaluate this position? There have been at least four basic kinds of arguments offered in favor of scientific realism. Due to space considerations, we can only state them briefly. Here is the first argument: Given that one must either embrace scientific realism or some form of antirealism, and given the fact that there are serious problems with each of the main forms of antirealism, then scientific realism, on balance, is to be preferred. Obviously, the strength of this argument turns on the case for the inadequacies of the various forms of antirealism. Later on in this chapter we will present the main an-

2.3.1 POSITIVE SUPPORT

tirealist position. At that time, you can get a feel for the various views. Hopefully, this will help you to begin to formulate your own evaluation of their strengths and weaknesses.

Second, a scientific realist can offer arguments in favor of SR1-SR5. For example, the scientific realist could offer arguments in favor of the correspondence theory of truth, in favor of the idea that rationality is intimately connected to truth, and against various forms of conceptual relativism. Similarly, the realist could also try to justify a reading of the history of science as a history of clear progress through the refinement and replacement of theories toward a better and better depiction of the way the world is. The first two issues (the correspondence theory of truth and the connection between rationality and truth) have already been discussed in chapters six and three, respectively. The third topic (conceptual relativism) was the subject of much of chapters four and six. The fourth factor would involve a detailed investigation of the history of science, among other things.

We cannot go into these debates here; however, one important point should not be missed. All of these topics are deeply philosophical in nature. Thus the defense or rebuttal of scientific realism illustrates the fact that the philosophy of science is presuppositional to science itself. That is, the question of how we should understand the existence claims of a given scientific theory will be answered, in part, by one's attitude toward scientific realism, and one's attitude about this will, in turn, be justified largely in philosophical terms. Thus the realism-antirealism debate serves as another illustration of the truth of an external philosophy of science that was discussed at the beginning of chapter fifteen.

The third argument for scientific realism is, perhaps, the main one. According to this argument, scientific realism is the best explanation for the fact that (1) our theories actually work (i.e., embody various epistemic virtues); (2) science makes progress in solving its problems; (3) often, a scientific theory will have a host of independent, empirical confirmations for it that converge together to support the theory, even if some of those empirical confirmations were not originally conceived as part of the domain for which the theory was thought to be responsible. Scientific realists claim that the best explanation for these three facts is that our theories succeed in laying hold of reality and giving at least approximately true descriptions of what really exists. For the scientific realist, it is because our theories *capture the way the world is* that those theories embody epistemic virtues, allow us to solve problems, obtain empirical confirmation and can be extended into new, previously unthought-of domains of investigation. If we abandon scientific realism, say its advocates, these facts about science can only be regarded as fortuitous miracles.

This argument places a burden of proof on antirealists, that is, realism should be assumed to be correct unless antirealists can show that their views are to be preferred to scientific realism. Among other things, this means that antirealists are required either to offer alternative accounts for these successful aspects of science or to deny that these successes really exist. As we will see later, Larry Laudan and Bas C. van Fraassen take the former approach and Thomas Kuhn takes the latter.

One final argument has been offered in favor of scientific realism, and it is theological in nature. According to some Christian philosophers of science, God has created us to know his creation and think his thoughts after him, given us cognitive and sensory faculties suited to be obtainers of truth for the world in which he placed us, and given us the desire to know his world. And these theological facts lend support to scientific realism. Other Christian philosophers of science do not agree. According to them, these points about God, our faculties and desires and the world only support the existence and availability of knowledge that comes from theology, philosophy and common sense. But they do not give support to such a technical enterprise as science which, they argue, is better understood in antirealist ways.

What are some of the main arguments against scientific realism? A number of them have been raised. First, antirealists have criticized the realist notion of truth in two different ways. To begin with, antirealists have criticized the correspondence theory of truth and/or the notion of a theory-independent external world to which we have access. Sometimes this latter point is supported by the claim that all observations are theory laden, there is no direct, theory-independent access to the external world, and thus the realist notion of such a world is either unintelligible or irrelevant. These criticisms have been the focus of much of chapters five and six, so we will not rehearse those issues here. But you should bear in mind that the epistemological and metaphysical topics mentioned in those chapters have a direct bearing on what view of science one will take.

2.3.2
OBJECTIONS TO
SCIENTIFIC
REALISM

A different way that antirealists have criticized realist notions of truth centers on the concept of approximate truth. Few would argue that our current theories are true in any complete or final way. Rather, scientific realists claim that our current well-established theories are approximately true to one degree or another. Another word for "approximate truth" is **verisimilitude**. Verisimilitude should not be confused with the epistemological notion that a given belief or set of beliefs has a high probability of being true, i.e., that our certainty regarding the belief or set of beliefs is probable, but not the belief itself, which is completely true if true at all. Verisimilitude means that a belief or set of beliefs is itself approximately true. Some critics of scientific realism point out that no one has been able to clarify sufficiently what approximate truth means, especially if a correspondence theory of truth is in view. Something is either true or false and truth does not come in degrees. A false proposition may serve certain purposes better than another false proposition, but it is still false. If a lunch box is on the kitchen floor, then the proposition that it is on the kitchen table may help you find the lunch box more than the proposition that it is in the den, but strictly speaking both propositions are false. Similarly, if we accept Einstein's laws of motion, space, time and mass, then Newton's laws of motion are literally false, even though at low velocities they are useful for a number of purposes (e.g., predicting where a projectile will land, flying an airplane). Thus antirealists claim that the realist notion of verisimilitude is an inadequate one.

A second antirealist criticism claims that theoretical terms in scientific laws or theories can be eliminated without loss of empirical content and we need not take those terms to be genuine referring terms. Remember, realists interpret the role of theoretical terms as referring to theoretical entities that actually exist. But if we can eliminate those terms without losing our ability to predict observations accurately and fit our theories and laws with the empirical world, then we can regard those terms as unnecessary.

An example may help clarify this antirealist argument. Some empirical generalizations are limited in their range of application and have exceptions, like the following:

1. Wood floats on water, iron sinks in water.

This generalization is limited to wood, water and iron (e.g., it doesn't apply to rocks), and it has exceptions: ebony chips sink and iron ships float. But we can fix the situation by introducing a theoretical concept, specific gravity, defined as the quotient of a solid body's weight divided by its volume. Now our generalization can be modified to remove exceptions and extend its application beyond wood, iron and water:

2. A solid body floats on a liquid if its *specific gravity* is less than that of the liquid.

If a scientific realist interprets specific gravity as a referring term, then the term would designate a real disposition or capacity of things in the world. We could understand this disposition as a type of drag or heaviness that an object possesses. However, an antirealist could claim that this makes specific gravity into an occult entity, an unobservable, metaphysical disposition that bodies possess. We can avoid such metaphysical excess baggage by treating the term *specific gravity* as a shorthand device for a set of calculations that enable us to predict what will float and what will sink. Thus specific gravity can be eliminated altogether as seen in this sentence:

3. A solid body floats on a liquid if *the quotient of its weight and volume is less than the corresponding quotient for the liquid.*

Some antirealists argue that most, or perhaps, all of the theoretical terms supposedly referring to unseen entities can be similarly eliminated without loss of empirical content or predictive ability for our laws and theories.

Third, antirealists claim that successful theories can turn out to be false such that the truth or approximate truth of a theory is not a necessary condition for the theory's being successful (its embodying various epistemic virtues), as scientific realists claim in SR4. In the history of science, many theories have explained phenomena, generated fruitful research and accurate predictions, yet were later abandoned as false. For example, Augustin Jean Fresnel (1788-1827) used optical aether theory to predict a novel test result: a small beam of light directed at a circular disk will undergo diffraction (bending around the edges of the object) in such a way that a bright spot at the center of the shadow of a circular disc should appear. When tested, the prediction proved correct. But we no longer believe in optical aether theory.

Fourth, antirealists claim that throughout the history of science, theories that would later be judged to have been approximately true based on a realist understanding of contemporary science (e.g., early atomic theory like that advocated by William Prout (1785-1850) have been unsuccessful for long periods of time compared to rival theories that we now consider false. Thus the truth or approximate truth of a theory is not a sufficient condition for its success. Arguments three and four directly attack SR4 by showing that the truth of a scientific theory is neither necessary nor sufficient for the theory to be successful.

A fifth and final objection to scientific realism claims that a proper understanding of the history of science shows that, surface appearances notwithstanding, science does not make progress toward truer and truer theories. Some antirealists like Thomas Kuhn support this contention by arguing that there is no progress whatever in science. We will look at Kuhn later in this chapter. But, briefly stated, his point is that the history of science is really a history of later theories completely replacing earlier theories and not refining them. This is clearly true in some cases, like theories that placed the earth at the center of the universe, but, Kuhn argues, it is even true when our current theories still use the language of earlier theories. For example, the shift from Newton's to Einstein's theory about space, time and mass represents a change in which the new theory still uses many of the same terms as did the older theory (*mass, space, time* are still used in Einstein's theory), but the entities represented by these terms are depicted as so radically different in the new theory compared to the old, that advocates of the two theories use the terms equivocally (both use the same terms but with very different meanings) and we no longer believe that Newtonian mass, space and time exist. Thus the history of science is a history of discarded theories, suggesting that our current theories will some day be discarded as well. Thus there is no reason to think that we now have or will have true theories.

Other antirealists, like Larry Laudan (also discussed later in this chapter), believe that science does, in fact, make progress through history, but that progress has nothing whatever to do with the notion that later theories are more true than earlier ones. Rather, our current theories represent progress compared to earlier ones in that our current theories are more pragmatically useful—they make better predictions, they help us explain more things, they allow us to generate better technology. But pragmatic usefulness should not be confused with truth, say some antirealists, and scientific progress, though real, is a function of the pragmatic usefulness of theories and not their truthfulness.

Other objections have been raised against scientific realism, but we have described the main ones. It is time now to take a look at antirealist alternatives to scientific realism. In what follows we will look at four rational nonrealist (i.e., instrumentalist) views in the order presented in figure 16.1 and then look at one nonrational nonrealist position.

3 ANTIREALISM

Rational nonrealism, also called **instrumentalism**, is a family of views that agree on two main points: (1) Science is an objectively rational enterprise, and conceptual relativism is false as a way of understanding the rationality of science. (2) Scientific theories do not give us true or approximately true pictures of the unobservable, theoretical entities and processes that are causally responsible for what we empirically observe, nor do the theoretical terms in those theories refer to actual entities in the theory-independent world (and even if, by

3.1
RATIONAL
NONREALISM
(INSTRUMEN-
TALISM)

accident, they do refer to existent entities, this would be utterly irrelevant for science). Rather, scientific theories are useful tools or instruments (thus the name *instrumentalism*) that help us accomplish certain things. But what, then, are the things that scientific theories help us to accomplish? Here, instrumentalists differ, and at least four answers have been given to this question.

1. Phenomenalism. Among other things, **phenomenalism** is an epistemological doctrine that includes a view about the nature of perception. It was discussed in chapter eight, and thus it will only be briefly treated here with special focus on the way phenomenalism relates to the nature of science. Phenomenalism is a view that was more popular earlier in this century. Major proponents of one form or another of phenomenalism have been Benjamin Brodie, Ernst Mach and A. S. Eddington. Essentially, phenomenalism is a radical empiricist theory of epistemology to the effect that all our knowledge is derived from and is about immediate sensory experiences. Applied to science, the view implies that scientific knowledge is about what can be directly observed. Any thing or process that cannot be perceived cannot be supposed to exist for science.

Second, the meaning of expressions that appear to be referring to unseen theoretical entities (e.g., electron, atom) must be taken as referring to sensory experience. Since only propositions about what is directly observable are meaningful or have the status of knowledge, claims about unobservable theoretical entities are really disguised statements about sensory experiences and must be translated or reduced to such. Science merely tries to **save the phenomena**, that is, to facilitate our ability to describe the successive sensory experiences we have of the world or to anticipate and predict future sensory experiences. As Mach put it, "it is the object of science to replace, or *save*, experiences, by the reproduction and anticipation of facts in thought."[1] Theoretical terms are merely summaries of data, labor-saving devices for classifying observations. A theory is a mnemonic device by which sensory facts are stored and recollected; it is an elliptical formula of the relations of dependence that regularly occur between observable events and properties. Thus theoretical terms can be translated without remainder into a set of statements about a potentially infinite set of actual or possible sensory experiences.

Furthermore, phenomenalists hold that experience is nothing more than a succession of immediately given, conscious states known by direct inspection or acquaintance with the flow of one's own consciousness. These conscious states are variously called ideas, sense data or impressions.

Some examples may help to clarify what all this means. According to phenomenalism, the word *hydrogen* refers not to an atom that exists but to a set of laboratory observations of "hydrogenated space" (i.e., a set of laboratory observations of colorlessness, weight and volume that are experienced after a series of prior sensory experiences occur that involve ways of preparing the "hydrogenated space"). The statement "There is presently an electric current in the wire on the table" does not refer to the theoretical entity, an electric current, but rather the statement can be translated into a set of statements like this: "If the

---

[1] Ernst Mach, *The Science of Mechanics* (La Salle, Ill.: Open Court, 1960), p. 577.

galvanometer on the desk there were introduced into the circuit, the pointer would be deflected from its present position." This statement can, in turn, be translated into a statement about a set of sensory experiences ("If one orients one's head in a certain direction at the right time, one will have a pointer type sense datum with a certain shape"). The law "$2H_2 + O_2 = 2H_2O$" merely asserts that, in the past and most likely in the future, two units of a certain observed volume, weight and odorlessness produced by certain techniques have been added to one unit of volume, weight, and odorlessness produced by certain other techniques, and a wet, colorless substance of two units has always followed. Note that the essential features of the law are all capable of being analyzed in terms of sensory experiences (e.g., observed volume, weight and odorlessness).

We cannot undertake a criticism of phenomenalism here, but one point should be made. There has always been a tension between the empirical aspects of science and the belief that science gives us the truth about the theoretical, unobservable entities and processes in the world. To the degree that one emphasizes the empirical aspects of science, to that degree it is difficult to sustain scientific realism. On the other hand, to the degree that one embraces scientific realism, to that degree one must allow that science goes beyond and involves itself in factors other than those that can be directly tested through immediate observation.

2. Operationalism. **Operationalism**, occasionally called operationism, is an approach to science very similar to phenomenalism. Its major proponent has been P. W. Bridgman (1882-1962). Whereas phenomenalism links scientific terms, laws and theories to actual or possible sensory experiences, operationalism links them to actual or possible laboratory operations. For the phenomenalist, scientific laws and theoretical terms really refer not to mind-independent entities and events but to mind-dependent sensations. For the operationalist, scientific laws and theoretical terms really refer to experimental activities and operations. Theoretical terms are like the term "the average family" that we discussed in conjunction with SR2 above.

Bridgman stated the central tenet of operationalism in this way: "In general, we mean by any concept nothing more than a set of operations; *the concept is synonymous with the corresponding set of operations*. . . . The proper definition of a concept is not in terms of its properties but in terms of actual operations."[2] For example, length is not an attribute that a physical body has; rather, it is defined as a set of operations of sliding rulers, marking coincidences and counting how many operations one has made. The "length" of a room is nothing but the operation of taking a stick with thirty-six markings (call them inch markings), starting at one end of the room, and laying the stick end after end until one crosses the room, and recording all one's activities. Similarly, the statement that x amount of some acid neutralizes y of some base means that if one pours a certain measurement of one liquid (which, in turn, is defined in terms of certain

---

[2]P. W. Bridgman, "The Logic of Modern Physics," in *The World of Physics*, ed. Jefferson Hane Weaver (New York: Simon & Schuster, 1987), 3:842.

operations used to obtain it) into a beaker and adds a certain measurement of another liquid, then certain measurements follow (e.g., the combined liquids change color when the measurements are done in a certain way).

Before we move on to the next instrumentalist view, a final observation about operationalism should be made. Operationalism is reductionistic in spirit and thus is an inadequate theory. Length is a property of bodies that may be measured by a set of measuring operations, but which is not identical to or the same thing as those measurements. Thus we should be careful to distinguish operationalism as a philosophy of science from the legitimate use of operational definitions. It is quite proper to come up with some **operational definition** for something—say *intelligence, depression* or *length*—in which a set of measurable, empirically testable operations are formulated as a test for the thing being studied. It is one thing to say that measurements x, y and z are good tests for the presence of some phenomenon P, which is what the legitimate use of operational definitions seeks to do. However, it is another thing altogether to claim, as operationalists do, that phenomenon P is identical to, is nothing other than, measurements x, y and z. Thus one can use operational definitions without being a full-blown operationalist.

3. Pragmatism. A third instrumentalist view is called **pragmatism**, and the main contemporary advocate of this view is philosopher Larry Laudan.[3] According to Laudan, any philosophy of science must take into account three features of the history of science: (1) At each period of science, one can find examples of agreement (where scientists agree about the adequacy of some theory) and disagreement (where various theories are competing for allegiance). (2) Science is an objectively rational, progressive discipline, but scientific progress has little or nothing to do with truth. We must, therefore, understand scientific progress in ways other than the scientific realist proposal expressed in proposition SR5. (3) Science tries to solve empirical and conceptual problems (see chap. 15). A solution to a problem need not be true; it must only remove our puzzlement about some phenomenon and allow us to make useful predictions about the natural world and harmonize our theories with what we observe.

Laudan's philosophy of science is an attempt to explain these three features of the history of science. For Laudan, then, the main goal of science is to solve problems. The solved problem is the basic unit of scientific progress. For example, if our theory of gravity helps us explain and predict the movement of the tides, then we have used our theory to remove puzzlement about this problem, and our solution is a good one because it works for us, irrespective of whether or not our solution is true. Thus scientific progress should be defined in terms of the relative rate, number and importance of solved problems accomplished by a theory or research program, not in terms of convergence toward the truth (a research program is, roughly, a group of theories focusing on the same issues,

---

[3]See Larry Laudan, *Progress and Its Problems* (Berkeley: University of California Press, 1977); *Science and Values: An Essay on the Aims of Science and their Role in Scientific Debate* (Berkeley: University of California Press, 1984); "A Confutation of Convergent Realism," *Philosophy of Science* 48 (1981): 19-49; "Explaining the Success of Science: Beyond Epistemic Realism and Relativism," in *Science and Reality*, ed. James T. Cushing, C. F. Delaney and Gary Gutting (Notre Dame, Ind.: University of Notre Dame Press, 1984), pp. 83-105.

e.g., all models of atomic theory through history would be part of the same research program). If theory *A* solves important problems more quickly than theory *B*, then it is more rational to accept theory *A* than *B*. The possession of various epistemic virtues (simplicity, predictive success, etc.) by a theory tells us merely that the theory is successful, that it works well in solving its problems, not that the theory is approximately true.

In sum, Laudan claims that problem solving is the fundamental feature of science, that scientific progress should be defined, not in terms of truth, but in terms of the rate and success of a theory's problem solving track record, and that scientific rationality should, in turn, be defined in terms of the progress of a theory—the more progressive a theory is the more rational it is to accept it. According to Laudan, the realist concept of truth is not relevant to any of these notions.

But the scientific realist will want to know how science can make progress in solving its problems if its theories are not at least approximately true. If the truth of our theories is not what is responsible for making them work, what is? Laudan's answer involves a coherence theory of epistemic justification (see chap. 5). The point of our theories is for them to work, and when a theory has problems we will continue to make adjustments in various ways. We may deny that the problematic data are really accurate (perhaps our instruments are not to be trusted), we may change the aims and methods we appropriate (e.g., start preferring theoretical simplicity to empirical accuracy, try different test methods that harmonize with our theory and abandon test methods that do not), or we may adjust part of our theory itself. The point is, we will find some way to reestablish coherence among our theories, the data and our aims and methods. But once we have obtained such coherence, that does not mean the theory is approximately true; it just means that scientists have become good at fitting things together until they work. For Laudan, this is all it takes to explain how science makes progress in solving its problems.

4. Constructive empiricism. Princeton philosopher Bas C. van Fraassen holds a view about science that he calls **constructive empiricism**.[4] According to van Fraassen, scientific realism is inadequate; the point of science is to "save the phenomena," that is, to develop theories that are consistent with empirical observations and predictions. Science aims at giving us theories that are empirically adequate, and acceptance of a theory only involves the belief that it is empirically adequate.

Van Fraassen calls his philosophy *constructive* because he sees the aim of science to be the construction of theoretical models, not the discovery of truth concerning unobservables. It is called *empiricism* because, as already mentioned, the main goal of science is to develop empirically adequate, predictively successful theories. Van Fraassen makes a distinction between believing and accepting a theory. Accepting a theory merely involves belief that the theory is empiri-

---

[4]Bas C. van Fraassen, *The Scientific Image* (Oxford: Oxford University Press, 1980); "To Save the Phenomena," in *Scientific Realism*, ed. Jarrett Leplin (Berkeley: University of California Press, 1984), pp. 250-59; Paul M. Churchland and Clifford Hooker, eds., *Images of Science: Essays on Realism and Empiricism, with a Reply from Bas C. van Fraassen* (Chicago: University of Chicago Press, 1985).

cally adequate, that it is true regarding what it says about what we can observe. It involves no commitment to the truth of the theoretical, unobservable entities and processes included in the theory, but merely the pragmatic commitment to act as if such entities and processes are real if such commitment leads us to better and better empirical success. Believing a theory, on the other hand, involves a commitment to the belief that a good theory truly describes both the observational *and unobservable* world. Scientific realists believe good theories; constructive empiricists merely accept them.

If scientific realism is false, then how is it that theories make progress in "saving the phenomena"? Van Fraassen's answer is similar to the one offered by Laudan: since the point of a theory is empirical adequacy in the first place, scientists will keep adjusting things until our models obtain such adequacy. Scientific theory competition is like natural selection: only the strong (i.e., the empirically adequate) survive.

This completes our brief overview of four instrumentalist views of science. All of them agree that science is an objectively rational set of disciplines. Nonrational nonrealists reject this notion. They agree with instrumentalists that truth about real, theoretical entities and processes is not the goal of science. But they also reject the notion that there is some objective sense of rationality that science embodies.

3.2	Thomas Kuhn is the best-known advocate of **nonrational nonrealism,** and we
NONRATIONAL	will look at his philosophy of science as a representative of the view.[5] Kuhn's
NONREALISM	view of science has two key aspects: the history of science and the epistemology

3.2
NONRATIONAL
NONREALISM

Thomas Kuhn is the best-known advocate of **nonrational nonrealism,** and we will look at his philosophy of science as a representative of the view.[5] Kuhn's view of science has two key aspects: the history of science and the epistemology of science. For Kuhn, the epistemic authority of science does not reside in the fact that scientists use something called the scientific method (he denies that there is such a thing) but rather in the scientific community itself, seen as a group of practitioners of a craft working within a shared paradigm.

The notion of a paradigm is central for understanding Kuhn's history and epistemology of science. What is a paradigm? Some have claimed that Kuhn has used as many as twenty-two different definitions of the term, but here are some of the main ones: the **paradigm** is an entire worldview, a specific scientific theory (like Newton's views of space, time, motion and mass), a pedagogical tool scientists use to indoctrinate new practitioners into a field (like the ideal gas equation $PV = nRT$, which teaches students how to view gases), a way of seeing the world and something that constitutes nature itself by telling us what the world in our theory amounts to (there are atomic corpuscles in some paradigms, waves in another, both in still different paradigms).

Regarding the history of science, there are periods in which science can be conceived of as normal science. These are times when a field is dominated by one, universally accepted paradigm. During this time, the paradigm is not questioned and scientific activity focuses on extending the range of application for the paradigm, making it more precise and so forth. However, if the paradigm

[5]Thomas Kuhn, *Structure of Scientific Revolutions,* 2d ed., enlarged (Chicago: University of Chicago Press, 1970); *The Essential Tension* (Chicago: University of Chicago Press, 1977); "Logic of Discovery or Psychology of Research?" and "Reflections on My Critics," in *Criticism and the Growth of Knowledge,* ed. Imre Lakatos and Alan Musgrave (Cambridge: Cambridge University Press, 1970), pp. 1-23 and 231-78, respectively.

develops a number of anomalies that it cannot adequately handle, then a period of crisis emerges when rival paradigms are formed. Eventually, a scientific revolution occurs by which the old paradigm is completely abandoned and a new paradigm is accepted, ushering in a new period of normal science. Accordingly, Kuhn rejects any notion of progress throughout the history of science or of theory refinement as a type of theory change. The history of science is a history of theory change and replacement through cycles of normal science, crisis, revolution and normal science.

Regarding the epistemology of science, Kuhn holds that there are no such things as neutral facts or data. Observation is theory laden and there are no data or epistemic virtues that could be used to justify a paradigm that are not themselves already dependent on that paradigm. Thus the notions of truth as correspondence and of an external, theory-independent world are bogus and irrelevant for science. Practitioners of two "rival" paradigms literally see a different world. Rival paradigms are **incommensurable**, that is, they cannot even be compared with each other to see which is more rational or closer to the facts because there is no common ground between them and nothing outside the paradigm that could serve, even in principle, as a basis of such a comparison. Different paradigms literally describe different worlds.

This means that the shift from one paradigm to another is like a conversion experience. It represents a different way of seeing things. Such paradigm shifts are not matters of gaining a more true or rational theory in favor of a discarded one. The rational-irrational distinction is itself relative to different paradigms. What is rational for one community of scientific practitioners defined by one paradigm will not necessarily be rational for another. Thus science is not objectively rational because such a notion is not applicable to science. The rational authority of science is primarily a cultural matter and relies on various types of persuasion; it is not a matter of objective rationality. Our current theories are not more rational than those of five hundred years ago, they are just more rational to those of us who accept them. It should be obvious that Kuhn's view of science has a postmodernist flavor to it in its rejection of truth as correspondence, of the notion of an objective theory-independent world and of the idea of objective rationality. It should also be obvious that it suffers from some of the problems that accrue to postmodernism in general (see chap. 6).

4 INTEGRATION AND THE REALIST-ANTIREALIST DEBATE

Christians have the desire, the responsibility, and the privilege of integrating their theological beliefs with justified beliefs from sources outside theology. We will take up the topic of the integration of science and theology in the next chapter, but for now, let us ask how the realist-antirealist debate informs the task of integration. Should Christians be realists or antirealists in light of their joint commitment to truth wherever it is found and to Christian teaching? In the introduction to this chapter we touched on the importance of this question. It is important for its own sake, since as Christians and simply as responsible human beings we want to know the truth about things, the realist-antirealist debate included.

This question is also important for the task of integration. For example, if some well-established scientific theory seems to be contrary to some well-established part of our Christian worldview, then one way to resolve this dilemma would be to take the scientific theory in question in antirealist terms. We could then accept that the theory is successful, but not take that to mean that the theory is true. Thus it would not constitute a direct challenge to the truth of the theological belief in question. Of course, such a strategy could easily be abused or charged with being a convenient way out of intellectual difficulties, so anyone who adopts such a strategy would need to use it with integrity. Moreover, such a recourse assumes that antirealism is an option, at least some of the time.

Should Christians adopt realism or antirealism as a philosophy of science? This is no easy question, and responsible Christian philosophers are divided on the issue, as we indicated earlier in this chapter. It would seem that, insofar as Christian doctrine is concerned, each position is a live and legitimate option. However, we need not leave the matter here because we think that there are some arguments against scientific realism that are not live options for Christians, while others are live options for Christians.

In our view, common sense, solid philosophical argument and Christian theology unite to justify belief in three things relevant to the realist-antirealist dialogue: (1) The notion of truth as correspondence is at least part of an adequate philosophical account of truth and is implicitly taught in and presupposed by the Bible, as is the notion of a theory- or (finite) mind-independent external world. (2) Our natural sensory and cognitive faculties, though fallen, are still adequate to give us justified true beliefs about the world, which is itself the sort of world suited for being known by creatures with the types of faculties we possess. Moreover, any attempt to limit human knowledge within the confines of strong forms of empiricism (as in phenomenalism or operationalism) is mistaken. (3) Rationality is intimately connected with truth in such a way that the main value or point of behaving rationally and of obtaining rational beliefs is that such behavior and beliefs put us in a better position to live and to have the truth. Thus antirealist arguments that run contrary to these three notions are to be rejected on rational and theological grounds.

On the other hand, three antirealist arguments do seem to carry weight: (1) The history of science clearly offers a number of cases where past theories now judged to have been false in light of realist interpretations of current science embodied several epistemic virtues, and theories judged as approximately true in light of realist interpretations of current theories failed to embody various epistemic virtues for some time compared to their rival theories. (2) Due to our finite and fallen condition, various psychological and sociological nonrational factors, while not making knowledge impossible, do, nevertheless, affect the processes by which we form and justify our belief. This is especially true in areas of life that have a high degree of social prestige, as does science. Thus the widespread acceptability of some theory by the scientific community (e.g., evolutionary theory) may well be due to various nonrational factors and not to the fact that the theory is a well-justified, approximately true view of the world. (3)

Much of the point of some areas of science, especially those that are highly mathematical (like theoretical physics and speculative cosmology), is to "save the phenomena" and not much is lost if the more metaphysical aspects of some theories in these areas are rejected.

Where, then, does this leave us? In our view, we are not forced to choose between realism or antirealism. Rather, we are free to adopt one or the other on a case by case basis. We should start with an examination of specific, actual scientific theories, assess the strengths and weaknesses of realist and antirealist interpretations of those theories in light of the comments just made, and make our choice accordingly. Note that one should start with particular cases in science and not with general criteria for choosing between realism and antirealism. General, though not universal, criteria for such choices emerge only after careful consideration of particular cases.

Are there any criteria that can be used to help us decide between a realist or antirealist view of some specific theory? We know of no complete set of adequate criteria, but the following are some criteria that, while admitting of exceptions, are still valuable. On the strength of the three points just mentioned in favor of scientific realism (truth as correspondence and the reality of the external world; the existence of knowledge beyond the empirical; the importance of truth for rationality), let us assume scientific realism and place the burden of proof on the antirealist. Then one should interpret a scientific theory in realist terms unless one or more of the following obtain:

1. A realist interpretation conflicts with a rationally well-established internal or external conceptual problem, but an antirealist view does not.

2. The history of theories in this area of study has exhibited a large proportion of theory replacements versus refinements, and thus there is no clear progress in converging on a widely shared theory in the area of study.

3. Nonrational factors can account for much of the theory's acceptance by the scientific community.

4. The main virtue of the theory is its empirical adequacy, and its more metaphysical, theoretical aspects can be understood as unnecessary, excess metaphysical baggage in our attempt to explain the success of the theory.

5. The theory has continued to be accepted largely through the use of inappropriate, ad hoc adjustments.

These criteria should be understood as mere guides and not as absolute rules. So understood, they can help inform any attempt to understand science and can be useful in the attempt to integrate science with theology. Principles (2) through (5) require little comment. (2) focuses on the realist emphasis on the progressive, refinement view of the history of science and asserts that, when absent or scarce in an area of science, this counts against realism. (3) captures the insight that if a theory's acceptance can be adequately explained by nonrational (e.g., sociological) factors, then we need not appeal to the approximate truth of the theory to explain why it is viewed as a success. (4) brings out the idea that in areas of science (perhaps some areas of mechanics, theoretical physics and speculative cosmology) where the epistemic virtue of empirical adequacy carries most of the weight for a theory (often these will be areas that are heavily mathematical or that depict a phenomenon in ways that are vastly different than the world of common sense, e.g., the quantum world), the more metaphysical aspects of the theory are less important for the rational acceptability of that theory. Finally, **ad hoc** adjustments of a theory are those solely designed to save it from being falsified by an anomaly and that accomplish little or nothing else. While it is not easy to tell when an ad hoc adjustment of a theory is appropriate or inappropriate, nevertheless, to the degree that a theory has been maintained through inappropriate ad hoc readjustments, to that degree it loses its claim to understand its success as a sign of its approximate truth.

That leaves us with (1), which may be the most important of the five for the task of integration. (1) tells us that if a theory, realistically interpreted, has problems of vagueness, circular definition or lack of clarity among its concepts, then if an antirealist understanding of the theory removes these problems, that counts in favor of the antirealist understanding. Moreover, if a realist understanding of a theory conflicts with rationally justified philosophical or theological beliefs whereas an antirealist view does not, this too counts in favor of the antirealist position. For example, if we have good philosophical or theological reasons for believing that the space-time universe had a beginning a finite time ago, then if a "successful" scientific model runs counter to this belief, it may be best to interpret the model in antirealist terms.

Principle (1), as well as principles (2) through (5) and, indeed, the realist-antirealist debate in general are important to keep in mind when we try to integrate our theological and scientific beliefs. Can more be said about how philosophy can be an aid to the task of integration? Most definitely, as the next chapter will illustrate.

CHAPTER SUMMARY

Science regularly uses terms that stand for unobservable, theoretical entities (e.g., electrons). Deciding whether or not to believe in these entities involves taking a position on the scientific realism-antirealism debate. Moreover, understanding this debate can also inform the task of integrating science and theology.

Scientific realism is the view that science is an objectively rational set of disciplines that progressively obtain truer and truer theories, whose central observational and theoretical terms genuinely refer to real entities and processes and whose theories embody epistemic virtues if and only if they are approximately true. Scientific realists argue that their view is superior to antirealist positions, that SR1-SR5 are rational to believe, that scientific realism explains the otherwise miraculous fact that scientific theories work, make progress and can be extended into new domains, and that scientific realism fits with certain theological beliefs. Antirealists reject these claims and argue that the notion of truth as correspondence and approximate truth are problematic, that theoretical terms can be eliminated from science without loss of empirical content, that successful theories can be false and theories taken as true by realists can be unsuccessful for a long time and that science either does not make progress or that its progress is unrelated to truth.

Antirealist alternatives come in two main groups. First, there is rational non-realism (instrumentalism). Instrumentalists agree that science is objectively rational, but they reject the realist claim about truth regarding theoretical entities. Rather, theories are useful instruments for summarizing sensations (phenomenalism) or laboratory operations (operationalism), for pragmatically solving problems (Laudan), or for constructing empirically adequate pictures of the world (van Fraassen). Second, there is nonrational nonrealism, represented by Thomas Kuhn, which rejects both the truthfulness and referential aspects of science, as well as the notion that science is objectively rational.

Regarding the task of integration, Christians are divided about this debate. Moreover, there are good and bad arguments against scientific realism. In light of this, an eclectic model may be the best. This model implies taking a realist or antirealist view on a case by case basis, guided by some useful principles to aid in such decision-making.

CHECKLIST OF BASIC TERMS AND CONCEPTS
ad hoc
alethic or truth realism
antirealism
commensurable
constructive empiricism
entity realism
epistemic virtues
incommensurable
nonrational nonrealism
observational terms
operational definition
operationalism (operationism)
paradigm
phenomenalism
pragmatism
rational nonrealism or instrumentalism
reductionism
refinement
replacement
save the phenomena
scientific realism
theoretical terms
verisimilitude

17

PHILOSOPHY
AND THE INTEGRATION
OF SCIENCE AND THEOLOGY

The theorist who maintains that science is the
be-all and end-all—that what is not in science textbooks
is not worth knowing—is an ideologist with a
peculiar and distorted doctrine of his own.
For him, science is no longer a sector of
the cognitive enterprise but an all-inclusive world-view.
This is the doctrine not of science but of scientism.
To take this stance is not to celebrate science but to distort it.
NICHOLAS RESCHER, *THE LIMITS OF SCIENCE*

1 INTRODUCTION

In the previous two chapters, we have peered through the lens of philosophy at various aspects of science. We have also seen in various places just how important it is for Christians to integrate their theological beliefs with their scientific ones. In this chapter, we shall probe more deeply into integrative issues and, in the process, will see once again just how important philosophy is for the task of integration and the formation of a Christian worldview.

In chapter sixteen, we saw how the realist-antirealist debate relates to integration. For the purposes of this chapter, let us assume scientific realism, though much of what will be said could equally apply to antirealist conceptions of science. In what follows, we will, first, examine an ideology, currently quite popular, known as scientism. Next, the chapter surveys various models for integrating science and theology. Finally, we will focus on the question of whether or not science must presuppose what is called methodological naturalism. In examining this question, the creation-evolution debate will be used to sharpen the issues.

2 SCIENTISM

Scientism, expressed in the quotation by Rescher at the beginning of the chapter, is the view that science is the very paradigm of truth and rationality. If something does not square with currently well-established scientific beliefs, if it is not within the domain of entities appropriate for scientific investigation, or if it is not amenable to scientific methodology, then it is not true or rational. Everything outside of science is a matter of mere belief and subjective opinion, of which rational assessment is impossible. Science, exclusively and ideally, is our model of intellectual excellence.

Actually, there are two forms of scientism: strong scientism and weak scientism. **Strong scientism** is the view that some proposition or theory is true and/or rational to believe if and only if it is a scientific proposition or theory; that is, if and only if it is a well-established scientific proposition or theory that, in turn, depends on its having been successfully formed, tested and used according to appropriate scientific methodology. There are no truths apart from scientific truths, and even if there were, there would be no reason whatever to believe them.

Advocates of **weak scientism** allow for the existence of truths apart from science and are even willing to grant that they can have some minimal, positive rationality status without the support of science. But advocates of weak scientism still hold that science is the most valuable, most serious and most authoritative sector of human learning. Every other intellectual activity is inferior to science. Further, there are virtually no limits to science. There is no field into which scientific research cannot shed light. To the degree that some issue or belief outside science can be given scientific support or can be reduced to science, to that degree the issue or belief becomes rationally acceptable. Thus we have an intellectual and perhaps even a moral obligation to try to use science to solve problems in other fields that, heretofore, have been untouched by scientific methodology. For example, we should try to solve problems about the mind by the methods of neurophysiology and computer science.

Note that advocates of weak scientism are not merely claiming that, for example, belief that the universe had a beginning, supported by good philosophical and theological arguments, gains *extra* support if that belief also has good scientific arguments for it. This claim is relatively uncontroversial because, usually, if some belief has a few good supporting arguments and later gains more good supporting arguments, then this will increase the rationality of the belief in question. But this is not what weak scientism implies, because this point cuts both ways. For it will equally be the case that good philosophical and theological arguments for a beginning of the universe will increase the rationality of such a belief initially supported only by scientific arguments. Advocates of weak scientism are claiming that fields outside science gain if they are given scientific support and not vice versa.

If either strong or weak scientism is true, this would have drastic implications for the integration of science and theology. If strong scientism is true, then theology is not a cognitive enterprise at all and there is no such thing as theological knowledge. If weak scientism is true, then the conversation between theology and science will be a monologue with theology listening to science and waiting for science to give it support. For thinking Christians, either of these alternatives is unacceptable. What, then, should we say about scientism?

Note first that strong scientism is self-refuting (see chap. 2 for a treatment of self-refutation). Strong scientism is not itself a proposition *of* science, but a second-order proposition *of* philosophy *about* science to the effect that only scientific propositions are true and/or rational to believe. And strong scientism is itself offered as a true, rationally justified position to believe. Now, propositions that are self-refuting (e.g., *There are no truths*) are not such that they just happen to be false but could have been true. Self-refuting propositions are necessarily false, that is, it is not possible for them to be true. What this means is that, among other things, no amount of scientific progress in the future will have the slightest effect on making strong scientism more acceptable.

There are two more problems that count equally against strong and weak scientism. First, scientism (in both forms) does not adequately allow for the task of stating and defending the necessary presuppositions for science itself to be practiced (assuming scientific realism). Thus scientism shows itself to be a foe and not a friend of science.

Science cannot be practiced in thin air. In fact, science itself presupposes a number of substantive philosophical theses which must be assumed if science is even going to get off the runway. Now each of these assumptions has been challenged, and the task of stating and defending these assumptions is one of the tasks of philosophy. The conclusions of science cannot be more certain than the presuppositions it rests on and uses to reach those conclusions.

Strong scientism rules out these presuppositions altogether because neither the presuppositions themselves nor their defense are scientific matters. Weak scientism misconstrues their strength in its view that scientific propositions have greater epistemic authority than those of other fields like philosophy. This would mean that the conclusions of science are more certain than the philosophical presuppositions used to justify and reach those conclusions, and that is absurd. In this regard, the following statement by John Kekes strikes at the heart of weak scientism:

> A successful argument for science being the paradigm of rationality must be based on the demonstration that the presuppositions of science are preferable to other presuppositions. That demonstration requires showing that science, relying on these presuppositions, is better at solving some problems and achieving some ideals than its competitors. But showing that cannot be the task of science. It is, in fact, one task of philosophy. Thus the enterprise of justifying the presuppositions of science by showing that with their help science is the best way of solving certain problems and achieving some ideals is a necessary precondition of the justification of science. Hence philosophy, and not science, is a stronger candidate for being the very paradigm of rationality.[1]

Here is a list of some of the philosophical presuppositions of science: (1) the existence of a theory-independent, external world; (2) the orderly nature of the external world; (3) the knowability of the external world; (4) the existence of truth; 5. the laws of logic; (6) the reliability of our cognitive and sensory faculties to serve as truth gatherers and as a source of justified beliefs in our intellectual environment; (7) the adequacy of language to describe the world; (8) the existence of values used in science (e.g., "test theories fairly and report test results honestly"); (9) the uniformity of nature and induction; (10) the existence of numbers.

Most of these assumptions are easy to understand and, in any case, are discussed in more detail in other parts of this book. It may be helpful, however, to

---

[1]John Kekes, *The Nature of Philosophy* (Totowa, N.J.: Rowman & Littlefield, 1980), p. 158.

say a word about (9) and (10). Regarding (9), scientists make inductive inferences from past or examined cases of some phenomenon (e.g., "All observed emeralds are green") to all cases, examined and unexamined, past and future, of that phenomenon (e.g., "All emeralds whatever are green"). The **problem of induction** is the problem of justifying such inferences. It is usually associated with David Hume. Here is his statement of it:

> It is impossible, therefore, that any arguments from experience can prove this resemblance of the past to the future, since all these arguments are founded on the supposition of that resemblance. Let the course of things be allowed hitherto ever so regular, that alone, without some new argument or inference, proves not that for the future it will continue so. In vain do you pretend to have learned the nature of bodies from your past experience. Their secret nature, and consequently, all their effects and influence, may change without any change in their sensible qualities. This happens sometimes, and with regard to some objects. Why may it not happen always, and with regard to all objects? What logic, what process of argument secures you against this supposition? My practice, you say, refutes my doubts. But you mistake the purport of my question. As an agent, I am quite satisfied in the point; but as a philosopher who has some share of curiosity, I will not say skepticism, I want to learn the foundation of this inference.[2]

We cannot look here at various attempts to solve the problem of induction except to note that inductive inferences assume what has been called the **uniformity of nature**: The future will resemble the past. And the uniformity of nature principle is one of the philosophical assumptions of science.

Regarding (10) (the existence of numbers), in general, if we accept as true a proposition like *The ball on the table is red*, we thereby are committed to the existence of certain things, e.g., a specific ball and the property of being red. Now science uses mathematical language much of the time and such usage seems to presuppose that mathematical language is true. This, in turn, seems to presuppose the existence of mathematical objects (e.g., numbers) that are truly described by those propositions. For example, the proposition *Two is an even number* seems to commit us to the existence of an entity, the number two (whatever our analysis of numbers turns out to be), which has the property of being even. The same theory of truth used outside of mathematics (the correspondence theory) applies within mathematics as well. Now the debate about the existence and nature of numbers is a philosophical one, and thus stating the debate and defending the existence of numbers is another philosophical task presuppositional to science.

There is a second problem that counts equally against strong and weak scientism: the existence of true and rationally justified beliefs outside of science. The simple fact is that true, rationally justified beliefs exist in a host of fields outside of science. Many of the issues in this book fall in that category. Strong scientism does not allow for this fact and therefore should be rejected as an inadequate account of our intellectual enterprise.

Moreover, some propositions believed outside science (e.g., *Red is a color,*

---

[2]David Hume, *An Inquiry Concerning Human Understanding* (1748; Indianapolis: Bobbs-Merrill, 1965), pp. 51-52 (section 4.2 in the original).

Torturing babies for fun is wrong, I am now thinking about science) are better justified than some believed within science (e.g., *Evolution takes place through a series of very small steps*). It is not hard to believe that many of our currently held scientific beliefs will and should be revised or abandoned in one hundred years, but it would hard to see how the same could be said of the extrascientific propositions just cited. Weak scientism does not account for this fact. In fact, weak scientism, in its attempt to reduce all issues to scientific ones, often has a distorting effect on an intellectual issue. Arguably, this is the case in current attempts to make the existence and nature of mind a scientific problem.

In sum, scientism in both forms is inadequate. There are domains of knowledge outside and independent of science, and while we have not shown this here, theology is one of those domains. How, then, should the domains of science and theology be integrated? To this question we now turn.

3 MODELS FOR INTEGRATING SCIENCE AND THEOLOGY

There are at least six different models for integrating science and theology. These models are not mutually exclusive unless, of course, one of them is taken to be the whole truth about integration. It is not always easy to identify clearly when some issue is a scientific or theological one. Still, there are clear cases where they can be differentiated, and in any case, there is an actual division of academic disciplines in the university. Thus the question may be fairly asked about how those disciplines, as they are actually practiced, should be integrated. According to these models:

A. Science and theology focus on two distinct, nonoverlapping areas of investigation, viz. the natural and the supernatural.

B. Science and theology involve two different, complementary approaches to and descriptions of the same reality from different perspectives. Each involves a different level of description, tells us different kinds of things, and uses a different vocabulary. Each level of description is complete at its own level without having gaps in its perspective. Nevertheless, each is only a partial description of the whole reality described. Science and theology do not directly interact with each other in epistemically positive or negative ways, but are complementary views of the total reality described. Science and theology only conflict if one field illicitly encroaches into the territory of the other field.

C. Science can fill out details in theology or help to apply theological principles and vice versa.

D. Theology provides the metaphysical and epistemological foundation for science by justifying or, at least, helping to justify the necessary presuppositions of science.

E. Science provides the boundaries within which theology must work. Theology can do its work only after consulting science. Thus science can inform theology but not vice versa.

F. Science and theology involve descriptions that can directly interact with each other in mutually reinforcing or competing ways.

Let us look at these in order. Position (A) surely accounts for certain areas of science and theology. For example, debates about the extent of the atonement or the nature of angels and debates about the structure of a methane molecule focus on very different areas of study and reality.

Position (B) is also useful, especially in areas where God operates via secondary causes. The distinction between primary and secondary causal action by God is important here. Roughly, what God did in parting the Red Sea was a primary causal act of God and what he did in guiding and sustaining that sea before and after that miracle involved a secondary causal act. **Secondary causes** are God's normal way of operating by which God sustains natural processes in existence and employs them mediately to accomplish some purpose through them. **Primary causes** are God's unusual way of operating, which involve direct, discontinuous, miraculous actions by God. The **complementarity view** (position B) is especially useful when God operates through secondary causes. For example, chemical descriptions of the synthesis of water from oxygen and hydrogen are complementary to a theological description of God's sustaining and providential governance of the chemicals during the reaction. Again, some aspects of conversion may be capable of complementary biological, psychological, sociological and theological descriptions.

Views (C) and (D) are relatively straightforward. One example of (C) is theology's assertion that fathers should not provoke their children to anger, and psychology can add important details to and practical application of this assertion by giving information about the nature and causes of anger in different personality types. Similarly, psychology can devise various tests for assessing whether one is or is not a mature person, and theology can help to fill in the details about what constitutes a mature person in the first place. Regarding view (D), the claim is that many or even most of the various presuppositions of science listed earlier in the chapter are quite at home in a Christian worldview, but are odd and without ultimate justification in a purely naturalistic worldview. Thus Christian theism is not only consistent with these presuppositions, but in some sense is also the best explanation of and justification for them as well.

An example of (E) would be the claim made by process theologians that science shows that events and not substances are the fundamental building blocks of reality and that everything is in process. Thus one ought to build his or her theological model of God on the basis of some form of process philosophy wherein God himself is constantly evolving and is not immutable. If taken at face value, position (E) is unacceptable for theological and philosophical reasons. It can be understood as an expression of weak scientism, which has already been subjected to criticism. Moreover, theological models, while certainly aided by insights from general revelation, nevertheless, ought not conflict with clear teachings of Scripture.

Does this mean that science can never contribute to a change in our understanding of theology? No, it does not, and a weakened form of view (E) can be helpful in integration. This weakened form implies that if two theological propositions are rivals, say two different interpretations of some text, A and B, and if A removes an intellectual tension with science and B does not, then A is to be preferred to B, *all other things being equal.* In particular, both interpretations would have to be exegetically justifiable on their own terms apart from scientific considerations and both would have to be consistent with good hermeneutics and with the nature of the Bible as an inspired, inerrant revelation from God. For example, passages that contain pictures of the earth having four corners should not be taken literally in light of modern science. This practice can be abused, though, and the appropriateness of this weakened form of (E) can be assessed only on a case-by-case basis.

This leaves us with position (F), labeled **theistic science**. This view, more than any of the others, allows for the possibility that science and theology may directly interact with each other in epistemically positive or negative ways. That is, (F) implies that some propositions of theology may support or gain support from science or they may conflict with and count against a scientific belief or vice versa. For example, the theological proposition that the universe had a beginning a finite time ago could gain support from the big bang model but would conflict with a scientific model (e.g., the oscillating universe model) that implies a beginningless universe with an actually infinite past. The degree of strength of support or conflict could vary.

For example, a theological and a scientific proposition may be logically incompatible with each other as in the oscillating universe case just mentioned. Or they may be logically consistent with each other but, nevertheless, odd bedfellows that are not mutually reinforcing. For example, the view that living organisms have natures (e.g., there is such a thing as human nature possessed by all and only human beings), while logically consistent with evolutionary accounts of their origins that are rooted in philosophical naturalism, is nevertheless not as reasonable to believe as it would be given some type of creationist account of the origins of living organisms. Evolutionary naturalism tends to reduce living organisms to property-things (see chap. 10). Position (F) implies that in the formation and testing of hypotheses and in explaining things in science, Christians ought to consult all they know or are justified in believing, and among the things they ought to consult are items of theological knowledge or justified theological beliefs. For example, if theology tells us that the universe had a beginning, that humans are sinful, that human beings arose in the Mideast, that life arose from a direct primary causal act of God and so forth, then these beliefs ought to be used by Christians in developing testable hypotheses, in evaluating whether or not to accept some scientific theory (e.g., that human life arose in China), and in explaining certain things.

Not everyone is happy with position (F). Some claim that (F) violates the complementary nature of science and theology and the fact that science must presuppose methodological naturalism, according to which answers to scientific questions are sought only within nature, within the contingent created order. Let us probe this dialogue more deeply.

4 THEISTIC SCIENCE AND METHODOLOGICAL NATURALISM

The main area where the debate about (F) has been focused is in the creation-evolution controversy. It may be helpful, therefore, to use that controversy as a way of spelling out the broader question of integration and the nature of science.

The term **evolution** has several meanings. It may simply mean "change over time." This sense of evolution is uncontroversial if taken to mean that microevolution has occurred, that is, that organisms can and have changed in various ways within certain limits. The second meaning of the term is the thesis of common descent: all organisms are related by common ancestry. This is sometimes called macroevolution, especially when coupled with the third meaning of evolution: the blind watchmaker thesis. This is a thesis about the mechanism of evolution, an explanation of how evolution in the first two senses has occurred. This thesis states that the processes of evolution are nonintelligent, purposeless and completely naturalistic (e.g., through mutation, natural selection, genetic drift).

There are three main camps (with different subgroups within each camp) among Christians regarding the creation-evolution controversy. First, there is **young earth creationism**. Advocates of this view, like Duane Gish, Henry Morris and John Morris, hold that God's work of creation took place in six literal, consecutive days of twenty-four hours and that the original creation of the universe took place recently, say ten to twenty thousand years ago. Moreover, most young earth creationists hold that the flood of Noah, understood as a universal deluge, is a major key for understanding the earth's geological column.

Second, there is **progressive creationism** (sometimes called "old earth creationists"), held by people such as Bernard Ramm, Walter Bradley and Hugh Ross, who hold that theistic evolution is scientifically and biblically inadequate. More positively, they hold that there is strong scientific and biblical evidence for the claim that God has acted through primary causation to create at various times. Progressive creationists differ over just how often God has done this, but many progressive creationists say that God directly created each "kind" of organism (which is in need of more clarification), and most of them agree that God directly created "the heavens and earth," first life (especially animal life) and Adam and Eve. Progressive creationists do not take the days of Genesis to be consecutive, literal twenty-four-hour periods, preferring instead to take them as long, unspecified periods of time or as six twenty-four-hour periods separated from each other by long periods of time. Either way, they view the age of the universe and earth in terms of billions of years, though most progressive creationists hold that Adam and Eve are recent creations. Progressive creationists are divided as to whether or not Noah's flood was a universal or a local flood, but they all agree that the flood is not the major factor to be consulted in understanding the earth's geology.

Finally, **theistic evolutionism**, represented by Howard J. Van Till and Richard Bube, generally holds that theology is complementary to science, that Scripture is not a science textbook, and that methodological naturalism (according to which answers to questions are sought only within nature, within the contingent created order) is the correct posture to take while doing science. Thus theistic

4.1
THEOLOGICAL
OPTIONS IN THE
CREATION-
EVOLUTION
CONTROVERSY

evolution is the proper view to take regarding origins. Accordingly, the general theory of evolution is to be taken as approximately true. Most theistic evolutionists accept all three senses of evolution listed above, except they would modify sense three. They would hold that naturalistic processes were, indeed, operative in the creation of all life and these are complementary to God's creative and providential activity. Some theistic evolutionists hold that when God created the world in the beginning, he caused it to have functional integrity—the created world had no gaps, no functional deficiencies that would require God to act through primary causation. Rather, God implanted potentialities in his original creation such that all the various kinds of creatures would arise through normal processes as these potentialities unfold. Others hold that God simply guides and sustains the widely accepted processes of evolution and creates through secondary causation solely by means of those processes.

The main debate between young earth and progressive creationists is over the use of the Hebrew word yom (day) in Genesis, and thus over the age of the universe and earth and over the usefulness of the flood for doing geology. They are agreed, however, that the general theory of evolution is false and that some sort of theistic science is appropriate. Theistic evolutionists, on the other hand, usually hold that science presupposes methodological naturalism, that science and theology are complementary to each other, and that evolution is only a problem for Christians when it is coupled with philosophical naturalism as a broad worldview, that is, the doctrine that the natural world is all there is. Thus the dialogue among these groups is not merely one about scientific fact. It never has been, because beginning with Darwin himself, the creation-evolution controversy has significantly been a debate about philosophy of science: Should theology directly interact and enter into the very fabric of science or should science adopt methodological naturalism?

4.2 THEISTIC SCIENCE

The idea behind theistic science is simple. When Christians engage in any intellectual activity, including science, they should consult all they know or have reason to believe is relevant to that activity, and theological beliefs should be among those consulted. Moreover, some theological propositions are clearly relevant to the practice of science and thus should be part of the Christian's scientific practices. For example, theological propositions that the universe had a beginning, that human beings (and animals) have souls and are not merely physical entities, that humans are fallen, that they arose within a certain time frame in the Mideast, that the basic kinds of life were directly created by God, that the flood of Noah was universal—these could all be used to form hypotheses with testable implications, to serve as background knowledge to evaluate the plausibility of various, especially competing scientific hypotheses and to explain certain things that are scientifically accessible. Thus theistic science can be understood as a research program that, among other things, utilizes the insights of theology, where appropriate, for doing science.

In chapter fifteen, we already saw some ways that theology can enter into scientific methodology and we have just listed some theological propositions that could be relevant for the practice of science. In addition, here is a brief list of some ways that theological ideas can and should enter into science according to advocates of theistic science. The list includes examples of the points being made, which often tend to be more debatable than the points they illustrate. Thus, even if the illustration is rejected, the point illustrated could still be reasonable.

1. Theology can provide propositions "from above" for guiding research and, in keeping with the hypothetico-deductive method, which can generate positive and negative test implications (e.g., that evidence of human origins should be found in the Mideast, that models of the universe entailing an infinite past like certain big bang models will be falsified).

2. Theology can provide and help solve external and internal conceptual problems (e.g., problems of overcoming the improbabilities of life originating by chance without a guiding intelligence).

3. Theology can provide explanations for certain scientific problems and data. Some of these explanations involve the use of a primary causal act of God, and thus the use of personal agency (e.g., in solving the problem of gaps in the fossil record by noting that they are to be expected due to God's primary causal activity in creating discrete "kinds" of organisms). Other explanations involve theological propositions that do not directly include personal agency (e.g., the notion of original sin to help explain different types of psychological defense mechanisms).

4. Theology can shed light on various issues in the confirmation of scientific hypotheses in at least four ways: (a) by providing rationally justified background beliefs against which rational assessment of a specific scientific theory can be made (e.g., given the belief that man was created by a primary causal act of God, then various evidences for prehuman ancestral forms will carry less weight than they would without this background belief); (b) by yielding positive and negative results that can be tested (see [1] above); (c) by recommending certain methodological rules over others (e.g., prefer explanations of living organisms on a substance model over those that treat them as machines and property-things when the two come into conflict—see chap. 10); (d) by specifying a certain ranking of epistemic virtues in certain cases (e.g., in origin of life research, prefer theories that solve external and internal conceptual problems theologically to theories that claim to offer avenues fruitful in guiding research for naturalistic mechanisms as to how life arose).

5. Theology can provide extrinsic goals for science (e.g., to glorify God, to show that our Scriptures are not in conflict with what it is reasonable to believe from sources outside them) and can help justify certain intrinsic goals for science (e.g., as we saw in chap. 16 with those Christian theists who use their theism to justify scientific realism and thus the goal of truth for scientific theories).

These are some of the ways theology can and should enter into the practice of science according to advocates of theistic science. The specific details of each aspect listed above will not be shared by all, and a choice of specific commitments will depend, in part, on one's understanding of just exactly what theology teaches in a certain area (e.g., whether first life arose by primary or by secondary causal action by God).

In recent years, a new movement has arisen called the **intelligent design (ID) movement**. Major participants in the ID movement are Phillip E. Johnson, Michael Behe, William Dembski, Jonathan Wells, Paul Nelson and Stephen Meyer. The ID movement rejects methodological naturalism and is committed to the in-principle legitimacy of theistic science. The ID movement is an entire approach to science, and as such it goes far beyond the topic of evolution. However, when applied to the issue of evolution, with a certain qualification to be mentioned shortly, the ID movement does not map neatly onto the three views mentioned above (young earth creationism, progressive creationism and theistic evolution). In principle, advocates of young earth and progressive creationism are participants of the ID movement, though there are intramural differences among those participants. But the converse is not true. Not all participants of the ID movement are young earth or progressive creationists. There is room for a qualified version of theistic evolution within the ID movement. To understand these issues more fully, we must probe more deeply the central intellectual commitments of the ID movement.

According to ID proponents, the central debate about evolution is not the age of the universe, it is not whether the history of the cosmos and life contains gaps due to the primary causal activity of God in creating various kinds of life, and it is not primarily a debate about science and theology. Regarding evolution, ID proponents are committed to two central claims: (1) The central issue is between an intelligent design hypothesis and the blind watchmaker thesis. According to the blind watchmaker thesis, there is no scientific evidence or intellectual justification for appealing to an intelligent designer in order to explain the history of life and the existence and nature of living things and their parts. Rather, nonintelligent, purposeless naturalistic processes are fully adequate to explain all the relevant scientific facts. Advocates of ID demur and believe an intelligent design model is superior to the blind watchmaker thesis. (2) The facts that justify an inference to an intelligent designer and the inference itself are properly construed as being within the domain of science. ID proponents reject methodological naturalism and accept theistic science.

In light of these two commitments, it becomes possible to clarify in what sense theistic evolution is and is not consistent with the ID movement. If theistic evolution is construed such that it includes a commitment to (1) the thesis of common descent (all life is related by a common ancestry), (2) the functional integrity of creation (subsequent to the initial creation of the universe, there are not gaps and God does not act in natural history by way of primary causal miracle) and (3) methodological naturalism, then theistic evolution is not compatible with ID theory. However, if theistic evolution is taken to include the first two commitments and not the third, then theistic evolution and ID theory are compatible.

The central aspect of ID theory is the idea that the designedness of some things that are designed can be identified as such in scientifically acceptable ways. ID theorist William Dembski has been the main figure in developing this aspect of ID theory.[3] We will revisit Dembski's analysis of design inferences in chapter twenty-four, but we close this section with a brief sketch of his theory. Dembski analyzes cases in which insurance employees, police and forensic scientists must determine whether a death was an accident (no intelligent cause) or brought about intentionally (done on purpose by an intelligent agent). According to Dembski, whenever three factors are present, scientific investigators are rationally obligated to draw the conclusion that the event was brought about intentionally: (1) The event was contingent, that is, even though it took place, it did not have to happen. (2) The event had a small probability of happening. (3) The event is capable of independent specifiability.

To illustrate, consider a game of bridge in which two people receive a hand of cards. Let one hand be a random set of cards—call it hand A—and the other be a perfect bridge hand dealt to the dealer himself. Now suppose that the dealer had announced he felt lucky that evening and wouldn't be surprised to get a perfect hand or that he received such a hand more than once that evening while dealing, we would immediately infer that while A was not dealt intentionally, the perfect bridge hand was, and it, in fact, represents a case of cheating on the part of the dealer. What justifies our suspicion?

First, neither hand had to happen. There are no laws of nature, logic or mathematics that necessitate that either hand had to come about in the history of the cosmos. In this sense, each hand—and, indeed, the very card game itself—is a contingent event that did not have to take place. Second, since hand A and the perfect bridge hand have the same number of cards, each is equally improbable. So while necessary, the small probability of an event is not sufficient to raise suspicions that the event came about by the intentional action of an agent.

The third criterion makes this clear. The perfect bridge hand can be specified as special independent of the fact that it happened to be the hand that came about, but this is not so for hand A. Hand A can be specified as "some random hand or other that someone happens to get." Now that specification applies to all hands whatever and does not mark out as special any particular hand that comes about. So understood, A is no more special than any other random deal. But this is not so for the perfect bridge hand, especially one preannounced or occurring more than once. This hand can be characterized as a special sort of combination of cards by the rules of bridge quite independent of the fact that it is the hand that the dealer received. It is the combination of contingency (this hand did not have to be dealt), small probability (this particular arrangement of cards was quite unlikely to have occurred) and independent specifiability (this is a pretty special hand for the dealer to receive , and he has announced that he expected to receive such a hand, or he has received such a hand more than once) that justifies us in accusing the dealer of cheating.

Similarly, if a spouse happens to die at a young age in an unlikely manner even though that spouse is healthy, and if this happens just after the other spouse took out a large insurance policy on him or her a week after agreeing to marry someone else, or if the remaining spouse repeatedly "lost" a spouse in a premature death, then the three factors that justify an intelligent design are present.

---

[3]William Dembski, *Intelligent Design* (Downers Grove, Ill.: InterVarsity Press, 1999).

Dembski and other ID theorists argue that the fine-tuning of the universe, the biological information in living organisms, and other phenomena justify the scientific inference of an intelligent designer. Thus ID theorists accept theistic science and reject methodological naturalism. But should theology directly interact with and enter into the very fabric of science or should science adopt methodological naturalism? Some thinkers have claimed the latter, and we turn to an investigation of their claims.

**4.3
NATURAL
SCIENCE AND
METHODO-
LOGICAL
NATURALISM**

Many Christian theists believe that in the **natural sciences** (defined ostensibly as the sciences of chemistry, physics, biology, geology and other branches of science usually taken to be the "hard" or "natural" sciences) one ought to adopt methodological naturalism. In one form or another, this position has been advanced by Howard J. Van Till, Charles Hummel, and Paul de Vries.[4] There are four main features of this view:

1. The goal of natural science: The goal of natural science is to explain contingent natural phenomena strictly in terms of other contingent natural phenomena. Explanations should refer only to natural objects and events and not to the personal choices and actions of human and divine agents. Natural science seeks knowledge of the physical properties, behavior and formative history of the physical world.

2. Methodological versus philosophical naturalism. Within science, we should adopt **methodological naturalism**, according to which answers to questions are sought within nature, within the contingent created order. For example, in describing how two charged electrodes separate hydrogen and oxygen gas when placed in water, the "God hypothesis" is both unnecessary and out of place. The physical universe—the world of atoms, subatomic particles and things made of atoms—is the proper object of scientific study, and methodological naturalism is the proper method for pursuing that study. **Philosophical naturalism**, on the other hand, is the philosophical doctrine that the natural world is all there is and that God, angels and the like do not exist. Science presupposes methodological naturalism but not philosophical naturalism, and the two should not be confused.

3. Natural scientific explanation: Natural science seeks to answer "what" questions and establish just what the facts are in some domain of study. But more importantly, science tries to explain by answering "how" questions. An answer to a "how" question will describe regular, empirically observable patterns in the natural world and explain them by describing a natural mechanism, understood in a scientific realist way, that accounts for those patterns.

4. A complementarian view of integration and agency. Advocates of methodological naturalism strongly promote the complementarian view of inte-

---

[4]See Howard J. Van Till, Robert E. Snow, John H. Stek and Davis A. Young, *Portraits of Creation* (Grand Rapids, Mich.: Eerdmans, 1990); Charles E. Hummel, *The Galileo Connection* (Downers Grove, Ill.: InterVarsity Press, 1986); Paul de Vries, "Naturalism in the Natural Sciences: A Christian Perspective," *Christian Scholar's Review* 15 (1986): 388-96.

gration mentioned above (position B). Moreover, they apply this model to divine and human actions. For example, an activity of raising one's hand to vote at a meeting can be given a complete description and explanation without any gaps at a physical level. Such an account will be formulated in terms of brain states, neurons and so on, and would be complete and true at its own level of approach. However, a complete noninteracting description of that event could be given at another level by appealing to the person's purposes and reasons for voting the way he or she did. These two levels of description of a human action (and of a divine one as well) will be complete at their own levels and complementary to one another.

What should we make of methodological naturalism as a philosophy of science? The view has certain strengths and weaknesses. Let us start with the latter. The first problem with methodological naturalism is this: It relies on a **line of demarcation** between science and nonscience or pseudo-science that consists in stating a set of necessary and/or sufficient conditions for something to count as science. No one has ever been able to draw such a line of demarcation and such a thing does not exist. Since theistic science was regarded as science by scientists and philosophers of science throughout most of the history of science, and since theistic science can be clearly illustrated in various ways (see above), then the burden of proof is on the one who would deny that theistic science is a science (a second-order philosophical claim). This burden of proof has not been met.

Various criteria have been offered as a line of demarcation, a set of necessary and sufficient conditions for something to count as science: It must focus on the natural or physical world, be guided by natural law, explain by reference to natural law, be empirically testable, be held tentatively and not as the last word, be falsifiable, be measurable or quantifiable, involve predictions and be repeatable. The problem is that no one or no set of these is necessary or sufficient for counting as science. There are examples of science that do not have the criterion in question (thus it is not necessary) and there are examples of nonscience that do have the criterion (thus it is not sufficient). For example, there are scientists that hold their views dogmatically and theologians that hold their views tentatively. Again, there are aspects of science that are not quantifiable (e.g., certain theories about viruses and how they work) and aspects of literary studies that are quantifiable (e.g., quantitative treatments of word frequency in determining how an author uses a word). And on it goes.

Focusing on methodological naturalism, advocates of this view need the four features of their theory to count as necessary conditions for science because that will allow them to conclude that theological concepts should not be part of science. For example, if it is a necessary condition for natural science that it explain things only in terms of natural objects, then explanations that use the notion of a primary causal act of God cannot be science. Let us look at the first two features of methodological naturalism—the goal of natural science and the description of methodological naturalism itself. Are these necessary features of science? To show they are not, we must simply give cases of natural science that do not exemplify the features deemed necessary in the descriptions listed above.

Consider first the goal of natural science. Advocates of methodological naturalism assume scientific realism in characterizing the goal of science. Now scientific realism may, in fact, be true. But if the goal of natural science is stated in realist terms, and if this goal is presented as a necessary condition for natural science, then antirealist statements of the goal of natural science (e.g., merely to save the phenomena) become impossible relative to this necessary condition. But this is a very strong claim and incorrect. Antirealist treatments of the goals of natural science are philosophies of *science* and they may be true. By employing realist notions in stating the necessary conditions for science, advocates of methodological naturalism do not allow for this possibility. Moreover, it is implausible to claim that there is only one goal or even a most important goal for science. In chapter sixteen we saw that several goals are consistent with the practice of science (e.g., gain simple theories, obtain empirically accurate theories, etc.) and these goals of science are capable of realist or antirealist interpretations.

Second, consider the characterization of methodological naturalism itself in contrast to philosophical naturalism. It is at least possible, and surely consistent with science, that a phenomenalistic understanding of science, in the spirit of Berkeley, Mach and certain logical positivists, is true (see chap. 16). But some of these approaches to science deny the existence of a material universe and reduce physical object statements (e.g., "There is an electron moving through the wire") to statements about actual or possible sense data which turn out to be private mental entities. If such views are even possible philosophies of science, then one cannot make the existence or study of matter a necessary condition for natural science. Furthermore, if certain antirealist views are true (e.g., those of Larry Laudan or Bas van Fraassen), then there most likely *is* no world of atoms; they are useful fictions. And even if we grant the existence of atoms, surely metaphysical views that take events or fieldlike entities to be real and atoms or other thinglike entities to be fictions are consistent with natural science. Thus we cannot make the existence of matter or atoms to be a necessary condition for the practice of science.

These difficulties with methodological naturalism illustrate the problem of drawing a line of demarcation between science and nonscience or pseudoscience in order to rule out something that is on the wrong side of the divide. As mentioned earlier, theistic science (also called **creationism** when applied to the theory of evolution, though this term is also frequently reserved for young earth creationism), which makes use of theological propositions in various ways, has been regarded as science for most of the history of science. Philip Kitcher, no friend of creationism, admits this:

> Moreover, *variants* of Creationism were supported by a number of eminent nineteenth-century scientists. . . . These Creationists trusted that their theories would accord with the Bible, interpreted in what they saw as a correct way. However, that fact does not affect the scientific status of those theories. Even postulating an unobserved Creator need be no more unscientific than postulating unobservable particles. What matters is the character of the proposals and the ways in which they are articulated and defended. The great scientific Creationists of the eighteenth and nineteenth centuries offered problem-solving strategies for many of the questions addressed by evolutionary theory.[5]

---

[5]Philip Kitcher, *Abusing Science: The Case Against Creationism* (Cambridge, Mass.: MIT Press, 1982), p. 125.

Even if creationist theories are false, that does not mean that they are not scientific; there is a difference between being a true or false scientific theory on the one hand and not being a scientific theory at all. Advocates of methodological naturalism make the latter claim, but they have not met the burden of proof necessary to sustain this charge.

What about the other two aspects of methodological naturalism: the picture of scientific explanation and the complementary view of divine and human agency? Regarding scientific explanation, advocates of methodological naturalism seem to rely too heavily on a covering-law model of scientific explanation and to focus too much attention on empirical as opposed to historical science. However, we have already seen that scientists do not simply answer "how" questions by subsuming things under natural laws. Scientists also explain by citing causal entities, processes, events and actions. For example, cosmologists explain certain aspects of the universe (the present location and motion of the stars) not only by citing natural laws (e.g., laws of motion), but also by citing the big bang as a single causal event.

Now some branches of science—for example, SETI (the search for extraterrestrial intelligence), archeology, forensic science, psychology and sociology—use personal agency and various internal states of agents (desires, willings, intentions, beliefs) as part of their description of the causal entities cited in their explanations of the things they try to explain. This is especially true in the historical sciences as opposed to the empirical sciences. Thus there is nothing nonscientific about appealing to divine agency in creationist explanations of certain phenomena such as the origin of the universe, first life and human beings. At the very least, such an appeal cannot be faulted as nonscientific on the grounds that it involves an agent causal explanation and not an explanation in terms of subsumption under natural law. Moreover, such an appeal to divine agency may be especially (but not solely) appropriate where there are theological reasons to believe God acted through primary and not secondary causes.

It may be objected that such appeals are permissible in the human sciences but not in the so-called natural sciences like biology or paleontology. But this response is clearly question begging in that it is an attempt to define and classify examples of "natural science" by smuggling methodological naturalism into the definition, rather than by using neutral ostensive definitions of natural science. It also distorts the history of at least some of the natural sciences. Scientists from Charles Darwin to Stephen Jay Gould have clearly seen that theological ideas can have scientifically testable implications, a fact that is not accounted for on the methodological naturalist view of scientific explanation.

For example, one often finds Darwin and other evolutionists making claims to the effect that if God were an optimal, efficient designer who was also free to use variety in his designing activities, then certain biological structures (e.g., homologous structures like the forelimbs of birds, porpoises and humans that have a similar structure but serve different purposes) would not be present because they are not very efficient nor do they show much creativity. The point here is not to evaluate the strength of such arguments or to examine the appropriateness of the model of God as designer they utilize. Rather, the point is to show that the history of biology and paleontology illustrate arguments of this sort time and again. And such arguments are not merely rhetorical devices but substantive claims that show how theological ideas, adequate or inadequate, can have implications for scientific explanation, evaluation, and testing.

What about the complementarity view of human and divine agency? We have already examined this view in previous chapters, so we will offer only a brief critique here. When God acts via secondary causes, when regularly recurring phenomena generated in part by natural mechanisms are in view (such as the production of water from hydrogen or oxygen), then theology may legitimately be seen as complementary to science. But such a picture of integration only allows for **event-event (or state-state) causation** where one state of affairs serves as a cause for another state of affairs (the moving of one ball causes the moving of a second ball). However, when God acts as a primary cause, God acts as an agent (and even when God acts through secondary causes, he somewhere or another must act in a primary causal way or else a vicious infinite regress of secondary causes will be required). You will recall that the important thing about **agent causation** is this. The cause of an action (e.g., raising my arm, voting for an election, directly creating first life) is a substance—the agent himself—and not a state of affairs in the agent. There is no sufficient set of prior conditions inside or outside the agent that guarantee the effect. The agent must exercise his or her causal powers as a substance and simply act.

This means that when it comes to states of affairs directly produced by agent causes (the hand being raised, life being created), there will be a gap between the state of affairs that existed prior to the effect and the state of affairs that is (or is correlated with) that effect. When a woman raises her arm, the state of affairs in her at the physical level just prior to her raising her arm, say, in her brain or central nervous system, and the physical state of affairs correlated with her arm being raised will not be smoothly continuous with that prior state of affairs. The former is not sufficient to account for the latter, and there is a causal gap in the production of the effect filled by the agent herself. A similar observation could be made for cases of God's primary causal agency and the resulting gaps (e.g., between inorganic materials and first life) could, at least in principle, be scientifically detectable, contrary to what advocates of the complementarity view claim.

In spite of these weaknesses, advocates of methodological naturalism have been correct to remind us of two things. First, God is constantly active in sustaining and directing the world, and it is theologically inappropriate to limit God's activity to primary causation. Second, we should be cautious in making appeals to God's primary causal activity, and such invocations should be done only where there are good theological, philosophical and scientific reasons for doing so. In general, methodological naturalism is most helpful in describing empirical or operational science where God acts through secondary causes and where our main purpose is to describe the natural mechanisms God uses to accomplish his activities.

Finally, we should consider two further objections that are often raised against theistic science.

Objection 1: The theistic science model utilizes an epistemically inappropriate "god-of-the-gaps" strategy in which God only acts when there are gaps in nature, one appeals to God merely to fill up gaps in our scientific knowledge of naturalistic mechanisms, these gaps are used in apologetic, natural theology arguments to support Christian theism, scientific progress is making these gaps increasingly rare, and thus this strategy is not a good one.

Reply: First, the model does not limit God's causal activity to gaps. God is constantly active in sustaining and governing the universe. Nature is not autonomous. Moreover, theistic science need not have *any* apologetical aim at all. A Christian theist may simply believe that he or she should consult all we know or have reason to believe is true—including theological beliefs—in forming, evaluating and testing scientific theories and in explaining scientific phenomena. And even if someone uses theistic science with apologetical intentions, creationists need not limit their apologetical case to gaps. The model merely recognizes a distinction between primary and secondary causes and goes on to assert that at least the former could have scientifically testable implications irrespective of the apologetic intentions of such a recognition.

Second, the model does not attempt to explain in light of God and his activities to cover our ignorance, but only when good theological or philosophical reasons are present, for instance, when certain theological or philosophical reasons cause us to expect a discontinuity in nature where God acted via primary causation or in cases where some doctrine like original sin sheds light on some psychological theory regarding human behavior.

Third, even if the gaps in naturalistic scientific explanations are getting smaller, this does not prove that there are no gaps at all. It begs the question to argue that just because most alleged gaps turn out to be explainable in naturalistic terms without gaps at that level of explanation, then all alleged gaps will turn out this way. After all, what else would one expect of gaps but that there would be few of them? Gaps due to primary divine agency are miracles, which are in the minority for two reasons. First, we have already seen that God's usual way of operating is through secondary causes, and primary causal gaps are God's extraordinary, unusual way of operating; by definition, these will be few and far between. Second, the evidential or sign value of a miraculous gap arises most naturally against a backdrop where the gaps are rare, unexpected and have a religious context (e.g., there are positive theological reasons to expect their presence).

Fourth, the distinction between empirical and historical science is helpful for answering the god-of-the-gaps problem. Recall that empirical science is a nonhistorical, empirical approach to the world that focuses on repeatable, regularly recurring events or patterns in nature (e.g., the relationship between pressure, temperature, volume in a gas). By contrast, historical science is historical in nature and focuses on past singularities that are not repeatable (e.g., the origin of the universe, first life, various kinds of life). Advocates of this distinction claim that appealing to God's primary causal activity is legitimate in historical science even if not in empirical science because the former deals with cases where,

4.4
TWO FINAL
OBJECTIONS TO
THEISTIC
SCIENCE

theologically speaking, God's primary causal activity is to be found, while the latter deals with God's secondary causal activity. Now, it could be argued that most cases in which God is appealed to as a cover for our ignorance about a gap are cases of issues involved in empirical science, not historical science. Thus, when those gaps are filled by naturalistic mechanisms, the conclusion to draw is not that God should never be appealed to as an explanatory notion of some scientifically discoverable phenomenon, but rather the notion of a primary causal act of God should be limited to cases in historical science precisely because of the differences between primary and secondary causation that is captured in the distinction between historical and empirical science.

Finally, as we noted above, advocates of ID theory practice theistic science without being committed one way or another to gaps in the history of the cosmos. According to ID advocates, one can use science to discover the products of intelligent design without having any idea how those products came about. Critics who raise a "god-of-the-gaps" objection against theistic science fail take into account ID theory.

Objection 2: The idea that some phenomenon is to be explained by a direct, primary causal activity of God is not a fruitful notion in guiding new research and yielding new empirically testable constructs in other areas of investigation. Thus the idea violates the epistemic virtue, "a scientific theory ought to be fruitful in guiding new research." Because of this, the practice of explaining something by an appeal to God's direct causation is not a scientific practice and should be excluded from natural science. As Richard Dickerson put it, "The most insidious evil of supernatural creationism is that it stifles curiosity and therefore blunts the intellect."[6]

Reply: First, something can be true without being fruitful. An appeal to God's primary causal activity could explain some scientific phenomenon (the origin of the universe) truly without suggesting new lines of research. It is true that such an appeal will stop investigation for further, more basic natural mechanisms used by God as secondary causes to perform such actions since appeals of this sort are made precisely because no such secondary causes are believed to exist. But the conclusion to draw from this is not that such appeals ought never to be made, but only that we should have good theological, philosophical and/or scientific reasons for making them.

Second, even if we grant that, say, theistic scientists' utilizations of theological concepts have not fruitfully suggested new lines of research (and this need not be granted), all that follows from this is that theistic scientists, where appropriate, need to do more work developing the infrastructure of their models, not that their models are not part of natural science. For example, in cases where a creationist wishes to explain geological phenomena by an appeal to the flood of Noah, it is important to develop detailed models of just how such a flood will do the job.

Third, an appeal to fruitfulness in cases of God's primary causal activity can be question-begging and may represent a naive understanding of the intricacies

[6]Richard E. Dickerson, "The Game of Science: Reflections After Arguing with Some Rather Overwrought People," *Perspectives on Science and Christian Faith* 44 (June 1992): 137.

of fruitfulness as a criterion for assessing the relative merits of rival hypotheses.

Two rivals may solve a problem differently depending on the way each theory depicts the phenomenon to be solved. Ptolemy solved the problem of planetary motion by a complicated set of orbitals with smaller orbitals (epicycles) contained within larger ones and by placing the earth in the center of the solar system. Copernicus solved the motion of the planets by removing the earth from the center of the universe and by employing epicycles as well. Though they shared certain features in common, each solution was different in important ways (and not necessarily of equal effectiveness).

Furthermore, the standards for what counts as a "good" solution, as well as the ranking of the relative merits of various epistemic virtues (e.g., prefer simplicity to empirical accuracy) may largely be determined differently by the competing paradigms. Thus often (though not always) the standards for adequacy in problem solving are set by the paradigm itself, and not by its rival.

Creationists and evolutionists do not need to attempt to solve a problem, say a gap in the fossil record, in precisely the same way, nor do they need to employ the same types of solutions or the same ranking of epistemic virtues in their solutions. Creationists may elevate the virtue "Solve theological or philosophical internal and external conceptual problems" above the virtue "Offer solutions yielding fruitful lines of new research." There is nothing unscientific about such a prioritization at all, and it is question-begging to claim that a criterion like "fruitfulness" set by one theory (say, the search for evolutionary mechanisms and transition forms to fill fossil gaps) should be most important for a rival theory and, if not, the rival is not even science.

Furthermore, sometimes one rival will consider a phenomenon basic and not in need of a solution. It may, therefore, disallow questions about how or why that phenomenon occurs and thus can hardly be faulted for not being fruitful in suggesting lines of research for mechanisms whose existence is not postulated by the theory, as Nicholas Rescher has pointed out:

> One way in which a body of knowledge S can deal with a question is, of course, by *answering* it. Yet another, importantly different, way in which S can deal with a question is by disallowing it. S *disallows* [Q] when there is some presupposition of Q that S does not countenance: given S, we are simply not in a position to raise Q.[7]

For example, motion was not natural in Aristotle's picture of the universe, and thus examples of motion posed problems in need of explanation. But on Newton's picture of the universe, uniform, linear motion is natural and only changes in motion pose problems in need of solution. Thus, suppose a Newtonian and an Aristotelian are trying to solve the observational problem of how and why a particular body is moving in uniform linear motion. The Aristotelian must tell how or why the body is moving to solve the problem. But the Newtonian can disallow the need for a solution by labeling the phenomenon as a basic given for which no solution in terms of a "how" question utilizing a more basic mechanism is possible.

Similarly, certain phenomena, like the origin of life or gaps in the fossil record,

---

[7]Nicholas Rescher, *The Limits of Science* (Berkeley: University of California Press, 1984), p. 22.

are not problems in need of solution for creationism beyond an appeal to the primary causal agency of God. But they are problems for evolutionary theory, so fruitful lines of research for new mechanisms must be sought. However, it is naive and question-begging to fault creationists for not developing fruitful problem-solving strategies for such gaps compared to their evolutionary rivals because such strategies are simply disallowed given that these phenomena are basic for creationists. In this case, it is enough for creationists to use theological notions to guide them in the research for scientific tests to establish the phenomena predicted by the theological constructs. Once the "what" question is answered, there is no further material or mechanistic "how" question that arises.

Finally, when they deem it appropriate in light of their models, advocates of theistic science do, in fact, develop conditions for the falsification of their theories. While more work needs to be done in this area, currently, proponents of theistic science are suggesting experiments that would falsify their models and which would corroborate those models in light of positive experimental evidence.

CHAPTER SUMMARY

The chapter began its study of the integration of science and theology by examining and rejecting strong and weak versions of scientism. The former claims that scientific knowledge is the only knowledge there is, the latter that it is the best, ideal form of knowledge. However, strong scientism is self-refuting, and both forms do not adequately allow for the task of stating and criticizing the presuppositions of science nor do they account for the existence and strength of rationally justified beliefs outside science.

Next, six models of science-theology integration were offered; the last of which allows for direct interaction between science and theology in epistemologically positive and negative ways. This position was given the name theistic science. Five different aspects of theistic science were offered, and the creation-evolution controversy was used to discuss and illustrate this model of integration. Many Christians reject theistic science in favor of a view called methodological naturalism. Four features of this position were stated and criticized and two positive aspects were mentioned. The chapter concluded with an examination of two final charges often leveled against theistic science: it represents an inappropriate "god-of-the-gaps" strategy, and theistic science is not a fruitful research tradition for guiding new research and yielding new empirically testable constructs in other areas of investigation.

CHECKLIST OF BASIC TERMS AND CONCEPTS

agent causation
complementarity view
creationism
event-event (or state-state) causation
evolution (three senses)
intelligent design (ID) movement
line of demarcation

methodological naturalism
natural science
philosophical naturalism
primary cause
problem of induction
progressive creationism
scientism
secondary cause
strong scientism
theistic evolution
theistic science
uniformity of nature
young earth creationism
weak scientism

18

PHILOSOPHY OF
TIME AND SPACE

And thus much concerning God,
to discourse of whom from the appearances of things
does certainly belong to Natural Philosophy.

ISAAC NEWTON,
MATHEMATICAL PRINCIPLES OF NATURAL PHILOSOPHY

1 INTRODUCTION

The philosophy of time and space has traditionally been a branch of metaphysics, but since the early twentieth century it has been subsumed as one of the subdisciplines of philosophy of science. Today mainstream philosophy of time and space is predominantly reflection on time and space as they are described in physics, particularly relativity theory (both special and general) and quantum theory.

Why this dramatic change occurred is itself a matter of considerable philosophical interest. Albert Einstein, in explaining the importance of Ernst Mach's radical empiricism for the development of the **special theory of relativity** (STR), once remarked that not even Mach's opponents realized how much of his philosophy they had imbibed, as it were, with their mother's milk.[1] Much the same could be said of contemporary philosophers of time and space with respect to the philosophy of **positivism**—a school of thought which was scientistic and deeply antimetaphysical—and its partner, **verificationism**, according to which an informative sentence, in order to be meaningful, must be capable in principle of being empirically verified. Though these radically empirical perspectives are today almost universally rejected, their legacy lives on in the physical theories predicated on them.

The edifice of twentieth-century physics rests on the twin pillars of relativity theory and quantum theory, and both of these mighty pillars stand on the decayed bases of a verificationist epistemology. Not that the mathematical cores of these theories are incorrect (though they are inconsistent with one another and will require some higher level theory to reconcile them); rather, it is the received physical interpretations of the mathematical equations which are verificationist in essence. This fact ought to arouse a good deal of sympathy for antirealist or instrumentalist construals of these theories. But neither philosophers nor physicists have by and large given up realist construals of these theories for that reason (though realist claims with respect to quantum theory do elicit a good deal of skepticism).

---

[1]Albert Einstein, "Ernst Mach," *Physikalische Zeitschrift* 17 (1916): 101; reprinted in Ernst Mach, *Die Mechanik in ihrer Entwicklung*, ed. Renate Wahsner and Horst-Heino Borzeszkowski (Berlin: Akademie-Verlag, 1988), pp. 683-89.

Moreover, philosophical discussion of time and space proceeds almost as if the epistemological revolution that brought about positivism's demise in the second half of the twentieth century had not occurred. In a survey article on "Philosophy of Space and Time" in an *Introduction to Philosophy of Science*, John Norton observes that this discipline exhibits some of the "clearest applications" of the ideas of logical positivism, such as (1) an application of the verification principle of meaning in Einstein's special theory of relativity in order to eliminate the state of absolute rest posited in Newton's classical theory of time and space, (2) conventionality claims concerning the metric of space and of time, as well as relations of simultaneity within a single reference frame and (3) reductionistic analyses of spatiotemporal relations to causal relations in the causal theory of time.[2] It is remarkable that while (2) and (3) have largely succumbed to criticism, (1) remains an almost unchallenged dogma. It is frequently said that the advent of relativity theory destroyed the classical conceptions of time and space, forcing us to abandon absolute rest, absolute simultaneity and even the separability of time and space.

2 RELATIVITY AND THE CLASSICAL CONCEPT OF TIME

In order to assess these claims, we must recur to the fount of the classical concept of time, Isaac Newton's epochal *Mathematical Principles of Natural Philosophy* (*Philosophiae naturalis principia mathematica*, 1687). In the scholium (annotation) to his set of definitions leading off the *Principia*, Newton explains his concepts of time and space. In order to clarify these concepts, Newton draws a distinction between **absolute time and space** and **relative time and space**:

I. Absolute . . . time, of itself, and from its own nature, flows equably without relation to anything external, and by another name is called duration: relative . . . time, is some sensible and external (whether accurate or unequable) measure of duration by the means of motion, which is commonly used instead of true time; such as an hour, a day, a month, a year.

II. Absolute space, in its own nature, without relation to anything external, remains always similar and immovable. Relative space is some movable dimension or measure of the absolute spaces; which our senses determine by its position to bodies; and which is commonly taken for immovable space; such is the dimension of a subterraneous, an aerial, or celestial space, determined by its position in respect of the earth.[3]

First and foremost, Newton is here distinguishing between time and space themselves and our *measures* of time and space. Relative time is the time determined or recorded by clocks and calendars of various sorts; relative space is the length or area or volume determined by instruments like rulers or measuring

---

[2]John D. Norton, "Philosophy of Space and Time," in *Introduction to the Philosophy of Science*, ed. Merrilee Salmon (Englewood Cliffs, N.J.: Prentice-Hall, 1992), p. 179.

[3]Isaac Newton, *Sir Isaac Newton's "Mathematical Principles of Natural Philosophy" and His "System of the World,"* trans. Andrew Motte, rev. with an appendix by Florian Cajori (Los Angeles: University of California Press, 1966), 1:6.

cups. As Newton says, these relative quantities may be more or less accurate measures of time and space themselves. Time and space themselves are absolute in the sense that they just are the quantities themselves, which we are trying to measure with our physical instruments.

There is a second sense in which Newton held time and space to be absolute, however. They are absolute in the sense that they are unique. There is one, universal time in which all events come to pass with determinate duration and in a determinate sequence and one, universal space in which all physical objects exist with determinate shapes and in a determinate arrangement. Thus Newton says that absolute time "of itself, and from its own nature, flows equably without relation to anything external," and absolute space "in its own nature, without relation to anything external, remains always similar and immovable." Relative times and spaces are many and variable, but not time and space themselves.

On the basis of his definitions of time and space, Newton went on to define absolute versus relative place and motion:

III. Place is a part of space which a body takes up, and is according to the space, either absolute or relative. . . .

IV. Absolute motion is the translation of a body from one absolute place into another; and relative motion, the translation from one relative place into another.[4]

By "translation" Newton means transporting or displacement. **Absolute place** is the volume of absolute space occupied by an object, and **absolute motion** is the displacement of a body from one absolute place to another. An object can be at relative rest and yet in absolute motion. Newton gives the example of a piece of a ship, say, the mast. If the mast is firmly fixed, then it is at rest relative to the ship; but the mast is in absolute motion if the ship is moving in absolute space as it sails along. Thus two objects can be at rest relative to each other, but both moving in tandem through absolute space (and thus moving absolutely).

In Newtonian physics there is already a sort of relativity. A body that is in **uniform motion** (that is, no accelerations or decelerations occur) serves to define an **inertial frame**, which is just a relative space in which a body at rest remains at rest and a body in motion remains in motion with the same speed and direction. Newton's ideal ship sailing uniformly along would thus define an inertial frame. Although Newton postulated the existence of an absolute inertial frame, namely, the reference frame of absolute space, nevertheless it is impossible for observers in inertial frames that are moving in absolute space to determine experimentally that they are in fact moving. If someone's relative space were moving uniformly through absolute space, that person could not tell whether he was at absolute rest or in absolute motion. By the same token, if his relative space were at rest in absolute space, he could not know that he was at absolute rest rather than in absolute motion. He could know that his inertial frame was in motion relative to some other observer's inertial frame (say, another passing ship), but he could not know if either of them were at absolute

---

[4]Ibid., 1:6-7.

rest or in absolute motion. Thus within Newtonian physics an observer could measure only the relative uniform motion of his inertial system, not its absolute uniform motion.

Newtonian physics prevailed all the way up through the end of the nineteenth century. The two great domains of nineteenth-century classical physics were **Newton's mechanics** (the study of the motion of bodies) and **Maxwell's electrodynamics** (the study of electromagnetic radiation, including light). The quest of physics at the end of the nineteenth century was to formulate mutually consistent theories of these two domains. The problem was that although Newton's mechanics was characterized, as we have mentioned, by relativity, Maxwell's electrodynamics was not. It was widely held that light consisted of waves, and, since waves had to be waves of something (e.g., sound waves are waves of the air, ocean waves are waves of the water), light waves had to be waves of an invisible, all-permeating substance dubbed the **aether**. As the nineteenth century wore on, the aether was divested of more and more of its properties until it became virtually characterless, serving only as the medium for the propagation of light. Since the **speed of light** had been measured and since light consisted of waves in the aether, the speed of light was absolute, that is to say, unlike moving bodies, light's velocity was determinable relative to an absolute frame of reference, the aether frame. To be sure, in the Newtonian scheme of things, moving bodies *possessed* absolute velocities relative to this frame, but within an inertial frame there was no way to *measure* what it was. By contrast, since waves move through their medium at a constant speed regardless of how fast the object that caused them is moving, light had a determinable, fixed velocity. So electrodynamics, unlike mechanics, was not characterized by relativity.

But now it seemed that one could use electrodynamics to eliminate relativity. Since light moved at a fixed rate through the aether, one could, by measuring the speed of light from different directions, figure out one's own velocity relative to the aether. For if one were moving through the aether toward the light source, the speed of light should be measured as being faster than if one were at rest (just as water waves would pass you more rapidly if you were swimming toward the source of the waves than if you were floating motionless in the water); whereas if one were moving through the aether away from the light source, the speed of light would be measured as being slower than if one were at rest (just as the water waves would pass you less rapidly if you were swimming away from the source of the waves than if you were floating). Thus it would be possible to determine experimentally within an inertial frame whether one is at rest in the aether or how fast one is moving through it.

Imagine, then, the consternation when experiments, such as the **Michelson-Morley experiment** in 1887, failed to detect any motion of the earth through the aether! Despite the fact that the earth is orbiting the sun, the measured speed of light was identical no matter what direction their measuring device was pointed. It needs to be underlined how weird the situation was. Waves travel at a constant speed regardless of the motion of their source and in this sense are unlike projectiles, which travel at a velocity that is a combination of the speed of their source plus their speed relative to the source. For example, a bullet fired ahead from a speeding police car travels at a combined speed of the car's speed plus the bullet's normal speed, in contrast to sound waves emitted from the car's siren, which travel through the air at the same velocity whether the car is stationary or in motion. Consequently, an observer who is moving in the same direction as a sound wave will observe it passing him at a slower speed than if he were at rest. If he goes fast enough, he can catch the wave and break the sound barrier. But light waves are different. Light's measured velocity is the *same* in all inertial frames, for *all* observers. This implies, for example, that if an observer in a rocket going 90% the speed of light sent a light beam ahead of him, both he and the recipient of the beam would measure the speed of the beam to be the same, and this whether the recipient were standing still or himself moving toward or away from the light source at 90% the speed of light.

Desperate for a solution, the Irish physicist FitzGerald and the great Dutch physicist Lorentz proposed the remarkable hypothesis that one's measuring devices shrink or contract in the direction of motion through the aether, so that light *appears* to traverse identical distances in identical times, when in fact the distances vary with one's speed. The faster one moves, the more his devices contract, so that the measured speed of light remains constant. Hence, in all inertial frames the speed of light appears the same. With the help of the British scientist Larmor, Lorentz also came to hypothesize that one's clocks slow down when in motion relative to the aether frame. One thus winds up with **Lorentzian relativity**: there exists absolute motion, absolute length and absolute time, but there is no way to discern these experimentally, since motion through the aether affects one's measuring instruments. Lorentz developed a series of equations called the **Lorentz transformations**, which show how to transform one's own measurements of the spatial and temporal coordinates of an event into the measurements that would be made by someone in another inertial frame. These transformation equations remain today the mathematical core of STR (special theory of relativity), even though Lorentz's physical interpretation of STR was different from Einstein's interpretation.

In 1905 Albert Einstein, then an obscure clerk in a patent office in Bern, Switzerland, published his own version of relativity. At this time in his young career, Einstein was still a disciple of the German physicist Ernst Mach. An ardent empiricist, Mach detested anything that smacked of metaphysics and thus sought to reduce statements about time and space to statements about sense perceptions and the connections between them. The young Einstein took what he called his "epistemological credo" from Mach, holding that knowledge is made up of the totality of sense experiences and the totality of concepts and propositions, which are related in the following way: "The concepts and propositions get 'meaning,' *viz.*, 'content,' only through their connection with sense experience."[5] Any proposition not so connected was literally without content, meaningless. Given such a verificationist criterion of meaning, Lorentz's absolute time, space and motion were "metaphysical" notions and therefore meaningless.

Einstein began his 1905 article by jettisoning the aether as superfluous, since, he says, it will not be necessary for the purposes of his paper. Now in order to

[5]Albert Einstein, "Autobiographical Notes," in *Albert Einstein: Philosopher-Scientist*, Library of Living Philosophers 7 (LaSalle, Ill.: Open Court, 1949), p. 13.

talk about motion in a physically meaningful way, Einstein claims, we must be clear what we mean by *time*. Since all judgments about time concern simultaneous events, what we need is a way to determine empirically the simultaneity of distant events. Einstein then proceeds to offer a method of determining, or rather defining, simultaneity for two spatially separated but relatively stationary clocks, that is, two distant clocks sharing the same inertial frame. This procedure will in turn serve as the basis for a definition of the time of an event. He asks us to assume that the time required for light to travel from point A to point B is the same as the time required for light to travel from B to A. Theoretically, light could travel more slowly from A to B and more quickly from B to A, even though the roundtrip velocity would always be constant. But Einstein says that we must assume that the **one-way velocity of light** is constant. Having made this assumption, he proposes to synchronize clocks at A and B by means of light signals from one to the other. Suppose A sends a signal to B, which is in turn reflected back from B to A. If A knows what time it was when he sent the signal to B and what time it was when he received the signal back from B, then he knows that the reading of B's clock when the signal from A arrived was exactly halfway between the time A sent the signal and the time A got the return signal. In this way A and B can arrange to synchronize their clocks. Events are declared to be simultaneous if they occur at the same clock times on synchronized clocks. Using clocks thus synchronized, Einstein defines the time of an event as "the reading simultaneous with the event of a clock at rest and located at the position of the event, this clock being synchronous . . . with a specified clock at rest."[6]

By means of these definitions Einstein laid the groundwork for a radically new understanding of time and space. For under the euphemism of disregarding the aether as unnecessary, Einstein abandoned not merely the aether, but, more fundamentally, the reference frame of the aether, or absolute space. Without absolute space there can be no absolute motion or absolute rest. Bodies are moving or at rest only relative to each other, and it would be meaningless to ask whether an isolated body was stationary or uniformly moving per se. Given the **constancy of the speed of light** in all inertial frames, bodies in motion will be related to each other electrodynamically in such a way that the use of electromagnetic signals to establish synchrony relations between them will play havoc with what we normally mean by *simultaneity*. What happens is that simultaneity becomes relative. Einstein writes, "Thus we see that we can attribute no *absolute* meaning to the concept of simultaneity, but that two events which, examined from a co-ordinate system, are simultaneous, can no longer be interpreted as simultaneous events when examined from a system which is in motion relatively to that system."[7] What this means is that events that are simultaneous as calculated from one inertial frame will not be simultaneous as calculated from another. An event that lies in A's future may be already present or past for B! In fact, events that are not causally connected can even be mea-

---

[6] Albert Einstein, "On the Electrodynamics of Moving Bodies," trans. Arthur Miller, in Arthur I. Miller, *Albert Einstein's Special Theory of Relativity* (Reading, Mass.: Addison-Wesley, 1981), p. 394.

[7] Ibid., p. 396.

sured to occur in a different temporal order in different inertial frames!

What Einstein did, in effect, was to shave away Newton's absolute time and space, and along with them the aether, thus leaving behind only their empirical measures. Since these are relativized to inertial frames, one ends up with the **relativity of simultaneity** and of **length**. What justification did Einstein have for so radical a move? How did he know that absolute time and space do not exist? The answer, in a word, is verificationism. The introductory sections of the 1905 paper are predicated squarely on verificationist assumptions. These come through most clearly in Einstein's operationalist redefinition of key concepts.[8] The meaning of *time* is made to depend on the meaning of **simultaneity**, which is defined locally in terms of occurrence at the same local clock reading. In order to define a common time for spatially separated clocks, we adopt the convention that the time it takes light to travel from A to B equals the time it takes light to travel from B to A—a definition that *presupposes* that absolute space does not exist. For if A and B are at relative rest but moving in tandem through absolute space, then it is not the case that a light beam will travel from A to B in the same amount of time it takes to travel from B to A, since the distances traversed will not be the same (figure 18.1).

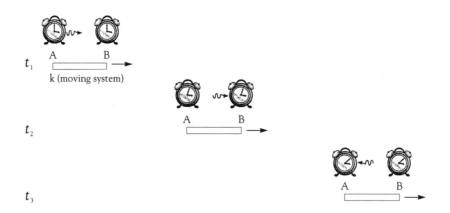

Fig. 18.1 Clock synchronization of relatively stationary clocks in absolute motion. A light signal is first sent A toward B. By the time the signal reaches B, both A and B will have moved together some distance from the point where A first released the signal. Finally, by the time the reflected signal from B reaches A again, both A and B will have moved still farther from the release point. Since the signal traveled farther from A to B than from B back to A, the time it took to travel from A to B is greater than the time it took to travel from B to A.

That is why Einstein's theory, far from disproving the existence of absolute space, actually presupposes its nonexistence. All of this is done by mere stipulation. Reality is reduced to what our measurements read; Newton's metaphysical time and space, which transcend operational definitions, are implied to be mere figments of our imagination.

---

[8]According to an **operationalist definition**, scientific laws and theoretical terms really refer to experimental activities and operations; the phenomenon is viewed as identical to the measurement of that phenomenon.

It was only by virtue of his verificationism that Einstein could ignore the metaphysical foundations of Newton's doctrine of absolute time and space. We have already seen that Newtonian time and space are absolute both in the sense that time and space are distinct from our measures of them and in the sense that there is a unique, all-embracing time and a unique, all-embracing space. But Newton also conceived of time and space as absolute in yet a third, more profound sense, namely, he held that time and space exist independent of any physical objects whatsoever. Usually, this is interpreted to mean that time and space would exist even if nothing else existed, that we can conceive of a logically possible world that is completely empty except for the container of absolute space and the flow of absolute time.

But here we must be very careful. Modern secular scholars tend frequently to forget how ardent a theist Newton was and how central a role this theism played in his metaphysical outlook. In fact, Newton makes quite clear in the General Scholium to the *Principia*, which he added in 1713, that absolute time and space are constituted by the divine attributes of **eternity** and **omnipresence**. He writes,

> He [God] is eternal and infinite; . . . that is, his duration reaches from eternity to eternity; his presence from infinity to infinity. . . . He is not eternity and infinity, but eternal and infinite; he is not duration or space, but he endures and is present. He endures forever, and is everywhere present; and, by existing always and everywhere, he constitutes duration and space. Since every particle of space is *always*, and every indivisible moment of duration is *everywhere*, certainly the Maker and Lord of all things cannot be *never* and *nowhere*.[9]

Because God is eternal, there exists an everlasting duration, and because he is omnipresent, there exists an infinite space. Absolute time and space are therefore relational in that they are contingent on the existence of God.

In his earlier treatise, "On the Gravity and Equilibrium of Fluids," Newton argued that space (and by implication time) is neither a substance, nor a property nor nothing at all. It cannot be nothing because it has properties, such as infinity and uniformity in all directions. It cannot be a property because it can exist without bodies. Neither is it a substance: "It is not substance . . . because it is not absolute in itself, but is as it were an emanent effect of God, or a disposition of all being."[10] Contrary to the conventional understanding, Newton here declares explicitly that space is *not* in itself absolute and therefore not a substance. Rather, it is an emanent—or emanative—effect of God. By this notion Newton meant to say that time and space were the immediate consequence of God's very being. God's infinite being has as its consequence infinite time and space, which represent the quantity of his duration and presence. Newton does not conceive of space or time as in any way attributes of God himself, but rather, as he says, concomitant effects of God.

In Newton's view God's "now" is thus the present moment of absolute time.

---

[9]Newton, *Mathematical Principles*, 2:545.

[10]Isaac Newton, "On the Gravity and Equilibrium of Fluids *[De gravitatione et aequipondio fluidorum]*," in *Unpublished Scientific Papers of Isaac Newton*, ed. A. Rupert Hall and Marie Boas Hall (Cambridge: Cambridge University Press, 1962), p. 132.

Since God is not "a dwarf-god" located at a particular place in space,[11] but is omnipresent, there is a worldwide moment that is absolutely present. Newton's temporal theism thus provides the foundation for absolute simultaneity. The absolute present and absolute simultaneity are features first and foremost of God's time, absolute time, and derivatively of measured or relative time.

Thus the classical Newtonian concept of time is firmly rooted in a theistic worldview. What Newton did not realize, nor could he have suspected, is that physical time is not only *relative*, but also *relativistic*, that the approximation of physical time to absolute time depends not merely on the regularity of one's clock, but also on its motion. Unless a clock were at absolute rest, it would not accurately register the passage of absolute time. Moving clocks run slowly. This truth, unknown to Newton, was finally grasped by scientists only with the advent of relativity theory.

Where Newton fell short, then, was not in his analysis of absolute or metaphysical time—he had theological grounds for positing such a time—but in his incomplete understanding of relative or physical time. He assumed too readily that an ideal clock would give an accurate measure of time independent of its motion. If confronted with relativistic evidence, Newton would no doubt have welcomed this correction and seen therein no threat at all to his doctrine of absolute time. In short, relativity corrects Newton's concept of relative time, not his concept of absolute time.

As a lingering effect of positivism, there is a great deal of antipathy in modern physics and philosophy of science toward such metaphysical realities as Newtonian space and time, primarily because they are not physically detectable. But Newton would have been singularly unimpressed with this verificationist equation between physical undetectability and nonexistence. The grounds for metaphysical space and time were not physical, but philosophical, or more precisely, theological. Epistemological objections fail to worry Newton because, as Oxford philosopher John Lucas nicely puts it, "he is thinking of an omniscient, omnipresent Deity whose characteristic relation with things and with space is expressed in the imperative mood."[12] Modern physical theories say nothing against the existence of such a God or the metaphysical time constituted, in Newton's thinking, by his eternity. What relativity theory did, in effect, was simply to remove God from the picture and to substitute in his place a finite observer. The theory thus represents, in the words of historian of science Gerald Holton, "the final secularization of physics."[13] But to a theist like Newton, such a secular outlook impedes rather than advances our understanding of the nature of reality.

How, then, shall we assess the claim that STR has eliminated absolute time and space? The first thing to be said is that the verificationism that characterized Einstein's original formulation of STR belongs essentially to the philosophical foundations of the theory. The whole theory rests on Einstein's redefinition

[11]Isaac Newton, "Place, Time, and God," in J. E. McGuire, "Newton on Place, Time, and God: An Unpublished Source," *British Journal for the History of Science* 11 (1978): 123.

[12]J. R. Lucas, *A Treatise on Time and Space* (London: Methuen, 1973), p. 143.

[13]Gerald Holton, "On the Origins of the Special Theory of Relativity," in *Thematic Origins of Scientific Thought: Kepler to Einstein* (Cambridge, Mass.: Harvard University Press, 1973), p. 171.

of simultaneity in terms of clock synchronization by light signals. But that redefinition assumes necessarily that the time it takes light to travel between two relatively stationary observers A and B is the same from A to B as from B to A in a roundtrip journey. That assumption presupposes that A and B are not both in absolute motion, or in other words that neither absolute space nor a privileged inertial frame exists. The only justification for that assumption is that it is empirically impossible to distinguish uniform motion from rest relative to such a frame, and if absolute space and absolute motion or rest are undetectable empirically, therefore they do not exist (and may even be said to be meaningless).

But if verificationism belongs essentially to the foundations of STR, the next thing to be said is that verificationism has proved to be completely untenable and is now outmoded. Verificationism provides no justification for thinking that Newton erred, for example, in holding that God exists in a time that exists independent of our physical measures of it and that may or may not be accurately registered by them. It matters not a whit whether we finite creatures know what time it is in God's absolute time; God knows, and that is enough.

We are not here endorsing Newton's views on divine eternity and omnipresence (see chap. 25), but we are contending that such metaphysical considerations as Newton adduced are crucial to a correct understanding of time and space. If we do suppose that God is in time, how then should we understand STR? In a fascinating passage in his essay "The Measure of Time," Henri Poincaré, the great French mathematician and precursor of relativity, briefly entertains the hypothesis of "an infinite intelligence" and considers the implications of such a hypothesis. Poincaré is reflecting on the problem of how we can apply one and the same measure of time to spatially distant events. What does it mean, for example, to say that two thoughts in two people's minds occur simultaneously? Or what does it mean to say that a supernova occurred before Columbus saw the New World? Like a good verificationist, Poincaré says, "All these affirmations have by themselves no meaning."[14] Then he remarks,

> We should first ask ourselves how one could have had the idea of putting into the same frame so many worlds impenetrable to one another. We should like to represent to ourselves the external universe, and only by so doing could we feel that we understood it. We know we can never attain this representation: our weakness is too great. But at least we desire the ability to conceive an infinite intelligence for which this representation could be possible, a sort of great consciousness which should see all, and which should classify all *in its time,* as we classify, *in our time,* the little we see.
>
> This hypothesis is indeed crude and incomplete, because this supreme intelligence would be only a demigod; infinite in one sense, it would be limited in another, since it would have only an imperfect recollection of the past; it could have no other, since otherwise all recollections would be equally present to it and for it there would be no time. And yet when we speak of time, for all which happens outside of us, do we not unconsciously adopt this hypothesis; do we not put ourselves in the place of this imperfect God; and do not even the atheists put themselves in the place where God would be if he existed?

---

[14]Henri Poincaré, "The Measure of Time," in *The Foundations of Science,* trans. G. B. Halstead (1913; reprint, Washington, D.C.: University Press of America, 1982), p. 228.

What I have just said shows us, perhaps, why we have tried to put all physical phenomena into the same frame. But that cannot pass for a definition of simultaneity, since this hypothetical intelligence, even if it existed, would be for us impenetrable. It is therefore necessary to seek something else.[15]

Poincaré here suggests that, in considering the notion of simultaneity, we instinctively put ourselves in the place of God and classify events as past, present or future according to his time. Poincaré does not deny that from God's perspective there would exist relations of absolute simultaneity. But he rejects the hypothesis as yielding a definition of simultaneity because we could not know such relations; such knowledge would remain the exclusive possession of God himself.

Clearly, Poincaré's misgivings are relevant to a definition of simultaneity only if one is presupposing some sort of verificationist theory of meaning, as he undoubtedly was. The fact remains that God knows the absolute simultaneity of events even if we grope in total darkness. Nor need we be concerned with Poincaré's argument that such an infinite intelligence would be a mere demigod, since there is no reason to think that a temporal being cannot have a perfect recollection of the past. There is no conceptual difficulty in the idea of a being that knows all past-tense truths. His knowledge would be constantly changing, as more and more events become past. But at each successive moment he could know every past-tense truth that there is at that moment. Hence, it does not follow that if God is temporal, he cannot have perfect recollection of the past.

Poincaré's hypothesis suggests, therefore, that if God is temporal, his present is constitutive of relations of absolute simultaneity. On this view the philosopher J. M. Findlay was wrong when he said, "the influence which harmonizes and connects all the world-lines is not God, not any featureless, inert, medium, but that living, active interchange called . . . Light, offspring of Heaven firstborn."[16] On the contrary, the use of light signals to establish clock synchrony would be a convention that finite and ignorant creatures have been obliged to adopt, but the living and active God, who knows all, would not be so dependent. In God's temporal experience, there would be a moment that would be present in absolute time, whether or not it were registered by any clock time. He would know, without any dependence on clock synchronization procedures or any physical operations at all, which events were simultaneously present in absolute time. He would know this simply in virtue of his knowing at every such moment the unique set of present-tense truths at that moment, without any need of physical observation of the universe.

So what would become of STR if God is in time? From what has been said, God's existence in time would imply that Lorentz, rather than Einstein, had the correct interpretation of relativity theory. That is to say, Einstein's clock synchronization procedure would be valid only in the preferred (absolute) reference frame, and measuring rods would contract and clocks slow down in the customary special relativistic way when in motion with respect to the preferred frame. Lorentzian relativity is admitted on all sides to be empirically equivalent to Ein-

---

[15]Ibid., pp. 228-29.

[16]J. M. Findlay, "Time and Eternity," *Review of Metaphysics* 32 (1978-1979): 6-7.

steinian relativity, and there are even indications on the cutting edge of science today that a Lorentzian view may be preferable in light of recent discoveries. Such an interpretation would be implied by divine temporality, for God in the "now" of absolute time would know which events in the universe are now being created by him and are therefore absolutely simultaneous with each other and with his "now." This startling conclusion shows that Newton's theistic hypothesis is not some idle speculation, but has important implications for our understanding of how the world is and for the assessment of rival scientific theories.

3 THE REALITY OF TENSE AND TEMPORAL BECOMING

We have seen that for Newton, "time, of itself, and from its own nature, flows equally without relation to anything external." By the metaphor of **time's flow**, Newton expresses his commitment to the objective reality of **tense**—that is, the moments of time are past, present or future in a mind-independent way—and likewise to the objective reality of **temporal becoming**, that things come into being and go out of existence as time elapses. Such a view of reality has been called a **dynamic** or **tensed** or (in J. M. E. McTaggart's influential terminology) **A-theory of time**. By contrast, many philosophers of science hold that tense and temporal becoming are subjective in character. All moments of time are equally existent and are related by the tenseless relations of *earlier than, simultaneous with* and *later than*. The distinction between past, present and future is not an objective distinction, being merely a subjective feature of consciousness. For the people located in 1868, for example, the events of 1868 are present, and we are future; by the same token, for the people living in 2050 it is the events of 2050 that are present, and we are past. If there were no minds, there would be no past, present or future. There would be just the four-dimensional space-time universe existing as a block. Such a view of time has been called a **static** or **tenseless** or **B-theory of time**. The question of whether an A- or a B-theory of time is correct has been called "the most fundamental question in the philosophy of time."[17]

It is admitted on both sides of the debate that the ordinary, commonsense view is that there is an objective distinction between past, present and future. We experience the reality of tense in a variety of ways that are so evident and so pervasive that the belief in the objective reality of tense is a universal feature of human experience. Psychologist William Friedman, who has made a career of the study of our consciousness of time, reports that "the division between past, present, and future so deeply permeates our experience that it is hard to imagine its absence."[18] He says that we have "an irresistible tendency to believe in a present. Most of us find quite startling the claim of some physicists and philosophers that the present has no special status in the physical world, that there is only a sequence of times, that the past, present, and future are only distinguishable in human consciousness."[19]

---

[17]Michael Tooley, *Time, Tense and Causation* (Oxford: Clarendon, 1997), p. 13.
[18]William Friedman, *About Time* (Cambridge, Mass.: MIT Press, 1990), p. 92.
[19]Ibid., p. 2.

Consequently, virtually all philosophers of time and space, even those who hold to a B-theory of time, admit that the view of the common man is that time involves a real distinction between past, present and future. One advocate of the static view grumps that the dynamic understanding of time is so deeply ingrained in us that it seems "programmed by original sin"![20] The advocate of the A-theory of time may plausibly contend that our experience of tense ought to be accepted as veridical, or trustworthy, unless we are given some more powerful reason for denying it.

The A-theorist might formulate an argument to the effect that the objective reality of tense is the best explanation of our experience of tense. But our belief in the reality of tense is much more fundamental than such an argument suggests. We do not adopt the belief in an objective difference between the past, present and future in an attempt to *explain* our experience of the temporal world. Rather, our belief in this case is what epistemologists call "a properly basic belief" (recall discussion in chap. 7).

A belief's being properly basic implies that one is justified in holding to that belief unless and until it is defeated. We may say that such a belief is justified at face value (prima facie). For example, take the belief "The external world is real." It is possible that you are really a brain in a vat of chemicals, being stimulated with electrodes by some mad scientist to believe that you are reading this book. Indeed, there is no way to prove this hypothesis wrong. But that does not imply that your belief in the reality of the external world is unjustified. On the contrary, it is a properly basic belief grounded in your experience and as such is justified until some defeater comes along. This belief is not defeated by the mere *possibility* that you are a brain in a vat. For there is no warrant for thinking that one is, in fact, a brain in a vat. Indeed, our belief in the reality of the external world is so deeply ingrained and strongly held that any successful defeater of this belief would have to possess enormous warrant. In the absence of any successful defeater, we are perfectly justified in taking our experience of the external world to be veridical.

Now the advocate of an A-theory of time may argue similarly concerning our belief in the past, present and future. Belief in the objective reality of tense is a properly basic belief that is universal among mankind. It therefore follows that anyone who denies this belief (and who is aware that he has no good defeaters of that belief) is irrational. For such a person fails to hold to a belief that is for him properly basic.

Sometimes advocates of a B-theory of time assert that our experience of past, present and future need not be taken as veridical, since we can imagine a universe exactly like this one that is a four-dimensional block universe containing individuals whose mental states correspond exactly to our mental states in this world. "But then surely our copies in the block universe would have the same experiences that we do—in which case they are not distinctive of a dynamic universe after all. Things would seem this way, even if we ourselves were elements of a block universe."[21] But this is like arguing that because a brain in a

---

[20]J. C. Smart, "Spacetime and Individuals," in *Logic and Art*, ed. Richard Rudner and Israel Scheffler (Indianapolis: Bobbs-Merrill, 1972), pp. 19-20.

[21]Huw Price, *Time's Arrow and Archimedes' Point* (New York: Oxford University Press, 1996), p. 15.

vat would have the same experiences of the external world that we do, therefore we no longer have any grounds for regarding our experiences as veridical! In the absence of some sort of defeater of beliefs grounded by such experiences, these experiences do provide warrant for those beliefs.

Is, then, belief in the objective reality of tense properly basic? To begin with the most obvious, we experience events as present. Our belief that events are happening presently is really no different than our belief that they are happening—and this latter belief is a basic belief grounded in our perceptual experience.

D. H. Mellor, as a proponent of the static view of time, does not believe that there really is a present. Therefore, we cannot, despite appearances, be experiencing it. Mellor thus goes to great lengths to explain away our experience of the present. First, he argues that we do not really observe the tense of events. He gives an illustration of observing astronomical events through a telescope. When we look at the stars, we seem to be observing the events as presently happening; but we know that they actually occurred millions of years ago. Thus what we see is the *order* in which events occurred, but our observations do not tell us the tense of the events. Therefore, when we think that we are observing any event to be present, we are simply confused. We do not observe the event itself to be present; rather, we observe our *experience* of the event to be present.

However, it seems that Mellor's objection is ineffective against the argument as we have framed it. For clearly one does not form a belief like "The phone is ringing" by inferring it from a more foundational belief like "My experience of the phone's ringing is present." Typically, one does not form any belief like the latter at all. One's beliefs about the tense of events is not inferred, but basic. As for the illustration of events viewed through a telescope, all that proves is that our beliefs about the tense of events is defeasible and sometimes wrong. One might as well argue that perceptual beliefs are not properly basic because things viewed through a microscope are observed to be larger than they are! Just because our sense perceptions are sometimes mistaken is no reason to think that we do not perceive things. In the same way, mistaken observations of the presentness of certain events do not prove that we make no such observations. In most cases, the events we observe fall within the limits of the psychological present, so that our observations of events as present are veridical and our judgments to that effect properly basic.

In any case, Mellor admits that we do observe our experiences to be present. This is the so-called **presentness of experience**. Even if we can be mistaken about the presentness of a supernova observed through a telescope, we cannot be mistaken about the presentness of our experience of observing the supernova. If we observe our experiences to be present, aren't we observing the tense of these mental events?

No, replies Mellor, for "although we observe our experience to be present, it really isn't."[22] This is a paradoxical statement. Mellor admits that when we make the judgment that our experience is present, we cannot be mistaken. He writes,

> So judging my experience to be present is much like my judging it to be painless. On the one hand, the judgment is not one I have to make. . . . But on the other

---

[22]D. H. Mellor, *Real Time* (Cambridge: Cambridge University Press, 1981), p. 26.

hand, if I do make it, I am bound to be right, just as when I judge my experience to be painless. The presence of experience . . . is something of which one's awareness is infallible.

. . . No matter who I am or whenever I judge my experience to be present, that judgment will be true.[23]

But if our observation of the presentness of our experience is analogous to our observation of whether our experiences are painful, if we are *bound to be right* in judging our experience to be present, if our awareness of the presentness of our experience is *infallible*, if our judgment that our experience is present will be *true every time*, then how can it be the case that, as Mellor says, "it really isn't?" If one's belief that "My experience of observing the supernova is present" is indefeasible, as Mellor admits, then how can that experience not be present, even if the supernova itself is not?

Mellor's answer is that while the belief that one's experience is present may have important cognitive significance, nonetheless the factual content of that belief is a tautology and therefore trivial. Mellor maintains that the following belief (A) is just true by definition:

A. The experiences that I am now having possess the property of being present.

He makes this claim because (A) is true if and only if (B):

B. The experiences that I have at the time of the utterance of (A) possess the property of existing at the time of the utterance of (A).

But (B) is trivially true, a mere tautology. Therefore, although (A) is true, its factual content, as disclosed by (B), does not imply the objective reality of presentness.

This response by Mellor is multiply flawed. First, Mellor's tautology is self-constructed, for he stipulates that it is "the experiences that I am now having" that are judged to be present. But there is no reason to describe one's experiences as those one is now having. The beliefs in question are not like (A); rather, they are like (A′):

A′. My experience of seeing the supernova is present.

And (A′) is not tautologous.

Second, even (A) can be read in a way that is not tautologous. Let the phrase "the experience that I am now having" pick out a specific, unique experience like observing the supernova. In that case, the ascription of presentness to that particular experience out of all the experiences one ever has is not trivial or true by definition.

Third, even if (A) is trivial, that does not imply that the presentness of experience is trivial. It may be trivial to assert that "My present experiences are present" or that "My present experiences are experiences." But that does nothing to explain away the fact that one does have present experiences or to defeat the belief in the presentness of one's experiences.

---

[23]Ibid., p. 53.

Fourth, stating tenseless truth conditions for one's belief in the presentness of his experience does not constitute even a prima facie defeater of that belief. Such truth conditions are just irrelevant to the proper basicality of that belief. For the object of one's belief is not the fact that is stated as the tenseless truth conditions of what one believes. In order for that to be the case, (B), the statement of the truth conditions, would have to have the same *meaning* as (A), the statement of the tensed belief—which Mellor himself denies. Since they are not synonymous, the triviality of the statement of the truth conditions does not imply the triviality of the tensed belief. Nor is there any reason to think that the factual content of the tensed belief is given exhaustively in the tenseless truth conditions.

It therefore seems that Mellor has not provided a successful defeater of our belief that our experiences are present. Not only does such a belief seem to be properly basic, but it even seems to be indefeasibly true.

A second way in which we experience the reality of tense is exhibited by our attitudes toward the past and future. We recall past events with nostalgia or regret, whereas we look forward to future events with either dread or anticipation. The beliefs that these attitudes express are tensed beliefs. As the late Oxford tense logician A. N. Prior once remarked, when we say, "Thank goodness that's over!" we certainly do not mean "Thank goodness the date of that thing's conclusion is June 15, 1954!" or "Thank goodness that thing's conclusion is simultaneous with this utterance!"—for why should anyone thank goodness for that?[24] Prior's point is that such attitudes cannot concern tenseless facts but are about tensed facts. The further point is that it is entirely rational to have such attitudes. Therefore, the tensed beliefs evinced by these attitudes must be rational as well. If it is rational for a person to be relieved that his visit to the dentist is past, then his belief that his visit is past is also rational.

On the B-theory of time, feelings of relief and anticipation must be ultimately regarded as irrational, since events really are not past or future. Yet one can safely say that no B-theorist has ever succeeded in divesting himself of such feelings. Indeed, anyone who did succeed in ridding himself of such feelings and the tensed beliefs they express would cease to be human.

In response B-theorists concede that such attitudes do express tensed beliefs; but they again try to strip those beliefs of any tensed factual content. They say that we thank goodness that our headache is over not because it is over but because we *believe* it to be over; and the content of this belief is fixed by its tenseless truth conditions, such as the headache's being earlier than the time of one's belief. Thus one's truly believing that his headache is over does not imply that one's headache is objectively past.

Now certainly B-theorists are correct that what our attitudes immediately express are tensed *beliefs*, not tensed *facts*. For an anticipated event may be avoided and so never come to pass at all. But all that proves is that one's tensed beliefs are defeasible. Many times, however, our tensed beliefs are correct. Indeed, sometimes they are indefeasibly correct, as when one believes that the pain he felt is over. In other words, the question comes down once more to the

---

[24]A. N. Prior, "Thank Goodness That's Over," *Philosophy* 34 (1959): 12-17.

presentness of experience. When one feels relief, what one is relieved about can be analyzed as a complex fact involving the beliefs that (1) one's experience is present and (2) some event is earlier than the present. One can be mistaken about (2), but one cannot be mistaken about (1), and thus the objectivity of tense remains.

There is a further feature of our attitudes toward the past and future which deserves to be highlighted, namely, the *difference* in how we regard an event depending on its pastness or futurity. An unpleasant experience that lies in the future occasions feelings of dread; but that very same experience, once past, evokes feelings of relief. On an A-theory of time these different attitudes are grounded in the reality of temporal becoming. A future event has yet to exist and will be present; but a past event no longer exists and was present. Therefore, it is rational to have different feelings about these events. But on a B-theory of time, this difference in attitude toward the past and future is groundless and, hence, irrational. As philosopher of time George Schlesinger points out, on the B-theory of time there is no more difference between an event's being located one hour later versus one hour earlier than now than there is in an event's being located one mile to the right versus one mile to the left of here, for neither "now" nor "here" is objective. Whether past or future, both events are equally real, there is no temporal becoming, nor are we moving toward one event and away from the other, and the distinction between past and future is purely subjective. Therefore, it just makes no sense to look upon these events differently. And yet, as Schlesinger observes, such a differential concern is a universal human experience.

Think, for example, of the difference in our attitude toward one's birth and one's death. On the B-theory of time the period of personal nonexistence that lies after one's death is of no more significance than the period of personal nonexistence that lies before one's birth. And yet we celebrate birthdays, whereas we typically dread dying, a dread that runs so deep that one's death, wholly in contrast to one's birth, seems to put a question mark behind the value of life itself. Many existentialist philosophers have said that life becomes absurd in light of "my death"; but no one has said this as a result of "my birth."

B-theorists have naturally been reluctant to dismiss as irrational our differential attitudes towards past and future events and so have instead tried to find some basis for this difference in the static theory. For example, Nathan Oaklander, an ardent defender of static time, insists that such a difference is rational because on the B-theory time is asymmetric, that is to say, there is a **direction of time** as determined by the ordering of events according to the relations *earlier than/later than*. Oaklander thinks that it makes all the difference in the world whether an event is later than one's location in time or earlier than one's location.

But it is evident that on a B-theory of time the mere **asymmetry of time**— its having direction according to the relations *earlier than/later than*—is not an adequate substitute for temporal becoming. Stripped of all tense, the relations of *earlier than/later than* with respect to some event no more justify differing attitudes on our part than would the relations *to the right of/to the left of*. Indeed, on the B-theory of time, there are really two directions to time: one the "earlier than" direction and the other the "later than" direction. In the absence of temporal becoming it is wholly arbitrary how these directions are laid on the series of events. The two arrows of time could be turned 180° without any inconsistency with the facts. Although some scientists try to appeal to the laws of thermodynamics or other physical processes to establish *the* single **arrow of time**, all such attempts *presuppose* a prior choice of direction—for example, that the direction of entropy increase is the *later than* direction. In the absence of temporal becoming, such a choice is wholly arbitrary. We could have called the direction of entropy increase *earlier than* if we had wanted to. Thus *earlier* and *later* simply do not have the significance on a B-theory of time that they do on a dynamic theory.

Our differing attitudes toward past and future events serve to underline how deeply ingrained and how strongly held our tensed beliefs are. If the B-theory of time is correct, feelings of relief, nostalgia, dread and anticipation are all irrational. Since such feelings are ineradicable, the B-theory would condemn us all to irrationality. In the absence of any defeater for our belief in the objective distinction between past, present and future, such a belief remains properly basic and the feelings they evoke entirely appropriate.

There are many other ways in which we experience the objective reality of tense and temporal becoming. Unless B-theorists are able to come up with some more powerful warrant for adopting a B-theory of time, we ought to stick with the A-theory. So what reasons are there for thinking that a B-theory of time is true?

Undoubtedly, the major motivation for the adoption of a B-theory of time by philosophers of science is the conviction that relativity theory demands it. As Einstein himself came to realize, his special theory makes the most sense if it is formulated in a geometry of four dimensions, and his **general theory of relativity** characterizes gravity, not as a force, but as the curvature of four-dimensional **space-time** (the union of space and time into a single reality which is presupposed by a **geometrical approach to gravitation**). But from what has already been said above, it is clear that such an argument is not at all compelling. First, there is an interpretation of the mathematical core of special relativity that is empirically equivalent to the Einsteinian interpretation and is fully compatible with an A-theory of time, namely, Lorentzian relativity. So what is wrong with a Lorentzian interpretation?

Verificationism aside, at the root of many physicists' aversion to Lorentzian relativity is the conviction that comes to expression in Einstein's aphorism: "Subtle is the Lord, but malicious He is not." That is to say, if there exists in nature a fundamental asymmetry, then nature will not conspire to conceal it from us. But Lorentzian relativity requires us to believe that although absolute simultaneity and length exist in the world, nature conceals these from us by slowing down our clocks (**clock retardation**) and shrinking our measuring rods (**length contraction**) when we try to detect them. D'Abro voices his objection to such a conspiracy of nature:

> If Nature was blind, by what marvelous coincidence had all things been so adjusted as to conceal a velocity through the ether? And if Nature was wise, she had surely other things to attend to, more worthy of her consideration, and would

scarcely be interested in hampering our feeble attempts to philosophize. In Lorentz's theory, Nature, when we read into her system all these extra-ordinary adjustments *ad hoc,* is made to appear mischievous; it was exceedingly difficult to reconcile one's self to finding such human traits in the universal plan.[25]

It must first be said that d'Abro greatly exaggerates the extent of the alleged conspiracy. After all, special relativity is a restricted theory: it is only uniform motion relative to the privileged reference frame that is concealed from us. But acceleration and rotation are absolute motions that nature does nothing to conceal. Furthermore, one must surely question the presupposition that if fundamental asymmetries exist, nature must disclose these to us. The empirical manifestation of an underlying state of nature may often appear altered as a result of distortions which intervene between theory and evidence, so that it is a nontrivial task to excavate the state of nature from its distorted manifestation. Tim Maudlin, a philosopher of science who has specialized in the implications of so-called quantum nonlocality for relativity theory, concludes after surveying all the attempts to integrate the results of Bell's theorem with relativity theory, "One way or another God has played us a nasty trick."[26] He maintains that the solution of Lorentzian relativity cannot be rejected on the grounds that it would be deceptive of nature, for the partisans of *all* the solutions say the same thing about all the others. In the end, he muses, "The real challenge falls to the theologians of physics, who must justify the ways of a Deity who is, if not evil, at least extremely mischievous."[27]

As for d'Abro's complaint about finding "human traits in the universal plan," the Lorentzian might in response appeal to the so-called **anthropic principle**. According to that principle, features of the universe can be seen in the correct perspective only if we keep in mind that certain features of the universe are necessary if observers like us are to exist. If the universe were not to have those features, then we would not be here to observe the ones it has. Now our very existence depends on the maintenance of certain states of equilibrium within us. But length contraction and clock retardation are, on the Lorentzian view, the result precisely of material systems' maintaining their equilibrium states while being in motion. Thus, if nature lacked this compensating behavior, we would not be here to observe the fact! Given that we could not exist without it, why should we be surprised at observing nature's "conspiracy"?

But why is nature structured in such a way? Given the theistic perspective from which we approach these questions, we should hardly be surprised at discovering that the universe is designed in such a way as to support our existence. We should expect that God will have chosen laws of nature that will maintain the equilibrium states essential to our existence. Even if, as d'Abro puts it, Nature is blind, God is not; and if Nature is not wise, God is. It is not Nature, then, who is concerned with our feeble selves, who deems us worthy subjects to attend to, but the Creator and Sustainer of the universe who is mindful of man (Ps 8:3-8). *Subtle is the Lord, merciful he is also.*

---

[25]A. d'Abro, *The Evolution of Scientific Thought,* 2d rev. ed. (1927; n.p.: Dover Publications, 1950), p. 138.

[26]Tim Maudlin, *Quantum Non-Locality and Relativity,* Aristotelian Society Series 13 (Oxford: Blackwell, 1994), p. 241.

[27]Ibid., p. 242.

As for the general theory of relativity, the question raised by Einstein's geometrical approach to gravitation is whether it is to be understood realistically or merely instrumentally. According to the noted philosopher of science Arthur Fine, few working, knowledgeable scientists give credence to the realist construal of general relativity. Rather, the theory is seen as "a magnificent organizing tool" for dealing with gravitational problems: "most who actually use it think of the theory as a powerful instrument, rather than as expressing a 'big truth.'"[28] It can be safely said that no scientific disadvantage arises from treating the geometrical approach to gravity as merely instrumental. Indeed, on the contrary, it can be argued that a realist understanding of space-time actually obscures our understanding of nature by substituting geometry for a physical gravitational force, thus impeding progress in connecting the theory of gravity to the theory of particles. In his *Gravitation and Cosmology*, the Nobel Prize winning physicist Steven Weinberg contends that taking gravity to be a real force is "a crucial link" between general relativity and **particle physics**, since there must then be a particle of gravitational radiation, the so-called graviton.[29] The geometrical approach of space-time realism is thus a positive impediment to our gaining a more integrated understanding of physics. Geometrical space-time, in Weinberg's view, should be understood "only as a mathematical tool" and "not as a fundamental basis for the theory of gravitation."[30]

What other reasons might be offered for adopting a B-theory of time? One of the most celebrated arguments is **McTaggart's paradox**. In 1908 the Cambridge idealist John Ellis McTaggart published a remarkable article in the journal *Mind* entitled "The Unreality of Time."[31] His argument consists of two parts. In the first part McTaggart argues that time is essentially tensed. In the second part he argues that tensed time is self-contradictory. It therefore follows that time is unreal.

Since our concern is with arguments for the B-theory of time, we shall focus on the second half of McTaggart's proof. His argument here is apt to appear bewildering unless we first understand its metaphysical presuppositions. The key to understanding the contradiction McTaggart sees in a tensed view of time is his presupposition that past, present and future events are all equally real or existent and that temporal becoming consists in the movement of the present along this series. McTaggart thinks of the series of temporal events as stretched out like a string of light bulbs that are each momentarily illuminated in succession, so that the light is seen to move across the series of bulbs. In the same way presentness moves across the series of events. Since all events are equally existent, the only respect in which they change is the change in tense that they undergo. First they are future, then they are present, then they are past. In every other respect they just *are*. Obviously, then, for McTaggart *becoming present* does not imply *becoming existent*.

[28]Arthur Fine, *The Shaky Game: Einstein, Realism and the Quantum Theory* (Chicago: University of Chicago Press, 1986), p. 123.

[29]Steven Weinberg, *Gravitation and Cosmology: Principles and Explications of the General Theory of Relativity* (New York: John Wiley & Sons, 1972), p. 251.

[30]Ibid., p. viii.

[31]J. Ellis McTaggart, "The Unreality of Time," *Mind* 17 (1908): 457-74.

McTaggart observes that pastness, presentness and futurity are mutually incompatible: no event can have all three. But given McTaggart's tenselessly existing series of temporal events, every event does have all three! Take an event tenselessly located at t_1. At t_1 that event is obviously present. But because all events are equally real, that same event also has pastness and futurity because at t_2 it is past and at t_0 it is future. The moment t_1 is not any more real or privileged than t_0 or t_2, and so the event in question must be characterized by the tenses it has at all these times, which is impossible. We can visualize the problem by imagining the people existing at each of these three moments. For the people at t_1, t_1 is present. Since neither t_1 nor these people pass away, it is still the case when it is t_2 that for the people at t_1 the moment t_1 is present. But for the people at t_2 the moment t_1 is past. The moment t_1 never sheds presentness and takes on pastness—just ask the people at t_1! But t_1 never exchanges its pastness for any other tense either, as the people at t_2 will tell you. Thus t_1 is changelessly both present and past, which is impossible. If someone should say, "But t_1 is present relative to t_1 and past relative to t_2, which is not contradictory," the advocate of tenseless time will say that such relational properties reduce to the tenseless relations *is simultaneous with* and *is earlier than*, which vindicates the tenseless theory.

After decades of discussion, a consensus seems to be emerging that McTaggart's paradox is based on a misguided attempt to marry a dynamic theory of temporal becoming to a static series of events. It is then no wonder that the dynamic-static theory of time he winds up with proves to be self-contradictory! Sharp-sighted critics of McTaggart such as C. D. Broad and A. N. Prior have insisted almost from the beginning that a tensed or A-theory of time implies a commitment to **presentism**, the doctrine that the only temporal entities that exist are present entities. According to presentism, past and future entities do not exist. Thus there really are no past or future events, except in the sense that there have been certain events and there will be certain others; the only real events are present events. Thus there can be no question of an event's swapping futurity for presentness or cashing in presentness for pastness. Temporal becoming is not the exchange of tense on the part of tenselessly existing events, but the coming into and going out of existence of the entities themselves. Events no more change tenses than they exchange properties of nonexistence and existence! An event possesses only the tense it has when it is present, namely, presentness. No event ever possesses pastness or futurity, for nonpresent events do not exist. Thus there can be no question of any event's possessing incompatible tense determinations. Thus McTaggart's paradox is ineffectual against the presentist. The paradox arises, not from a contradiction within a tensed theory of time, but from a misconceived union of the A- and B-theories of time.

Presentism is not infrequently rejected because it is thought to imply, in conjunction with STR, a sort of **solipsism** (the view that I alone exist), which no sane person can believe. This unwelcome consequence is due to the absence of absolute time and space within the context of STR, which makes it impossible to define any plausible coexistence relation between oneself and other things. Anyone who has followed our argument thus far, however, will realize that this objection to presentism is not difficult to answer. It is predicated on an Einsteinian interpretation of relativity theory, which one may reject on wholly independent grounds in favor of a Lorentzian interpretation. A Lorentzian understanding of relativity preserves relations of absolute simultaneity and so confronts no challenge concerning coexistence relations among temporal beings. The presentist who accepts Lorentzian relativity is thus not threatened by the specter of solipsism.

In conclusion, we have good grounds for accepting an A-theory of time in view of the proper basicality of our belief in the objective reality of tense and temporal becoming. By contrast, arguments for a B-theory of time tend to rely on a physical interpretation of relativity theory that is founded on an untenable verificationist epistemology. In general, contemporary philosophy of time and space has, as a result of the positivist era, been thoroughly infected by an unhealthy scientism. It is high time for philosophy of time and space to be restored to the domain of philosophy where it properly belongs: metaphysics, where theistic considerations, such as Newton adduced, cannot be ignored.

CHAPTER SUMMARY

Traditionally a topic handled in metaphysics, philosophy of time and space as practiced today has been absorbed into philosophy of science. This is the lingering effect of the acid bath of verificationism and positivism, which dominated philosophy during the first half of the twentieth century. In particular, verificationist analyses of key concepts like time and simultaneity lie essentially at the epistemological foundations of relativity theory, the principal domain of physics addressing problems of time and space. The demise of positivism reopens the traditional metaphysical problems of time and space. In dealing with such questions one cannot ignore the philosophical impact of the existence of God, which lies at the metaphysical foundations of the classical concept of time and space.

One of the most important metaphysical questions about the nature of time concerns the status of tense and temporal becoming. Partisans of a tensed or A-theory of time can plausibly argue that in light of our temporal experience our belief in the objective difference between past, present and future is a properly basic belief. Advocates of a tenseless or B-theory of time appeal in vain to relativity theory to defeat this conclusion, since there are plausible interpretations of that theory that are consistent with an A-theory. Moreover, objections based on McTaggart's paradox may be turned back by adoption of a metaphysic of presentism.

CHECKLIST OF BASIC TERMS AND CONCEPTS

A-theory of time (dynamic or tensed theory of time)
absolute motion
absolute place
absolute space
absolute time
aether

anthropic principle
arrow of time
asymmetry of time
B-theory of time (static or tenseless theory of time)
clock retardation
clock synchronization
constancy of the speed of light
direction of time
eternity
general theory of relativity
geometrical approach to gravitation
inertial frame
length contraction
Lorentz transformations
Lorentzian relativity
McTaggart's paradox
Maxwell's electrodynamics
Michelson-Morley experiment
Newton's mechanics
omnipresence
one-way velocity of light
operationalist definition
particle physics
positivism
presentism
presentness of experience
relative space
relative time
relativity of length
relativity of simultaneity
simultaneity
solipsism
space-time
special theory of relativity
speed of light
temporal becoming
tense
time's flow
uniform motion
verificationism

PART V

ETHICS

19

ETHICS, MORALITY
AND METAETHICS

A knowledge of ethical theory has enormous practical benefits.
It can free us from prejudice and dogmatism.
It sets forth the comprehensive systems
from which to orient our individual judgments.
It carves up the moral landscape so that we can sort out the issues
in order to think more clearly and confidently about moral problems.
LOUIS P. POJMAN, *DISCOVERING RIGHT AND WRONG*

There can be no complete non-personal,
objective justification for acting morally rather than nonmorally.
KAI NIELSEN, "WHY SHOULD I BE MORAL?"
IN *READINGS IN ETHICAL THEORY*

1 INTRODUCTION

What exactly is morality and why does it seem to matter so much to us? Is there really an objective difference between good and evil, right and wrong, virtue and vice, and if so, how can we tell the difference? Is some form of moral relativism the best ethical theory? Is there a broad ethical theory that is most consistent with Scripture, and if so, what is it? These and many other questions arise when one begins to think deeply about ethical issues. In the next four chapters, many of these questions will be addressed. This important exploration of ethical topics will be launched in this chapter by looking at an overview of the field of ethics, examining the main options in metaethics regarding the meaning of moral terms and the nature of moral propositions, such as *Persons have intrinsic value* or *It is wrong to steal*, and probing the question, "Why should I be moral?"

2 MORALITY AND THE FIELD OF ETHICS

Ethics can be understood as the philosophical study of morality, which is concerned with our beliefs and judgments regarding right and wrong motives, attitudes, character and conduct. When an ethicist studies morality, certain **value concepts** are the center of focus: "right," "wrong," "good," "bad," "ought," "duty," "virtuous," "blameworthy" and so on.

But there is a problem. Most of these value concepts have a nonmoral as well as a moral usage. For example, given certain evidence regarding weather patterns, one "ought" to believe that it will rain in the next twenty-four hours.

2.1
THE NATURE OF
MORALITY

But the "ought" here is a rational ought, not a moral one. One may be irrational not to hold this belief, but one would not be immoral. Again, some paintings are good and others bad, but these terms express aesthetic evaluations, not moral ones. Religion, law, custom, etiquette, politics and other fields use value terms. Is there any way to state a set of necessary and sufficient conditions that can be used to draw a line between the moral and nonmoral uses of these value terms? Among other things, such a set of conditions could be used to define ethics more precisely.

In general, it is very difficult to state an airtight set of necessary and sufficient conditions for almost anything. For example, it would be difficult to state such a set for defining *play, sport, love, history, friendship, justice* or *anxiety.* But in each of these examples people can recognize clear cases of the term in question and clear cases that are not examples of the term. What Mickey Mantle did with the New York Yankees is sport, but what a mailman does in delivering letters is not.

In epistemology, there is a view called particularism (see chap. 4). According to **particularism**, one does not always need a set of necessary and sufficient conditions before one can know clear cases of a thing in question; instead, we first recognize particular cases of that thing. By way of application, we can all recognize clear cases of a moral and nonmoral use of value terms without having criteria for such differentiations. Actually, we start with clear cases: "Stealing is wrong" is a moral statement, and "Eating peas with a knife is wrong" is a statement of etiquette. Then we use these to test alternative formulations of necessary and sufficient conditions. These conditions can, in turn, be helpful in shedding light on borderline cases that are more difficult. "It is wrong to drive on the left side of the street in the United States" may use "wrong" as a moral term, a legal term or both. However, knowledge of the clear cases provides justification for the conditions, not conversely.

The following have been offered by a number of philosophers as a set of necessary (and/or sufficient) conditions for defining morality:

1. A judgment is moral only if it is accepted as a supremely authoritative, overriding guide to conduct, attitudes and motives.

The point of this criterion is that morality must have top priority over all else in our lives. In this way, morality is contrasted with mere custom, etiquette and, perhaps, law. This criterion certainly captures much of what we want to say about morality. However, some would argue that it is inadequate as a necessary (or sufficient) condition for morality on the grounds that it is possible to have other duties, such as religious duties, that might override mere ethical duties. For example, some would claim that the worship of a divine being takes precedence over a moral duty to obey the state or the moral duty not to offend others. A rejoinder to this argument could point out that these religious duties and moral duties are not mutually exclusive and are, instead, both within the realm of morality. However, it is not at all clear that religious duties are exhausted by their moral dimension. Thus the argument is inconclusive. Whereas this criterion may not be necessary for addressing all cases of morality, in a weakened form it is helpful in many moral contexts. Moral judgments are extremely important, they carry a great deal of authority, and they override considerations of mere etiquette, custom and law.

2. A judgment is moral only if it is a prescriptive imperative that recommends actions, attitudes and motives and not merely a factual description about actions, attitudes and motives.

This criterion expresses the distinction between a mere **descriptive, factual "is"** and a **prescriptive, evaluative "ought"** and identifies morality with the latter. It should be clear that this criterion is not a sufficient condition for morality, since there are aesthetic oughts (the piece ought to be played at this tempo for maximum beauty) and rational oughts (in light of the evidence, one ought to believe what Smith said). Furthermore, there are other points to morality besides providing prescriptive action guides for conduct; for example, some moral statements are used to praise and blame, some merely to describe what is right without necessarily commanding that one do what is right. Nevertheless, this criterion does capture an important aspect of moral judgments. They do prescribe our moral duties rather than merely describe what people actually do.

3. A judgment is moral only if it is **universalizable**, that is, if it applies equally to all relevantly similar situations.

The main point of this criterion is to express the conviction that moral judgments must be impartially applied to moral situations by taking into account all of the morally relevant features of the situation. If someone claimed that one act is right and a second act is wrong, but that person was unable to cite a relevant distinction between the two acts, then the judgment would seem arbitrary and without adequate foundation. This criterion points to an important aspect of morality: Moral judgments are not arbitrary expressions of personal preference. They are rationally justifiable claims that, if true, are binding on all cases that fit the relevant conditions on which the claim is based. If one act of lying is wrong, then in the absence of relevant features (e.g., a certain act of lying may be the only way to save a life), all acts of lying are wrong.

4. A judgment is moral only if it makes reference to proper human flourishing, human dignity, the welfare of others, the prevention of harm and the provision of benefit.

Inasmuch as this criterion makes exclusive reference to human beings, it is clearly inadequate as a necessary condition for morality. Animals and the environment are, arguably, appropriate objects of moral concern in their own right and not merely because such concern is of benefit to human flourishing. But if this caveat is kept in mind, criterion (4) *is* a good one. It focuses attention on the fact that much of the point of morality is to preserve the dignity, welfare and richness of human life.

In summary, we can all recognize examples of moral and nonmoral judgments without possessing a set of necessary and/or sufficient conditions for drawing a line of demarcation between them. And while perhaps no airtight set of conditions exists, the same situation obtains when we try to define other areas of our intellectual and cultural life. Nevertheless, the four features above do seem to capture much of what we mean by morality. For the most part, morality is supremely authoritative, prescriptive, universalizable and makes reference to human dignity, welfare and flourishing.

We have seen that ethics is the study of morality. In addition, we have looked briefly at the nature of morality. Now let us survey the various branches of ethics as a field of study.

2.2
THE FIELD OF
ETHICS

At least four different areas of study focus on morality. Two are nonnormative in that they do not seek to prescribe what ought or ought not to be done. On the other hand, the two areas of **normative ethics** do seek to offer guides for determining right or wrong actions, attitudes and motives.

The two nonnormative approaches to the study of morality are descriptive ethics and metaethics. **Descriptive ethics** is a factual study of moral attitudes, behaviors, rules and motives that are embodied in various individuals and cultures. As such, descriptive ethics is not really a branch of ethics, but a sociological, anthropological, historical or psychological view about ethics.

Metaethics involves two main areas of investigation. First, metaethics focuses on the meaning and reference of crucial ethical terms, such as *right* and *wrong, good* and *bad, ought* and *ought not, duty,* and so on. For example, metaethics investigates the meaning of a statement like "Love is a virtue." **Emotivism** is a view in metaethics which translates this statement as follows: "Hurrah! Love!" According to emotivists, moral statements are not indicative statements that can be true or false, but are mere expressions of feelings that seek to evoke similar feelings in others. A second view is **metaethical relativism**, which translates "Love is a virtue" to mean "Love is preferred by those in our culture." Some ethical naturalists treat the statement as making this claim: "Love is what most people desire" or "Acts of love tend to promote survival." Ethical nonnaturalists claim that the statement ascribes a second-order nonphysical property—virtuousness—to a first-order nonphysical property—love. In this way, ethical nonnaturalists treat "Love is a virtue" as analogous to "Red is a color." If the latter is true, it commits us to the existence of two properties: redness and coloredness. If the former is true, it commits us to the existence of two moral properties: love and virtuousness.

The important thing here is not to survey all the options in metaethics. Later in the chapter, the most prominent options will be examined. Rather, the present point is that metaethics does not provide explicit principles to aid us in determining what is the right or wrong course of action to take in a given situation. Instead, metaethics primarily focuses on giving a conceptual analysis of the meanings of moral terms and moral sentences.

A second area of metaethical investigation is the question of the structure of moral reasoning and justification. Are reasoning and justification relevant in morality? If so, is moral justification the same as scientific justification or is it different? For example, if one is an emotivist (moral statements are mere expressions of feelings), then rational, moral justification for a moral statement is impossible, for one does not give a justification for an expression of emotion. Such an expression is neither true nor false.

On the other hand, if one is an ethical naturalist (e.g., moral statements describe what most people, in fact, happen to desire), then scientific methodology would be the appropriate model for moral justification. One can determine what most people desire by a scientifically controlled survey. Again, if one is an ethical nonnaturalist, one may argue that moral reasoning ultimately appeals to a basic, irreducible intuition of a moral property or moral proposition in justifying moral positions. For example, it seems to be intuitively self-evident that persons have value and that mercy as such is a virtue.

Neither descriptive ethics nor metaethics is the central focus of this section of the book, except where certain moral positions will be evaluated. The next few chapters focus on the normative ethics. **Normative ethics proper** seeks to formulate and defend basic moral principles, rules, systems and virtues which serve as guides for what actions ought or ought not to be taken, what motives ought or ought not to be embraced, and what kinds of persons we ought or ought not seek to be. Utilitarianism, deontological ethical theories and virtue ethics are examples of normative ethical theories. **Applied ethics** is the area of study that centers its investigation on specific moral issues, such as abortion, euthanasia and capital punishment, and seeks to bring normative ethics to bear on them.

3 METAETHICS AND THE MEANING OF MORAL STATEMENTS

In the previous section, metaethics was defined as that branch of philosophy that analyzes the meaning of certain moral terms (right, wrong, good, bad, ought, worth and so forth). Certain moral statements make reference to persons or actions. With regard to persons, one might affirm the moral statement "Persons ought to be treated as ends in themselves" or "Persons have intrinsic value and dignity." With regard to actions, one might affirm that "The act of loving your neighbor is morally right" or "Murder is wrong." In general, many moral statements are of this form: X is right (or wrong). X has value (or fails to have value).

Different metaethical views have been offered which analyze statements like these differently. The major options in metaethics can be summarized as follows:

I. Noncognitivist Theories
   A. Emotivism
   B. Imperativalism/Prescriptivism

II. Cognitivist Theories
   A. Subjectivist Theories
     1. Private Subjectivism
     2. Cultural Relativism

   B. Objectivist Theories
     1. Ethical Naturalism
     2. Ethical Nonnaturalism

Noncognitivism denies that moral statements (e.g., "X is right") are indicative statements that can be either true or false. Consider the statement "The apple is red." This is an indicative statement. It asserts an alleged fact which has ontological implications. It asserts that there is an apple that exists and has an existent property, redness, in it. So indicative statements have ontological implications. Further, they can be either true or false. In this case, if the apple really is red, the statement is true. If the apple were green, it would be false. So indicative statements are cognitive in the sense that they can be either true or false, and they have ontological implications because they assert that some state of affairs obtains in the world.

Noncognitivist theories or moral statements, however, deny that moral statements are either true or false and that moral statements have ontological implications. Emotivists hold that the meaning of moral statements consists in the expression of emotions: "X is right" really means "Hurrah for x!" Statements like "X is wrong" really mean "Ugh! x!" For example, when someone says that murder is wrong, emotivists hold that the person is merely expressing the feeling "Ugh! I hate murder!"

Imperativalism/prescriptivism agrees with emotivists that moral statements are not indicative statements of fact. But they do not think that moral statements are expressions of feeling. Rather, they hold that moral statements are merely moral commands whose sole function is to guide action. "X is right" is merely the command "Do x!"

Noncognitivist theories of moral statements fail to do justice to the nature of morality. At least three objections can be raised against both views. First, moral judgments can occur in the absence of feelings or in the absence of commands, and some expressions of feelings or some commands are not moral judgments. For example, one can form the judgment "Killing rats is wrong" without feeling or commanding anything. But if a moral judgment is just an expression of a feeling or the issuing of a command, then it would be impossible to have a moral judgment without feeling or without commanding. Feelings and commands may be a part of a general theory of morality, but they do not exhaust the nature of morality. Similarly, someone can express a feeling when he stubs his toe on a table ("Ugh! I hate tables!"), but this expression is not a moral judgment. So moral judgments can occur without feelings or commands and vice versa. Thus they cannot be identical.

Second, emotivism and imperativalism imply that there is no such thing as moral education (since there is no cognitive information to learn) and there is no such thing as a moral disagreement. Consider two people who appear to be having a moral disagreement about abortion. Person A says "Abortion is right," and person B says "Abortion is wrong." Emotivists analyze these statements such that A is saying, "Hurrah! I (A) love abortion!" and B is saying, "Ugh! I (B) hate abortion!" According to emotivist (and imperativalist) translations of the statements, there is no disagreement occurring, since neither person is making a factual claim that could be true or false. Disagreements occur when one person asserts that some claim is true and another asserts that it is false. So emotivism and imperativalism imply the impossibility of moral disagreement. But any view that implies such an implausible assertion as this is inadequate as a general theory of moral meaning.

Finally, some moral statements seem to stand in logical relations with other moral statements. For example, the statement "I have a duty to do *x*" seems logically to imply the statement "I have a right to do *x*." But emotional utterances or mere imperatives do not stand to other emotional utterances or mere imperatives in logical relationships. Only indicative statements can stand in logical relationships to one another. So emotivism and imperativalism fail to account for this feature of morality.

An imperativalist may respond to this last argument as follows. Consider this syllogism:

Syllogism A:
1. All promises being kept, please.
2. This is a promise.
3. This promise being kept, please.

The imperativalist may argue that moral imperatives may be expressed by sentences like (1) which contain two components: a descriptive component to the left of the comma ("All promises being kept") and an imperative component to the right of the comma ("please"). The descriptive component describes a state of affairs, in this case, a world in which all promises are kept. Now a possible world in which all promises are, in fact, kept, would logically imply that some specific promise is kept. So in a sense, (1) and (2) do imply (3) even though, strictly speaking, none of these propositions is either true or false. But if we allow that there seems to be a sense in which the first two premises imply the conclusion, then the imperativalist can argue that this is enough to show that moral imperatives stand in logical relations to other moral imperatives.

Does this imperativalist rejoinder work? The answer seems to be no. As the argument stands, given that (1) through (3) are neither true nor false, it is not clear that (1) and (2) logically entail (3). The only sense in which this could be true is if one removes "please" from (1) and (3) to form the following:

Syllogism B:
1'. All promises are kept.
2'. This is a promise.
3'. This promise is kept.

In this case, (3') does follow from the premises. However, syllogism B no longer contains moral statements because on the imperativalist view, what makes a proposition a moral one is its imperatival force expressed in the word *please*. It is "please" that gives (1) through (3) their action-guiding potential. Thus the only way that the moral propositions in syllogism A can be said to stand in logical relations to each other is if we drop their distinctively moral component to generate syllogism B. Since B is no longer composed of moral propositions, this response fails.

Cognitivism holds that moral statements make truth claims because they are indicative statements that convey descriptive factual information: the statement "X is right" can be either true or false. Nevertheless, cognitivist theories of the meaning of moral statements differ in what they identify as the object that ethical statements describe.

Subjectivism holds that moral statements convey information about the speaker of the moral statement. According to **private subjectivism**, "X is right" states the psychological fact that "I dislike x." This differs from emotivism. Emotivism holds that moral statements merely express feelings. Private subjectivism, however, holds that moral statements do not express feelings but describe the psychological state of the speaker. An expression of feeling cannot be false. But if person A says "I dislike x," then this can be false if A really likes x but does not want to admit it. **Cultural relativism** is the view that statements like "X is right" state the sociological fact that "We in our culture dislike x."

Cultural relativism and private subjectivism are very much alike and will be criticized more fully in chapters twenty and twenty-one. But for now, it should be pointed out that few philosophers hold that these metaethical theories are adequate treatments of morality. The main reason is that they make moral statements into nonmoral statements. The statement "X is right" appears to be a moral statement that makes a normative claim about right and wrong, and it implies a statement about what one ought to do. But the psychological and sociological translations of this statement, "I like x" and "We in our culture like x," make no normative claims whatever. They assert what people happen to like. So they do not translate moral statements; they transform them inappropriately into nonmoral statements. Thus private subjectivism and cultural relativism cannot be adequate understandings of moral meaning.

Objectivist theories agree with subjectivist theories of moral meaning in holding that moral statements assert true or false statements of fact. However, rather than focusing on the speakers of moral statements, **objectivism** holds that moral statements are stating facts about the acts of morality themselves or the objects that are said to have value.

The statement "The apple is red" says something about the apple. The statements "Persons have value" and "Murder is wrong" say something about persons and acts of murder. Just as "The apple is red" asserts that the apple has a property (redness), so moral statements assert that persons or moral acts have certain properties. In short, objectivist theories hold that moral statements convey information about persons or moral acts by describing properties of those persons or acts.

It is here that agreement among objectivists ends. The two major versions of objectivism—ethical naturalism and ethical nonnaturalism—disagree over the nature of the moral properties that moral judgments ascribe to persons or acts. The debate between them is over the issue of moral reductionism (i.e., over whether or not moral properties can be reduced to or identified with nonmoral properties). Ethical naturalists say that such a reduction is correct, and ethical nonnaturalists say that moral properties are unique and cannot be reduced to nonmoral properties.

Ethical naturalism is a reductionist view that holds that ethical terms (*goodness, worth* and *right*) can be defined by or reduced to natural, scientific properties that are biological, psychological, sociological or physical in nature. For example, according to ethical naturalism the term *right* in "X is right" means one of the following: "What is approved by most people"; "What most people desire"; "What is approved by an impartial, ideal observer"; "What maximizes desire or interest"; "What furthers human survival." The important point here is that these moral terms and moral properties are not irreducibly moral in nature. Moral properties (e.g., worth, goodness or rightness) turn out to be properties that are biological or psychological.

Furthermore, according to ethical naturalism, these properties can be measured by science by giving them operational definitions. Consider an example. Suppose "X is right" means "X is what most people desire," and one goes on to argue that the presence of pleasure and the absence of pain is what most people desire. A scientist could measure the presence of pleasure and the absence of pain by defining such a state in physiological terms—the presence of a certain heart rate, the absence of certain impulses in the nervous system, slight coloration of the skin. "Rightness" means what is desired by most people; what is desired by most people is the presence of pleasure and the absence of pain; and pleasure and pain can be defined by certain physical traits of the body. Thus the moral property of rightness has been reduced to a natural property that can be measured.

Two major objections can be raised against ethical naturalism both based on its **moral reductionism**. First, it confuses an *is* with an *ought* by reducing the latter to the former. Moral properties are normative properties. They carry with them a moral "ought." If some act has the property of rightness, then one ought to do that act. But natural properties like the ones listed do not carry normativeness. They just are. Second, every attempted reduction of a moral property to a natural one has failed because there are cases where an act is right even if it does not have the natural property, and an act can have the natural property and not be right. For example, suppose one reduces the moral property of rightness in "X is right" to "X is what is approved by most people." This reduction is inadequate. For one thing, the majority can be wrong. What most people approve of can be morally wrong. If most people approved of torturing babies, then according to this version of ethical naturalism, this act would be right. But even though it was approved by most people, it would still be wrong. On the other hand, some acts can be right even if they are not approved of (or even thought of, for that matter) by most people.

Ethical nonnaturalism is the only view we have considered that holds that irreducible moral facts and properties really *exist* as part of the furniture of the universe. In addition to natural properties (redness and so forth), there are moral properties (rightness, goodness, worth), which persons and acts have and which moral statements ascribe to persons and acts. "X is right" ascribes an unanalyzable, irreducible moral property to X, just as "The apple is red" ascribes the natural property redness to the apple. Most Christian theists have advocated some form of ethical nonnaturalism since they hold that God himself has certain morally relevant value properties (goodness, holiness and so forth), that persons made in his image have worth and dignity (as he does) and that some acts have the property of moral rightness.

Critics of nonnaturalism often use what J. L. Mackie has called the argument from queerness, which has both a metaphysical and an epistemological component. Mackie argues:

> If there were objective values, then they would be entities or qualities or relations of a very strange sort, utterly different from anything else in the universe. Correspondingly, if we were aware of them, it would have to be by some special faculty of moral perception or intuition, utterly different from our ordinary ways of knowing everything else.[1]

Mackie is arguing—asserting might be a better word, for this is not much of an argument as it stands—that moral values are so odd that their existence would be strange and our ability to know them would be odd. But why should anyone agree with Mackie about this? If morals do exist, why would anyone expect them to be like other kinds of things? Mackie appears to be faulting moral values for not behaving like physical objects. But this is an absurd example of fault-finding. If moral values are not physical objects, then why should people expect them to be like physical objects? If Mackie is correct in his view, then a host of entities—numbers, persons, laws of logic, universals, sets and any other nonphysical entity—go by the boards because they are "queer."

Mackie's objection is a mere assertion of bias in favor of naturalism. It seems reasonable to say that if a physicalist version of philosophical naturalism is true, then objective moral values do not exist. But it is often the case in philosophy that one person's *modus ponens* is another's *modus tollens*. Mackie would affirm the antecedent and deny the objectivity of moral values. However, an opponent would deny the consequence and thus deny that a physicalist version of philosophical naturalism is true. In chapter twenty-four we will revisit this dialectic and see that the objectivity of moral values provides grounds for believing in the existence of God.

In sum, these are the major options in metaethics. In addition to the analysis of moral terms and assertions, another important issue in metaethics is the problem of justifying the moral point of view itself.

4 WHY SHOULD I BE MORAL?

A mature philosophy of life should include an answer to the question of why one should be moral. But the question "Why should I be moral?" needs clarification. Three points should help to clarify the question.

First, one can distinguish specific moral acts (an act of kindness, an act of self-sacrifice) from what philosophers call the moral point of view. The question "Why should I be moral?" is really asking, "Why should I adopt the moral point of view?" So it is important to understand what the moral point of view is. If one adopts the **moral point of view**, then one does the following: One subscribes to normative judgments about actions, things (persons, the environ-

[1]J. L. Mackie, *Ethics: Inventing Right and Wrong* (New York: Penguin, 1977), p. 38.

ment) and motives; one is willing to universalize his judgments; one seeks to form his moral views in a free, unbiased, enlightened way; one seeks to promote the good. In other words, if one adopts the moral point of view, one submits to and seeks to promote the dictates of normative, universalizable morality in a mature, unbiased, impartial way. One embraces the dictates of morality and seeks to live in light of the moral point of view. Such a viewpoint governs one's life and priorities. So understood, the question "Why should I be moral?" becomes the question "Why should I adopt the moral point of view as a guiding force over my life?"

Second, one can distinguish between motives and reasons for adopting the moral point of view. Regarding the former, the question asks what motivates one to adopt the moral point of view. Motives do not need to be rational factors. For example, one could say that he was motivated to adopt the moral point of view because it gave him approval from his parents and society or simply because of a certain urge or feeling to do so. Regarding reasons, the question asks what rational justification can be given for adopting the moral point of view. The question is usually framed in terms of reasons, but both reasons and motives are relevant to a full discussion of why one adopts the moral point of view.

Third, it is not clear what kind of justification the question is seeking. What kind of "should" is involved in "Why should I be moral?" If it is a **moral "should,"** then the question is asking for a moral justification for adopting the moral point of view. If a moral "should" is used in the question, then some philosophers think the question involves a pointless self-contradiction. For one is then asking for a moral reason for accepting moral reasons. In other words, if one is using a moral "should" in the question, then one is already reasoning from *within* the moral point of view, since one is already willing to acknowledge a moral answer to a moral question. But if one has already adopted the moral point of view, then there is not much point in asking for a moral reason for doing so. About the only answer one could give to the question would be that it is just morally right to adopt the moral point of view. But if one is willing to adopt the moral point of view because such an act is morally right, then one has already adopted the moral point of view without knowing it. So the question "Why should I be moral?" is not really using a moral sense of "should," and if it is, the only answer is that such an act is just the morally right thing to do.

But there is a different notion of "should" that is better suited as a part of the question. This is a **rational "should."** According to this sense of "should," one is not asking the question "Why should I be moral?" from within the moral point of view, but from outside the moral point of view altogether. In other words, one is asking the question "What rational justification can be given to me as to why it would be reasonable for me to adopt the moral point of view rather than some other point of view, say, an egoistic self-interested point of view by which I govern my life for my own best interests without regard for the moral point of view at all?" As one seeks to formulate a **rational life plan** for oneself, a well thought-out, reasonable approach to the way one will live one's life so as to be a rational person, why should the moral point of view be a part of that rational life plan? In sum, the question "Why should I be moral?" is asking for the motives, but more important, the reasons why someone should adopt the moral point of view as a part of a rational plan of life.

Part of the rational assessment of an ethical theory or, more generally, an entire worldview is the evaluation of the answer that theory or worldview provides to the question "Why should I be moral?" Different answers have been given to the question, but the two most prominent have been the egoistic and theistic replies. Roughly, the egoistic response says that one ought to be moral just in the case that it is in one's best interests to do so. In one way or another, theistic responses incorporate reference to the existence of God. For example, one ought to be moral because the moral law is true and is constituted by the nonarbitrary commands of a good, just, wise, loving God or because the moral law is grounded in the way we were designed by such a God to function properly. Ethical egoism will be examined in chapter nineteen and God's relationship to moral obligation will be analyzed in chapter twenty-seven. The question "Why should I be moral?" should be kept in mind while reflecting on those discussions.

CHAPTER SUMMARY

Ethics can be understood as the philosophical study of morality, but because value concepts such as "ought" have a nonmoral and moral usage, there is need to clarify the nature of morality. Certain conditions have been offered for characterizing a judgment as moral: It must be accepted as a supremely authoritative guide to conduct, attitudes and motives; it must be a prescriptive imperative; it must be universalizable; and it must make reference to things such as proper human flourishing, human dignity and so forth.

There are at least four different areas of study that focus on morality. Two are nonnormative: descriptive ethics and metaethics. Two are normative: normative ethics proper and applied ethics.

Various noncognitivist and cognitivist metaethical theories were analyzed. The former deny that moral statements are either true or false. Emotivism and imperativalism/prescriptivism are the main versions of noncognitivism. Cognitivist theories depict moral statements as indicatives. Subjective cognitivist theories (private subjectivism and cultural relativism) imply that moral statements convey information about the speaker of the moral statement. Objectivist theories imply that moral statements convey information about moral acts themselves or the objects (e.g., human persons), which are said to have value. Ethical naturalists claim that moral properties can be reduced to nonmoral properties, and ethical nonnaturalists disagree with this claim.

When properly understood, the question "Why should I be moral?" amounts to the question "What rational justification can be given to me as to why it would be reasonable for me to adopt the moral point of view rather than some other point of view, say, an egoistic self-interested point of view where I govern my life for my own best interests without regard for the moral point of view at all?"

CHECKLIST OF BASIC TERMS AND CONCEPTS

applied ethics
cognitivism
cultural relativism
descriptive ethics
descriptive, factual "is"
emotivism
ethical naturalism
ethical nonnaturalism
ethics
imperativalism/prescriptivism
metaethical relativism
metaethics (two areas of investigation)
moral point of view
moral reductionism
moral "should"
noncognitivism
normative ethics
normative ethics proper
objectivism
particularism
prescriptive, evaluative "ought"
private subjectivism
rational "should"
rational life plan
subjectivism
universalizable
value concepts

20

ETHICAL RELATIVISM
AND ABSOLUTISM

Man is the measure of all things:
of things that are, that they are;
of things that are not, that they are not.
PROTAGORAS ON TRUTH

[Protagoras] was saying, in other words,
that each individual's private impression is absolutely true.
But if that position is adopted, then it follows
that the same thing is and is not, that it is both good and bad,
and similarly for other contradictions;
because, after all, a given thing will seem beautiful to one group of people
and ugly to another, and by the theory in question
each of the conflicting appearances will be "the measure."
ARISTOTLE METAPHYSICS 1062^{B}13

1 INTRODUCTION

When a person approaches specific issues in applied ethics, such as abortion, capital punishment or euthanasia, he or she brings to those issues a set of background beliefs about general ethical topics. This is the way it should be. In any field of study, specific debates are argued within the framework of broad theories that are relevant to those debates. For example, if two historians are going to discuss the causes for the decline of the Roman Empire, they will utilize arguments rooted in broader theories about history, civilizations and so forth: Do historians create facts or discover them? Do we have good records about ancient Rome? How does one determine for a civilization the relative importance of economic factors compared to other factors? And so on.

Similarly, when we attempt to analyze specific ethical issues, certain broad topics are important. What is the difference between a factual judgment (e.g., people disapprove of murder) and a value judgment (e.g., people ought to disapprove of murder). Are all values relative, or are some absolute? What does it mean to say that some moral value is an absolute? The debate between moral relativism and absolutism is of central importance to ethical reasoning, and this debate is especially pressing in contemporary culture. Louis Pojman observes,

Eskimos allow their elderly to die by starvation, whereas we believe that this practice is morally wrong. The Spartans of ancient Greece believed, and Dobu of New Guinea believe today, that stealing is morally right, but we believe that it is wrong. The Nuer of East Africa throw deformed infants to the hippopotamus, but we abhor infanticide. Ruth Benedict describes a tribe in Melanesia that views cooperation and kindness as vices, and Colin Turnbull had documented that the Ik in Northern Uganda have no sense of duty toward their children or parents. Some societies make it a duty for children to kill (sometimes strangle) their aging parents. Eskimos sometimes abandon their elderly as they move on to new locations. Sexual practices vary over time and clime. Some cultures permit homosexual behavior, whereas others condemn it. Some cultures practice cannibalism, whereas we detest it. Cultural relativism is well documented, and custom seems "king o'er all."[1]

In this chapter, we will do two things: state and evaluate different theses that have been associated with ethical relativism, and state and evaluate different forms of ethical absolutism.

2 ETHICAL RELATIVISM

In this section we will clarify and evaluate six different theses that, in one way or another, have been associated with relativism. But first, let us look briefly at an important philosophical distinction between facts and values.

Consider two cultures, A and B. In culture A, it is thought to be a moral duty to benefit an elderly person by taking his or her life when that person gets old. In culture B, such an act is morally forbidden. Do cultures A and B differ over the values they embrace? Maybe not. They may both agree on the truth of the moral proposition *Do not murder an innocent human being.* However, because of a difference in factual beliefs, culture A (in contrast to culture B) may not consider taking the life of an elderly parent to be murder. Suppose culture A believes that one must take one's body into the afterlife and hunt for food with it forever. In such a case, one's happiness and safety in the afterlife would depend on the condition of one's body at death, and taking an elderly person's life would not be murder, but an example of morally justifiable life taking. Or so claim members of A. In culture B, no such beliefs about the afterlife are present, and thus taking the life of an elderly person is an act of murder. Cultures A and B agree about moral values (murdering an innocent human being is wrong), but they differ in their factual beliefs about what the world is like.

2.1
FACTS AND
VALUES

In general, a **fact** or factual belief involves a **description** about the way the world *is:* empirically, metaphysically, religiously. Some descriptions have nothing to do with morality, such as, "The lamp is on the desk." If a descriptive statement does involve morality, then it is a statement *about* morality; for example, "Most people in America think racism is wrong." In contrast, a **value** or value belief involves the adherence to some moral proposition that *prescribes* what morally *ought* to be. An "ought" statement makes a **prescription**. Moral, prescriptive statements are statements *of* morality, e.g., "Racism is wrong" or "Racism is morally permissible." These differences are summarized in table 20.1.

---

[1]Louis P. Pojman, *Ethics: Discovering Right and Wrong* (Belmont, Calif.: Wadsworth, 1990), p. 19.

Table 20.1 Distinctions between facts and values

fact	is	description	statement *about* morality
value	ought	prescription	statement *of* morality

While the distinction between facts and values is fairly clear, nevertheless, this distinction has been used in two very different ways. Some have used *fact* to stand for any state of affairs that is real and part of the mind-independent world. For them, values are not facts, and thus they are not objectively real in the mind-independent world. Values turn out to be subjective in one way or another. For example, to say that friendship has value merely says that I subjectively value friendship. A second, more adequate way of viewing the distinction between facts and values is as follows. First, values are real entities in the world. For example, to say that humans have intrinsic value is to say they have the property of intrinsic worth and this is true of them irrespective of what people believe to be so. Second, there are **value facts**—descriptions of what ought to be—and **nonvalue** or **"mere" facts**—descriptions of what simply is—since both kinds of facts are real. On this view, the distinction between facts and values is the distinction between value facts and "mere" facts. Thus the importance of the distinction amounts to the idea that just because something *is* the case, it doesn't automatically follow that it *ought* to be the case. We are using the distinction in the second sense and will use *fact* for nonvalue or "mere" fact.

Differences in factual beliefs can play a decisive role in ethical disagreements. For example, when a Jehovah's Witness refuses a blood transfusion and dies, does this imply that he or she accepts the moral appropriateness of suicide? Not at all. Jehovah's Witnesses may agree with others that suicide is morally forbidden. But because they believe that God disapproves of eating blood and transfusions are examples of eating blood, these religious factual beliefs lead them to the following position: An act of refusing a blood transfusion is not an act of suicide but rather an act of sacrificing one's life for God.

The distinction between facts and values can give us insight into **three different sources for moral disagreements**, which can be illustrated with the abortion controversy. First, a moral dispute can be about a factual difference. For example, debates about abortion sometimes involve debates about whether the fetus is a person or a human being. Such a debate is a factual debate, not primarily a moral one, though of course it has serious moral implications. Both sides in the debate can agree that murder or manslaughter is wrong, but they differ about whether abortion is murder or manslaughter because they have different factual beliefs about the status of the fetus.

The next two sources of moral disagreements involve value differences. To begin with, a value difference can occur when one side affirms and the other side denies a moral proposition, such as the proposition that it is wrong to intentionally kill an innocent human being. On the other hand, a value difference can occur when both sides accept two or more moral principles, but weigh their relative strengths differently. For example, the right to life and the right to choice could both be embraced by each side of the abortion debate, but the two sides weigh them differently. Pro-life advocates could hold that the right to life takes precedence over the right to choose, and pro-choice advocates could reverse this order. In general, then, there are three important sources of moral disagreement. A test for when such a disagreement is rooted in a value difference is this: Is there a moral principle one side affirms and the other denies or are there two or more principles being weighed differently?

We have seen that ethical disputes involve disagreements about facts and values, and one should try to understand precisely what is being debated in a particular ethical dispute. The distinction between facts and values is also helpful in understanding six different theses often associated with ethical relativism.

First, there is **cultural** or **descriptive relativism**. This is the descriptive, factual thesis, often expressed by anthropologists, sociologists and historians, that societies do, in fact, have disparate views on basic ethical judgments. A **basic ethical disagreement** is one that remains when all the factual issues are agreed upon and when two cultures mean the same thing by the same ethical concepts like "right" or "wrong," but disagree as to what acts are right and wrong. Thus a basic ethical disagreement will be a value difference. Cultural relativism, then, amounts to the thesis that what is considered right and wrong or the way moral principles are weighed relative to each other varies from culture to culture. There is an individual version of this thesis—right and wrong varies from individual to individual—but we will focus here only on the cultural version.

2.2
Six Theses
Associated
with Ethical
Relativism

2.2.1
Cultural or
Descriptive
Relativism

Two things should be kept in mind when evaluating cultural relativism. First, it is not a moral thesis at all. It is not a prescriptive statement of morality, but a descriptive, factual statement about morality. As such it entails no substantive moral thesis whatever. In particular, it does not follow from cultural relativism that there are no moral absolutes that are true for all people, nor does it follow that these absolutes cannot be known. Different cultures differ over the shape of the earth, but this does not imply that no one is right about the earth's shape or that no one is rational in believing one's view about the earth's shape. The same line of reasoning applies to cultural relativism.

Someone could respond that sometimes the fact that people cannot agree about something shows that there is no real fact of the matter at stake, that is, that no one is right and no one is wrong. On the other hand, from the simple existence of unresolved disagreements about something it still does not follow that no one is right. This further conclusion needs to be argued for, not merely asserted. Moreover, if a case can be made for true moral values (see below), then the presence of disagreements in moral views shows something other than the relative truth value of moral statements—for example, that people often form their moral views for self-serving, sinful reasons. Finally, ethical differences may not be as widespread as many people think. This leads to a second observation.

Cultural relativism may even be a weak factual thesis. When due consideration is given to factual clarification, many apparent moral differences turn out to be merely factual, not moral. This lends support to the claim that cultures exhibit widespread agreement regarding basic values; for instance, no culture has valued cowardice in battle. So it may well be that many cultural differences turn out to be factual differences. The Christian doctrine of general revelation and the idea of **natural moral law**—the notion that there are true, universally binding moral principles knowable by all people and rooted in creation and the way things are made—lead us to suspect at least some widespread agreement about moral values. On the other hand, there do appear to be genuine disputes among cultures about basic ethical judgments. And the biblical doctrine of original sin should lead us to suspect that cultures can become morally twisted and repugnant depending on the degree to which that culture lives and thinks in light of general or special revelation.

2.2.2
NORMATIVE OR
ETHICAL
RELATIVISM

A second ethical thesis is called **normative relativism** or **ethical relativism**. This substantive moral thesis holds that everyone ought to act in accordance with the agent's own society's code. What is right for one society is not necessarily right for another society. For example, society A may have in its code "Adultery is morally permissible," and society B may have "Adultery is morally forbidden." A and B mean the same thing by "adultery," "morally permissible" and "morally forbidden," and thus these societies genuinely differ over the rightness of adultery.

Put differently, normative relativism implies that moral propositions are not simply true or false. Rather, the truth values of moral principles themselves are relative to the beliefs of a given culture. For example, "Murder is wrong" is not true plain and simply; it is "true for culture A," but, perhaps, "false for culture B." The point here is not just that there is a certain relativity in the *application* of moral principles. For example, two cultures could both hold that "One should maintain sexual fidelity in marriage," but apply this differently due to factual differences about what counts as a marriage (e.g., one wife or several wives). Factual diversity can lead to differences in the way a moral rule is applied.

Normative relativism goes beyond this type of diversity and asserts that the truth values of moral principles themselves are relative to a given culture, e.g., whether or not one ought to maintain sexual fidelity itself could be true relative to one culture and false relative to another culture. As with cultural relativism, there is a difference between individual and cultural versions. Individual normative relativism (also called **subjectivism**) says that the truth of moral rules is relative to the beliefs of each individual; cultural normative relativism (also called **conventionalism**) makes moral truth relative to entire cultures or societies.

The majority of moral philosophers and theologians do not embrace normative relativism because of the seriousness of the criticisms raised against it. First, it is difficult to define what a society is or to specify in a given case what the relevant society is. Consider societies A and B above. If a man from A has sex with a woman from B in a hotel in a third society C with a different view from either A or B, which is the relevant society for determining whether the act was right or wrong? Second, a related objection is the fact that we are often simultaneously a member of several different societies that may hold different moral values: our nuclear or extended family; our neighborhood, school, church or social clubs; our place of employment; our town, state, country and the international community. Which society is the relevant one? What if I am simultaneously members of two societies and one allows but the other forbids a certain moral action? What do I do in this case?

Third, normative relativism suffers from a problem known as the reformer's dilemma. If normative relativism is true, then it is logically impossible for a society to have a virtuous, moral reformer like Jesus Christ, Gandhi or Martin Luther King Jr. Why? Moral reformers are members of a society who stand outside that society's code and pronounce a need for reform and change in that code. However, if an act is right if and only if it is in keeping with a given society's code, then the moral reformer is by definition an immoral person, for his views are at odds with those of his society. Moral reformers must always be wrong because they go against the code of their society. But any view that implies moral reformers are impossible is defective.

Put differently, normative relativism implies that neither cultures (if conventionalism is in view) nor individuals (if subjectivism is in view) can improve their moral code. The only thing they can do is change it. Why? Consider any change in a code from believing, say, racism is right to racism is wrong. How should we evaluate this change? All the normative relativism can say is that, from the perspective of the earlier code, the new principle is wrong and from the perspective of the new code, the old principle is wrong. In short, there has merely been a change in perspective. No sense can be given to the idea that a new code reflects an improvement on an old code because this idea requires a vantage point outside of and above the society's (or individual's) code from which to make that judgment. And it is precisely such a vantage point that normative relativism denies.

Some relativists respond to this by claiming that moral reformers are allowed in their view because all moral reformers do is to make explicit what was already implicit but overlooked in the society's code. Thus, if a society already has a principle that persons ought to be treated equally, then this implicitly contains a prohibition against racism even though it may not be explicitly noted. The moral reformer merely makes this explicit by calling people to think more carefully about their code. Unfortunately, this claim is simply false. Many moral reformers do, in fact, call people to alter their codes. They do not merely make clear what was already contained in preexisting codes.

Other relativists claim that they can allow for the existence of moral reformers by recognizing that societies may contain, implicitly or explicitly, a principle in their code that says "Follow the advice of moral reformers." But, again, this response does not work. For one thing, what does it mean to call these reformers "moral" if they do not keep the rest of their society's code? If, on the other hand, the reformer does keep and believe in the rest of his or her society's code, how could a change in that code count as a moral improvement? A reformer could have the *power* to bring change, but how could he or she have the moral *authority* to do so? And why call the change a moral improvement? Second, moral reformers can exist without any such principle being in a society's code, so the presence or absence of such a principle is irrelevant. Third, what if there are two or more moral reformers with mutually exclusive agendas operating at the same time? Which one do we follow? Finally, the presence of such a principle in a society's code would place all the other moral principles in jeopardy, for they would be temporary principles subject to the whims of the next moral reformer. In fact, before someone could honestly follow a principle in their society's code, they would have to make a good faith effort to make sure a moral reformer had not changed that part of the code that day.

Fourth, some acts are wrong regardless of social conventions. Advocates of this criticism usually adopt the standpoint of epistemological particularism (see chap. 4) and claim that all people can know that some things are wrong, such as torturing babies for fun, stealing as such, greed as such without first requiring criteria for knowing how it is that they do, in fact, know such things. Thus an act (e.g., torturing babies for fun) can be wrong even if society says it is right, and an act can be right even if society says it is wrong. In fact, an act can be right or wrong even if society says nothing whatever about that act.

Fifth, it is difficult to see how one society could be justified in morally blaming another society in certain cases. According to normative relativism, one should act in keeping with his society's code and others should act in keeping with their societies' codes. If Smith does an act that is right in his code but wrong in mine, how can I criticize his act as wrong?

One could respond to this objection by pointing out that society A may have in its code the principle that one should criticize acts of, say, murder, regardless of where they occur. So members of A could criticize such acts in other societies. But such a rule further reveals the inconsistency in normative relativism. Given this rule and the fact that normative relativism is true and embraced by members of A, those in A seem to be in the position of holding that members of B ought to murder (since their code says it is right) and I ought to criticize members of B because my code says I should. Thus I criticize members of B as immoral and at the same time hold that their acts should have been done. Further, why should members of B care about what members of A think? After all, if normative relativism is true, there is nothing intrinsically right about the moral views of society A.

2.2.3
METAETHICAL
RELATIVISM

A third version of ethical relativism is called metaethical relativism. According to normative relativism, cultures A and B mean the same thing by moral terms of appraisal such as *right* and *wrong*. Relativism does not enter into the picture at the level of conceptual meaning, but at the level of judgment as to what counts as right and wrong. In this view, two societies can genuinely differ over the moral worth of some action or practice.

However, according to **metaethical relativism** (also called **conceptual relativism**), the meanings of moral terms of appraisal are themselves relative. Put metaphysically, there is no such property as goodness or rightness. Rather, goodness or rightness is a relation between an act and a society. Put linguistically, the statement "X is right" is shorthand for the statement "X is right for society A." The very meaning of *right* (and other moral terms) is relative to a particular culture.

Metaethical relativism is even more radical than normative relativism. It suffers from some of the same problems that were raised against normative relativism—problems of defining a society and determining the relevant society for the act and agent, the reformer's dilemma, and the fact that some acts are intuitively wrong regardless of what societies mean by *right* and *wrong*.

Metaethical relativism also suffers from an additional objection that makes it highly implausible. If metaethical relativism is true, then it is impossible for two societies to even have a moral difference. Suppose society A holds that "Murder is right" and B holds that "Murder is wrong." According to metaethical relativism, these two statements are incomplete translations. What is really being said by A is "What counts as murder-to-us is right-to-us"; what is said by B is "What counts as murder-to-us is wrong-to-us." In this case, no moral dispute is occurring, for both statements could be true. Societies A and B equivocate regarding the meaning of *murder, right* and *wrong*. Now any moral theory that rules out the possibility of crosscultural moral conflict appears to be mistaken, for it is a basic feature of the moral life that, at least occasionally, societies do in fact differ. In fact, some fail in their ethical duties (e.g., Hitler and the Nazis). Thus moral statements do not mean what metaethical relativists tell us they mean.

A fourth thesis often associated with ethical relativism is **ethical skepticism**. This is the view that no one's ethical beliefs are true, or even if they are, no one is ever in a position to know that they are true. There are two main versions of ethical skepticism: an epistemological version and an ontological one. The **epistemological version** does not state that there are no objective moral values that are true; it merely holds that even if such values exist, we can never know what they are. The **ontological version** of ethical skepticism claims that there is no moral knowledge because there are simply no objective moral truths to be known. We will not look specifically at the ontological version of ethical skepticism except to note that there are two main reasons why someone could hold it. First, someone could hold it because of one's ethical views in general. Someone could embrace ontological ethical skepticism because that person is a normative or metaethical relativist, since both deny that moral principles have objective truth values or meanings. Similarly, one could hold it because one was a noncognitivist in metaethics (see chap. 19). Second, someone could hold the view because of his or her position regarding what it means to exist. For example, someone could hold that everything that exists is composed of matter and since values are not composed of matter, then they cannot exist. Theories of existence, and other related metaphysical themes are studied in part three of this text.

2.2.4
ETHICAL
SKEPTICISM

The epistemological version of ethical skepticism is usually embraced because one's overall theory of epistemology (see part I) does not leave room for moral knowledge. For example, one could embrace skepticism in general, including moral skepticism. Or one could hold to a strict form of empiricism—a statement *P* is knowable if and only if it can be verified by one of the five senses—and go on to claim that moral knowledge is not empirically verifiable.

Three things can be said against ethical skepticism. First, one could adopt the standpoint of particularism and claim that it is self-evidently true that some things are simply right or wrong—mercy as such is a virtue; rape as such is wrong. The skeptic could respond that this claim is question-begging. He could ask us how we know these things are wrong. The particularist could reply that one does not need a criterion that tells us how we know the above claims before we are rationally entitled to make them. Further, we have more grounds for believing that mercy as such is a virtue than we have for believing that ethical skepticism is true. Thus the burden of proof seems to be on the skeptic in this case.

A second problem with ethical skepticism is this. It often happens that the philosophical reasons that motivate ethical skepticism in the first place turn out to be self-refuting. A statement is self-refuting if it falsifies itself and thus cannot be true. The statements "I do not exist," "There are no truths whatever," "I cannot utter a sentence in English" (uttered in English) are all self-refuting. Sometimes ethical skepticism is an outgrowth of views, like strict empiricism, that are self-refuting if one claims to know them. The empiricist principle stated above cannot itself be verified by the senses and thus is unknowable by its own standards.

Finally, if ethical skepticism is true, one cannot recommend any moral behavior whatever, including toleration of different moral opinions or even the alleged moral obligation to be skeptical. One cannot deny the existence or knowability of moral "oughts" in one breath and affirm a moral "ought" in the next breath; at least one cannot do this and remain consistent.

2.2.5 COMBINATORIAL RELATIVISM

A different form of relativism is called combinatorial relativism because it involves a combination of absolutism and relativism. To understand this position, we need to make a distinction between a formal and a material moral principle. A **formal principle** states necessary conditions for the thing in question and gives the structure of that thing. It can be likened to the mold used to form a statue. It provides the necessary structure for what that statue will be like, but by itself it is not a statue. A **material principle** states a sufficient condition for the thing in question and gives its content. The material principle is like the content you pour into the mold to get the statue. The whole statue is a combination of its formal and material principle.

Here is another illustration. The formal principle of justice states that equals ought to be treated equally and unequals ought (or at least may) be treated unequally. This is true as far as it goes, but it gives no material content, no specification of the respect by which people may be treated unequally. Different answers to this question constitute different material principles of justice: to each an equal share (egalitarianism), to each according to need (Marxism), to each according to individual effort or merit (libertarianism), to each according to social contribution (utilitarianism). The formal principle of justice states necessary conditions for any further specification of a complete principle of justice. It provides the mold into which various material principles of justice, various contents, are poured.

Now one of the main purposes of a moral rule is that it serve as an action guide. It must be specific enough to specify for us what actions we are and are not to do. Thus adequate moral rules must be combinations of formal principles (e.g., pursue the good and avoid the evil, respect persons) and material principles (e.g., one way to respect persons is to tell them the truth). Formal principles alone lack the substance necessary to serve as action guides.

Combinatorial relativism is view that combines a formal principle, taken as a moral absolute, with a material principle that is taken to be relative. For example, some versions of combinatorial relativism state that we ought to respect creatures with biographical lives, or that we have a duty to pursue the good life and to allow others to do the same, or we have a duty not to harm others. Note that these principles, as stated, are formal principles only. Combinatorial relativists take them to be absolute formal principles, that is, principles that are objectively true and binding without exception. However, as they stand, they do not give enough content to qualify as action guides because the terms "biographical lives," "the good life" and "harm," as used by combinatorial relativists, do not have the content necessary to give the principles substance. When material content is given to these notions by combinatorial relativists, the resulting action guides become relative to the values, interests and desires of each individual. For example, a "biographical life" is the sum of one's aspirations, goals, desires, plans, etc. *that are considered worthwhile from the individual's own personal standpoint.* "The good life" is the notion of happiness and flourishing that *each individual freely, autonomously chooses for himself or herself.* And a "harm," in this context, is *whatever would count as a loss for an individual from his or her own point of view.*

The main problem with combinatorial relativism is that it collapses into individual subjectivism. Why? Because the action guide formed by giving material content (what it is to have biographical life, to pursue the good life, to be harmed) to the formal principle (pursue the good life, don't harm others) is relativized to individual subjective preferences. Thus combinatorial relativism suffers from the objections that can be raised against individual normative relativism. For example, there is no room in combinatorial relativism to value objectively some understandings of the good life over others. Thus a person who freely chooses to spend his life pushing a wooden block around the sidewalk has as much of a life of flourishing as does the person like Mother Teresa who freely chooses to devote her life to Jesus Christ and the service of the poor and needy. However, some forms of "the good life" are better than others and, indeed, some choices of "the good life" (e.g., one devoted to self-mutilation and narcissism) are bad forms of life. The simple fact is that some lifestyles are objectively more valuable than others and some lifestyles are actually worthless even if they are chosen freely. Combinatorial relativism does not leave room for this fact and this counts against it.

Finally, the principle of tolerance is often associated with the debate about relativism in the following way: it is often thought that the principle is implied by relativism but is at odds with some form of absolutism because the latter is dogmatic and judgmental and the former is more tolerant in orientation. In order to evaluate this claim, we need to get clear on what the **principle of tolerance** is. Actually, it has been defined in different ways, but two senses can be distinguished. According to the **classical sense of the principle of tolerance**, a person holds that his own moral views are true and those of his opponent are false. But he still respects his opponent as a person and his right to make a case for his views. Thus someone has a duty to tolerate a different moral view, not in the sense of thinking it is morally correct, but quite the opposite, in the sense that a person will continue to value and respect one's opponent, to treat him with dignity, to recognize his right to argue for and propagate his ideas and so forth. Strictly speaking, on the classic view, one tolerates persons, not their ideas. In this sense, even though someone disapproves of another's moral beliefs and

2.2.6
THE PRINCIPLE
OF TOLERANCE

practices, he or she will not inappropriately interfere with them. However, it is consistent with this view that a person judges his opponent's views to be wrong and dedicates himself to doing everything morally appropriate to counteract those views, such as using argument and persuasion. It should be clear that the classic sense of tolerance is really an absolutist position and is inconsistent with normative and metaethical relativism and ethical skepticism. If a person does not hold another position to be morally false, what is there to tolerate? Surely, it is not just the fact that one doesn't like the view in question, but that he judges it mistaken.

The **modern version of tolerance**, popular in the general culture, goes beyond the classical version in claiming that one should not even judge that other people's viewpoints are wrong. How does this view square with relativism? It is not at all clear. For one thing, this principle of tolerance does not follow from cultural relativism. From the fact that cultures differ in basic ethical judgments, no moral duties whatever follow. Second, normative relativism implies that one ought to be tolerant if the principle of tolerance is in that person's social code and one ought to be intolerant if the principle of intolerance is in that person's social code. So the morality of tolerance does not clearly follow from normative or metaethical relativism for that matter. Normative relativism does allow for the principle of tolerance, but it also allows for the principle of intolerance in the same way. Combinatorial relativism does, in fact, imply that we ought not to pass judgment on the freely chosen understanding of the good life of others. But since some forms of "the good life" are actually worthless or less valuable than others, this feature of combinatorial relativism is a vice and not a virtue. Finally, the moral duty to be tolerant does not follow from ethical skepticism because no moral duties whatever follow from ethical skepticism. It seems, then, that the modern notion of tolerance is not an easy fit with different versions of relativism, in spite of what many people think.

In sum, the various versions of relativism are extremely problematic. Relativism does not appear to be a defensible moral doctrine, and hence, some form of absolutism would seem to follow. Let us look briefly at the nature of absolutism.

3 ABSOLUTISM

3.1
THE NATURE OF
ABSOLUTISM

What does it mean to claim that some moral principle P is an absolute? There are at least three answers to this question. First, one can mean that P is objectively and unchangingly true irrespective of the beliefs of individuals or cultures. Someone who holds this form of **absolutism** would embrace one or more of the following: (1) Moral statements have truth values which make no reference to the beliefs of individuals or cultures. (2) There are objectively good/bad arguments for the truth of moral positions people take. (3) Nonmoral facts (e.g., persons exist) and moral facts (irreducibly moral properties like goodness) are relevant to the assessment of the truth value of moral statements. (4) When two moral statements conflict, only one can be true. (5) There is a single true morality. The main thing to keep in mind here is that this first understanding of *absolute* emphasizes the fact that we discover moral values, we do not merely invent moral beliefs. This is the most fundamental sense of the term used by moral absolutists.

A second understanding of an absolute is as follows. A moral absolute is true and completely exceptionless. This is sometimes put by saying that a moral absolute is **universalizable**: it is equally binding on all people at all times in relevantly similar circumstances. An **exception** to a moral principle is a case in which that principle normally applies, but for some reason it does not apply in this particular instance. On this understanding of a moral absolute, moral principles have no exceptions.

There are two important issues related to this notion of an absolute. The first one is the question of whether or not the definition of moral terms like *lying* or *suicide* are purely descriptive or evaluative. In **descriptive definitions of moral terms**, the definition merely describes a certain behavior without including a moral evaluation (positive or negative) as part of the definition. *Lying* could be defined as intentionally deceiving another. *Suicide* could be defined as "directly terminating one's life regardless of the circumstances." By contrast, a more widely held view implies that moral definitions are essentially **evaluative definitions**—they include a positive or negative evaluation as part of moral definitions themselves. Thus *lying* is defined as intentionally deceiving another in an immoral way. *Suicide* could be defined as immorally and directly terminating one's own life.

How are these different approaches to moral terms related to the second sense of a moral absolute? In this way: if moral terms are defined in purely descriptive ways, then it is hard to avoid the existence of exceptions to moral rules because in this case, faking in basketball, bluffing in a card game or tricking someone to come to a surprise birthday party would all be cases of lying and therefore exceptions to the rule "Do not lie." Similarly, a soldier who takes a pill to cause his death to avoid giving away secrets to the enemy, a monk who burns himself in protest, a truck driver who drives off a bridge to his death to avoid hitting children all commit suicide, but these would be morally appropriate exceptions to the rule "Do not commit suicide." If, on the other hand, we take an evaluative approach to moral definitions, these cases would not be exceptions to their respective moral rules because they would not count as legitimate examples of those rules in the first place. For example, faking in basketball would not be counted as a lie, the truck driver case would not be counted as a suicide.

A second issue of related importance is the relevance of the exceptionless nature of moral principles to various slippery slope arguments. In one way or another, **slippery slope arguments** attempt to show someone that if they take a first step, they will find themselves unavoidably heading in the direction of embracing an unacceptable consequence. Slippery slope arguments are often used to shift the burden of proof onto one's opponent in a debate. There are different types of slippery slope arguments. First, there is a **logical slippery slope argument**. This argument starts by asserting that practice A is wrong and it goes on to claim that practice B is similar to practice A in morally relevant ways and, therefore, practice B is wrong as well. An opponent of capital punishment could use this against an advocate of capital punishment as follows: Practice A (intentionally killing a human being) is wrong. Practice B (capital punishment) is similar to practice A in morally relevant ways, and thus practice B (capital punishment) is wrong.

The main issue in logical slippery slope arguments is whether or not practices A and B are similar in morally relevant ways. In the example just cited, the advocate of capital punishment could try to show that it is relevantly different from intentionally killing a human being, e.g., the former is done by the state against a person guilty of a capital offense, the latter is done by an individual acting on his own against an innocent person. Logical slippery slope arguments are applications to moral debate of the insight that moral principles are exceptionless and universalizable.

There are at least three other types of slippery slope arguments.[2] These arguments can be appropriate, but they are not clearly related to the notion of an absolute as a universalizable principle. First, there is a **precedent slippery slope**: If practice A is allowed, it will function as a precedent, which will set up a further precedent and so on, until you reach a point of no return. Once you let the camel's nose in the tent, there will be no stopping him. For example, some have argued that if we start an affirmative action, quota system of hiring based on factor X (e.g., race), then this will set a precedent for affirmative action based on factor Y (e.g., sexual orientation), then on factor Z, and so on.

Second, there is a **sorites slippery slope**: A sorites argument (from Greek *sōros*, meaning "heap") focuses on paradoxes that arise from minor variations is some situation. For example, one cannot take a single grain of sand and form a large heap of sand by adding one grain to the original, nor can one form a large heap of sand by adding one grain to the twosome formed from the original and the second grain of sand. Generalizing, it would seem that no matter how many single grains of sand are added to form a new whole, one will never arrive at a large heap of sand, yet this is absurd and the paradox needs to be solved. Often, sorites paradoxes are generated by the presence of a vague, variable term ("large heap") that is hard to make precise in a nonarbitrary way. Likewise, in a moral sorites slippery slope argument, a certain moral practice is characterized by a vague term that is hard to make precise in a nonarbitrary way. In this case, there is no clear cut-off point for when the practice is no longer allowable. For example, some have argued that if we allow the termination of life because that life does not have a "sufficient quality of life" or is not "a meaningful life" or is not a "life with biological worthiness," then there will be no nonarbitrary way to limit this practice due to the vagueness of the terms in question.

Third, there is a **causal slippery slope**: practice A is wrong; if practice B is allowed it will contribute to an increase in practice A, and thus practice B should be forbidden. For example, some argue that child molestation is wrong and that if pornography is allowed it will lead to an increase in child molestation, and thus pornography should be forbidden.

In sum, the second view of a moral absolute implies that it is a true, universally valid and exceptionless principle binding on all people at all times in circumstances similar in a morally relevant way. Sometimes this position is called **objectivism**. Objectivism is sometimes considered a version of absolutism (as we are doing) and sometimes it is treated as a rival to absolutism. In that case, the term *absolutism* is not used for each of the three views we are currently

---

[2]See Douglas Walton, *Slippery Slope Arguments* (Oxford: Clarendon, 1992), chap. 1.

discussing, but rather it is reserved solely for the next view.

A third, more stringent understanding of an absolute is the notion that an absolute is such that it is a true, exceptionless moral principle that has the **highest degree of incumbency**. In this view, a moral statement only qualifies as an absolute if it cannot be overridden by a more weighty principle. An absolute is like an ace. It can trump (override) all rivals but cannot itself be trumped. Put differently, all moral principles are equally weighty.

It would seem that this understanding of an absolute is too strong. Surely, if a moral statement did have the highest degree of incumbency, it would be an absolute. But we do seem to have absolute (objectively true, exceptionless) duties that can be overridden by more important duties. The notion of weightier and less weighty absolutes is not unintelligible, and in fact, it plays an important role in the moral life. To see this, consider what philosophers call a prima facie duty. A **prima facie duty** is an objectively true, exceptionless moral duty that can be overridden by a weightier duty in a specific instance. When this occurs, the prima facie duty does not disappear, but continues to apply to the specific instance in question and make its presence felt. An **exemption** to a moral absolute occurs when that absolute is overridden by a weightier duty.

The difference between an exemption and an exception is this. When there is an exemption, the overridden principle continues to apply. With an exception, the excepted principle no longer applies at all. Suppose a professor stipulates that all papers must be handed in exactly on time and gives a due date for the first paper. Suppose, further, that Sally has overriding grounds for getting the paper in late (say, she was seriously ill). If the situation envisioned amounts to an exception to the tardiness rule, then the rule simply vanishes, and Sally starts from scratch with the professor. She could just as easily argue that the paper could be turned in two years or two weeks later because there is no principle of tardiness any longer relevant. It has been set aside. However, if the tardiness rule is exempted in the envisioned situation, then while overridden by Sally's illness, it still informs the situation and, in this case, grounds the professor's requirement that the paper be turned in as soon as Sally is well. Arguably, exemptions do happen to moral duties but exceptions do not.

Prima facie duties can be clarified by an illustration. In medical ethics, a number of prima facie moral absolutes are often relevant to ethical dilemmas. Here are some of those principles:

- **The principle of autonomy**: A competent person has the right to determine his or her own course of medical action in accordance with a plan he or she chooses. We have a duty to respect the wishes and desires expressed by a competent patient and securing informed consent is a way of doing this.

- **The principle of nonmaleficence**: One should refrain from inflicting harm (or unduly risking the infliction of harm) on another. Nonmaleficence requires me to refrain from doing something harmful to another.

- **The principle of beneficence**: One should act in order to further the welfare and benefits of another and to prevent evil or harm to that person. Beneficence requires me to do something for someone else.

- **The principle of honesty**: We have a duty to deal honestly with others.

- **The principle of life preservation**: We have a duty to preserve and protect human life whenever possible.

Sometimes these duties can come into conflict and one can override another. For example, a woman at a nursing home can request to forego her kidney dialysis treatments and be allowed to die. Here the principle of autonomy
requires us to honor her request, but the principles of nonmaleficence, beneficence and life preservation require us to deny her request.

Here is another example: On the way to the emergency room, an ambulance
nurse was monitoring the vital signs of a thirty-five-year-old man who had just
had a heart attack. Suddenly, he asked her if he had undergone a heart attack.
Based on her medical knowledge and his anxious state, she knew that if she told
him the truth, it would place him at risk. Here the principle of autonomy was
conflicting with nonmaleficence and beneficence. She judged that autonomy
was a prima facie duty, so she exempted it by changing the subject. This was an
exemption, because the principle implies that she needed his informed consent
to continue and she did not inform him of what was going on. He asked her
again so she told him a half truth by saying that things were going to be fine at
the hospital. Finally, he said if she did not answer his question straightforwardly, he would assume that he had a heart attack. At this point the nurse lied
to the patient. Regardless of your assessment of her actions, this case illustrated
how autonomy was a prima facie duty. Note that even though the nurse exempted it at first, she did so as gently as needed to honor the higher principles
of nonmaleficence and beneficence. Autonomy was not excepted (she did not
feel free to ignore it altogether), but it was exempted (it continued to make its
presence felt even though overridden). If the situation were an exception to autonomy, then the principle would not be applicable and there would be no reason to regard the principle at all.

This third view of an absolute does not recognize the existence of prima facie
duties and, for this reason, many believe it to be too strong. We have examined
three views regarding the nature of a moral absolute. In the process, we have
entered into a discussion of cases where, at least on the surface, two or more
moral absolutes seem to come into unavoidable conflict. How should we view
situations like these? Our discussion of the various understandings of an absolute puts us in a position to understand the differences between three different
answers to this question.[3]

First, there is **unqualified absolutism**. This is the view that all moral duties
are equally weighty, that the third sense of an absolute above is correct, and
thus that there are no prima facie duties. All supposed inescapable moral dilemmas are only apparently unavoidable; there will always be a way to escape the
dilemma. The second and third views are called **conflicting absolutism** (also
called the **lesser of two evils view**) and **graded absolutism** (also called the
greater of two goods view). Both positions accept the existence of prima facie

---

[3]For more on this, see Norman L. Geisler, *Christian Ethics: Options and Issues* (Grand Rapids, Mich.: Baker, 1989),
chaps. 5-7.

duties and the notion that there are weightier and less weighty duties. Thus advocates of these points of view reject the third understanding of an absolute as adequate. Further, both positions believe that genuine moral conflicts occur. However, they differ as to how we should view the action performed in such conflict situations.

For example, take the nurse and heart attack victim case above. Both views would most likely say that the nurse should honor beneficence and nonmaleficence over autonomy and honesty in this case. But the conflicting absolutist would say that the nurse who withheld information from (and later lied to) the patient did a moral evil, whereas the graded absolutist would say that the nurse did a morally good act. We cannot undertake an evaluation of these three views here and each is held by well-informed, well-intentioned thinkers. We note only that light can be shed on this debate by looking at it in view of the third sense of an absolute above. The unqualified absolutist accepts this third sense as adequate, and the conflicting and graded absolutists do not.

There are three general strategies for defending the existence of moral absolutes. First, since one must either be a relativist or an absolutist, then arguments against relativism count as arguments for absolutism. An absolutist can try to show that the various forms of relativism are inadequate and use this as evidence for absolutism. For example, one can point out that if absolutes are denied, then morally unacceptable and irrational consequences follow. For example, if there are no absolutes, one could argue, then what Hitler and the Nazis did to the Jews was not plain and simply wrong, but only wrong in some lesser, relative sense. If this conclusion is unacceptable, then the premise that led to it (there are no absolutes) must be false.

3.2
STRATEGIES FOR
DEFENDING THE
EXISTENCE OF
MORAL
ABSOLUTES

Second, one can try to show that absolutes are to be expected, given that a certain worldview is judged reasonable. For example, theists or Platonists (those who hold that objective properties and propositions, including moral ones, exist whether or not they come from some divine being) could cite the fact that their worldview has this result: Absolute morality is at home in their conceptions of the world and is to be expected. On the other hand, physicalistic or naturalistic worldviews labor to justify moral absolutes in a way not necessary for theism or Platonism, because objective moral properties and propositions that refer to human beings are odd and surprising within their worldview. This type of argument moves the debate to the level of general worldview and the relationship between a worldview and objective morality.

Finally, one can seek to justify belief in the existence of moral absolutes by appealing to fundamental, basic, moral intuitions. We have already had occasion to see examples of this strategy. The moral relativist can respond that such appeals are question-begging. The issue boils down to different views of the burden of proof regarding moral relativism (cf. chap. 4). The absolutist believes that there are more grounds for believing these basic intuitions than there are for believing that relativism is true. The mere fact that it is logically possible that he or she is wrong is not sufficient to grant victory to the relativist. The relativist holds the opposite view and claims that the possibility of error is sufficient to justify abandonment of the claim to know that certain moral propositions are objectively true.

Our discussion of absolutes provides a fitting occasion to mention the role of intuitions in ethical theory. Princeton philosopher Saul Kripke once remarked that it was difficult to see what could be said more strongly for a view than that it squared with one's basic, reflective intuitions. Kripke's remark reminds us that in philosophy, ethical theory included, intuitions play an important role. What is an intuition? The philosophical use of **intuition** does not mean a mere hunch or a prereflective expression of, say, a moral attitude. Nor is it a way of playing it safe, as when one says, "My intuition tells me that P is true but I really don't know, and if you chose to accept P, you do so at your own risk." While philosophers differ over a precise definition of intuitions, a common usage defines an intuition as an immediate, direct awareness or acquaintance with something. An intuition is a mode of awareness—sensory, intellectual or otherwise—in which something seems or appears to be directly present to one's consciousness. For example, one can have a sensory intuition of a table or an intellectual intuition of a conceptual truth, for instance, that $2 + 2 = 4$.

Intuitions are not infallible, but they are prima facie justified. That is, if one carefully reflects on something, and a certain viewpoint intuitively seems to be true, then one is justified in believing that viewpoint in the absence of overriding counterarguments (which will ultimately rely on alternative intuitions). Furthermore, an appeal to intuitions does not rule out the use of additional arguments that add further support to that appeal. One can claim to know that a brown chair is present by appealing to a basic, sensory intuition of being appeared to in a brown, chair-type way. But one could also support the claim that there is a chair by further arguments; for example, the testimony of others or the fact that if we postulate a chair in the room, then we have an explanation for why people walk around a certain spatial location where the chair is postulated. Similarly, an appeal to intuitions in ethics is not a claim to infallibility or a substitute for further arguments.

In ethics, appeals to intuition occur in four main areas. First, there are specific cases or judgments (e.g., Dr. Jones ought not to lie to the patient in room 10 tomorrow morning). Second, there are moral rules and principles (e.g., promises should be kept, persons ought to be respected). Third, there are general, normative theories (e.g., deontological theories are to be preferred to utilitarian theories or vice versa; see chaps. 21-22). Finally, there are background philosophical or religious factual beliefs (e.g., a human has a property of intrinsic value). Again, such appeals to intuition claim prima facie justification and do not rule out further argumentation. Appeals to reflective, considered intuitions occur throughout one's intellectual life, and ethics is no exception, nor is the debate about relativism and absolutism.

CHAPTER SUMMARY

Factual statements describe what is the case, and value statements prescribe what ought to be the case. There are six different theses that, in one way or another, have been associated with relativism, which were each stated and criticized. Cultural or descriptive relativism is the view that cultures have basic ethical differences. Normative or ethical relativism asserts that one ought to follow his or her society's code and that societies differ in the content of their codes. Metaethical or conceptual relativism says that the meanings of moral terms are themselves relative to culture. Ethical skeptics assert that moral truths do not exist and, even if they do, no one knows what they are. Combinatorial relativism combines an absolute, formal principle with a relative, material principle to yield a relative action guide. The classical principle of tolerance was an absolute and the modern principle does not clearly follow from any form of relativism.

Ethical absolutists disagree with moral relativists and assert the existence of absolutes. A moral absolute has three different meanings: (1) it is objectively true; (2) it is exceptionless; and (3) it is a principle with the highest degree of incumbency. Most absolutists (also called objectivists) accept the first two principles but reject the third one and embrace prima facie duties. The three views about conflict situations are unqualified, conflicting and graded absolutism. Only the first view rejects prima facie duties.

Absolutes can be defended by (1) arguing against relativism; (2) showing that it is at home in a Platonic or theistic worldview, but not in a naturalistic one, and claiming the superiority of the former over the latter; (3) appealing to intuitions.

CHECKLIST OF BASIC TERMS AND CONCEPTS
absolutism
basic ethical disagreement
combinatorial relativism
conflicting absolutism (or lesser of two evils view)
conventionalism
cultural or descriptive relativism
description
descriptive definitions of moral terms
normative or ethical relativism
ethical skepticism (ontological and epistemological versions)
evaluative definitions of moral terms
exception
exemption
fact
formal principle
graded absolutism (or greater of two goods view)
highest degree of incumbency
intuition
material principle
metaethical or conceptual relativism
natural moral law
nonvalue or "mere" facts
objectivism
prescription
prima facie duty
principle of autonomy
principle of beneficence

principle of honesty
principle of life preservation
principle of nonmaleficence
principle of tolerance (classical and modern)
slippery slope arguments (logical, precedent, sorites, causal)
subjectivism
three different sources for moral disagreements
universalizable
unqualified absolutism
value
value facts

21

NORMATIVE ETHICAL THEORIES
Egoism and Utilitarianism

Each person should seek to maximize his own interests
(whatever these may be)—usually "in the long run" or over a life-span.
JOHN HOSPERS, "RULE-EGOISM"

The creed which accepts as the foundation of morals,
Utility, or the Greatest Happiness Principle,
holds that actions are right in proportion as they tend to promote happiness,
wrong as they tend to produce the reverse of happiness.
JOHN STUART MILL, *UTILITARIANISM*

1 INTRODUCTION

Normative theories in ethics seek to provide an account of what actions are right and wrong and why. In current discussions of ethics, normative theories are usually grouped into two basic and mutually exclusive groups—teleological and deontological.

There are two different senses of the term *teleological* when it is used to identify teleological normative theories in ethics. First, teleological ethics can refer to certain types of natural moral law theories that depict the purpose of human life in general, and moral rules in particular, to be that of moving toward and promoting the end or goal (the *telos*) for which we were made—ideal human flourishing in accordance with our human nature. This sense of "teleological ethics" is not the one we are using in this chapter. Virtue ethics is closely related to this type of teleological theory, and this way of thinking will be examined in the next chapter. The second notion of a teleological ethical theory is the one we have in mind here. Roughly, this notion of **teleological ethics** holds that the rightness or wrongness of an act is exclusively a function of the goodness or badness of the consequences of that act. Ultimately, consequences and consequences alone are crucial. So understood, teleological ethics is in conflict with deontological theories of ethics. **Deontological ethics** deny the claim that consequences are the sole determinant of rightness or wrongness. It places limits on the relevance of teleological considerations. Deontologists hold that some acts are intrinsically right or wrong from a moral point of view. This approach will be studied in the next chapter.

Utilitarianism is clearly the most widely accepted teleological theory. Some, however, have accepted another teleological view—ethical egoism. Thus in what follows we will state and evaluate ethical egoism and different forms of utilitarianism, in that order.

2 ETHICAL EGOISM

The most plausible form of **ethical egoism**, embraced by such philosophers as Ayn Rand and John Hospers, is called **universal** or **impersonal rule egoism** (hereafter, ethical egoism): each person has a moral duty to follow those and only those moral rules that will be in the agent's maximal self-interest over the long haul. For the ethical egoist, one has a duty to follow "correct" moral rules. And the factor that makes a rule a "correct" one is that, if followed, it will be in the agent's own best interests in the long run. Each person ought to advance his/her own self-interests and that is the sole foundation of morality.

Ethical egoism is sometimes confused with various distinct issues. First, there is **individual** or **personal ethical egoism**, which says everyone has a duty to act so as to serve *my* self-interests. Here, everyone is morally obligated to serve the speaker's long-term best interests. Second, there is **psychological egoism**, roughly, the idea that each person can only do an act that the person takes to maximize his or her own self-interest. Psychological egoism is a descriptive thesis about motivation to the effect that we can only act on motives that are in our own self-interests. Psychological egoism is sometimes used as part of an argument for ethical egoism, but the two are distinct theses.

Third, ethical egoism is not the same thing as **egotism**—an irritating character trait of always trying to be the center of attention. Nor is it the same as being what is sometimes called a wanton. A **wanton** has no sense of duty at all, but only acts to satisfy his own desires. The only conflict the wanton knows is that between two or more desires he cannot simultaneously satisfy (e.g., to eat more and lose weight). He knows nothing about duty. Fifth, ethical egoism is not to be confused with being an **egoist**, that is, being someone who believes that the sole worth of an act is its fairly immediate benefits to the individual himself or herself.

Among the arguments for ethical egoism, two have become most prominent. First, some argue that ethical egoism follows from psychological egoism. The argument goes like this. Psychological egoism is true, and this implies that we always and cannot help but act egoistically. This is a fact about human motivation and action. Further, ought implies can. If I ought to do *x*, if I have a duty to do *x*, then I must be able to do *x*. If I cannot do something, then I have no duty or responsibility to do it. Applied to egoism, this means that since I can only act egoistically, whatever account of moral action must be consistent with this fact of human psychology, and ethical egoism is the best of these accounts. Moreover, since I cannot act nonegoistically, then I have no duty to do so. Thus ethical egoism is the correct picture of moral obligation since it is consistent with and best captures the nature of human motivation and action.

Does this argument work? Most philosophers have not thought so. First, the principle of psychological egoism—that we always act to maximize our own self-interest—is ambiguous. So stated, the principle fails to make a distinction between the *result* of an act versus the *intent* of an act. If it is understood in one way it is irrelevant, and if it is taken in the second way it is false. If the statement merely asserts that, as a matter of fact, the result of our actions is the maximization of self-interest, then this does not imply ethical egoism. Ethical egoism is the view that the thing which morally justifies an act is the agent's intent to maximize his own self-interest. So the mere psychological fact (if it is a fact) that people only do those acts that result in their own satisfaction proves nothing.

On the other hand, if the statement claims that we always act solely with the intent to satisfy our own desires, then this claim is simply false. Every day we are aware of doing acts with the sole intent of helping someone else, of doing something just because we think it is the right thing to do and of expressing virtuous, other-centered behavior. As Christian philosopher Joseph Butler (1692-1752) argued,

> Mankind has various instincts and principles of action as brute creatures have; some leading most directly and immediately to the good of the community, and some most directly to private good. . . . [I]t is not a true representation of mankind, to affirm that they are wholly governed by self-love, the love of power and sensual appetites. . . . it is manifest fact, that the same persons, the generality, are frequently influenced by friendship, compassion, gratitude; . . . and liking of what is fair and just, takes its turn amongst the other motives of action.[1]

Furthermore, it is not even true that we always *try* to do what we want. We sometimes experience *akrasia* (weakness of will) when we fail to do or even try to do what we want (see Rom 7:15-25). And we sometimes do (or try to do) our duty even when we don't want to do it.

Second, this argument for ethical egoism suffers from what has been called the **paradox of hedonism**. Often, the best way to get happiness and the satisfaction of desire is not to aim at it. Happiness is not usually achieved as an intended goal, but rather it is a by-product of a life well lived and of doing what is right. If people always act in order to gain happiness, then it will remain forever elusive. Now a major purpose of a moral theory of rules and actions, ethical egoism included, is to specify and offer a justifying account of what one should intend to do in moral actions. Seen in this light, ethical egoism requires us to act with the intent of maximizing our own self-interests, and it is the actual maximization of our own self-interests that justifies an act. However, the paradox of hedonism brings to light the fact that the goal specified by ethical egoism (actual maximization of one's self-interests) is often thwarted by the proper moral intentions (acting with the intent of maximizing one's self-interests) indicated by ethical egoism. Thus psychological egoism presents a paradox for advocates of ethical egoism when viewed as a model of human intention and action.

Finally, as a model of human action, psychological egoism rules out the possibility of libertarian freedom of the will. Libertarian freedom was discussed in chapter thirteen, so a detailed exposition will not be presented here. For present purposes, it should be noted that if libertarian freedom is the correct

---

[1]Joseph Butler, "Fifteen Sermons," in *British Moralists: 1650-1800*, vol. 1, ed. D. D. Raphael (Oxford: Clarendon, 1969), pp. 328-29 (originally published in 1726).

account of human action, then these propositions follow: (1) No amount of internal states (e.g., desires, beliefs, emotions) are sufficient to produce behavior. (2) The agent himself or herself must spontaneously exercise his or her causal powers and act for the sake of a reason that functions as the end or teleological goal for the sake of which the action was performed. On this view, psychological egoism is false if taken as a total account of human action because psychological egoism is a version of compatibilism and libertarianism is the preferred account of human agency. Psychological egoism (as a theory about unexceptionable human action or motivation) cannot underwrite any moral theory since "ought" (S ought to do x) implies "may not" (S may not do x). Libertarian freedom is controversial and not everyone accepts this model of action, but for those who do, this argument has force.

A second argument for ethical egoism may be called the **closet utilitarian argument**. It is pointed out that if everyone acted in keeping with ethical egoism, then the result of this would be the maximization of happiness for the greatest number of people. If acted upon, ethical egoism, as a matter of fact, leads to the betterment of humanity. There are two main problems with this argument. First, it amounts to a utilitarian justification of ethical egoism. As we shall see shortly, utilitarianism is a rival normative theory. It is problematic, therefore, for someone to use a rival theory, in this case utilitarianism, as the moral justification for ethical egoism. If one is an ethical egoist, why should he/she care about the greatest good for the greatest number for its own sake, and not merely because such "caring" would itself lead to greater satisfaction of one's individual desires? Second, the claim seems to be factually false. Is it really the case that if everyone acted according to ethical egoism, it would maximize everyone's happiness? Surely not. Sometimes self-sacrifice and personal denial is needed to maximize happiness for the greatest number, and this argument for ethical egoism cannot allow for that to be the case.

2.3
Arguments
Against
Ethical Egoism

Among the arguments against ethical egoism, three are most prominent. First, there is the **publicity objection**. Moral principles must serve as action guides that inform moral situations. Most moral situations involve more than one person and, in this sense, are public situations. Thus moral action guides must be teachable to others so they can be publicly-used principles that help us in our interpersonal moral interactions. According to ethical egoism itself, however, it may be immoral for me to teach others to embrace ethical egoism because that could easily turn out not to be in my own self-interest. It may be better for me if others always acted altruistically. Thus it could be immoral for one to go public and teach ethical egoism to others and, if so, this would violate one of the necessary conditions for a moral theory, namely, that it be teachable to others.

In response, some have claimed that we have no good reason to believe that a moral doctrine needs to be consistently promulgatable. Why, it is asked, should we have to be able to teach a moral doctrine to others? Couldn't someone consistently hold to the following moral notion, P: "It is never right to promulgate anything." Unfortunately, this response fails because it does not capture the public nature of moral principles insofar as they serve as action guides to adjudicate interpersonal moral conflict. How could principle P serve as an action guide sufficient to deal with the various aspects of duty, virtue and rights that constitute much of the point of action guides in the first place?

Moreover, this response fails to take into account the universalizability of moral rules. If I should never promulgate anything, then this implies that I should not teach something to someone else. But there does not seem to be a clear moral difference in this case between others and myself. To be consistent, then, I should not promulgate this moral principle to myself. Is it possible to promulgate a principle to oneself? It would seem so. All that is involved here is that one seek to instruct oneself about the principle in view through reading and other means in order to strengthen one's commitment to the principle. Now if I should not promulgate this moral principle to myself, then this implies, among other things, that if I hold to P as a moral principle that should be universalized, then, applying P to myself, I would no longer have moral grounds for embracing P. On the other hand, if I do not think P should be universalized, then in what sense is P a moral principle (since universalizability is most likely a necessary condition for a principle to count as *moral*)?

A second argument against ethical egoism is called the **paradox of egoism**. Some things—for example, altruism, deep love, genuine friendship—are inconsistent with ethical egoism. Why? Because these features of a virtuous, moral life require us not to seek our own interests but rather those of the other. Moreover, ethical egoism seems to imply, for example, that helping others at one's own expense (where there is no long-term payoff for the actor) is wrong. Thus egoism would seem to rule out important, central features of the moral life. The main point of a normative moral theory is to explain and not to eliminate what we already know to be central facets of morality. Furthermore, in order to reach the goal of egoism (personal happiness), one must give up egoism and be altruistic in love, friendship and other ways. Thus egoism is paradoxical in its own right and it eliminates key aspects of the moral life.

Some respond by claiming that **altruism** is fully consistent with ethical egoism. In fact, say egoists, we ought to do acts that benefit others because that is in our own self-interest. But this response fails to distinguish pseudo-altruism from genuine altruism. **Genuine altruism** requires that an altruistic act have, as its intent, the benefit of the other. An act whose sole intent is self-interest but which, nevertheless, does result in the benefit of others is **pseudo-altruism**. If you found out that someone "loved" you or did an "altruistic" act toward you solely with the intent of benefiting himself and not you, then you would not count that as genuine love or altruism even if the act happened to benefit you in some way. Thus "egoistic altruism" is a contradiction in terms. Ethical egoism is consistent with pseudo-altruism but not with genuine altruism.

Finally, a third objection claims that ethical egoism leads to inconsistent outcomes. A moral theory must allow for moral rules that are public and universalizable. But ethical egoism could lead to situations where this is not the case. How? Consider two persons, A and B, both of whom are themselves ethical egoists and who are in a situation involving a conflict of interest. For example, suppose that there was only one kidney available for transplant, that A and B both need it, and that the one who does not get the kidney will die. According to ethical egoism, A ought to act in his own self-interests and prescribe that his desires come out on top. A has a duty to secure the kidney and thwart B's attempts to do the same. This would seem to imply that A should prescribe that B has a duty to act in A's self-interest since A's getting the kidney is the correct, universalizable moral outcome. Of course B, according to ethical egoism, has from his perspective a duty to act in B's own self-interests. But now a contradiction arises because ethical egoism implies that B both has a duty to give the kidney to A and to get it himself.

Ethical egoists respond by claiming that this objection fails to capture adequately the nature of ethical egoism. They claim that as an ethical egoist, A should not hold that B should act in A's self-interest, but in B's *own* self-interest. This would seem to solve the problem of contradictory duty above. But this way of stating ethical egoism does not seem to capture the egoistic spirit of ethical egoism because it leaves open the question of why egoist A would need to hold that B should act in B's interests and not in A's.

Moreover, there is yet another problem for this formulation of ethical egoism, which can be brought out as follows: A holds that B has a duty to get the kidney for B himself, have his own (B's) interests come out on top, and thus do an act that actually harms A even if this were not B's intent. But in this case, ethical egoism still seems to imply an inconsistent posture on A's (and B's) part, namely, that A thinks that B has a duty to get the kidney for himself since A thinks that B should act in B's own self-interests. But if B does so act, the results will actually harm the maximization of A's self-interest. Thus A, acting in his own self-interest, will have a duty to thwart B from doing his own duty. Any moral theory that implies that someone has a moral duty to keep others from doing their moral duty is surely in trouble, so the objection goes. And it is hard to see how an ethical egoist A could claim that someone else had a duty to harm A himself.

Not everyone accepts this argument. Some claim that we often find it to be the case that we have a duty to thwart what is the duty of others. For example, in war, one soldier has a duty to thwart another's efforts to do his duty to win. If we separate beliefs about ethical situations from desires, so the response goes, then A can believe B has a duty to win the war or get the kidney, but A can at the same time desire these objectives for himself and act on those desires. In general, the belief that B ought to do x does not imply that A wants B to do x.

What should we make of this response? First, the soldier example fails because it does not distinguish between subjective and objective duty. **Subjective duty** is a duty someone has when one has done one's best to discover what is and is not the right thing to do. If someone sincerely and conscientiously tries to ascertain what is right and acts on this, then one has fulfilled one's subjective duty, and in a sense, he is, therefore, praiseworthy. But people can be sincerely wrong and fail to live up to their **objective duty**—the truly correct thing to do from a God's-eye perspective—even if they have tried to do their best. Soldier A could only claim that soldier B has a subjective duty to obey his country. But A could also believe that B has an objective duty to do so only if B's country is, in fact, conducting a morally justified war. Now either A or B is on the right side of the war even though it may be hard to tell which side is correct. Thus A and B could believe that only one of them actually has an objective duty to fight and thwart the other. So the war example may not give a genuine case in which A believes B has a(n) (objective) duty to fight and that he has a(n) (objective) duty to thwart B.

Second, what about the point of separating beliefs from desires? For one thing, a desirable feature of any moral theory is that it describe what a virtuous person is and how virtue can be achieved. Now one aspect of a virtuous person is that there is a harmony between desire and duty. A virtuous person desires to see the good prosper and moral duty honored. With this in mind, it becomes clear that ethical egoism, if consistently practiced, could produce fragmented, nonvirtuous persons who believe one thing about duty (for example, A believes B ought to do x) but who desire something else altogether (for example, A does not *desire* B to do x).

If we grant, however, that the ethical egoist's distinction between beliefs and desires is legitimate from a moral point of view, then this distinction does resolve the claim that ethical egoism leads to a conflict of desire, where, for example, A desires the kidney for himself and A also desires that B get the kidney. Given this distinction between beliefs and desires, ethical egoism implies that A believes that B has a duty to get the kidney while allowing that A desires that he himself have it. Nevertheless, this response misses the real point of the objection to ethical egoism. That point is not that ethical egoism straightforwardly leads to a conflict of desire. Rather, the objection shows that ethical egoism leads to an unresolvable conflict of moral beliefs and moral duty. If A and B are ethical egoists, then A believes that it is wrong for B to get the kidney but also that it is B's duty to try to get it. But how can A consistently believe that B has a duty to do something wrong? And how can A have an *objective* duty to thwart B's *objective* duty?

Before we move on to utilitarianism, we need to look at one more issue. Some claim that the Bible, with its emphasis on avoiding hell and going to heaven and on securing eternal rewards for life on earth, implicitly affirms ethical egoism as an appropriate moral theory. This is supposed to count as an argument against Christianity since, granting the inadequacy of ethical egoism, Christianity implies an incorrect moral theory. What should we make of this claim? It is clear that legitimate self-interest is part of biblical teaching. But does this mean that Scripture implies ethical egoism as a moral theory?

To begin with, we need to distinguish between achieving what is in my self-interest as a by-product of an act versus self-interest as the sole intent of an act. Scriptural passages that appeal to self-interest may simply be pointing out that if you intentionally do the right thing, then a good by-product of this will be rewards of various kinds. It could be argued that these passages do not clearly use self-interest as the sole legitimate intent of a moral action. For example, Exodus 20:12 says, "Honor your father and your mother, so that your days may be long in the land that the LORD your God is giving you." Clearly, the Ten Commandments, of which this verse is a part, are to be obeyed largely because they are the correct moral commands of a holy God, not solely because they are in the self-interests of the believer.

This observation relates to a second distinction between a motive and a reason. Roughly, a motive is some state within a person that influences and moves that per-

2.4
CHRISTIANITY
AND ETHICAL
EGOISM

son to believe something or to act in a certain way. By contrast, a reason is something that serves rationally to justify some belief one has or action one has done. Citing a reason for believing x is an attempt to cite something that makes it likely that x be true. Citing a reason for doing x is an attempt to cite something that makes x the thing that I rationally or morally ought to do. In this context, just because something, say self-interest, serves as a motive for an action, it does not follow that it also serves as the reason that justifies the action in the first place. Self-interest may be a legitimate motive for moral action, but, it could be argued, God's commands, the objective moral law, etc. could be rationally cited as the things that make an act our duty in the first place. The Scriptures may be citing self-interest as a motive for action and not as the reason for what makes the act our duty.

Moreover, even if Scripture is teaching that self-interest is a reason for doing some duty, it may be offering self-interest as a prudential and not a moral reason for doing the duty. In other words, the Bible may be saying that it is wise, reasonable and a matter of good judgment to avoid hell and seek rewards without claiming that these considerations are *moral* reasons for acting according to self-interest. In sum, it could be argued that Scripture can be understood as advocating self-interest as a by-product and not an intent for action, as a motive and not a reason or as a prudential and not a moral reason. If this is so, then these scriptural ideas do not entail ethical egoism.

Second, even if Scripture teaches that self-interest contributes to making something my moral duty, ethical egoism still does not follow. For one thing, ethical egoism as a normative ethical theory teaches that an act is moral if and only if it maximizes my own self-interests. Ethical egoism teaches that self-interest is both necessary and sufficient for something to be my duty. It could be argued, however, that egoistic factors, while not the sole factors that are morally relevant to an act (other things like self-sacrifice and obeying God because it is intrinsically right may also be relevant), nevertheless, are at least one feature often important for assessing the moral worth of an act. Moral duty is not exhausted by self-interest as ethical egoism implies, but self-interest can be a legitimate factor in moral deliberation, and Scripture may be expressing this point.

In addition, it is likely that the precise nature of self-interest contained in Scripture is different in two ways from the self-interest that forms part of ethical egoism. For one thing, according to ethical egoism, the thing that makes an act right is that it is in *my* self-interest. The important value-making property here is the fact that something promotes the first-person interests of the actor. Here, the moral agent attends to himself precisely as being identical to himself and to no one else.

By contrast, the scriptural emphasis on self-interest most likely grounds the appropriateness of that self-interest, not in the mere fact that such interests are *mine*, but in the fact that I am a creature of intrinsic value made in God's image and, as such, I ought to care about what happens to me. Here I seek my own welfare not because it is my own, but because of what I am, namely, a creature with high intrinsic value. Consider a possible world where human persons have no value whatever. In that world, ethical egoism would still legislate self-interest, but the second view under consideration (that self-interest follows from the fact that I am a creature of value) would not because the necessary condition for self-interest (being a creature of intrinsic value) does not obtain in that world.

Both Kantian and teleological views have to take the self into consideration no less than others. My self is relevant in universalizability considerations. Also, there may be special contexts in which my own interests are a fundamental consideration—for example, where my own eternal destiny is at stake. Furthermore, for the gift of heaven to be significant, it must answer some personal interest or desire for salvation. Could God be glorified for his provision of salvation if it was not something in which we had an interest?

There is a second way that the nature of self-interest in Scripture and in ethical egoism differ. As C. S. Lewis argued, there are different kinds of rewards, and some are proper because they have a natural connection with the things we do to earn them and because they are expressions of what God made us to be by nature.[2] Money is not a natural reward for love (one is mercenary to marry for money) because money is foreign to the desires that ought to accompany love. By contrast, victory is a natural reward for battle. It is a proper reward because it is not tacked on to the activity for which the reward is given, but rather victory is the consummation of the activity itself.

According to Lewis, the desire for heaven and rewards is a natural desire expressing what we, by nature, are. We were made to desire honor before God, to be in his presence and to hunger to enjoy the rewards he will offer us, and these things are the natural consummations of our activity on earth. Thus the appropriateness of seeking heaven and rewards derives from the fact that these results are genuine expressions of our natures and are the natural consummation of our activities for God. By contrast, according to ethical egoism, the value of results has nothing to do essentially with our natures or with natural consummations of activities. Rather, the worth of those outcomes is solely a function of the fact that they benefit the agent himself. And that's all there is to it.

This completes our discussion of ethical egoism. We now turn to a far more popular version of teleological ethics, namely, utilitarianism.

3 UTILITARIANISM

Utilitarians view the moral life in terms of means-to-ends reasoning. The essence of **utilitarianism** can be stated in this way: *the rightness or wrongness of an act or moral rule is solely a matter of the nonmoral good produced directly or indirectly in the consequences of that act or rule.* Utilitarianism can be clarified and criticisms of it sharpened by probing three different aspects of theories bearing this name: utilitarian theories of value, the principle of utility itself, and different forms of utilitarianism.

We first need to distinguish between moral and nonmoral values. In clarifying the notion of **nonmoral value** (sometimes called **goodness**), a utilitarian can correctly point out that a number of things can have intrinsic value without that value being moral. In this context, **moral value**, sometimes called **rightness**, refers to moral rules (do not steal) or individual moral actions (an act of

3.1
UTILITARIAN
THEORIES OF
VALUE

[2]C. S. Lewis, *The Weight of Glory* (Grand Rapids, Mich.: Eerdmans, 1949), pp. 1-15; *The Problem of Pain* (New York: Macmillan, 1962), pp. 144-54.

stealing) or kinds of actions (for example, stealing-type actions in general). Examples of nonmoral intrinsic value (things with intrinsic value apart from moral rules and actions) are these: health, beautiful art, friendship, mathematical knowledge. What is meant by intrinsic value here? If something has **intrinsic value**—for example, joy—then it is valuable in and of itself, it is an end in itself, it is good and worthy of being desired for its own sake. By contrast, if something has **instrumental value**—money, for example—then its sole value is as a means to intrinsic value. Note that there could be intrinsic values without instrumental ones, but there could be no instrumental values without intrinsic ones. Finally, something has **mixed value** (e.g., health) if it has both intrinsic and instrumental value.

Utilitarians differ about what values we should seek to produce as consequences of our actions; this is a disagreement about what has intrinsic nonmoral value. There are three major utilitarian views regarding intrinsic value. First, **hedonistic utilitarianism** conceives of utility solely in terms of happiness or pleasure. All other things are valuable only insofar as they are means to gaining happiness or pleasure and avoiding unhappiness and pain. One of the earliest utilitarians, Jeremy Bentham (1748-1832), was a **quantitative hedonist**. According to Bentham, the amount of pleasure versus pain is what matters, and he tried to develop a hedonic calculus whereby one can calculate the total amount of pleasure versus pain likely to be produced by an act. His calculus relied on considerations of the intensity, duration, nearness and purity of the pleasure that an act would have as its consequences.

Another early utilitarian, John Stuart Mill (1806-1873), rejected this approach. Mill pointed out that it is better to be a human being dissatisfied than a pig satisfied; better to be Socrates dissatisfied than a fool satisfied. On Bentham's views a satisfied pig had a larger quantity of pleasure than a dissatisfied Socrates and thus would exemplify more value. But, Mill argued, something is wrong with this notion. Bentham failed to distinguish different kinds of pleasure and neglected or overlooked the fact that some kinds of pleasure are of more value than others—for example, intellectual pleasure versus a full stomach. Moreover, it is difficult to know how to calculate the duration and intensity of various pleasures as envisaged by Bentham. Thus the application of the hedonic calculus in concrete situations of moral action/decision-making is extremely problematic. Mill embraced **qualitative hedonism** wherein it is still pleasure versus pain that constitutes utility, but now room is made for different kinds of pleasure. For example, on this view it is not such things as friendship or beautiful art themselves that have intrinsic value, but the pleasure that comes from them. A problem for Mill's view is that it fails adequately to specify just how we are to rank the relative value of different kinds of pleasure.

A second view, in opposition to hedonism, is called **pluralistic utilitarianism**. In this view, not only do pleasure and happiness have intrinsic, nonmoral value, but a number of other things do as well. Other intrinsic, nonmoral values countenanced by pluralistic utilitarians include knowledge, love, beauty, health, freedom, courage, self-esteem and so on. For example, according to pluralistic utilitarianism, it is not merely the pleasure produced by friendship that is of value, but friendship itself. Advocates of this approach claim that it is intuitively obvious that the items listed above do, indeed, have intrinsic value, and no one has offered any single feature that all these diverse items have in common.

A number of modern utilitarians have rejected pluralistic utilitarianism. The main problem they point out is that the aforementioned values are relatively useless in determining what one should do. Widely different views exist about the relative merits of the items listed above. Furthermore, no common scale seems to exist for comparing and ranking, say, friendship, including the various kinds of friendship that can take place, with such values as aesthetic experience or courage. For this and other reasons, most contemporary utilitarians embrace a third theory of value—**subjective preference utilitarianism**. Because it seems to many to be futile and presumptuous to attempt to develop a general theory of value, this position holds that an act ought to maximize the satisfaction of individual desires and preferences. The goal of moral actions is the satisfaction of desires or wants that express individual preferences.

Unfortunately, this theory seems to be a version of combinatorial relativism (see chap. 20); it thus collapses into a form of relativism when it is used to specify goodness for action-guiding purposes. Why? Because when one attempts to use the principle to determine what action to take, any act whatever can be justified as long as it satisfies an individual's private preferences. If someone desires to be a child molester or to practice some form of self-deprecation, then, in this view, such an act is appropriate because it could maximize the satisfaction of individual desires. The theory cannot account for the simple fact that people can have morally unacceptable preferences such as the desire for genocide.

Utilitarians have responded to this charge in the following way. They supplement the principle of subjective preference with a condition of rationality: the good consists in the satisfaction of individual desires that it is rational to desire. They claim that utilitarianism is not responsible for solving the problem of universal idiocy. In other words, the subjective preference view only takes into account rational preferences. Neither child molestation nor acts of self-deprecation are rational, so they do not count as "appropriate" preferences.

But what is meant by rationality here? Let us distinguish between prescriptive rationality and descriptive rationality. **Prescriptive rationality** involves two things: (1) the ability to have justified beliefs about what is intrinsically valuable and (2) having those beliefs inform appropriately one's desires. This type of rationality cannot be what the utilitarian has in mind, for such a rationality either implies pluralistic utilitarianism (the ability to have justified beliefs about what has nonmoral value) or it is deontological (the ability to have justified beliefs about what has intrinsic moral value). Either way, the definition of *rationality* would be circular: the "good" is defined as what it is rational to desire, and "rational" is defined as what people desire when they desire the good.

The only type of rationality available to the subjective preference form of utilitarianism is **descriptive rationality**, which necessarily involves two things: first, the ability to use efficient means to accomplish certain ends, once those ends are posited. But this alone is not adequate to save subjective preference utilitarianism, for one could posit morally abhorrent ends and still be rational if one knew efficient means to accomplish those ends. So a second thing must be included in descriptive rationality: One is rational if and only if one desires what all psychologically normal (i.e., statistically usual) people desire. If one is psychologically balanced, then one presumably will not choose to be a child molester. Our human natures are contingent—they could have turned out to have been different, say, if evolutionary progression had taken a different turn. Given the contingent human natures that we happen to have, whatever statistically usual people desire is what it is rational to desire. And as a contingent matter of fact, such people happen not to desire to be child molesters.

But the question is why a normal person would not choose such a way of life. The answer cannot be that such acts are simply wrong, for in this case the advocate of subjective preference utilitarianism would be arguing in a circle. It could have turned out that psychologically "normal" (i.e., typical) people would prefer to have satisfied a number of highly immoral desires. No contradiction is involved in this claim. There are possible worlds (including the future of the actual world) where people, as a contingent matter of fact, typically desire to molest children. But if this were the case, the satisfaction of these desires would be morally appropriate in the subjective preference view. For this reason, such a view must be judged inadequate. Any view that even allows for the logical possibility that child molestation and a host of other immoral acts could be morally justified has a wrong conception of value. And because human preferences may change as time goes by, we may not be raising worries about what is merely logically possible.

By way of conclusion, two important things must be kept in mind when contemplating a utilitarian theory of value. First, moral value (moral acts and rules) only have instrumental value. They are solely a means to an end. Utilitarians differ over what that end, called "the good," amounts to. The "right" is to the "good" as a means is to an end. This can be pictured as in table 21.1.

Table 21.1 Utilitarian theories of value

The Right	The Good
moral acts and rules	pleasure (quantity or quality), pluralistic value, "rational" subjective preference
instrumental value	intrinsic value

Second, most utilitarians are objectivists regarding the nature of nonmoral value. For hedonist and pluralist utilitarians, the good is objective and not dependent on the beliefs or desires of individuals. By contrast, for subjective preference utilitarians, the good is relative to individual beliefs and desires, and thus it is subjective.

3.2
THE PRINCIPLE
OF UTILITY

As we have just seen, utilitarians differ about what value counts in defining utility, where **utility** stands for whatever the good is that we should seek to maximize in the consequences of our moral acts and rules. Utilitarians also differ about the form of the principle of utility itself. The **principle of utility** states the goal or test for what one ought to do. According to utilitarianism, most generally, a moral act (or moral rule) is right if and only if consequences of the right kind and/or in the right measure are (actually) produced by the action (or are a result of following the moral rule). But this is still too general, and utilitarians are divided about the best way to characterize this principle more pre-cisely. Each of the following have peen proposed:

   a. It produces only good consequences.
   b. It maximizes good consequences.
   c. It avoids all bad consequences.
   d. It minimizes bad consequences.
   e. It produces the greatest happiness for the greatest number.
   f. It maximizes the net balance of good versus bad consequences.

Clearly, these principles can easily come into conflict with each other. So utilitarians disagree significantly about what is right and wrong in precisely the same situation. Principles (a), (b), (c), (d) are self-explanatory and need no spe-cial comment, but it may be helpful to clarify principles (e) and (f).

To simplify, suppose we have a society of ten persons and we have ten pieces of candy to distribute. Let *hedon* stand for one unit on the pleasure-pain scale or continuum, with pleasure on the positive side and pain on the negative side. Further, suppose eight people in our society derive +1 hedon from a piece of candy, one person hates candy and gets -1 hedon from eating a piece, and one candy connoisseur derives a whopping +5 hedons from each piece. Principle (e) states that in considering what is right and wrong in a given circumstance, one must estimate the amount of utility (i.e., the good versus bad consequences) produced as a function of two things: the total number of positive versus nega-tive hedons generated and the total number of people involved.

Principle (f) makes no reference to the latter factor and only focuses on the total hedons generated. Principle (f) would require that we give all ten pieces to the candy connoisseur because this generates 50 hedons (5 hedons for each of 10 pieces of candy). Compare this to each individual getting one piece. The first eight people contribute one hedon each, the connoisseur contributes five he-dons, and the candy hater yields minus one for a total of 12 hedons. Since this is less than 50 hedons, principle (f) requires that our moral duty is to give all ten pieces to the connoisseur. Principle (e), however, is more complicated because it requires that the number of people be factored into the equation. If all ten pieces are given to the connoisseur, that only includes one person compared to ten people involved in an equal distribution. Principle (e) dictates that we bal-ance the amount of hedons with the number of people included, and thus dif-fers from (f) in its orientation.

It is beyond the scope of our present discussion to analyze further these alterna-tive formulations of the principle of utility. The point to be emphasized here is that utilitarians are not agreed about how to state the principle of utility. This dis-agreement has often been presented as a criticism of the theory. Furthermore, each individual formulation of the principle of utility is subject to criticism. Con-sider principle (e) above, the formulation most often associated with utilitarianism. The difficulty with formula (e) is that (e) attempts to balance two different scales used to evaluate the morality of an act or rule: the number of people affected and the total amount of utility produced. This can easily lead to conflicting answers as to what is or is not one's duty in a given case because one action could be better for more people while the alternative action produces more overall utility.

Another more general criticism of the principle of utility involves the way it is used by utilitarians. Utilitarians emphasize that what we should try to do in our actions is maximize the utility in the consequences of those actions *in the long run*. They are not interested in the short-term consequences of an act; what matters is the total utility produced by that act, and this must take into account the long-range affects of that act.

But now a problem enters the picture. It is difficult, if not impossible, to know the comparative long-term consequences of alternative acts one could perform. Short of being (nearly) omniscient, one could hardly judge accurately that alternative A is his duty and action B is morally forbidden. Keep in mind that the agent's intentions have no bearing on the moral character of the agent's action. Someone could sincerely do A, thinking that it would produce the most utility, but actually do the immoral thing if B turned out in the long run to maximize utility vis-à-vis A. Some utilitarians respond to this by claiming that one merely has a duty to do an act in light of what it is reasonable to expect will be the consequences of an act, and has no duty to do what actually maximizes utility in the long run. Further, doing one's best to act in light of reasonable expectations about consequences will itself maximize utility compared to not acting at all or acting in ways that do not reasonably offer the expectation of maximizing utility.

But this response misses the point. The point is not that moral agents are responsible to do the best they can in their actions and, since they are not omniscient, they will sometimes make mistakes. This point is correct and applies to all moral theories. The real issue surfaced in the objection is that utilitarian approaches to morality and moral decision-making have a defect that is central to the theory. The very factor that makes an action right or wrong—the long-term utility produced by that act compared to alternative acts—often (if not typically) has an uncertainty that paralyzes moral decision-making and that brings to center stage a tentativeness about duty that is not conducive to the development of conviction and character (see chap. 22).

As Solomon noted in Ecclesiastes 2:18-19, "I must leave [the fruit of my labor] to those who come after me—and who knows whether they will be wise or foolish? Yet they will be master of all for which I toiled and used my wisdom under the sun. This also is vanity." Solomon's point is this: If the worth of my labor and its fruits derives from the long-term consequences of that labor, then there is a certain emptiness and paralyzing uncertainty to my current actions because I could actually be contributing to something with bad long-term effects. Thus, if my current labor is to have value, then that worth must derive from something in addition to its long-term consequences.

The paralyzing impact of utilitarian views of the principle of utility has also been highlighted by what is called the **no-rest objection**. According to utilitarianism, one is to do that act which maximizes utility in the long run. But for any act one could perform, there will always be a potentially infinite set of alternative acts. How is one effectively to take into account all the relevant alternatives? And how can one even approximately evaluate the long-term consequences of each of these alternatives?

Before we look at different forms of utilitarianism, we need to examine one more question regarding the principle of utility: Does the principle of utility commit utilitarianism to a form of moral relativism? Many people mistakenly believe the answer to be yes. In order to see why this is mistaken, let us make a distinction between something being a *relation* versus something being *relative*. Being red is a simple property. It takes only one thing, say an apple, to have it. By contrast, a relation is an objective feature of the world that obtains between two or more things. For example, "larger than" or "between" are relations. Note that it is an objective feature of the world whether or not some object A is larger than some object B or some object C is between two other objects D and E. Such facts do not depend on the beliefs of people. Believing that A is larger than B is not what makes it so. On the other hand, something (a belief) is relative if its truth or falsity is dependent on the beliefs of individuals or cultures. It is sometimes said that P is true-for-me but false-for-you. Such a statement expresses the idea that the truth of P is subjective—its truth depends on P being believed.

Now utilitarianism makes the morality of an act (or rule) a relation between the act and the consequences produced in that specific circumstance. For act utilitarians (see below), an act of stealing by Smith on Tuesday is right or wrong in relation to the consequences of that specific act. The same could be said for an act of stealing by Jones on Wednesday. In each case, moral rightness or wrongness is a relation to those and only those circumstances involved in that very case. Thus moral rightness or wrongness is not invariant; it changes as consequences and circumstances change. Some people think that this variation makes utilitarianism a form of relativism. But this is mistaken for, in any given situation, it will be an objective feature of the world (not always easy to discover) as to which action will actually maximize utility in that case. So even though utilitarianism does turn rightness or wrongness into a relation, which this makes moral value something that can vary as circumstances vary, utilitarianism does not make moral value dependent on the beliefs of individuals. It, therefore, is not a form of relativism.

Finally, there are two major versions of utilitarianism: act utilitarianism and rule utilitarianism. Act utilitarianism focuses on the utility produced by particular concrete acts, and rule utilitarianism focuses on the utility produced by adopting rules governing kinds of acts. Before we can understand the difference between these two approaches, we must first take into account two preliminary distinctions: (1) an act type versus an act token and (2) a summary concept of rules versus a practice concept of rules.

3.3
DIFFERENT
FORMS OF
UTILITARIANISM

An **act type** is a kind of act that can take place in different places at the same time or at different times. Act types are repeatable. A promise-keeping kind of act, a promise-breaking kind of act and a stealing type act are all examples of act types. An **act token**, however, is a particular, concrete instance of a type of act. If Smith breaks a promise at noon on Tuesday and Jones does the same thing at noon the next day, then these are two act tokens of the same kind of act. If Roth steals at noon on Thursday, this is a third act token, but it is an instance of a different type of act (a stealing type act and not a promise-breaking type act).

So much for the difference between act types and tokens. What about the second distinction between summary and practice conceptions of rules, in this case moral rules like "Do not steal" or "Do not break promises"? According to the **summary conception of rules**, such moral rules are like a scientific generalization. For example, the scientific rule "All ravens are black" is a generalization reached by starting with the examination of several individual cases—raven$_1$ is black, raven$_2$ is black and so on, such that all ravens examined so far are black—and then generalizing to the conclusion that, probably, all ravens whatsoever (both examined and unexamined) are black. Note two things about this example. To begin with, individual cases (e.g., each specific raven) are more fundamental and important than the rule. The rule is justified by the cases, not vice versa. Further, the rule is merely a useful summary of what has been found to be true so far (All examined ravens have been black) and a guiding rule of thumb for future cases (Ravens examined in the future will most likely be black). What would happen if we came upon a white raven? Our rule (All ravens are black) does not tell us that ravens *must* be black. If that were the case, we would be forced to classify our new bird as a nonraven simply because it is white. No, we would affirm that we have before us a white raven and we would change the rule to "In most cases, ravens are black." The rule would still be a convenient, generally correct guide in most cases, but it would not be universally true.

The **practice conception of rules** is a very different one. A practice is a form of activity specified by rules (and offices, roles, duties, etc.). The game of baseball, the system of tort law, the insurance industry are examples of institutions or practices in this sense. Here, if one wants to engage in activity within a practice (e.g., pitch in baseball, sue someone in court), then he or she must follow the rules of the game that constitute the very essence of that practice. The rules of a practice already exist prior to individual activities that take place within that practice. If one is going to pitch, then he or she must get a baseball (not a javelin), go to a baseball diamond (not a pool hall), and throw the ball according to certain rules. These rules are not useful summaries of past observations of what pitchers have so far done. Rather, they are definitional. Rules determine the practice. If someone was throwing a javelin in a pool hall and claimed to be pitching in baseball, we would not think that our rule "All pitchers throw a baseball over home plate in such and such a way" needed to be altered slightly like we do when we find a white raven. No, we simply would not count the javelin thrower as an example of pitching in baseball regardless of what he or she calls it. With these distinctions in mind, we are in a better position to understand the difference between act and rule utilitarianism.

1. Act Utilitarianism. According to **act utilitarianism**, an act is right if and only if no other act available to the agent maximizes utility more than the act in question. Here, each moral act is treated atomistically; that is, it is evaluated in complete isolation from other acts. Act utilitarians regard act tokens, not act types as the proper object of moral evaluation. Each individual moral situation (Should Smith break his promise on Tuesday?) is more important than the rule relevant to that situation (In general, keep your promises). Moreover, act utilitarians employ a summary notion of moral rules, not a practice conception. General moral rules like "Don't steal," "Don't break promises" or "Don't punish innocent people" are mere rules of thumb; summaries of how people up to this moment have generally experienced the consequences of acts similar to the one under consideration. If I am considering the morality of an act of stealing, then the rule "Don't steal" reminds me that such acts usually do not maximize utility. But such rules have no intrinsic moral value, nor do they dictate to me how I must view the present act. That is, moral rules like "Don't steal" do not constitute the very moral essence of specific actions of stealing. Instead, they are mere rules of thumb and as such are fallible aides in reflecting the actual moral character of a specific act under consideration.

A number of objections have been raised against act utilitarianism. First, act utilitarianism makes it possible to justify morally a number of acts that seem to be immoral. For example, if it would maximize utility to break a promise, for the police to punish a man they know to be innocent (perhaps to show the efficiency of the police and to serve as a deterrent, provided of course that they keep this a secret to prevent social chaos resulting from a lowering of respect for the police), or for a few to be enslaved for the benefit of the majority, then there are no grounds within act utilitarianism to judge these acts as immoral. Sometimes actions of this kind will produce the "morally desirable consequences." But any doctrine that treats these immoral acts as morally justifiable is wrong.

The idea behind these points is that we start our moral theorizing—in this case, our attempt to state a normative theory like act utilitarianism—with rational intuitions about what is and is not morally appropriate. It is wrong to punish an innocent person, period. If a theory like act utilitarianism could imply that such an act would be morally obligatory or even permissible, then that theory must be rejected because we have better grounds for believing that we should not punish an innocent person than we have for accepting act utilitarianism. If something has to go it is the theory, not our intuitions. Of course, utilitarians can respond that, in this case, we should simply adjust our intuitions in light of the theory. But the critic of act utilitarianism is using intuitional knowledge of specific moral cases in roughly the same way that scientists use facts, namely, as an important factor to use in evaluating alternative theories, and it is hard to see how this can be mistaken. Moreover, making an exception to a rule may not in the long run be such a good thing. Thus act utilitarianism threatens to collapse into rule utilitarianism.

The criticisms listed above tend to show that act utilitarianism does not accord with our conviction that individuals have intrinsic value with individual rights and that persons are not merely bundles of social utility. In these cases, people are treated as means to an end, sometimes on the grounds that doing so will have great social utility. But this fails to treat these persons as intrinsically valuable ends with individual rights. Put differently, it is difficult to derive a robust, intuitively acceptable principle of justice that respects the intrinsic rights of individuals from a principle of utility.

Third, act utilitarianism turns trivial acts into moral acts. Consider the choice of what cereal to eat for breakfast. Suppose three cereals were available to you and that one of these would produce slightly more utility than the others if it were selected, perhaps because it is slightly better in flavor, texture and so on. In this case, act utilitarianism would imply that you were morally obligated to eat this cereal because that act would maximize utility. But in spite of act utilitarian claims, such an act does not seem to be a moral act at all. Thus act utilitarianism fails because it turns trivial acts like this into issues of moral obligation.

Other objections, which apply equally to act utilitarianism and rule utilitarianism, will be considered below. In light of the objections just mentioned, some utilitarians have formulated different versions of rule utilitarianism, which they believe handle these objections in a way not possible within an act utilitarian framework.

2. Rule Utilitarianism. According to **rule utilitarianism**, an act is right if and only if it falls under a correct moral rule that covers that generic type of act. And a rule is a correct moral rule if and only if everyone's acting on this rule would maximize utility compared to everyone's acting on an alternative rule. Rule utilitarians emphasize act types (not act tokens) and a practice conception of moral rules.

Here acts are no longer evaluated in isolation from moral rules. The reason act utilitarianism failed was that one could sever a particular act of keeping a promise or punishing an innocent person from general moral rules ("Keep promises," "Punish only guilty people") and evaluate the utility produced by that particular act directly. In act utilitarianism, if breaking a promise does not weaken respect for the moral rule to keep promises (in which case chaos would result and bad utility would be produced), then the act can be justified. Rule utilitarians tighten the connection between rules and acts. An act token (a specific case of stealing) is viewed in light of the act type (stealing types of acts in general) of which it is an example. And an act type is evaluated by reference to the correctness of a moral rule relevant to that act type taken as a moral practice. Utility calculations enter into the process at the level of evaluating alternative moral rules governing alternative moral practices and act types. For example, if everyone followed the rule "Punish only guilty people," then this would lead to greater utility than if everyone followed the rule "Punish innocent people as well as guilty people."

Thus rule utilitarianism cannot be used to justify the problematic acts cited against act utilitarianism. Further, it is claimed that it would not maximize utility if we treated trivial acts like what to eat for breakfast as moral issues. Utility is maximized if areas of individual freedom are maintained, or so say rule utilitarians.

But is it really the case that we do not treat choices of breakfast food as moral questions because doing so would fail to maximize utility? On the contrary, it seems that such acts are just not moral by their very nature. Further, act utilitarians argue that when faced with any moral situation, we should always follow this rule: When faced with a moral dilemma, then maximize utility. This is the correct moral rule for everyone to adopt, for if one does, then utility will be maximized, and thus rule utilitarianism would entail the adoption of this particular rule. But, say act utilitarians, this rule is just another way of expressing act utilitarianism. So in reality rule utilitarianism collapses back into act utilitarianism. After all, act utilitarians claim that producing utility is what matters, and acts, not rules, produce utility in the concrete, actual world.

Three further objections have been raised against both rule and act utilitarianism. First, there is the publicity objection we encountered earlier in our treatment of ethical egoism. It is surely possible that if people adopt a deontological approach (see chap. 22) to ethics, then this could actually maximize utility compared to people adopting utilitarianism. If people simply acted out of pure respect for the moral law and believed that moral rules have objective, intrinsic moral value, this could maximize utility more effectively compared to people consciously acting as utilitarians. In this case, utilitarian theory would imply that it would be morally wrong to teach others to be utilitarians. Any moral doctrine that allows for the possibility that it could be immoral to teach that doctrine to others is surely flawed.

Second, rule (and act) utilitarianism denies the existence of supererogatory acts whereas there does seem to be such acts. A **supererogatory act** is one that is not morally obligatory (one is not immoral for failing to do such an act) but nevertheless is morally praiseworthy. A supererogatory act is thus an act of moral heroism done above and beyond the call of moral duty. Examples included giving half of one's income to the poor, throwing oneself on a bomb to save another person and so on. In each of these cases one could act in supererogatory way or fail to. Either option would produce a certain amount of utility, and the option that produced the greater utility would be morally obligatory according to both rule and act utilitarianism. So supererogatory acts become impossible. But in spite of utilitarianism, such acts not only seem possible, they sometimes actually occur.

Finally, both rule and act utilitarianism are inadequate in their treatment of motives. We rightly praise good motives and blame bad ones. But utilitarianism implies that motives have no intrinsic moral worth. All that matters from a moral point of view are the consequences of actions, not the motives for which they are done.

Utilitarians have a response to these last two criticisms, which further clarifies the nature of utilitarianism as a moral position. They argue that it maximizes utility if we allow areas of moral freedom (recall the breakfast example). Thus any rule requiring that one must do supererogatory acts would not itself maximize utility. So supererogatory acts should be preserved because that would itself produce the best consequences. Similarly, we should praise good motives and blame bad ones because such acts of praise and blame will maximize utility compared with praising bad motives and blaming good ones or failing to discuss motives altogether.

At this point, the real difficulty with utilitarianism seems obvious: it misconstrues the real nature and source of our moral obligations. Contrary to what utilitarianism implies, some acts just appear to be intrinsically right or wrong (torturing babies for fun), some rules seem to be intrinsically right or wrong (punishing only guilty people), some areas of life seem to be intrinsically trivial (what to eat for breakfast) or supererogatory (giving half your income to the poor). From a moral point of view, some motives (morally) should be blamed or praised for what they are intrinsically and not because such acts of praise or blame produce utility, and humans seem to have intrinsic value and rights, which ground what is just and unjust treatment regarding them. In our opinion, utilitarianism fails to explain adequately these features of the moral life.

CHAPTER SUMMARY

There are two main types of normative ethical theories: teleological and deontological. A teleological theory can either be a natural law position or a theory implying that the rightness or wrongness of an act is exclusively a function of the good or bad consequences of that act. This chapter focuses on two main examples of this latter usage: ethical egoism and utilitarianism.

Ethical egoism is the view that each person has a moral duty to follow those rules that will be in the agent's self-interest over the long haul. It should not be confused with certain other ideas (for example, egotism) discussed in the chapter. Two main arguments for ethical egoism are the argument from psychological egoism and the closet utilitarian argument. The publicity objection, the paradox of egoism and the fact that ethical egoism leads to inconsistent outcomes are debilitating problems for the theory. Ethical egoism was also compared to biblical teachings related to it.

Utilitarians claim that the rightness or wrongness of an act or moral rule is solely a matter of the nonmoral good directly or indirectly produced in the consequences of that act or rule. Different utilitarian theories of value (quantitative and qualitative hedonism, pluralistic and subjective preference utilitarianism) were examined, followed by a survey of various statements of the principle of utility. The most popular statement of this principle is the claim that one ought to act so as to produce the greatest happiness for the greatest number. Act and rule utilitarianism are two different forms of this teleological theory. The former focuses on act tokens and a summary concept of rules; the latter focuses on act types and a practice concept of rules. The chapter concluded with criticisms of utilitarianism in all of its major formulations.

CHECKLIST OF BASIC TERMS AND CONCEPTS
act token
act type
act utilitarianism
altruism (pseudo versus genuine)
closet utilitarian argument
deontological ethics
descriptive rationality
egoist
egotism
ethical egoism (universal or impersonal rule egoism)
hedonistic utilitarianism (quantitative and qualitative)
individual or personal ethical egoism
instrumental value

intrinsic value
mixed value
moral value (rightness)
nonmoral value (goodness)
no-rest objection
objective duty
paradox of egoism
paradox of hedonism
pluralistic utilitarianism
practice conception of rules
prescriptive rationality
principle of utility
psychological egoism
publicity objection
rule utilitarianism
subjective duty
subjective preference utilitarianism
summary conception of rules
supererogatory act
teleological ethics
utilitarianism
utility
wanton

22

NORMATIVE
ETHICAL THEORIES
Deontological and Virtue Ethics

Now, I say, man and, in general, every rational being
exists as an end in himself and not merely as a
means to be arbitrarily used by this or that will.
In all his actions, whether they are directed
to himself or to other rational beings,
he must always be regarded at the same time as an end.
IMMANUEL KANT,
FOUNDATIONS OF THE METAPHYSICS OF MORALS

The virtues are those excellences which enable a human being
to attain the furthest potentialities of his nature.
GILBERT MEILAENDER,
THE THEORY AND PRACTICE OF VIRTUE

1 INTRODUCTION

The vast majority of Christian thinkers throughout the history of the church have embraced either deontological or virtue ethics or some combination of the two. The Ten Commandments and, more generally, the Old Testament law seems most naturally to be an example of deontological ethics. The book of Proverbs and the Sermon on the Mount seem to be expressions of a virtue approach to ethics. Moreover, these two normative ethical theories appear to capture what most people take to be a commonsense approach to the nature of ethics.

Roughly, **deontological ethics** focuses on right and wrong moral actions and moral laws and holds that some moral acts and rules are intrinsically right or wrong irrespective of the consequences produced by doing those acts or following those rules. According to deontological ethics, morality is its own point, at least in part, and moral duty should be done for its own sake. By contrast, **virtue ethics** focuses on the nature and formation of a good person, and the sort of dispositions and character traits that constitute the good person. According to virtue ethics, the good person is the one who is functioning properly, that is, as a human ought to function and thus is one who is skilled at life.

In this chapter, deontological and virtue ethics will be examined and evaluated in that order. The chapter will close with a brief examination of different ways the two theories can be united into a comprehensive vision of the moral life.

2 DEONTOLOGICAL ETHICS

In order to grasp the deontological theory of morality, three aspects of the theory should be understood: the deontological theory of value, the nature of a moral rule and the arguments for and against the theory.

The term **deontology** comes from the Greek word *deon*, which means "binding duty." Accordingly, the essence of deontological approaches to ethics lies in the notion that duty should be done for duty's sake. Moral rightness or duty is, in part, independent of the nonmoral good realized in the consequences of moral acts. On this view, a moral act is right when it conforms to the relevant, correct principle of moral duty. A correct principle of moral duty is one that is intrinsically right or derived from a principle that is intrinsically right. Consider the moral law "Do not murder." A deontologist may take this to be an intrinsically correct moral rule or he may take it to be derived from the more basic rule "Respect persons as things with intrinsic value." On this latter approach, "Do not murder" is justified as an important way of respecting the more basic rule and, in this sense, it is derived from that basic rule. Either way, true moral rules are intrinsically right from a moral standpoint. Thus acts are right or wrong, not solely due to the consequences produced by following those acts, but in virtue of the type of act under which the individual acts fall. A specific act of breaking a promise is wrong because the type of act—a promise-breaking act—violates an intrinsically correct moral rule, "One ought to keep one's promises."

A deontological theory of value may be clarified by comparing it to utilitarianism, beginning with the general utilitarian theory of value. Note first, that there is a distinction between intrinsic and instrumental value. Something has **intrinsic value** just in case it is valuable as an end in itself—for example, friendship. Something has **instrumental value** just in case it is valuable as a means to an end—for example, money. Some things can exemplify both kinds of value. Thus friendship is intrinsically good and also a means to pleasure. Second, there is a distinction between moral and nonmoral value. **Moral value**, sometimes called **rightness**, is the value possessed by moral acts and rules. **Nonmoral value**, sometimes called **goodness**, is the value possessed by things besides moral acts and rules—for example, pleasure, beauty, health, friendship.

Now according to utilitarianism, rightness is merely an instrumental value, that is, rightness is simply a means for obtaining goodness, namely, the maximization of utility, which, as we saw in chapter twenty-one, has been defined differently by various advocates of utilitarianism. On this view, morality is not its own point; rather, it is a means to an end. Many utilitarians believe in objective, intrinsic nonmoral value (for example, friendship, pleasure). However, they do not believe that moral value is intrinsic. By contrast, advocates of deontological ethics believe that moral value stands to value in general as part to whole, not as means to end. For them, there are, indeed, things that have nonmoral value, but moral acts and rules also have intrinsic value. Rightness is intrinsically valuable and not solely a means to goodness. Morality is, at least in part, its own point. To behave morally solely as a means to something else is not to behave morally at all.

In addition to competing general theories of value, deontological and utilitar-

2.1
DEONTOLOGICAL
THEORY OF
VALUE

ian ethical theories may be compared fruitfully in four other areas: persons, social relations, the past and the features of an act relevant to moral appraisal. To begin with, deontological and utilitarian ethical theories have different views of the value of persons. On a deontological theory, persons have intrinsic value simply as such and ought not be treated solely as a means to an end. According to utilitarianism, persons do not have intrinsic value; rather, they have value as units that contain utility. On this view, persons do not have intrinsic value simply as persons. Rather, they are in some sense "bundles of nonmoral good," and as such they have value insofar as they exemplify pleasure, health and so forth. It is beyond the scope of this chapter to pursue the issue, but some critics of utilitarianism have argued that because it does not depict persons as ends in themselves, it lacks the resources to support a robust doctrine of human rights.

Regarding social relationships, utilitarianism implies that there is one fundamental moral relationship between people, namely, the relationship of benefactor to beneficiary. On this view, people relate to each other morally as recipients or creators of utility. On a deontological view, there is a wide range of special social relationships that create their own special, intrinsic moral duties: parent-child, promisor-promisee, employer-employee and so forth.

Regarding the past, deontological ethics holds that past events place moral obligations on people, and thus moral reasoning should include looking into the past for those morally relevant human transactions. For example, it is because Jerry promised Jim a week ago that he would help him with his homework today, that Jerry has a moral obligation to provide that help. By contrast, utilitarian moral reasoning is applicable to present and future states of affairs. In assessing a moral duty, the utilitarian looks for the moral act that maximizes utility in the present or future, and the past is consulted simply as part of the context to be taken into consideration in attempting to predict present or future utility.

Finally, deontological and utilitarian ethical theories differ regarding their analysis of the features of a moral act relevant for assessing the moral worth of that act. To get at this difference, consider two people, Jack and Jill, who spend an afternoon with their grandmother. Jack, motivated by love for his grandmother, intends to show kindness to her by spending the afternoon visiting with her. As a result, Jack's grandmother is cheered by the company. Jill, motivated by greed, intends to secure a place in her grandmother's will by spending an afternoon visiting with her and Jill is successful in hiding her intention from her grandmother. As a result, Jill's grandmother is cheered by the company.

In these moral actions, we may distinguish four things: a motive, an intent, a means, and a consequence. A **motive** is why one acts. Jack's motive was a feeling of love; Jill's was greed. An **intent** is what act one actually performs. The intent answers the question "What sort of act was it?" Jack's intent was to show kindness toward his grandmother and he performed an act of kindness. Jill's intent was to secure a place in the will, and her act was one of attempting to secure that place. The **means** is the way an agent purposely carries out his or her intention. Jack and Jill each perform the same means, namely, each spends the afternoon visiting with the grandmother. Finally, the **consequence** is the state of affairs produced by the act. In each case, the grandmother was cheered up.

For the utilitarian, the consequences of the act are the sole intrinsic factor that determines its moral worth. Means are evaluated according to their effectiveness in securing the maximization of utility. Intentions and motives are assessed morally in the same way. Intentions and motives receive moral praise and blame not because some are intrinsically right or wrong, but on the basis of whether or not those acts of moral praise or blame will themselves maximize utility.

For the deontologist, the end does not justify the means, and it is appropriate to assess the intrinsic moral worth of means as well as ends. The same thing may be said for motives and intentions, but for the deontologist, the latter are more important than the former. Why? An intention is the key factor in deciding what sort of act a particular action is, and thus the intention is what places the act in the relevant class of acts that is defined by a certain act type. Motives are also important, but they are more relevant to the assessment of the character of the moral actor than of the moral nature of the act itself. Finally, while a deontologist may see consequences as part of the relevant factors for assessing an action, they are less important than the intrinsic features of the act itself.

In the history of philosophy, there have been act and rule deontologists. According to **act deontology**, a moral agent should intuitively grasp the right thing to do in each specific moral situation without relying on moral rules. Act deontology has never gained widespread acceptance because it is too subjective and it fails to capture the nature of moral rules and their role in the moral life. **Rule deontology** is the view that types of acts are right or wrong depending on their conformity or nonconformity to one or more correct moral rules. The most important advocate of rule deontology is the eighteenth-century German philosopher Immanuel Kant. Even though contemporary advocates of deontological ethics have expanded on or abandoned certain aspects of Kant's moral philosophy, he is still regarded as the most important advocate of the position. At the core of Kant's deontological ethics is his notion of a **categorical imperative**, which, according to many interpreters of Kant, has at least three different formulations:

2.2
DEONTOLOGICAL
ETHICS AND THE
NATURE OF
MORAL RULES

CI_1: Act only according to that **maxim** (i.e., principle) by which you can at the same time will that it should become a universal law.

CI_2: Act so that you treat humanity, whether in your own person or in that of another, always as an end and never as a means only.

CI_3: Act only so that the will through its maxim could regard itself at the same time as universally law-giving such that in performing the act, the agent follows the law autonomously.

CI_1 is sometimes called the universalizability formulation of the categorical imperative, and it exhibits two important features. First, a moral rule is **universalizable** in the sense that it is equally binding on all people at all times in relevantly similar situations. Among other things, this principle expresses the principle of consistency: one ought to be consistent about one's moral judgments. If some act X is judged right for some person P, then X is right for anyone relevantly similar to P. Second, moral rules are categorical imperatives, not hypothetical indicatives. For utilitarians, moral rules are **hypothetical indicatives**, that is, they are "if-then" conditional statements such that the consequent that follows the "then" describes a means for attaining the antecedent that follows the "if." For example, "If you want to maximize happiness, then keep your promises." Here, the moral rule "Keep your promises!" is a description of an effective means for maximizing happiness, and the moral rule is to be followed on the condition that one is trying to maximize happiness. By contrast, CI_1 implies that moral rules are categorical imperatives such as "Do not steal!" or "Keep your promises!" Moral rules present themselves to us as categorical statements that apply across the board and not as statements conditioned on the acceptance of some hypothetical goal. Further, moral rules present themselves as imperatives, not as simple means-ends indicatives.

CI_2 expresses the fact that human persons are members of the **kingdom of ends**, that is, that human persons have intrinsic value. Thus human persons should never be treated merely as a means to some other end. People sometimes treat others as means to an end and this is entirely appropriate. A student may treat a professor as a means to an education. But CI_2 implies that human persons should never be treated *solely* as a means to an end. Arguably, the most plausible way to justify this principle is in light of the biblical doctrine that human persons are created in the image of God.

CI_3 expresses what is sometimes called the **principle of autonomy**: duty should be done for duty's sake. For an act to count as a morally correct one, it is not enough for it to be done in accordance with duty; it should be done for the sake of duty. In this way, a human being as moral agent acts as a rational being by treating his own will as a legislator of moral action in this sense: the moral action is done autonomously for no reason other than simple respect for moral duty. Such an act is called an **autonomous act**. In contrast, Kant described what he called a **heteronomous act**, that is, one done to satisfy some inclination, desire or impulse. Heteronomous acts treat moral rules as means to some end—the satisfaction of desire—and thus they fail to count as genuinely moral acts done out of mere respect for the moral law and moral duty. In heteronomous acts, rationality enters the picture as an instrument for desire since reason simply engages in means-to-ends deliberation in the service of satisfaction. But in autonomous action, however, reason serves to produce a will good in itself, one that acts solely for the sake of moral duty.

2.3
ASSESSMENT OF
DEONTOLOGICAL
ETHICS

It is safe to say that deontological ethics captures the commonsense and considered moral intuitions of most people when they reflect about the nature of moral actions and rules. Indeed, it was deontological ethical intuitions that served as the basis for the counterexamples raised against ethical egoism and utilitarianism in chapter twenty-one. It is also safe to say that deontological ethics captures at least part of the core of biblical ethics, especially the Old Testament law, including the Ten Commandments. Critics claim that it is a troublesome feature of deontological ethics that it must rely so heavily on moral intuition. In response, deontologists point out that all philosophical views, including all ethical theories, sooner or later must appeal to intuitions, and the fact that deontological intuitions harmonize so well with the insights of most human beings counts heavily in its favor. This fact places a burden of proof on alternative theories such as utilitarianism, and that burden has not been met.

Besides the issue of the role of moral intuitions in justifying an ethical theory, there are at least four objections that have been raised against deontological ethical theories. First, some argue that while CI_1 may be a necessary condition for a moral rule, it is not sufficient because a maxim could satisfy CI_1 yet still not qualify as a moral rule. In this way, CI_1 is, at best, a formally empty principle without sufficient material content to serve as an action guide which is required of an adequate moral rule. As an illustration of this argument, consider the following maxim M: Everyone should always tie one's left shoe before one's right shoe. Clearly M can be universalized without contradiction, and thus M could be consistently willed as a universal law. But, equally clearly, M does not rise to the level of a moral maxim even though it satisfies CI_1. In response, some deontologists, especially Christian ones, appeal to natural moral law and Scripture as sources of material content for the moral law. Roughly, **natural moral law** consists in true moral principles grounded in the way things are and, in principle, knowable by all people without the aid of Scripture. Many Christian theists see natural moral law as part of God's **general revelation**, truths God has revealed in the creation itself. Both natural moral law and the commands of Scripture provide material content that supplements CI_1, say some deontologists.

A second objection amounts to the claim that deontological approaches to ethics fail to provide adequate consideration for the consequences of moral acts and, it is argued, those consequences, if not the sole determining moral factor, are extremely important in evaluating alternative actions available to an agent. For example, consider a physician who has several medical interventions he could employ in attempting to benefit his patient. Surely, the doctor should select that medical means that would maximize benefit for his patient and all those affected by the moral act. Since deontological ethics fails to weigh adequately the consequences of moral acts, it fails as an ethical theory.

In response, deontologists point out that deontological theories vary in the considerations they give to consequences of moral acts, but it is clearly false that they disregard them altogether. Consider the medical case in the last paragraph. A physician may subscribe to the deontological principle "One ought to benefit and not harm one's patient." Given this principle, different medical interventions may honor this principle to varying degrees. All things being equal, the doctor should perform that intervention which most exemplifies the moral rule. In this case, the moral rule is intrinsically correct and not justified on the basis of consequences, but consequences enter the picture as factual considerations which help the doctor decide the best way to respect a moral rule justified independent of those consequences. By contrast, if the moral rule is interpreted in a utilitarian way, then not only are the consequences of the various medical interventions evaluated morally solely in terms of the utility they produce, but the moral rule itself is justified relative to alternative rules on the grounds that if most people follow that rule it will maximize utility compared to most people following an alternative rule. In a particular situation, it may well be that a deontological and utilitarian approach will justify the same medical action, but they will do so for different reasons and, in any case, the deontologist does, in fact, have room for consequences in his overall depiction of morality.

A third objection to deontological theories is that they fail to deal adequately with moral conflicts in which more than one moral rule is at stake and one cannot honor all the relevant rules. The utilitarian has no such problem because in such cases, utilitarianism implies that one ought to perform that action or follow that rule that maximizes utility compared to alternative actions or rules. But deontological theories provide no guidance in such cases and this counts against deontological theories.

Deontologists claim that however much this objection counts against Kant's particular version of deontological ethics, it is not a sufficient defeater of deontological theories in general since those theories have, in fact, provided a response to conflict situations.

To understand the deontological response to this objection, it is necessary to review some important ideas discussed in chapter twenty: three views of an absolute moral rule and three deontological systems. First, consider the following three analyses of a moral absolute P:

1. P is a moral absolute just in case P is a moral proposition that is objectively true irrespective of the beliefs of individuals or cultures.

2. P is a moral absolute just in case P satisfies (1) above and is universalizable, i.e., equally binding on all people at all times in relevantly similar situations.

3. P is a moral absolute just in case P satisfies (1) and (2) and P has the highest degree of incumbency within its scope of application.

(1) is the most fundamental sense of a moral absolute. It is sometimes called moral **objectivism**, and it amounts to a rejection of **subjectivism**, roughly, the idea that believing a moral proposition is what makes it true relative to those who believe it. (2) is also a crucial notion of a moral absolute. Most deontological ethicists would accept (1) and (2), or since (1) is incorporated into (2), they would simply accept the objectivity and universalizability of moral rules. (2) entails that moral rules do not have exceptions. An **exception** to a moral rule is a case where the rule should apply but, for some reason, it is judged inapplicable and has no relevance to the moral case under consideration.

(3) is controversial and it expresses a more stringent understanding of an absolute: an absolute is such that it is a true, exceptionless moral principle that has the **highest degree of incumbency**, that is, it cannot be overridden by a more weighty principle. In this view, only those absolutes with the maximum weight qualify as moral statements. An absolute is like an ace. It can trump (override) all rivals but cannot itself be trumped. Put differently, (3) implies that all moral absolutes are equally weighty.

It would seem that this understanding of an absolute is too strong. Surely, if a moral statement did have the highest degree of incumbency, it would be an absolute. But we seem to have absolute (objectively true, exceptionless) duties that can be overridden by more important duties. The notion of weightier and less weighty absolutes is not unintelligible, and in fact, it plays an important role in the moral life (see chap. 20). To see this, consider what philosophers call a prima facie duty. A **prima facie duty** is an objectively true, exceptionless moral duty that can be overridden by a weightier duty in a specific instance. When this occurs, the prima facie duty does not disappear, but continues to apply to the specific instance in question and make its presence felt. An **exemption** to a moral absolute occurs when that absolute is overridden by a weightier duty. The difference between an exemption and an exception is this. With an exemption, the overridden principle continues to apply. In the latter case, the excepted principle no longer applies at all. Arguably, exemptions do happen to moral duties but exceptions do not.

Given the distinction between exemptions and exceptions, many absolutists believe that while objectively true moral rules are universalizable and thus do not admit of exceptions within the relevant range of situations to which those rules apply (there are no cases in which, for example, the moral rule "Do not lie" should apply but where it simply vanishes and may be completely disregarded), moral rules do admit of exemptions. In those cases, the rule still applies, it may be overridden by a weightier rule, but the exempted principle still makes its presence felt and must be honored by being overridden only to the degree necessary to honor the weightier principle.

Besides these three different understandings of an absolute moral rule, there are three different deontological systems regarding how to treat moral conflict situations. First, there is **unqualified absolutism**, the view that all moral duties are equally weighty, that the third sense of an absolute above is correct, and thus that there are no prima facie duties. All supposed inescapable moral dilemmas are only apparently unavoidable and there will always be a way to escape the dilemma. The second and third views are called conflicting absolutism and graded absolutism. Both positions accept the existence of prima facie duties and the notion that there are weightier and less weighty duties. Thus advocates of these points of view reject the third understanding of an absolute. Further, both positions believe that genuine moral conflicts occur. However, they differ as to how we should view the action performed in such conflict situations. According to **graded absolutism** (also called the **greater of two goods view**), when one does the greater good, one performs a morally correct act even if one went against a lesser moral rule. For example, if one lies to save a life, then what one did was a good thing. According to **conflicting absolutism** (also called the **lesser of two evils view**), if one lies to save a life, then one still does something wrong, because a moral rule was violated, even though one did the lesser of two evils. Given these different understandings of an absolute moral rule and these three deontological systems, advocates of deontological ethics believe they have, indeed, provided guidance for handling moral conflict cases, and thus this objection has been rebutted.

Finally, some have criticized deontological theories on the grounds that they are preoccupied with moral actions and rules, they fail to give due consideration to the nature of virtue and the good person, and they do not give any advice as to how to develop character. In fact, on at least one reading of Kant, if one does a morally correct act because he desired to do so, that actually counts against the moral worth of the act, and this is highly implausible. According to Kantian deontology, a moral act is one done solely out of respect for moral duty. If an act is done for the sake of satisfying desire, it is a heteronomous act and, to that extent, it falls short of moral worth. Consider two people, Frank and Joe, who are considering whether or not to commit adultery. Frank very much wants to commit adultery and struggles a great deal with his decision, but in the end, he refrains, not because he wants to, but because it is his moral duty. By contrast, Joe, having developed a pure heart through years of virtuous living, deeply desires to honor his wife and has a great moral distaste for adultery. With no struggle at all, Joe refrains. On one interpretation of Kant, Joe's act is worth less than Frank's from a moral point of view because it is done out of desire and thus is heteronomous, while Frank's act of refraining is strictly an autonomous act. But surely this is backward. Joe's act is at least of equal value to Frank's and, arguably more morally worthy, so deontological ethical theory fails on this score.

It is open to a deontologist to respond by drawing a distinction between two kinds of desires: **morally relevant desire** is a desire to do one's duty that results from a cultivation of a desire for moral holiness. In contrast, **heteronomous self-interest** is a form of desire that seeks "moral" action solely as a means to the satisfaction of a desire—for example, a desire to be liked, that is not directed towards holiness and moral rightness. Given this distinction, a deontologist could argue that an autonomous act can and, in fact, ought to be done according to a morally relevant desire, and a heteronomous act is one done for morally irrelevant self-interest. By way of application, the deontologist could claim that Joe's act is superior to Frank's because it was done according to a stronger morally relevant desire and, in this way, Joe actually showed more respect for morality as such than did Frank.

Even if this response is a good one, it still seems true that deontological ethics does not provide an adequate analysis of virtue, character and the good person. This problem raises the question of the relative merits of deontological and virtue ethics. So to address this problem sufficiently, it is important to turn to an analysis of virtue ethics.

3 VIRTUE ETHICS

Virtue theory, also called **aretaic ethics** (from the Greek word *aretē*, "virtue"), has a long and distinguished pedigree, going back to Aristotle and Plato, running through Thomas Aquinas, and including many contemporary advocates. Virtue ethicists sometimes claim that deontological ethics fails because it abstracts from the moral agent himself, it focuses entirely on doing the right things instead of on being a good person, and it provides little guidance for understanding how to develop ethical character and moral motivation. By contrast, central to virtue ethics is the question of what a good person is and how a good person is developed. Further, the claim is made that deontological ethics places too much emphasis on moral autonomy, whereas virtue theory includes an emphasis on community and relationships. The remainder of this section will survey an exposition and evaluation of virtue ethics.

Virtue ethics is teleological in nature. The sort of **teleology** (focus upon goals or ends) involved in virtue ethics is not like that of utilitarianism. Utilitarianism is teleological in the sense that it focuses on what sort of action will maximize utility. Virtue ethics focuses on the overall purpose of life, namely, to live well and achieve excellence and skill as a human person. In this sense, virtue ethics is deeply connected to a vision of life as a whole and of the ideal human person. Given an understanding of the purpose of life and of ideal human flourishing and skillful living that is part of that purpose, an ethics of virtue is an attempt to clarify the nature of a good person and how one is developed in light of this overarching vision of life. Put differently, virtue ethics aims at defining and developing the good person and the good life, and virtues are those character traits that enable people to achieve **eudaimonia** or **happiness**, not understood as a state of pleasurable satisfaction, but rather as a state of well-being, of excellence and skill at life.

3.1
EXPOSITION OF
VIRTUE ETHICS

Classic virtue ethics includes a commitment to **essentialism**, roughly, the idea that human beings have an essence or nature. An essence is a set of properties—for humans, those that constitute what it is to be human—that define the kind of thing an entity is and are such that if the entity in question loses them, it ceases to exist. To illustrate, Socrates has humanness as his essence, and has the property of being white as an accidental feature. Socrates could lose his skin color and still exist, but if he lost his humanness, he would cease to be. Moreover, being human tells us what Socrates is by his very nature. According to **classic virtue ethics**, human nature provides the grounds for ideal human functioning; one who functions ideally and skillfully in life is one who functions properly in accordance with human nature. Human nature defines what is unique and proper for human flourishing, and a bad person is one who lives contrary to human nature. Thus, in Romans 1:26-27, Paul argues that homosexuality is wrong because it is "unnatural," literally, "against nature," that is, it is contrary to proper human functioning in accordance with the essence of being human.

An illustration may help to clarify this notion further. A bad or dysfunctional carburetor is one that is not functioning the way it ought to function, that is, according to the way it was designed to function by its very nature. Similarly, a dysfunctional sexual life is one that is not functioning the way it ought to function, that is, according to the way humans were designed to function by their very nature.

In **contemporary virtue ethics**, some, such as Alasdair MacIntyre, have rejected essentialism and sought to explicate virtue ethics in an antiessentialist context. Roughly, virtues are features judged to be skills relevant to the good life as that is understood relative to the narrative embodied in different traditions. A tradition is a community whose members are united by a core of shared beliefs and a commitment to them. Thus virtues are not grounded in an objective human nature; rather, they are linguistic constructions relative to the valuations and commitments of different traditions. Whether this contemporary understanding of virtue ethics is adequate is something to be considered later.

Given a vision of ideal human functioning and skill, virtue ethics places great importance on character and habit. **Character** is the sum total of an individual's habits, and a **habit** is a disposition to think, feel, desire and act in a certain way without having to will consciously to do so. A **virtue** is a habit of excellence, a beneficial tendency, a skilled disposition that enables a person to realize the crucial potentialities that constitute proper human flourishing according to ideal human nature. Put more simply, a virtue is a skill that suits one for excellence at life.

Virtues go beyond moral virtues. For example, there are rational virtues such as the desire to seek truth, to be rational and so forth. Traditionally, virtue theory included a commitment to the four cardinal virtues of prudence, justice, courage and temperance. Christianity added the so-called distinctively Christian virtues of faith, hope and love.

Finally, there have been a number of different views as to how to develop virtue, but the spiritual disciplines have been central to a Christian understanding of character development for some time and they are reemerging as important aspects of sanctification. So understood, a **spiritual discipline**, such as fasting, solitude or silence, is a repeated bodily activity, done in submission to the Holy Spirit, aimed at developing habits that train a person in a life of virtue. A spiritual discipline is very much like playing the scales on a piano. One does not play the scales to get good at playing the scales. Rather, one plays the scales to form the habits necessary for being a skillful piano player. Similarly, one does not perform spiritual disciplines to get good at them, but rather to get good at life. A spiritual discipline is a means to habit formation relevant to the development of character and virtue.

3.2 EVALUATION OF VIRTUE ETHICS	Virtue ethics has secured a wide following throughout the history of ethics, and it is easy to see why. Its core notions of the purpose of life, the good person, character and virtue capture much of what is central to the moral life. In fact, it is often easier to secure agreement among people about what a good person is and who fits that category than it is to reach consensus about the correct thing to do in a particular situation or about the correct set of moral rules.

Still, virtue ethics is not without its critics and two objections are often raised against it. The first one, touched on above, is the claim that given naturalistic evolutionary theory, several notions at the core of virtue theory, while not logically impossible, are nevertheless implausible. Such things as an overarching purpose to life, genuine natures, normative proper and improper function and a general teleological outlook are hard to harmonize with a view that depicts humans as creatures that have evolved through a blind process of chance and necessity.

Virtue ethicists may offer two responses to this. First, they can admit the force of the objection and build a theory of virtue ethics without the traditional metaphysical framework. Most often, this strategy is taken by those who adopt some form of postmodernism. On this view, virtues are those habits a tradition or linguistic community takes to be valuable and skillful relative to the shared narrative and belief commitments of that tradition or community. While this approach does preserve some sort of virtue ethics, it is not clear that this community-relative version is worthy of the title. On the classic view, there really is a difference between a good person and a bad one, a skillful, functional life of virtue and a dysfunctional life of vice. Thus the whole point of virtue theory is to help clarify and develop people who are really functioning the way they were intended to function. However, on the community-relative view, a virtue or vice turns out to be what a group chooses to count as such, perhaps by embedding certain terms of appraisal in the group's distinctive form of life. But it seems neither necessary nor sufficient for something genuinely to be a virtue that it be regarded as such by a tradition or community. It is not necessary because something such as humility is actually a virtue even if no community regards it to be one. It is not sufficient because if the community is a gang, it may treat the ability to steal or hate members outside the gang as a virtue, but this would not make it so. In the final analysis, community-relative virtues or values reduce moral notions to those of mere custom. As a result, they trivialize the moral life and fail to provide the resources for something to rise to the level of a real virtue.

Second, an advocate of virtue ethics can argue that since, strictly speaking, it is logically possible to embrace classic virtue theory and the metaphysics that is part of it along with naturalistic evolutionary theory, then there is no good reason to be forced to choose one or the other. This response may be convincing to some, but given the metaphysics of both naturalistic evolution and classic virtue theory, the two do not seem to sit easily with each other. Naturalistic evolutionary theory makes the existence of purpose in life, essentialism, teleology and the like fairly implausible, and since these are central to classic virtue theory, this move will not be persuasive to many. A more promising line of approach may be seen by considering the following syllogism:

P: If naturalistic evolutionary theory is true, than classic virtue ethics is false.

Q: Naturalistic evolutionary theory is true.

Therefore,

R: Classic virtue ethics is false.

It is open to a defender of classic virtue ethics to embrace the *modus ponens* form of the argument, accept *Q* ("Classic virtue ethics is true") and conclude with *R* ("Naturalistic evolutionary theory is false"). In this way, classic virtue ethics provides a defeater for naturalistic evolutionary theory.

The second objection to virtue ethics may fairly be called the classic criticism of the theory. According to this objection, virtue ethics simply fails to give guidance in resolving moral dilemmas and in knowing what to do in various moral situations. This is especially true when virtue ethics is compared with rule-based ethical theories such as deontological ethics. Rule-based theories are far better suited for providing such guidance than is virtue ethics.

This objection may be somewhat overstated if it means that virtue theory provides no guidance for the moral life. Asking questions such as "What would Jesus do in this situation?" or trying to imitate virtuous people does provide guidance for leading a morally superior life. Still, the objection does carry some force because virtue ethics does not seem to provide the sort of clarity that rule-based theories do when it comes to assessing difficult moral situations.

If one grants that this objection carries weight, does that mean that one ought to abandon virtue ethics? One's answer to this question will depend on one's view about how virtue and deontological ethical theories should be integrated. Many theorists hold that virtues and moral rules should coexist in some way. They claim that virtues without rules are blind, but rules without virtues are motivationally impotent. There are three different positions on how virtue and deontological ethics should be integrated:

1. **Pure virtue ethics**: The virtues are basic and have intrinsic value; deontological moral rules are derived from the virtues. For example, the duty to behave justly towards others derives from the virtue of being fair. In this sense, moral rules are both expressions of what virtuous people typically do in certain circumstances and they are instrumentally valuable as means for developing virtues.

2. The **standard deontic view** or the **correspondence thesis**: Moral rules are intrinsically valuable and basic, and they obligate people to perform certain actions regardless of whether they possess the required virtues. Virtues are dispositions to obey correct moral rules. As such, virtues have only instrumental value as motivators and aids that help people obey the moral law.

3. The **complementary thesis**: Both virtue and deontological ethics are necessary for an adequate moral system. Neither virtues nor moral rules is basic; rather, each has intrinsic value and they complement each other. A person has a duty to be a certain kind of person and to obey correct moral rules. The virtues refer to the character traits that should characterize a good person and moral rules provide guidance for defining right and wrong moral actions. Thus each has a different focus—virtues focus on the agent and rules on the action—and a comprehensive moral theory will include elements, as basic elements, from each theory.

Each position has had its share of advocates and there is no clear winner in this debate. However, it may be that the complementary view best expresses the ethics of the Bible since Scripture seems to give weight and intrinsic value both to moral commands and virtues of character.

CHAPTER SUMMARY

The vast majority of Christian thinkers throughout the history of the church have embraced either deontological or virtue ethics or some combination of the two. Deontological ethics focuses on right and wrong moral actions and moral laws, and it holds that some moral acts and rules are intrinsically right or wrong irrespective of the consequences produced by doing those acts or following those rules. According to deontological ethics, morality is its own point, at least in part, and moral duty should be done for its own sake. By contrast, virtue ethics focuses on the nature and formation of a good person and on the sort of dispositions and character traits that constitute the good person. According to virtue ethics, the good person is one who is functioning properly, that is, as a human ought to function, and thus is one skilled at life.

Act and rule deontological theories were contrasted and emphasis was placed on the latter. Rule deontology is the view that types of acts are right or wrong depending on their conformity or nonconformity to one or more correct moral rules. Central to rule deontology is the notion of a categorical imperative. Three different formulations of a categorical imperative were given, and five objections to deontological ethics were evaluated. Along the way, three different senses of an absolute moral rule were offered, and three different deontological systems were described.

Virtue ethics focuses on the overall purpose of life, namely to live well and achieve excellence and skill as a human person. In this sense, virtue ethics is deeply connected to a vision of life as a whole and of the ideal human person. Given an understanding of the purpose of life and of ideal human flourishing and skillful living that is part of that purpose, an ethics of virtue is an attempt to clarify the nature of a good person and how one is developed in light of this overarching vision of life. Classic virtue ethics was described, and a brief characterization of a contemporary postmodern virtue theory was presented.

An evaluation of two main arguments against virtue ethics was provided: the problem of harmonizing it with naturalistic evolutionary theory and the claim that it fails to give adequate guidance in morally difficult situations. The chapter closed with a presentation of three different ways of integrating deontological and virtue ethics: pure virtue ethics, the correspondence thesis and the complementary thesis.

CHECKLIST OF BASIC TERMS AND CONCEPTS

act deontology
aretaic ethics
autonomous act
categorical imperative
character
classic virtue ethics
complementary thesis
conflicting absolutism (or lesser of two evils view)
consequence
contemporary virtue ethics
deontological ethics
deontology
essentialism
eudaimonia or happiness
exception
exemption
general revelation
graded absolutism (or greater of two goods view)
habit
heteronomous act
heteronomous self-interest
highest degree of incumbency

hypothetical indicative
instrumental value
intent
intrinsic value
kingdom of ends
maxim
means
moral value or rightness
morally relevant desire
motive
natural moral law
nonmoral value or goodness
objectivism
prima facie duty
principle of autonomy
pure virtue ethics
rule deontology
spiritual discipline
standard deontic view or correspondence thesis
subjectivism
teleology
universalizable
unqualified absolutism
virtue
virtue ethics

PART VI

PHILOSOPHY OF RELIGION AND PHILOSOPHICAL THEOLOGY

23

THE EXISTENCE OF GOD
I

For it is owing to their wonder that men
both now begin and at first began to philosophize;
they wondered originally at the obvious difficulties,
then advanced little by little
and stated difficulties about the greater matters,
e.g., about the phenomena of the moon
and those of the sun and the stars, and about the origin of the universe.
ARISTOTLE METAPHYSICS A.2.982ᴮ10-15

No question is more sublime than why there is a Universe:
why there is anything rather than nothing.
DEREK PARFIT, "WHY ANYTHING? WHY THIS?"
LONDON REVIEW OF BOOKS, JANUARY 22, 1998

1 INTRODUCTION

One of the second-order disciplines of philosophy which is of special interest to the Christian is **philosophy of religion**. As it appears on the contemporary scene, there are actually two rather different disciplines going under the name of philosophy of religion. What we shall be concerned with here is the second-order discipline pursued by professional philosophers, who typically participate in a professional society like the American Philosophical Association. Philosophy of religion is also a second-order discipline of religious studies, where it is typically carried out by professors of religion or theology who are active professionally in societies like the American Academy of Religion. These two approaches to philosophy of religion have a very different texture. Loosely speaking, we may say that the former is concerned with philosophizing about problems raised by religious truth claims, whereas the latter tends to philosophize about the phenomenon of religion itself. The latter therefore resembles more closely than the former the discipline of comparative religion, and when its practitioners do reflect on a problem of philosophical significance, they often lack the conceptual tools furnished by training in analytic philosophy, which is the dominant tradition in philosophy of religion as it is pursued by professional philosophers today. Although philosophy of religion has been recognized as a delineated second-order discipline of philosophy as far back as the German philosopher G. W. F. Hegel, who lectured on the subject, analytic philosophy of religion is a recent movement of the last half century or so, which is one of the most exciting and burgeoning areas of contemporary Anglo-American philosophy.

Within the discipline of philosophy of religion certain standard topics have emerged, such as the nature of religious language (Do sentences having religious content make factual assertions which are either true or false?); religious epistemology (How can one can be justified or warranted in believing religious truth claims?); the existence of God (Is there such a being as God?); the coherence of theism (Does the concept of God make sense?); the problem of evil (Does the suffering in the world preclude God's existence?); comparative religions (How are the religious truth claims of other religious faiths to be evaluated?); the problem of miracles (How should divine action in the natural world be understood?); the soul and immortality (What is the nature of man and life after death?); religious experience (Can we experience God and how?); and revealed religious doctrines (How are we to understand doctrines such as the Trinity, the Incarnation, heaven and hell, providence, predestination, biblical inspiration and a host of other doctrines?).

It is evident that philosophy of religion not only overlaps with several other disciplines of philosophy, but also with the concerns of systematic theology. Indeed, it is difficult to see how the task of the *Christian* philosopher of religion differs greatly from that of the systematic theologian. Although some Christian thinkers would say that **systematic theology** differs from philosophy of religion in that the systematic theologian alone presupposes the truth of Scripture, it is difficult to see why the Christian philosopher should be peculiarly hamstrung, restricted to natural reason alone rather than permitted to avail himself of all sources of truth, of which he believes Scripture to be one. Insofar as he philosophizes as a Christian rather than affects an epistemological stance that misrepresents his actual beliefs, he is, in effect, indistinguishable from the systematic theologian, at least insofar as the latter is engaged in the formulation and defense of Christian doctrine. Indeed, the most interesting and important work in exploring issues in systematic theology today is increasingly being done, not by theologians, but by analytic philosophers of religion.

In this section we shall, due to constraints of space, restrict ourselves to the discussion of some of the most central topics in philosophy of religion insofar as these topics have not already been addressed elsewhere in this book. Specifically, in this and the succeeding chapter we shall explore the question of the existence of God.

2 THE EXISTENCE OF GOD

It has become conventional wisdom that in light of the critiques of Hume and Kant there are no good arguments for the existence of God. But insofar as we mean by a "good argument" an argument that is formally and informally valid and consists of true premises that are more plausible than their negations, there do appear to be good arguments for God's existence, and there are on the contemporary scene many philosophers who think so. Indeed, it would be fair to say that the rise of analytic philosophy of religion has been accompanied by a resurgence of interest in **natural theology**, that branch of theology that seeks to prove God's existence apart from the resources of authoritative divine revelation. Alvin Plantinga, perhaps the most important philosopher of religion now writing, has defended what he calls "Two Dozen (or so) Arguments for God's Existence."[1] In the space of these chapters we shall examine four of the most important.

The **cosmological argument** is a family of arguments that seek to demonstrate the existence of a Sufficient Reason or First Cause of the existence of the cosmos. The roll of the defenders of this argument reads like a *Who's Who* of western philosophy: Plato, Aristotle, ibn Sina, al-Ghazali, Maimonides, Anselm, Aquinas, Scotus, Descartes, Spinoza, Leibniz and Locke, to name but some. The arguments can be grouped into three basic types: the *kalam* cosmological argument for a First Cause of the beginning of the universe, the Thomist cosmological argument for a sustaining Ground of Being of the world, and the Leibnizian cosmological argument for a Sufficient Reason why something exists rather than nothing.

2.1
THE
COSMOLOGICAL
ARGUMENT

The *kalam* **cosmological argument** derives its name from the Arabic word designating medieval Islamic scholasticism, the intellectual movement largely responsible for developing the argument. It aims to show that the universe had a beginning at some moment in the finite past and, since something cannot come out of nothing, must therefore have a transcendent cause, which brought the universe into being. Classical proponents of the argument sought to demonstrate that the universe began to exist on the basis of philosophical arguments against the existence of an infinite, temporal regress of past events. Contemporary interest in the argument arises largely out of the startling empirical evidence of astrophysical cosmology for a beginning of space and time. Today the controlling paradigm of cosmology is the **standard big bang model**, according to which the space-time universe originated *ex nihilo* about fifteen billion years ago. Such an origin *ex nihilo* seems to many to cry out for a transcendent cause.

2.1.1
EXPOSITION
OF THE
ARGUMENTS

By contrast the **Thomist cosmological argument**, named for the medieval philosophical theologian Thomas Aquinas, seeks a cause that is first, not in the temporal sense, but in the sense of rank. Aquinas agreed that "if the world and motion have a first beginning, some cause must clearly be posited for this origin of the world and of motion" (*Summa contra gentiles* 1.13.30). But since he did not regard the *kalam* arguments for the past's finitude as demonstrative, he argued for God's existence on the more difficult assumption of the eternity of the world. On Aquinas's Aristotelian-inspired metaphysic, every existing finite thing is composed of essence and existence and is therefore radically contingent. A thing's **essence** is an individual nature which serves to define what that thing is. Now if an essence is to exist, there must be conjoined with that essence an **act of being.** This act of being involves a continual bestowal of being, or the thing would be annihilated. Essence is in potentiality to the act of being, and therefore without the bestowal of being the essence would not exist. For the

---

[1]Alvin Plantinga, "Two Dozen (or so) Theistic Arguments," lecture presented at the 33d Annual Philosophy Conference, Wheaton College, Wheaton, Ill., October 23-25, 1986.

same reason no substance can actualize itself; for in order to bestow being on it-self it would have to be already actual. A pure potentiality cannot actualize it-self but requires some external cause. Now although Aquinas argued that there cannot be an infinite regress of causes of being (because in such a series all the causes would be merely instrumental and so no being would be produced, just as no motion would be produced in a watch without a spring even if it had an infi-nite number of gears) and that therefore there must exist a First Uncaused Cause of being, his actual view was that there can be no intermediate causes of being at all, that any finite substance is sustained in existence immediately by the Ground of Being. This must be a being that is not composed of essence and existence and, hence, requires no sustaining cause. We cannot say that this be-ing's essence includes existence as one of its properties, for existence is not a property, but an act, the instantiating of an essence. Therefore, we must con-clude that this being's essence just *is* existence. In a sense, this being has no es-sence; rather, it is the pure act of being, unconstrained by any essence. It is, as Thomas says, *ipsum esse subsistens*, the act of being itself subsisting. Thomas identifies this being with the God whose name was revealed to Moses as "I am" (Ex 3:14).

The German polymath Gottfried Wilhelm Leibniz, for whom the third form of the argument is named, sought to develop a version of the cosmological argu-ment from **contingency** without the Aristotelian metaphysical underpinnings of the Thomist argument. In his essay "The Principles of Nature and of Grace, Based on Reason," Leibniz wrote, "The first question which should rightly be asked is this: why is there something rather than nothing?" Leibniz meant this question to be truly universal, not merely to apply to finite things. On the basis of his **principle of sufficient reason**, as stated in his treatise *The Monadology*, that "no fact can be real or existent, no statement true, unless there be a suffi-cient reason why it is so and not otherwise," Leibniz held that his question must have an answer. It will not do to say that the universe (or even God) just exists as a **brute fact**, a simple fact that cannot be explained. There must be an expla-nation why it exists. He went on to argue that the sufficient reason cannot be found in any individual thing in the universe, nor in the collection of such things which comprise the universe, nor in earlier states of the universe, even if these regress infinitely. Therefore, there must exist an ultramundane being that is **metaphysically necessary** in its existence, that is to say, its nonexistence is impossible. It is the sufficient reason for its own existence as well as for the exis-tence of every contingent thing.

**2.1.2
EVALUATION
OF THE
ARGUMENTS**

In evaluating these arguments, let us consider them in reverse order. A simple statement of a **Leibnizian cosmological argument** runs as follows:

1. Every existing thing has an explanation of its existence, either in the ne-cessity of its own nature or in an external cause.

2. If the universe has an explanation of its existence, that explanation is God.

3. The universe is an existing thing.

4. Therefore the explanation of the existence of the universe is God.

Is this a good argument? One of the principal objections to Leibniz's own formulation of the argument is that the principle of sufficient reason as stated in
The Monadology seems evidently false. There cannot be an explanation of why
there are any contingent states of affairs at all, for if such an explanation is contingent, then it too must have a further explanation, whereas if it is necessary,
then the states of affairs explained by it must also be necessary. Some theists
have responded to this objection by agreeing that one must ultimately come to
some explanatory stopping point that is simply a brute fact, a being whose existence is unexplained. For example, Richard Swinburne claims that in answering
the question "Why is there something rather than nothing?" we must finally
come to the brute existence of some contingent being. This being will not serve
to explain its own existence (and, hence, Leibniz's question goes unanswered),
but it will explain the existence of everything else. Swinburne argues that God
is the best explanation of why everything other than the brute Ultimate exists
because as a unique and infinite being God is simpler than the variegated and finite universe.

But the above formulation of the Leibnizian argument avoids the objection
without retreating to the dubious position that God is a contingent being.
Premise (1) merely requires any existing *thing* to have an explanation of its existence, either in the necessity of its own nature or in some external cause. This
premise is compatible with there being brute *facts* about the world. What it precludes is that there could exist things—substances exemplifying properties—
that just exist inexplicably. This principle seems quite plausible, at least more so
than its contradictory, which is all that is required for a successful argument. On
this analysis, there are two kinds of being: **necessary beings**, which exist of their
own nature and so have no external cause of their existence, and **contingent
beings**, whose existence is accounted for by causal factors outside themselves.

Premise (2) is, in effect, the contrapositive of the typical atheist response to
Leibniz that on the atheistic worldview the universe simply exists as a brute
contingent thing. Atheists typically assert that, there being no God, it is false
that everything has an explanation of its existence, for the universe, in this
case, just exists inexplicably. In so saying, the atheist implicitly recognizes that if
the universe has an explanation, then God exists as its explanatory ground.
Since, as premise (3) states, the universe is obviously an existing thing (especially evident in its very early stages when its density was so extreme), it follows
that God exists.

It is open to the atheist to retort that while the universe has an explanation
of its existence, that explanation lies not in an external ground but in the necessity of its own nature. In other words, (2) is false; the universe is a metaphysically necessary being. This was the suggestion of David Hume, who demanded,
"Why may not the material universe be the necessarily existent being?" Indeed,
"How can anything, that exists from eternity, have a cause, since that relation
implies a priority in time and a beginning of existence?" (*Dialogues Concerning
Natural Religion*, part 9).

This is an extremely bold suggestion on the part of the atheist. We have, we
think we can safely say, a strong intuition of the universe's contingency. A possible world in which no concrete objects exist certainly seems conceivable. We

generally trust our modal intuitions on other matters; if we are to do otherwise with respect to the universe's contingency, then atheists need to provide some reason for such skepticism other than their desire to avoid theism. But they have yet to do so.

Still, it would be desirable to have some stronger argument for the universe's contingency than our modal intuitions alone. Could the Thomist cosmological argument help us here? If successful, it would show that the universe is a contingent being causally dependent on a necessary being for its continued existence. The difficulty with appeal to the Thomist argument, however, is that it is very difficult to show that things are, in fact, contingent in the special sense required by the argument. Certainly things are naturally contingent in that their continued existence is dependent on a myriad of factors including particle masses and fundamental forces, temperature, pressure, entropy level and so forth, but this natural contingency does not suffice to establish things' metaphysical contingency in the sense that being must continually be added to their essences lest they be spontaneously annihilated. Indeed, if Thomas's argument does ultimately lead to an absolutely simple being whose essence is existence, then one might well be led to deny that beings are metaphysically composed of essence and existence if the idea of such an absolutely simple being proves to be unintelligible (see discussion of divine simplicity in chap. 26).

But what about the *kalam* cosmological argument? An essential property of a metaphysically necessary and ultimate being is that it be eternal, that is to say, without beginning or end. If the universe is not eternal, then it could not be, as Hume suggested, a metaphysically necessary being. But it is precisely the aim of the *kalam* cosmological argument to show that the universe is not eternal but had a beginning. It would follow that the universe must therefore be contingent in its existence. Not only so, the *kalam* argument shows the universe to be contingent in a very special way: it came into existence out of nothing. The atheist who would answer Leibniz by holding that the existence of the universe is a brute fact, an exception to the principle of sufficient reason, is thus thrust into the very awkward position of maintaining not merely that the universe exists eternally without explanation, but rather that for no reason at all it magically popped into being out of nothing, a position which might make theism look like a welcome alternative. Thus the *kalam* argument not only constitutes an independent argument for a transcendent Creator but also serves as a valuable supplement to the Leibnizian argument.

The *kalam* cosmological argument may be formulated as follows:

1. Whatever begins to exist has a cause.

2. The universe began to exist.

3. Therefore, the universe has a cause.

Conceptual analysis of what it means to be a cause of the universe then aims to establish some of the theologically significant properties of this being.

Premise (1) seems obviously true—at the least, more so than its negation. It is rooted in the metaphysical intuition that something cannot come into being from nothing. Moreover, this premise is constantly confirmed in our experience. Nevertheless, a number of atheists, in order to avoid the argument's conclusion, have denied the first premise. Sometimes it is said that **quantum physics** furnishes an exception to premise (1), since on the subatomic level events are said to be uncaused (according to the so-called **Copenhagen interpretation**). In the same way, certain theories of cosmic origins are interpreted as showing that the whole universe could have sprung into being out of the subatomic vacuum. Thus the universe is said to be the proverbial free lunch.

This objection, however, is based on misunderstandings. In the first place, not all scientists agree that subatomic events are uncaused. A great many physicists today are quite dissatisfied with the Copenhagen interpretation of subatomic physics and are exploring deterministic theories like that of David Bohm. Thus subatomic physics is not a proven exception to premise (1). Second, even on the traditional, indeterministic interpretation, particles do not come into being out of nothing. They arise as spontaneous fluctuations of the energy contained in the subatomic **vacuum**, which constitutes an indeterministic cause of their origination. Third, the same point can be made about theories of the origin of the universe out of a primordial vacuum. Popular magazine articles touting such theories as getting "something from nothing" simply do not understand that the vacuum is not nothing but rather a sea of fluctuating energy endowed with a rich structure and subject to physical laws. Thus there is no basis for the claim that quantum physics proves that things can begin to exist without a cause, much less that universe could have sprung into being uncaused from literally nothing.

Other critics have said that premise (1) is true only for things *in* the universe, but it is not true *of* the universe itself. But the argument's defender may reply that this objection misconstrues the nature of the premise. Premise (1) does not state merely a physical law like the law of gravity or the laws of thermodynamics, which are valid for things within the universe. Premise (1) is not a physical principle. Rather, premise (1) is a metaphysical principle: being cannot come from nonbeing; something cannot come into existence uncaused from nothing. The principle therefore applies to all of reality, and it is thus metaphysically absurd that the universe should pop into being uncaused out of nothing. This response seems quite reasonable: for on the atheistic view, there was not even the *potentiality* of the universe's existence prior to the big bang, since nothing is prior to the big bang. But then how could the universe become actual if there was not even the potentiality of its existence? It makes much more sense to say that the potentiality of the universe lay in the power of God to create it.

Recently some critics of the *kalam* cosmological argument have denied that in beginning to exist the universe *became actual* or *came into being*. They thereby focus attention on the theory of time underlying the *kalam* argument (see chap. 18). On a static or so-called **B-theory of time** (according to which all moments of time are equally existent) the universe does not in fact come into being or become actual at the big bang; it just exists tenselessly as a four-dimensional space-time block that is finitely extended in the *earlier than* direction. If time is tenseless, then the critics are right that the universe never really comes into being, and therefore the quest for a cause of its coming into being is misconceived. Although Leibniz's question, "Why is there (tenselessly) something rather than nothing?" should still rightly be asked, there would be no reason to look for a cause of the universe's beginning to exist, since on tenseless theories of time the universe did not truly begin to exist by virtue of its having a first event, any more than a meter stick begins to exist by virtue of its having a first centimeter. In affirming that things which begin to exist need a cause, the proponent of the *kalam* cosmological argument assumes the following understanding of that notion, where x ranges over any entity and t ranges over times, whether instants or moments of nonzero finite duration:

A. x begins to exist at t if and only if x comes into being at t.

B. x comes into being at t if and only if (i) x exists at t, and the actual world includes no state of affairs in which x exists timelessly, (ii) t is either the first time at which x exists or is separated from any $t' < t$ at which x existed by an interval during which x does not exist, and (iii) x's existing at t is a tensed fact.

The key clause in (B) is (iii). By presupposing a dynamic or so-called **A-theory of time**, according to which temporal becoming is real, the proponent of the *kalam* cosmological argument justifiably assumes that the universe's existing at a first moment of time represents the moment at which the universe came into being. Thus the real issue separating the proponent of the *kalam* cosmological argument and critics of the first premise is the objectivity of tense and temporal becoming.

Premise (2),*The universe began to exist,* has been supported by both deductive philosophical arguments and inductive scientific arguments. The first of four arguments for this premise that we will consider is the argument based on *the impossibility of the existence of an actual infinite.* It may be formulated as follows:

1. An actual infinite cannot exist.

2. An infinite temporal regress of physical events is an actual infinite.

3. Therefore an infinite temporal regress of physical events cannot exist.

In order to assess this argument, it will be helpful to define some terms. By an **actual infinite**, the argument's defender means any collection having at a time t a number of definite and discrete members that is greater than any natural number $\{0, 1, 2, 3, \ldots\}$. This notion is to be contrasted with a **potential infinite**, which is any collection having at any time t a number of definite and discrete members that is equal to some natural number but which over time increases endlessly toward infinity as a limit. By *exist* proponents of the argument mean "have extra-mental existence," or "be instantiated in the real world." By a "physical event," they mean any change occurring within the space-time universe. Since any change takes time, there are no instantaneous events. Neither could there be an infinitely slow event, since such an "event" would in reality be a changeless state. Therefore, any event will have a finite, nonzero duration. In order that all the events comprising the temporal regress of past events be of equal duration, one arbitrarily stipulates some event as our standard and, taking as our point of departure the present standard event, we consider any series of such standard events ordered according to the relation *earlier than*. The question is whether this series of events is comprised of an actually infinite number of events or not. If not, then since the universe is not distinct from the series of past physical events, the universe must have had a beginning, in the sense of a first standard event. It is therefore not relevant whether the temporal series had a beginning *point* (a first temporal instant). The question is whether there was in the past an event occupying a nonzero, finite temporal interval that was absolutely first, that is, not preceded by any equal interval.

Premise (1) asserts, then, that an actual infinite cannot exist in the real, spatiotemporal world. It is usually alleged that this sort of argument has been invalidated by Georg Cantor's work on the actual infinite and by subsequent developments in set theory. But this allegation misconstrues the nature of both Cantor's system and modern set theory, for the argument does not in fact contradict a single tenet of either. The reason is this: Cantor's system and **set theory** are simply a universe of discourse, a mathematical system based on certain adopted axioms and conventions. The argument's defender may hold that while the actual infinite may be a fruitful and consistent concept within the postulated universe of discourse, it cannot be transposed into the spatiotemporal world, for this would involve counterintuitive absurdities. This can be shown by concrete examples that illustrate the various absurdities that would result if an actual infinite were to be instantiated in the real world.

Take, for example, **Hilbert's Hotel**, a product of the mind of the great German mathematician David Hilbert. As a warm-up, let us first imagine a hotel with a finite number of rooms. Suppose, furthermore, that all the rooms are full. When a new guest arrives asking for a room, the proprietor apologizes, "Sorry, all the rooms are full," and that is the end of the story. But now let us imagine a hotel with an infinite number of rooms and suppose once more that *all the rooms are full.* There is not a single vacant room throughout the entire infinite hotel. Now suppose a new guest shows up, asking for a room. "But of course!" says the proprietor, and he immediately shifts the person in room #1 into room #2, the person in room #2 into room #3, the person in room #3 into room #4 and so on, out to infinity. As a result of these room changes, room #1 now becomes vacant, and the new guest gratefully checks in. But remember, before he arrived, all the rooms were full! Equally curious, according to the mathematicians, there are now no more persons in the hotel than there were before: the number is just infinite. But how can this be? The proprietor just added the new guest's name to the register and gave him his keys—how can there not be one more person in the hotel than before?

But the situation becomes even stranger. For suppose an infinity of new guests show up at the desk, asking for a room. "Of course, of course!" says the proprietor, and he proceeds to shift the person in room #1 into room #2, the person in room #2 into room #4, the person in room #3 into room #6 and so on out to infinity, always putting each former occupant into the room number twice his own. Because any natural number multiplied by two always equals an even number, all the guests wind up in even-numbered rooms. As a result, all the odd-numbered rooms become vacant, and the infinity of new guests is easily accommodated. And yet, before they came, all the rooms were full! And again, strangely enough, the number of guests in the hotel is the same after the infinity of new guests check in as before, even though there were as many new guests as old guests. In fact, the proprietor could repeat this process *infinitely many times,* and yet there would never be one single person more in the hotel than before.

But Hilbert's Hotel is even stranger than the German mathematician made it out to be. For suppose some of the guests start to check out. Suppose the guest in room #1 departs. Is there not now one fewer person in the hotel? Not according to the mathematicians! Suppose the guests in rooms #1, 3, 5, . . . check out. In this case an infinite number of people have left the hotel, but according to the mathematicians, there are no fewer people in the hotel! In fact, we could have every other guest check out of the hotel and repeat this process infinitely many times, and yet there would never be any fewer people in the hotel. Now suppose the proprietor doesn't like having a half-empty hotel (it looks bad for business). No matter! By shifting occupants as before, but in reverse order, he transforms his half-vacant hotel into one that is jammed to the gills. You might think that by these maneuvers the proprietor could always keep this strange hotel fully occupied. But you would be wrong. For suppose that the persons in rooms #4, 5, 6, . . . checked out. At a single stroke the hotel would be virtually emptied, the guest register would be reduced to three names, and the infinite would be converted to finitude. And yet it would remain true that the same number of guests checked out this time as when the guests in rooms #1, 3, 5, . . . checked out! Can anyone believe that such a hotel could exist in reality?

Hilbert's Hotel certainly seems absurd. Since nothing hangs on the illustration's involving a hotel, the argument, if successful, would show in general that it is impossible for an actually infinite number of things to exist in spatiotemporal reality. Students sometimes react to such illustrations as Hilbert's Hotel by saying that we really do not understand the nature of infinity and, hence, these absurdities result. But this attitude is simply mistaken. Infinite set theory is a highly developed and well-understood branch of mathematics, and these absurdities can be seen to result precisely because we *do* understand the notion of a collection with an actually infinite number of members.

Sometimes it is said that we can find counterexamples to the claim that an actually infinite number of things cannot exist, so that premise (1) must be false. For instance, is not every finite distance capable of being divided into 1/2, 1/4, 1/8, . . . , on to infinity? Does that not prove that there are in any finite distance an actually infinite number of parts? The defender of the argument may reply that this objection confuses a potential infinite with an actual infinite. He will point out that while you can continue to divide any distance for as long as you want, such a series is merely potentially infinite, in that infinity serves as a limit that you endlessly approach but never reach. If you assume that any distance is *already* composed out of an actually infinite number of parts, then you are begging the question. You are assuming what the objector is supposed to prove, namely that there is a clear counterexample to the claim that an actually infinite number of things cannot exist.

Again, it is worth reiterating that nothing in the argument need be construed as an attempt to undermine the theoretical system bequeathed by Cantor to modern mathematics. Indeed, some of the most eager enthusiasts of the system of transfinite mathematics are only too ready to agree that these theories have no relation to the real world. Thus Hilbert, who exuberantly extolled Cantor's greatness, nevertheless held that the Cantorian paradise exists only in the ideal world invented by the mathematician and is nowhere to be found in reality. The case against the existence of the actual infinite need say nothing about the use of the idea of the infinite in conceptual mathematical systems.

The second premise states that *an infinite temporal regress of events is an actual infinite*. The second premise asserts that if the series or sequence of changes in time is infinite, then these events considered collectively constitute an actual infinite. The point seems obvious enough, for if there has been a sequence composed of an infinite number of events stretching back into the past, then an actually infinite number of events have occurred. If the series of past events were an actual infinite, then all the absurdities attending the real existence of an actual infinite would apply to it.

In summary: if an actual infinite cannot exist in the real, spatiotemporal world and an infinite temporal regress of events is such an actual infinite, we can conclude that an infinite temporal regress of events cannot exist, that is to say, the temporal series of past physical events had a beginning. And this implies the second premise of the original syllogism of the *kalam* cosmological argument.

The second argument against the possibility of an infinite past that we will consider is the argument based on *the impossibility of forming an actual infinite by successive addition*. It may be formulated as follows:

1. The temporal series of physical events is a collection formed by successive addition.

2. A collection formed by successive addition cannot be an actual infinite.

3. Therefore, the temporal series of physical events cannot be an actual infinite.

Here one does not assume that an actual infinite cannot exist. Even if an actual infinite can exist, it is argued that the temporal series of events cannot be such, since an actual infinite cannot be formed by successive addition, as the temporal series of events is.

Premise (1) presupposes once again an A-theory of time. On such a theory the collection of all past events prior to any given event is not a collection whose members all tenselessly coexist. Rather, it is a collection that is instantiated sequentially or successively in time, one event coming to pass on the heels of another. Since temporal becoming is an objective feature of the physical world, the series of past events is not a tenselessly existing continuum, all of whose members are equally real. Rather, the members of the series come to be and pass away one after another.

Premise (2) asserts that a collection formed by successive addition cannot be an actual infinite. Sometimes this is described as the impossibility of **traversing the infinite**. In order for us to have "arrived" at today, temporal existence has, so to speak, traversed an infinite number of prior events. But before the present event could arrive, the event immediately prior to it would have to arrive, and before that event could arrive, the event immediately prior to it would have to arrive, and so on ad infinitum. No event could ever arrive, since before it could elapse there will always be one more event that had to have happened first. Thus, if the series of past events were beginningless, the present event could not have arrived, which is absurd.

This argument brings to mind Betrand Russell's account of Tristram Shandy, who, in the novel by Sterne, writes his autobiography so slowly that it takes him a whole year to record the events of a single day. Were he mortal, he would never finish, asserts Russell, but if he were immortal, then the entire book could be completed, since to each day there would correspond a year, and both are infinite. Russell's assertion is untenable on an A-theory of time, however, since the future is in reality a potential infinite only. Though he write forever, Tristram Shandy would only get farther and farther behind, so that instead of finishing his autobiography, he will progressively approach a state in which he would be *infinitely* far behind. But he would never reach such a state because the years and hence the days of his life would always be finite in number though indefinitely increasing.

But let us turn the story about: Suppose Tristram Shandy has been writing from eternity past at the rate of one day per year. Should not Tristram Shandy now be infinitely far behind? For if he has lived for an infinite number of years, Tristram Shandy has recorded an equally infinite number of past days. Given the thoroughness of his autobiography, these days are all consecutive days. At any point in the past or present, therefore, Tristram Shandy has recorded a beginningless, infinite series of consecutive days. But now the question inevitably arises: *Which* days are these? Where in the temporal series of events are the days recorded by Tristram Shandy at any given point? The answer can only be that *they are days infinitely distant from the present.* For there is no day on which Tristram Shandy is writing that is finitely distant from the last recorded day.

If Tristram Shandy has been writing for one year's time, then the most recent day he could have recorded is one year ago. But if he has been writing two years, then that same day could not have been recorded by him. For since his intention is to record *consecutive* days of his life, the most recent day he could have recorded is the day immediately after a day at least two years ago. This is because it takes a year to record a day, so that to record two days he must have two years. Similarly, if he has been writing three years, then the most recent day recorded could be no more recent than three years ago plus two days. In fact, the recession into the past of the most recent recordable day can be plotted according to the formula: (present date − n years of writing) + (n − 1) days. In other words, the longer he has written the further behind he has fallen. But what happens if Tristram Shandy has, *ex hypothesi,* been writing for an infinite number of years? The first day of his autobiography recedes to infinity, that is to say, to a day infinitely distant from the present. Nowhere in the past at a finite distance from the present can we find a recorded day, for by now Tristram Shandy is infinitely far behind. The beginningless, infinite series of days which he has recorded are days which lie at an infinite temporal distance from the present. What therefore follows from the Tristram Shandy story is that an infinite series of past events is absurd, for there is no way to traverse the distance from an infinitely distant event to the present, or, more technically, for an event that was once present to recede to an infinite temporal distance.

But now a deeper absurdity bursts into view. For if the series of past events is an actual infinite, then we may ask, why did Tristram Shandy not finish his autobiography yesterday or the day before, since by then an infinite series of moments had already elapsed? Given that in infinite time he would finish the book, then at any point in the infinite past he should already have finished. No matter how far along the series of past events one regresses, Tristram Shandy would have already completed his autobiography. Therefore, at no point in the infinite series of past events could he be finishing the book. We could never look over Tristram Shandy's shoulder to see if he were now writing the last page. For at any point an actually infinite sequence of events would have transpired and the book would have already been completed. Thus at no time in eternity will we find Tristram Shandy writing, which is absurd, since we supposed him to be writing from eternity. And at no point will he finish the book, which is equally absurd, because for the book to be completed, he must at some point have finished. What the Tristram Shandy story really tells us is that an actually infinite temporal regress is absurd.

Sometimes critics indict this argument as a sleight-of-hand trick like **Zeno's paradoxes of motion**. Zeno argued that before Achilles could cross the stadium, he would have to cross halfway; but before he could cross halfway, he would have to cross a quarter of the way; but before he could cross a quarter of the way, he would have to cross an eighth of the way, and so on to infinity. It is evident that Achilles could not even move! Therefore, Zeno concluded, motion is impossible. Now even though Zeno's argument is very difficult to refute, nobody really believes that motion is impossible. Even if Achilles must pass through an infinite number of halfway points in order to cross the stadium, somehow he manages to do so! The argument against the impossibility of traversing an infinite past, some critics allege, must commit the same fallacy as Zeno's paradox.

But such an objection fails to reckon with two crucial disanalogies of an infinite past to Zeno's paradoxes: whereas in Zeno's thought experiments the intervals traversed are *potential* and *unequal*, in the case of an infinite past the intervals are *actual* and *equal*. The claim that Achilles must pass through an infinite number of halfway points in order to cross the stadium is question-begging, for it already assumes that the whole interval is a composition of an infinite number of points, whereas Zeno's opponents, like Aristotle, take the line as a whole to be conceptually prior to any divisions which we might make in it. Moreover, Zeno's intervals, being unequal, sum to a merely finite distance, whereas the intervals in an infinite past sum to an infinite distance. Thus his thought experiments are crucially disanalogous to the task of traversing an infinite number of equal, actual intervals to arrive at our present location.

It is frequently objected that this sort of argument illicitly presupposes an infinitely distant starting point in the past and then pronounces it impossible to travel from that point to today. But if the past is infinite, then there would be no starting point whatever, not even an infinitely distant one. Nevertheless, from any given point in the past, there is only a finite distance to the present, which is easily "traversed." But in fact no proponent of the *kalam* argument of whom we are aware has assumed that there was an infinitely distant starting point in the past. (Even the **Tristram Shandy paradox** does not assert that there was an infinitely distant first day, but merely that there were days infinitely distant in the past.) The fact that there is *no beginning* at all, not even an infinitely distant one, seems only to make the problem worse, not better. To say that the infinite past could have been formed by successive addition is like saying that someone has just succeeded in writing down all the negative numbers, ending at -1. And, we may ask, how is the claim that from any given moment in the past there is only a finite distance to the present even relevant to the issue? The defender of the *kalam* argument could agree to this happily. For the issue is how the *whole* series can be formed, not a finite portion of it. Does the objector think that because every *finite* segment of the series can be formed by successive addition that the whole *infinite* series can be so formed? That is as logically fallacious as saying because every part of an elephant is light in weight, the whole elephant is light in weight. The claim is therefore irrelevant.

In summary: If a collection formed by successive addition cannot be an actual infinite, then since the temporal series of events is a collection formed by successive addition, it follows that the temporal series of events cannot be an actual infinite. This implies, of course, that the temporal series of past physical events is not beginningless.

The third argument for the universe's beginning advanced by contemporary proponents of the *kalam* cosmological argument is an inductive argument based on the expansion of the universe. In 1917, Albert Einstein made a cosmological application of his newly discovered gravitational theory, the **general theory of relativity** (GTR). In so doing he assumed that the universe exists in a steady state, with a constant mean mass density and a constant curvature of space. To his chagrin, however, he found that GTR would not permit such a model of the universe unless he introduced into his gravitational field equations a certain "fudge factor" in order to counterbalance the gravitational effect of matter and so ensure a static universe. Unfortunately, Einstein's static universe was balanced on a razor's edge, and the least perturbation would cause the universe either to implode or to expand. By taking this feature of Einstein's model seriously, the Russian mathematician Alexander Friedman and the Belgian astronomer Georges Lemaître were able to formulate independently in the 1920s solutions to the field equations which predicted an expanding universe.

In 1929 the astronomer Edwin Hubble showed that the red-shift in the optical spectra of light from distant galaxies was a common feature of all measured galaxies and was proportional to their distance from us. This red-shift was taken to be a Doppler effect indicative of the recessional motion of the light source in the line of sight. Incredibly, what Hubble had discovered was the isotropic expansion of the universe predicted by Friedman and Lemaître on the basis of Einstein's GTR.

According to the Friedman-Lemaître model, as time proceeds, the distances separating galactic masses become greater. It is important to understand that as a GTR-based theory, the model does not describe the expansion of the material content of the universe into a preexisting, empty space, but rather the expansion of space itself. The ideal particles of the cosmological fluid constituted by the galactic masses are conceived to be at rest with respect to space but to recede progressively from one another as space itself expands or stretches, just as buttons glued to the surface of a balloon would recede from one another as the balloon inflates. As the universe expands, it becomes less and less dense. This has the astonishing implication that as one reverses the expansion and extrapolates back in time, the universe becomes progressively denser until one arrives at a state of "infinite density"[2] at some point in the finite past. This state represents a **singularity** at which space-time curvature, along with temperature, pressure and density, becomes infinite. It therefore constitutes an edge or boundary to space-time itself. The term "big bang" is thus potentially misleading, since the expansion cannot be visualized from the outside (there being no "outside," just as there is no "before" with respect to the big bang).

The standard big bang model, as the Friedman-Lemaître model came to be called, thus describes a universe that is not eternal in the past but that came into being a finite time ago. Moreover—and this deserves underscoring—the origin it posits is an absolute origin *ex nihilo*. For not only all matter and energy, but space and time themselves come into being at the initial cosmological singularity. There can be no natural, physical cause of the big bang event, since, in Quentin Smith's words, "it belongs analytically to the concept of the cosmological singularity that it is not the effect of prior physical events. The definition of a singularity . . . entails that it is *impossible to extend the spacetime manifold beyond the singularity*. . . . This rules out the idea that the singularity is an effect of some prior natural process."[3] Sir Arthur Eddington, contemplating the beginning of the universe, opined that the expansion of the universe was so preposterous and incredible that "I feel almost an indignation that anyone should believe in it—except myself."[4] He finally felt forced to conclude, "The beginning seems to present insuperable difficulties unless we agree to look on it as frankly supernatural."[5]

Sometimes objectors appeal to scenarios other than the standard model of the expanding universe in an attempt to avert the absolute beginning predicted by the standard model. But while such theories are possible, it has been the overwhelming verdict of the scientific community than none of them is more probable than the big bang theory. The devil is in the details, and once you get down to specifics you find that there is no mathematically consistent model that has been so successful in its predictions or as corroborated by the evidence as the traditional big bang theory. For example, some theories, like the **oscillating universe** (which expands and recontracts forever) or the **chaotic inflationary universe** (which continually spawns new universes), do have a potentially infinite future but turn out to have only a finite past. **Vacuum fluctuation**

---

[2]This should not be taken to mean that the density of the universe takes on a value of $\aleph_0$ but rather that the density of the universe is expressed by a ratio of mass to volume in which the volume is zero; since division by zero is impermissible, the density is said to be infinite in this sense.

[3]Quentin Smith, "The Uncaused Beginning of the Universe," in *Theism, Atheism and Big Bang Cosmology*, by William Lane Craig and Quentin Smith (Oxford: Clarendon, 1993), p. 120.

[4]Arthur Eddington, *The Expanding Universe* (New York: Macmillan, 1933), p. 124.

[5]Ibid., p. 178.

universe theories (which postulate an eternal vacuum out of which our universe is born) cannot explain why, if the vacuum was eternal, we do not observe an infinitely old universe. The **quantum gravity universe** theory propounded by the famous physicist Stephen Hawking, if interpreted realistically, still involves an absolute origin of the universe even if the universe does not begin in a so-called singularity, as it does in the standard big bang theory. The recent speculative **cyclic ekpyrotic scenario** championed by Paul Steinhardt not only leaves unresolved the difficulties facing the old oscillating universe but has also been shown to require a singular beginning in the past. In sum, according to Hawking, "Almost everyone now believes that the universe, and *time itself*, had a beginning at the Big Bang."[6]

The fourth argument for the finitude of the past is also an inductive argument, this time on the basis of the thermodynamic properties of the universe. According to the **second law of thermodynamics**, processes taking place in a closed system always tend toward a state of equilibrium. Now our interest in the law concerns what happens when it is applied to the universe as a whole. The universe is, on a naturalistic view, a gigantic closed system, since it is everything there is and there is nothing outside it. This seems to imply that, given enough time, the universe and all its processes will run down, and the entire universe will come to equilibrium. This is known as the **heat death of the universe**. Once the universe reaches this state, no further change is possible. The universe is dead.

There are two possible types of heat death for the universe. If the universe will eventually recontract, it will die a "hot" death. As it contracts, the stars gain energy, causing them to burn more rapidly so that they finally explode or evaporate. As everything in the universe grows closer together, the black holes begin to gobble up everything around them, and eventually begin themselves to coalesce. In time, all the black holes finally coalesce into one large black hole that is coextensive with the universe, from which the universe will never reemerge.

On the other hand if, as is more likely, the universe will expand forever, then its death will be cold, as the galaxies turn their gas into stars, and the stars burn out. At 10^{30} years the universe will consist of 90% dead stars, 9% supermassive black holes formed by the collapse of galaxies, and 1% atomic matter, mainly hydrogen. Elementary particle physics suggests that thereafter protons will decay into electrons and positrons so that space will be filled with a rarefied gas so thin that the distance between an electron and a positron will be about the size of the present galaxy. Eventually all black holes will completely evaporate and all the matter in the ever-expanding universe will be reduced to a thin gas of elementary particles and radiation. Equilibrium will prevail throughout, and the entire universe will be in its final state, from which no change will occur.

Now the question that needs to be asked is this: if given enough time the universe will reach heat death, then why is it not in a state of heat death now, if it has existed forever, from eternity? If the universe did not begin to exist, then it should now be in a state of equilibrium. Like a ticking clock, it should by now have run down. Since it has not yet run down, this implies, in the words of

---

[6]Stephen Hawking and Roger Penrose, *The Nature of Space and Time,* The Isaac Newton Institute Series of Lectures (Princeton, N.J.: Princeton University Press, 1996), p. 20.

one baffled scientist, "In some way the universe must have been *wound up.*"[7]

Some people have tried to escape this conclusion by adopting an oscillating model of the universe which never reaches a final state of equilibrium. But even apart from the physical and observational problems plaguing such a model, the thermodynamic properties of this model imply the very beginning of the universe that its proponents sought to avoid. Because entropy increases from cycle to cycle in such a model, it has the effect of generating larger and longer oscillations with each successive cycle. Thus, as one traces the oscillations back in time, they become progressively smaller until one reaches a first and smallest oscillation. Hence, the oscillating model has an infinite future, but only a finite past. In fact, it is estimated on the basis of current entropy levels that the universe cannot have gone through more than 100 previous oscillations.

Even if this difficulty were avoided, a universe oscillating from eternity past would require an infinitely precise tuning of initial conditions in order to last through an infinite number of successive bounces. A universe rebounding from a single, infinitely long contraction is, if entropy increases during the contracting phase, thermodynamically untenable and incompatible with the initial low-entropy condition of our expanding phase. Postulating an entropy decrease during the contracting phase in order to escape this problem would require us to postulate inexplicably special low-entropy conditions at the time of the bounce in the life of an infinitely evolving universe. Such a low-entropy condition at the beginning of the expansion is more plausibly accounted for by the presence of a singularity or some sort of quantum creation event.

So whether one adopts a recontracting model, an ever-expanding model or an oscillating model, thermodynamics suggests that the universe had a beginning. The universe appears to have been created a finite time ago, and its energy was somehow simply put in at the creation as an initial condition.

On the basis of these four arguments for the finitude of the past, the proponent of the *kalam* argument seems to have good grounds for affirming the second premise of the *kalam* cosmological argument: that the universe began to exist. It therefore follows that the universe has a cause. Conceptual analysis enables us to recover a number of striking properties that must be possessed by such an ultramundane being. For as the cause of space and time, this entity must transcend space and time and therefore exist atemporally and nonspatially, at least without the universe. This transcendent cause must therefore be changeless and immaterial, since timelessness entails changelessness, and changelessness implies immateriality. Such a cause must be beginningless and uncaused, at least in the sense of lacking any antecedent causal conditions. Ockham's razor will shave away further causes, since we should not multiply causes beyond necessity. This entity must be unimaginably powerful, since it created the universe without any material cause.

Finally, and most remarkably, such a transcendent cause is plausibly taken to be personal. Three reasons can be given for this conclusion. First, there are two types of causal explanation: scientific explanations in terms of laws and initial conditions and personal explanations in terms of agents and their volitions. A

---

[7]Richard Schlegel, "Time and Thermodynamics," in *The Voices of Time*, ed. J. T. Fraser (London: Penguin, 1948), p. 511.

first state of the universe *cannot* have a scientific explanation, since there is nothing before it, and therefore it can be accounted for only in terms of a personal explanation. Second, the personhood of the cause of the universe is implied by its timelessness and immateriality, since the only entities we know of that can possess such properties are either minds or abstract objects, and abstract objects do not stand in causal relations. Therefore, the transcendent cause of the origin of the universe must be of the order of mind. Third, this same conclusion is also implied by the fact that we have in this case the origin of a temporal effect from a timeless cause. If the cause of the origin of the universe were an impersonal set of necessary and sufficient conditions, it would be impossible for the cause to exist without its effect. For if the necessary and sufficient conditions of the effect are timelessly given, then their effect must be given as well. The only way for the cause to be timeless and changeless but for its effect to originate anew a finite time ago is for the cause to be a personal agent who freely chooses to bring about an effect without antecedent determining conditions. Thus we are brought, not merely to a transcendent cause of the universe, but to its Personal Creator. He is, as Leibniz maintained, the Sufficient Reason why anything exists rather than nothing.

CHAPTER SUMMARY

The cosmological argument is a family of arguments that seek to demonstrate the existence of a Sufficient Reason or First Cause of the existence of the cosmos. The arguments can be grouped into three basic types: the *kalam* cosmological argument for a First Cause of the beginning of the universe, the Thomist cosmological argument for a sustaining Ground of Being of the world, and the Leibnizian cosmological argument for a Sufficient Reason why something exists rather than nothing. A plausible version of the Leibnizian argument can be formulated on the basis of the following premises:

1. Every existing thing has an explanation of its existence, either in the necessity of its own nature or in an external cause.

2. If the universe has an explanation of its existence, that explanation is God.

3. The universe is an existing thing.

Premise (2) might be challenged by contending that the universe is a necessary being. Implausible as this might seem, an argument for the universe's contingency would be desirable. Although the Thomist argument proffers such a proof, it is difficult to justify the real distinction between essence and existence at the heart of the argument. The *kalam* argument is more promising: through the demonstration that the universe began to exist its contingency is revealed. This central premise in the argument may be supported by philosophical arguments against the possibility of an infinite past based on either the impossibility of the existence of an actual infinite or on the impossibility of forming an actual infinite by successive addition and by scientific evidence for a beginning of the universe from astrophysical cosmology and thermodynamics. Taken together with the plausible premise that whatever begins to exist has a cause, the beginning of the universe implies the existence of an ultramundane being which is the cause of the universe. A conceptual analysis of what it is to be a cause of the universe enables us to deduce a number of the traditional divine attributes, including the personhood of the First Uncaused Cause.

CHECKLIST OF BASIC TERMS AND CONCEPTS

A-theory of time
act of being
actual infinite
B-theory of time
brute fact
chaotic inflationary universe
contingency
contingent beings
Copenhagen interpretation
cosmological argument
cyclic ekpyrotic scenario
essence
expansion of the universe
general theory of relativity
heat death of the universe
Hilbert's Hotel
kalam cosmological argument
Leibnizian cosmological argument
metaphysically necessary
natural theology
necessary being
oscillating universe
philosophy of religion
potential infinite
principle of sufficient reason
quantum gravity universe
quantum physics
second law of thermodynamics
set theory
singularity
standard big bang model
systematic theology
Thomist cosmological argument
traversing the infinite
Tristram Shandy paradox
vacuum
vacuum fluctuation universe
Zeno's paradoxes of motion

24
THE EXISTENCE OF GOD
II

There are five ways in which one can prove that there is a God.
THOMAS AQUINAS SUMMA THEOLOGIAE 1A.2.3

I believe also that nearly all the means which have been employed to prove the existence of God are good and might be of service, if we perfect them.
G. W. LEIBNIZ, NEW ESSAYS ON HUMAN UNDERSTANDING

1 THE TELEOLOGICAL ARGUMENT

Widely thought to have been demolished by Hume and Darwin, the **teleological argument** for God's existence has come roaring back into prominence in recent years. The explanatory adequacy of the neo-Darwinian mechanisms of random mutation and natural selection with respect to observed biological complexity has been sharply challenged, as advances in microbiology have served to disclose the breathtaking complexity of the micromachinery of a single cell, not to speak of higher level organisms. The field of origin of life studies is in turmoil, as all the old scenarios of the chemical origin of life in the primordial soup have collapsed, and no new, better theory is on the horizon. And the scientific community has been stunned by its discovery of how complex and sensitive a nexus of initial conditions must be given in order for the universe even to permit the origin and evolution of intelligent life.

Undoubtedly, it is this last discovery that has most served to reopen the books on the teleological argument. Due to sociological factors surrounding the neo-Darwinian theory of biological evolution, captured most poignantly in the public image of the Scopes trial, biologists have been for the most part extremely loath so much as even to contemplate a design hypothesis, lest they let a creationist foot in the door; but cosmologists, largely untainted by this controversy, have been much more open to entertain seriously the alternative of design. The discovery of the cosmic fine-tuning has led many scientists to conclude that such a delicate balance of physical constants and quantities as is requisite for life cannot be dismissed as mere coincidence but cries out for some sort of explanation.

What is meant by **fine-tuning**? The physical laws of nature, when given mathematical expression, contain various constants or quantities, such as the gravitational constant or the density of the universe, whose values are not mandated by the laws themselves; a universe governed by such laws might be characterized by any of a wide range of values for such variables. By "fine-tuning" one typically means that the actual values assumed by the constants and quantities in question are such that small deviations from those values would render the universe life-prohibiting. Various examples of cosmic fine-tuning can be cited. The world is conditioned principally by the values of the fundamental constants—α (the fine structure constant, or electromagnetic interaction), α_G (gravitation), α_w (the weak force), α_s (the strong force) and m_p/m_e (proton to electron mass ratio). When one assigns different values to these constants or forces, one discovers that the number of observable universes, that is to say, universes capable of supporting intelligent life, is very small. Just a slight variation in some of these values would render life impossible. For example, according to British physicist Paul Davies, changes in either α_G or electromagnetism by only one part in 10^{40} would have spelled disaster for stars like the sun, thereby precluding the existence of planets.

In investigating the initial conditions of the big bang, one also confronts two arbitrary parameters governing the expansion of the universe: Ω_0, related to the density of the universe, and H_0, related to the speed of the expansion. Observations indicate that at 10^{-43} seconds after the big bang the universe was expanding at a fantastically special rate of speed with a total density close to the critical value on the borderline between recollapse and everlasting expansion. Stephen Hawking estimates that even a decrease of one part in a million million when the temperature of the universe was 10^{10} degrees would have resulted in the universe's recollapse long ago; a similar increase would have precluded the galaxies from condensing out of the expanding matter. At the Planck time, 10^{-43} seconds after the big bang, the density of the universe must have apparently been within about one part in 10^{60} of the critical density at which space is flat. Classical cosmology serves to highlight another parameter, S, the entropy per baryon in the universe. The structure of the big bang must have been severely constrained in order that thermodynamics as we know it should have arisen. Not only so, but S is itself a consequence of the baryon asymmetry in the universe, which arises from the inexplicable, built-in asymmetry of quarks over anti-quarks prior to 10^{-6} seconds after the big bang. Oxford physicist Roger Penrose calculates that the odds of the special low-entropy condition having arisen sheerly by chance in the absence any constraining principles is at least as small as about one part in $10^{10(123)}$ in order for our universe to exist. Penrose comments, "I cannot even recall seeing anything else in physics whose accuracy is known to approach, even remotely, a figure like one part in $10^{10\,(123)}$."[1]

In a sense more easy to discern than to articulate, this fine-tuning of the universe seems to manifest the presence of a designing intelligence. The inference to design is best thought of, not as an instance of reasoning by analogy (as it is often portrayed), but as a case of **inference to the best explanation**.[2] John Leslie, the philosopher who has most occupied himself with these matters, speaks of the need for what he calls a "tidy explanation." A **tidy explanation** is one that not only explains a certain situation but also reveals in doing so that there is something to be explained. Leslie provides a whole retinue of charming illus-

[1]Roger Penrose, "Time-Asymmetry and Quantum Gravity," in *Quantum Gravity 2*, ed. C. J. Isham, R. Penrose and D. W. Sciama (Oxford: Clarendon, 1981), p. 249.

[2]See Peter Lipton, *Inference to the Best Explanation* (London: Routledge, 1991).

trations of tidy explanations at work. Suppose, for example, that Bob is given a new car for his birthday. There are millions of license plate numbers, and it is therefore highly unlikely that Bob would get, say, CHT 4271. Yet that plate on his birthday car would occasion no special interest. But suppose Bob, who was born on August 8, 1949, finds BOB 8849 on the license plate of his birthday car. He would be obtuse if he shrugged this off with the comment, "Well, it had to have *some* license plate, and any number is equally improbable . . ." But what makes this case different than the other?

A full-fledged theory of **design inference** has recently been offered by William Dembski. He furnishes a ten-step generic chance elimination argument, which delineates the common pattern of reasoning that he believes underlies chance-elimination arguments. Dembski's analysis can be used to formalize what Leslie grasped in an intuitive way. What makes an explanation a tidy one is not simply the fact that the *explanandum* (the thing to be explained) is some improbable event, but the fact that the event also conforms to some independently given pattern, resulting in what Dembski calls "specified complexity." It is this **specified complexity** (high improbability plus an independent pattern) that tips us off to the need for an explanation in terms of more than mere chance.

Regardless of whether one adopts Dembski's analysis of design inferences,[3] the key to detecting design is to eliminate the two competing alternatives of physical necessity and chance. Accordingly, a teleological argument appealing to cosmic fine-tuning might be formulated as follows:

1. The fine-tuning of the universe is due to either physical necessity, chance or design.

2. It is not due to physical necessity or chance.

3. Therefore, it is due to design.

Since premise (1) seems to exhaust the alternatives, the soundness of this argument will depend on the plausibility of premise (2).

Can the cosmic fine-tuning be plausibly attributed to **physical necessity**? According to this alternative, the constants and quantities must have the values they do, and there was really no chance or little chance of the universe's not being life-permitting. Now on the face of it this alternative seems extraordinarily implausible. It requires us to believe that a life-prohibiting universe is virtually physically impossible. But surely it does seem possible. If the primordial matter and antimatter had been differently proportioned, if the universe had expanded just a little more slowly, if the entropy of the universe were marginally greater, any of these adjustments and more would have prevented a life-permitting universe, yet all seem perfectly possible physically. The person who maintains that the universe must be life-permitting is taking a radical line that requires strong proof. But as yet there is none; this alternative is simply put forward as a bare possibility.

---

[3]An alternative approach is offered by Robin Collins. He employs Bayes's theorem (recall chap. 2) to argue that the cosmic fine-tuning is much more probable on the hypothesis of theism than on the hypothesis of a single, atheistic universe and that therefore the evidence of fine-tuning strongly confirms theism over its rival hypothesis.

Sometimes physicists do speak of a yet-to-be-discovered **theory of everything** (T.O.E.), but such nomenclature is, like so many of the colorful names given to scientific theories, quite misleading. A T.O.E. actually has the limited goal of providing a unified theory of the four fundamental forces of nature, to reduce gravity, electromagnetism, the strong force and the weak force to one fundamental force carried by one fundamental particle. Such a theory will, we hope, explain why these four forces take the values they do, but it will not even attempt to explain literally everything. For example, in the most promising candidates for a T.O.E. to date, **super-string theory** or M-theory, the physical universe must be 11-dimensional, but why the universe should possess just that number of dimensions is not addressed by the theory. Hence, one must not be misled by talk of a T.O.E. into thinking that the universe possesses all its fundamental constants and quantities by physical necessity.

On the contrary, there is good reason to reject this alternative. For it would require us to say that only one set of constants and quantities is compatible with the laws of nature, which seems false. Even if the laws of nature were themselves necessary, one would still have to supply initial conditions. As Davies states,

> Even if the laws of physics were unique, it doesn't follow that the physical universe itself is unique. . . . The laws of physics must be augmented by cosmic initial conditions. . . . There is nothing in present ideas about "laws of initial conditions" remotely to suggest that their consistency with the laws of physics would imply uniqueness. Far from it. . . .
>
> It seems, then, that the physical universe does not have to be the way it is: it could have been otherwise.[4]

The extraordinarily low-entropy condition of the early universe provides a good example of an arbitrary quantity that seems to have just been put in at the creation as an initial condition.

Moreover, it seems likely that any attempt to significantly reduce fine-tuning will itself turn out to involve fine-tuning. This has certainly been the pattern in the past. For example, attempts to eliminate the fine-tuning of the parameters Ω_0 and H_0 by appeal to so-called **inflationary models** of the early universe only suppressed fine-tuning at this point to have it pop up again at another, namely, the fine-tuning of the cosmological constant Λ. This constant, which is hypothesized to drive the inflationary expansion, must be tuned to a precision of at least one part in 10^{53}. There is no reason to think that showing every constant and quantity to be physically necessary is anything more than a pipe dream.

What, then, of the alternative of chance? One may seek to eliminate this hypothesis either by appealing to the specified complexity of cosmic fine-tuning or by arguing that the fine-tuning is significantly more probable on design (theism) than on the chance hypothesis (atheism). It is sometimes objected that it is meaningless to speak of the probability of our finely tuned universe's existing because there is, after all, only one universe. But the following illustration clarifies the sense in which a life-permitting universe is improbable. Take a sheet of

---

[4]Paul Davies, *The Mind of God* (New York: Simon & Schuster, 1992), p. 169.

paper and place upon it a red dot. That dot represents our universe. Now alter slightly one or more of the finely-tuned constants and physical quantities which have been the focus of our attention. As a result we have a description of another universe, which we may represent as a new dot in the proximity of the first. If that new set of constants and quantities describes a life-permitting universe, make it a red dot; if it describes a universe that is life-prohibiting, make it a blue dot. Now repeat the procedure arbitrarily many times until the sheet is filled with dots. One winds up with a sea of blue with only a few pin-points of red. That is the sense in which it is overwhelmingly improbable that the universe should be life-permitting. There are simply vastly more life-prohibiting universes in our local area of possible universes than there are life-permitting universes.

It might be objected that we do not know if all these possible universes are equally probable. This amounts, in effect, to the claim that the actual range of possible values for a certain constant or quantity may be very narrow. But even if that were the case, when one has many variables requiring fine-tuning, the probability of a life-permitting universe's existing is still very small. Moreover, in the absence of any physical reason to think that the values are constrained, we are justified in assuming a **principle of indifference** to the effect that the probability of our universe's existing will be the same as the probability of any other universe's existing that is represented on our sheet.

It might be demanded why we should consider only universes represented on the sheet. Perhaps universes are possible that have wholly different physical variables and natural laws and are life-permitting. Perhaps these would contain forms of life vastly different from life as we know it. The teleologist need not deny the possibility, for such worlds are irrelevant to his argument. His claim is that within the local group of possible universes any life-permitting universe is highly improbable. John Leslie gives the illustration of a fly, resting on a large, blank area of the wall. A single shot is fired, and the bullet strikes the fly. Now even if the rest of the wall outside the blank area is covered with flies, such that a randomly fired bullet would probably hit one, nevertheless it remains highly improbable that a single, randomly fired bullet would strike the solitary fly within the large, blank area. In the same way, we need only concern ourselves with the universes represented on our sheet in order to determine the probability of the existence of a life-permitting universe.

Issues pertinent to the so-called anthropic principle also arise here. As formulated by Barrow and Tipler, the **anthropic principle** states that any observed properties of the universe that may initially appear astonishingly improbable can be seen in their true perspective only after we have accounted for the fact that certain properties could not be observed by us, were they to be exemplified, because we can only observe those compatible with our own existence. The implication is that we ought not to be surprised at observing the universe to be as it is and that therefore no explanation of its fine-tuning need be sought. The argument is, however, based on confusion. Barrow and Tipler have confused the true claim (A) with the false claim (A′):

A. If observers who have evolved within a universe observe its fundamental constants and quantities, it is highly probable that they will observe them to be fine-tuned to their existence.

A'. It is highly probable that a universe exist that is finely-tuned for the evolution of observers within it.

An observer who has evolved within the universe should regard it as highly probable that he will find the basic conditions of the universe fine-tuned for his existence; but he should not infer that it is therefore highly probable that such a fine-tuned universe exist at all.

Most anthropic theorizers now recognize that the anthropic principle can only legitimately be employed when it is conjoined to a **many worlds hypothesis**, according to which a world ensemble of concrete universes exists, actualizing a wide range of possibilities. The many worlds hypothesis is essentially an effort on the part of partisans of the chance hypothesis to multiply their probabilistic resources in order to reduce the improbability of the occurrence of fine-tuning. The very fact that they must resort to such a remarkable hypothesis is a sort of backhanded compliment to the design hypothesis in that they recognize that the fine-tuning does cry out for explanation. But is the many worlds hypothesis as plausible as the design hypothesis?

It seems not. In the first place, it needs to be recognized that the many worlds hypothesis is no less metaphysical than the hypothesis of a cosmic designer. As the physicist-theologian John Polkinghorne says, "People try to trick out a 'many universe' account in sort of pseudo-scientific terms, but that is pseudo-science. It is a metaphysical guess that there might be many universes with different laws and circumstances."[5] But as a metaphysical hypothesis, the many worlds hypothesis is arguably inferior to the design hypothesis because the design hypothesis is simpler. According to **Ockham's razor**, we should not multiply causes beyond what is necessary to explain the effect. But it is simpler to postulate one cosmic designer to explain our universe than to postulate the infinitely bloated and contrived ontology of the many worlds hypothesis. Only if the many worlds theorist could show that there exists a single, comparably simple mechanism for generating a world ensemble of randomly varied universes would he be able to elude this difficulty. But no one has been able to identify such a mechanism. Therefore, the design hypothesis is to be preferred.

Second, there is no known way of generating a world ensemble. No one has been able to explain how or why such a collection of varied universes should exist. Lee Smolin made the ingenious suggestion that if we suppose that black holes spawn other universes beyond our own, then universes that produce large numbers of black holes would have a selective advantage in producing offspring, so that a sort of cosmic evolution would take place. If each new universe is not an exact reproduction of its parent universe but varies in its fundamental constants and quantities, then universes that are proficient in producing black holes would have a selective advantage over those less proficient. Thus in the course of cosmic evolution universes whose fundamental parameters are fine-tuned to the production of black holes would proliferate. Since black holes are

---

[5]John C. Polkinghorne, *Serious Talk: Science and Religion in Dialogue* (London: SCM Press, 1996), p. 6.

the residue of collapsed stars, cosmic evolution has the unintended effect of producing more and more stars and hence, more and more planets where life might form. Eventually observers would appear who marvel at the fine-tuning of the universe for their existence. The fatal flaw in Smolin's scenario, wholly apart from its ad hoc and even disconfirmed conjectures, was his assumption that universes fine-tuned for black hole production would also be fine-tuned for the production of stable stars. In fact, the opposite is true: the most proficient producers of black holes would be universes that generate them prior to star formation, so that life-permitting universes would actually be weeded out by Smolin's cosmic evolutionary scenario.

Other suggested mechanisms for generating a world ensemble turn out to require fine-tuning themselves. For example, although some cosmologists appeal to inflationary theories of the universe to generate a world ensemble, we have seen that inflation itself requires fine-tuning. The total cosmological constant Λ_{tot} is usually taken to be zero. But this requires that the energy density of the true vacuum be tuned to zero *by hand*; there is no understanding of why this value should be so low. Worse, inflation requires that Λ_{tot} was once quite large, though zero today; this assumption is without any physical justification. Moreover, in order to proceed appropriately, inflation requires that the two components of Λ_{tot} cancel each other out with an enormously precise though inexplicable accuracy. A change in the strengths of either α_G or α_w by as little as one part in 10^{100} would destroy this cancellation on which our lives depend. In these and other respects, inflationary scenarios actually require rather than eliminate fine-tuning.

Third, there is no evidence for the existence of a world ensemble *apart from the fine-tuning itself*. But the fine-tuning is equally evidence for a cosmic designer. Indeed, the hypothesis of a cosmic designer is again the better explanation because we have independent evidence of the existence of such a designer in the form of the other arguments for the existence of God.

Fourth, the many worlds hypothesis faces a severe challenge from biological evolutionary theory. By way of background, the nineteenth-century physicist Ludwig Boltzmann proposed a sort of many worlds hypothesis in order to explain why we do not find the universe in a state of "heat death" or thermodynamic equilibrium. Boltzmann hypothesized that the universe as a whole *does*, in fact, exist in an equilibrium state, but that over time fluctuations in the energy level occur here and there throughout the universe, so that by chance alone there will be isolated regions where disequilibrium exists. Boltzmann referred to these isolated regions as "worlds." We should not be surprised to see our world in a highly improbable disequilibrium state, he maintained, since in the ensemble of all worlds there must exist by chance alone certain worlds in disequilibrium, and ours just happens to be one of these.

The problem with Boltzmann's daring many worlds hypothesis was that if our world were merely a fluctuation in a sea of diffuse energy, then it is overwhelmingly more probable that we should be observing a much tinier region of disequilibrium than we do. In order for us to exist, a smaller fluctuation, even one that produced our world instantaneously by an enormous accident, is inestimably more probable than a progressive decline in entropy over fifteen billion years to fashion the world we see. In fact, Boltzmann's hypothesis, if adopted, would force us to regard the past as illusory, everything having the mere appearance of age, and the stars and planets as illusory, mere "pictures" as it were, since that sort of world is vastly more probable given a state of overall equilibrium than a world with genuine, temporally and spatially distant events. Therefore, Boltzmann's many worlds hypothesis has been universally rejected by the scientific community, and the present disequilibrium is usually taken to be just a result of the initial low-entropy condition mysteriously obtaining at the beginning of the universe.

Now a precisely parallel problem attends the many worlds hypothesis as an explanation of fine-tuning. According to the prevailing theory of biological evolution, intelligent life like ourselves, if it evolves at all, will do so as late in the lifetime of the sun as possible. The less the time span available for the mechanisms of genetic mutation and natural selection to function, the lower the probability of intelligent life's evolving. Given the complexity of the human organism, it is overwhelmingly more probable that human beings will evolve late in the lifetime of the sun rather than early. In fact Barrow and Tipler list ten steps in the evolution of *Homo sapiens, each of which* is so improbable that before it would occur the sun would have ceased to be a main sequence star and incinerated the earth![6] Hence, if our universe is but one member of a world ensemble, then, assuming for the sake of argument that the prevailing evolutionary account of biological complexity is correct, it is overwhelmingly more probable that we should be observing a very old sun rather than a relatively young one. If we are products of biological evolution, we should find ourselves in a world in which we evolve much later in the lifetime of our star. (This is the analogue to its being overwhelmingly more probable that we should exist in a smaller region of disequilibrium on the Boltzmann hypothesis.) In fact, adopting the many worlds hypothesis to explain away fine-tuning also results in a strange sort of illusionism: it is far more probable that all our astronomical, geological and biological estimates of age are wrong, that we really do exist very late in the lifetime of the sun and that the sun and the earth's appearance of youth is a massive illusion. (This is the analogue of its being far more probable that all the evidence of the old age of our universe is illusory on the Boltzmann hypothesis.) Thus the many worlds hypothesis is no more successful in explaining cosmic fine-tuning than it was in explaining cosmic disequilibrium.

For these four reasons the many worlds hypothesis faces a severe challenge as a candidate for the best explanation of the observed cosmic fine-tuning. It therefore seems that the fine-tuning of the universe is plausibly due neither to physical necessity nor to chance. It follows that the fine-tuning is therefore due to design, unless the design hypothesis can be shown to be even more implausible that its competitors.

The implication of the design hypothesis is that there exists a Cosmic Designer who fine-tuned the initial conditions of the universe for intelligent life. Such a hypothesis supplies a personal explanation of the fine-tuning of the universe. Is this explanation implausible? Detractors of design sometimes object that on this hypothesis the Cosmic Designer himself remains unexplained. It is

---

[6]John Barrow and Frank Tipler, *The Anthropic Cosmological Principle* (Oxford: Clarendon, 1986), pp. 561-65.

said that an intelligent mind also exhibits complex order, so that if the universe needs an explanation, so does its Designer. If the Designer does not need an explanation, why think that the universe does?

This popular objection is based on a misconception of the nature of explanation. It is widely recognized that in order for an explanation to be the best, one need not have an explanation of the explanation (indeed, such a requirement would generate an infinite regress, so that everything becomes inexplicable). If astronauts should find traces of intelligent life on some other planet, for example, we need not be able to explain such extraterrestrials in order to recognize that they are the best explanation of the artifacts. In the same way, the design hypothesis's being the best explanation of the fine-tuning does not depend on our being able to explain the Designer.

Moreover, the complexity of a mind is not really analogous to the complexity of the universe. A mind's *ideas* may be complex, but a mind itself is a remarkably simple thing, being an immaterial entity not composed of pieces or separable parts. Moreover, properties like intelligence, consciousness and volition are not contingent properties which a mind might lack, but are essential to its nature. Thus postulating an uncreated mind behind the cosmos is not at all like postulating an undesigned cosmos. Thus the teleological argument based on the fine-tuning of the initial state of the universe fares well as a sound and persuasive argument for a Designer of the cosmos.

2 THE AXIOLOGICAL ARGUMENT

Can we be good without God? At first the answer to this question may seem so obvious that even to pose it arouses indignation. For while theists undoubtedly find in God a source of moral strength and resolve which enables them to live lives that are better than those they would otherwise live, nevertheless it would be arrogant and ignorant to claim that those who do not share a belief in God do not often live good moral lives. But wait! It would, indeed, be arrogant and ignorant to claim that people cannot be good without *belief* in God. But that was not the question. The question was, can we be good without God? When we ask that question, we are posing in a provocative way the metaethical question of the objectivity of moral values (see chaps. 19-20). Are the values we hold dear and guide our lives by mere social conventions akin to driving on the left versus right side of the road or mere expressions of personal preference akin to having a taste for certain foods? Or are they valid independent of our apprehension of them, and if so, what is their foundation? Moreover, if morality is just a human convention, then why should we act morally, especially when it conflicts with self-interest? Or are we in some way held accountable for our moral decisions and actions?

Many philosophers have argued that if God exists, then the objectivity of moral values, moral duties and moral accountability is secured, but that in the absence of God, that is, if God does not exist, then morality is just a human convention, that is to say, morality is wholly subjective and nonbinding. We might act in precisely the same ways that we do in fact act, but in the absence of God, such actions would no longer count as good (or evil), since if God does not exist, objective moral values do not exist. Thus we cannot truly be good without God. On the other hand, if we do believe that moral values and duties are objective, that provides moral grounds for believing in God. We should thus have an **axiological argument** for the existence of God.

Consider the hypothesis that God exists. According to classical theism, objective moral values are rooted in God. To say that there are **objective moral values** is to say that something is right or wrong independent of whether anybody believes it to be so. It is to say, for example, that Nazi anti-Semitism was morally wrong, even though the Nazis who carried out the Holocaust thought that it was good, and it would still be wrong even if the Nazis had won World War II and succeeded in exterminating or brainwashing everybody who disagreed with them. On classical theism God's own holy and perfectly good nature supplies the absolute standard against which all actions and decisions are measured. God's moral nature is what Plato called the "Good." He is the locus and source of moral value. He is by nature loving, generous, just, faithful, kind and so forth.

Moreover, God's moral nature is expressed in relation to us in the form of **divine commands**, which constitute our **moral duties** or obligations. Far from being arbitrary, these commands flow necessarily from his moral nature. On this foundation we can affirm the objective goodness and rightness of love, generosity, self-sacrifice and equality, and condemn as objectively evil and wrong selfishness, hatred, abuse, discrimination and oppression.

Finally, on classical theism God holds all persons morally accountable for their actions. Evil and wrong will be punished; righteousness will be vindicated. **Moral accountability** implies that despite the inequities of this life, in the end the scales of God's justice will be balanced. Thus the moral choices we make in this life are infused with an eternal significance. We can with consistency make moral choices that run contrary to our self-interest and even undertake acts of extreme self-sacrifice, knowing that such decisions are not empty and ultimately meaningless gestures. Rather, our moral lives have a paramount significance. Thus it seems evident that theism provides a sound foundation for morality.

Contrast the atheistic hypothesis. If God does not exist, then what is the foundation for moral values? More particularly, what is the basis for the value of human beings? If God does not exist, then it is difficult to see any reason to think that human beings are special or that their morality is objectively valid. Moreover, why think that we have any moral obligations to do anything? Who or what imposes any moral duties upon us? Philosopher of science Michael Ruse writes,

> The position of the modern evolutionist . . . is that humans have an awareness of morality . . . because such an awareness is of biological worth. Morality is a biological adaptation no less than are hands and feet and teeth. . . .
>
> Considered as a rationally justifiable set of claims about an objective something, ethics is illusory. I appreciate that when somebody says "Love thy neighbour as thyself," they think they are referring above and beyond themselves. . . . Nevertheless, . . . such reference is truly without foundation. Morality is just an aid to survival and reproduction, . . . and any deeper meaning is illusory.[7]

---

[7]Michael Ruse, "Evolutionary Theory and Christian Ethics," in *The Darwinian Paradigm* (London: Routledge, 1989), pp. 262, 268-69.

As a result of **sociobiological pressures**, there has evolved among *Homo sapiens* a sort of "herd morality," which functions well in the perpetuation of our species in the struggle for survival. But there does not seem to be anything about *Homo sapiens* that makes this morality objectively binding.

Now it is important that we remain clear in understanding the issue before us. The question is *not:* Must we believe in God in order to live moral lives? There is no reason to think that atheists and theists alike may not live what we normally characterize as good and decent lives. Similarly, the question is *not:* Can we formulate a system of ethics without reference to God? If the nontheist grants that human beings do have objective value, then there is no reason to think that he cannot work out a system of ethics with which the theist would also largely agree. Or again, the question is *not:* Can we recognize the existence of objective moral values without reference to God? The theist will typically maintain that a person need not believe in God in order to recognize, say, that we should love our children. Rather, as humanist philosopher Paul Kurtz puts it, "The central question about moral and ethical principles concerns their ontological foundation. If they are neither derived from God nor anchored in some transcendent ground, are they purely ephemeral?"[8]

If there is no God, then any ground for regarding the herd morality evolved by *Homo sapiens* as objectively true seems to have been removed. Human beings are just accidental by-products of nature that have evolved relatively recently on an infinitesimal speck of dust lost somewhere in a hostile and mindless universe and which are doomed to perish individually and collectively in a relatively short time. Some action, say, rape, may not be socially advantageous and so in the course of human evolution has become taboo; but on the atheistic view it is difficult to see why there is anything really *wrong* about raping someone. Crudely put, on the atheistic view human beings are just animals, and animals are not moral agents.

Some philosophers, unwilling to affirm that acts like rape or torturing a child are morally neutral actions, have tried to affirm objective moral values in the absence of God. Let us call this view **atheistic moral realism**. Atheistic moral realists affirm that objective moral values and duties do exist and are not dependent on evolution or human opinion, but they also insist that they are not grounded in God. Indeed, moral values have no further foundation. They just exist.

It is difficult, however, even to comprehend this view. What does it mean to say, for example, that the moral value *justice* just exists? It is hard to know what to make of this. It is clear what is meant when it is said that a person is just; but it is bewildering when it is said that in the absence of any people, *justice* itself exists. Moral values seem to exist as properties of persons, not as mere abstractions—or at any rate, it is hard to know what it is for a moral value to exist as a mere abstraction. Atheistic moral realists seem to lack any adequate foundation in reality for moral values but just leave them floating in an unintelligible way.

Second, the nature of moral duty or obligation seems incompatible with atheistic moral realism. Let us suppose for the sake of argument that moral val-

---

[8]Paul Kurtz, *Forbidden Fruit* (Buffalo, N.Y.: Prometheus, 1988), p. 65.

ues do exist independent of God. Suppose that values like *mercy, justice, love, forbearance* and the like just exist. How does that result in any moral obligations for me? Why would I have a moral duty, say, to be merciful? Who or what lays such an obligation on me? As the ethicist Richard Taylor points out, "A duty is something that is owed. . . . But something can be owed only to some person or persons. There can be no such thing as duty in isolation."[9] God makes sense of moral obligation because his commands constitute for us our moral duties. Taylor writes, "Our moral obligations can . . . be understood as those that are imposed by God. . . . But what if this higher-than-human lawgiver is no longer taken into account? Does the concept of a moral obligation . . . still make sense? . . . the concept of moral obligation [is] unintelligible apart from the idea of God. The words remain but their meaning is gone."[10] As a nontheist, Taylor therefore thinks that we literally have no moral obligations, that there is no right or wrong. The atheistic moral realist rightly finds this abhorrent, but, as Taylor clearly sees, on an atheistic view there simply is no ground for duty, even if moral values somehow exist.

Third, it is fantastically improbable that just that sort of creatures would emerge from the blind evolutionary process who correspond to the abstractly existing realm of moral values. This seems to be an utterly incredible coincidence when one thinks about it. It is almost as though the moral realm *knew* that we were coming. It is far more plausible to regard both the natural realm and the moral realm as under the hegemony of a divine Creator and Lawgiver than to think that these two entirely independent orders of reality just happened to mesh.

Thus it seems that atheistic moral realism is not as plausible a view as theism, but serves as a convenient halfway house for philosophers who do not have the stomach for the **moral nihilism** that atheism seems to imply. Some philosophers, equally averse to abstractly existing moral values as to theism, try to salvage the existence of objective moral principles or properties in the context of a naturalistic worldview. But the advocates of such theories are typically at a loss to justify their starting point. If their approach to metaethical theory is to be serious metaphysics rather than just a shopping list approach, whereby one simply helps oneself to the supervenient moral properties or principles needed to do the job, then some sort of explanation is required for why moral properties supervene on certain natural states or why such principles are true. It is insufficient for the naturalist to point out that we do, in fact, apprehend the goodness of some feature of human existence, for that only goes to establish the objectivity of moral values and duties, which the proponent of the axiological argument is eager to affirm.

Finally, if atheism is true, there is no moral accountability for one's actions. Even if there were objective moral values and duties under naturalism, they are irrelevant because there is no moral accountability. If life ends at the grave, it makes no difference whether one lives as a Stalin or as a saint. As the Russian writer Fyodor Dostoyevsky rightly said, if there is no immortality, then all things are permitted. Given the finality of death, it really does not matter how

[9]Richard Taylor, *Ethics, Faith and Reason* (Englewood Cliffs, N.J.: Prentice-Hall, 1985), p. 83.
[10]Ibid., pp. 83-84.

we live. So what do we say to someone who concludes that we may as well just live as we please, out of pure self-interest? This presents a pretty grim picture for an atheistic ethicist like Kai Nielsen. He writes,

> We have not been able to show that reason requires the moral point of view, or that all really rational persons should not be individual egoists or classical amoralists. Reason doesn't decide here. The picture I have painted for you is not a pleasant one. Reflection on it depresses me. . . . Pure practical reason, even with a good knowledge of the facts, will not take you to morality.[11]

Somebody might say that it is in our **best self-interest** to adopt a moral lifestyle. But clearly, that is not always true: we all know situations in which self-interest runs smack in the face of morality. Moreover, if one is sufficiently powerful, like a Ferdinand Marcos or a Papa Doc Duvalier or even a Donald Trump, then one can pretty much ignore the dictates of conscience and safely live in self-indulgence. Finally, as we saw in chapters nineteen and twenty-one, anyone who tries to adopt the moral point of view *solely* on the grounds of self-interest fails in so doing to adopt the moral point of view. It therefore follows that it is impossible to adopt a truly moral lifestyle out of pure self-interest.

Acts of self-sacrifice become particularly inept on a naturalistic worldview. Why should you sacrifice your self-interest and especially your life for the sake of someone else? Considered from the sociobiological point of view, such **altruistic behavior** is merely the result of evolutionary conditioning that helps to perpetuate the species. A mother rushing into a burning house to rescue her children or a soldier throwing his body over a hand grenade to save his comrades does nothing more significant or praiseworthy, morally speaking, than a fighter ant which sacrifices itself for the sake of the ant hill. Good sense dictates that we should resist, if we can, the sociobiological pressures to such self-destructive activity and choose instead to act in our best self-interest. Life is too short to jeopardize it by acting out of anything but pure self-interest. Sacrifice for another person is just stupid. Thus the absence of moral accountability from the philosophy of naturalism makes an ethic of compassion and self-sacrifice a hollow abstraction.

We thus come to radically different perspectives on morality depending on whether or not God exists. If God exists, there is a sound foundation for morality. If God does not exist, then, as Nietzsche claimed, we seem to be ultimately landed in nihilism.

But the choice between the two need not be arbitrarily made. On the contrary, the very considerations we have been discussing can constitute moral justification for the existence of God.

For example, if we do think that objective moral values exist, then we shall be led logically to the conclusion that God exists. And surely we do apprehend a realm of objective moral values. There is no more reason to deny the objective reality of moral values than the objective reality of the physical world. The reasoning of Ruse that morality is only a biological adaptation is at worst a textbook example of the **genetic fallacy** (the fallacy of arguing that a belief is mistaken or false because of the way that belief originated) and at best only proves that our

---

[11]Kai Nielsen, "Why Should I Be Moral?" *American Philosophical Quarterly* 21 (1984): 90.

subjective perception of objective moral values has evolved. But if moral values are gradually discovered, not invented, then our gradual and fallible apprehension of the moral realm no more undermines the objective reality of that realm than our gradual, fallible perception of the physical world undermines the objectivity of that realm. Most of us think that we do apprehend objective values. As Ruse himself confesses, "The man who says that it is morally acceptable to rape little children is just as mistaken as the man who says, $2 + 2 = 5$."[12]

Furthermore, consider the nature of moral obligation. The international community recognizes the existence of universal human rights, and many persons are willing to speak of **animal rights** as well. But the best way to make sense of such rights is in terms of agreement or disagreement of certain acts with the will or commands of a holy, loving God.

Finally, take the problem of moral accountability. Here we find a powerful **practical argument** for believing in God. According to William James, practical arguments can only be used when theoretical arguments are insufficient to decide a question of urgent and pragmatic importance. But it seems obvious that a practical argument could also be used to back up or motivate acceptance of the conclusion of a sound theoretical argument. To believe, then, that God does not exist and that there is thus no moral accountability would be quite literally de-moralizing, for then we should have to believe that our moral choices are ultimately insignificant, since both our fate and that of the universe will be the same regardless of what we do. By "de-moralization" we mean a deterioration of moral motivation. It is hard to do the right thing when that means sacrificing self-interest and resisting temptation to do wrong when desire is strong; and the belief that ultimately it does not matter what you choose or do is apt to sap your moral strength and so undermine your moral life. By contrast, there is nothing so likely to strengthen the moral life as the beliefs that you will be held accountable for your actions and that your choices do make a difference in bringing about the good. Theism is thus a morally advantageous belief, and this, in the absence of any theoretical argument establishing atheism to be the case, provides practical grounds to believe in God and motivation to accept the conclusions of the theoretical arguments in support of theism.

In conclusion, if God does not exist, then it is plausible to think that there are no objective moral values, that we have no moral duties and that there is no moral accountability for how we live and act. If, on the other hand, we hold, as it seems rational to do, that objective moral values and duties do exist, then we have good grounds for believing in the existence of God. We can formulate this argument simply as follows:

1. If God did not exist, objective moral values and duties would not exist.

2. Objective moral values and duties do exist.

3. Therefore, God exists.

In addition, we have seen powerful practical reasons for embracing theism in view of the morally bracing effects that belief in moral accountability produces.

---

[12]Michael Ruse, *Darwinism Defended* (London: Addison-Wesley, 1982), p. 275.

We cannot, then, truly be good without God; but if we can in some measure be good, then it follows that God exists.

3 THE ONTOLOGICAL ARGUMENT

By 1077 Anselm of Canterbury had already written his *Monologium*, a treatise in which he argued for the existence of God by means of axiological and cosmological arguments. But Anselm remained dissatisfied with the complexity of his demonstration and yearned to find a single argument that would on its own prove that God exists. It was then that he hit upon the conception of God as "the greatest conceivable being," which provided the key to his new argument. Anselm argued that once a person truly understands the notion of a **greatest conceivable being**, then he will see that such being must exist, since if it did not, it would not be the *greatest* conceivable being. God's existence, then, is truly inconceivable for him who rightly understands God (*Proslogium* 2-3).

Anselm's argument, which has come to be known as the **ontological argument**, went on to assume a variety of forms, being defended by Duns Scotus, Descartes, Spinoza, Leibniz and others. Although Graham Oppy in his very thorough book identifies six basic types of ontological argument, his classification of an argument as ontological is based on a criterion far too vague for useful classification (namely, an argument is a form of the ontological argument if it proceeds from considerations that are entirely internal to the theistic worldview). Rather, the common thread in ontological arguments is that they try to deduce the existence of God from the very concept of God, together with certain other necessary truths. Proponents of the argument claim that once we understand what God is—the greatest conceivable being or the most perfect being or the most real being—then we shall see that such a being must in fact exist.

The ontological argument tends to sharply polarize philosophers. Many would agree with Schopenhauer's dismissal of the argument as "a charming joke," but a number of recent, prominent philosophers such as Norman Malcolm, Charles Hartshorne and Alvin Plantinga not only take the argument seriously but consider it to be sound.

In his version of the argument, Plantinga appropriates Leibniz's insight that the argument assumes that the concept of God is possible, that is to say, that it is possible that a being falling under that concept exists or, employing the semantics of possible worlds (see chap. 2), that there is a **possible world** in which God exists. Plantinga conceives of God as a being that is "maximally excellent" in every possible world, where **maximal excellence** entails such excellent-making properties as omniscience, omnipotence and moral perfection. Such a being would have what Plantinga calls "maximal greatness." Now **maximal greatness**, Plantinga avers, is possibly instantiated, that is to say, there is a possible world in which a maximally great being exists. But then this being must exist in a maximally excellent way in every possible world, including the actual world. Therefore, God exists.

Although Plantinga thinks that the ontological argument is sound and non-question-begging, still he did not initially regard it as "a successful piece of natural theology" because the key premise, "Possibly, maximal greatness is exemplified," can be rationally denied. Plantinga later confessed that he had set the bar for "success" in natural theology unreasonably high, for he believes that "the ontological argument provides as good grounds for the existence of God as does any serious philosophical argument for any important philosophical conclusion."[13] As George Mavrodes muses, "But if natural theology can be *that* good, as good as the best arguments anywhere in serious philosophy, . . . why should we not put forward these powerful arguments as *proofs* of God?"[14]

The principal issue to be settled with respect to Plantinga's ontological argument concerns the warrant for thinking the key premise to be true. It is crucial in this regard to keep in mind the difference between **metaphysical possibility** (roughly understood as actualizability) and mere **epistemic possibility** (that is, imaginability). One is tempted to say, "It's possible that God exists, and it's possible that he doesn't exist!" But this is true only with respect to epistemic possibility; if God is conceived as a maximally great being, then his existence is either metaphysically necessary or impossible, regardless of our epistemic uncertainty. Thus the epistemic entertainability of the key premise (or its denial) does not guarantee its metaphysical possibility.

It might be said that the idea of a maximally great being is intuitively a coherent notion and, hence, possibly instantiated. In this respect, the idea of God differs from supposedly parallel notions traditionally put forward by the argument's detractors like the idea of a maximally great island or of a necessarily existent lion. The properties that make up maximal excellence have **intrinsic maxima**, that is, they have peak values, so to speak, whereas the excellent-making properties of things like islands do not. There could always be more palm trees or native dancing girls! Moreover, it is far from clear that objective excellent-making properties even exist for things like islands, for the excellence of islands seems to be relative to one's interests—does one prefer a desert island or an island boasting the finest resort hotels? The idea of something like a necessarily existent lion also seems incoherent. For as a **necessary being**, such a beast would have to exist in every possible world we can conceive. But any animal that could exist in a possible world in which the universe is comprised wholly of a singularity of infinite density just is not a lion. In contrast, a maximally excellent being could transcend such physical limitations and so be conceived as necessarily existent.

Perhaps the greatest challenge to the appeal to intuition to warrant the premise that maximal greatness is possibly exemplified is that it seems intuitively coherent in the same way to conceive of a quasi-maximally great being, say, one which is in every other respect maximally excellent save that it does not know truths about future contingents. Why is the key premise of the ontological argument more plausibly true than a parallel premise concerning **quasi-maximal greatness**? Are we not equally warranted in thinking that a quasi-maximally great being exists? Perhaps not; for maximal greatness is logically incompatible with

---

[13]Alvin Plantinga, "Reason and Belief in God," typescript dated October 1981, pp. 18-19. This paragraph was inadvertently omitted in the published version of the essay, with the result that Mavrodes's reference to it has no referent. Fortunately, a nearly identical paragraph appears in Alvin Plantinga, "Self-Profile," in *Alvin Plantinga*, ed. James E. Tomberlin and Peter van Inwagen, Profiles 5 (Dordrecht: D. Reidel, 1985), p. 71. Cf. idem, *Warranted Christian Belief* (Oxford: Oxford University Press, 2001), p. 69.

[14]George Mavrodes, "Jerusalem and Athens Revisited," in *Faith and Rationality*, ed. A. Plantinga and N. Wolterstorff (Notre Dame, Ind.: University of Notre Dame Press, 1983), pp. 205-6.

quasi-maximal greatness. Since a maximally great being is omnipotent, no concrete object can exist independent of its creative power. As an omnipotent being, a maximally great being must have the power to freely refrain from creating anything at all, so that worlds must exist in which nothing other than the maximally great being exists. But that entails that if maximal greatness is possibly exemplified, then quasi-maximal greatness is not. A quasi-excellent being may exist in many worlds (worlds in which the maximally great being has chosen to create it), but such a being would lack necessary existence and thus not be quasi-maximally great. Hence, if maximal greatness is possibly exemplified, quasi-maximal greatness is impossible. Thus our intuition that a maximally great being is possible is not undermined by the claim that a quasi-maximally great being is also intuitively possible, for we see that the latter intuition depends on the assumption that maximal greatness is not possibly exemplified, which begs the question.

Still, **modal skeptics** (skeptics about the knowability of necessary and possible truths) will insist that we have no way of knowing a priori whether maximal greatness or quasi-maximal greatness is possibly exemplified. It cannot be both, but we have no idea if either is possible. Our intuitions about modality are unreliable guides. Can anything more be said in defense of the ontological argument's key premise? Plantinga provides a clue when he says that if we "carefully ponder" the key premise and the alleged objections to it, if we "consider its connections with other propositions we accept or reject" and we still find it compelling, then we are within our rational rights in accepting it. Such a procedure is a far cry from the sort of a priori speculations decried by the modal skeptic. Even if we cannot determine a priori whether maximal greatness is possibly exemplified, we may come to believe on the basis of a posteriori considerations that it is possible that a maximally great being exist. For example, other theistic arguments like the Leibnizian cosmological argument and the axiological argument may lead us to think that it is plausible that a maximally great being exists. The one argument leads to a metaphysically necessary being that is the ground of existence for any conceivable finite reality and the other to a locus of moral value that must be as metaphysically necessary as the moral values it grounds.

Moreover, we may find ourselves persuaded by a **conceptualist argument** for God's existence that the best metaphysical grounding for the existence of abstract objects is an omniscient mind whose concepts they are. Considerations of simplicity might also come into play here. For example, it is simpler to posit one metaphysically necessary, infinite, omniscient, morally perfect being than to think that three separate necessary beings exist instantiating these respective excellent-making properties. Similarly, with respect to quasi-maximally great beings, Swinburne's contention seems plausible that it is simpler (or perhaps less ad hoc) to posit either zero or infinity as the measure of a degreed property than to posit some inexplicably finite measure. Thus it would be more plausible to think that maximal greatness is possibly instantiated than quasi-maximal greatness. On the basis of considerations like these, we might well consider ourselves to be warranted in believing that it is possible that a maximally great being exists.

The question that arises at this point is whether the ontological argument has not then become **question-begging**, that is, a case in which one's only reason for thinking a premise in an argument to be true is one's belief that the conclusion is true. It might seem that the reason one thinks that it is possible that a maximally great being exists is that one has good reasons to think that a maximally great being does exist. But this misgiving may arise as a result of thinking of the project of natural theology in too linear a fashion. The theistic arguments need not be taken to be like links in a chain, in which one link follows another so that the chain is only as strong as its weakest link. Rather, they are like links in a coat of chain mail, in which all the links reinforce one another so that the strength of the whole exceeds that of any single link. The ontological argument might play its part in a cumulative case for theism, in which a multitude of factors simultaneously conspire to lead one to the global conclusion that God exists. In that sense Anselm was wrong in thinking that he had discovered a single argument which, standing independent of all the rest, served to demonstrate God's existence in all his greatness. Nevertheless, his argument does encapsulate the thrust of all the arguments together to show that God, the Supreme Being, exists.

CHAPTER SUMMARY

The teleological argument for the existence of God has come back into prominence today due to the discovery of the fine-tuning of the universe for intelligent life. The presence of the finely-tuned initial conditions of the universe must be explained as the result of either physical necessity, chance or design. The hypothesis that a life-permitting universe is physically necessary is not merely a baseless speculation but actually goes against the evidence. The chance hypothesis can only be reasonably defended by the postulation of a world ensemble of an infinite number of randomly varied universes in which our universe appears by chance alone. But such a hypothesis is arguably inferior to the design hypothesis because (1) it is less simple, (2) there is no known way of generating a world ensemble, (3) there is no independent evidence for the existence of a world ensemble, and (4) it is incompatible with contemporary biological evolutionary theory. Design is therefore the best explanation.

The axiological argument provides moral justification for theism. If God exists, then a sound foundation for objective moral values, moral duties and moral accountability exists. If God does not exist, then human beings seem to be mere animals and so have no moral value, moral duties or moral accountability. If we believe, as seems reasonable, that moral values and duties do exist, then it follows logically that God exists. Finally, we have a practical argument for theism in view of its morally advantageous nature in contrast to the de-moralization wrought by atheism.

The ontological argument seeks to show that once we grasp the concept of God as the greatest conceivable being, then it becomes clear that God must exist. If a maximally great being is possible, it follows that such a being exists in every possible world with maximal excellence and so exists in the actual world. It seems intuitively clear that maximal greatness is possibly exemplified, in contrast to chimeras like a maximally great island or a necessarily existent lion. Moreover, if maximal greatness is possibly exemplified, then quasi-maximal greatness is not possibly exemplified, so that one cannot undercut the ontological argument by appeal to the possible existence of a quasi-maximally great being. The possibility of maximal greatness's being exemplified is rendered plausible by various a posteriori arguments for the existence of such a being.

CHECKLIST OF BASIC TERMS AND CONCEPTS

altruistic behavior
animal rights
anthropic principle
atheistic moral realism
axiological argument
best self-interest
conceptualist argument
cosmic fine-tuning
design inference
divine commands
epistemic possibility
genetic fallacy
greatest conceivable being
inference to the best explanation
inflationary models
intrinsic maxima
many worlds hypothesis
maximal excellence
maximal greatness
metaphysical possibility
modal skeptics
moral accountability
moral duties
moral nihilism
necessary being
objective moral values
Ockham's razor
ontological argument
physical necessity
possible world
practical argument
principle of indifference
quasi-maximal greatness
question-begging
sociobiological pressures
specified complexity
super-string theory
teleological argument
theory of everything (T.O.E.)
tidy explanation

25

THE COHERENCE
OF THEISM
I

It has been said by someone that the proper study of mankind is man.
I will not oppose the idea, but I believe it is equally true
that the proper study of God's elect is God;
the proper study of a Christian is the Godhead.
The highest science, the loftiest speculation, the mightiest philosophy,
which can ever engage the attention of a child of God,
is the name, the nature, the person, the work, the doings,
and the existence of the great God whom he calls his Father.

CHARLES SPURGEON, SUNDAY MORNING SERMON, JANUARY 7, 1855

1 INTRODUCTION

One of the central concerns of contemporary philosophy of religion is the **coherence of theism**, or the analysis of the attributes of God. During the generation previous to our own the concept of God was often regarded as fertile ground for antitheistic arguments. The difficulty with theism, it was said, was not merely that there are no good arguments for the existence of God, but, more fundamentally, that the notion of God is incoherent.

This antitheistic critique has evoked a prodigious literature devoted to the philosophical analysis of the concept of God. Two controls have tended to guide this inquiry into the divine nature: Scripture and **perfect being theology**. For thinkers in the Judeo-Christian tradition, God's self-revelation in Scripture is obviously paramount in understanding what God is like. In addition, the Anselmian conception of God as the greatest conceivable being or most perfect being—perfect being theology—has guided philosophical speculation on the raw data of Scripture, so that God's biblical attributes are to be conceived in ways that would serve to exalt God's greatness. Since the concept of God is underdetermined by the biblical data and since what constitutes a "great-making" property is to some degree debatable, philosophers working within the Judeo-Christian tradition enjoy considerable latitude in formulating a philosophically coherent and biblically faithful doctrine of God. Theists thus found that antitheistic critiques of certain conceptions of God could actually be quite helpful in framing a more adequate conception. Thus, far from undermining theism, the antitheistic critiques have served mainly to reveal how rich and challenging is the concept of God, thereby refining and strengthening theistic belief.

2 NECESSITY

Ever since Aristotle, God has been conceived in Western philosophical theology as a **necessarily existent being** (*ens necessarium*). Christian theologians interpreted the revelation of the divine name "I am that I am" (Ex 3:14 KJV) to express the same idea of God's **necessity**. For Aristotle, God's necessary existence probably meant simply his immunity to generation and corruption. The Aristotelian conception finds its counterpart among those contemporary philosophers who defend the idea of God's **"factual" necessity**: according to this notion, God exists necessarily in the sense that, given that God exists, it is impossible that he ever came into or will go out of existence. He is uncaused, eternal, incorruptible, and indestructible. During the Middle Ages, however, Islamic philosophers such as al-Farabi began to enunciate an even more powerful conception of God's necessity: God's nonexistence is logically impossible. This conception of necessary existence lay at the heart of Anselm's ontological argument: if God's nonexistence is logically impossible, it follows that he must exist. On this view God is not merely factually necessary, but **logically necessary** in his being.

Powerful theological and philosophical reasons can be given for taking God's existence to be logically necessary. Philosophically, the conception of God as the greatest conceivable being implies his necessary existence in this sense, since logically contingent existence is not as great as necessary existence. Certain forms of the contingency argument for God's existence terminate in a logically necessary being, for only such a being can supply an adequate answer to the question, Why is there something rather than nothing? The conceptualist argument for God's existence also entails the existence of a logically necessary being in order to ground the realm of abstract objects. The axiological argument leads naturally to such a being, since moral values and principles are not plausibly logically contingent. Theologically speaking, a God who just happens to exist (even eternally and without cause) seems less satisfactory religiously than one whose nonexistence is impossible. Mere factual necessity thus does not seem to capture the fullness of divine being.

Since the critiques of Hume and Kant, however, philosophers have until recently widely rejected the notion of God as a logically necessary being. It was often said that to speak of a logically necessary being is flatly a category mistake; propositions are logically necessary or contingent with respect to their truth value, but beings are no more necessary or contingent than they are true or false. If one replied that the theist means to hold that the proposition *God exists* is necessarily true, then the response was that existential propositions (that is, those which assert the existence of something) are uniformly contingent. Besides, the proposition *God does not exist* is not itself a contradiction, so that *God exists* cannot be logically necessary. Moreover, many philosophers insisted that the distinction between necessary and contingent truth is merely a result of linguistic convention, so that it becomes merely conventional to assert that God necessarily exists.

Philosophical reflection over the last quarter century has largely overturned these critiques. The development of **possible worlds semantics** has provided a useful means of expressing the theist's claim: To say that God is a logically necessary being is to say that God exists in every possible world (*God* in this case being a proper name and, hence, rigidly designating its referent, that is to say, picking out the same entity in every possible world in which it exists). In other words, the proposition *God exists* is true in every possible world. There is no good reason to think that such an existential proposition cannot be true in every possible world, for many philosophers make precisely similar claims about the necessary existence of various abstract objects like numbers, properties, propositions and so forth. Though abstract, such objects are thought by many philosophers to exist, in Plantinga's words, just as serenely as your most solidly concrete object.[1] Thus it would be special pleading to privilege these objects with necessary existence while denying the possibility of God's existing necessarily.

Furthermore, the modality operative in possible worlds semantics is not **strict logical necessity/possibility**, but **broad logical necessity/possibility**. With regard to the first there is no logical impossibility, strictly speaking, in the proposition *The Prime Minister is a prime number*; but we should not want to say, therefore, that there is a possible world in which this proposition is true. In contrast, broad logical possibility is usually construed in terms of **actualizability** and is therefore often understood as **metaphysical possibility**. There are no clear criteria which can be applied mechanically to determine whether a proposition is metaphysically necessary or impossible. One chiefly has to rely on intuition or conceivability. Propositions that are not strictly logically contradictory may nonetheless be metaphysically impossible—for example, *This table could have been made of ice* or *Socrates could have been a hippopotamus*. Similarly, propositions need not be tautologous (*If it is raining, then it is raining*) or analytic (*Even numbers are divisible by two*) in order to be metaphysically necessary; for example, *Gold has the atomic number 79, Whatever begins to exist has a cause* or *Everything that has a shape has a size*. Intuitions may differ over whether some proposition is metaphysically necessary or impossible. Thus, with respect to the proposition *God exists*, the fact that the negation of this proposition is not a contradiction in no way shows that the proposition is not metaphysically necessary. Similarly, the proposition that *Nothing exists* is not a logical contradiction, but that does not show that the proposition is broadly logically possible. If one has some reason to think that a metaphysically necessary being exists, then it would be question-begging to reject this conclusion solely on the grounds that it seems possible that nothing should exist.

Finally, as for the **conventionalist theory of necessity**, according to which the distinction between necessary and contingent truth is based merely on linguistic convention, such a construal of modal notions is not only unjustified but enormously implausible. As Plantinga points out,[2] the linguistic conventionalist confuses sentences with propositions. **Sentences** are linguistic entities composed of words; **propositions** are the information content expressed by declarative sentences. We can imagine situations in which the sentence "Either God exists or he does not" would not have expressed the proposition it in fact does and so might have been neither necessary nor true. But that goes no distance

---

[1]Alvin Plantinga, *The Nature of Necessity*, Clarendon Library of Logic and Philosophy (Oxford: Clarendon, 1974), p. 132.
[2]See remarks of Alvin Plantinga, "Self-Profile," in *Alvin Plantinga*, ed. James E. Tomberlin and Peter van Inwagen, Profiles 5 (Dordrecht: D. Reidel, 1985), pp. 71-73.

toward proving that the proposition it does express is neither necessary nor true. Moreover, it seems quite incredible to think that the necessity of this proposition is in any wise affected by our determination to use words in a certain way. Could it really be the case that God both exists and does not exist?

The conception of God as a necessary being in a broadly logical sense thus seems a coherent notion which properly belongs to Christian theism.

3 ASEITY

Aseity (from the Latin *a se,* "by itself") refers to God's self-existence or independence. God does not merely exist in every possible world (as great as that is) but, even more greatly, he exists in every world wholly independent of anything else. The Scriptures affirm the preexistence of the divine Word: "All things came into being through him, and without him not one thing came into being" (Jn 1:3). God is unique in his aseity; all other things exist *ab alio* (through another).

Divine aseity confronts a serious challenge from one of the oldest and most persistent of philosophical doctrines: **Platonism**, which holds that in addition to concrete objects like people and planets there also exist separate realms of abstract objects like numbers and sets and propositions and properties. These objects, though abstract and usually held to exist beyond time and space, are nonetheless every bit as real as the familiar physical objects of our daily experience. They exist necessarily, for it is inconceivable that there should exist, for example, a possible world lacking in numbers or propositions, even if that world were altogether devoid of concrete objects other than God himself. Moreover—and this is the crucial point—they exist *a se.* There is no cause of the existence of such entities; they each exist independent of one another and of God. It is this feature of Platonism, more than any other, that has troubled many Christian theists. Not only is there an infinite number of such objects (there is an infinite number of natural numbers alone), but there are higher and higher orders of infinities of such objects, infinities of infinities, so that God is utterly dwarfed by their unimaginable multitude. God finds himself amid uncreated, infinite realms of beings that exist just as necessarily and independently as he. The dependence of physical creation upon God for its existence becomes an infinitesimal triviality in comparison with the existence of the infinitude of beings that exist independent of him. Platonism thus entails a **metaphysical pluralism** that is incompatible with the unique aseity of God.

Some contemporary Christian philosophers have sought to reconcile the existence of such abstract objects with divine aseity by denying that these objects exist *a se,* even if they exist necessarily. According to this **modified Platonism**, while such objects exist in every possible world, they are nonetheless created beings, just as are physical objects. They are not created by God at any time but rather are timelessly created by him. God is not temporally prior to the existence of such objects, but he is causally or **explanatorily prior** to their existence.

But two problems threaten to spoil this simple solution: (1) Since such entities exist necessarily, they are obviously independent of the divine will. God is not free to refrain from creating such beings. But central to the Christian doctrine of **creation** is the conviction that creation is the freely willed act of God, that God, had he wished, could have remained alone without any exigency of producing a world of creatures. (2) Even more seriously, the solution seems incoherent. For in order to create, say, properties, God must already exemplify certain properties. In order to create the property *being powerful,* for example, God must already have the property of being powerful. (Recall that according to Platonism properties exist apart from their instances or abstract particulars.) God cannot coherently be said to create his own properties, since in order to create them, he must already possess them. Of course, God and properties both exist timelessly on the proposed view, but it turns out that God's properties must be explanatorily prior to their own existence, which is incoherent.

How might modified Platonism handle these difficulties? With respect to the first, the modified Platonist must admit that, while God is free to refrain from creating contingent beings, he is not free to refrain from sustaining abstract objects in existence. But he will probably deny that this is really a serious problem, insisting that it merely amounts to the claim that God cannot refrain from making it the case that red is a color, say, by making red into a taste or the number two, that he cannot make red be brighter than yellow, that he cannot make $2 + 2 = 7$, and so forth. Virtually all Christian theists have held that mathematical and logical truths do not lie within the scope of God's will, and the same is true for the nature of and relations among various abstract objects. It may be said that all these "limitations" on God's freedom are actually pseudo-tasks and thus not real limitations.

The problem of the causal or explanatory priority of God relative to abstract objects is a more serious difficulty. Some contemporary Christian philosophers have appealed to divine simplicity as a solution, for if God is identical to his properties, they are not explanatorily prior to him. But the classical doctrine of divine simplicity never envisioned making God identical with his properties as the Platonist construes them, for that would be to turn God into an abstract object. Perhaps the modified Platonist might maintain that all the properties that God exemplifies as part of his nature—for example, *being loving, being powerful* and so on—do not exist in a "realm" outside the being of God, as do other properties. Rather, as a brute fact, God, along with his nature, simply exists *a se.* Other properties, such as *being red,* are sustained by God, either by his intellect, will or in some other way. Thus only these other properties that are not constituents of God are timelessly created by God. This distinction among properties might appear to be ad hoc and therefore unacceptable, but the modified Platonist might respond as follows: we have good, independent grounds for believing in God's existence and aseity and in the existence of abstract objects construed along Platonic lines. The modified Platonist solution provides a way to reconcile these two justified beliefs, and that is a virtue of the approach.

Historically, the majority of Christian theologians have not embraced modified Platonism. Rather, most have followed Augustine in adopting some form of **conceptualism** as an account of the existence of abstract objects. Augustine identified the Platonic forms with the **divine ideas,** holding that abstract objects have a conceptual reality as the contents of God's mind. Thus they do not exist independent of God nor even outside of God but only within his mind. Thus the number seven, the proposition that $2 + 2 = 4$, and the property of *redness*, for example, are all ideas conceived by God.

Conceptualism offers quite different responses to the difficulties raised in connection with modified Platonism. (1) Since the divine ideas belong to the divine mind and are not externally existing abstract objects, they are not part of the created order. Thus their necessary existence is not incompatible with the freely-willed character of creation. Even in possible worlds in which God refrains from creation, he still exists with his ideas. Just as moral values are rooted in the moral nature of God such that his moral commands are necessary expressions of his nature, so the divine mind operates in accord with logically necessary truths. The necessity of logic and mathematics may be seen as grounded in the necessity of God's intellect. (2) If abstract objects have a conceptual reality, then they do not exist explanatorily prior to God's conception of them. That does not entail that God is not in that explanatorily prior moment omnipotent, omniscient, eternal and all the rest. Just as medieval theologians like Boethius, Aquinas and Ockham thought of a conceptualized universal property as explanatorily posterior to the relevant abstract particular, so God's being in a certain way need not be construed in terms of instantiating a universal; rather, the universal is conceptually abstracted from the particular. Thus, in order for properties and other abstract objects to be the result of divine intellection, they need not exist prior to themselves.

Modified Platonists claim that there are two main problems with the conceptualist account. First, it confuses a concept with its object. To understand this problem, consider someone who is thinking about the color red, say, as it is exemplified on the surface of an apple. The red color of the apple is "in" the mind only in the sense that it is an object towards which the mind is directed. Such mental objects are not constituents within the mind. By contrast, the concept of being red is a constituent that is in the mind of the person thinking about redness. Thus a concept in the mind is not identical to the object of the mind that has the concept. God's various concepts of abstract objects are within his mind, but the objects of those concepts—various abstract objects themselves—are not. On this point, the critic sides with those that believe that universals are instantiated by their possessors, God included, against the conceptualist notion that the universal is abstracted from the particular.

Second, the conceptualist solution seems vulnerable to the same difficulty that its advocates press against modified Platonism, namely, that if God is the creator of properties, then he must be causally or explanatorily prior to those properties, and this becomes problematic with respect to that range of properties that God himself possesses. The modified Platonist will charge that the conceptualist is hoist on his own petard. For the divine mind is not identical to its concepts; the divine mind has or contains them. One way this can be seen is to notice that while the divine mind is one, its concepts are many. Now if properties are identified as concepts in God's mind, then the attributes of God—for example, *omnipotence*—are themselves concepts in God's mind. But God and his mind must exist causally and explanatorily prior to his concepts. Thus conceptualism seems to face the same problem raised against modified Platonism.

How might conceptualists respond to these objections? With respect to the first, conceptualists will recognize the distinction between the redness that exists in an apple as an abstract particular and is independent of the conceiving mind and the universal property *redness* that is an abstract entity. Only the latter is identified as a conceptual reality and so is mind-dependent. *Redness* is the divine concept of the mind-independent reality, which exists in the apple as an abstract particular. Such concepts may or may not have mind-independent correlates, as is evident in cases in which one thinks of creatures of fiction or logically impossible entities like a square circle. Abstract objects are God's concepts, and if he has concepts of abstract objects, then those are concepts of his concepts.

As for the second difficulty, conceptualists will agree that the universal properties that God exemplifies are concepts in God's mind. But it is not evident why in that moment explanatorily prior to God's conceptualization of omnipotence, God cannot be omnipotent. There simply will not be in that explanatorily prior moment any conceptualization of the universal *omnipotence*, but there will be an omnipotent God.

These are extremely difficult and unresolved issues, and we can look forward to further discussion of modified Platonist and conceptualist perspectives on divine aseity on the part of Christian philosophers. For now, we can agree that God is uniquely self-existent, and abstract objects should be thought of as in some way grounded in God.

4 INCORPOREALITY

"God is spirit" (Jn 4:24), that is to say, a living, immaterial substance. God's **immateriality** entails the divine attribute of **incorporeality**, that God is neither a body nor embodied. As a personal being, God is therefore of the order of unembodied Mind.

Scientific naturalism and, in particular, physicalism cannot abide the doctrine of divine incorporeality. Since all that exists is physical in nature or at least supervenient or dependent on the physical, there can be no such entity as an unembodied Mind existing beyond the universe. How such a Mind could causally affect the world, so as to be its Creator and Sustainer, is said to be wholly mysterious. Thus, if incorporeality belongs to the concept of God, it follows that God does not exist.

This challenge to divine incorporeality is reminiscent of the physicalist critique of mind-body dualism with respect to philosophical anthropology, and, doubtlessly, the most effective way to meet this challenge will be to recall the arguments offered in support of the mind as a mental substance (see chaps. 11-12, 14). For if the coherence of finite minds distinct from the body can be defended, so analogously can the coherence of an infinite Mind distinct from the world. It is noteworthy therefore that the failure of reductive materialism has become patent to most thinkers in contemporary philosophy of mind and that the leading views are therefore either nonreductive versions of physicalism or not physicalist at all. But nonreductive physicalism, which arguably must view mental states as mere epiphenomena of brain states, cannot be plausibly squared with our firsthand experience of ourselves. Moreover, since there is no enduring self on such theories, but just a temporal succession of mental states, personal identity across time (diachronic identity) is impossible. And yet I do grasp myself as an enduring self (recall chap. 14). We should rightly hold someone deranged who really believed that he has not existed longer than the present instant, that his memories are not in fact his, that he himself has never before done or said or thought anything. On such theories moral praise or blame become meaningless, since one's present mental state cannot be held responsible or praised for prior actions associated with quite distinct mental states. Moreover, given the causal impotence of epiphenomenal mental states, no one can be held accountable anyway for actions carried out by the body alone. For the same reason epiphenomenalism squeezes out freedom of the will, since the direction of causal influence between consciousness and the body is exclusively a one-way street (see chap. 13).

Not only does such a view fly in the face of our firsthand experience of ourselves as causally efficacious agents, but it raises two further problems as well. (1) Such a deterministic view of human agency cannot be rationally affirmed. For if our thought life is merely the byproduct of our material make-up and external stimuli, then the decision to believe that determinism is true can be no more rational than having a toothache. (2) Such a view is incompatible with evolutionary biology, since causally impotent mental states, which merely ride along, as it were, on physical states, can confer no advantage in the struggle for survival. Indeed, we might be led to question whether anything at all that we believe is veridical, given that the bodily states on which our beliefs supervene have evolved only under the pressure of survival, not success in grasping truth. For all these reasons, the view that minds are immaterial substances is at the very least coherent, in which case theism stands unconvicted of incoherence in affirming God's incorporeality.

The problem of divine interaction with the world also mirrors the issue raised by dualist-interactionist views of the mind and the body. In chapter eleven we saw that our inability to explain *how* the mind influences the body should not lead us to doubt our firsthand knowledge *that* it does. We apprehend ourselves as causes; indeed, our grasp of the notion of causation probably comes primarily from our acquaintance with ourselves as causally efficacious agents. Moreover, we saw that the question itself may well be malposed, for it seems to assume the necessity of some intermediate causal linkage between cause and effect, which is precluded by the nature of the case. Because God, in particular, acts immediately in creating, there can in principle be no intermediate, since creation constitutes in being its object (see chap. 28).

The parallel of dualism-interactionism and God-world relations suggests that God's actions in the world are like the basic actions we undertake in our bodies. In a basic action we do not perform some action by means of undertaking to do something else; rather, we undertake to perform some action immediately, as when I will to raise my arm. Just as I, as an immaterial substance, can perform basic actions with respect to my body, so God can by merely willing bring about effects in the world. The world is, as it were, the instrumental equivalent of God's body.

Should we push the analogy further and affirm with **process theism** that God then does have a body after all, that the world is the body of God and God the soul the world? Is the analogy so entire as to suggest that although God has created the world *ex nihilo*, it nonetheless has come to embody him? It seems not. For the crucial disanalogy between the world and the body is that the world does not function for God either as a material substratum of consciousness or as a sense organ through which he perceives the external world. Our souls, while embodied, are somehow and in some respects dependent on our bodily states as a physical grounding for consciousness and as a means of perceiving reality outside ourselves. But nothing comparable to this is true in God's case. The human brain is the most complex structure in the universe, and there is nothing in the physical world which could serve as a substratum for an omniscient Mind. Moreover, God's knowledge, as we shall see, should not be construed along the lines of perception.

In short, while the soul-body relation works nicely as an analogy for God-world relations in an active sense, it is not analogous in the passive sense. God is ontologically distinct from his creation.

5 OMNIPRESENCE

The comparison of the God-world relation and the mind-body relation naturally raises the question of how we are to understand God's presence in creation. As an incorporeal being, God is clearly not to be thought of as localized in space, having a certain circumscribed size and shape. The Scriptures present God as having the attribute of **omnipresence**; he is everywhere present in his creation in virtue of his incorporeality:

> Where can I go from your spirit?
>> Or where can I flee from your presence?
> If I ascend to heaven, you are there;
>> if I make my bed in Sheol, you are there.
> If I take the wings of the morning
>> and settle at the farthest limits of the sea,
> even there your hand shall lead me,
>> and your right hand shall hold me fast. (Ps 139:7-10)

But how are we to understand this? Just as we do not think of God as localized in space neither should we conceive of him as extended throughout space like some sort of an all-pervasive ether. Just as incorporeality is incompatible with a locally circumscribed deity, so it is incompatible with such a universally extended deity, who would be imbued with the size and shape of space itself (which would be constantly changing as space expands) and who could not be wholly present at all places simultaneously but could only have parts which would occupy corresponding parts of space. In some way God must be wholly present to all points in space at once.

Again, analogies of the soul-body relation are instructive. Some philosophers of mind hold that the soul is spatially present in the body. Our selves seem to have spatial location: I, for example, am here in this room and not at the bottom of the Marianas Trench or struggling on the steeps of Patagonia. Nonetheless, as an incorporeal entity, my soul does not have spatial extension. So according to these thinkers, the soul has a spatial location but lacks spatial extension. It is present in its respective body but is not extended throughout it like a humanoid ghost. Nor is it confined to some part of the body, such as the brain, but is somehow wholly present at all points in its body. On the other hand, some mind-body theorists deny that the soul is spatially located at all. Its perceptions are relative to a certain vantage point, the location of its body, through which it experiences and acts in the world. For that reason it appears that our selves are spatially located; indeed, each of us fancies himself to be the center of the universe. But the mind itself is not a spatial entity and so lacks either location or extension in space.

Similarly, we can say either that God is spatially located in the universe but is wholly present at every point in it or else that God is not spatially located in the universe but is causally active at every point in it. Are there any reasons for preferring one of these conceptions of divine omnipresence over the other? Divine **spacelessness** could be easily deduced from certain construals of other divine attributes. For example, if God is timeless or immutable, he could not exist in space, since any spatially located entity will be constantly changing in relation to other spatial things. But since timelessness and immutability are very controversial doctrines, we ought to ask if there are independent arguments for our interpretation of divine omnipresence. The idea that a concrete entity can be wholly present at spatially separated points is certainly a difficult conception. It might seem to require us to say that God, wholly present at every point, would believe that two points separated by billions of light years are both "here," which is incoherent. But perhaps one could avoid a multiplicity of "heres" for God by stipulating that God's "here" is coextensive with the entire universe, so that space as a whole is "here" for him.

A better reason for thinking that God transcends space is that we know, in virtue of the doctrine of creation, that God existing alone without creation is spaceless. For on a **relational view of space**, space does not exist in the utter absence of any physical reality, and on a **substantival view of space**, space is a thing or substance and therefore must have been created by God. In either case, then, God brings space into being at the moment of his creation of the universe. Without creation, therefore, God exists spacelessly. But the creation of space would do nothing to "spatialize" God, that is to say, to draw him into space. The creating of space is not itself a spatial act (as is, say, bumping something). Hence, there is just no reason to think that divine spacelessness is surrendered in the act of creation. If not, then omnipresence should be understood in terms of God's being immediately cognizant of and causally active at every point in space. He knows what is happening at every spatial location in the universe and he is causally operative at every such point, even if nothing more is going on there than quantum fluctuations in the vacuum of "empty" space.

God's spacelessness would be the functional equivalent of an embedding **hyperdimension** of space. Just as a three-dimensional being could act in the two-dimensional plane in ways that would appear mysterious to the inhabitants of Flatland, so the transcendent God can act immediately at any point in our three-dimensional world. Charmed by this image, a few thinkers have even thought to construe God as literally a hyperdimensional being existing in an embedding space-time. But this metaphysical extravagance actually gives up what has been achieved by our construing divine omnipresence in terms of spacelessness without accruing any new advantage. Talk of an embedding hyperspace inhabited by God should be taken as an illustrative device without ontological significance. It seems best to say that God literally exists spacelessly but is present at every point in space in the sense that he is cognizant of and causally active at every point in space.

6 ETERNITY

The question of God's relationship to space naturally raises the question of his relationship to time as well. That God is eternal is the clear teaching of the Judeo-Christian Scriptures (Ps 90:2), and God's eternality also follows from divine necessity. For if God exists necessarily, it is impossible that he not exist; therefore he can never go out of or come into being. God just exists, without beginning or end, which is a minimalist definition of what it means to say that God is eternal.

But there is considerable disagreement concerning the nature of divine **eternity**. Plato, Plotinus, Augustine, Boethius, Anselm and Aquinas argued that God transcends time, just as he does space, and therefore has his whole life at once (*tota simul*). Such thinkers often say that from the standpoint of eternity (*sub specie aeternitatis*) the entire series of temporal events is real to God and thus available for his causal influence at any point in history through a single timeless act. On the other hand, Aristotle may well have taken God's eternity to be everlasting temporal duration, and Duns Scotus sharply criticized the atemporalist view of Aquinas on the grounds that time, being dynamic by nature, cannot coexist as a whole with God. Isaac Newton, the father of modern physics, in his General Scholium to his great *Mathematical Principles of Natural Philosophy* (*Principia Mathematica*), founded his doctrine of absolute time upon God's infinite temporal duration, and in our day process philosophers and theologians like Whitehead and Hartshorne have vigorously asserted the temporalist view.

Why think that God exists timelessly? God's atemporality could be successfully deduced from his simplicity and immutability, for if God is absolutely simple, he stands in no real relations whatsoever—including temporal relations of *earlier than/later than*—and if God is absolutely immutable, then he cannot change in any way, which, if he is in time, he must do, at least extrinsically, as things copresent with him change. But as we shall see in the next chapter, these extrabiblical doctrines are highly controversial and now widely rejected, so that one needs to look for other grounds of one's doctrine of divine eternity.

Perhaps the most persuasive argument in favor of divine timelessness is based on the incompleteness of temporal life. Shakespeare's melancholy lines,

> Tomorrow and tomorrow and tomorrow
> Creeps in this petty pace from day to day
> To the last syllable of recorded time. (*Macbeth* 5.5.21)

are a poignant reminder of the evanescence of temporal life. Our yesterdays are gone, and our tomorrows we do not yet have. The fleeting present is our only claim on existence. There is thus a transiency and incompleteness to temporal life that seems incompatible with the life of a most perfect being.

On the other hand, there do seem to be good reasons, too, for affirming divine temporality. If God is really related to the world, then it is extraordinarily difficult to see how God could remain untouched by the world's temporality. For simply in virtue of his being related to changing things (even if he himself somehow managed to remain intrinsically changeless), there would exist a *before* and *after* in God's life. Aquinas escaped the force of this reasoning only by insisting that God stands in no real relation to the world—a position that seems fantastic in light of God's being the Creator and Sustainer of the universe.

Eleonore Stump and Norman Kretzmann try to craft an **eternal-temporal simultaneity relation** between God and creatures to preserve God's atemporality. Their basic idea is as follows: Take some atemporal being x and some temporal being y. These two are ET-simultaneous just in case, relative to some hypothetical observer in the eternal reference frame, x is eternally present and y is observed as temporally present, and relative to some hypothetical observer in any temporal reference frame, y is temporally present and x is observed as eternally present. The problem with this account is that the notion of observation employed in the definition is wholly obscure. No hint is given as to what is meant, for example, by x's being observed as eternally present relative to some moment of time. In the absence of any procedure for determining ET-simultaneity, the definition reduces to the assertion that, relative to the reference frame of eternity, x is eternally present and y is temporally present and that, relative to some temporal reference frame, y is temporally present and x is eternally present—which is only a restatement of the problem! Stump and Kretzmann later revised their definition of ET-simultaneity so as to free it from observation language. Basically, their new account tries to define ET-simultaneity in terms of causal relations. On the new definition, x and y are ET-simultaneous just in case, relative to an observer in the eternal reference frame, x is eternally present and y is temporally present, and the observer can enter into direct causal relations with both x and y, and relative to an observer in any temporal reference frame, x is eternally present and y is at the same time as the observer, and the observer can enter into direct causal relations with both x and y. The fundamental problem with this new account of ET-simultaneity is that it is viciously circular. For ET-simultaneity was originally invoked to explain how a timeless God could be causally active in time; but now ET-simultaneity is defined in terms of a timeless being's ability to be causally active in time. This amounts to saying that God can be causally active in time because he can be causally active in time!

Brian Leftow tries to remedy the defects in the Stump-Kretzmann theory by proposing a theory according to which temporal entities exist in timeless eternity as well as in time and so can be causally related to God. Leftow argues as follows: there can be no change of place relative to God because the distance between the transcendent God and everything in space is zero. But if there is no change of place relative to God, there can be no change of any sort on the part of spatial things relative to God. Moreover, since anything that is temporal is also spatial, it follows that there are no temporal, nonspatial beings. The only temporal beings there are exist in space, and none of these changes relative to God. Assuming, then, some relational view of time, according to which time cannot exist without change, it follows that all temporal beings exist timelessly relative to God. Thus relative to God all things are timelessly present and so can be causally related to God.

The fundamental problem with this reasoning is that it commits a serious category mistake. When we say that there is no distance between God and creatures, we do not mean that there is a distance and its measure is zero. Rather, we mean that the category of distance does not even apply to the relations between a nonspatial being like God and things in space. Hence, it does not follow that things in space are changeless relative to God; but without this premise the rest of Leftow's theory collapses. In short, God's real relation to a temporal, changing world implies divine temporality.

A second powerful argument for divine temporality is based on God's being all-knowing. In order to know the truth of propositions expressed by tensed sentences like "Christ is risen from the dead" God must exist temporally. For such knowledge locates the knower relative to the present. Hermetically sealed in timeless eternity, God could not know such tensed facts as whether Christ has died or has yet to be born. God's knowledge of the history of the world would be like the knowledge a film producer has of a movie as it lies in the can: he knows what is on every frame, but he has no idea what is now being projected on the screen. Similarly, all a timeless God could know would be tenseless truths like *Christ dies in* A.D. *30*, but he would have no idea whether Christ has actually died yet or not. Such ignorance is inconsistent with the standard account of omniscience, which requires that God know all truths, and is surely incompatible with God's maximal cognitive excellence. To date no satisfactory account of how a timeless God could know tensed truths has been forthcoming. The proposals advanced by thinkers like Leftow, Jonathan Kvanvig and Edward Wierenga, upon examination, all turn out to deny God knowledge of tensed facts.

We thus have comparatively weak grounds for affirming divine timelessness but two powerful arguments in favor of divine temporality. It would seem, then, that we should conclude that God is temporal. But such a conclusion would be premature. For there does remain one way of escape still open for defenders of divine timelessness. The argument based on God's real relation to the world assumed the objective reality of temporal becoming, and the argument based on God's knowledge of the temporal world assumed the objective reality of tensed facts. If one denies the objective reality of temporal becoming and tensed facts, then the arguments are undercut. For in that case, nothing to which God is related ever changes, and all facts are tenseless, so that God undergoes neither relational nor intrinsic change. He can be the immutable, omniscient Sustainer and Knower of all things and, hence, exist timelessly.

In short, the defender of divine timelessness can escape the two arguments by embracing the static or B-theory of time. Divine timelessness thus stands or falls with the static theory of time. The competing A- and B-theories of time have been assessed in chapter eighteen.[3] If we adopt a dynamic or A-theory of time, as we think we ought, we should conclude that God is temporal.

But if God is temporal in virtue of his relation to and knowledge of a tempo-

---

[3]See further William Lane Craig, *The Tensed Theory of Time: A Critical Examination*, Synthese Library 293 (Dordrecht: Kluwer Academic, 2000); idem, *The Tenseless Theory of Time: A Critical Examination*, Synthese Library 294 (Dordrecht: Kluwer Academic, 2000).

ral world, what about his state without the world? Although we shall treat this
question in more detail in chapter twenty-eight in discussing the concept of
creation, it is also appropriate to pause to reflect on the question at this junc-
ture. Did God exist literally before creation? Has he existed for infinite time,
from eternity past? Is not such a hypothesis contradicted by the *kalam* cosmological argument against the infinitude of the past?

Strictly speaking, the argument for the finitude of the past did not reach the
conclusion "Therefore, time began to exist." Rather, what it proved, if successful, is that there cannot have been an infinite past, that is to say, a past that is
composed of an infinite number of equal temporal intervals. But some philosophers have argued that in the absence of any empirical measures, there is no objective fact that one interval of time is longer or shorter than another distinct
interval. Prior to creation it is impossible to differentiate between a tenth of a
second and ten trillion years. There is no moment, say, one hour before creation. Time literally lacks any **intrinsic metric**; God existing alone without the
universe would thus not endure through an infinite number of, say, hours, prior
to the moment of creation.

Such an understanding of God's time prior to creation seems quite attractive.
Nevertheless, a close inspection of the view reveals difficulties. Even in a **metrically amorphous time** (that is, time without any intrinsic metric), there are objective factual differences of length for certain temporal intervals. For in the case of
intervals that are enclosed in other intervals, the enclosed intervals are factually
shorter than their encompassing intervals. But this implies that if God existed
temporally prior to creation, then he has in fact endured through a beginningless
series of longer and longer intervals. In fact, we can even say that such a precre-
ation time must be infinite. The past is infinite if and only if there is no first finite
interval of time and time is not circular. Thus the amorphous time prior to creation would be infinite, even though we cannot compare the lengths of nonnested
intervals of it. Thus all the difficulties of an infinite past return to haunt us.

What must be done is to dissolve the linear geometrical structure of precre-
ation time. One must maintain that prior to creation there literally are no intervals of time at all. There would be no earlier and later, no enduring through
successive intervals, and, hence, no waiting, no temporal becoming. This
changeless state would pass away, not successively, but as a whole, at the moment of creation, when metric time begins.

But such a changeless, undifferentiated state looks suspiciously like a state of
timelessness! Imagine God existing changelessly alone in a possible world in
which he refrains from creation. In such a world, God is reasonably conceived
to be timeless. But God, existing alone without creation in the actual world, is
no different than he would be in such a possible world, even though in the actual world he becomes temporal by creating. To claim that time would exist
without the universe in virtue of the beginning of the world seems to postulate
a sort of backward causation: the occurrence of the first event not only causes
time to exist with the event, but also before it. But on a dynamic theory of
time, such retrocausation is metaphysically impossible, for it amounts to something's being caused by nothing, since at the time of the effect the retro-cause
in no sense exists. Apart from backward causation, there seems to be nothing

that would produce a time prior to the moment of creation. Time would simply begin with the occurrence of the first event, the act of creation.

It seems, therefore, that it is not only coherent but also plausible that God existing changelessly alone without creation would be timeless and that he enters time at the moment of creation in virtue of his real relation to the temporal universe. The image of God existing temporally prior to creation is just that: a figment of the imagination. Given that time began to exist, the most plausible view of God's relationship to time is that he is timeless without creation and temporal subsequent to creation.

CHAPTER SUMMARY

Philosophical analysis of the concept of God has proceeded under the controls of Scripture and perfect being theology.

God's necessity has been construed as either broadly logical necessity or as merely factual necessity. Several of the theistic arguments support God's being necessary in the broadly logical sense, as do theological sensibilities. To say that God is a logically necessary being is to say that God exists in every possible world. There is no more reason to think that God cannot be necessary in this sense that to think that abstract objects cannot be necessary in the same sense.

Aseity refers to God's self-existence or independence. The doctrine of divine aseity confronts a serious challenge from Platonism, which holds that there exist separate realms of abstract objects. Platonism entails a metaphysical pluralism that is incompatible with the unique aseity of God. Possible solutions to this challenge include a modified Platonism, which conceives God to timelessly create abstract objects, or some form of conceptualism, according to which abstract objects have a conceptual reality as the contents of God's mind.

Incorporeality is the property of being neither a body nor embodied. As a personal being, God is therefore of the order of unembodied Mind. The challenge to divine incorporeality is reminiscent of the physicalist critique of mind-body dualism with respect to philosophical anthropology, and the most effective way to meet this challenge is to utilize the arguments in support of the mind as a mental substance. The parallel of dualism-interactionism and God-world relations suggests that God's actions in the world are like the basic actions we undertake in our bodies. But the crucial disanalogy between the world and our bodies is that the world does not function for God either as a material substratum of consciousness or as a sense organ through which he perceives the external world.

Omnipresence is God's being present at every point in space. Just as incorporeality is incompatible with a locally circumscribed deity, so it is incompatible with such a universally extended deity, who could not be wholly present at all places simultaneously but could only have parts which would occupy corresponding parts of space. God can be conceived to be spatially located but not spatially extended and thus wholly present at every point in the universe, or else as not spatially located in the universe at all but cognizant of and causally active at every point in it. The latter alternative seems preferable because God existing alone without creation is spaceless. On this view God brings space into being at the moment of his creation of the universe, but the creation of space does nothing to "spatialize" God, that is to say, to draw him into space.

Eternity is minimally defined as the state of existing without beginning or end. It can be construed as either timelessness or omnitemporality. God's real relation to a temporal, changing world and his omniscience seem to necessitate a temporalist construal of divine eternity. This conclusion could be avoided, however, by adopting a static or B-theory of time. On a dynamic or A-theory of time, the beginning of time would entail that God without creation exists either timelessly or in an amorphous time in which temporal intervals cannot be distinguished. Such an amorphous time is dubiously called "time" at all, so that God is atemporal without creation and temporal since creation.

CHECKLIST OF BASIC TERMS AND CONCEPTS

actualizability
aseity
broad logical necessity/possibility
coherence of theism
conceptualism
conventionalist theory of necessity
creation
divine ideas
eternal-temporal simultaneity relation
eternity
explanatorily prior
"factual" necessity
hyperdimension
immateriality
incorporeality
intrinsic metric
logical necessity
metaphysical necessity/possibility
metaphysical pluralism
metrically amorphous time
modified Platonism
necessarily existent being
necessity
omnipresence
perfect being theology
Platonism
possible worlds semantics
process theism
propositions
relational view of space
sentences
spacelessness
strict logical necessity/possibility
substantival view of space

26

THE COHERENCE
OF THEISM
II

If the object of worship in the Judeo-Christian tradition
is indeed intended to be God—the ultimate reality
responsible for the existence and activity of all else—
and if the Anselmian conception is coherent,
then it can be quite reasonable to hold that the God of Anselm
is one and the same as the God of Abraham, Isaac, and Jacob,
the God and Father of Jesus the Christ.

THOMAS V. MORRIS,
"THE GOD OF ABRAHAM, ISAAC, AND ANSELM,"
ANSELMIAN EXPLORATIONS

1 OMNISCIENCE

On the standard account of **omniscience**, for any person S, S is omniscient if and only if S knows every true proposition and believes no false proposition. The standard account entails that if there are true propositions expressed by future tense sentences, then God, since he is omniscient, must know those propositions. If God exists in time, then he has literal **foreknowledge** of the events described by such propositions. So if it is true that "Jones will mow his lawn Saturday," then God, being omniscient, must know and have always known the proposition expressed by this sentence. But this raises two difficult questions: (1) If God has always believed this proposition and God cannot be mistaken, then is not Jones fated to mow his lawn on Saturday? (2) If Jones's action is truly free, then how can God foreknow it?

The first question raises the issue of **fatalism**, the view that everything that happens happens of necessity (see chap. 13). Ancient Greek thought was infected with fatalism, and the church fathers felt obliged stoutly to resist it. Greek fatalism was purely logical: if it is true that some event will happen, then it will necessarily happen. For the church fathers fatalism took on a theological coloring: if God foreknows that some event will happen, then it will necessarily happen. Almost every major Christian philosophical theologian after Origen had something to say about this question, the vast majority defending freedom and contingency, but some like Martin Luther and Jonathan Edwards, who denied libertarian freedom, endorsing it.

Aristotle had sought to avoid fatalism by denying the validity of the **princi-**

ple of bivalence for future contingent propositions; that is to say, he held that propositions about future contingents are neither true nor false. Such a position would be compatible with divine omniscience, since no truths remain unknown by God; but such a solution was not open to the church fathers in light of the biblical doctrine that God has foreknowledge (Greek: *prognosis* [Acts 2:23; 1 Pet 1:1-2, 19-20]) and the many biblical examples of detailed prophecies of future events (e.g., Mk 14:18, 30). Some contemporary philosophers, notably the Polish logician Łukasiewicz, have followed Aristotle's lead, but few have found this course attractive in view of the logical dislocations and implausibilities attending this position.[1]

Theists who deny God's knowledge of future contingents have therefore felt obliged to redefine omniscience in such a way that God's ignorance of true future contingent propositions does not count against his being omniscient. For example, it is typically proposed that S is omniscient if and only if S knows only and all true propositions which are such that it is logically possible for them to be known. But it is not clear what more beyond truth is required for a proposition to be logically possible to know, in which case the revision is pointless. Revisionists will say that true future contingent propositions are logically impossible to know, for if one knows them, then they are not contingently true. But the revisionist's reasoning is fallacious, as can be shown by the following: For any future contingent proposition p, even if one grants that

1. Not-possibly (God knows p, and p is contingently true)

and

2. p is contingently true,

it does not logically follow that

3. Not-possibly (God knows p).

(Recall our discussion of modal fallacies in chap. 2.) It only follows that God does not in fact know p. But it is still possible for him to know p. Thus, even on the revisionist definition of omniscience, God must know future contingent propositions, since it is logically possible for him to know them.

But if God knows future contingent propositions, does this not imply fatalism? The question here is why we should think that (1) is true. The basic form of the fatalistic argument on behalf of (1) is as follows:

4. Necessarily (If God knows p, then p).
5. God knows p.

Therefore,

6. Necessarily (p).

Since p is necessarily true, it does not describe a contingent event. In virtue of God's foreknowledge everything is fated to occur.

---

[1]For discussion, see William Lane Craig, *Divine Foreknowledge and Human Freedom: The Coherence of Theism: Omniscience*, Brill's Studies in Intellectual History 19 (Leiden: E. J. Brill, 1991), chap. 4.

The problem with the argument is that it is just logically fallacious. What is validly implied by (4) and (5) is not (6) but

6′. *p.*

It is correct that in a valid deductive argument the conclusion follows necessarily from the premises. That is to say, it is impossible for the premises to be true and the conclusion to be false. But the conclusion itself need not be necessary. The fatalist illicitly transfers the necessity of the *inference* to the conclusion *itself*. What necessarily follows from (4) and (5) is just the contingent proposition (6′). But the fatalist confusedly thinks that the conclusion is itself necessarily true and so winds up with (6). In so doing, he simply commits a common logical fallacy.

Undoubtedly a major source of the fatalist's confusion is his conflating *certainty* with *necessity*. One frequently finds in the writings of contemporary theological fatalists statements which slide from affirming that something is *certainly* true to affirming that it is *necessarily* true. This is a mistake. **Certainty** is a property of persons and has nothing to do with truth, as is evident from the fact that we can be absolutely certain about something and yet turn out to be wrong. By contrast, **necessity** is a property of propositions, indicating that a proposition cannot possibly have a different truth value. We can be wholly uncertain about propositions which are, unbeknownst to us, necessarily true (imagine some complex mathematical equation or theorem). Thus, when we say that some proposition is "certainly true," this is but a manner of speaking indicating that we are certain that the proposition is true. People are certain; propositions are necessary.

By confusing certainty and necessity, the fatalist makes his logically fallacious argument deceptively appealing. For it is correct that from premises (4) and (5) we can be absolutely certain that the events described by *p* will happen. But it is muddle-headed to think that because they will certainly happen they will necessarily happen. We can be certain, given God's foreknowledge, that the events foreknown will not fail to happen, even though it is entirely possible that they fail to happen. They could fail to occur, but God knows that they will not. Therefore, we can be sure that they will happen—yet happen contingently.

Contemporary theological fatalists recognize the fallaciousness of the above form of the argument and therefore try to remedy the defect by making premise (5) also necessarily true:

4. Necessarily (If God knows *p*, then *p*).
5′. Necessarily (God knows *p*).

Therefore,

6. Necessarily (*p*).

Thus formulated, the argument is no longer logically fallacious, and so the question becomes whether (5′) is true. Now at face value, (5′) is obviously false. Christian theology has always maintained that God's creation of the world is a free act, that God could have created a different world, where *p* is false, or even no world at all. To say that *necessarily* God knows *p* implies that this is the only world God could have created and thus denies divine freedom.

But theological fatalists have a different sort of necessity in mind when they say that necessarily God knows *p*. What they are talking about is **temporal necessity**, or the necessity of the past. Often this is expressed by saying that the past is unpreventable or unchangeable. If some event is in the past, then it is now too late to do anything to affect it. It is in that sense necessary. Since God's foreknowledge of future events is now part of the past, it is now fixed and unalterable. Therefore, it is said, (5′) is true. Unfortunately, theological fatalists have never provided an adequate account of this peculiar modality. What is temporal necessity anyway, and why think that God's past beliefs are now temporally necessary? We have yet to encounter an explanation of temporal necessity, according to which God's past beliefs are temporally necessary, which does not reduce to either the *unalterability* or the *causal closedness* of the past.

But interpreting the necessity of the past as its unalterability (or unchangeability or unpreventability) is clearly inadequate, since the future, by definition, is just as unalterable as the past. By definition the future is what will occur, and the past is what has occurred. To *change* the future would be to bring it about that an event which will occur will not occur, which is self-contradictory. It is purely a matter of definition that the past and future cannot be changed, and no fatalistic conclusion follows from this truth. For we need not be able to *change* the future in order freely to *determine* the future. If our actions are freely performed, then it lies within our power to determine causally what the course of future events will be, even if we do not have the power to change the future.

The fatalist will insist that the past is necessary in the sense that we do not have a similar ability to determine causally the past. The orthodox theologian may happily concede the point: backward causation is impossible. But the causal closedness of the past does not imply fatalism. For freedom to refrain from doing as God knows one will do does not involve backward causation. The orthodox theologian may grant that there is nothing I can now do to cause or bring about the past. In particular, I cannot cause God to have had in the past a certain belief about my future actions. Nevertheless, as the medieval theologian William Ockham saw, it may well lie within my power to freely perform some action A, and if A were to occur, then the past would have been different than it in fact is. Suppose, for example, that God has always believed that on August 23, 2010, Jones would mow his lawn. Let us suppose that up until the time arrives Jones has the ability to mow or not mow his lawn. If Jones were to decide not to mow his lawn, then God would have always held a different belief than the one he in fact holds. For if Jones were to decide not to mow his lawn, then different future contingent propositions would have been true, and God, being omniscient, would have known them. Thus he would have had different foreknowledge than that which he in fact has. Neither the relation between Jones's action and a corresponding future contingent proposition about it nor the relation between a true future contingent proposition and God's believing it is a causal relation. Thus the causal closedness of the past is irrelevant. If temporal necessity is merely the causal closedness of the past, then it is insufficient to support fatalism.

No fatalist has successfully explicated a conception of temporal necessity that does not amount to either the unalterability or the causal closedness of the past. Typically, fatalists just assert some sort of "fixed past principle" to the effect that it is not within my power to act in such a way that, if I were to do so, the past would have been different—which begs the question. On analyses of temporal necessity that are not reducible to either the unalterability or the causal closedness of the past, God's past beliefs always turn out *not* to be temporally necessary.[2] Thus (5') is false, and the argument for theological fatalism is unsound.

If divine foreknowledge and future contingency are compatible, the question remains as to *how* could God know future contingent propositions. Process theologians typically deny divine foreknowledge because, given the contingency of the future, it is impossible for anyone, even God, to have knowledge about what will happen. In assessing this objection, it will be helpful to distinguish two models of divine cognition: the *perceptualist* model and the *conceptualist* model. The **perceptualist model** construes divine knowledge on the analogy of sense perception. God looks and sees what is there. Such a model is implicitly assumed when people speak of God's "foreseeing" the future or having "foresight" of future events. Given a dynamic theory of time, the perceptualist model of divine cognition does run into real problems when it comes to God's knowledge of the future, for, since future events do not exist, there is nothing there to perceive.

By contrast on a **conceptualist model** of divine knowledge, God does not acquire his knowledge of the world by anything like perception. His knowledge of the future is not based on his "looking" ahead and "seeing" what lies in the future (a terribly anthropomorphic notion in any case). Rather, God's knowledge is self-contained; it is more like a mind's knowledge of innate ideas. As an omniscient being, God has essentially the property of knowing all true propositions; there are true propositions about future contingents; ergo, God knows all true propositions concerning future contingents. So long as we are not seduced into thinking of divine foreknowledge on the model of perception, it is no longer evident why knowledge of future events should be impossible. Unless the detractor of divine foreknowledge can show some incoherence in the notion of innate knowledge, his objection cannot even get off the ground.

We can push the conceptualist analysis a step further. According to the Counter-Reformation theologian Luis Molina, logically prior to the divine decree to create a world, God possesses not only knowledge of everything that *could* happen (**natural knowledge**) but also everything that *would* happen in any appropriately specified set of circumstances (**middle knowledge**). God's natural knowledge is his knowledge of all necessary truths. By means of it God knows what is the full range of possible worlds. He knows, for example, that in some possible world Peter freely denies Christ three times and that in another world Peter freely affirms Christ under identical circumstances, for both are possible. God's middle knowledge is his knowledge of all contingently true

---

[2]See, for example, Alfred J. Freddoso, "Accidental Necessity and Logical Determinism," *Journal of Philosophy* 80 (1983): 257-78. The implications of this, though startling, are not unique to divine foreknowledge but also follow from retrocausation, time travel, precognition and the special theory of relativity.

counterfactual propositions, including propositions about creaturely free actions. A **counterfactual proposition** is a conditional proposition in the subjunctive mood. For example, logically prior to his creative decree, God knew that *If Peter were in circumstances C, he would freely deny Christ three times.* These counterfactuals serve to delimit the range of possible worlds to worlds that are **feasible** for God to actualize. For example, there is a possible world in which Peter freely affirms Christ in precisely the same circumstances in which he in fact denied him; but given the counterfactual truth that if Peter were in precisely those circumstances he would freely deny Christ, then the possible world in which Peter freely affirms Christ in those circumstances is not feasible for God. God could *make* Peter affirm Christ in those circumstances, but then his confession would not be free. By means of his middle knowledge, God knows what is the proper subset of possible worlds that are feasible for him, given the counterfactuals that are true. God then decrees to create certain free creatures in certain circumstances and thus on the basis of his middle knowledge and his knowledge of his own **decree**—that is, his decree to create the world—God has foreknowledge of everything that *will* happen (**free knowledge**). In that way, he knows, simply on the basis of his own internal states and without any need of any sort of perception of the external world, that Peter will freely deny Christ three times. Thus on the Molinist scheme, we have the logical order illustrated in figure 26.1.

Moment 1 . . . O   O   O   O   O   O   O . . .

Natural Knowledge: God knows the range of possible worlds

Moment 2 . . .   O   O   O   . . .

Middle Knowledge: God knows the range of feasible worlds

Divine Creative Decree

Moment 3   O

Free Knowledge: God knows the actual world

Fig. 26.1 The Molinist scheme

Of course, basing divine foreknowledge in divine middle knowledge raises inevitably the question of the basis of God's middle knowledge. The Molinist can respond either that God knows the **individual essence** of every possible creature so well that he knows just what that creature would do under any set of circumstances God might place him in, or that God, being omniscient, simply discerns all the truths there are and, prior to the divine decree, there are not only necessary truths, but counterfactual truths and therefore God possesses not only natural knowledge, but middle knowledge as well. Thus a conceptualist model along the lines of middle knowledge furnishes a perspicuous basis for God's knowledge of future contingents.

Does God, then, have middle knowledge? Consider the following argument:

1. If there are true counterfactuals about creaturely free choices, then God knows these truths.

2. There are true counterfactuals about creaturely free choices.

3. If God knows true counterfactuals about creaturely free choices, God knows them either logically prior to the divine creative decree or only logically posterior to the divine creative decree.

4. Counterfactuals about creaturely free choices cannot be known only logically posterior to the divine creative decree.

5. Therefore, God knows true counterfactuals about creaturely free choices. (MP, 1, 2)

6. Therefore, God knows true counterfactuals about creaturely free choices either logically prior to the divine creative decree or only logically posterior to the divine creative decree. (MP, 3, 5)

7. Therefore, God knows true counterfactuals about creaturely free choices logically prior to the divine creative decree. (DS, 4, 6)

—which is the essence of the doctrine of divine middle knowledge.

The truth of (1) is required by the standard definition of omniscience. As for (2), a little reflection reveals how pervasive and indispensable such counterfactual truths are to rational conduct and planning. We sometimes base our very lives on them. Moreover, Scripture itself gives examples of such true counterfactuals (1 Cor 2:8).

The most common objection urged against (2) is the so-called **grounding objection**. Detractors of middle knowledge typically claim that if such counterfactuals have any truth value, they are uniformly false, since there is no ground of their truth. Grounding objectors have never clearly articulated or defended the theory of truth the objection tacitly presupposes. It appears to assume some version of what is called **truth-maker theory**, according to which true propositions are made to be true by certain entities in the world. Truth-maker theory is a controversial position, however, and even its proponents typically reject **truth-maker maximalism**, the doctrine that all types of true propositions have truth-makers. No grounding objector has yet to answer Plantinga's retort: "It seems to me much clearer that some counterfactuals of freedom are at least possibly true than that the truth of propositions must, in general, be grounded in this way."[3] Moreover, acceptable truth-makers for counterfactuals of creaturely freedom are available. Alfred Freddoso suggests, for example, that counterfactuals of creaturely freedom are grounded by the fact that a relevant indicative proposition would have grounds of its truth. Thus the truth-maker of the counterfactual *If Peter were in C, he would deny Christ three times* is the fact

---

[3]Alvin Plantinga, "Reply to Robert Adams," in *Alvin Plantinga,* ed. James E. Tomberlin and Peter van Inwagen, Profiles 5 (Dordrecht: D. Reidel, 1985), p. 378.

or state of affairs that the proposition *Peter denies Christ three times* would have a truth-maker under the relevant condition.

Premise (3) of the argument states logically exhaustive alternatives for an omniscient deity and so must be true. Finally, (4) must be true because if counterfactuals of creaturely freedom were known only posterior to the divine decree, then it is God who determined what every creature would do in every circumstance. Augustinian/Calvinist thinkers bear witness to the truth of this premise in their affirmation of compatibilist theories of creaturely freedom. They thereby testify that God's all-determining decree precludes libertarian freedom, which is the sort of freedom with which we are here concerned. Thus, if God knows counterfactual truths about us only posterior to his decree, then there really are no counterfactuals about creaturely free choices. If there are such counterfactuals, they must be true logically prior to the divine decree.

Given the truth of the premises, the conclusion follows that prior to his creative decree God knows all true counterfactuals of creaturely freedom, which is to say that he has middle knowledge. If this conclusion is correct, then we have a theological tool of remarkable fecundity when we come to deal with other questions, such as the nature of divine providence.

2 SIMPLICITY

Divine **simplicity** is a doctrine inspired by the neo-Platonic vision of the ultimate metaphysical reality as the absolute One. It holds that God, as the metaphysical ultimate, is an undifferentiated unity, that there is no complexity in his nature or being. As such, this is a radical doctrine that enjoys no biblical support and even is at odds with the biblical conception of God in various ways. According to the doctrine of divine simplicity God has no distinct attributes, he stands in no real relations, his essence is not distinct from his existence, he just is the pure act of being subsisting. All such distinctions exist only in our minds, since we can form no conception of the absolutely simple divine being. While we can say what God is not like, we cannot say what he is like, except in an **analogical sense**. But these predications must in the end fail, since there is no **univocal** element in the predicates we assign to God, leaving us in a state of genuine agnosticism about the nature of God. Indeed, on this view God really has no nature; he is simply the inconceivable act of being.

Why should we adopt so extraordinary a doctrine? It will be recalled that Thomas Aquinas argued for the existence of such a simple being by means of his cosmological argument. But Thomas's famous argument from contingent beings (beings whose essence is distinct from their existence), forces us at most to postulate the existence of a being whose essence is such that it exists necessarily, a metaphysically necessary being. It need not commit us to divine simplicity.

The doctrine is open, moreover, to powerful objections. For example, to say that God does not have distinct properties seems patently false: omnipotence is not the same property as goodness, for a being may have one and not the other. It might be said that God's omnipotence and goodness differ in our conception only, as manifestations of a single divine property, just as, say, "the morning star" and "the evening star" have different senses but both refer to the same reality, namely, Venus. But this response is inadequate. For *being the morning star* and *being the evening star* are distinct properties both possessed by Venus; the same entity has these two distinct properties. In the same way *being omnipotent* and *being good* are not different senses for the same property (as are, say, *being even* and *being divisible by two*) but are clearly distinct properties. In God's case the same entity possesses both of these distinct properties.

Moreover, if God is identical with his essence, then God cannot know or do anything different from what he knows and does. He can have no contingent knowledge or action, for everything about him is essential to him. But in that case all modal distinctions collapse and everything becomes necessary. Since *God knows that p* is logically equivalent to *p is true*, the necessity of the former entails the necessity of the latter. Thus divine simplicity leads to an extreme fatalism, according to which everything that happens does so, not with temporal necessity, but with logical necessity.

It might be said that Thomas could escape this unwelcome conclusion by his doctrine that God stands in no real relations to creatures. As a simple being, God transcends all the Aristotelian distinctions among **substance** and **accidents**. Since relations are one type of accident, God has no relational properties and stands in no real relations to things outside himself. Things stand in real relations to God, but the situation is not symmetrical: God's relations to creatures are just in our minds, not in reality. Thus God is perfectly similar in all logically possible worlds we can imagine, but in some worlds either different creatures stand in relation to God or no creatures at all exist and are related to God. Thus the same simple cognitive state counts as knowledge of one conjunction of propositions in one world and another conjunction of propositions in a another world. Similarly, the same act of power (which just is the divine being) has in one world effects really related to it in the form of creatures and in another world no such effects. But Thomas's doctrine only serves to make divine simplicity more incredible. For it is incomprehensible how the same cognitive state can be knowledge that "I exist alone" in one world and that "I have created myriads of creatures" in another. Moreover, *what God knows* is still different, even if God's cognitive state is the same; and since God is his knowledge, contingency is introduced into God. It is equally unintelligible why a universe of creatures should exist in some worlds and not others if God's act of power is the same across worlds (for more on this see chap. 28 on the doctrine of creation). The reason cannot be found in God, since he is absolutely the same. Neither can the reason be found in creatures themselves, for the reason must be explanatorily prior to creatures. Thus to contend that God stands in no real relations to things is to make the existence or nonexistence of creatures in various possible worlds independent of God and utterly mysterious.

Finally, to say that God's essence just is his existence seems wholly obscure, since then there is in God's case no entity that exists; there is just the existing itself without any subject. Things exist; but it is unintelligible to say that *exists* just exists.

In short, we have no good reason to adopt and many reasons to reject a full-blown doctrine of divine simplicity. Still, that does not mean that the doctrine is wholly without merit. For example, it is surely correct to emphasize that God is not composed of mind and body; rather, he is pure mind. As such, God is remarkably simple in that such an immaterial substance is not composed of pieces, or separable parts in the way that a material object is. Moreover, some thinkers such as William Alston, while rejecting complete simplicity, have advocated that God's knowledge be construed as simple. On Alston's view God has a simple intuition of all of reality, which we human cognizers represent to ourselves propositionally. Such a view is in line with Aquinas's adaptation of the Augustinian notion of the divine ideas. In order to preserve divine aseity in the face of Platonism, Augustine located the Platonic forms in God's mind as the divine ideas. Aquinas went further by contending that God does not, strictly speaking, have a plurality of divine ideas but rather an undifferentiated knowledge of truth. We finite knowers break up God's undivided intuition into separate ideas. Similarly, Alston maintains that God's knowledge is strictly nonpropositional, though we represent it to ourselves as knowledge of distinct propositions. Thus we say, for example, that God knows that *Mars has two moons*, and he does indeed know that, but the representation of his knowing this proposition is a merely human way of stating what God knows in a nonpropositional manner. Such a conception of divine knowledge has the advantage that it enables us to embrace conceptualism without committing us to an actual infinite of divine cognitions or divine ideas.

A modified doctrine of divine simplicity might be useful in other ways. For example, we might think of God's act of creation or of conservation of the world, not as a multiplicity of individual acts of creating this or that thing, but as a single act comprising all that exists outside himself. This is an area which deserves further exploration by Christian thinkers.

3 IMMUTABILITY

For Aristotle, God was the Unmoved Mover, the unchanging source of all change. God's **immutability** is also attested in Scripture (Mal 3:6; Jas 1:17). But the biblical authors did not have in mind the radical changelessness contemplated by Aristotle nor the immutability required by the doctrines of essential divine timelessness or simplicity. They were speaking primarily of God's unchanging character and fidelity. But if God is essentially timeless and simple, he must be utterly incapable of change. We can distinguish usefully between two types of change: intrinsic change and extrinsic change. An **intrinsic change** is a nonrelational change, involving only the subject. For example, an apple changes from green to red. An **extrinsic change** is a relational change, involving something else in relation to which the subject changes. For example, Jones becomes shorter than his son, not by undergoing an intrinsic change in his height, but by being related to his son as his son undergoes intrinsic change in his height. Jones changes extrinsically from being taller than his son to being shorter than him because his son is growing. Divine timelessness or divine simplicity would require that God undergo neither intrinsic nor extrinsic change. For in either case a relation of before and after would be generated by such changes which would serve to locate God temporally with respect to those changes. Thus God would have to incapable of even the slightest alteration.

We have seen reason, however, to reject God's essential timelessness and simplicity. Is there some other reason for thinking God to be immutable? Sometimes divine immutability is said to be a necessary correlate of divine perfection: if God were to change, it could only be for the worse. Being essentially perfect, God must therefore be changeless. But this reasoning seems clearly incorrect. A perfect being need not change "vertically," so to speak, on the scale of perfection and, hence, for the worse, but could change "horizontally," remaining equally perfect in both states. For example, for God to change from knowing "It is now t_1" to knowing "It is now t_2" is not a change for the worse in God; on the contrary, it is a sign of his perfection that he always knows what time it is.

We have argued that in virtue of his real, causal relation to the temporal world, God must minimally undergo extrinsic change and therefore be temporal—at least since the moment of creation. Moreover, God's knowledge of tensed facts, implied by his omniscience, requires that since the moment of creation he undergoes intrinsic change as well, since he knows what is now happening in the universe. Thus God is not immutable in a strong sense.

Rejection of radical immutability nonetheless leaves it open for us to affirm that God is immutable in the biblical sense of being constant and unchangeable in his character. Moreover, he is immutable in his existence (necessity, aseity, eternity) and his being omnipresent, omniscient and omnipotent. These essential attributes are enough to safeguard God's perfection without freezing him into immobility.

Finally, if we do adopt our proposed construal of divine eternity as timelessness without creation and temporality with creation, then we can affirm God's changelessness, if not his immutability, in the timeless state of existing alone without the world. It bespeaks God's freedom and condescension that he should quit such a state for the sake of the creation and the salvation of temporal creatures like us. God could have remained changeless had he wished to; the fact that he did not is testimony to both his love and freedom.

4 OMNIPOTENCE

Although one of the biblical names of God is *El-Shaddai* (God Almighty), the concept of **omnipotence** has remained poorly understood due to its recalcitrance to analysis. Few thinkers, aside from Descartes, have been willing to affirm that the doctrine means that God can do just *anything*—for example, make a square triangle. Such a view has been construed as affirming **universal possibilism**, the doctrine that there are no necessary truths. For on this view an omnipotent deity could have brought it about that even logical contradictions be true and tautologies be false, as inconceivable as this may seem to us. But such a doctrine seems incoherent: is the proposition *There are no necessary truths* itself necessarily true or not? If so, then the position is self-refuting. If not, then that proposition is possibly false, that is to say, God could have brought it about that there are necessary truths. Using possible worlds semantics, we may say that there is, therefore, a possible world in which God brings it about that there are propositions that are true in every possible world. But if there are such propositions, then there is no world in which it is the case that there are no propositions true in every possible world, that is, it is not possible that there are no necessary truths, which contradicts universal possibilism.

Moreover, Descartes's position is incredible. It asks us to believe, for example, that God could have brought it about that he created all of us without his existing, that is to say, there is a possible world in which both God does not exist and he created all of us. This is simply nonsense.

One must therefore delineate more carefully what is understood as omnipotence. Unfortunately this has not been easy. Philosophical discussion appeared to be stalled until the remarkable piece "Maximal Power" by Thomas Flint and Alfred Freddoso appeared in 1983.[4] Their analysis is closely connected with the Ockhamist solution to theological fatalism and Molina's doctrine of middle knowledge. A key insight into the concept of omnipotence is that it should be defined in terms of the ability to actualize certain **states of affairs**, rather than in terms of raw power. Thus omnipotence should not be understood as power that is unlimited in its quantity or variety. Such an understanding leads immediately to the hoary problem of whether God can make a stone too heavy for him to lift. If God possesses the power to do the one, then he lacks the power to do the other. Such conundrums arise, not from some lack of power on God's part, but from a faulty concept of omnipotence. If we understand omnipotence in terms of ability to actualize states of affairs, then it is no attenuation of God's omnipotence that he cannot make a stone too heavy for him to lift, for, given that God is essentially omnipotent, "a stone too heavy for God to lift" describes as logically impossible a state of affairs as does "a square triangle," and thus it describes nothing at all.

Shall we say, then, that an agent S is omnipotent if and only if S can actualize any state of affairs that is broadly logically possible? No, for certain states of affairs may be logically possible but due to the passage of time may no longer be possible to actualize. For example, *the Cubs' winning the 1968 World Series* describes a logically possible state of affairs; but it is no longer possible to actualize this state of affairs, at least directly. To actualize directly such a state of affairs now would be tantamount to changing the past or to backward causation, both of which are broadly logically impossible. Therefore, the inability of S to actualize directly such a state of affairs at this time should not count against S's omnipotence. But could S perhaps actualize such a state of affairs indirectly? Suppose there were some action A that S could take, and if S were to take A, then God would have foreknown this and brought about a Cubs victory in 1968. Then S would now seem to have the power to actualize the state of affairs *the Cubs' winning the 1968 World Series* indirectly. Whether S in fact has such a power depends on whether certain **backtracking counterfactuals**, that is, counterfactuals that involve the past's being different than it was, happen to be true. Let us call past states of affairs that are indirectly actualizable by someone the "soft" past, and states that are not indirectly actualizable by someone the "hard" past. Accordingly, we must amend our analysis of omnipotence in such a

---

[4]Thomas P. Flint and Alfred J. Freddoso, "Maximal Power," in *The Existence and Nature of God* (Notre Dame, Ind.: University of Notre Dame Press, 1983), pp. 81-113.

way that S's inability to actualize states of affairs inconsistent with the hard past does not count against S's omnipotence.

Shall we say, then, that an agent S is omnipotent at a time t if and only if S can at t actualize any state of affairs that is broadly logically possible for someone sharing the same hard past with S to actualize at t? It seems not. For counterfactuals about creaturely free actions raise a further problem. The counterfactual *If Jones were in C, he would freely write to his wife* is within Jones's control, that is to say, how Jones freely decides to behave in C entails whether that counterfactual is true or not. By contrast that counterfactual does not lie within Smith's control: if that counterfactual is true, then it is logically impossible for Smith to do anything that would entail its falsity. He could prevent Jones from being in C, but he can do nothing that would entail the falsity of the counterfactual. Thus one has control over counterfactuals about one's own free decisions but not over counterfactuals about the free decisions of others. That implies that an adequate definition of omnipotence cannot require S to be able to actualize states of affairs described by counterfactuals about the free decisions of other agents. If the above counterfactual is true, S cannot be expected to actualize a world in which Jones is in C and freely refrains from writing to his wife, for this is to demand the logically impossible of S. Our provisional definition would require S to have the ability to actualize all the same states of affairs as Jones if they share the same hard past at t, which is to ask the logically impossible of S. We must therefore amend our analysis of omnipotence so as not to require such an ability in S.

Shall we say, then, that S is omnipotent at a time t if and only if S can at t actualize any state of affairs that is broadly logically possible for S to actualize, given the same hard past at t and the same true counterfactuals about free acts of others? This seems almost right. But it is open to the complaint that if S is essentially incapable of any particular action, no matter how trivial, than S's inability to perform that action does not count against his omnipotence. For in that case it is logically impossible for S to perform the act in question, since he is essentially incapable of it. Therefore we need to broaden the definition so as to require S to perform any action that any agent in his situation could perform. The trick is that we must not thereby require S to actualize states of affairs described by counterfactuals about the free acts of others.

The following analysis would seem to do the trick: S is omnipotent at a time t if and only if S can at t actualize any state of affairs that is not described by counterfactuals about the free acts of others and that is broadly logically possible for someone to actualize, given the same hard past at t and the same true counterfactuals about free acts of others. Such an analysis successfully sets the parameters of God's omnipotence without imposing any nonlogical limit on his power.

5 GOODNESS

Believers in the monotheistic tradition have always held that God is perfectly good, and Christians have thought of God as the fount of all varieties of goodness, whether moral, metaphysical, aesthetic and so forth. Here our interest is in God's **moral goodness**. Some versions of the axiological argument for God's existence imply that goodness is somehow rooted in God himself. But ever since Plato the claim that moral values and duties are founded in God has been criticized as problematic. In a famous dilemma in his dialogue *Euthyphro*, Plato asks, in effect, whether something is good because it is approved by God or whether something is approved by God because it is good. Either horn of this dilemma has been said to lead to untenable consequences. If we say that some action is good or right for the mere reason that God wills it, then morality is fundamentally arbitrary. God could have willed that cruelty be good and love evil, and we should have been obliged to hate others and seek to do them harm. Not only is this unconscionable, but it appears to make the claim that God is good vacuous. To claim that God is good seems to mean no more than that God does whatever he wants! On the other hand, if God wills that we perform some action because it is the right or a good thing to do, then moral values are not based in God after all but exist independent of him. Such an alternative is taken to be incompatible with classical theism because it compromises the sovereignty and aseity of God. God is himself duty-bound to obey certain moral principles not of his own creation, but, as it were, imposed on him. Evidence that moral value is independent of God is sometimes said to be found in the fact that we can apprehend moral values and duties quite independent of belief in God.

In sorting through the tangle of issues raised by this objection, we shall find it helpful to distinguish clearly various areas of moral theory as depicted in figure 26.2 (see further chap. 19).[5]

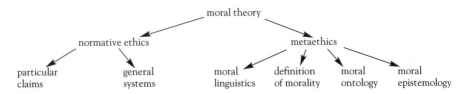

Fig. 26.2 Various areas of moral theory

The claim that moral values and duties are rooted in God is a metaethical claim about **moral ontology**. It is not fundamentally a claim about **moral linguistics** or about **moral epistemology**. It is fundamentally a claim about the metaphysical status of moral properties, not a claim about the meaning of moral sentences or about the justifcation or knowledge of moral principles.

These distinctions serve to sweep away in a single stroke all those objections to theistic metaethics based on linguistic or epistemological considerations. For example, the theist should not be understood as offering a definition of *good* or *right* in theistic terms (e.g., "willed by God"). The theist does offer a **definition of morality** in the sense that moral values and duties are to be explicated in terms of God's nature and will rather than of self-interest, social contract, common happiness or what have you. But the aim of theists is not to analyze the

[5]See Walter Sinnott-Armstrong, "Moral Skepticism and Justification," in *Moral Knowledge?* ed. Walter Sinnott-Armstrong and Mark Timmons (New York: Oxford University Press, 1996), pp. 4-5.

meaning of moral terms; rather, they aim to provide an ontological grounding for objective moral values and duties. Therefore objections to the effect that we can understand the meaning of statements like "Torture of political prisoners is wrong" without reference to God are quite beside the point. Similarly, when it is said that the statement "God is good" becomes trivial on theistic metaethics, this objection misconstrues the theistic position as a meaning-claim. A statement like "God is good" may be taken as a synthetic statement expressing a proposition that is metaphysically necessary both in the sense that the proposition is true in all possible worlds and in the sense that goodness is an essential property of God. Or again, the theist will agree quite readily (and, if he is a proponent of the axiological argument for God's existence, will even insist) that we do not need to know or even believe that God exists in order to discern objective moral values or to recognize our moral duties.

Although theistic metaethics assumes a rich variety of forms, there has been in recent years a resurgence of interest in **divine command morality**, which understands our moral duties as our obligations to God in light of his moral commands; for example, "You shall love the LORD your God with all your heart," "You shall love your neighbor as yourself" and so on. Our moral duties are constituted by the **commands of a just and loving God**. For any action A and moral agent S, we can explicate the notions of **moral requirement, permission** and **forbiddenness** of A for S as follows:

A is required of S if and only if a just and loving God commands S to do A.

A is permitted for S if and only if a just and loving God does not command S not to do A.

A is forbidden to S if and only if a just and loving God commands S not to do A.

Since our moral duties are grounded in the divine commands, they are not independent of God nor, plausibly, is God bound by moral duties, since he does not issue commands to himself.

If God does not fulfil moral duties, then what content can be given to the claim that he is good? Here Kant's distinction between *following a rule* and acting *in accordance with a rule* has proved helpful. God may act naturally in ways which for us would be rule-following and so constitutive of goodness in the sense of fulfilling our moral duties, so that God can be said similarly to be good in an analogical way. This fact also supplies the key to the arbitrariness objection. For our duties are determined by the commands, not merely of a supreme potentate, but of a just and loving God. God is essentially compassionate, fair, kind, impartial and so forth, and his commandments are reflections of his own character. Thus they are not arbitrary, and we need not trouble ourselves about counterfactuals with impossible antecedents like "If God were to command child abuse, . . ." God may be said to be good in the sense that he possesses all these **moral virtues** (recall chap. 22)—and he does so essentially and to the maximal degree! Thus God's axiological perfection should not be understood in terms of **duty-fulfillment**, but in terms of virtue. This conception helps us to understand the sense in which God is to be praised: not in the sense of commendation for fully executing his duties or even for his acts of supererogation, but rather in the sense of adoration for his axiological perfection.

Nonetheless, the fact that God is not duty-bound should alert us to the fact that he may well have prerogatives (for example, taking human life at his discretion) that are forbidden to us. Taking the life of an innocent person is something we have no right to do; but God is not similarly restricted. God's having no duties also helps to explain how God can command a person to perform an action that would be sinful were the person to undertake such an action on his own initiative, but that is his moral duty in virtue of God's command. The most celebrated example is Abraham's sacrificing his son Isaac, an act which would have been murder in the absence of any command of God but which became Abraham's moral duty in light of the divine command given him. This is not to say that God can bring it about that murder be good, but rather that he can command an act that would have been murder had it been undertaken in the absence of a divine command. This also not to say that God could have brought it about that it be a general moral duty for people to kill one another. The case of Abraham and Isaac is the exception that proves the rule. Issuing a general command that we should seek one another's harm would be contrary to God's loving nature, but in the extraordinary case of Abraham and Isaac, it was not unloving of God to so try Abraham's devotion, and God had good reasons for testing him so severely.

The question might be pressed as to why God's nature should be taken to be definitive of goodness. But unless we are nihilists, we have to recognize some ultimate standard of value, and God seems to be the least arbitrary stopping point. Moreover, God's nature is singularly appropriate to serve as such a standard. For by definition, God is a being *worthy of worship.* And only a being that is the locus and source of all value is worthy of worship.

CHAPTER SUMMARY

Omniscience is the property of knowing every true proposition and believing no false proposition. This standard definition entails that if there are true propositions expressed by future tense sentences, then God, since he is omniscient, must know those propositions. This conclusion raises the problem of theological fatalism: Since God cannot be mistaken in his beliefs, must not everything that happens come to pass necessarily? On the other hand, if events do come to pass contingently, how can God possess knowledge of future contingent events? Attempts to redefine omniscience in such a way that God does not know future contingents rest on a logical fallacy, with the result that even on the revisionary definition God must know future contingents if he is omniscient. Such revisionary efforts are unnecessary, however, since the argument for fatalism is also based on a logical fallacy. Attempts to eliminate this fallacy by appeals to temporal necessity have been unsuccessful because no explication of this peculiar modality has been found on which propositions about God's beliefs concerning future contingents are necessary in any sense other than being unchangeable or causally inaccessible, which are irrelevant to fatalism. Dynamic time theorists have also asked how God could have knowledge of future contingent events in light of the future's unreality and indeterminacy. But if we adopt a conceptualist as opposed to a perceptualist model of divine cognition, it is not evident why God cannot simply possess innate knowledge of all true propositions, including propositions expressed by future tense sentences. A particularly striking version of a conceptualist model of divine cognition is afforded by the theory of middle knowledge, according to which God possesses knowledge of all true counterfactuals of creaturely freedom logically prior to his decree to create the world. The so-called grounding objection to middle knowledge seems to presuppose the controversial theory of truth-makers, as well as truth-maker maximalism, a widely rejected doctrine. In any case, plausible truth-makers for counterfactuals of creaturely freedom have been offered.

Divine simplicity is God's attribute of being an undifferentiated unity, so that there is no complexity in his nature or being. The doctrine faces powerful objections. To say that God does not have distinct properties seems patently false; to say that God is his essence implies that God cannot know or do anything different than what he knows and does, and to say that God's essence just is his existence seems wholly obscure. Still, the doctrine is not wholly without merit. God is not composed of mind and body, and as such, God is remarkably simple in that an immaterial substance is not composed of parts in the way that a material object is. Moreover, some thinkers have advocated that God's knowledge be construed as simple. We finite knowers represent to ourselves God's undivided intuition of truth as knowledge of distinct propositions. Such a conception of divine knowledge has the advantage that it enables us to embrace conceptualism without committing us to an actual infinite of divine cognitions or divine ideas.

Immutability is the property of being unsusceptible to change. Medieval theologians interpreted God's immutability to mean that he could undergo neither intrinsic not extrinsic change. But not only are there no good reasons for adopting so radical a doctrine, there are also good grounds for rejecting it. In virtue of his real, causal relation to the temporal world, God must minimally undergo extrinsic change. Moreover, God's knowledge of tensed facts, implied by his omniscience, requires that since the moment of creation he undergoes intrinsic change as well. God is immutable in the biblical sense of being constant and unchangeable in his character. Moreover, he is immutable in his existence (necessity, aseity, eternity) and his being omnipresent, omniscient and omnipotent. Finally, if we do think of divine eternity as implying timelessness without creation, then we can affirm God's changelessness, if not his immutability, in the timeless state of existing alone without the world.

Omnipotence is the property of being almighty. But the property has been very difficult to define. The doctrine that God can do just anything is incoherent and unbelievable. A rigorous analysis of the conditions for being omnipotent issue in the definition that an agent S is omnipotent at a time t if and only if S can at t actualize any state of affairs that is not described by counterfactuals about the free acts of others and that is broadly logically possible for someone to actualize, given the same hard past at t and the same true counterfactuals about free acts of others.

God's goodness has to do with God's moral perfection. Some versions of the axiological argument for God's existence imply that goodness is somehow rooted in God himself. The claim that moral values and duties are rooted in God is a claim about the metaphysical status of moral properties, not a claim about the meaning of moral sentences or about the justification or knowledge of moral principles. Divine command morality understands our moral duties as our obligations to a just and loving God in light of his commands. Since our moral duties are grounded in the divine commands, they are not independent of God nor, plausibly, is God bound by moral duties, since he does not issue commands to himself. God may be said to be good, not in the sense of duty-fulfillment, but in the sense that he possesses all the moral virtues essentially and to the maximal degree. The fact that God is not duty-bound should alert us to the fact that he may well have prerogatives which are forbidden to us. It can also help to explain how God can command a person to perform an action which would be sinful were the person to undertake such an action on his own initiative but which is his moral duty in virtue of God's command. As a being worthy of worship God is singularly appropriate to serve as the ultimate standard of value.

CHECKLIST OF BASIC TERMS AND CONCEPTS
accidents
analogical sense
backtracking counterfactuals
certainty
commands of a just and loving God
conceptualist model
counterfactual proposition
decree
definition of morality
divine command morality
duty-fulfillment
extrinsic change
fatalism
feasible
foreknowledge
free knowledge
grounding objection
immutability
individual essence
intrinsic change
middle knowledge
moral epistemology
moral goodness
moral linguistics
moral ontology
moral requirement, permission and forbiddenness
moral virtues
natural knowledge

necessity
omnipotence
omniscience
perceptualist model
principle of bivalence
simplicity
states of affairs
substance
temporal necessity
truth-maker maximalism
truth-maker theory
universal possibilism
univocal

27

THE PROBLEM
OF EVIL

Epicurus's old questions are yet unanswered.
Is he willing to prevent evil, but not able? then he is impotent.
Is he able, but not willing? then he is malevolent.
Is he both able and willing? whence then is evil?
DAVID HUME, *DIALOGUES CONCERNING NATURAL RELIGION*, PART 10

1 INTRODUCTION

Undoubtedly the greatest intellectual obstacle to belief in God is the so-called **problem of evil**. That is to say, it seems unbelievable, if an omnipotent and omnibenevolent God exists, that he would permit so much pain and suffering in the world.

The amount of human misery and pain in the world is, indeed, incalculable. On the one hand, there are all the evils that are the result of man's own inhumanity to man. Such **moral evil** is bad enough, but perhaps even more difficult to reconcile with the existence of an omnipotent and omnibenevolent God is the suffering brought on by natural causes in the world, disasters such as floods, earthquakes or tornadoes; different sorts of diseases such as smallpox, polio, cancer or leukemia; congenital disabilities such as muscular dystrophy, cerebral palsy or encephalitis; accidents and injuries such as being burned, crushed or drowned. Sometimes **natural evil** is intertwined with human evil: for example, millions of East Africans face famine and starvation, not because there are inadequate relief supplies to meet their need, but because dictatorial governments use food as a political weapon to crush rebel resistance by interdicting those supplies. In light of the quantity and nature of the suffering brought on by human or natural causes, how can it be that an omnipotent, omnibenevolent God exists?

During the last quarter century or so, an enormous amount of philosophical analysis has been poured into the problem of evil, with the result that genuine philosophical progress on the age-old question has been made. We may begin our inquiry by making a number of distinctions to help keep our thinking straight. Most broadly speaking, we must distinguish between the intellectual problem of evil and the emotional problem of evil. The **intellectual problem of evil** concerns how to give a rational explanation of the coexistence of God and evil. The **emotional problem of evil** concerns how to comfort those who are suffering and how to dissolve the emotional dislike people have of a God who would permit such evil. The intellectual problem lies in the province of the philosopher; the emotional problem lies in the province of the counselor. It is important to keep this distinction clear because the solution to the intellectual problem is apt to appear dry, uncaring and uncomforting to someone who is going through suffering, whereas the solution to the emotional problem is apt to appear superficial and deficient as an explanation to someone contemplating the question abstractly. Keeping this distinction in mind, let us turn first to the intellectual problem of evil.

2 THE INTELLECTUAL PROBLEM OF EVIL

Here again, further distinctions will be helpful. Contemporary thinkers recognize that there are significantly different versions of the intellectual problem of evil and have assigned various labels to them, such as "deductive," "inductive," "logical," "probabilistic," evidential" and so on. Although there is no uniformly accepted terminology on this score, it seems to us that it will be most helpful to distinguish two ways in which the intellectual problem of evil may be cast, either as an internal problem or as an external problem. That is to say, the **internal problem of evil** is presented in terms of premises to which the Christian theist is or ought to be committed as a Christian, so that the Christian worldview is somehow at odds with itself. On the other hand, the **external problem of evil** is presented in terms of premises to which the Christian theist is not committed as a Christian but which we nonetheless have good reason to regard as true. The first approach tries to expose an inner tension within the Christian worldview itself; the second approach attempts to present evidence against the truth of the Christian worldview.

Now the internal problem of evil takes two forms: the logical version and the probabilistic version. In the **logical version of the problem of evil**, the objector's goal is to show that it is logically impossible for both God and evil to exist. There is no possible world in which God and evil coexist, any more than there is a possible world in which an irresistible force and an immovable object both exist. The two are logically incompatible. If one exists, the other does not. Yet the Christian faith (unlike certain types of Hinduism, for example) is committed to the reality of evil, just as it is to the reality of an omnipotent and omnibenevolent God. Since we know that evil exists, the argument goes, it follows logically that God must not exist.

The **probabilistic version of the problem of evil** admits that it is possible that God and evil coexist, but it insists that it is highly improbable that both God and the evil in the world exist. Thus the Christian theist is stuck with two beliefs which tend to undermine each other. Given that the evil in the world is real, it is highly improbable that God exists.

Let us examine each of these versions of the argument in turn.

As we have noted, the logical version of the internal problem of evil holds that the following two statements are logically incompatible:

1. An omnipotent, omnibenevolent God exists.
2. Evil exists.

2.1
THE INTERNAL
PROBLEM OF
EVIL

2.1.1
THE LOGICAL
VERSION

This has for centuries been the form usually assumed by the problem, going back, as Hume notes, as far as Epicurus and, in Hume's opinion still unresolved in his day. Indeed, as late as the mid-twentieth-century atheists like J. L. Mackie propounded the problem in this form.

It is largely due to the work of Alvin Plantinga that discussion of this version of the problem of evil was pushed significantly forward. Plantinga distinguished between what he called a "defense" and a "theodicy." As he employs these terms, a theodicy aims to provide an account of why God actually permits the evils in the world. By contrast a defense offers no such account but seeks merely to show that atheists have failed to carry their case that evil is incompatible with God's existence. The advocate of a defense thus seeks merely to undercut the atheist's case, not to explain why the evils in the world exist. A successful defense will have defeated the atheist's argument, while still leaving us in the dark as to why God permits evil and suffering in the world.

Plantinga believes that the proponent of the logical version of the problem of evil has assumed an enormous burden of proof which he cannot sustain. For at face value, statements (1) and (2) are not logically inconsistent. There is no explicit contradiction between them. If the atheist thinks that they are implicitly contradictory, then he must be assuming some hidden premises that would serve to bring out the contradiction and make it explicit. But what are those premises? There seem to be two:

3. If God is omnipotent, then he can create any world that he desires.
4. If God is omnibenevolent, then he prefers a world without evil over a world with evil.

The atheist reasons that since God is omnipotent, he could create a world containing free creatures who always freely choose to do the right thing. Such a world would be a sinless world, free of all human, moral evils. By the same token, being omnipotent, God could as well create a world in which no natural evils ever occurred. It would be a world free of evil, pain and suffering. Notice that the atheist is not saying that people would be mere puppets in such a world. Rather, he is saying that there is a possible world in which everyone always freely makes the right decision. Such a world must be possible, for if it were not, that would imply that sin is necessary, which the Christian cannot admit. Thus, whenever a moral decision is made, it is logically possible for the person involved to decide to do the right thing. So we can conceive a world in which everyone freely chooses every time to do right, and since God is omnipotent, he must be able to create it.

But since God is also omnibenevolent, the objector continues, he would, of course, prefer such a world to any world infected with evil. If God had the choice between creating a flawless world and a world with evil in it like this one, he would surely choose the flawless world. Otherwise, he would himself be evil to prefer that his creatures experience pain and suffering when he could have given them happiness and prosperity. David Hume summarized the logical version of the internal problem of evil nicely when he asked concerning God, "Is he willing to prevent evil, but not able? then he is impotent.

Is he able, but not willing? then he is malevolent. Is he both able and willing? whence then is evil?"[1]

Plantinga opposes this version of the problem of evil with what he calls the **free will defense**. He argues that if it is even *possible* that creatures have libertarian freedom (even if in fact they do not), then the two assumptions made by the objector are not necessarily true, which they must be if the atheist is to show that there is no possibility of the coexistence of God and evil. In the first place, if libertarian free will is possible, it is not necessarily true that an omnipotent God can create just any possible world that he desires. As we saw in our discussion of divine omnipotence, God's being omnipotent does not imply that he can do logical impossibilities, such as make a round square or make someone freely choose to do something. For if one causes a person to make a specific choice, then the choice is no longer free in the libertarian sense. Thus, if God grants people genuine freedom to choose as they like, then it is impossible for him to guarantee what their choices will be. All he can do is create the circumstances in which a person is able to make a free choice and then, so to speak, stand back and let the person make that choice. Now this implies that there are worlds which are possible in and of themselves, but which God is incapable of creating. Recalling our discussion of divine middle knowledge, we may say that such worlds are not feasible for God. Suppose, then, that in every feasible world where God creates free creatures some of those creatures freely choose to do evil. In such a case, it is the creatures themselves who bring about evil, and God can do nothing to prevent their doing so, apart from refusing to actualize any such worlds. Thus it is possible that every world feasible for God which contains free creatures is a world with sin and evil.[2] Moreover, as for natural evils, Plantinga points out that these could be the result of demonic activity in the world. Demons can have freedom just like human beings, and it is possible that God could not preclude natural evil without removing the free will of demonic creatures. Now one might think that such a resolution to the problem of natural evil is ridiculous and even frivolous, but that would be to confuse the *logical* problem of evil with the *probabilistic* problem of evil. Admittedly, ascribing all evil to demonic beings is improbable, but that is strictly irrelevant here. All one needs to show now is that such an explanation is possible and that, as a consequence, the objector's argument that God and evil are logically incompatible fails. So the first assumption made by the objector, namely, that an omnipotent God can create any world that he desires, is just not necessarily true. Therefore, the objector's argument on this ground alone is invalid.

But what about the second assumption, that if God is omnibenevolent, then he prefers a world without evil over a world with evil? Again, such an assumption is not necessarily true. The fact is that in many cases we allow pain and suffering to occur in a person's life in order to bring about some greater good or because we have some sufficient reason for allowing it. Every parent knows this

---

[1] David Hume, *Dialogues Concerning Natural Religion*, ed. with an introduction by Norman Kemp Smith (Indianapolis: Bobbs-Merrill, 1980), part 10, p. 198.

[2] Does not the sinlessness of the blessed in heaven show that the Christian is committed theologically to the feasibility of a world without sin? No, for heaven is only part of a world, so to speak, not a maximal state of affairs, and in any case the will of the blessed may no longer be free to sin once they are beatified.

fact. There comes a point at which a parent can no longer protect a child from every mishap; and there are other times when discipline must be inflicted on the child in order to teach him to become a mature, responsible adult. Similarly, God may permit suffering in our lives in order to build us or to test us, or to build and test others, or to achieve some other overriding end. Thus, even though God is omnibenevolent, he might well have morally sufficient reasons for permitting pain and suffering in the world. Consequently, the second assumption of our objector, that an omnibenevolent God prefers a world with no evil over a world with evil, is also not necessarily true. The argument is thus doubly invalid.

Those who propound the logical version of the problem of evil can regroup and return for a second wave of attack. They can admit that there is no inconsistency between God and evil in general but still argue that the existence of God is inconsistent with the quantity and quality of evil in the world. In other words, although abstractly speaking there is no inconsistency between God and evil, there is an inconsistency between God and the amount and kinds of evil that actually exist. For example, even if God's existence is compatible with, say, the fact that innocent persons are sometimes murdered, it is not compatible with the fact that so many people are killed and that they are killed in such tortuous, gruesome ways. An omnibenevolent and omnipotent God would not permit such things to happen.

But the crucial assumption behind this reasoning is the notion that God cannot have morally sufficient reasons for permitting the amount and kinds of evil that exist. But it is again not clear that this assumption is necessarily true. Consider first the amount of evil in the world. As terrible a place as the world is, there is still on balance a great deal more good in the world than evil. Despite life's hardships, people generally agree that life is worth living, and when things are going bad, people characteristically look to the future in the hope that things will get better. Now it is possible, given creaturely freedom, that in any other world of free creatures feasible for God, the balance between good and evil would have been no better than in this world. That is to say, any world containing less evil might also have contained less good. Maybe the actual world has in it the most good God could get for the least amount of evil. The same goes for the kinds of evil in the world. It is possible that God has overriding reasons for permitting the world's most terrible atrocities to occur. It might be objected that God could have created a world of free creatures in which they committed fewer atrocities. But then the same answer applies as before: it is possible that if the world had fewer atrocities then it would also have been lacking in important, overriding goods.

Now one might say that that seems pretty unlikely. But then one would be confusing once again the logical problem of evil with the probabilistic problem of evil. To refute the logical version of the internal problem of evil, the theist does not have to suggest a plausible or likely solution—all he has to do is suggest a possible one. All he needs to do is undercut the objector's claim to have shown that God and the amount of evil in the world are not compossible, and that he seems to have done. The point is, if atheists aim to show that it is logically impossible for both God and the evil in the world to exist, then they have to prove that God cannot have morally sufficient reasons for permitting the amount and kinds of evil that exist. And no one has offered any proof for that assumption.

Plantinga argues that we can go even further than this. Not only has the atheist failed to prove that God and evil are inconsistent, but we can, on the contrary, prove that they are consistent. In order to do that, all we have to do is provide some possible explanation of the evil in the world that is compatible with God's existence. And the following is such an explanation:

5. God could not have created a world that had so much good as the actual world but had less evil, both in terms of quantity and quality; and, moreover, God has morally sufficient reasons for permitting the evil that exists.

The "could not" in (5) should be understood to mean that such a world is infeasible for God. There are doubtless logically possible worlds that are sinless and exceed the actual world in goodness, but such worlds may not be feasible for God. So long as this explanation is even possible, it proves that God and the evil in the world are logically compatible.

The difficulty with this further move emerges when we recall the distinction between epistemic and metaphysical possibility discussed in connection with the ontological argument. While (5) is clearly epistemically possible (for all we know, it may be true), the atheist might insist that it has not been shown that (5) is metaphysically possible (that there is a possible world where [5] is true). The atheist could insist that perhaps (1) and (5) are after all logically incompatible in some way which we cannot discern. Perhaps in every possible world in which God exists the counterfactuals of creaturely freedom that are true in that world permit him to create a world having more good but less evil than the actual world. Now this might strike us as an extraordinarily bold hypothesis; indeed, most atheists today do concede that (5) is metaphysically possible. Nonetheless, the dogmatic atheist cannot be forced, it seems, from his stronghold.

But this shortcoming of the argument is of little significance. Because it is the atheist who claims to have discerned a contradiction within theistic truth claims, it is the atheist who bears the burden of proof to show that there is no possible world in which (1) and (2) are true. That is an enormously heavy burden, which has proved to be unbearable. After centuries of discussion, contemporary philosophers, including most atheists and agnostics, have come to recognize this fact. It is now widely admitted that the logical problem of evil has been solved.

When we consider the probabilistic problem of evil, however, things are not so easy. For even though the account of evil given above is possible, still it seems wildly improbable. Explaining all natural evil as the result of demonic activity, for example, seems ridiculous. And could not God reduce the evil in the world without reducing the good? The world is filled with so many seemingly pointless or unnecessary evils that it seems doubtful that God could have any sort of morally sufficient reason for permitting them. Accordingly, it might be argued that given the evil in the world, it is improbable, even if not impossible, that God exists.

Now this is a much more powerful argument than the purely logical problem

2.1.2
THE
PROBABILISTIC
VERSION

of evil. Since its conclusion is more modest ("It is improbable that God exists"), it is much easier to prove. What shall we say about this argument? Is it improbable that God exists? Four points present themselves in response.

1. Relative to the full scope of the evidence God's existence is probable. If the logical version of the internal problem of evil were a sound argument, then God would not exist, case closed. But probabilities are relative to one's background information. Thus, with a probability argument, we have to ask: probable with respect to what? To give an illustration, suppose that Joe is a college student. Suppose, further, that 90 percent of college students drink beer. With respect to that information, it is highly probable that Joe drinks beer. But suppose we find out that Joe is a Biola University student and that 90 percent of Biola students do not drink beer. Suddenly the probability of Joe's being a beer drinker has changed dramatically! The point is that probabilities are relative to the **background information** one considers.

Now apply this principle to the probabilistic problem of evil. The objector claims to prove that God's existence is improbable. But with respect to what? To the evil in the world? If that is all the background information one considers, then it is hardly surprising if God's existence should appear improbable relative to that alone. Indeed, it would be a major philosophical achievement if theists could demonstrate that relative to the evil in the world alone, God's existence is not improbable. But the Christian theist need not be committed to such an arduous task. He will insist that we consider, not just the evil in the world, but all the evidence relevant to God's existence, including the cosmological argument for a Creator of the universe, the teleological argument for an intelligent Designer of the cosmos, the axiological argument for an ultimate, personally embodied Good, the ontological argument for a maximally great being, as well as evidence concerning the person of Christ, the historicity of the resurrection, the existence of miracles and, in addition, existential and religious experience. When we take into account the full scope of the evidence, the Christian theist might maintain, then the existence of God becomes quite probable. Hence, the theist could actually admit that the problem of evil, taken in isolation, does make God's existence improbable. But he will insist that when the total scope of the evidence is considered, then the scales are at least evenly balanced or tip in favor of theism.

Indeed, the theist might insist that insofar as the probabilistic problem of evil is taken to be an internal problem for the theist, there is nothing whatsoever objectionable or irrational in believing statements that are improbable with respect to each other, so long as one knows them both to be true. For example, relative to the background information of human reproductive biology, one's own personal existence is astronomically improbable. Yet there is nothing irrational about believing both the facts of human reproductive biology and that one exists. Similarly, if one is warranted in believing that God exists, then there is no problem occasioned by the fact that this belief is improbable relative to the evil in the world.

2. We are not in a good position to assess with confidence the probability that God has no morally sufficient reasons for permitting the evils that occur.

Whether God's existence is improbable relative to the evil in the world depends on how probable it is that God has morally sufficient reasons for permitting the evil that occurs. What makes the probability here so difficult to assess is that we are not in a good epistemic position to make these kinds of probability judgments with any sort of confidence. As finite persons, we are limited in space and time, in intelligence and insight. But the transcendent and sovereign God sees the end of history from its beginning and providentially orders history so that his purposes are ultimately achieved through human free decisions. In order to achieve his ends God may well have to put up with certain evils along the way. Evils that appear pointless or unnecessary to us within our limited framework may be seen to have been justly permitted from within God's wider framework.

To borrow an illustration from a developing field of science, chaos theory, scientists have discovered that certain macroscopic systems—for example, weather systems or insect populations—are extraordinarily sensitive to the tiniest perturbations. A butterfly fluttering on a branch in West Africa may set in motion forces that would eventually issue in a hurricane over the Atlantic Ocean. Yet it is impossible in principle for anyone observing that butterfly palpitating on a branch to predict such an outcome.

The brutal murder of an innocent man or a child's dying of leukemia could send a ripple effect through history so that God's morally sufficient reason for permitting it might not emerge until centuries later or perhaps in another country. Our discussion of divine middle knowledge (chap. 26) stressed that only an omniscient mind could grasp the complexities of directing a world of free creatures toward one's previsioned goals. One has only to think of the innumerable, incalculable contingencies involved in arriving at a single historical event, say, the Allied victory at D-Day. This has relevance to the probabilistic problem of evil, for we have no idea of the natural and moral evils that might be involved in order for God to arrange the circumstances and free agents in them requisite to some intended purpose, nor can we discern what reasons such a provident God might have in mind for permitting some evil to enter our lives. Certainly many evils seem pointless and unnecessary to us—but we are simply not in a position to judge.

To say this is not to appeal to mystery, but rather to point to the inherent cognitive limitations that frustrate attempts to say that it is improbable that God has a morally sufficient reason for permitting some particular evil. Ironically, in other contexts nonbelievers recognize these cognitive limitations. One of the most damaging objections to utilitarian ethical theory, for example, is that it is quite simply impossible for us to estimate which action that we might perform will ultimately lead to the greatest amount of happiness or pleasure in the world (see chap. 21). Because of our cognitive limitations, actions that appear disastrous in the short term may redound to the greatest good, while some short-term boon may issue in untold misery. Once we contemplate God's providence over the whole of history, than it becomes evident how hopeless it is for limited observers to speculate on the probability of God's having morally sufficient reasons for the evils that we see. We are simply not in a good position to assess such probabilities with any confidence.

3. *Christian theism entails doctrines that increase the probability of the coexistence of God and evil.* The objector maintains that if God exists, then it is improbable that the world would contain the evil it does. Now what the Christian can do in response to such an assertion is to offer various hypotheses that would tend to raise the probability of evil given God's existence: Pr (Evil/God & Hypotheses) > Pr (Evil/God). The Christian can try to show that if God exists and these hypotheses are true, then it is not so surprising that evil exists. This in turn reduces any improbability that evil might be thought to throw upon God: Pr (God & Hypotheses/Evil) > Pr (God/Evil). Now, of course, the Christian cannot beg the question here by simply taking as his hypothesis the statement "Evil exists," which would trivially make evil more probable on God & Hypothesis than on God alone! Rather, he will appeal to certain key Christian doctrines in order to show that evil is not so improbable on Christian theism as on some bare-boned theism. Thus it turns out that answering the probabilistic problem of evil is easier from the Christian perspective than from the perspective of mere theism. Since the problem is being presented as an internal problem for the Christian theist, there is nothing illicit about the Christian theist's availing himself of all the resources of his worldview in answering the objection. We shall mention four Christian doctrines in this connection.

First, *the chief purpose of life is not happiness, but the knowledge of God.* One reason that the problem of evil seems so intractable is that people tend naturally to assume that if God exists, then his purpose for human life is happiness in this world. God's role is to provide a comfortable environment for his human pets. But on the Christian view, this is false. We are not God's pets, and the goal of human life is not happiness per se, but the knowledge of God—which in the end will bring true and everlasting human fulfillment. Many evils occur in life that may be utterly pointless with respect to the goal of producing human happiness; but they may not be pointless with respect to producing a deeper knowledge of God. Innocent human suffering provides an occasion for deeper dependency and trust in God, either on the part of the sufferer or those around him. Of course, whether God's purpose is achieved through our suffering will depend on our response. Do we respond with anger and bitterness toward God, or do we turn to him in faith for strength to endure?

Because God's ultimate goal for humanity is the knowledge of himself—which alone can bring eternal happiness to creatures—history cannot be seen in its true perspective apart from considerations pertinent to the kingdom of God. The British divine Martyn Lloyd-Jones has written,

> The key to the history of the world is the kingdom of God. . . . From the very beginning, . . . God has been at work establishing a new kingdom in the world. It is His own kingdom, and He is calling people out of the world into that kingdom: and everything that happens in the world has relevance to it. . . . Other events are of importance as they have a bearing upon that event. The problems of today are to be understood only in its light. . . .
>
> Let us not therefore be stumbled when we see surprising things happening in the world. Rather, let us ask, "What is the relevance of this event to the kingdom of God?" Or, if strange things are happening to you personally, don't complain but say, "What is God teaching me through this?". . . We need not become bewil-

dered and doubt the love or the justice of God. . . . We should . . . judge every event in the light of God's great, eternal and glorious purpose.[3]

It may well be the case that natural and moral evils are part of the means God uses to draw people into his kingdom. A reading of a missions handbook such as Patrick Johnstone's *Operation World* reveals that it is precisely in countries that have endured severe hardship that evangelical Christianity is growing at its greatest rates, while growth curves in the indulgent West are nearly flat. Consider, for example, the following reports:[4]

China:

It is estimated that 20 million Chinese lost their lives during Mao's Cultural Revolution. Christians stood firm in what was probably the most widespread and harsh persecution the Church has ever experienced. The persecution purified and indigenized the Church. Since 1977 the growth of the Church in China has no parallels in history. Researchers estimate that there were 30-75 million Christians by 1990. Mao Zedong unwittingly became the greatest evangelist in history.

El Salvador:

The 12-year civil war, earthquakes, and the collapse of the price of coffee, the nation's main export, impoverished the nation. Over 80% live in dire poverty. An astonishing spiritual harvest has been gathered from all strata of society in the midst of the hate and bitterness of war. In 1960 evangelicals were 2.3% of the population, but today are around 20%.

Ethiopia:

Ethiopia is in a state of shock. Her population struggles with the trauma of millions of deaths through repression, famine, and war. Two great waves of violent persecution refined and purified the Church, but there were many martyrs. There have been millions coming to Christ. Protestants were fewer than 0.8% of the population in 1960, but by 1990 this may have become 13% of the population.

Examples such as these could be multiplied. The history of mankind has been a history of suffering and war. Yet it has also been a history of the advance of the kingdom of God. Figure 27.1 is a chart released in 1990 by the U.S. Center for World Mission documenting the growth in evangelical Christianity over the centuries.

According to Johnstone, "We are living in the time of the largest ingathering of people into the kingdom of God that the world has ever seen."[5] It is not at all improbable that this astonishing growth in God's kingdom is due in part to the presence of natural and moral evils in the world.

Second, *mankind is in a state of rebellion against God and his purpose.* Rather than submit to and worship God, people rebel against God and go their own way and so find themselves alienated from God, morally guilty before him, grop-

---

[3]D. Martyn Lloyd-Jones, *From Fear to Faith* (London: Inter-Varsity Press, 1953), pp. 23-24.
[4]Patrick Johnstone, *Operation World* (Grand Rapids, Mich.: Zondervan, 1993), pp. 164, 207-8, 214.
[5]Ibid., p. 25.

THE DIMINISHING TASK

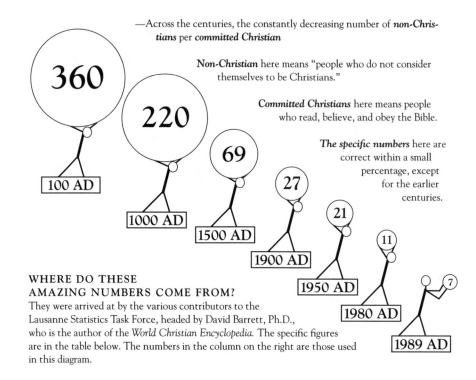

—Across the centuries, the constantly decreasing number of *non-Christians* per *committed Christian*

Non-Christian here means "people who do not consider themselves to be Christians."

Committed Christians here means people who read, believe, and obey the Bible.

The specific numbers here are correct within a small percentage, except for the earlier centuries.

WHERE DO THESE AMAZING NUMBERS COME FROM?

They were arrived at by the various contributors to the Lausanne Statistics Task Force, headed by David Barrett, Ph.D., who is the author of the *World Christian Encyclopedia*. The specific figures are in the table below. The numbers in the column on the right are those used in this diagram.

These are the numbers in the diagram above. Despite the rapid increase of world population, Christianity is simply growing faster than any other global religion when what is measured is its most relevant type of growth—the growth of committed adherents.

Column 1 DATE	Column 2 Non-Christians	Column 3 Com. Christians	Astounding Trend
100 AD	180	0.5	360
1000 AD	220	1	220
1500 AD	344	5	69
1900 AD	1,062	40	27
1950 AD	1,650	80	21
1980 AD	3,025	275	11
1989 AD	3,438	500	7
	The above numbers are published by the Lausanne Statistics Task Force. Note: figures in these two columns are millions		(Column 2 divided by Column 3)

Fig. 27.1 Ratio of non-Christians to committed Christians over history. Chart adapted from *Mission Frontiers*, November 1990 <www.missionfrontiers.org>. Reprinted with permission.

ing in spiritual darkness and pursuing false gods of their own making. The terrible human evils in the world are testimony to man's depravity in our state of spiritual alienation from God. Moreover, there is a realm of beings higher than man also in rebellion against God, demonic creatures, incredibly evil, in whose power the creation lies and who seek to destroy God's work and thwart his purposes. Christians are thus not surprised at the moral evil in the world; on the contrary, we *expect* it. The Scriptures indicate that God has given mankind over to the sin it has freely chosen; he does not interfere to stop it but lets human depravity run its course (Rom 1:24, 26, 28). This only serves to heighten mankind's moral responsibility before God, as well as our wickedness and our need of forgiveness and moral cleansing.

Third, *God's purpose is not restricted to this life but spills over beyond the grave into eternal life.* According to Christian theism, this life is but the cramped and narrow foyer opening up into the great hall of God's eternity. God promises eternal life to all those who place their trust in Christ as Savior and Lord. When God asks his children to bear horrible suffering in this life, it is only with the prospect of a heavenly joy and recompense that is beyond all comprehension. The apostle Paul underwent a life of incredible suffering which included both natural and moral evils. His life as an apostle was a life punctuated by "afflictions, hardships, calamities, beatings, imprisonments, riots, labors, sleepless nights, hunger" (2 Cor 6:4-5). Yet he wrote,

> So we do not lose heart. . . . For this slight momentary affliction is preparing us for an eternal weight of glory beyond all comparison, because we look not to the things that are seen but to the things that are at unseen; for the things that are seen are transient, but the things that are unseen are eternal. (2 Cor 4:16-18 RSV)

Paul lived this life in the perspective of eternity. He understood that the length of this life, being finite, is literally infinitesimal in comparison with the eternal life we shall spend with God. The longer we spend in eternity, the more the sufferings of this life will shrink toward an infinitesimal moment. That is why Paul called the sufferings of this life a "slight momentary affliction": he was not being insensitive to the plight of those who suffer horribly in this life—on the contrary, he was one of them—but he saw that those sufferings were simply overwhelmed by the ocean of everlasting joy and glory that God will give to those who trust him. It may well be that there are evils in the world that serve no earthly good at all, that are entirely gratuitous from a human point of view, but which God permits simply that he might overwhelmingly reward in the afterlife those who undergo such evils in faith and confidence in God.

Fourth, *the knowledge of God is an incommensurable good.* The passage cited from Paul also serves to make this point. Paul imagines, as it were, a scale, in which all the suffering of this life is placed on one side, while on the other side is placed the glory God will bestow on his children in heaven. The weight of glory is so great that it is beyond comparison with the suffering. For to know God, the locus of infinite goodness and love, is an incomparable good, the fulfillment of human existence. The sufferings of this life cannot even be compared to it. Thus the person who knows God, no matter what he suffers, no matter how awful his pain, can still truly say, "God is good to me!" simply in virtue of the fact that he knows God, an incommensurable good.

These four Christian doctrines increase the probability of the coexistence of God and the evils in the world. They thereby serve to decrease any improbability that these evils might seem to cast on the existence of God.

So it seems that the probabilistic problem of evil is far from unanswerable. Even if God's existence is improbable relative to the evil in the world alone, that does not make God's existence improbable, for balancing off the negative evidence from evil is the positive evidence for God's existence. Moreover, it is extremely difficult to establish from the evil in the world that God's existence is improbable, for God could have morally sufficient reasons for permitting such evil. We do not find ourselves in a good epistemic position to judge with any confidence that this is improbable. Finally, we can render the coexistence of God and evil more probable by adopting certain hypotheses inherent in the Christian worldview—for example, that the purpose of life is the knowledge of God, that mankind is in a state of rebellion against God and his purpose, that God's purpose extends beyond the grave to eternal life and that the knowledge of God is an incommensurable good. Taken together, these considerations make it not improbable that God and the evil in the world should both exist.

| 2.2 | But if the problem of evil fails as an internal problem for Christian theism, does it present an insuperable external problem? In recent years, the debate among philosophers has turned to examining this question. The versions of the problem thus far discussed have tried to show that two beliefs held by Christians, namely, that God exists and that the world contains the evils we observe, are either inconsistent or improbable with respect to one another. Most nontheists have now abandoned that project. Instead they claim that the apparently pointless and unnecessary evils in the world constitute *evidence* against God's existence. That is to say, they argue that the following two propositions are incompatible with each other.

2.2
The External
Problem of
Evil

6. An omnipotent, omnibenevolent God exists.
7. Gratuitous evil exists.

What makes this an external problem is that the Christian is not committed by his worldview to admitting the truth of (7). The Christian is committed to the truth that *evil exists*, but not that *gratuitous evil exists*. The objector is therefore presenting an argument against (Christian) theism of the following form:

8. If God exists, gratuitous evil does not exist.
9. Gratuitous evil exists.
10. Therefore, God does not exist.

The key question will be the warrant offered for (9). The theist will readily admit that much of the evil we observe in the world *appears* to be pointless and unnecessary and, hence, **gratuitous evil**. But he will challenge the objector's inference from the appearance of gratuitous evil to the reality of gratuitous evil. Here much of what has already been said with respect to the probabilistic internal problem of evil will be relevant. For example, the objector must assume that if we do not discern God's morally sufficient reason for allowing certain evils to occur, then it is probable that there is no such reason, that is to say, that such evils are gratuitous. But we have already seen how uncertain and tenuous such probability judgments on our part are. Our failure to discern the morally justifying reason for the occurrence of various evils gives very little ground for thinking that God—especially a God equipped with middle knowledge—could not have morally sufficient reasons for permitting the evils we observe in the world. Moreover, our insistence on considering the full scope of the evidence is also relevant. For in asking whether the evil we observe really is gratuitous, the most important question to consider is, ironically, whether God exists. That is, the theist may argue:

8. If God exists, gratuitous evil does not exist.
11. God exists.
12. Therefore, gratuitous evil does not exist.

It has been said that one man's *modus ponens* is another man's *modus tollens*. Thus the conclusion that follows from (8), which is the same in both the atheist and the theist's arguments, will depend on whether (9) or (11) has the greater warrant. As Daniel Howard-Snyder points out, the problem of evil is thus a problem only for "the theist who finds all its premises and inferences compelling and who has lousy grounds for believing theism"; but if one has more compelling grounds for theism, then the problem of evil "is not a problem."[6]

These same sorts of consideration will doubtlessly be relevant to the various permutations assumed by the external problem of evil as the discussion continues among philosophers. For example, Paul Draper has argued that naturalism is more probable than theism relative to the evolution of biological organisms and the distribution of pain/pleasure in the world. But Draper's argument hinges on three probability estimates which seem dubious in light of our discussion. First, he assumes that naturalism and theism are equally probable with respect to our general background knowledge ($\text{Pr}(N) = \text{Pr}(T)$), which we have seen reason to dispute (recall chaps. 23-24). Second, he believes that the probability of the distribution of pain/pleasure in the world is greater on naturalism and evolution than it is on theism and evolution ($\text{Pr}(P/E \& N) > \text{Pr}(P/E \& T)$). But we have seen reason to question whether we are in an epistemic position to make justifiably this sort of probability judgment. Finally, he argues that the probability of evolution on naturalism is greater than the probability of evolution on theism ($\text{Pr}(E/N) > \text{Pr}(E/T)$). For if naturalism is true, evolution is the only game in town; but if theism is true, God had more alternatives. But this assessment is confused. What Draper's argument supports is the assessment that evolution is more probable relative to naturalism *and* the existence of biological organisms than to theism and the existence of biological organisms ($\text{Pr}(E/N \& B) > \text{Pr}(E/T \& B)$). But we have seen from our discussion of the teleological argument (chap. 23) that the existence of biological organisms (and, hence, their evolution) is virtually impossible relative to naturalism alone and that we should therefore expect a lifeless world given naturalism, which cannot be said of theism. Without his three crucial probability estimates, Draper's evidential argument from evil founders.

It should also be noted that premise (8) itself is not obviously true. Some the-

---

[6]Daniel Howard-Snyder, "Introduction," in *The Evidential Argument from Evil*, ed. Daniel Howard-Snyder (Bloomington, Ind.: Indiana University Press, 1996), p xi.

ists have suggested that while God could eliminate this or that specific evil without decreasing the goodness of the world, nevertheless there must exist a certain amount of gratuitous evil in the world if the goodness of the world is not to be impaired. Thus the probability that a certain specified evil is gratuitous would not aversely affect theism. Considerations pertinent to divine middle knowledge of counterfactuals of creaturely freedom also arise at this point. It is epistemically possible that only in a world in which gratuitous natural and moral evils exist that the relevant counterfactuals of creaturely freedom are true to enable God to bring the optimal number of persons freely to salvation and the knowledge of himself. The atheist might say that in that case the evils are not really gratuitous after all: they serve the greater good of securing people's eternal salvation. But if one allows a greater good of that sort to count against the gratuity of some evil, then that makes it all the more difficult for the atheist to prove that truly gratuitous evil exists, for how could he possibly surmise what in God's providential plan for history does or does not contribute to the ultimate salvation of the greatest number of people?

Finally, one last point reamins to be made that constitutes a defeater of any argument from evil against the existence of God, namely, that moral evil proves that God exists. For in our discussion of the axiological argument for God's existence, we saw that it is plausible that apart from God objective moral values do not exist. But then we can employ the atheist's own premise as part of a sound argument for the existence of God:

13. If God did not exist, then objective moral values would not exist.
14. Evil exists.
15. Therefore, objective moral values exist. (from 14 by definition of *evil*)
16. Therefore, God exists. (MT, 13, 15)

Premise (13) was the key premise of the axiological argument, which is accepted by many theists and nontheists alike. Premise (14) is furnished by the problem of evil itself, since it appeals in part to moral evils in the world. (15) follows by definition from (14), for if one grants that some things are truly evil, then one has admitted the objectivity of moral truths. Since objective values cannot exist without God and objective values do exist (as shown by the evil in the world), it follows that God exists. Therefore, evil in the world actually proves that God exists. This argument demonstrates the coexistence of God and evil without attempting to give any explanation at all for why evil exists—we, like Job, may be totally ignorant of that—but it nonetheless shows that the existence of evil in the world does not call into question, but on the contrary, implies God's existence.

In summary, the intellectual problem of evil—whether in its internal or external versions—can be satisfactorily solved.

3 THE EMOTIONAL PROBLEM OF EVIL

But, of course, when one says "solved" one means "philosophically resolved." All these mental machinations may be of little comfort to someone who is intensely suffering from some undeserved evil in life. This leads us to the second aspect of the problem mentioned earlier: the emotional problem of evil.

For many people, the problem of evil is not really an intellectual problem: it is an emotional problem. They are hurting inside and perhaps bitter against a God who would permit them or others to suffer so. Never mind that there are philosophical solutions to the problem of evil—they do not care and simply reject a God who allows such suffering as we find in the world. It is interesting that in Dostoyevsky's *Brothers Karamazov*, in which the problem of evil is presented so powerfully, this is what the problem really comes down to. Ivan Karamazov never refutes the Christian solution to the problem of evil. Instead, he just refuses to have anything to do with the Christian God. "I would rather remain with my unavenged suffering and unsatisfied indignation, *even if I am wrong*," he declares. His is simply an atheism of rejection.

What can be said to those who are laboring under the emotional problem of evil? In one sense, the most important thing may not be what one says at all. The most important thing may be just to be there as a loving friend and sympathetic listener. But some people may need counsel, and we ourselves may need to deal with this problem when we suffer. Does Christian theism also have the resources to deal with this problem as well?

It certainly does! For it tells us that God is not a distant Creator or impersonal ground of being, but a loving Father who shares our sufferings and hurts with us. Alvin Plantinga has written,

> As the Christian sees things, God does not stand idly by, coolly observing the suffering of his creatures. He enters into and shares our suffering. He endures the anguish of seeing his son, the second person of the Trinity, consigned to the bitterly cruel and shameful death of the cross. Some theologians claim that God cannot suffer. I believe they are wrong. God's capacity for suffering, I believe, is proportional to his greatness; it exceeds our capacity for suffering in the same measure as his capacity for knowledge exceeds ours. Christ was prepared to endure the agonies of hell itself; and God, the Lord of the universe, was prepared to endure the suffering consequent upon his son's humiliation and death. He was prepared to accept this suffering in order to overcome sin, and death, and the evils that afflict our world, and to confer on us a life more glorious that we can imagine. So we don't know why God permits evil; we do know, however, that he was prepared to suffer on our behalf, to accept suffering of which we can form no conception.[7]

Christ endured a suffering beyond all understanding: he bore the punishment for the sins of the whole world. None of us can comprehend that suffering. Though he was innocent, he voluntarily underwent incomprehensible suffering for us. Why? Because he loves us so much. How can we reject him who gave up everything for us?

When we comprehend his sacrifice and his love for us, this puts the problem of evil in an entirely different perspective. For now we see clearly that the true problem of evil is the problem of *our* evil. Filled with sin and morally guilty before God, the question we face is not how God can justify himself to us, but how we can be justified before him.

---

[7]Alvin Plantinga, "Self-Profile," in *Alvin Plantinga*, ed. James E. Tomberlin and Peter van Inwagen, Profiles 5 (Dordrecht: D. Reidel, 1985), p. 36.

When God asks us to undergo suffering that seems unmerited, pointless and unnecessary, meditation on the cross of Christ can help to give us the moral strength and courage needed to bear the cross that we are asked to carry. So, paradoxically, even though the problem of evil is the greatest objection to the existence of God, at the end of the day God is the only solution to the problem of evil. If God does not exist, then we are locked without hope in a world filled with gratuitous and unredeemed suffering. God is the final answer to the problem of evil, for he redeems us from evil and takes us into the everlasting joy of an incommensurable good, fellowship with himself.

CHAPTER SUMMARY

In order to deal with the problem of evil, it is helpful to distinguish between the intellectual problem of evil and the emotional problem of evil. The intellectual problem of evil may be cast as either an internal or an external problem for theism. As an internal problem, it comes in two versions: the logical version and the probabilistic version. The logical version of the problem of evil asserts that the coexistence of God and evil (or the observed quantity and kinds of evil) is logically impossible. Today this version of the problem has been almost universally given up because the burden of proof of demonstrating that there is no possibility at all of the coexistence of God and (the observed) evil is just too heavy for the atheist to bear. The probabilistic version of the problem of evil involves a burden of proof that is less heavy, since it asserts that God's existence is merely improbable relative to the evil in the world. But at least three considerations show that atheists have not been able to shoulder even this burden of proof: (1) God's existence is still probable relative to the full scope of the evidence; (2) we are not in a good position to assess with confidence the probability that God has no morally sufficient reasons for permitting the evils that occur; (3) Christian theism entails doctrines that increase the probability of the coexistence of God and evil. More recently atheists have argued that evil presents, not an internal, but an external problem for theism. The presence of gratuitous evil in the world is alleged to be incompatible with the existence of God. But the key move in the atheist's reasoning will be the demonstration that evil which appears to be gratuitous really is gratuitous. The same considerations raised in considering the probabilistic version of the internal problem of evil return to haunt the atheist, for it is extraordinarily difficult to prove that the evil in the world is gratuitous. Moreover, some theists maintain that theism is not incompatible with gratuitous evil in the first place, that God, in order to achieve his ends, may have to permit evils which in themselves are gratuitous. Finally, Christian theism in its doctrine of Christ's vicarious suffering and death has the resources to meet the emotional problem occasioned by evil.

CHECKLIST OF BASIC TERMS AND CONCEPTS

background information
emotional problem of evil

external problem of evil
free will defense
gratuitous evil
intellectual problem of evil
internal problem of evil
logical version of the problem of evil
moral evil
natural evil
probabilistic version of the problem of evil
problem of evil

28

CREATION, PROVIDENCE
AND MIRACLE

The leaf hanging from the tree does not fall,
nor does either of the two sparrows sold for a farthing fall to the ground,
nor does anything else whatever happen without God's providence
and will either intending it as a particular or permitting it as a particular.
LUIS MOLINA, CONCORDIA 4.53.3.17

1 CREATIO EX NIHILO

"In the beginning God created the heavens and the earth" (Gen 1:1 RSV). With majestic simplicity the author of the opening chapter of Genesis thus differentiated his viewpoint, not only from that of the ancient creation myths of Israel's neighbors, but also effectively from pantheism, such as is found in Eastern religions like Hinduism and Taoism, from panentheism, whether of classical neo-Platonist vintage or twentieth-century process theology, and from polytheism, ranging from ancient paganism to contemporary Mormonism. For the author of Genesis 1, no preexistent material seems to be assumed, no warring gods or primordial dragons are present—only God, who is said to "create" (*bara*, a word used only with God as its subject and which does not presuppose a material substratum) "the heavens and the earth" (*eth hassamayim we'eth ha'arets*, a Hebrew expression for the totality of the world or, more simply, the universe). Moreover, this act of creation took place "in the beginning" (*bereshith*, used here as in Is 46:10 to indicate an absolute beginning). The author thereby implies **creatio ex nihilo** (creation out of nothing) in the temporal sense that God brought the universe into being without a **material cause** at some point in the finite past.

Later biblical authors so understood the Genesis account of creation (e.g., Is 44:24; cf. Is 45:12, 18). The doctrine of *creatio ex nihilo* is also implied in various places in early extrabiblical Jewish literature. And the church fathers, while heavily influenced by Greek thought, dug in their heels concerning the doctrine of creation, sturdily insisting, with few exceptions, on the temporal creation of the universe *ex nihilo* in opposition to the eternity of matter. In the form of the *kalam* cosmological argument, a tradition of robust argumentation against the past eternity of the world and in favor of *creatio ex nihilo* continued for centuries in Islamic, Jewish and Christian thought. In 1215, the Catholic church promulgated temporal *creatio ex nihilo* as official church doctrine at the Fourth Lateran Council, declaring God to be "Creator of all things, visible and invisible, . . . who, by his almighty power, from the beginning of time has created both orders in the same way out of nothing." This remarkable declaration not only affirms that God created everything without any material cause, but even that time itself had a beginning. The doctrine of creation is thus inherently bound up with temporal considerations and entails that God brought the universe into being at some point in the past without any antecedent or contemporaneous material cause.

At the same time, the Christian Scriptures also suggest that God is engaged in a sort of ongoing creation, sustaining the universe in being. Christ "reflects the glory of God and bears the very stamp of his nature, upholding the universe by his word of power" (Heb 1:3 RSV). Although relatively infrequently attested in Scripture in comparison with the abundant references to God's original act of creation, this idea of **continuing creation** came to constitute an important aspect of the doctrine of creation as well. For Thomas Aquinas, for example, this aspect becomes the core doctrine of creation, and the question of whether the world's reception of being from God had a temporal beginning or not has only secondary importance. For Aquinas creation is the immediate bestowal of being and as such belongs only to God, the universal principle of being; therefore, creation is *ex nihilo* in that God's causing a creature to exist is immediate. Even if that creature has existed from eternity, it is still created *ex nihilo* in this metaphysical sense.

Thus God is conceived in Christian theology to be the cause of the world both in his initial act of bringing the universe into being and in his ongoing conservation of the world in being. These two actions have been traditionally classed as species of *creatio ex nihilo*, namely, **creatio originans** (originating creation) and **creatio continuans** (continuing creation). While this is a handy rubric, it unfortunately quickly becomes problematic if pressed to technical precision. For if we say that a thing is created at a time *t* only if *t* is the first moment of the thing's existence, then the doctrine of *creatio continuans* implies that at each instant God creates a brand new individual, numerically distinct from its chronological predecessor. We are thus landed us in a bizarre doctrine called **occasionalism**, according to which no persisting individuals exist, so that personal agency and identity over time are precluded.

One could elude this problem by reinterpreting creation in such a way that it does not involve a thing's first beginning to exist at the time of its creation. But something important about the concept of creation would then seem to be lost. It is therefore preferable to take "continuing creation" as but a manner of speaking and to distinguish **creation** from **conservation**. As John Duns Scotus observed,

> Properly speaking . . . it is only true to say that a creature is created at the first moment (of its existence) and only after that moment is it conserved, for only then does its being have this order to itself as something that was, as it were, there before. Because of these different conceptual relationships implied by the words "create" and "conserve" it follows that one does not apply to a thing when the other does.[1]

It has been objected that trying to differentiate creation and conservation in this way wrongly presupposes that the power required to create something *ex nihilo*

---

[1] John Duns Scotus, *God and Creatures*, trans. E. Alluntis and A. Wolter (Princeton, N.J.: Princeton University Press, 1975), p. 276.

is different from the power needed to keep it from lapsing back into nonbeing once it has been created. Since God's power and action in creation and conservation are the same, there is no intrinsic difference between the two. But we need not find the intrinsic difference between creation and conservation in God's power or action. Rather, we may find it in the object of that action. Intuitively, creation involves God's bringing something into being. Thus, if God creates some entity e (whether a thing or an event) at a time t (whether an instant or finite interval), then e **comes into being** at t. We can analyze this last notion as follows:

> E_1: e comes into being at t if and only if (a) e exists at t, (b) t is the first time at which e exists, and (c) e's existing at t is a tensed fact.

Accordingly,

> E_2: God creates e at t if and only if God brings it about that e comes into being at t.

God's creating e involves e's coming into being, which is an absolute beginning of existence, not a transition of e from nonbeing into being. In creation there is no entity on which the agent acts to bring about its effect. It follows that creation is not a type of **change**, since there is no enduring subject that persists from one state to another. It is precisely for this reason that conservation cannot be properly thought of as essentially the same as creation. For conservation does presuppose a subject which is made to persist from one state to another. In creation God does not act on a subject, but constitutes the subject by his action. In contrast, in conservation God acts on an existing subject to perpetuate its existence. This is the meaning of Scotus's remark that only in conservation does a creature "have this order to itself as something that was, as it were, there before." In conservation there is an existing entity on which the agent acts to produce its effect.

To analyze God's conservation of e as God's re-creation of e anew at each instant or moment of e's existence is to run the risk of falling into the radical occasionalism of certain medieval Islamic theologians, who denied that the atoms out of which things are made endure from one instant to another. Rather, atoms were said to be created in new states of being by God at every successive instant. The Islamic theologians therefore denied the reality of **secondary causation**, leaving God as the sole cause of change.

The fundamental difference between creation and conservation, as we have seen, lies in the fact that in conservation, as opposed to creation, there is presupposed an object on which God acts. Intuitively, conservation involves God's preservation of that object in being over time. Conservation ought therefore to be understood in terms of God's preserving some entity e from one moment of its existence to another. A crucial insight into conservation is that unlike creation, it involves transition and therefore cannot occur at an instant. We may therefore provide the following analysis of divine conservation:

> E_3: God conserves e if and only if God acts upon e to bring about e's existing from t until some $t^* > t$ through every subinterval of the interval $t \to t^*$.

In this light, when it is said that God's creating and conserving the world are indistinguishable with respect to the act itself, that statement is misleading. For creating and conserving cannot be adequately analyzed with respect to the act alone but involve relations to the object of the act. The act itself (the causing of existence) may be the same in both cases, but in one case may be instantaneous and presupposes no prior object, whereas in the other case it occurs over an interval and does involve a prior object.

The doctrine of creation also involves an important metaphysical feature which is underappreciated: it commits one to a tensed or dynamic or A-theory of time. For if one adopts a tenseless or B-theory of time, then things do not literally come into existence. Things are four-dimensional objects that tenselessly subsist and begin to exist only in the sense that their extension along their temporal dimension is finite in the *earlier than* direction. The whole four-dimensional, space-time manifold exists coeternally with God. The universe thus does not come into being on a B-theory of time, regardless of whether it has a finite or an infinite past relative to any time. Hence, clause (iii) in E_2 represents a necessary feature of creation. In the absence of clause (iii) God's creation of the universe *ex nihilo* could be interpreted along tenseless lines to postulate merely the finitude of cosmic time in the *earlier than* direction.

What about conservation? At first blush this notion would seem to be much more amenable to a tenseless construal. God can be conceived to act tenselessly on e to sustain it from t_1 to t_2. But a moment's reflection reveals this construal to be problematic. What if e exists only at t? Or what if e is the whole, four-dimensional space-time block? In neither case can God be said to conserve e, according to our analysis, since e does not persist from one time to another. Yet on a tenseless view of time God is the source of being for such entities and therefore in some sense sustains them. Similarly, if we allow timeless entities in our ontology, such as abstract objects, then God must be the source of their being as well. In their case there is properly speaking no conservation, no preserving them in existence from one moment to another. The existence of such entities would seem to necessitate a third category of creation not contemplated by the classical theologians, a sort of static creation. Static creation is the relation appropriate to a tenseless theory of time. We use **sustenance** as the technical term for such divine action and explicate it as follows:

> E_4: God sustains e if and only if either e exists tenselessly at t or e exists timelessly, and God brings it about that e exists.

The very idea of the need for conservation in being thus also implies an A-theory of time, according to which temporal becoming is real and moments of time do elapse. Conservation of an entity is necessary if that entity is to endure from one moment to another and not to lapse into nonbeing. On a B-theory of time, no such lapse occurs, and so conservation is unnecessary, indeed, excluded. Rather, God is engaged in sustaining the four-dimensional universe as a whole and every entity in it, whether that entity has a temporal extension or exists merely at an instant. Thus even conservation is compromised if definitions of it are given that are compatible with a B-theory of time.

Since a robust doctrine of *creatio ex nihilo* commits us to an A-theory of time, we are brought face to face with what has been called "one of the most neglected, but also one of the most important questions in the dialogue between theology and science," namely, the relation between the concept of eternity and that of the spatiotemporal structure of the universe.[2] We have already discussed this problem briefly in our handling of the divine attribute of eternity (chap. 25). Here we may enter into more detail.

Since the rise of modern theology with Schleiermacher, the doctrine of *creatio originans* has been allowed to atrophy, while the doctrine of *creatio continuans* has assumed supremacy. Undoubtedly this was largely due to theologians' fear of a conflict with science, which *creatio continuans* permitted them to avoid by ignoring the realities of the physical, space-time world. But the discovery in the early twentieth century of the expansion of the universe, coupled with the Hawking-Penrose singularity theorems of 1968, which demonstrated the inevitability under very general conditions of a past, cosmic singularity as an initial boundary to space-time, forced the doctrine of *creatio originans* back into the spotlight. As physicists Barrow and Tipler observe, "At this singularity, space and time came into existence; literally nothing existed before the singularity, so, if the Universe originated at such a singularity, we would truly have a creation *ex nihilo*."[3]

Of course, various and sometimes heroic attempts have been made to avert the beginning of the universe posited in the standard big bang model and to regain an infinite past. But none of these alternatives has commended itself as more plausible than the standard model. The old steady state model, the oscillating model, and vacuum fluctuation models are now generally recognized among cosmologists to have failed as plausible attempts to avoid the beginning of the universe.[4] Most cosmologists believe that a final theory of the origin of the universe must await the as-yet-undiscovered quantum theory of gravity. Such quantum gravity models may or may not involve an initial singularity, although attention has tended to focus on those that do not. But even those that eliminate the initial singularity, such as the Hartle-Hawking model, still involve a merely finite past and, on any physically realistic interpretation of such models, imply a beginning of the universe. Such theories, if successful, thus enable us to model the origin of the universe without an initial cosmological singularity and, by positing a finite past time on a closed geometrical surface of space-time rather than an infinite time on an open surface, actually support temporal *creatio ex nihilo*.

But if the spatiotemporal structure of the universe exhibits an origination *ex nihilo*, then the difficulty concerns how to relate that structure to divine eternity. For given the reality of tense and God's causal relation to the world, it is difficult to think that God could remain untouched by the world's temporality. Imagine God existing changelessly alone without creation, with a changeless and eternal determination to create a temporal world. Since God is omnipotent, his will is done, and a temporal world begins to exist. (We may set aside the

---

[2]Wolfhart Pannenberg, "Theological Questions to Scientists," in *The Sciences and Theology in the Twentieth Century*, ed. A. R. Peacocke, Oxford International Symposia (Stocksfield, England: Oriel Press, 1981), p. 12.

[3]John D. Barrow and Frank J. Tipler, *The Anthropic Cosmological Principle* (Oxford: Clarendon, 1986), p. 442.

[4]See William Lane Craig, "Naturalism and Cosmology," in *Naturalism: A Critical Appraisal*, ed. W. L. Craig and J. P. Moreland, Routledge Studies in Twentieth-Century Philosophy (London: Routledge, 2000), pp. 215-52.

question whether this beginning of a temporal creation would require some additional act of intentionality or exercise of power other than God's timeless determination.) Now in such a case, either God existed temporally prior to creation or he did not. If he did exist alone temporally prior to creation, then God is not timeless, but temporal, and the question is settled. Suppose, then, that God did not exist temporally prior to creation. In that case he exists timelessly without creation. But once time begins at the moment of creation, God either becomes temporal in virtue of his real, causal relation to time and the world or else he exists as timelessly with creation as he does without it. But this second alternative seems quite impossible. At the first moment of time, God stands in a new relation in which he did not stand before (since there was no *before*). We need not characterize this as an intrinsic change in God; but there is a real, causal relation that is at that moment new to God and that he does not have in the state of existing without creation. At the moment of creation, God comes into the relation of *causing the universe* or at the very least that of *coexisting with the universe*, relations which he did not before have. Since he is free to refrain from creation, God could have never stood in those relations, but in virtue of his decision to create a temporal universe God comes into a relation with the temporal world the moment the temporal world springs into being. As God successively sustains each subsequent moment or event in being, he experiences the flow of time and acquires a growing past, as each moment elapses. Hence, even if God remains intrinsically changeless in creating the world, he nonetheless undergoes an extrinsic, or relational, change, which, if he is not already temporal prior to the moment of creation, draws him into time at that very moment in virtue of his real relation to the temporal, changing universe. So even if God is timeless without creation, his free decision to create a temporal world constitutes also a free decision on his part to enter into time and to experience the reality of tense and temporal becoming.

The classic response to the above argument is to deny that God is really related to the world. Aquinas tacitly agrees that if God were really related to the temporal world, then he would be temporal. For in the coming to be of creatures, certain relations accrue to God anew and thus, if these relations are real for God, he must be temporal in light of his undergoing relational change. So Thomas denies that God has any **real relation** to the world. According to Aquinas, while the temporal world does have the real relation of *being created by God*, God does not have a real relation of *creating the temporal world*. Since God is immutable, the new relations predicated of him at the moment of creation are just in our minds; in reality the temporal world itself is created with a relation inhering in it of *dependence on God*. Hence, God's timelessness is not jeopardized by his creation of a temporal world.

This unusual doctrine of creation becomes even stranger when we reflect on the fact that, on Thomas's view, God in creating the world does not perform some act extrinsic to his nature; God just *is*, and creatures simply begin to exist with a relation to God of *being created by God*. According to this doctrine, then, God in freely creating the universe does not really do anything different than he would have, had he refrained from creating. The only difference is to be found in the universe itself: instead of God existing alone without the universe, we have a universe springing into being at the first moment of time possessing the property *being created by God,* even though God, for his part, bears no real reciprocal relation to the universe made by him.

It hardly needs to be said that Thomas's solution, despite its daring and ingenuity, is extraordinarily implausible. "Creating" clearly describes a relation that is founded on something's intrinsic properties concerning its causal activity, and therefore *creating the world* ought to be regarded as a real property acquired by God at the moment of creation. It seems unintelligible, if not contradictory, to say that one can have real effects without real causes. Yet this is precisely what Aquinas affirms with respect to God and the world.

Moreover, bizarre as it may sound, it is the implication of Aquinas's position that God is perfectly similar across possible worlds, the same even in worlds in which he refrains from creation as in worlds in which he creates. For in none of these worlds does God have any relation to anything other than himself. In all these worlds God never acts differently, he never cognizes differently, he never wills differently. He is just the simple, unrelated act of being. Even in worlds in which he does not create, his act of being, by which creation is produced, is no different in these otherwise empty worlds than in worlds chock-full of contingent beings of every order. Thomas's doctrine thus makes it unintelligible why the universe exists rather than nothing. The reason obviously cannot lie in God, either in his nature or his activity (which are only conceptually distinct anyway), for these are perfectly similar in every possible world. Nor can the reason lie in the creatures themselves, in that they have a real relation to God of *being freely willed by God.* For their existing with that relation cannot be explanatorily prior to their existing with that relation. Therefore, Thomas's solution, based in the denial of God's real relation to the world, cannot succeed in hermetically sealing off God in atemporality.

The above might lead one to conclude that God existed temporally prior to his creation of the universe in a sort of metaphysical time. But as we have seen in chapter twenty-three, the notion of an actual infinity of past events or intervals of time seems strikingly counterintuitive. Moreover, on such a view of time, we should have to answer the difficult question that Leibniz lodged against Samuel Clarke: why did God delay for infinite time the creation of the world? In view of these perplexities, it seems more plausible to adopt the view that time begins at the first event, which, for simplicity's sake, we may take to be the big bang (on the plausibility of a metrically amorphous time prior to creation, see chap. 25 on divine eternity). God's bringing the initial cosmological singularity into being is simultaneous (or coincident) with the singularity's coming into being, and therefore God is temporal from the moment of creation onward. Though we might think of God as existing, say, one hour prior to creation, such a picture is purely the product of our imagination.

Why, then, did God create the world? It has been said that if God is essentially characterized by self-giving love, creation becomes necessary. But the Christian doctrine of the Trinity suggests another possibility. Insofar as he exists without creation, God is not, on the Christian conception, a lonely monad, but in the tri-unity of his own being, God enjoys the full and unchanging love relationships among the persons of the Trinity. Creation is thus unnecessary for

God and is sheer gift, bestowed for the sake of creatures, that we might experience the joy and fulfillment of knowing God. He invites us, as it were, into the intratrinitarian love relationship as his adopted children. Thus creation, as well as salvation, is *sola gratia*.

2 PROVIDENCE

The biblical worldview involves a very strong conception of divine sovereignty over the world and human affairs, even as it presupposes human freedom and responsibility. While too numerous to list here, biblical passages affirming God's **sovereignty** have been grouped by D. A. Carson under four main heads: (1) God is the Creator, Ruler and Possessor of all things; (2) God is the ultimate personal cause of all that happens; (3) God elects his people; and (4) God is the unacknowledged source of good fortune or success.[5] No one taking these passages seriously can embrace currently fashionable revisionist or "open" views, which deny God's complete sovereignty over the contingent events of history. On the other hand, the conviction that human beings are free moral agents also permeates the Hebrew way of thinking, as is evident from passages listed by Carson under nine heads: (1) People face a multitude of divine exhortations and commands; (2) people are said to obey, believe and choose God; (3) people sin and rebel against God; (4) people's sins are judged by God; (5) people are tested by God, (6) people receive divine rewards; (7) the elect are responsible to respond to God's initiative; (8) prayers are not mere showpieces scripted by God; and (9) God literally pleads with sinners to repent and be saved.[6] These passages rule out a traditional deterministic understanding of divine providence, which precludes human freedom (for a discussion of which see chap. 13).

Reconciling these two streams of biblical teaching without compromising either has proven extraordinarily difficult. Nevertheless, a startling solution to this enigma emerges from Molina's doctrine of divine middle knowledge. Molina, it will be recalled from chapter twenty-six, proposes to furnish an analysis of divine knowledge in terms of three logical moments. Although whatever God knows, he knows eternally, so that there is no temporal succession in God's knowledge, nonetheless there does exist a sort of logical succession in God's knowledge in that his knowledge of certain truths is conditionally or explanatorily prior to his knowledge of certain other truths. In the first, unconditioned moment, God knows all possibilities, not only all the creatures he could possibly create, but also all the orders of creatures that are possible. Molina calls such knowledge "natural knowledge" because the content of such knowledge is essential to God and in no way depends on the free decisions of his will. By means of his natural knowledge, then, God has knowledge of every contingent state of affairs that could possibly obtain and of what any free creature could freely choose to do in any such state of affairs that should be actual.

In the second moment, God possesses knowledge of all true counterfactual

---

[5]D. A. Carson, *Divine Sovereignty and Human Responsibility: Biblical Perspectives in Tension*, New Foundations Theological Library (Atlanta, Ga.: John Knox Press, 1981), pp. 24-35.

[6]Ibid., pp. 18-22. One should mention also the striking passages that speak of God's repenting in reaction to a change in human behavior (e.g., Gen 6:6; 1 Sam 15:11, 35).

propositions, including counterfactuals of creaturely freedom. Whereas by his natural knowledge God knew what any free creature *could* do in any set of circumstances, now in this second moment God knows what any free creature *would* do in any set of circumstances. This is not because the circumstances causally determine the creature's choice, but simply because this is how the creature would freely choose. God thus knows that were he to actualize certain states of affairs, then certain other contingent states of affairs would obtain. This so-called "middle" knowledge is like natural knowledge in that such knowledge does not depend on any decision of the divine will; God does not determine which counterfactuals of creaturely freedom are true or false. Thus, if it is true that "If some agent S were placed in circumstances C, then he would freely perform action *a*," then even God in his omnipotence cannot bring it about that S would freely refrain from *a* if he were placed in C. On the other hand, middle knowledge is unlike natural knowledge in that the content of his middle knowledge is not essential to God. True counterfactuals are contingently true; S could freely decide to refrain from *a* in C, so that different counterfactuals could be true and be known by God than those that are. Hence, although it is essential to God that he have middle knowledge, it is not essential to him to have middle knowledge of those particular propositions that he does in fact know.

Intervening between the second and third moments of divine knowledge stands God's free decree to actualize a world known by him to be realizable on the basis of his middle knowledge. By his natural knowledge, God knows what is the entire range of logically possible worlds; by his middle knowledge he knows, in effect, what is the proper subset of those worlds which it is feasible for him to actualize. By a free decision, God decrees to actualize one of those worlds known to him through his middle knowledge. In so doing he also decrees how he himself would act in any set of circumstances, so that **counterfactuals of divine freedom** become true coincidentally with the divine decree.

Given God's free decision to actualize a world, in the third and final moment God possesses knowledge of all remaining propositions that are in fact true in the actual world, including future contingent propositions. The content of such "free knowledge" is clearly not essential to God, since he could have decreed to actualize a different world. Had he done so, the content of his free knowledge would be different.

Molina's scheme is a doctrine of remarkable theological fecundity that resolves in a single stroke most of the traditional difficulties concerning divine providence and human freedom. Molina defines **providence** as God's ordering of things to their ends, either directly or mediately through secondary agents. But he distinguishes between God's **absolute intentions** and his **conditional intentions** concerning creatures. It is, for example, God's absolute intention that no creature should ever sin and that all should reach heaven. But it is not within God's power to determine what decisions creatures would freely take under various circumstances. In certain circumstances, creatures will freely sin, despite the fact that it is God's will that they not sin. If then God for whatever reason wants to bring about those circumstances, he has no choice but to allow the creature to sin, though that is not his absolute intention. God's absolute intentions are thus often frustrated by sinful creatures, though his conditional intention, which takes into account the creatures' free actions, is always fulfilled. Now obviously in this world it is God's providential plan to permit sin to occur. But even sin serves God's conditional intentions in that it manifests his over-flowing goodness in the incarnation of Christ for the purpose of rescuing humanity from sin, his power in his redeeming people from sin, and his justice in punishing sin.

While God's providence, then, extends to everything that happens, it does not follow that God wills positively everything that happens. God wills positively every good creaturely decision, but evil decisions he does not will, but merely permits. Molina explains,

> All *good* things, whether produced by causes acting from a necessity of nature or by free causes, depend upon divine predetermination . . . and providence in such a way that each is *specifically intended* by God through His predetermination and providence, whereas the *evil* acts of the created will are subject as well to divine predetermination and providence to the extent that the causes from which they emanate and the general concurrence on God's part required to elicit them are granted through divine predetermination and providence—though not in order that *these particular acts* should emanate from them, but rather in order that *other, far different, acts* might come to be, and in order that the innate freedom of the things endowed with a will might be preserved for their maximum benefit; in addition evil acts are subject to that same divine predetermination and providence to the extent that they cannot exist in particular unless God by His providence *permits them in particular* in the service of some greater good. It clearly follows from the above that all things without exception are *individually* subject to God's will and providence, which intend certain of them *as particulars* and permit the rest *as particulars*. (Molina *On Divine Foreknowledge* 4.53.3.17)

Everything that happens, therefore, occurs either by God's will or God's permission and thus falls under his providence.

This serves to bring into focus Molina's doctrine of simultaneous concurrence, which together with middle knowledge supplies the underpinnings of his doctrine of providence. Since God is the first cause, medieval theologians traditionally held that God not only conserves the universe in being, but that he concurs with the operation of every secondary cause in the universe so that he is quite literally the cause of everything that happens. Aquinas interpreted the notion of divine concurrence to mean that God not only supplies and conserves the power of operation in every secondary cause, but that he acts on the secondary causes in order to produce their actual operations, a view that came to be known as the **doctrine of pre-motion**. With regard to contingent acts of the will, this doctrine meant that the free decisions of creatures are produced by God's causing a person's will to turn itself this way or that.

Molina, however, rejects this interpretation of divine concurrence in terms of pre-motion as in reality utterly deterministic and incompatible with the existence of sin. Instead he proposes to regard divine concurrence as **simultaneous concurrence**; that is to say, God acts, not *on*, but *with* the secondary cause to produce its effect. Thus, when a person wills to produce some effect, God concurs with that person's decision by also acting to produce that effect; but he does not act on the person's will to move it to its decision. In sinful decisions, God concurs by acting to produce the effect, but he is not to be held responsible for the sinfulness of the act, since he did not move the creature's will to do it. Rather, out of his determination to allow human freedom, he merely permitted the decision to be made. In thus either willing or permitting everything that happens, therefore, God acts to produce every event in the actual world.

In reconciling divine sovereignty and human freedom, Molina appeals both to middle knowledge and simultaneous concurrence. By his middle knowledge God knows an infinity of orders that he could create because he knows how the creatures in them would in fact respond given the various circumstances. He then decides by the free act of his will how he would respond in these various circumstances and simultaneously wills to bring about one of these orders. He directly causes certain circumstances to come into being and brings about others indirectly through causally determined secondary causes. Free creatures, however, he allows to act as he knew they would when placed in such circumstances, and he concurs with their decisions in producing in being the effects they desire. Some of these effects God desired unconditionally and so wills positively that they occur. Others he does not unconditionally desire, but he nevertheless permits due to his overriding desire to allow creaturely freedom, knowing that even these sinful acts will fit into the overall scheme of things, so that God's ultimate ends in human history will be accomplished. God has thus providentially arranged for everything that happens by either willing or permitting it, and he causes everything that does happen, yet in such a way as to preserve freedom and contingency.

Molinism thus effects a dramatic reconciliation between divine sovereignty and human freedom. What account of divine providence can be given in the absence of middle knowledge? Advocates of revisionist views, such as the openness view of God that denies divine middle knowledge and foreknowledge, freely admit that without middle knowledge a strong doctrine of divine providence becomes impossible. But such a viewpoint consequently has real difficulty in making sense of the scriptural emphases summarized above. The Augustinian/Calvinist perspective interprets divine providence in terms of predetermination. God knows what will happen because he makes it happen. It is hard to see how this interpretation can avoid making God the author of sin, since it is he who moved Judas, for example, to betray Christ. But how can a holy God move people's wills to commit moral evil, and moreover, how can he then hold these people morally responsible for acts over which they had no control? The proponent of simple foreknowledge in the absence of middle knowledge has difficulty making sense of God's providential planning of a world of free creatures. For on this view, logically prior to the divine decree God has only natural knowledge of all possibilities, but no knowledge of what would happen under any circumstances. Thus, logically posterior to the divine decree, God must be astonished to find himself existing in a world, out of all the possible worlds he could have created, in which mankind falls into sin and God himself enters human history as a substitutionary sacrificial offering to rescue them! Of course, one is speaking anthropomorphically here; but the point remains that without middle knowledge, God cannot know prior to the creative decree what the world would be like. Thus none of Molinism's competitors seems equipped to offer so robust a doctrine of divine providence and human freedom as Molinism.

What objections might be raised against a Molinist account? Surveying the literature, one discovers that the detractors of Molinism tend not so much to criticize the Molinist doctrine of providence as to attack the concept of middle knowledge on which it is predicated. These objections, however, have been repeatedly answered by defenders of middle knowledge. What objection, then, might be raised, not to middle knowledge per se, but to a Molinist account of providence?

Perhaps the most compelling objection to what revisionists sometimes call "meticulous providence" is that the Molinist account makes the problem of evil all the more intractable. For we must then say that God planned even the most horrendous evils that occur in the world. For example, he planned down to the last detail that the brutal beating and rape of a small child should take place. The problem of innocent suffering might seem less difficult if we adopt the revisionist view that God is ignorant of future contingents and so did not plan that such horrors should occur.

A little reflection reveals, however, that the objection cannot stand. For on the revisionist view, God, so to speak, sits idly by wringing his hands while allowing horrendous evils to occur without intervening to stop them. Any reason to which the revisionist might appeal for God's allowing such evils to go on is also available to the Molinist. In fact, the Molinist is better positioned to defend the claim that God has morally sufficient reasons for allowing horrendous evils to occur. For given his middle knowledge, God knows all the myriad consequences throughout the rest of human history of any given evil. The revisionist God can only take into account such consequences as are immediate and predictable. Those might well be insufficient to justify his inaction in permitting the evil to go on. But as we saw in our discussion of the problem of evil, given divine middle knowledge, we are not in a good position to claim that God has no morally sufficient reasons for permitting any given evil to occur. God's reasons for permitting the evil might involve consequences that lie centuries into the future and are inextricably intertwined with other events in other parts of the world. For the same reason, our willingness or obligation to prevent or to stop certain evils that we observe does not automatically translate into God's obligation to prevent them. Hence, while we can rightly question the goodness of the revisionist's God for his lack of intervention, we are not in a position to judge a truly omniscient God. Molinism thus seems to provide the most illuminating and biblically faithful account of divine providence available today.

3 MIRACLE

It hardly needs to be demonstrated that the biblical narrative of divine action in the world is a narrative replete with miraculous events. God is conceived to bring about events that natural things, left to their own resources, would not bring about. Hence, **miracles** are able to function as signs of divine activity. "Here is an astonishing thing!" exclaims the man born blind, when confronted with the Pharisees' skepticism concerning Jesus' restoration of his sight,

"Never since the world began has it been heard that anyone opened the eyes of a person born blind. If this man were not from God, he could do nothing" (Jn 9:30, 32-33).

In order to differentiate between the customary way in which God acts and his special, miraculous action, theologians have traditionally distinguished within divine providence between God's *providentia ordinaria* (ordinary providence) and his *providentia extraordinaria* (extraordinary providence), the latter being identified with miracles. But our exposition of divine providence based on God's middle knowledge suggests a category of nonmiraculous, **special providence**, which it will be helpful to distinguish. We have in mind here events that are the product of natural causes but whose context is such as to suggest a special divine intention with regard to their occurrence. For example, just as the Israelites approach the Jordan River, a rockslide upstream blocks temporarily the water's flow, enabling them to cross into the Promised Land (Josh 3:14-17); or again, as Paul and Silas lie bound in prison for preaching the gospel, an earthquake occurs, springing the prison doors and unfastening their fetters (Acts 16:25-26). By means of his middle knowledge, God can providentially order the world so that the natural causes of such events are, as it were, ready and waiting to produce such events at the propitious time, perhaps in answer to prayers that God knew would be offered. Of course, if such prayers were not to be offered or the contingent course of events were to go differently, then God would have known this and so not arranged the natural causes, including human free volitions, to produce the special providential event. Events wrought by special providence are no more outside the course and capacity of nature than are events produced by God's ordinary providence, but the context of such events—such as their timing, their coincidental nature and so forth—points to a special divine intention to bring them about. Such events seem to deserve more appropriately than miracles the appellation *providentia extraordinaria.*

If, then, we distinguish miracles from both God's *providentia ordinaria* and *extraordinaria,* how should we characterize miracles? Since the dawning of modernity, miracles have been widely understood to be **violations of the laws of nature**. In his *Philosophical Dictionary* article "Miracles," for example, Voltaire states that according to accepted usage, "a miracle is the violation of mathematical, divine, immutable, eternal laws" and is therefore a contradiction. Voltaire is in fact quite right that such a definition is a contradiction, but this ought to have led him to conclude, not that miracles can thus be defined out of existence, but that the customary definition is defective. Indeed, an examination of the chief competing schools of thought concerning the notion of a **natural law** in fact reveals that on each theory the concept of a violation of a natural law is incoherent and that miracles need not be so defined. Broadly speaking, there are three main views of natural law today: the regularity theory, the nomic necessity theory and the causal dispositions theory.

According to the **regularity theory**, the "laws" of nature are not really laws at all, but just generalized descriptions of the way things happen in the world. They describe the regularities we observe in nature. Now since on such a theory a natural law is just a generalized description of *whatever* occurs in nature, it follows that no event that occurs can violate such a law. Instead, it just becomes part of the description. The law cannot be violated, because it describes in a certain generalized form everything that does happen in nature.

According to the **nomic necessity theory**, natural laws are not merely descriptive, but tell us what can and cannot happen in the natural world. They allow us to make certain counterfactual judgments, such as "If the density of the universe were sufficiently high, it would have recontracted long ago," which a purely descriptivist theory would not permit. Again, however, since natural laws are taken to be **universal inductive generalizations**, a violation of a natural law is no more possible on this theory than on the regularity theory. So long as natural laws are *universal* generalizations based on experience, they must take account of anything that happens and so would be revised should an event occur that the law does not encompass.

Of course, in practice proponents of such theories do not treat natural laws so rigidly. Rather, natural laws are assumed to have implicit in them certain assumptions about all things' being equal, so that a law states what is the case under the assumption that no other natural factors are interfering. When a scientific anomaly occurs, it is usually assumed that some unknown natural factors are interfering, so that the law is neither violated nor revised. But suppose the law fails to describe or predict accurately what happens because some *supernatural* factors are interfering? Clearly the implicit assumption of such laws is that no supernatural factors as well as no natural factors are interfering. If the law proves inaccurate in a particular case because God is acting, the law is neither violated nor revised. If God brings about some event that a law of nature fails to predict or describe, such an event cannot be characterized as a violation of a law of nature, since the law is valid only on the assumption that no supernatural factors in addition to the natural factors come into play.

On such theories, then, miracles ought to be defined as **naturally impossible events**, that is to say, events that cannot be produced by the natural causes operative at a certain time and place. Whether an event is a miracle is thus relative to a time and place. Given the natural causes operative at a certain time and place, for example, rain may be naturally inevitable or necessary, but on another occasion, rain may be naturally impossible. Of course, some events, say, the resurrection of Jesus, may be absolutely miraculous in that they are at every time and place beyond the productive capacity of natural causes.

According to the **causal dispositions theory**, things in the world have different natures or essences, which include their causal dispositions to affect other things in certain ways, and natural laws are metaphysically necessary truths about what causal dispositions are possessed by various natural kinds of things. For example, "Salt has a disposition to dissolve in water" would state a natural law. If, due to God's action, some salt failed to dissolve in water, the natural law is not violated, because it is still true that salt has such a disposition. As a result of things' causal dispositions, certain deterministic natural propensities exist in nature, and when such a propensity is not impeded (by God or some other free agent), then we can speak of a natural necessity. On this theory, an event that is naturally necessary must and does actually occur, since the natural propensity will automatically issue forth in the event if it is not impeded. By the same token, a naturally impossible event cannot and does not actually occur. Hence, a miracle cannot be characterized on this theory as a naturally impossible event. Rather, a miracle is an event that results from causal interference with a natural propensity that is so strong that only a supernatural agent could impede it. The concept of miracle is essentially the same as under the previous two theories, but one just cannot call a miracle "naturally impossible" as those terms are defined in this theory; perhaps we could adopt instead the nomenclature "physically impossible" to characterize miracles under such a theory.

On none of these theories, then, should miracles be understood as violations of the laws of nature. Rather, they are naturally (or physically) impossible events, events which at certain times and places cannot be produced by the relevant natural causes.

Now the question is, what could conceivably transform an event that is naturally impossible into a real historical event? Clearly, the answer is the personal God of theism. For if a transcendent, personal God exists, then he could cause events in the universe that could not be produced by causes within the universe. Given a God who created the universe, who conserves the world in being, and who is capable of acting freely, miracles are evidently possible. Indeed, if it is even (epistemically) possible that such a transcendent, personal God exists, then it is equally possible that he has acted miraculously in the universe. Only to the extent that one has good grounds for believing atheism to be true could one be rationally justified in denying the possibility of miracles. In this light, arguments for the impossibility of miracles based on defining them as violations of the laws of nature are vacuous.

The more interesting question concerns the **identification of miracles**: whether it is possible to identify any event as a miracle. On the one hand, it might be argued that a convincing demonstration that a purportedly miraculous event has occurred would only succeed in forcing us to revise natural law so as to accommodate the event in question. But as Swinburne has argued, a natural law is not abolished because of one exception; the anomaly must occur repeatedly whenever the conditions for it are present.[7] If an anomalous event occurs and we have reason to believe that this event would not occur again under similar circumstances, then the law in question will not be abandoned. One may regard an anomalous event as repeatable if another formulation of the natural law better accounts for the event in question and if it is no more complex than the original law. If any doubt exists, the scientist may conduct experiments to determine which formulation of the law proves more successful in predicting future phenomena. In a similar way, one would have good reason to regard an event as a nonrepeatable anomaly if the reformulated law were much more complicated than the original without yielding better new predictions or by predicting new phenomena unsuccessfully where the original formulation predicted successfully. If the original formulation remains successful in predicting all new phenomena as the data accumulate, while no reformulation does any better in predicting the phenomena and explaining the event in question, then the event should be regarded as a nonrepeatable anomaly. Hence, the admitted occurrence of a miraculous event would not serve to upset the natural law.

---

[7]R. G. Swinburne, "Miracles," *Philosophical Quarterly* 18 (1968): 321-23.

On the other hand, it might be urged that if a purportedly miraculous event were demonstrated to have occurred, we should conclude that the event occurred in accordance with **unknown natural causes** and laws. The question is, what serves to distinguish a genuine miracle from a mere scientific anomaly?

Here the **religio-historical context** of the event becomes crucial. A miracle without a context is inherently ambiguous. But if a purported miracle occurs in a significant religio-historical context, then the chances of its being a genuine miracle are increased. For example, if the miracles occur at a momentous time (say, a man's leprosy vanishing when Jesus speaks the words, "Be clean!") and do not recur regularly in history, and if the miracles are numerous and various, then the chances of their being the result of some unknown natural causes are reduced. In Jesus' case, moreover, his miracles and resurrection ostensibly took place in the context of and as the climax to his own unparalleled life and teachings and produced so profound an effect on his followers that they worshiped him as Lord.

The central miracle of the New Testament, the resurrection of Jesus, was, if it occurred, doubtlessly a miracle. In the first place, the resurrection so exceeds what we know of the productive capacity of natural causes that it can only be reasonably attributed to a supernatural cause. The more we learn about cell necrosis, the more evident it becomes that such an event is naturally impossible. If it were the effect of unknown natural causes, then its uniqueness in human history would be inexplicable. Secondly, the supernatural explanation is given immediately in the religio-historical context in which the event occurred. Jesus' resurrection was not merely an anomalous event, occurring without context; it came as the climax to Jesus' own life and teachings and serves as the divine vindication of Jesus' allegedly blasphemous claims for which he was crucified. We therefore have good reason to regard Jesus' resurrection, if it occurred, as truly miraculous. Thus, while it is, indeed, difficult to know in some cases whether a genuine miracle has occurred, that does not imply pessimism with respect to all cases.

But perhaps the very natural impossibility of a genuine miracle precludes our ever identifying an event as a miracle. As Hume notoriously argued, perhaps it is always more rational to believe that some mistake or deception is at play than to believe on the basis of testimony that a genuine miracle has occurred.[8] This conclusion is based on Hume's principle that it is always more probable that the testimony to a miracle is false than that the miracle occurred. But Hume's claim is doubly erroneous. First, it fails to take into account all the probabilities involved. Stimulated by Hume's original argument against miracles, there arose a discussion among probability theorists over what evidence is required in order to establish the occurrence of highly improbable events.[9] It was soon realized that if one simply weighed the probability of the event against the reliability of the witness, then we should be led into denying the occurrence of events which, though highly improbable, we reasonably know to have occurred. For

---

[8]David Hume, *An Enquiry Concerning Human Understanding*, ed. L. A. Selby-Bigge, 3d ed. rev. P. H. Nidditch (Oxford: Clarendon, 1975), chap. 10.

[9]See S. L. Zabell, "The Probabilistic Analysis of Testimony," *Journal of Statistical Planning and Inference* 20 (1988): 327-54; for an outstanding discussion see John Earman, *Hume's Abject Failure* (Oxford: Oxford University Press, 2000).

example, if on the morning news you hear reported that the pick in last night's lottery was 7492871, this is a report of an extraordinarily improbable event, one out of several million, and even if the morning news's accuracy is known to be 99.99%, the improbability of the event reported will swamp the probability of the witness's reliability, so that we should never believe such reports. In order to believe the report, Hume's principle would require us to have enough evidence in favor of the morning news' reliability to counterbalance the improbability of the winning pick, which is absurd.

Probability theorists saw that what also needs to be considered is the probability that if the reported event has *not* occurred, the witness's testimony is still the same as it is. Thus, to return to our example, the probability that the morning news would announce the pick as 7492871 if some other number had been chosen is so incredibly small, given that the newscasters had no preference for the announced number, that it counterbalances the high improbability of the event reported. What Hume would have to say in the case of the resurrection, for example, is that if Jesus did not rise from the dead then it is highly probable that we should have exactly the testimony we do to the facts of his empty tomb, postmortem appearances and the disciples' belief in his resurrection. But clearly if Jesus had not risen, then the testimonial evidence, rather than being what it is, might be to any of a wide range of envisionable scenarios. A further factor neglected by Hume is the remarkable increase in probability that results from multiple, independent testimony to some event. Charles Babbage, in his Ninth Bridgewater Treatise, points out that if two witnesses are each 99% reliable, then the odds of their both independently testifying falsely to some event are only one out of 10,000; the odds of three such witnesses' being wrong is one out of 1,000,000; and the odds of six such witnesses' being mistaken is one out of 1,000,000,000,000, which, he points out, is five times as great as the improbability that Hume assigns to the resurrection of Jesus. In fact, the cumulative power of independent witnesses is such that individually they could be *un*reliable more than 50% of the time and yet their testimony combine to make an event of apparently enormous improbability quite probable in light of their testimony. With respect to Jesus' resurrection, it is difficult to know how independent some of the witnesses are—though in the cases of people like Peter, James and Saul independence is well-established—but we have a similar accumulation of probability from the fact that the evidence of the empty tomb, the postmortem appearances and the disciples' belief in Jesus' resurrection are themselves three independent lines of evidence pointing to the fact of the resurrection.

In order to show that a miracle M has probably occurred on the basis of specific evidence E and our background information B, we shall need to show that Pr (M/B & E) > Pr (¬M/B & E). Even this needs some finessing, however. If we let M = the resurrection of Jesus, then we need not even show that the probability of the resurrection on the evidence and background information is greater than the probability of no resurrection on the same evidence and information. Rather, what we must show is that the probability of the resurrection is greater than any one of its alternatives. For the collective probability of all these alternatives taken together is meaningless, since the disjunction formed of all these alternatives is not itself an alternative. Thus the hypothesis of the resurrection will be preferable if it is more probable than any one of its alternatives.

The second problem with Hume's argument is that he incorrectly assumes that miracles are intrinsically highly improbable. With respect to the resurrection of Jesus, for example, there is no reason to think that the hypothesis "God raised Jesus from the dead" is highly improbable relative to our background information. What is improbable relative to our background information is the hypothesis "Jesus rose naturally from the dead." Given what we know of cell necrosis, that hypothesis is fantastically, even unimaginably, improbable. Conspiracy theories, apparent death theories, hallucination theories, twin brother theories—almost any hypothesis, however unlikely, seems more probable than the hypothesis that all the cells in Jesus' corpse spontaneously came back to life again. But such naturalistic hypotheses are not more probable than the hypothesis that God raised Jesus from the dead. The evidence for the laws of nature relevant in this case makes it probable that a resurrection from the dead is naturally impossible, which renders improbable the hypothesis that Jesus rose naturally from the grave. But such evidence is simply irrelevant to the probability of the hypothesis that God raised Jesus from the dead. There is no reason a priori to expect that it is more probable that the testimony to the resurrection is false than that the hypothesis of resurrection is true.

Although it would be fair to say that the fallaciousness of Hume's reasoning has been recognized by the majority of philosophers writing on the subject today, still a widespread assumption persists that if historical inquiry is to be feasible, then one must adopt a sort of **methodological naturalism** as a fundamental historiographical principle (see chap. 17). According to this outlook, historians must adopt as a methodological principle a sort of "historical naturalism" that excludes the supernatural.

This viewpoint is simply a restatement of Ernst Troeltsch's **principle of analogy**.[10] According to Troeltsch, one of the most basic of historiographical principles is that the past does not differ essentially from the present. Though events of the past are of course not the same events as those of the present, they must be the same *in kind* if historical investigation is to be possible. Troeltsch realized that this principle was incompatible with miraculous events and that any history written on this principle will be skeptical with regard to the historicity of the events of the gospels.

Pannenberg, however, has persuasively argued that Troeltsch's principle of analogy cannot be legitimately employed to banish from the realm of history all nonanalogous events.[11] Properly defined, analogy means that in a situation that is unclear, the facts ought to be understood in terms of known experience; but Troeltsch has elevated the principle to constrict all past events to purely natural events. But that an event bursts all analogies cannot be used to dispute its historicity. When, for example, myths, legends, illusions and the like are dis-

---

[10]Ernst Troeltsch, "Über historische und dogmatische Methode in der Theologie," in *Gesammelte Schriften* (Tübingen: J. C. B. Mohr, 1913), 2:729-53.

[11]Wolfhart Pannenberg, "Redemptive Event and History," in *Basic Questions in Theology*, trans. G. H. Kehm (Philadelphia: Fortress, 1970), 1:40-50.

missed as unhistorical, it is not because they are nonanalogous, but because they *are* analogous to present forms of consciousness having no objective referent. When an event is said to have occurred for which no analogy exists, its reality cannot be automatically dismissed; to do this we should require an analogy to some known form of consciousness lacking an objective referent that would suffice to explain the situation. Pannenberg has thus upended Troeltsch's principle of analogy such that it is not the *want* of an analogy that shows an event to be unhistorical, but the *presence* of a positive analogy to known thought forms that shows a purportedly miraculous event to be unhistorical. Thus he has affirmed that if the Easter traditions were shown to be essentially secondary constructions analogous to common comparative religious models, the Easter appearances were shown to correspond completely to the model of hallucinations, and the empty tomb tradition were evaluated as a late legend, then the resurrection would be subject to evaluation as unhistorical. In this way, the lack of an analogy to present experience says nothing for or against the historicity of an event. Troeltsch's formulation of the principle of analogy attempts to squeeze the past into the mold of the present without providing any warrant for doing so. It thus destroys genuine historical reasoning, since the historian must be open to the uniqueness of the events of the past and cannot exclude a priori the possibility of events like the resurrection simply because they do not conform to his present experience. But Pannenberg's formulation of the principle preserves the analogous nature of the past to the present or to the known, thus making the investigation of history possible, without thereby sacrificing the integrity of the past or distorting it.

Given, then, the God of creation and providence described in classical theism, miracles are possible and, when occurring under certain conditions, plausibly identifiable.

CHAPTER SUMMARY

The biblical doctrine of creation may be explicated in terms of God's bringing something into being at a certain time without a material cause. Conservation is God's action on an entity to preserve it in being from one time to another. Both these notions involve commitment to an A-theory of time. God's timeless or tenseless production of an entity in being may be referred to as his sustaining that entity. God's creation of the world plausibly involved a creation of time as well. Given his real relation to the world, God undergoes extrinsic change in creating the world and is therefore temporal since the beginning of time. Without the world God is most plausibly thought of as timeless.

The most adequate reconciliation of divine sovereignty and human freedom is to be found in a Molinist doctrine of providence based on God's middle knowledge and simultaneous concurrence. Logically prior to his creative decree God knows what every possible free creature would do in any circumstances in which God might place him. By decreeing to place particular creatures in particular circumstances God providentially orders a world and by concurring with the actions of creatures God causes everything that happens. Everything that occurs does so either by God's will or permission. God can thus so order the world that even sinful actions of creatures, which God does not positively will, turn out for the achievement of God's ultimate ends.

Miracles are to be distinguished from God's special providences, which are unusually propitious events having secondary causes. Miracles are events that do not have secondary causes but are produced directly by God. On none of the current theories of natural laws should miracles be understood as violations of the laws of nature. Rather, they are events beyond the productive capacity of the natural causes extant at the time and place at which the event occurs. Given the God of classical theism, miracles are obviously possible. Hume's argument against the identification of a miracle neglects to take into account the probability that the evidence should be just as it is in a particular case if the miracle did not occur; moreover, he wrongly assumes miracles to be intrinsically improbable. Troeltsch's appeal to methodological naturalism in history is subverted by a proper understanding of analogy: events are deemed unhistorical, not because they are nonanalogous, but because they are analogous to present forms of consciousness lacking an objective referent.

CHECKLIST OF BASIC TERMS AND CONCEPTS
absolute intentions
causal dispositions theory
change
comes into being
conditional intentions
conservation
continuing creation
counterfactuals of divine freedom
creatio continuans
creatio ex nihilo
creatio originans
creation
doctrine of pre-motion
identification of miracles
material cause
methodological naturalism
miracles
natural law
naturally impossible events
nomic necessity theory
occasionalism
principle of analogy
providence
providentia extraordinaria
providentia ordinaria
real relation
regularity theory
religio-historical context

secondary causation
simultaneous concurrence
sovereignty
special providence
sustenance
universal inductive generalizations
unknown natural causes
violations of the laws of nature

29

CHRISTIAN DOCTRINES
I
The Trinity

Let me ask of my reader, wherever, alike with myself,
he is certain, there to go on with me;
wherever, alike with myself, he hesitates,
there to join with me in inquiring;
wherever he recognizes himself to be in error,
there to return to me; wherever he recognizes me to be so,
there to call me back. . . . And I would make this pious and safe agreement, . . .
above all, in the case of those who inquire into the unity of the Trinity,
of the Father and the Son and the Holy Spirit;
because in no other subject is error more dangerous,
or inquiry more laborious, or the discovery of truth more profitable.
AUGUSTINE ON THE TRINITY 1.3.5

1 INTRODUCTION

One of the most noteworthy developments in contemporary philosophy of religion has been the ingress of Christian philosophers into areas normally considered the province of systematic theologians. In particular, many Christian philosophers have taken up a share of the task of formulating and defending coherent statements of Christian doctrine. In the next three chapters we shall examine briefly a few of the most important peculiarly Christian doctrines which have attracted philosophical attention.

It is remarkable that despite the fact that its founder and earliest protagonists were to a man monotheistic Jews, Christianity, while zealous to preserve Jewish monotheism, came to enunciate a nonunitarian concept of God. On the Christian view, God is not a single person, as traditionally conceived, but is **tripersonal**. There are three persons, denominated the **Father**, the **Son** and the **Holy Spirit**, who deserve to be called God, and yet there is but one God, not three. This startling rethinking of Jewish **monotheism** doubtless grew out of reflection on the radical self-understanding of Jesus of Nazareth himself and on the charismatic experience of the early church. Although many New Testament critics have called into question the **historical Jesus'** use of explicit christological titles, a very strong historical case can be made for **Jesus' self-understanding** as the Son of man (a divine-human eschatological figure in

Daniel 7) and the unique Son of God (Mt 11:27; Mk 13:32; Lk 20:9-19). More-over, something of a consensus has emerged among New Testament critics that in his teachings and actions—such as his assertion of personal authority, his re-vising of the divinely given Mosaic Law, his proclamation of the in-breaking of God's reign or kingdom into history in his person, his performing miracles and exorcisms as signs of the advent of that kingdom, his messianic pretensions to restore Israel, and his claim to forgive sins—Jesus enunciated an **implicit Christology,** putting himself in God's place. The German theologian Horst Georg Pöhlmann asserts,

> This unheard of claim to authority, as it comes to expression in the antitheses of the Sermon on the Mount, for example, is implicit Christology, since it presup-poses a unity of Jesus with God that is deeper than that of all men, namely a unity of essence. This . . . claim to authority is explicable only from the side of his deity. This authority only God himself can claim. With regard to Jesus there are only two possible modes of behavior; either to believe that in him God encounters us or to nail him to the cross as a blasphemer. *Tertium non datur.*[1]

Moreover, the post-Easter church continued to experience the presence and power of Christ among them, despite his physical absence. Jesus himself had been a charismatic, imbued with the Spirit of God; and the Jesus movement which followed him was likewise a charismatic fellowship that experienced indi-vidually and corporately the supernatural filling and gifts of the Holy Spirit. The Spirit was thought to stand in the place of the risen and ascended Christ and to continue in his temporary absence his ministry to his people (Jn 7:39; 14:16-17; 15:26; 16:7-16; Rom 8:9-10; Gal 4:6).

In the pages of the New Testament, then, we find the raw data that the doctrine of the Trinity later sought to systematize. The New Testament church remained faithful to its heritage of Jewish monotheism in affirming that there is only one God (Mk 12:29; Rom 3:29-30; 1 Cor 8:4; 1 Tim 2:5; Jas 2:19). In accord with the portrayal of God in the Old Testament (Is 63:16) and the teaching of Jesus (Mt 6:9), Christians also conceived of God as Father, a distinct person from Jesus his Son (Mt 11:27; 26:39; Mk 1:9-11; Jn 17:5-26). In-deed, in New Testament usage, *God* (*ho theos*) typically refers to God the Fa-ther (e.g., Gal 4:4-6). Now this occasioned a problem for the New Testament church: If *God* designates the Father, how can one affirm the deity of Christ without identifying him as the Father? In response to this difficulty the New Testament writers refer to Jesus principally as "Lord" (*kyrios*), the same word which the Septuagint translators used in place of God's name Yahweh. The New Testament writers applied to Jesus Old Testament proof texts concerning Yahweh (e.g., Rom 10:9, 13). Indeed, the confession "Jesus is Lord" was the central confession of the early church (1 Cor 12:3), and they not only called Jesus "Lord" but also addressed him in prayer as Lord (1 Cor 16:22). This dif-ference-in-sameness can lead to odd locutions like Paul's confession "yet for us there is one God, the Father, from whom are all things and for whom we exist, and one Lord, Jesus Christ, through whom are all things and through whom we exist" (1 Cor 8:6).

---

[1]Horst Georg Pöhlmann, *Abriss der Dogmatik*, 3d rev. ed. (Gütersloh, Germany: Gerd Mohn, 1980), p. 230.

Furthermore, the New Testament church, not content with use of divine nomenclature for Christ, also ascribed to him God's role as the Creator and Sustainer of all reality apart from God (Col 1:15-20; Heb 1:1-4; Jn 1:1-3). In places restraint is thrown to the winds, and Jesus is explicitly affirmed to be (*ho*) *theos* (Jn 1:1, 18; 20:28; Rom 9:5; Tit 2:13; Heb 1:8-12; 1 Jn 5:20). Noting that the oldest Christian sermon, the oldest account of a Christian martyr, the oldest pagan report of the church, and the oldest liturgical prayer (1 Cor 16:22) all refer to Christ as Lord and God, Jaroslav Pelikan, the great historian of Christian thought, concludes, "Clearly it was the message of what the church believed and taught that 'God' was an appropriate name for Jesus Christ."[2]

Finally, the Holy Spirit, who is also identified as God (Acts 5:3-4) and the Spirit of God (Mt 12:28; 1 Cor 6:11), is conceived as personally distinct from both the Father and the Son (Mt 28:19; Lk 11:13; Jn 14:26; 15:26; Rom 8:26-27; 2 Cor 13:13; 1 Pet 1:1-2). As these and other passages make clear, the Holy Spirit is not an impersonal force, but a personal reality who teaches and intercedes for believers, who possesses a mind, who can be grieved and lied to, and who is ranked as an equal partner with the Father and the Son.

In short, the New Testament church was sure that only one God exists. But they also believed that the Father, Son and Holy Spirit, while personally distinct, all deserve to be called God. The challenge facing the postapostolic church was how to make sense of these affirmations. How could the Father, Son and Holy Spirit each be God without there being either three Gods or only one person?

2 HISTORICAL BACKGROUND

The stage for both the later **trinitarian controversy** and the **christological controversies**, in which the doctrines of the Trinity and Incarnation were forged and given creedal form, was set by the early **Greek Apologists** of the second century, such as Justin Martyr, Tatian, Theophilus and Athenagoras. Connecting the divine Word (*Logos*) of the prologue of John's Gospel (Jn 1:1-5) with the divine **Logos** (Reason) as it played a role in the system of the Hellenistic Jewish philosopher Philo of Alexandria (c. 20 B.C.-c. A.D. 50), the Apologists sought to explain Christian doctrine in Philonic categories. For good or ill, their appropriation of Hellenistic thought is one of the most striking examples of the profound and enduring influence of philosophy on Christian theology. For Philo, the Logos was God's reason, which is the creative principle behind the creation of the world and which, in turn, informs the world with its rational structure. Similarly, for the Christian Apologists, God the Father, existing alone without the world, had within himself his Word or Reason or Wisdom (cf. Prov 8:22-31), which somehow proceeded forth from him, like a spoken word from a speaker's mind, to become a distinct individual who created the world and ultimately became incarnate as Jesus Christ. The procession of the Logos

2.1
LOGOS
CHRISTOLOGY

---

[2]Jaroslav Pelikan, *The Christian Tradition: A History of the Development of Doctrine*, vol. 1: *The Emergence of the Catholic Tradition (100-600)* (Chicago and London: University of Chicago Press, 1971), p. 173.

from the Father was variously conceived as taking place either at the moment of creation or, alternatively, eternally. Although christological concerns occupied center stage, the Holy Spirit too might be understood to proceed from God the Father's mind. Here is how Athenagoras describes it:

> The Son of God is the Word of the Father in Ideal Form and energizing power; for in his likeness and through him all things came into existence, which presupposes that the Father and the Son are one. Now since the Son is in the Father and the Father in the Son by a powerful unity of Spirit, the Son of God is the mind and reason of the Father. . . . He is the first begotten of the Father. The term is used not because he came into existence (for God, who is eternal mind, had in himself his word or reason from the beginning, since he was eternally rational) but because he came forth to serve as Ideal Form and Energizing Power for everything material. . . . The . . . Holy Spirit . . . we regard as an effluence of God which flows forth from him and returns like a ray of the sun. (*A Plea for the Christians* 10)

According to this doctrine, then, there is one God, but he is not an undifferentiated unity. Rather, certain aspects of his mind become expressed as distinct individuals. The Logos doctrine of the Apologists thus involves a fundamental reinterpretation of the fatherhood of God: God is not merely the Father of mankind or even, especially, of Jesus of Nazareth; rather, he is the Father from whom the Logos is begotten before all worlds. Christ is not merely the only-begotten Son of God in virtue of his Incarnation; rather, he is begotten of the Father even in his preincarnate divinity.

2.2
MODALISM

The Logos-doctrine of the Greek Apologists was taken up into Western theology by Irenaeus, who identifies God's Word with the Son and his Wisdom with the Holy Spirit (*Against Heresies* 4.20.3; cf. 2.30.9). During the following century a quite different conception of the divine personages emerged in contrast to the Logos doctrine. Noetus, Praxeus and Sabellius espoused a **unitarian** view of God, variously called **modalism, monarchianism,** or **Sabellianism,** according to which the Son and Spirit are not distinct individuals from the Father. Either it was the Father who became incarnate, suffered and died—the Son being at most the human aspect of Christ—or else the one God sequentially assumed three roles as Father, Son and Holy Spirit in relation to his creatures. In his refutation of modalism, *Against Praxeas*, the North African church father Tertullian brought greater precision to many of the ideas and much of the terminology later adopted in the creedal formulations of the doctrine of the Trinity. While anxious to preserve the divine **monarchy** (a term employed by the Greek Apologists to designate monotheism), Tertullian insisted that we dare not ignore the divine **economy** (a term borrowed from Irenaeus), by which Tertullian seems to mean the way in which the one God exists. The error of the monarchians or modalists is their "thinking that one cannot believe in one only God in any other way than by saying that the Father, the Son, and the Holy Spirit are the very selfsame person." But while "all are of one, by unity (that is) of substance," Tertullian insists that

> the mystery of the economy . . . distributes the unity into a Trinity, placing in their order the three persons—the Father, the Son and the Holy Spirit: three, however, not in condition, but in degree; not in substance, but in form; not in

power, but in aspect; yet of one substance, and of one condition, and of one power, inasmuch as He is one God, from whom these degrees and forms and aspects are reckoned, under the name of the Father, and of the Son, and of the Holy Spirit. (*Against Praxeas* 2)

In saying that the Father, Son and Holy Spirit are one in **substance**, Tertullian employs the word *substance* in both the senses explained by Aristotle. First, there is, as Tertullian affirms, just "one God," one thing which is God. But Tertullian also means that the three distinct persons share the same essential **nature**. Thus, in his exegesis of the monarchian proof text "I and my Father are one" (Jn 10:30), Tertullian points out (1) that the plural subject and verb intimate that there are two entities, namely, two **persons**, involved, but (2) that the predicate is an abstract (not a personal) noun—*unum*, not *unus*. He comments, "*Unum*, a neuter term, . . . does not imply singularity of number, but unity of essence, likeness, conjunction, affection on the Father's part, . . . and submission on the Son's. . . . When He says, 'I and my Father are one' in essence—*unum*—He shows that there are two, whom He puts on an equality and unites in one" (22).

So when Tertullian says that the one substance is distributed into three forms or aspects, he is not affirming modalism, but the diversity of three persons sharing the same nature. Indeed, he is so bold in affirming the distinctness of the persons, even calling them "three beings" (13; cf. 22), that he seems at times to court **tritheism**. Comparing the Father and the Son to the sun and a sunbeam, he declares, "For although I make not two suns, still I shall reckon both the sun and its ray to be as much two things and two forms of one undivided substance, as God and His Word, as the Father and the Son" (13). Thus he conceives the Son to be "really a substantive being, by having a substance of his own, in such a way that he may be regarded as an objective thing and a person, and so able . . . to make two, the Father and the Son, God and the Word" (7). Tertullian even seems to think of the Father and Son as distinct parcels of the same spiritual stuff out of which, in his idiosyncratic view, he believed God to be constituted (7).

Conventional wisdom has it that in affirming that God is three persons, church fathers like Tertullian meant at most three **individuals**, not three persons in the modern, psychological sense of three **centers of self-consciousness**. We shall return to this issue when we look at the creedal formulation of trinitarian doctrine, but for now we may note that an examination of Tertullian's statements suggests that such a claim is greatly exaggerated. In a remarkable passage aimed at illustrating the doctrine of the Son as the immanent Logos in the Father's mind, Tertullian invites his reader, who, he says, is created in the image and likeness of God, to consider the role of reason in the reader's own self-reflective thinking. "Observe, then, that when you are silently conversing with yourself, this very process is carried on within you by your reason, which meets you with a word at every movement of your thought, at every impulse of your conception" (5). Tertullian envisions one's own reason as a sort of dialogue partner when one is engaged in self-reflective thought. No doubt every one of us has carried on such an internal dialogue, which requires not merely consciousness but self-consciousness. Tertullian's point is that "in a certain sense, the word is a second person within you" through which you generate thought. He realizes, of course, that no human being is literally two persons, but he holds that "all this is much more fully transacted in God," who possesses his immanent Logos even when he is silent. Or again, in proving the personal distinctness of the Father and the Son, Tertullian appeals to scriptural passages employing first- and second-person indexical words distinguishing Father and Son. Alluding to Psalm 2:7, Tertullian says to the modalist, "If you want me to believe Him to be both the Father and the Son, show me some other passage where it is declared, 'The Lord said unto himself, I am my own Son, today I have begotten myself'" (11). He quotes numerous passages that, through their use of **personal indexicals**, illustrate the I-Thou relationship in which the persons of the Trinity stand to one another. He challenges the modalist to explain how a Being who is absolutely one and singular can use first-person plural pronouns, as in "Let us make man in our image." Tertullian clearly thinks of the Father, Son and Spirit as individuals capable of employing first-person indexicals and addressing one another with second-person indexicals, which entails that they are self-conscious persons. Hence, "in these few quotations the distinction of persons in the Trinity is clearly set forth" (11). Tertullian thus implicitly affirms that the persons of the Trinity are three distinct, self-conscious individuals.

The only qualification that might be made to this picture lies in a vestige of the Apologists' Logos doctrine in Tertullian's theology. He not only accepts their view that there are relations of derivation among the persons of the Trinity, but that these relations are not eternal. The Father he calls "the fountain of the Godhead" (29); "the Father is the entire substance, but the Son is a derivation and portion of the whole" (9). The Father exists eternally with his immanent Logos; and at creation, before the beginning of all things, the Son proceeds from the Father and so becomes his first begotten Son, through whom the world is created (19). Thus the Logos only becomes the Son of God when he proceeds from the Father as a substantive being (7). Tertullian is fond of analogies such as the sunbeam emitted by the sun or the river by the spring (8, 22) to illustrate the oneness of substance of the Son as he proceeds from the Father. The Son, then, is "God of God" (15). Similarly, the Holy Spirit proceeds from the Father through the Son (4). It seems that Tertullian would consider the Son and Spirit to be distinct persons only after their procession from the Father (7), but it is clear that he insists on their personal distinctness from at least that point.

Through the efforts of church fathers like Tertullian, Hippolytus, Origen and Novatian, the church came to reject modalism as a proper understanding of God and to affirm the distinctness of the three persons called Father, Son and Holy Spirit. During the ensuing century, the church was confronted with a challenge from the opposite end of the spectrum: Arianism, which affirmed the personal distinctness of the Father and the Son, but only at the sacrifice of the Son's deity.

2.3
ARIANISM

In 319 an Alexandrian presbyter named Arius began to propagate his doctrine that the Son was not of the same substance with the Father, but was rather created by the Father before the beginning of the world. This marked the beginning of the great trinitarian controversy, which lasted through the end of the century and gave us the **Nicene** and **Constantinopolitan Creeds**. Although Alexandrian theologians like Origen, in contrast to Tertullian, had argued that the begetting of the Logos from the Father did not have a beginning but is from eternity, the reason most theologians found Arius's doctrine unacceptable was not, as Arius fancied, so much because he affirmed "The Son has a beginning, but God is without beginning" (*Letter to Eusebius of Nicomedia* 4-5). Rather, what was objectionable was that Arius denied even that the Logos preexisted immanently in God before being begotten or was in any sense from the substance of the Father, so that his beginning was not, in fact, a begetting but a creation *ex nihilo* and that therefore the Son is a creature. As Athanasius, bishop of Alexandria, was later to protest, on Arius's view, God without the Son lacked his Word and his Wisdom, which is blasphemous (*Orations Against the Arians* 1.6.17), and the Son is "a creature and a work, not proper to the Father's essence" (1.3.9). In 325 a council at Antioch condemned anyone who says that the Son is a creature or originated or made or not truly an offspring or that once he did not exist; later that year the ecumenical **Council of Nicaea** issued its creedal formulation of trinitarian belief.

The creed states,

> We believe in one God, the Father All Governing, creator of all things visible and invisible;
>
> And in one Lord Jesus Christ, the Son of God, begotten of the Father as only begotten, that is, from the essence of the Father, God from God, Light from Light, true God from true God, begotten not created, of the same essence as the Father, through whom all things came into being, both in heaven and in earth; Who for us men and for our salvation came down and was incarnate, becoming human. He suffered and the third day he rose, and ascended into the heavens. And he will come to judge both the living and the dead.
>
> And [we believe] in the Holy Spirit.
>
> But, those who say, Once he was not, or he was not before his generation, or he came to be out of nothing, or who assert that he, the Son of God, is a different *hypostasis* or *ousia*, or that he is a creature, or changeable, or mutable, the Catholic and Apostolic Church anathematizes them.

Several features of this statement deserve comment: (1) The Son (and by implication the Holy Spirit) is declared to be of the same essence (***homoousios***) as the Father. This is to say that the Son and Father both share the same divine nature. Therefore, the Son cannot be a creature, having, as Arius claimed, a nature different (***heteroousios***) from the divine nature. (2) The Son is declared to be begotten, not made. This anti-Arian affirmation is said with respect to Christ's divine nature, not his human nature, and represents the legacy of the old Logos Christology. In the creed of Eusebius of Caesarea, used as a draft of the Nicene statement, the word *Logos* stood where *Son* stands in the Nicene Creed, and the Logos is declared to be "begotten of the Father before all ages." The condemnations appended to the Nicene Creed similarly imply that this begetting is eternal. Athanasius explains through a subtle word play that while both the Father and the Son are *agenetos* (that is, did not come into being at some moment), nevertheless only the Father is *agennetos* (that is, unbegotten), whereas the Son is *gennetos* (begotten) eternally from the Father

(*Four Discourses Against the Arians* 1.9.31). (3) The condemnation of those who say that Christ "is a different **hypostasis** or **ousia**" from the Father occasioned great confusion in the church. For Western, Latin-speaking theologians the Greek word *hypostasis* was etymologically parallel to, and hence synonymous with, the Latin *substantia* ("substance"). Therefore, they denied a plurality of *hypostaseis* in God. Although the Nicene Creed was drafted in Greek, the meaning of the terms is Western. For many Eastern, Greek-speaking theologians *hypostasis* and *ousia* were not synonymous. *Ousia* meant "substance," and *hypostasis* designated a concrete individual, a property-bearer. As Gregory of Nyssa, one of three Cappadocian church fathers renowned for their explication of the Nicene Creed, explains, a *hypostasis* is "what subsists and is specially and peculiarly indicated by [a] name," for example, Paul, in contrast to *ousia*, which refers to the universal nature common to things of a certain type—for example, man (*Epistle* 38.2-3). The Father and Son, while sharing the same substance, are clearly distinct *hypostaseis*, since they have different properties (only the Father for example, has the property of being unbegotten). Therefore, the Nicene Creed's assertion that the Father and Son are the same *hypostasis* sounded like modalism to many Eastern thinkers. After decades of intense debate, this terminological confusion was cleared up at the Council of Alexandria in 362, which affirmed *homoousios* but allowed that there are three divine *hypostaseis*.

What were these *hypostaseis*, all sharing the divine nature? The unanimous answer of orthodox theologians was that they were three *persons*. It is customarily said, as previously mentioned, that we must not read this affirmation anachronistically, as employing the modern psychological concept of a person. This caution must, however, be qualified. While *hypostasis* does not mean "person," nevertheless a rational *hypostasis* comes very close to what we mean by a "person." For Aristotle the generic essence of man is captured by the phrase "rational animal." Animals have souls but lack rationality, and it is the property of rationality that serves to distinguish human beings from other animals. Thus a rational *hypostasis* can only be what we call a person. It is noteworthy that Gregory of Nyssa's illustration of three *hypostaseis* having one substance is Peter, James and John, all exemplifying the same human nature (*To Ablabius That There Are Not Three Gods*). How else can this be taken than as an intended illustration of three persons with one nature? Moreover, the Cappadocians ascribe to the three divine *hypostaseis* the properties constitutive of personhood, such as mutual knowledge, love and volition, even if, as Gregory of Nazianzus emphasizes, these are always in concord and so incapable of being severed from one another (*Third Theological Oration: On the Son* 2). Thus Gregory boasts that his flock, unlike the Sabellians, "worship the Father and the Son and the Holy Spirit, One Godhead; God the Father, God the Son and (do not be angry) God the Holy Spirit, One Nature in Three Personalities, intellectual, perfect, self-existent, numerically separate, but not separate in Godhead" (*Oration* 33.16). The ascription of personal properties is especially evident in the robust defense of the full equality of the Holy Spirit with the Father and the Son as a divine *hypostasis*. Basil states that the Holy Spirit is not only "incorporeal, purely immaterial, and indivisible," but that "we are compelled to direct our thoughts on high, and to think of an intelligent being, boundless in power" (*On the Holy Spirit* 9.22). Quoting 1 Corinthians 2:11, he compares God's Spirit to the human spirit in each of us (16.40) and states that in his sanctifying work the Holy Spirit makes people spiritual "by fellowship with Himself" (9.23). The Cappadocians would have resisted fiercely any attempt to treat the Holy Spirit as an impersonal, divine force. Thus their intention was to affirm that there really are three persons in a rich psychological sense who are the one God.

In sum, while modalism affirmed the equal deity of the three persons at the expense of their personal distinctness, orthodox Christians maintained both the equal deity and personal distinctness of the three persons. Moreover, they did so while claiming to maintain the commitment of all parties to monotheism. There exists only one God, who is three persons, Father, Son and Holy Spirit.

Does the doctrine of the Trinity make sense? Enlightenment thinkers denounced the doctrine as incoherent, but during the twentieth century many theologians came to a fresh appreciation of trinitarian theology, and in recent decades a number of Christian philosophers have sought to formulate philosophically defensible versions of the doctrine of the Trinity. Two broad models or approaches are typically identified: **social trinitarianism**, which lays greater emphasis on the diversity of the persons, and **Latin trinitarianism**, which places greater stress on the unity of God. This nomenclature, however, is misleading, since the great Latin church fathers Tertullian and Hilary were both social trinitarians, as was Athanasius, a fount of Latin theology. Therefore, we shall instead contrast social trinitarianism with what one wag has called **anti social trinitarianism**. The central commitment of social trinitarianism is that in God there are three distinct centers of self-consciousness, each with its proper intellect and will. The central commitment of anti social trinitarianism is that there is only one God, whose unicity of intellect and will is not compromised by the diversity of persons. Social trinitarianism threatens to veer into tritheism; anti social trinitarianism is in danger of lapsing into unitarianism.

2.4
MODELS OF
THE TRINITY

Social trinitarians typically look to the Cappadocian Fathers as their champions. As we have seen, they explain the difference between substance and *hypostasis* as the difference between a generic essence, say, *man*, and particular instances of it, in this case, several men like Peter, James and John. This leads to an obvious question: if Peter, James and John are three men each having the same nature, then why would not the Father, Son and Holy Spirit similarly be three Gods each having the divine nature?

In his letter *To Ablabius That There Are Not Three Gods*, Gregory of Nyssa struggled to answer this question. He emphasizes the primacy of the universal, which is one and unchangeable in each of the three men. This is merely to highlight a **universal property**, which Gregory holds to be one in its many instantiations, rather than the **property instance** of that universal in each man. Gregory, like Plato, thinks of the universal as the primary reality. He advises that rather than speaking of three Gods, we ought instead to speak of one man. But this answer solves nothing. Even if we think of the universal as the primary reality, still it is undeniable that there are three instances of that reality who, in the one case, are three distinct men, as is obvious from the fact that one man can cease to exist without the others ceasing to do so. Similarly, even if the one divine nature is the primary reality, still it is undeniably exemplified by three *hypostaseis*, who should each be an instance of deity.

In order to block the inference to three Gods, Gregory also appeals to the ineffability of the divine nature and to the fact that all the operations of the Trinity toward the world involve the participation of all three persons. But even granted his assumptions, one cannot justifiably conclude that there are not three cooperatively acting individuals who each share this ineffable nature, and any remaining indistinguishability seems purely epistemic, not ontological.

Gregory goes on to stress that every operation between God and creation finds its origin in the Father, proceeds through the Son and is perfected by the Holy Spirit. Because of this, he claims, we cannot speak of those who conjointly and inseparably carry out these operations as three Gods. But Gregory's inference seems unjustified. Simply because we creatures cannot distinguish the persons who carry out such operations, one cannot therefore conclude that there are not three instances of the divine nature at work; moreover, the very fact that these operations originate in the Father, proceed through the Son and are perfected by the Spirit seems to prove that there are three distinct if inseparable operations in every work of the Trinity toward creation.

Finally, Gregory appears to deny that the divine nature can be multiply instantiated. He identifies the principle of individuation as "bodily appearance, and size, and place, and difference in figure and color"—"That which is not thus circumscribed is not enumerated, and that which is not enumerated cannot be contemplated in multitude." Therefore, the divine nature "does not admit in its own case the signification of multitude." But if this is Gregory's argument, not only is it incompatible with there being three Gods, but it precludes there being even one God. The divine nature would be uninstantiable, since there is no principle to individuate it. If it cannot be enumerated, there cannot even be one. On the other hand, if Gregory's argument intends merely to show that there is just one generic divine nature, not many, then he has simply proved too little: for the universal nature may be one, but multiply instantiated. Given that there are three *hypostaseis* in the Godhead, distinguished according to Gregory by the intratrinitarian relations, then there should be three Gods. The most pressing task of contemporary social trinitarians is to find some more convincing answer to why, on their view, there are not three Gods.

Anti social trinitarians typically look to Latin-speaking theologians like Augustine and Aquinas as their champions. To a considerable extent the appeal to Augustine rests on a misinterpretation that results from taking in isolation his analogies of the Trinity in the human mind, such as the lover, the beloved and love itself (*On the Trinity* 8.10.14; 9.2.2) or memory, understanding and will (or love) (10.11.17-18). Augustine explicitly states that the persons of the Trinity are not identified with these features of God's mind; rather, they are "an image of the Trinity in man" (14.8.11; 15.8.14). "Do we," he asks, "in such manner also see the Trinity that is in God?" He answers, "Doubtless we either do not at all understand and behold the invisible things of God by those things that are made, or if we behold them at all, we do not behold the Trinity in them" (15.7.10). In particular, Augustine realizes that these features are not each identical to a person but rather are features which any single human person possesses (15.7.11). Identifying the Father, Son and Holy Spirit with the divine memory, understanding and love, Augustine recognizes, would lead to the absurd conclusion that the Father knows himself only by the Son or loves himself only by the Holy Spirit, as though the Son were the understanding of the Father and the Spirit, and the Father the memory of the Spirit and the Son! Rather, memory, understanding and will (or love) must belong to each of the individual persons (15.7.12). Augustine concludes with the reflection that having found in one human person an image of the Trinity, he had desired to illuminate the relation among the three divine persons; but in the end three things which belong to one person cannot suit the three persons of the Trinity (15.24.45).

Anti social trinitarians frequently interpret Augustine to hold that the persons of the Trinity just are various relations subsisting in God. But this is not what Augustine says (5.3.4—5.5.6). Arians had objected that if the Father is essentially unbegotten and the Son essentially begotten, then the Father and Son cannot share the same essence or substance (*homoousios*). In response to this ingenious objection Augustine claims that the distinction between Father and Son is a matter neither of different essential properties nor of different accidental properties. Rather, the persons are distinguished in virtue of the relations in which they stand. Because "Father" and "Son" are relational terms implying the existence of something else, Augustine thinks that properties like *begotten by God* cannot belong to anything's essence. He evidently assumes that only intrinsic properties go to constitute something's essence. But if *being begotten* is not part of the Son's essence, is it not accidental to him? No, says Augustine, for it is eternally and immutably the case for the Son to be begotten. Augustine's answer is not adequate, however, since eternality and immutability are not sufficient for necessity; there could still be possible worlds in which the person who in the actual world is the Father does not beget a Son and so is not a Father. Augustine should instead claim that *Father* and *Son* imply internal relations between the persons of the Godhead, so that there is no possible world in which they do not stand in that relation. The Father and Son would share the same intrinsic essential properties, but they would differ in virtue of their differing relational properties or the different internal relations in which they stand. Note what Augustine does not say, namely, that the Father and Son just are relations. It is true that Augustine felt uneasy about the terminology of "three persons" because this seems to imply three instances of a generic type and hence three Gods (5.9.10; 7.4.7-8). He accepted the terminology somewhat grudgingly for want of a better word. But he did not try to reduce the persons to mere relations.

For a bona fide example of anti social trinitarianism, we may turn to Thomas Aquinas, who pushes the Augustinian analogy to its apparent limit. Aquinas holds that there is a likeness of the Trinity in the human mind insofar as it understands itself and loves itself (*Summa contra gentiles* 4.26.6). We find in the mind the mind itself, the mind conceived in the intellect, and the mind beloved in the will. The difference between this human likeness and the Trinity is, first, that the human mind's acts of understanding and will are not identical with its being and, second, that the mind as understood and the mind as beloved do not

subsist and so are not persons. By contrast, Aquinas's doctrine of divine simplicity implies that God's acts of understanding and willing are identical with his
being, and he further holds (paradoxically) that God as understood and God as
beloved do subsist and therefore count as distinct persons from God the Father.
According to Aquinas, since God knows himself, there is in God the one who
knows and the object of that knowledge, which is the one known. The one
known exists in the one knowing as his Word. They share the same essence and
are indeed identical to it, but they are relationally distinct (4.11.13). Indeed,
Aquinas holds that the different divine persons just are the different relations
in God, like *paternity (being father of)* and *filiation (being son of)* (*Summa theologiae* 1a.40.2). Despite his commitment to divine simplicity, Aquinas regards
these relations as subsisting entities in God (*Summa contra gentiles* 4.14.6, 11).
Because the one knowing generates the one known and they share the same essence, they are related as Father to Son. Moreover, God loves himself, so that
God as beloved is relationally distinct from God as loving (4.19.7-12) and is
called the Holy Spirit. Since God's knowing and willing are not really distinct,
the Son and Holy Spirit would be one person if the only difference between
them were that one proceeds by way of God's knowing himself and the other by
way of God's loving himself. But they are distinct because only the Holy Spirit
proceeds from both the Father and the Son.

3 ASSESSMENT OF THE MODELS

Is Thomistic anti social trinitarianism viable? Thomas's doctrine of the Trinity is
doubtless inconsistent with his doctrine of divine simplicity. Intuitively, it seems
obvious that a being that is absolutely without composition and transcends all
distinctions cannot have real relations subsisting within it, much less be three
distinct persons. More specifically, Aquinas's contention that each of the three
persons has the same divine essence entails, given divine simplicity, that each
person just is that essence. But if two things are identical with some third thing,
they are identical with each other. Therefore, the Father, Son and Holy Spirit
cannot be distinct persons or relations. Since this unwelcome conclusion arises
not so much from Aquinas's trinitarian doctrine as from the doctrine of divine
simplicity, and since we have already found reason to call that doctrine seriously
into question, let us ask whether Thomas's account of anti social trinitarianism
is viable once freed of the constraints of the simplicity doctrine.

It seems not. Without begging the question in favor of social trinitarianism,
it can safely be said that on no reasonable understanding of *person* can a person
be equated with a **relation**. Relations do not cause things, know truths or love
people in the way the Bible says God does. Moreover, to think that the intentional objects of God's knowing himself and loving himself constitute in any
sense really distinct persons is wholly implausible. Even if God the Father were
a person and not a mere relation, there is no reason, even in Aquinas's own
metaphysical system, why the Father as understood and loved by himself would
be different persons. The distinction involved here is merely that between oneself as subject ("I") and as object ("me"). There is no more reason to think that
the individual designated by "I", "me" and "myself" constitutes a plurality of

persons in God's case than in any human being's case. Anti social trinitarianism seems to reduce to classical modalism.

Suppose the anti social trinitarian insists that in God's case the subsistent relations within God really do constitute distinct persons in a sufficiently robust sense. Then two problems present themselves. First, there arises an infinite regress of persons in the Godhead. If God as understood really is a distinct person called the Son, then the Son, like the Father, must also understand himself and love himself. There are thereby generated two further persons of the Godhead, who in turn can also consider themselves as intentional objects of their knowledge and will, thereby generating further persons ad infinitum. We wind up with a fractal-like infinite series of Trinities within Trinities in the Godhead. Aquinas actually considers this objection, and his answer is that "just as the Word is not another god, so neither is He another intellect; consequently, not another act of understanding; hence, not another word" (*Summa contra gentiles* 4.13.2). This answer only reinforces the previous impression of modalism, for the Son's intellect and act of understanding just are the Father's intellect and act of understanding; the Son's understanding himself is identical with the Father's understanding himself. The Son seems but a name given to the Father's *me*. Second, one person does not exist in another person. On Aquinas's view the Son or Word remains in the Father (4.11.180). While we can make sense of a relation's existing in a person, it seems unintelligible to say that one person exists in another person. (Two persons' inhabiting the same body is obviously not a counterexample.) Classic trinitarian doctrine affirms that more than one person may exist in one being, but persons are not the sort of entity that exists in another person. It is true that the classic doctrine involves a *perichoresis* (*circumincessio*) or mutual indwelling of the three persons in one another, which is often enunciated as each person's existing in the others. But this may be understood in terms of complete harmony of will and action, of mutual love, and full knowledge of one another with respect to the persons of the Godhead; beyond that it remains obscure what literally could be meant by one person's being in another person. Again, we seem forced to conclude that the subsisting relations posited by the anti social trinitarian do not rise to the standard of personhood.

Are there brighter prospects for a viable social trinitarianism? Brian Leftow has distinguished three forms of social trinitarianism on offer: **Trinity monotheism, group mind monotheism** and **functional monotheism**.

To consider these in reverse order, functional monotheism appeals to the harmonious, interrelated functioning of the divine persons as the basis for viewing them as one God. For example, Richard Swinburne considers God to be a logically indivisible, collective substance composed of three persons who are also substances. He sees the Father as the everlasting active cause of the Son and Spirit, and the latter as permissive causes, in turn, of the Father. Because all of them are omnipotent and perfectly good, they cooperate in all their volitions and actions. It is logically impossible that any one person should exist or act independent of the other two. Swinburne considers this understanding sufficient to capture the intention of the church councils, whose monotheistic affirma-

3.2
SOCIAL
TRINITARIANISM

3.2.1
FUNCTIONAL
MONOTHEISM

tions, he thinks, meant to deny that there were three independent divine beings who could exist and act without one another.

Leftow blasts Swinburne's view as "a refined paganism," a thinly veiled form of polytheism.[3] Since, on Swinburne's view, each person is a discrete substance, it is a distinct being, even if that being is causally dependent on some other being for its existence. Indeed, the causal dependence of the Son on the Father is problematic for the Son's being divine. For on Swinburne's account, the Son exists in the same way that creatures exist—only due to a divine person's conserving him in being and not annihilating him. Indeed, given that the Son is a distinct substance from the Father, the Father's begetting the Son amounts to *creatio ex nihilo*, which as Arius saw, makes the Son a creature. If we eliminate from Swinburne's account the causal dependence relation among the divine persons, then we are stuck with the surprising and inexplicable fact that there just happen to exist three divine beings all sharing the same nature, which seems incredible. As for the unity of will among the three divine persons, there is no reason at all to see this as constitutive of a collective substance, for three separate Gods who were each omnipotent and morally perfect would similarly act cooperatively, if Swinburne's argument against the possibility of dissension is correct. Thus there is no salient difference between functional monotheism and polytheism.

<table>
<tr><td>3.2.2
GROUP MIND
MONOTHEISM</td><td>Group mind monotheism holds that the Trinity is a **mind** that is composed of the minds of the three persons in the Godhead. If such a model is to be theologically acceptable, the mind of the Trinity cannot be a self-conscious self in addition to the three self-conscious selves who are the Father, Son and Holy Spirit, for otherwise we have not a Trinity but a Quaternity, so to speak. Therefore, the Trinity itself cannot be construed as an agent, endowed with intellect and will, in addition to the three persons of the Trinity. The three persons would have to be thought of as **subminds** of the mind of God. In order to render such a view intelligible, Leftow appeals to thought experiments involving surgical operations in which the cerebral commissures, the network of nerves connecting the two hemispheres of the brain, are severed. Such operations have been performed as a treatment for severe epilepsy, and the results are provocative. Patients sometimes behave as though the two halves of their brain were operating independent of each other. The interpretation of such results is controversial, but one interpretation, suggested by various thought experiments, is that the patients come to have two minds. Now the question arises whether in a normally functioning human being we do not already have two separable subminds linked to their respective hemispheres that cooperate together in producing a single human consciousness. In such a case the human mind would itself be a group mind.</td></tr>
</table>

Applying this notion of a group mind to the Trinity, we must, if we are to remain biblically orthodox, maintain that the minds of the persons of the Trinity are more than mere subminds which either never come to self-consciousness or else share a common mental state as a single self-consciousness. For such a view is incompatible with the persons' existing in I-Thou relationships with one

---

[3]Brian Leftow, "Anti Social Trinitarianism," in *The Trinity*, ed. Stephen T. Davis, Daniel Kendall and Gerald O'Collins (Oxford: Oxford University Press, 1999), p. 232.

another; on such a view God really is only one person.

In order to be theologically acceptable, group mind monotheism will have to be construed dynamically, as a process in which the subminds emerge into self-consciousness to replace the single trinitarian self-consciousness. In other words, what group mind monotheism offers is a strikingly modern version of the old Logos doctrine of the Greek Apologists. The divine monarchy (the single self-consciousness of the Trinity) contains within itself an immanent Logos (a submind) that at the beginning of the creation of the world is deployed into the divine economy (the subminds emerge into self-consciousness in replacement of the former single self-consciousness).

This provocative model gives some sense to the otherwise very difficult idea of the Father's begetting the Son in his divine nature. On the other hand, if we think of the primal self-consciousness of the Godhead as the Father, then the model requires that the person of the Father expires in the emergence of the three subminds into self-consciousness (cf. Athanasius *Four Discourses Against the Arians* 4.3). In order to avoid this unwelcome implication, one would need to think of some way in which the Father's personal identity is preserved through the deployment of the divine economy, just as a patient survives a commissurotomy.

The whole model, of course, depends on the very controversial notion of subminds and their emergence into distinct persons. If we do not equate minds with persons, then the result of the deployment of the divine economy will be merely one person with three minds, which falls short of the doctrine of the Trinity. But if, as seems plausible, we understand minds and persons to exist in a one-to-one correspondence, then the emergence of three distinct persons raises once again the specter of tritheism. The driving force behind group mind monotheism is to preserve the unity of God's being in a way functional monotheism cannot. But once the divine economy has been deployed, the group mind has lapsed away, and it is unclear why we do not now have three Gods in the place of one.

We turn finally to Trinity monotheism, which holds that while the persons of the Trinity are divine, it is the Trinity as a whole that is properly God. If this view is to be orthodox, it must hold that the Trinity alone is God and that the Father, Son and Holy Spirit, while divine, are not Gods. Leftow presents the following challenge to this view:

3.2.3
TRINITY
MONOTHEISM

> Either the Trinity is a fourth case of the divine nature, in addition to the Persons, or it is not. If it is, we have too many cases of deity for orthodoxy. If it is not, and yet is divine, there are two ways to be divine—by being a case of deity, and by being a Trinity of such cases. If there is more than one way to be divine, Trinity monotheism becomes Plantingian Arianism. But if there is in fact only one way to be divine, then there are two alternatives. One is that only the Trinity is God, and God is composed of non-divine persons. The other is that the sum of all divine persons is somehow not divine. To accept this last claim would be to give up Trinity monotheism altogether.[4]

---

[4]Ibid., p. 221.

Leftow's dilemma is graphically exhibited in figure 29.1.

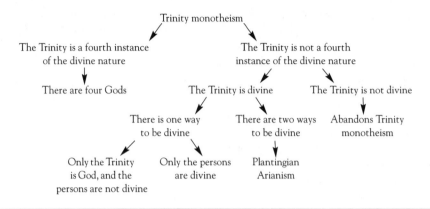

Fig. 29.1 Leftow's dilemma for Trinity monotheism

How should the Trinity monotheist respond to this dilemma? Starting with the first disjunction, he will clearly want to say that the Trinity is not a fourth instance of the divine nature, lest there be four divine persons. Moving then to the next set of options, he must say that the Trinity is divine, since that is entailed by Trinity monotheism. Now if the Trinity is divine but is not a fourth instance of the divine nature, this suggests that there is more than one way to be divine. This alternative is said to lead to Plantingian Arianism. What is that? Leftow defines it merely as "the positing of more than one way to be divine."[5] This is uninformative, however; what we want to know is why the view is objectionable. Leftow responds, "If we take the Trinity's claim to be God seriously, . . . we wind up downgrading the Persons' deity and/or [being] unorthodox."[6] The alleged problem is that if only the Trinity exemplifies the complete divine nature, then the way in which the persons are divine is less than fully divine.

This inference would follow, however, only if there were but one way to be divine (namely, by instantiating the divine nature); but the position asserts that there is more than one way to be divine. The persons of the Trinity are not divine in virtue of instantiating the divine nature. For presumably *being triune* is a property of the divine nature (God does not just happen to be triune); yet the persons of the Trinity do not have that property. It now becomes clear that the reason that the Trinity is not a fourth instance of the divine nature is that there are no other instances of the divine nature. The Father, Son and Holy Spirit are not instances of the divine nature, and that is why there are not three Gods. The Trinity is the sole instance of the divine nature, and therefore there is but one God. So while the statement "The Trinity is God" is an identity statement, statements about the persons like "The Father is God" are not identity statements. Rather, they perform other functions, such as ascribing a title or office to a person (like "Belshazzar is king," which is not incompatible with there being coregents) or ascribing a property to a person (a way of saying, "The

[5]Ibid., p. 208.
[6]Ibid.

Father is divine," as one might say, "Belshazzar is regal").

So if the persons of the Trinity are not divine in virtue of being instances of the divine nature, in virtue of what are they divine? Consider an analogy. One way of being feline is to instantiate the nature of a cat. But there are other ways to be feline as well. A cat's DNA or skeleton is feline, even if neither is a cat. Nor is this a sort of downgraded or attenuated felinity: A cat's skeleton is fully and unambiguously feline. Indeed, a cat just is a feline animal, as a cat's skeleton is a feline skeleton. Now if a cat is feline in virtue of being an instance of the cat nature, in virtue of what is a cat's DNA or skeleton feline? One plausible answer is that they are parts of a cat. This suggests that we could think of the persons of the Trinity as divine because they are parts of the Trinity, that is, parts of God. Now obviously, the persons are not parts of God in the sense in which a skeleton is part of a cat; but given that the Father, for example, is not the whole Godhead, it seems undeniable that there is some sort of **part-whole relation** obtaining between the persons of the Trinity and the entire Godhead.

Far from downgrading the divinity of the persons, such an account can be very illuminating of their contribution to the divine nature. For parts can possess properties which the whole does not, and the whole can have a property because some part has it. Thus, when we ascribe omniscience and omnipotence to God, we are not making the Trinity a fourth person or agent; rather, God has these properties because the persons do. Divine attributes like omniscience, omnipotence and goodness are grounded in the persons' possessing these properties, while divine attributes like necessity, aseity and eternity are not so grounded. With respect to the latter, the persons have these properties because God as a whole has them. For parts can have some properties in virtue of the wholes of which they are parts. The point is that if we think of the divinity of the persons in terms of a part-whole relation to the Trinity that God is, then their deity seems in no way diminished because they are not instances of the divine nature.

Is such a solution unorthodox? It is true that the church fathers frequently insisted that the expression "from the substance of the Father" should not be understood to imply that the Son is formed by division or separation of the Father's substance. But the concern here was clearly to avoid imagining the divine substance as a sort of "stuff" which could be parceled out into smaller pieces. Such a stricture is wholly compatible with our suggestion that no one person is identical to the whole Trinity, for the part-whole relation at issue here does not involve separable parts. It is simply to say that the Father, for example, is not the whole Godhead. The Latin church father Hilary seems to capture the idea nicely when he asserts, "Each divine person is in the Unity, yet no person is the one God" (*On the Trinity* 7.2; cf. 7.13, 32).

On the other hand, it must be admitted that a number of post-Nicene creeds, probably under the influence of the doctrine of divine simplicity, do include statements that can be construed to identify each person of the Trinity with God as a whole. For example, the Eleventh Council of Toledo (675) affirms, "Each single person is wholly God in Himself," the so-called Athanasian Creed (fifth century) enjoins Christians "to acknowledge every Person by himself to be God and Lord," and the Fourth Lateran Council, in condemning the idea of a divine Quaternity, declares, "each of the Persons is that reality, *viz.*, that divine substance, essence, or nature . . . what the Father is, this very same reality is also the Son, this the Holy Spirit." If these declarations are intended to imply that statements like "The Father is God" are **identity statements**, then they threaten the doctrine of the Trinity with logical incoherence. For the logic of identity requires that if the Father is identical with God and the Son is identical with God, then the Father is identical with the Son, which the same councils also deny.

Peter van Inwagen has sought to defend the coherence of such creedal affirmations by appeal to **relative identity**. According to this notion, the identity relation is not absolute but is relative to a sort of thing. For example, we say, "The couch is the same color as the chair" (not "The couch is the chair") or "The Lord Mayor John is the same person as the schoolboy Johnny" (not "The Lord Mayor is the schoolboy Johnny"). Given certain assumptions, van Inwagen shows that we can coherently affirm not only statements like "The Father is the same being as the Son," "The Father is not the same person as the Son," but even paradoxical statements like "God is a person," "God is the same person as the Father," "God is the same person as the Son," and "The Son is not the same person as the Father." The fundamental problem with the appeal to relative identity, however, is that the very notion of relative identity is widely recognized to be spurious. Van Inwagen himself admits that apart from trinitarian theology, there are no known cases of allegedly relative identities that cannot be analyzed in terms of classical identity. Our example of the couch and the chair is not any kind of identity statement at all, for neither piece of furniture literally is a color; rather, they have the same color as a property. The example of the Lord Mayor is solved by taking seriously the tense of the sentence; we should say, "The Lord Mayor was the schoolboy Johnny." Not only are the alleged cases of relative identity spurious, but there is a powerful theoretical argument against making identity relative. Suppose that two things x and y could be the same N but could not be the same P. In such a case x could not fail to be the same P as x itself, but y could. Therefore, x and y are discernible and so cannot be the same thing. But then it follows that they cannot be the same N, since they cannot be the same anything. Identity must therefore be absolute.

Finally, even granted relative identity, its application to trinitarian doctrine involves highly dubious assumptions. For example, it must be presupposed that x and y can be the identical being without being the identical person. Notice how different this is from saying that x and y are parts of the same being but are different persons. The latter statement is like the affirmation that x and y are parts of the same body but are different hands; the former is like the affirmation that x and y are the identical body but are different hands. Van Inwagen confesses that he has no answer to the questions of how x and y can be the same being without being the same person or, more generally, how x and y can be the same N without being the same P. It seems, then, that the ability to state coherently the trinitarian claims under discussion using the device of relative identity is a hollow victory.

Protestants bring all doctrinal statements, even conciliar creeds, especially creeds of nonecumenical councils, before the bar of Scripture. Nothing in Scripture warrants us in thinking that God is simple and that each person of the Trinity is identical to the whole Trinity. Nothing in Scripture prohibits us from maintaining that the three persons of the Godhead stand in some sort of part-whole relation to the Trinity. Therefore, Trinity monotheism cannot be condemned as unorthodox in a biblical sense. Trinity monotheism seems therefore to be thus far vindicated.

All of this still leaves us wondering, however, how three persons could be parts of the same being, rather than be three separate beings. What is the salient difference between three divine persons who are each a being and three divine persons who are together one being?

Perhaps we can get a start at this question by means of an analogy. (There is no reason to think that there must be any analogy to the Trinity among created things, but analogies may prove helpful as a springboard for philosophical reflection and formulation.) In Greco-Roman mythology there is said to stand guarding the gates of Hades a three-headed dog named Cerberus. We may suppose that Cerberus has three brains and therefore three distinct states of consciousness of whatever it is like to be a dog. Therefore, Cerberus, while a sentient being, does not have a unified consciousness. He has three consciousnesses. We could even assign proper names to each of them: Rover, Bowser and Spike. These centers of consciousness are entirely discrete and might well come into conflict with one another. Still, in order for Cerberus to be biologically viable, not to mention in order to function effectively as a guard dog, there must be a considerable degree of cooperation among Rover, Bowser and Spike. Despite the diversity of his mental states, Cerberus is clearly one dog. He is a single biological organism having a canine nature. Rover, Bowser and Spike may be said to be canine, too, though they are not three dogs, but parts of the one dog Cerberus. If Hercules were attempting to enter Hades and Spike snarled at him or bit his leg, he might well report, "Cerberus snarled at me" or "Cerberus attacked me." Although the church fathers rejected analogies like Cerberus, once we give up divine simplicity, Cerberus does seem to represent what Augustine called an image of the Trinity among creatures.

We can enhance the Cerberus story by investing him with rationality and self-consciousness. In that case Rover, Bowser and Spike are plausibly personal agents and Cerberus a tripersonal being. Now if we were asked what makes Cerberus a single being despite his multiple minds, we should doubtless reply that it is because he has a single physical body. But suppose Cerberus were to be killed and his minds survive the death of his body. In what sense would they still be one being? How would they differ intrinsically from three exactly similar minds that have always been unembodied? Since the divine persons are, prior to the Incarnation, three unembodied minds, in virtue of what are they one being rather than three individual beings?

The question of what makes several parts constitute a single object rather than distinct objects is a difficult one. But in this case perhaps we can get some insight by reflecting on the nature of the soul. We have argued that souls are immaterial substances and have seen that it is plausible that animals have souls (see chap. 11). Souls come in a spectrum of varying capacities and faculties.

Higher animals such as chimpanzees and dolphins possess souls more richly endowed with powers than those of iguanas and turtles. What makes the human soul a person is that the human soul is equipped with rational faculties of intellect and volition that enable it to be a self-reflective agent capable of self-determination. Now God is very much like an unembodied soul; indeed, as a mental substance God just seems to be a soul. We naturally equate a rational soul with a person, since the human souls with which we are acquainted are persons. But the reason human souls are individual persons is because each soul is equipped with one set of rational faculties sufficient for being a person. Suppose, then, that God is a soul which is endowed with three complete sets of rational cognitive faculties, each sufficient for personhood. Then God, though one soul, would not be one person but three, for God would have three centers of self-consciousness, intentionality and volition, as social trinitarians maintain. God would clearly not be three discrete souls because the cognitive faculties in question are all faculties belonging to just one soul, one immaterial substance. God would therefore be one being that supports three persons, just as our own individual beings each support one person. Such a model of Trinity monotheism seems to give a clear sense to the classical formula "three persons in one substance."

Finally, such a model does not feature (though it does not preclude) the derivation of one person from another, enshrined in the confession that the Son is "begotten of the Father before all worlds, Light of Light, very God of very God, begotten, not made" (Constantinopolitan Creed). God could simply exist eternally with his multiple cognitive faculties and capacities. This is, in our view, all for the better. For although creedally affirmed, the doctrine of the generation of the Son (and the procession of the Spirit) is a relic of Logos Christology which finds virtually no warrant in the biblical text and introduces a **subordinationism** into the Godhead which anyone who affirms the full deity of Christ ought to find very troubling.[7]

Finally, although the doctrine of the Trinity belongs to revealed theology rather than to natural theology, we may ask if there are any positive arguments which might be offered on behalf of the plausibility of that doctrine. We close with an argument that a number of Christian philosophers have defended for God's being a plurality of persons. God is by definition the greatest conceivable being. As the greatest conceivable being, God must be perfect. Now a perfect being must be a loving being. For love is a moral perfection; it is better for a person to be loving rather than unloving. God therefore must be a perfectly loving being. Now it is of the very nature of love to give oneself away. Love reaches out to another person rather than centering wholly in oneself. So if God is perfectly loving by his very nature, he must be giving himself in love to another. But who is that other? It cannot be any created person, since creation is a result of God's free will, not a result of his nature. It belongs to God's very essence to love, but it does not belong to his essence to create. So we can imagine a possible world in which God is perfectly loving and yet no created persons exist. So created per-

---

[7]For a systematic theologian's argument for abandoning eternal generation of the Son and the procession of the Spirit, see John S. Feinberg, *No One Like Him: The Doctrine of God* (Wheaton, Ill.: Crossway, 2001), pp. 488-92. Feinberg stands in the tradition of evangelical theologians like J. Oliver Buswell Jr. who have expressed misgivings about this doctrine.

sons cannot sufficiently explain whom God loves. Moreover, contemporary cosmology makes it plausible that created persons have not always existed. But God is eternally loving. So again created persons alone are insufficient to account for God's being perfectly loving. It therefore follows that the other to whom God's love is necessarily directed must be internal to God himself.

In other words, God is not a single, isolated person, as unitarian forms of theism like Islam hold; rather, God is a plurality of persons, as the Christian doctrine of the Trinity affirms. On the unitarian view God is a person who does not give himself away essentially in love for another; he is focused essentially only on himself. Hence, he cannot be the most perfect being. But on the Christian view, God is a triad of persons in eternal, self-giving love relationships. Thus, since God is essentially loving, the doctrine of the Trinity is more plausible than any unitarian doctrine of God.

CHAPTER SUMMARY

The doctrine of the Trinity arises from reflection on the scriptural data affirming the personal distinctness and deity of the Father, Son and Holy Spirit. Early Logos Christology sought to explain the person of the Son in terms of the external projection of God's immanent reason. Rejecting modalism's denial of the distinctness of the persons and Arianism's denial of the full deity of the persons, the church articulated the position that there exist three persons and one substance in God. Contemporary thought on the Trinity tends to divide between two camps: social trinitarianism and anti social trinitarianism. According to the former there are three centers of self-consciousness in God, whereas the latter tends to think of God in terms of a unitary consciousness. Anti social trinitarianism finds it difficult to avoid modalism, while the danger facing social trinitarianism is tritheism. Of the various forms of social trinitarianism, such as functional monotheism, group mind monotheism and Trinity monotheism, the latter has the best prospects for facilitating an orthodox account of how the one God can be three persons. Since God is essentially self-giving love, the doctrine of the Trinity is more plausible than any unitarian doctrine of God.

CHECKLIST OF BASIC TERMS AND CONCEPTS

anti social trinitarianism
center of self-consciousness
christological controversies
Constantinopolitan Creed
Council of Nicaea
economy
Father
functional monotheism
Greek Apologists
group mind monotheism
heteroousios
historical Jesus

Holy Spirit
homoousios
hypostasis
identity statements
implicit Christology
individual
Jesus' self-understanding
Latin trinitarianism
Logos
mind
modalism
monarchianism
monarchy
monotheism
nature
Nicene Creed
ousia
part-whole relation
person
personal indexicals
property instance
relation
relative identity
Sabellianism
social trinitarianism
Son
subminds
subordinationism
substance
tripersonal
tritheism
trinitarian controversy
Trinity monotheism
unitarian
universal property

30

CHRISTIAN DOCTRINES II

The Incarnation

The Person of Christ is the bankruptcy of logic.
H. MAURICE RELTON, *A STUDY IN CHRISTOLOGY*

In the course of thinking about the Incarnation for some years now,
I have come to see that a few simple metaphysical distinctions
and a solid dose of logical care will suffice to explicate and defend
the doctrine against all extant criticisms of a philosophical nature.
THOMAS V. MORRIS, *THE LOGIC OF GOD INCARNATE*

1 INTRODUCTION

The New Testament affirms both the humanity and deity of Jesus Christ. As a
human being Jesus was born (Lk 2:7, 11), experienced physical and mental limitations (Lk 2:52; cf. Mt 4:2; Mk 4:38; 13:32; Jn 4:6), was tempted (Mt 4:1-11),
increased in moral perfection through suffering (Heb 5:7-10), and was tortured
and executed (Mk 15:15). Nevertheless, the New Testament authors affirm
that Jesus was God (Jn 1:1-3, 14, 18; 20:26-29; Rom 9:5; Tit 2:13; Heb 1:8; 2 Pet
1:1) and describe him as the fullness of deity in bodily form (Col 1:15-20; 2:9;
Phil 2:5-8). The New Testament church called him *kyrios* ("Lord"), the same
word used in the Greek translation of the Old Testament in place of *Yahweh*,
and applied to Jesus Old Testament passages concerning Yahweh (1 Cor 16:22;
Rom 10:8, 13).

But if anything appears to be a contradiction, surely this is it! How can Jesus
be both God and man, infinite and finite, Creator and creature? How can we
unite in a single person both omniscience and ignorance, omnipotence and
weakness, moral perfection and moral perfectibility? The attributes of deity
seem to drive out the attributes of humanity, so that it seems logically inconsistent to affirm with the historic Christian church that Jesus is truly God and
truly man (*vere Deus/vere homo*).

2 THE CHRISTOLOGICAL CONTROVERSIES

As a result of the trinitarian controversy culminating in the Councils of Nicaea
(325) and Constantinople (381), the full deity of Christ, along with his humanity, was declared nonnegotiable. With the final formulation of the doctrine of

the Trinity in place, the **christological controversies** of the fourth through the seventh centuries opened a new chapter in the intellectual history of the church. The central question of this new epoch was how we should understand the affirmation that Jesus Christ is both human and divine.

Two broad schools of christological thought emerged among the church fathers. Often labeled **Logos-flesh** versus **Logos-man Christology** or **Alexandrian** versus **Antiochene Christology**, these competing schools are perhaps best seen as a struggle between one-nature (**monophysite**) versus two-nature (**dyophysite**) **Christology**. The presupposition of both schools is that members of **natural kinds** of things do have **natures**, or essential properties that make the things what they are (see chap. 10). Thus there is such a thing as **human nature**, and this differs from the **divine nature.** According to Aristotle the nature of man is that he is a rational animal, so that being truly human involves having both an intellectual soul and a physical body, and the church fathers seem to have accepted this view. At the same time, they believed that God possesses certain essential attributes, such as omnipotence, omniscience, eternity, moral perfection and so forth. The question was how to understand the Incarnation of the divine Logos, the Second Person of the Trinity, in the man Jesus of Nazareth. The fathers were unanimous in thinking that the **Incarnation** did not involve the Logos's divesting himself of certain divine attributes in order to turn himself into a human being. Such a conception would be akin to pagan, mythological ideas, such as Zeus's transforming himself into a bull or swan. The notion of the Incarnation was not that the Logos turned himself into a human being, thereby ceasing to be God, but that Jesus Christ was both God and man simultaneously. Since the divine nature was not abandoned by the Logos, the Incarnation could only be conceived as the acquisition by the Logos of the additional, essential properties of human nature. The question was how this acquisition of a human nature by the Logos is to be understood.

Advocates of a one-nature Christology held that after the Incarnation the Logos possessed a single divine-human nature. Some understood the Incarnation to be the Logos's clothing himself in flesh, assuming as his own a human body. Christ's flesh was sometimes taken to be deified in virtue of its union with the Logos. By contrast, proponents of a two-nature Christology emphasized that in the Incarnation the Logos took on not merely human flesh but a complete human nature, and therefore a rational soul and body. The Logos was joined at conception to the human being borne by Mary the mother of Christ. The Incarnation thus involved the existence of a complete human being and a complete divine being.

One of the most creative christological thinkers, and a seminal influence throughout the christological controversies, was Apollinarius (d. c. 390), bishop of Laodicea during the mid-fourth century. Apollinarius argued that it is impossible that Christ should have both a complete divine nature and a complete human nature, for that would amount to a mere **indwelling** of God in a human being, which falls short of a true Incarnation (*Fragments*). If, in addition to the divine intellect of the Logos, there was in Christ a human intellect, then the Logos did not achieve a full Incarnation. The key to Apollinarius's ingenious solution to the problem of achieving a true Incarnation lay in his **anthropology.**

Each human being consists of a **body** (*sōma*), an **animal soul** (*psychē*) and a **rational soul** (*nous*). The *nous* was conceived to be the seat of the sinful instincts. In Jesus, the divine Logos took the place of the human *nous* and thus became embodied. As a result, in Christ God was constitutionally conjoined with man. Just as the soul and the body are essentially different but in man are combined in one human nature, so also in Christ there exists one nature composed of a part coessential with God and another part coessential with human flesh. The Logos came to experience the world through his flesh and to act through the flesh as his instrument. Having only a single intellect and will belonging properly to the Logos, Christ was without sinful desires and incapable of sin.

In advocating such an understanding of the Incarnation, Apollinarius stood in the train of the great Alexandrian theologians. Athanasius always spoke of the Logos's taking on flesh and never refers to the human soul of Jesus. Athanasius typically affirms: "in nature the Word himself is impassible, and yet because of that flesh which He put on, these things are ascribed to Him, since they belong to the flesh, and the body itself belongs to the savior" (Athanasius *Orations Against the Arians* 34). **Apollinarianism** achieved a genuine Incarnation that, given anthropological dualism, is no more inherently implausible than the soul's union with the body. It combated **Arianism's** fallible Christ, it insured the unity of his person, and it explained how God through the assumption of a body could participate in suffering.

Nevertheless, Apollinarianism was inadequate as it stood. Two deficiencies of Apollinarian Christology seemed especially serious. First, a body without a mind is a truncation of human nature. By merely clothing himself with flesh, the Logos did not truly become a man. For essential to human nature is a rational soul, which Christ lacked. He was like us only with respect to his flesh, which is a mere animal nature. Gregory of Nyssa thus charged that Apollinarius had reduced the Incarnation to God's becoming an animal! Apollinarianism is thus unacceptable, since it denies the true humanity of Christ. Second, if Christ lacked a human mind, then he did not redeem the human mind. This inference was based on the fundamental principle that underlay the doctrine of the Incarnation: that which is not assumed is not saved (*quod non est assumptum non est sanatum*). Apart from the truth of this principle, there is no rationale for the Incarnation at all. Thus Apollinarius's Christology undermined Christian soteriology. Because of these deficiencies, Apollinarianism was condemned as heretical at a synod in Rome in 377.

The Antiochene theologians who opposed Apollinarius insisted on Christ's possession of two complete natures, human and divine. Such a doctrine implied that Christ possessed all the elements essential to a complete human nature, including a soul and a body. Theodore of Mopsuestia, the most prominent of these thinkers, conceived of the Incarnation as a special sort of indwelling by means of which the Logos attached himself to the man Jesus at the moment of his conception in Mary's womb (*On the Incarnation* 7, Fragments 2-3). Because he is omnipresent and provident, God is present according to his essence to all things in their existence and operation, but by his good pleasure he chooses to be more intimately related to some things than to others. In Christ God was pleased to dwell as in a Son. Theodore affirmed that there is but one person in

Christ, but he also held that each nature considered in itself is complete and has its own *hypostasis*. Moreover, he thought of the union of the Logos with the man Jesus in terms of a **functional unity** of will and mutual love, so that they constitute a person in the sense that they present a functionally unified "face" (*prosōpon*) to the world. Thus his affirmation that there is in Christ one person was viewed with suspicion by his detractors. However, it was Nestorius, who became patriarch of Constantinople in 428, whose name came to be associated with the view that there are two persons in Christ. Nestorius affirmed that in Christ there are two complete natures. He objected to Mary's being called *theotokos* ("bearer," or "mother," "of God"), since Mary bore only the man Jesus, not the divine Logos. What was formed in her womb, crucified and buried was not God; but the one assumed in the womb is called God because of the divinity of the One who assumed him (*First Sermon Against the Theotokos*).

The Alexandrian theologians believed that Nestorius was committed to the view that there are in Christ two persons or Sons, despite his protestations to the contrary. It is easy to see why they thought so. If each of Christ's two natures is complete, each having its full complement of rational faculties, then it is difficult to see why, indeed, one does not have two persons, two Sons. Alexandrians, now forced by the condemnation of Apollinarius to admit the existence of a human soul in Christ, could not supply a solution to the dilemma, but they were certain that the Bible does not teach two Sons. Cyril of Alexandria insisted, "when he was made flesh, we do not define the indwelling in him in precisely the same manner as that in which one speaks of an indwelling in the saints; but being united by nature and not changed into flesh, he effected such an indwelling as the soul of man might be said to have in its own body" (*Second Letter to Nestorius*). The problem of the analogy is apparent: It either supports Apollinarianism (the soul being equivalent to the Logos and the body to Jesus' body) or **Nestorianism** itself (the Son assumes a whole person, body and soul). Condemned at Ephesus in 431, Nestorianism is fundamentally flawed in positing no real **union** of God and man in Christ but simply an ontological juxtaposition, or at best an indwelling. But if the concept of personhood is bound up with that of a complete human nature, then it seems very difficult, given the rejection of Apollinarianism, to affirm two natures in Christ while avoiding Nestorianism.

In 451 the Emperor Marcion convened the **Council of Chalcedon** at the request of Pope Leo the Great. Heavily dependent on the *Tome* of Leo (449), in which the pope following the lead of Tertullian (*Against Praxeas*) declared Christ to be **one person having two natures**, the settlement marked the zenith of the early church's christological speculations. Formulated in the light of the numerous controversies over the person of Christ, the Chalcedonian statement carefully charts a middle course between the competing schools preceding it:

> We . . . confess one and the same Son, our Lord Jesus Christ, the same perfect in Godhead and also perfect in manhood, truly God and truly man, of a reasonable soul and body; consubstantial [*homoousios*] with the Father according to the Godhead, and consubstantial [*homoousios*] with us according to the manhood, like us in all things except sin; begotten before all ages of the Father according to the Godhead, and in these latter days, for us and for our salvation, born of the Virgin Mary,

the Mother of God *[theotokos]*, according to the manhood, one and the same Christ, Son, Lord, Only-Begotten, to be acknowledged in two natures without confusion, without change, without division, without separation, the difference of the natures being by no means taken away because of the union, but rather the property of each nature being preserved, and concurring in one Person *[prosopon]* and one Subsistence *[hypostasis]*, not divided or separated into two Persons, but one and the same Son and only-begotten God, Word, Lord Jesus Christ.

The settlement is a ringing endorsement of dyophysite Christology. Christ is declared to exist in two natures, whose distinction remains real even in their union in Christ. Moreover, Apollinarianism is implicitly rejected in the statement that Christ is not only perfect in his deity and truly God but is also perfect in his humanity and truly man, having both a rational soul and body. At the same time, however, in agreement with monophysite Christology, the settlement insists on there being only one person, one Son, in Christ. Thus the excesses of Nestorianism are proscribed. *Person* and *hypostasis* are taken as having the same referent, so that the Incarnation becomes a sort of mirror image of the Trinity. Just as in the Trinity there are multiple persons in one nature, so in Christ there are multiple natures in one person. The famous series of the four adjectives *asynchytōs, atreptōs, adiairetōs, achōristōs* (**without confusion, without change, without division, without separation**) serves as a reminder that the **two natures** of Christ must be kept distinct and that the **unity of his person** must not be compromised. The first two adjectives are aimed at the Alexandrian tendency to blend the two natures together as a result of the Incarnation; the last two are directed at the Antiochene failure to achieve a real union of the two natures so that they are "divided or separated into two Persons." As result of Chalcedon, it has become an imperative of orthodox Christology that we must "neither **confuse the natures** nor **divide the person**" of Christ.

The Chalcedonian formula itself does not tell us how to do this. It does not seek to explain the Incarnation but sets up, as it were, channel markers for legitimate christological speculation; any theory of Christ's person must be one in which the distinctness of both natures is preserved and both meet in one person, one Son, in Christ. It admirably fulfilled the purpose for which it was drawn up; namely, to exclude two possible but unacceptable explanations of the Incarnation and to provide a convenient summary of essential facts that must be borne in mind by all those who attempt to penetrate further into the mystery.

Although the apex of christological formulation was reached at Chalcedon, two more councils were yet needed to refine more closely the limits of christological speculation: in 553, the Second Council of Constantinople moderated the Chalcedonian stance against monophysitism by condemning certain Nestorian tendencies; however, in 680 the Third Council of Constantinople condemned both **monophysitism** and **monotheletism**. The Council of Chalcedon had alienated a multitude of Greek-speaking Christians sympathetic to Alexandria. Their disquietude with the notion of two complete natures in Christ arose from a quite legitimate concern. How does one have two complete natures without two persons? The Second Council of Constantinople did not answer the question; the council merely anathematized anyone who does not confess that "the ineffable union took place without confusion, neither the Word being changed into the nature of the flesh, nor the flesh transferred into the nature of the Word—for each remains what it was by nature, even when the union by *hypostasis* has taken place" (*The Anathemas of the Second Council of Constantinople*).

The question troubling monophysites became even more acute in the controversy over the will of Christ. Monothelites contended that he possessed one will, that of his unique person. But the Third Council of Constantinople held that each nature, to be complete, must have a will of its own. It declared, "We proclaim two natural willings or wills in him and two natural operations . . . not contrary [to each other], God forbid, . . . but his human will following, and not resisting or opposing, but rather subject to his divine and all-powerful will" (*The Statement of Faith of the Third Council of Constantinople*). But no explanation is given of how one can have two separate wills and operations without two persons. By condemning monotheletism, the church seemed in danger of dividing the person of Christ.

3 LATER CHRISTOLOGICAL CONTROVERSIES

3.1
LUTHERAN
CHRISTOLOGY

During the **Protestant Reformation** the old dispute between Alexandria and Antioch was replayed in the debates between Lutheran and Reformed theologians, especially in their interpretation of Christ's presence in the Lord's Supper. Luther himself found the traditional doctrine of two distinct natures united in one person in Christ entirely congenial. But Luther also insisted that Christ's human nature was filled and permeated by the Godhead. Like the Alexandrian theologians, he compared this union with that of the body and soul or an iron glowing with heat. Luther notes that the Bible "often so interchanges the words that both are attributed to each nature because of the personal union. This they call *communicationem idiomatem* (communication of the attributes). Thus one may say: The man Christ is God's eternal Son. . . . On the other hand, this, too, may be said: Christ, God's Son (that is, the Person who is true God), was conceived and born by the Virgin Mary."[1] This communication is not a verbal exchange only, however; Luther believed that actual attributes of deity were communicated to Christ's humanity. This conviction is most clearly evident in his discussion of the **ubiquity** (omnipresence) **of Christ's body** and thus its **real presence** in the Lord's Supper. Luther explained it by appeal to the Scholastic notion of the three ways in which a thing may be in place. In the first sense, called *localiter* or circumscriptive, the place and the body correspond exactly, occupying the same space, as, for example, in the case of the volume displaced by an object submerged in water. The second sense is definitive, wherein a thing occupies space, but illocally, as, for example, in the case of an angel who may be in a house or a nutshell. The third sense is repletive, in which a thing fills all places but is contained by none; this sense belongs to God alone. Now it was Luther's contention that all three senses are applicable to the body of Christ simultaneously. The first was evident "when He went about bodily on earth,

---

[1] Martin Luther, *What Luther Says*, comp. Ewald M. Plass, 3 vols. (St. Louis: Concordia Publishing House, 1959), 1:174.

when, according to His size, He occupied and vacated space." The second manner of presence is that in which his body neither occupies nor vacates space but "penetrates all creatures, wherever He pleases, just as light and heat penetrate and are in air, water, and the like, and also do not occupy space." In this manner, his body is present in the Lord's Supper and is masticated by the communicant. Finally, he is present in the third sense in that all creation does not circumscribe or comprehend him, but rather he circumscribes and comprehends it, so that everything is present before him.

Lutheran Christology through its doctrine of the **communication of the attributes** seems to violate Chalcedon's prohibition of confusing the two natures of Christ and thus threatens the reality of Christ's humanity. While Lutheran theologians were zealous to maintain the distinctness of the two natures, it is very difficult to see how a human nature can really share all the attributes of deity without actually being deity. Moreover, it is not explained how such a communication is possible. The illustration of the fire and the iron, wielded with enthusiasm by Lutheran divines, is in the end unhelpful because the fire may communicate to the iron only such properties as are consistent with the iron's nature, such as heat and light; in the same way, deity may communicate to humanity only those attributes that are consistent with the nature of humanity. But this is merely to restate the very problem of the Incarnation: how is it that the infinite and the finite, the absolute and the relative, can be one?

In 1581, the Reformed church published its views on the person of Christ in a doctrinal statement designed to reply to the Lutheran *Formula of Concord.* In the Reformed statement, the traditional view of the two natures and one person is set forth, the **hypostatic union** of the natures being declared more intimate than that of the soul and body. But in this union each nature retains its essential properties, even to the extent of there being a twofold mind in Christ, one knowing all things in an eternal intuition, the other possessing limited, discursive knowledge. There is also a twofold will and operation, the human following the divine. Predicates addressed to Christ are true of his undivided person with respect to both natures or to one alone. As for attributes belonging to the divine nature, such as omniscience or omnipresence, Christ did not manifest these properties openly during his **state of humiliation** (from conception to ascension), but they were hidden. In his **state of exaltation**, these are openly disclosed and his humanity perfected with its infirmities being left behind.

3.2
REFORMED
CHRISTOLOGY

Unlike the Lutheran doctrine, such a Christology preserves clearly the humanity of Christ. But the most marked problem of **Reformed Christology** is that it tends toward Nestorianism. When one speaks of two minds, two wills and two operations in Christ, how is it that one does not wind up with two persons, a human person subordinate to a divine person? One might also ask what is meant by the "hiddenness" of the divine attributes in Christ. The emptying of the Incarnation was not an actual abandonment of the attributes, but an *occultatio*, a concealment of them, much as clouds obscure the sun. But if Christ actually possessed such attributes in his incarnate state, then how is it that as a man he did not in fact possess them? This problem seems to exacerbate the charge of Nestorianism, for it seems as though we are left again with two individuals, one possessing attributes of deity and the other merely human, bolted together like two pieces of wood.

During the nineteenth century a radical, new school of Christology emerged: **kenotic Christology** (from the Greek word *kenōsis* used in Phil 2:5 to characterize Christ's Incarnation as an "emptying"). Kenoticism can be thought of as an extension of either Lutheran or Reformed Christology: it is on the one hand simply a reversal of the Lutheran doctrine of *communicatio idiomatum* in which human attributes are now communicated to the divine nature; on the other hand, it is the heightening of the Reformed doctrine of *occultatio* into a real and positive emptying of the divine nature. We may define kenoticism as that christological view which contends that in the Incarnation Christ ceased to possess certain attributes of deity so that he might become truly human. Of course, this view raises several questions concerning the extent of the *kenosis*, the relationship between the Logos and the man Jesus, and the status of the divine attributes. A. B. Bruce identifies four main schools of kenotic Christology which emerged in answer to these questions, each represented by a prominent exponent: Thomasius, Gess, Ebrard and Martensen.

Thomasius argued that unless the Son of God truly limited himself, there could be no Incarnation; there would only be the divine Logos hovering over the human Jesus. The Son of God must, therefore, enter into human finitude, becoming subject to the limits of space, time and human development. This is a self-limitation, and the essence of deity is not destroyed nor are the two natures confused. The Son of God becomes a divine-human ego, and he continues to be himself. But he is human as well, for he has a reasonable soul and body; his ego has a human consciousness as well as a divine. He has merely stripped away those attributes not essential to deity—omniscience, omnipotence, omnipresence. These are only relational attributes of the Creator to the world. Essential attributes, such as absolute truth, holiness and love, are retained.

Gess conceived of the *kenosis* as a loss of the eternal self-consciousness on the part of Jesus, only to be gradually regained, and as a cessation of the flow of life from the Father into the Son so that the Son was no longer self-sufficient. The Logos is metamorphosed into a human soul. He did not *assume* a human soul; rather, he *became* a human soul. The only difference between a human soul and the Logos is that he became one by *kenosis*, whereas the other is the result of a creative act. As a result, he was capable of sinning; he had lost his eternal holiness. If asked how God can thus all but extinguish himself, Gess would say simply because he is God—he would not be omnipotent if he did not have power over himself. The theory involves four consequences for the Trinity: (1) Only the Father has aseity and the Son does not experience its "overflow" during *kenosis*, (2) during *kenosis*, the Spirit cannot proceed from the Son, (3) during *kenosis*, the Son no longer upholds the universe, and (4) in glorification a man is taken up into the Trinity.

Ebrard agrees with Gess in giving the Logos the place of the human soul. But this is not a loss of divinity; rather, it is a disguise. The *kenosis* consisted in an exchange of an eternal mode of being for a temporal. Omniscience, omnipotence and so forth are not surrendered but are now capable of being expressed only in a way consistent with space and time, that is, toward particular objects. For example, omnipotence remained in an applied form in Christ's ability to perform miracles. Ebrard accepted the doctrine of two natures, but only as abstract ways of viewing the one divine-human person. The divine person has become subject to the space-time world, and his attributes are displayed in the powers of his humanity, not *contrary* to them, in the applied form. Nevertheless, he believed that Christ could actually sin. He also seemed to believe that this *kenosis* was a decision to renounce permanently the eternal mode of being.

Martensen held to a real but relative *kenosis*. The preexistent Logos did not cease to be the sustainer and ground of the universe when he limited himself to become a man. In Jesus we see God revealed in humanity in the form of human consciousness. Thus the Logos lives a *double life:* He at the same time upholds the universe and enters into our finitude. But Martensen never attempts to explain the relationship between these roles of the Logos, nor how such a duality is possible.

Kenoticism represents a distinctively non-Chalcedonian approach to Christology, since it holds that the Logos in becoming incarnate changed in his nature. This fact raises the question as to whether kenoticism does not in fact amount to a denial of the deity of the incarnate Christ. Baillie demands,

> Does Christianity, then, teach that God changed into a Man? . . . That at a certain point of time, God . . . was transformed into a human being for a period of about thirty years? It is hardly necessary to say that the Christian doctrine of the Incarnation means nothing like that. . . . It would be grotesque to suggest that the Incarnation has anything in common with the *metamorphoses* of ancient pagan mythology. . . . The deity and humanity of Christ are not merely successive stages . . . as if He had first been God, then Man, then after the days of His flesh were past, God again, with manhood left behind.[2]

The Incarnation is the doctrine that Christ is both God and man simultaneously. But Baillie charges that kenoticists, while affirming that the Son of God keeps his personal identity in becoming the subject of the human attributes which he assumes, nevertheless hold that he has divested himself of the distinctively divine attributes, so that in becoming human he ceased to be divine. If Jesus is in every sense human, then the kenotic theologian is in the position of saying that God has turned himself into a human being, which seems absurd.

The question raised by kenotic Christology is the content of the divine nature, that is to say, which properties are essential to deity. Baillie holds that any change in God is a **substantial change** from deity. But it is exactly at this point that kenoticists question the traditional doctrine, for they argue that many of God's most prominent attributes are, in fact, merely contingent properties of God and therefore that he may yield up these nonessential properties and yet continue to be God. We have already argued that not every change in God is a substantial change, that God may change in certain accidental ways while remaining unchanged in his essence or nature (chap. 26). The decisive question, then, will be whether so profound a change as kenoticists envision is a merely **accidental change** compatible with God's nature.

---

[2] D. M. Baillie, *God Was in Christ* (New York: Charles Scribner's Sons, 1948), p. 82.

4 A PROPOSED CHRISTOLOGY

Having reviewed briefly some high points of the history of doctrine with respect to the Incarnation, we believe that from these precedents one may formulate a rational doctrine of the person of Christ. Before we present such a Christology, let us remind ourselves that we are attempting to provide a *possible* model of the Incarnation. We cannot presume to dogmatize; but if we can expound a plausible model of the Incarnation, then objections to the coherence of that doctrine will have been defeated.

1. *We postulate with Chalcedon that in Christ there is one person who exemplifies two distinct and complete natures, one human and one divine.* In one sense the Alexandrian theologians were right in postulating a single nature in Christ, in the sense, that is, of an **individual essence** that serves to designate the unique individual who is Jesus Christ. But when the framers of Chalcedon affirmed two natures in Christ, they were not talking about abstract individual essences, but **kind essences** or natures that serve to demarcate certain natural kinds of things. For example, according to Aristotle, every human being belongs to the natural kind designated "rational animal." In affirming that the incarnate Christ had two natures, the church fathers were stating that Christ exemplified all the properties that constitute humanity and all the properties that make up deity. In that sense, he had two natures and so belonged to two natural kinds, man and God. These natures are distinct in that they do not combine to make up a single "theanthropic" essence belonging to Christ, for that would make the Incarnation essential to the Second Person of the Trinity, which we know to be false, since the Logos preexisted as a member of the Trinity in incorporeal form. Only the divine nature belongs essentially to the Logos, and in the Incarnation he assumed contingently a human nature as well. Thus Christ's individual essence, while including some of the properties that serve to constitute humanity (for example, rationality), does not include all of them (for example, animality), for any property that he might lack cannot belong to his individual essence. The Logos possesses his human nature only contingently.

Our first point entails a rejection of any form of kenotic Christology which suggests that in the Incarnation the Logos surrendered various attributes belonging to the divine nature. For if Christ divested himself of any attribute essential to divinity, then he thereby ceased to be God, which is incompatible with the biblical data and therefore unacceptable as a Christian doctrine of the Incarnation. On such kenotic views the Logos would be the same *person* after *kenosis* as before, but that person would no longer be God, since it is one's nature, not one's person, that determines one's deity. Hence, if the Logos's nature were changed, his deity would change and he would no longer be divine. Moreover, **typical members of natural kinds** are plausibly taken to be essentially members of that kind. Thus, if an individual undergoes a substantial change (that is, a change of substance or essence), it ceases to exist as that individual and becomes something else. For example, a man who is cremated and ground to dust has undergone a substantial change and so is no longer a human being. Although Christ is not a typical member of the natural kind "man," he is a typical member of the kind "deity" and therefore cannot cease to be God without ceasing to exist. (Of course, God cannot cease to exist, since he is necessary and eternal.) Therefore Christ could not have ceased to be God. Should the kenoticist assert that to not grant Christ this prerogative is to limit his omnipotence, we should reply that this is no more a limitation on God's omnipotence than denying that God can make a stone heavier than he can lift. These are logical absurdities, and to appeal to God's omnipotence in such instances is to fail to understand that attribute.

Now the kenoticist might avert the above problems by denying that attributes such as omnipotence, omniscience, omnipresence and so on are essential to deity and therefore argue that the Logos could have abandoned them without thereby ceasing to be God. Such a Christology, however, entails a concept of God that might strike one as far too thin to be acceptable. We have seen that various theistic arguments imply that a being exists which is necessary in a broadly logical sense, as well as omniscient and wholly good. Moreover, it seems theologically untenable to think that a being could lack such properties and be God. On kenotic theology there is a possible world in which a being exists which is no more powerful, no more intelligent, no less limited spatially, no less logically contingent than an ordinary human being (like Jesus of Nazareth), and yet that being is God and is worthy of worship. That seems incredible.

Some contemporary kenoticists have tried to avert this objection by claiming that God, while lacking the essential properties of omnipotence, omniscience, omnipresence and so on, does have essential properties like being-omniscient-except-when-kenotically-incarnate, which he never surrenders and which are sufficient for deity. This answer, however, seems to be explanatorily vacuous. In answer to the question "How can God remain God if he gives up omniscience?" we are told that it is because he retains the essential property of being-omni-scient-unless-he-gives-up-omniscience! Imagine a case in which a human being is said to have abandoned all properties incompatible with becoming an ant and yet to have remained a human being. If we objected that rationality is essential to being human and that therefore he had ceased to be human, would it be a satisfactory answer to be told that only rationality-except-when-kenotically-an-ant is essential to being human and that he retains this property? Such an answer merely reasserts the problem. Ontologically speaking, it is not clear that there even are such properties as being-omniscient-except-when-kenotically-incarnate. These contrived properties are not attributes in the sense of capacities or qualities but are really statements masquerading as attributes. They are really assertions like "Christ remains divine even if he temporarily gives up omniscience"—which is precisely the issue under dispute.

Moreover, it is not clear that the problem of the Incarnation is solved even by postulating such gerrymandered properties of Christ. For it seems that certain divine attributes cannot be temporarily divested in the way envisioned by kenoticists. For example, it seems incoherent to say that Christ had the essential property being-omnipotent-except-when-kenotically-incarnate, for if, having relinquished omnipotence, he retained the power to get omnipotence back again, then he never in fact ceased to be omnipotent, since omnipotence is a modal property concerning what one *can* do. But if he lacked the power to get omnipotence back again, then how is it that he was only temporarily not omnipotent? Or consider the divine attributes of necessity, aseity and eternality. It makes no sense to say that these were given up temporarily, for by their very nature if one has such properties, one has them permanently. But then how could Christ die unless these were given up? One seems forced to say that Christ died only in his human nature, while these attributes are preserved in the divine nature—but then why not say the same for the other divine attributes as well? Christ can be omniscient, omnipotent, omnipresent and so on in his divine nature but not in his human nature—which is to revert to Chalcedonian orthodoxy.

2. *We postulate with Apollinarius that the Logos was the rational soul of Jesus of Nazareth.* What Apollinarius correctly discerned was that if we are to avoid a duality of persons in Christ, the man Jesus of Nazareth and the divine Logos must share some common constituent which unites their two individual natures. Chalcedon states that there is a single *hypostasis* that exemplifies the human and divine natures. That *hypostasis* is identified as the person Christ is. The question is how to make sense of this. If there exists a complete, **individual human nature** in Christ and a complete, individual divine nature who is the Logos, then how can there not be two persons? Apollinarius proposed that the Logos replaced the human mind of Jesus, so that there was in Christ a single person, the Logos, who was united with a human body, much as the soul is united with a body in an ordinary human being. On Apollinarius's view, it is easy to see how a single *hypostasis* can exemplify the properties proper to each nature.

Unfortunately, Apollinarius's view was radically defective as it stood. For a complete human nature involves more than a hominid body, so that on Apollinarius's view the Incarnation was really a matter of the Logos's assuming, not humanity, but mere animality. Moreover, Apollinarius's opponents rightly charged that such a view undercut Christ's work as well as his person, since Christ did not have a truly human nature, but only an animal nature, and so could not have redeemed humanity.

But are these defects irremediable? Can we appropriate Apollinarius's insight without falling into his errors? Let us see. Apollinarius may have been misunderstood when his critics charged him with giving Christ a truncated human nature. When Apollinarius argued that the Logos was not only the image of God but also the **archetypal man** and in this latter sense already possessed human nature in his preexistent form, his opponents like Gregory of Nazianzus understood him to mean that the *flesh* of Christ was preexistent. Apollinarius may have been more subtle than this; what he may have meant is that the Logos contained perfect human personhood archetypically in his own nature. The result was that in assuming a hominid body the Logos brought to Christ's animal nature just those properties that would serve to make it a complete human nature. Thus the human nature of Christ was complete precisely in virtue of the union of his flesh with the Logos. As a result of the union Christ did, indeed, possess a complete, individual human nature comprised of body and soul; for that nature was made complete by the union of the flesh with the Logos, the archetype of humanity.

Such an interpretation of the Incarnation draws strong support from the doctrine of man as created in the **image of God** (*imago Dei*). Human beings do not bear God's image in virtue of their animal bodies, which they have in common with other members of the biosphere. Rather, in being persons they uniquely reflect God's nature. God himself is personal, and inasmuch as we are persons we resemble him. Thus God already possesses the properties sufficient for human personhood even prior to the Incarnation, lacking only corporeality. The Logos already possessed in his preincarnate state all the properties necessary for being a human self. In assuming a hominid body, he brought to it all that was necessary for a complete human nature. For this reason, in Christ the one self-conscious subject who is the Logos possessed divine and human natures that were both complete.

This reformulation (or rehabilitation!) of Apollinarius's insight nullifies the traditional objections lodged against his original formulation of it. For on our view Christ is both fully God and fully man, that is to say, he is all that God is and all that man ought to be. He has two complete natures, human and divine. All he lacks is sin, since his individual human nature, like Adam's, is uncorrupted by sin. Because Christ has a complete human nature and has thus fully identified with our humanity, his atoning work our behalf is efficacious. Our proposed Christology thus lies safely within the boundaries of orthodoxy marked out at Chalcedon.

This second point of our Christology illuminates a doctrine implicit in the Chalcedonian formula and which later came to be called **enhypostasia**. Developed by Leontius of Byzantium (485-543), the doctrine states that Christ's individual human nature, that body-soul composite which was the man Jesus of Nazareth, did not have its own *hypostasis*, that is to say, it did not subsist on its own but became hypostatic only in its union with the Logos. Monophysites argued that if Christ had two individual natures, then each would have its own proper *hypostasis*, thereby destroying the unity of Christ's person. Leontius agreed with the monophysites that an individual nature without a *hypostasis* (*anhypostasia*) is impossible, but he escaped the Nestorian conclusion of two *hypostaseis* by postulating in Christ a human nature which is enhypostatic, that is, a nature which receives subsistence from another. In the case of Christ, the *hypostasis* of the divine Logos already exists prior to the Incarnation and then comes to possess the human nature as well. Hence, the individual human nature of Christ supervenes on the individual divine nature of the Logos. The two natures of Christ do not possess two separate *hypostaseis*, but they share one common *hypostasis*. The *hypostasis* of the human nature is identical with the divine person. Thus neither of the individual natures is without a *hypostasis* nor does each possess a *hypostasis* peculiar to it, but they have one and the same *hypostasis* that belongs properly to the divine Logos, the Second Person of the Trinity.

When *enhypostasia* is combined with our christological proposal, we have an illuminating explanation of how Christ can have a fully human nature and a fully divine nature and yet be one person. For the Logos is both the *hypostasis* which serves as the subsistent property-bearer for each abstract kind-nature and the person who is the self-conscious ego of both individual natures. The reason Christ's human nature is enhypostatic is that it is incomplete apart from its union with the Logos. Apart from this insight, the doctrine of *enhypostasia* remains mysterious and perhaps incoherent. On the present proposal the Logos completes the individual human nature of Christ by furnishing it with a rational soul, which is the Logos himself. The considerable theological advantage to be gained from this is that it aborts the suggestion that the Logos could have assumed just any human nature, so that Ronald Reagan or even J. P. Moreland could have been the Son of God. The individual human nature that is the man Jesus of Nazareth could not have existed apart from its union with the Logos, and were the Logos to be united with the body of, say, J. P. Moreland, the resultant person would not have been J. P. Moreland but someone else who merely looked like him.

The principal difficulty with our christological proposal as described thus far is that it seems to founder on the human limitations evinced by Jesus of Nazareth according to the Gospel accounts. The church has typically dealt with the problem of Christ's evident limitations by means of the device of **reduplicative predication**, that is to say, by predicating certain properties of the person of Christ with respect to one nature or the other. Thus, for example, Christ is said to be omniscient with respect to his divine nature but limited in knowledge with respect to his human nature, to have been omnipotent with regard to his divine nature but limited in power with regard to his human nature and so on. Such a device seems to work well with respect to certain properties like omnipotence and necessity. It is easy to see how Christ could have limited strength and mortality relative to his humanity in virtue of his having an ordinary human body, though he is omnipotent and imperishable in his divine nature. But for other attributes, reduplicative predication, especially on our proposed scheme, does not seem to work so well. How could Christ be omniscient and yet limited in knowledge if there is a single conscious subject in Christ? How could he be **impeccable** (incapable of sin) with respect to his divine nature and yet peccable in his humanity? Regarding Apollinarianism, A. B. Bruce objects, "There is no human *nous*, no freedom, no struggle; . . . the so-called temptations and struggles recorded in the Gospels are reduced to a show and a sham, and a cheap virtue results, devoid of all human interest, and scarcely deserving the name."[3] If one stops with the model as thus far described, then Bruce's objection will surely prove decisive. But as we shall see, the model can be enhanced in such a way as to turn back this criticism.

3. *We postulate that the divine aspects of Jesus' personality were largely subliminal during his state of humiliation.* We suggest that what William James called the **"subliminal self"** is the primary locus of the superhuman elements in the consciousness of the incarnate Logos. Thus Jesus possessed a normal human conscious experience. But the human consciousness of Jesus was underlain, as it were, by a divine subconsciousness. This understanding of Christ's personal experience draws on the insight of depth psychology that there is vastly more to a person than waking consciousness. The whole project of psychoanalysis is based

---

[3] A. B. Bruce, *The Humiliation of Christ* (New York: George H. Doran Company, n.d.), p. 46.

on the conviction that some of our behaviors have deep springs of action of which we are only dimly, if at all, aware. Multiple personality disorders furnish a particularly striking example of the eruption of subliminal facets of a single person's mind into distinct conscious personalities. In some cases there is even a dominant personality who is aware of all the others and who knows what each of them knows but who remains unknown by them. Hypnotism also furnishes a vivid demonstration of the reality of the subliminal. As Charles Harris explains, a person under hypnosis may be informed of certain facts and then instructed to forget them when he "awakens," but

> the knowledge is truly in his mind, and shows itself in unmistakable ways, especially by causing him to perform . . . certain actions, which, but for the possession of this knowledge, he would not have performed. . . . What is still more extraordinary, a sensitive hypnotic subject may be made both to see and not to see the same object at the same moment. For example, he may be told not to see a lamp-post, whereupon he becomes (in the ordinary sense) quite unable to see it. Nevertheless, he does see it, because he avoids it and cannot be induced to precipitate himself against it.[4]

Similarly, in the Incarnation—at least during his state of humiliation—the Logos allowed only those facets of his person to be part of Christ's waking consciousness which were compatible with typical human experience, while the bulk of his knowledge and other cognitive perfections, like an iceberg beneath the water's surface, lay submerged in his subconscious. On the model we propose, Christ is thus one person, but in that person conscious and subconscious elements are differentiated in a theologically significant way. Unlike Nestorianism our view does not imply that there are two persons, anymore than the conscious aspects of one's life and the subconscious aspects of one's life constitute two persons.

The model here proposed implies monotheletism, since the Logos, as the mind of Jesus of Nazareth, has but a single will. The subliminal facets of a person's personality do not possess a distinct faculty of the will, even though those subconscious aspects of one's personality may, indeed, powerfully influence what one wills in ways that one does not suspect. This implication of the model is in our view unobjectionable, since dyotheletism, despite its conciliar support, finds no warrant in Scripture. Passages in the Gospels usually used as proof texts of this doctrine—such as Jesus' prayer in Gethsemane, "Yet, not my will but yours be done" (Lk 22:42)—do not contemplate a struggle of Jesus' human will with his divine will (he is not, after all, talking to himself!), but have reference to the interaction between Jesus' will ("my will") and the Father's will ("yours"). Possessing a typical human consciousness, Jesus had to struggle against fear, weakness and temptation in order to align his will with that of his heavenly Father. The will of the Logos had in virtue of the Incarnation become the will of the man Jesus of Nazareth. This implication of the model is, in our view, one of its advantages, since it is extraordinarily difficult to preserve the unity of Christ's person once distinct wills are ascribed to the Logos and to the individual human nature of Christ.

---

[4] Charles Harris, cited in A. M Stibbs, *God Became Man* (London: Tyndale Press, 1957), p. 12.

Such a model provides a satisfying account of the Jesus we see in the Gospel portrait. In his conscious experience, Jesus grew in knowledge and wisdom, just as a human child does. One does not have the monstrosity of the baby Jesus lying in the manger possessing the full divine consciousness. In his conscious experience, we see Jesus genuinely tempted, even though he is, in fact, impeccable. The enticements of sin were really felt and could not be blown away like smoke; resisting temptation required spiritual discipline and moral resoluteness on Jesus' part. In his waking consciousness, Jesus is actually ignorant of certain facts, though kept from error and often supernaturally illumined by the divine subliminal. Even though the Logos possesses all knowledge about the world from quantum mechanics to auto mechanics, there is no reason to think that Jesus of Nazareth would have been able to answer questions about such subjects, so low had he stooped in condescending to take on the human condition. Moreover, in his conscious life, Jesus knew the whole gamut of human anxieties and felt physical hurt and fatigue. The model also preserves the integrity and sincerity of Jesus' prayer life, and it explains why Jesus was capable of being perfected through suffering. He, like us, needed to be dependent on his Father moment by moment in order to live victoriously in a fallen world and to carry out successfully the mission with which he had been charged. The agonies in Gethsemane were no mere show but represented the genuine struggle of the incarnate Logos in his waking consciousness. All the traditional objections against the Logos's being the mind of Christ melt away before this understanding of the Incarnation, for here we have Jesus who is not only divine but truly shares the human condition as well.

Some Christian philosophers, such as Thomas Morris, have postulated an independent conscious life for the incarnate Logos in addition to the conscious life of Jesus of Nazareth, what Morris calls a **"two minds"** view of the Incarnation. He provides a number of intriguing analogies in which asymmetrical accessing relations exist between a subsystem and an encompassing system, such that the overarching system can access information acquired through the subsystem but not vice versa. He gives a psychological analogy of dreams in which the sleeper is himself a person in the dream, and yet the sleeper has an awareness that everything that he is experiencing as reality is in fact merely a dream. Morris proposes that the conscious mind of Jesus of Nazareth be conceived as a subsystem of a wider mind which is the mind of the Logos. Such an understanding of the consciousness of the Logos stands in the tradition of Reformed theologians like Zwingli, who held that the Logos continued to operate outside the body of Jesus of Nazareth. The main difficulty of this view is that it threatens to lapse into Nestorianism, since it is very difficult to see why two self-conscious minds would not constitute two persons.

If the model here proposed makes sense, then it serves to show that the classic doctrine of the Incarnation of Christ is coherent and plausible. It also serves religiously to elicit praise to God for his self-emptying act of humiliation in taking on our human condition with all its struggles and limitations for our sakes and for our salvation. The Christian philosopher's heart rejoices with the words of Charles Wesley:

Veiled in flesh the Godhead see!
Hail the incarnate deity!
Pleased as man with men to dwell,
Jesus our Emmanuel!
Hark! The herald angels sing,
"Glory to the new-born King!"

CHAPTER SUMMARY

In response to the biblical data affirming both Christ's true humanity and true deity, the church fathers came to confess that in Christ there is one person who possesses two natures. They insisted that one must neither confuse the natures nor divide the person of Christ. This traditional doctrine is coherent if we differentiate between kind natures or essences and individual essences and affirm that Christ contingently exemplified two kind natures. Kenotic theology represents an unnecessary and, in the end, unsuccessful alternative to the classical view that Christ retained in his divine nature the traditional attributes of God. A plausible model of the Incarnation affirms that the mind of the incarnate Christ was the Logos, the Second Person of the Trinity. The individual human nature of Christ would be incomplete apart from its possession by the Logos, so that the individual Jesus of Nazareth could not have existed apart from the Incarnation. The Logos's acquisition of a hominid body brings the human nature of Christ to completion, since the Logos already possesses in his preexistent form the properties of personhood. Thus Christ's human nature is enhypostatic, finding its subsistence in the person of the Logos. Such a Christology implies monotheletism. If we conceive of the superhuman facets of Christ's person as largely subliminal, we achieve a plausible portrait of the historical Jesus that is faithful to the biblical record.

CHECKLIST OF BASIC TERMS AND CONCEPTS
accidental change
Alexandrian Christology
animal soul
anthropology
Antiochene Christology
Apollinarianism
archetypal man
Arianism
body
christological controversies
communication of the attributes
confuse the natures
Council of Chalcedon
divide the person
divine nature
dyophysite Christology
enhypostasia

functional unity
human nature
hypostatic union
image of God
impeccable
Incarnation
individual essence
individual human nature
indwelling
kenotic Christology
kind essence
Logos-flesh Christology
Logos-man Christology
Lutheran Christology
monophysite Christology
monophysitism
monotheletism
natural kinds
natures
Nestorianism
one person having two natures
Protestant Reformation
rational soul
Reformed Christology
real presence
reduplicative predication
state of exaltation
state of humiliation
subliminal self
substantial change
theotokos
two minds
two natures of Christ
typical member of a natural kind
ubiquity of Christ's body
union
unity of Christ's person
without confusion, without change, without division, without separation

31

CHRISTIAN DOCTRINES III

Christian Particularism

There is salvation in no one else,
for there is no other name under heaven given among men
by which we must be saved.

ACTS 4:12 RSV

1 INTRODUCTION

The apostles of Jesus Christ believed and preached that there was no salvation apart from Christ. Indeed, the conviction that **salvation** is available through Christ alone permeates the New Testament. Paul, for example, invites his Gentile converts to recall their pre-Christian days: "Remember that you were at that time without Christ, being aliens from the commonwealth of Israel, and strangers to the covenants of promise, having no hope and without God in the world" (Eph 2:12). It is the burden of the opening chapters of the book of Romans to show that this desolate condition is the general situation of mankind. Paul explains that God's power and deity are made known through the created order around us, so that men are without excuse (Rom 1:20), and that God has written his moral law upon all men's hearts, so that they are morally responsible before him (Rom 2:15). Although God offers eternal life to all who will respond in an appropriate way to God's **general revelation** in nature and conscience (Rom 2:7), the sad fact is that rather than worship and serve their Creator, people ignore God and flout his moral law (Rom 1:21-32). The conclusion: All men are under the power of sin (Rom 3:9-12). Worse, Paul goes on to explain that no one can redeem himself by means of righteous living (Rom 3:19-20). Fortunately, however, God has provided a means of escape: Christ has died for the sins of mankind, thereby satisfying the demands of God's justice and facilitating reconciliation with God (Rom 3:21-26). By means of his **atoning death** salvation is made available as a gift to be received by faith.

The logic of the New Testament is clear: The universality of sin and the uniqueness of Christ's atoning death entail that there is no salvation apart from Christ. This particularistic doctrine was just as scandalous in the polytheistic world of the Roman Empire as in contemporary Western culture. In time, however, the scandal receded, as Christianity grew to supplant the religions of Greece and Rome and became the official religion of the Roman Empire. Indeed, for medieval thinkers like Augustine and Aquinas, one of the marks of the true church was its **catholicity**, that is, its universality. To them it seemed incredible that the great edifice of the Christian church, filling all of civilization, should be founded on a falsehood.

The demise of Christian particularism came with the so-called **expansion of Europe**, the three centuries of exploration and discovery from about 1450 until 1750. Through the travels and voyages of men like Marco Polo, Christopher Columbus and Ferdinand Magellan, new civilizations and whole new worlds were discovered, which knew nothing of the Christian faith. The realization that much of the world lay outside the bounds of Christianity had a twofold impact on people's religious thinking. First, it tended to relativize religious beliefs. It was seen that far from being the universal religion of mankind, Christianity was largely confined to Western Europe, a corner of the globe. No religion, it seemed, could make a claim to universal validity; each society seemed to have its own religion suited to its peculiar needs. Second, it made Christianity's claim to be the only way of salvation seem narrow and cruel. Enlightenment rationalists like Voltaire taunted the Christians of his day with the prospect of millions of Chinese doomed to hell for not having believed in Christ, when they had not so much as even heard of Christ. In our own day, the influx into Western nations of immigrants from former colonies and the advances in telecommunications that have served to shrink the world to a global village have heightened our awareness of the **religious diversity** of mankind. It is estimated that somewhere between 15-25% of the world's population have still not yet heard the gospel of Christ.

The missiological and theological consequences of the challenge posed by religious diversity have been major. Mainline churches have largely lost a sense of calling to **world evangelization**. No longer is the task of missions to carry the life-giving message of the gospel to a lost and dying world; rather, the missionary task is reinterpreted as social improvement of the Third World. The task at hand is to bring assistance to developing countries in agriculture, medicine and economic development—a sort of Christian Peace Corps. The theological fallout has been just as serious: it has marginalized the person of Christ. This development is epitomized in the pilgrimage of the philosophical theologian John Hick. Hick began his career as a relatively conservative theologian. His first book was entitled *Christianity at the Centre*. But as Hick became acquainted with adherents to other world religions, it seemed inconceivable to him that these people should all be destined to hell. Their own religions must be equally efficacious avenues of salvation. But then Christ can no longer be at the center; somehow he must be marginalized. Hick therefore came to edit the book *The Myth of God Incarnate*, in which he rejects the incarnation and divinity of Christ as a myth. Thus the missiological and theological consequences of the challenge posed by religious diversity have been serious, indeed.

2 THE PROBLEM POSED BY RELIGIOUS DIVERSITY

But what exactly is the problem arising from religious diversity supposed to be? How is traditional Christianity undermined by the existence of other world religions? In exploring this problem, it will be useful to draw some distinctions. First, we may distinguish between universalism and particularism. **Universalism** is the doctrine that every human being will partake of God's salvation; **particularism** is the view that only some, but not all, human beings will partake of

God's salvation. Obviously, from this definition particularism may range from a narrow particularism, according to which comparatively few persons will be saved, to a broad particularism, according to which comparatively few will be lost. A second distinction is that between accessibilism and restrictivism. Christian **restrictivism** maintains that salvation is available only through an appropriate response to God's **special revelation** concerning Christ, which requires a faith response to the message of the gospel of Christ. Christian **accessibilism**, on the other hand, maintains that for those who have not had the benefit of special revelation, salvation is available through their appropriate response to God's general revelation in nature and conscience. Finally, we may distinguish between exclusivism, inclusivism and pluralism. Christian **exclusivism** is the view that people actually appropriate God's salvation only on the basis of Christ's work and through explicit faith in him. Christian **inclusivism** is the view that people actually appropriate God's salvation only on the basis of Christ's work but not always through explicit faith in him. Again, inclusivism may range from broad inclusivism, which endorses universalism, to narrow inclusivism, which implies a narrow particularism. **Pluralism** is the view that people actually appropriate God's salvation through a multiplicity of conditions and means in various religions.

These different schools of thought are obviously closely related, but it is important, if confusion is not to result, that we do not conflate these distinctions. For example, although we are apt to associate restrictivism with particularism, this is not always the case: some restrictivists are universalists because they envision the possibility of postmortem proclamation and reception of the gospel. Or again, we are apt to think that pluralism implies universalism; but that need not be the case, since the pluralist may regard some religions—for example, those that practice human sacrifice, cultic prostitution or satanic worship—as inefficacious channels of salvation.

The question, then, is what problem is posed by the reality of religious diversity and for whom? When one reads the literature on this problem, the recurring challenge seems to be laid at the doorstep of the Christian particularist. The phenomenon of religious diversity is taken to require the truth of universalism, and the main debate then proceeds to the question of which form of that doctrine is the most plausible. But why think that Christian particularism is untenable in the face of religious diversity?

When one examines the arguments on behalf of universalism, one finds them to be of very uneven worth, some objections being little more than ad hominem attacks on particularists. For example, it is frequently asserted that it is arrogant and immoral to hold to any doctrine of religious particularism because one must then regard all persons who disagree with one's own religion as mistaken. This is an odd objection, since the truth of a position is quite independent of the moral qualities of those who believe it. Even if all Christian particularists were arrogant and immoral, that would do nothing to prove that their view is false. In any case, it is not only incorrect to say that arrogance and immorality are necessary conditions of being a particularist—the Christian particularist may have done all he can to discover the religious truth about reality and humbly embraces Christian faith as an undeserved gift—but, even more fundamentally, those who make such accusations find themselves hoist on their own petard. For the universalist believes that his own view is right and that all those adherents to particularistic religious traditions are wrong. Thus he himself would be convicted of arrogance and immorality if he were right that holding to a view with which many others disagree is arrogant and immoral.

Or again, it is frequently alleged that Christian particularism cannot be correct because religious beliefs are culturally relative; for example, if a Christian believer had been born in Pakistan during the Abbassid Dynasty, he would likely have been a Muslim. But such a claim simply has no relevance to the truth of Christian particularism or to one's justification in accepting it. If one had been born in ancient Greece, one would likely have believed that the sun orbits the earth; but is our belief in heliocentrism therefore false or unjustified? Evidently not! And once again, the universalist finds the rug pulled from beneath his own feet: for had he been born in medieval Spain he would likely have been a Christian particularist. Thus on his own analysis his universalism is merely the product of his being born in late twentieth-century Western society.

Or again, it is sometimes alleged that the Christian particularist cannot be warranted in believing that Christianity alone of all the world religions is the truth. But that is a matter for Christian apologetics to decide. In any case, this fact in and of itself would not show that Christian particularism is false. And, we may ask, what warrant is there for believing that universalism is the truth? The alleged failure of arguments for the Christian worldview is in itself no reason to think that universalism is true.

Thus many of the arguments against Christian particularism frequently found in the literature are unimpressive. When these objections are answered by defenders of Christian particularism, however, then the real issue separating universalists and particularists tends to emerge in the discussion. That issue is the fate of unbelievers outside one's particular religious tradition. Christian particularism consigns such persons to hell, which universalists take to be unconscionable.

But what exactly is the problem here supposed to be? Is it supposed to be simply the allegation that a loving God would not send people to hell? It seems not. The Scriptures indicate that God wills the salvation of every human being. "The Lord is . . . not wishing that any should perish, but that all should reach repentance" (2 Pet 3:9 RSV). He "desires all men to be saved and to come to the knowledge of the truth" (1 Tim 2:4 RSV). Thus, for example, God speaks through the prophet Ezekiel:

> Have I any pleasure in the death of the wicked, says the Lord GOD, and not rather that he should turn from his way and live? . . . For I have no pleasure in the death of any one, says the Lord GOD; so turn, and live. (Ezek 18:23, 32 RSV)

> Say to them, As I live, says the Lord GOD, I have no pleasure in the death of the wicked, but that the wicked turn from his way and live; turn back, turn back from your evil ways; for why will you die? (Ezek 33:11 RSV)

Here God literally pleads with people to turn back from their self-destructive course of action and be saved. Thus, in a sense, the biblical God does not send any person to hell. His desire is that everyone be saved, and he seeks to draw all persons to himself. If we make a free and well-informed decision to reject Christ's sacrifice for our sin, then God has no choice but to give us what we deserve. God will not send us to hell—but we shall send ourselves. Our eternal destiny thus lies in our own hands. It is a matter of our free choice where we shall spend eternity. The lost, therefore, are self-condemned; they separate themselves from God despite God's will and every effort to save them, and God grieves over their loss.

Now the universalist might admit that given human freedom God cannot guarantee that everyone will be saved. Some people might freely condemn themselves by rejecting Christ's offer of salvation. But, he might argue, it would be unjust of God to condemn people *forever*. For even grievous sins like those of the Nazi torturers in the death camps still deserve only a finite punishment. Therefore, at most hell could be a sort of purgatory, lasting an appropriate length of time for each person before that person is released and admitted into heaven. Eventually hell would be emptied and heaven filled. Thus, ironically, hell is incompatible, not with God's love, but with his justice. The objection charges that God is unjust because the punishment does not fit the crime.

Some Christian thinkers have sought to avoid this objection by adopting the doctrine of **annihilationism**. They hold that hell is not endless separation from God, but rather the annihilation of the damned. The damned simply cease to exist, whereas the saved are given eternal life. Other Christian philosophers have denied that hell involves **retributive justice**, that is, appropriate punishment for our deeds, on God's part. Rather, it is simply the result of God's allowing free creatures, out of respect for their moral autonomy, to separate themselves from God forever rather than to coerce submission on their part. God would permit the damned to leave hell and go to heaven, but they freely refuse to do so. Rather than repent and ask God for forgiveness, persons in hell continue to curse him and reject him. They grow only more implacable in their hatred of God as time goes on. God thus has no choice but to leave them where they are. In such a case, the door to hell is locked, as Jean Paul Sartre said, from the inside. The damned thus choose eternal separation from God.

Such views are rather difficult to square with the biblical data, however, which do seem to present hell as everlasting punishment (Mt 25:46; 2 Thess 1:9). Such modifications of the traditional understanding do not seem to be necessary, however. At least two responses to the objection are in fact available on the traditional view.

1. The objection that eternal punishment does not fit the crime equivocates between *every* sin we commit and *all* the sins we commit. We could agree that every individual sin a person commits deserves only a finite punishment. But it does not follow from this that all of a person's sins taken together as a whole deserve only a finite punishment. If a person commits an infinite number of sins, then the sum total of all such sins deserves infinite punishment. Now, of course, nobody commits an infinite number of sins in the earthly life. But what about in the afterlife? Insofar as the inhabitants of hell continue to hate God and reject him, they continue to sin and so accrue to themselves more guilt and more punishment. In a real sense, then, hell is self-perpetuating. In such a case,

every sin has a finite punishment, but because sinning goes on forever, so does the punishment.

2. Why think that every sin does have only a finite punishment? We could agree that sins like theft, lying, adultery and so forth, are only of finite consequence and so only deserve a finite punishment. But, in a sense, these sins are not what serves to separate someone from God, since Christ has died for those sins; the penalty for those sins has been paid. One has only to accept Christ as Savior to be completely free and clean of those sins. But the refusal to accept Christ and his sacrifice seems to be a sin of a different order altogether. This sin repudiates God's provision for sin and so decisively separates one from God and his salvation. To reject Christ is to reject God himself. And in light of God's status, this is a sin of infinite gravity and proportion and therefore plausibly deserves infinite punishment. What makes sin against God so serious? We can think of the seriousness of sin against God either in terms of God's being wholly other than finite moral agents in moral virtue—for example, of his being the locus and source of all moral value and obligation—or else in terms of a universally applicable moral principle—for example, that the more loving a person's overtures the more morally reprehensible it is to reject him. We ought not, therefore, to think of hell primarily as punishment for the array of sins of finite consequence that we have committed, but as the just due for a sin of infinite consequence, namely, the rejection of God himself. Thus it seems that the problem raised by mankind's religious diversity cannot be reduced simply to objections to the doctrine of hell.

Is the problem perhaps supposed to be that a loving God would not send people to hell because they were uninformed or misinformed about Christ? Again, the answer would seem to be no. Here the Christian particularist may endorse some form of accessibilism. He may argue that according to the Christian view, God does not judge people who have never heard of Christ on the basis of whether they have placed their faith in Christ. Rather, God judges them on the basis of the light of God's general revelation in nature and conscience that they do have. The offer of Romans 2:7—"To those who by patiently doing good seek for glory and honor and immortality, he will give eternal life"—is a bona fide offer of salvation. This is not to say that people can be saved apart from Christ. Rather, it is to say that the benefits of Christ's atoning death could be applied to people without their conscious knowledge of Christ. Such persons would be similar to certain figures mentioned in the Old Testament like Job and Melchizedek, who had no conscious knowledge of Christ and were not even members of the covenant family of Israel and yet clearly enjoyed a personal relationship with God. Similarly, there could be modern-day Jobs living among that percentage of the world's population that have yet to hear the gospel of Christ.

Unfortunately, the testimony of the New Testament, as we have seen, is that people do not in fact measure up to these much lower standards of general revelation. So there are little grounds for optimism about there being many, if any at all, who will actually be saved through their response to general revelation alone. At best a narrow inclusivism might be true. Nonetheless, the point remains that salvation is universally accessible for anyone who will respond to

God's general revelation in nature and conscience, so that the problem posed by religious diversity cannot be simply that God would not condemn persons who are uninformed or misinformed about Christ.

Rather, the real problem seems to be this: If God is omniscient, then even logically prior to his decree to create the world, he knew who would freely receive the gospel and who would not. But then certain very difficult questions arise:

1. Why did God not bring the gospel to people who he knew *would* accept it if they heard it, even though they reject the light of general revelation that they do have? To illustrate: imagine a North American Indian living prior to the arrival of Christian missionaries. Let us call him Walking Bear. Let us suppose that as Walking Bear looks up at the heavens at night and sees the beauty of nature around him, he senses that all of this has been made by the Great Spirit. Furthermore, as Walking Bear looks into his own heart, he senses there the moral law, telling him that all men are brothers made by the Great Spirit, and he therefore realizes that we ought to live in love for one another. But suppose that instead of worshiping the Great Spirit and living in love for his fellow man, Walking Bear ignores the Great Spirit and creates totems of other spirits and that rather than loving his fellow man he lives in selfishness and cruelty toward others. In such a case Walking Bear would be justly condemned before God on the basis of his failure to respond to God's general revelation in nature and conscience. But now suppose that if only the missionaries had arrived, then Walking Bear would have believed the gospel and been saved! In that case his salvation or damnation seems to be the result of bad luck. Through no fault of his own he just happened to be born at a time and place in history when the gospel was as yet unavailable. His condemnation is just; but would an all-loving God allow people's eternal destiny to hinge on historical and geographical accident?

2. More fundamentally, why did God even create the world, when he knew that so many people would not believe the gospel and be lost?

3. Even more radically, why did God not create a world in which everyone freely believes the gospel and is saved?

What is the Christian particularist supposed to say in answer to these questions? Does Christianity make God out to be cruel and unloving?

3 THE PROBLEM ANALYZED

In order to answer these questions it will be helpful to examine more closely the logical structure of the problem before us. The universalist seems to be alleging that it is impossible for God to be all-powerful and all-loving and yet for some people to never hear the gospel and be lost, that is to say, that the following statements are logically inconsistent:

1. God is all-powerful and all-loving.

2. Some people never hear the gospel and are lost.

The problem thus has the same logical structure as the logical version of the internal problem of evil; indeed, it is a sort of **soteriological problem of evil**. Accordingly, the free will defense ought to be relevant to this problem as well as to the general problem of evil. For we can ask, why think that (1) and (2) are logically incompatible? After all, there is no explicit contradiction between them. But if the universalist is claiming that (1) and (2) are implicitly contradictory, he must be assuming some hidden premises that would serve to bring out this contradiction and make it explicit. The question is, what are those hidden premises?

Although universalists have not been very forthcoming about their hidden assumptions, the logic of the problem of evil suggests that they must be something akin to the following:

3. If God is all-powerful, he can create a world in which everybody hears the gospel and is freely saved.

4. If God is all-loving, he prefers a world in which everybody hears the gospel and is freely saved.

Since, according to (1), God is both all-powerful and all-loving, it follows that he both can create a world of universal salvation and prefers such a world. Therefore, such a world must exist, which is in contradiction to (2).

As in the logical version of the internal problem of evil, both of the hidden premises must be necessarily true if the logical incompatibility of (1) and (2) is to be demonstrated. But are these premises necessarily true?

Consider (3). It seems uncontroversial that God could create a world in which everybody hears the gospel. But so long as people are free, there is no guarantee that everybody in such a world would be freely saved. In fact, there is no reason to think that the balance between saved and lost in such a world would be any better than the balance in the actual world! It is possible that in any world of free creatures that God could create, some people would freely reject his saving grace and be lost. Hence, (3) is not necessarily true, and the universalist's argument is fallacious.

But what about (4)? Is it necessarily true? Let us suppose for the sake of argument that there are possible worlds that are feasible for God in which everyone hears the gospel and freely accepts it. Does God's being all-loving compel him to prefer one of these worlds over a world in which some persons are lost? Not necessarily; for these worlds might have other, overriding deficiencies that make them less preferable. For example, suppose that the only worlds in which everybody freely believes the gospel and is saved are worlds with only a handful of people in them. If God were to create any more people, then at least one of them would have freely rejected his grace and been lost. Must he prefer one of these sparsely populated worlds over a world in which multitudes believe in the gospel and are saved, even though that implies that other persons freely reject his grace and are lost? This is far from obvious. So long as God gives sufficient grace for salvation to all persons he creates, God seems no less loving for preferring a more populous world, even though that implies that some people would freely resist his every effort to save them and be damned. Thus the universalist's second assumption is not necessarily true, so that his argument is revealed to be doubly fallacious.

So neither of the universalist's assumptions seems to be necessarily true. Unless the universalist can suggest some other premises, we have no reason to think that (1) and (2) are logically incompatible.

But we can push the argument a notch further. We may try to show positively that it is entirely possible that God is all-powerful and all-loving and that many persons never hear the gospel and are lost. All we have to do is find a possibly true statement that is compatible with God's being all-powerful and all-loving and that, together with (1), entails that some people never hear the gospel and are lost. Can such a statement be formulated? Let us see.

As a good and loving God, God wants as many people as possible to be saved and as few as possible to be lost. His goal, then, is to achieve an optimal balance between these, to create no more of the lost than is necessary to attain a certain number of the saved. But it is possible that the actual world (which includes the future as well as the present and past) has such a balance. It is possible that in order to create this many people who will be saved, God also had to create this many people who will be lost. It is possible that had God created a world in which fewer people go to hell, then even fewer people would have gone to heaven. It is possible that in order to achieve a multitude of saints, God had to accept a multitude of sinners.

It might be objected that an all-loving God would not create people who he knew will be lost, but who would have been saved if only they had heard the gospel. But how do we know there *are* any such persons? It is reasonable to assume that many people who never hear the gospel would not have believed the gospel if they had heard it. Suppose, then, that God has so providentially ordered the world that *all* persons who never hear the gospel are precisely such people. In that case, anybody who never hears the gospel and is lost would have rejected the gospel and been lost even if he had heard it. No one could stand before God on the judgment day and complain, "All right, God, so I didn't respond to your general revelation in nature and conscience! But if I had just heard the gospel, then I would have believed!" For God will say, "No, I knew that even if you had heard the gospel, you would not have believed it. Therefore, my judgment of you on the basis of nature and conscience is neither unfair nor unloving." Thus (5) is possible:

5. God has created a world that has an optimal balance between saved and lost, and those who never hear the gospel and are lost would not have believed in it even if they had heard it.

So long as (5) is even *possibly true*, it shows that there is no incompatibility between an all-powerful, all-loving God and some people's never hearing the gospel and being lost.

On this basis we are now prepared to offer *possible* answers to the three difficult questions that prompted this inquiry. To take them in reverse order:

a. Why did God not create a world in which everyone freely believes the gospel and is saved?

Possible answer: It may not be either feasible or preferable for God to create such a world. If such a world were feasible and did not have overriding deficiencies, God would have created it. But given his will to create free creatures, God had to accept that some would freely reject him and his every effort to save them and be lost.

   b. Why did God even create the world, when he knew that so many people would not believe the gospel and be lost?

Possible answer: God wanted to share his love and fellowship with created persons. He knew this meant that many would freely reject him and be lost. But he also knew that many others would freely receive his grace and be saved. The happiness and blessedness of those who would freely embrace his love should not be precluded by those who would freely spurn him. Persons who would freely reject God and his love should not be allowed, in effect, to hold a sort of veto power over which worlds God is free to create. In his mercy God has providentially ordered the world to achieve an optimal balance between saved and lost by maximizing the number of those who freely accept him and minimizing the number of those who would not.

   c. Why did God not bring the gospel to people who he knew would accept it if they heard it, even though they reject the light of general revelation that they do have?

Possible answer: There are no such people. God in his providence has so arranged the world that those who would respond to the gospel if they heard it, do hear it. The sovereign God has so ordered human history that as the gospel spreads out from first-century Palestine, he places people in its path who would believe it if they heard it. Once the gospel reaches a people, God providentially places there persons who he knew would respond to it if they heard it. In his love and mercy, God ensures that no one who would believe the gospel if he heard it is born at a time and place in history where he fails to hear it. Those who do not respond to God's general revelation in nature and conscience and never hear the gospel would not respond to it if they did hear it. Hence, no one is lost because of historical or geographical accident. Anyone who wants or even would want to be saved will be saved.

   These are *possible* answers to the questions we posed. But so long as they are even possible, they show that there is no incompatibility between God's being all-powerful and all-loving and some people's never hearing the gospel and being lost. Furthermore, these answers are attractive because they also seem quite biblical as well. In his open-air address to the Athenian philosophers gathered on the Areopagus Paul declared:

> The God who made the world and everything in it is the Lord of heaven and earth. . . . He himself gives all men life and breath and everything else. From one man he made every nation of men, that they should inhabit the whole earth; and he determined the times set for them and the exact places where they should live. God did this so that men would seek him and perhaps reach out for him and find him, though he is not far from each one of us. For in him we live and move and have our being. As some of your own poets have said, "We are his offspring." (Acts 17:24-28 NIV)

Now the universalist might concede the logical compatibility of God's being all-powerful and all-loving and some people's never hearing the gospel and being lost but insist that these two facts are nonetheless improbable with respect to each other. People by and large seem to believe in the religion of the culture in which they were raised. But in that case, the universalist may argue, it is highly probable that if many of those who never hear the gospel had been raised in a Christian culture, they would have believed the gospel and been saved. Thus the hypothesis we have offered is highly implausible.

Now it would, indeed, be fantastically improbable that by happenstance alone it just turns out that all those who never hear the gospel and are lost are persons who would not have believed the gospel even if they had heard it. But that is not the hypothesis. The hypothesis is that a provident God has so arranged the world. Given a God endowed with middle knowledge of how every free creature would respond to his grace in whatever circumstances God might place him, it is not at all implausible that God has ordered the world in the way described. Such a world would not look outwardly any different from a world in which the circumstances of a person's birth are a matter of happenstance. The particularist can agree that people generally adopt the religion of their culture and that if many of those born into non-Christian cultures had been born in a Christian society instead, they would have become nominally or culturally Christian. But that is not to say that they would have been saved.

The universalist might claim that such a world would look significantly different than the actual world, that persons who would have been no more than nominal Christians had they been born in a Christian culture would be perceptibly different from people who would have become regenerate Christians. But this claim would be manifestly untrue. It is a simple empirical fact that there are no distinguishing psychological or sociological traits between persons who become Christians and persons who are nonbelievers. There is no way to predict accurately by examining a person whether and under what circumstances that person would believe in Christ for salvation. Since a world providentially ordered by God would appear outwardly identical to a world in which one's birth is a matter of historical and geographical accident, it is hard to see how the hypothesis we have defended can be deemed improbable apart from a demonstration that the existence of a God endowed with middle knowledge is implausible. But objections to middle knowledge have been shown to be inconclusive at best.

In short, there is no logical incompatibility in the biblical view of Christian particularism, and with the resources of a doctrine of divine middle knowledge a plausible account can be given of God's universal salvific will and the perdition of those who never hear the gospel. Therefore, the fact of mankind's religious diversity does not undermine the Christian gospel of salvation through Christ alone. On the contrary, the view here expressed helps to put the proper perspective on Christian missions: it is our duty as Christians to proclaim the gospel to the whole world, trusting that God has so providentially ordered things that through us the good news will come to persons who God knew would accept it if they heard it. Our compassion toward those in other world religions is expressed, not in pretending they are not lost and dying without Christ, but by supporting and making every effort ourselves to communicate to them the life-giving message of Christ.

CHAPTER SUMMARY

The problem posed by religious diversity has to do with the fate of those who stand outside the community of Christian faith. The problem is not simply the claim that the existence of hell is incompatible with a just and loving God, for on the Christian view people freely separate themselves from a loving God despite his every effort to save them, and the retribution they suffer for this sin is consonant with God's justice. Nor is the problem the claim that persons who are uninformed or misinformed about Christ are unjustly judged by God, for the New Testament suggests that persons will be judged on the basis of the information they have and that salvation is universally accessible through God's general revelation in nature and conscience, even if, unfortunately, it is rarely so accessed. Rather, the real challenge posed by religious diversity is a soteriological problem of evil: the fact that some persons never hear the gospel and are lost seems incompatible with the existence of an all-loving and all-powerful God. But the key assumptions presumed by the universalist have not been shown by him to be necessarily true, so that this argument is defeated. Moreover, we can construct a scenario to show that the facts of God's existence and the perdition of the unevangelized are consistent. God could so providentially order the world that all those who would believe the gospel and be saved if they heard it are born at times and places in history such that they do hear it. Given that such a world would be empirically indistinguishable from a world in which the facts of a person's birth are the result of historical and geographical accident, such a scenario is not merely possible but is also not improbable as well.

CHECKLIST OF BASIC TERMS AND CONCEPTS

accessibilism
annihilationism
atoning death
catholicity
exclusivism
expansion of Europe
general revelation
inclusivism
particularism
pluralism
religious diversity
restrictivism
retributive justice
salvation
soteriological problem of evil
special revelation
universalism
world evangelization

SUGGESTIONS FOR FURTHER READING

*Students will find useful further reading
among the following resources for each chapter.*

CHAPTER 1: WHAT IS PHILOSOPHY?

Some of the most important resource tools in philosophy are the following:

Audi, Robert, ed. *The Cambridge Dictionary of Philosophy*. Cambridge: Cambridge University Press, 1995.

Blackburn, Simon. *The Oxford Dictionary of Philosophy*. Oxford: Oxford University Press, 1996.

Burkhardt, Hans, and Barry Smith, eds. *Handbook of Metaphysics and Ontology*. 2 vols. Munich: Philosophia Verlag, 1991.

Copleston, F. C. *A History of Philosophy*. 9 vols. Garden City, N.Y.: Doubleday & Company, 1962.

Craig, Edward, ed. *Routledge Encyclopedia of Philosophy*. 10 vols. London: Routledge, 1998. (The *Concise Routledge Encyclopedia of Philosophy* is a 1999 abridged volume based on the 10-volume set.)

Edwards, Paul, ed. *The Encyclopedia of Philosophy*. 8 vols. New York: Macmillan, 1967.

Grayling, A. C., ed. *Philosophy: A Guide Through the Subject*. Oxford: Oxford University Press, 1995.

Honderich, Ted, ed. *The Oxford Companion to Philosophy*. Oxford: Oxford University Press, 1995.

Kenny, Anthony. *A Brief History of Western Philosophy*. Malden: Blackwell, 1998.

Kenny, Anthony, ed. *The Oxford History of Western Philosophy*. Oxford: Oxford University Press, 1994.

Mautner, Thomas, ed. *A Dictionary of Philosophy*. Oxford: Blackwell, 1996.

Solomon, Robert C., and Kathleen M. Higgins. *A Passion for Wisdom: A Very Brief History of Philosophy*. New York: Oxford University Press, 1997.

———. *A Short History of Philosophy*. New York: Oxford University Press, 1996.

Sparkes, A. W. *Talking Philosophy: A Wordbook*. London: Routledge, 1991.

Stumpf, Samuel Enoch. *Socrates to Sartre: A History of Philosophy*. Rev. 5th ed. New York: McGraw-Hill, 1993.

There is also an important series of volumes called the Blackwell Companions to Philosophy (Oxford: Blackwell).

Three important Christian professional societies are as follows: (1) Evangelical Philosophical Society, c/o Dr. Craig Hazen, Executive Committee member and editor of the EPS journal *Philosophia Christi*, c/o Biola University, 13800 Biola Ave., La Mirada, CA 90639; email: <philchristi@biola.edu>. (2) Society of Christian Philosophers, c/o Kelley James Clark, secretary, Department of Philosophy, Calvin College, Grand Rapids, MI 49546-4388 (journal: *Faith and Philosophy*). (3) American Catholic Philosophical Association, Room 403, Administration Building, The Catholic University of America, Washington, DC 20064 (journal: *American Catholic Philosophical Quarterly*).

CHAPTER 2: ARGUMENTATION AND LOGIC

Copi, Irving M., and Carl Cohen. *Introduction to Logic*. 11th ed. Upper Saddle River, N.J.: Prentice Hall, 2002.

Gorowitz, Samuel, et al. *Philosophical Analysis*. 3d ed. New York: Random House, 1979.

Hacking, Ian. *An Introduction to Probability and Inductive Logic*. Cambridge: Cambridge University Press, 2001.

Hughes, G. E., and M. J. Cresswell. *A New Introduction to Modal Logic*. London: Routledge, 1996.

Kneale, William, and Martha Kneale. *The Development of Logic*. Oxford: Clarendon, 1985.

Lewis, David K. *Counterfactuals*. Malden, Mass.: Blackwell, 2001.

Lipton, Peter. *Inference to the Best Explanation*. London: Routledge, 1991.

Purtill, Richard L. *Logic for Philosophers*. New York: Harper & Row, 1971.

Salmon, Wesley C. *Logic*. 3d ed. Foundations of Philosophy. Englewood Cliffs, N.J.: Prentice-Hall, 1984.

CHAPTER 3: KNOWLEDGE AND RATIONALITY

BonJour, Laurence. *In Defense of Pure Reason*. Cambridge: Cambridge University Press, 1998.

Crumley, Jack S., II. *An Introduction to Epistemology*. Mountain View, Calif.: Mayfield, 1999.

DePaul, Michael R., and William Ramsey, eds. *Rethinking Intuition: The Psychology of Intuition and Its Role in Philosophical Inquiry*. Lanham, Md.: Rowman & Littlefield, 1998.

Gettier, Edmund L. "Is Justified True Belief Knowledge?" *Analysis* 23 (1963): 121-23.

Moser, Paul K., Dwayne H. Mulder and J. D. Trout. *The Theory of Knowledge*. New York: Oxford University Press, 1998.

Plantinga, Alvin. *Warrant: The Current Debate*. New York: Oxford University Press, 1993.

———. *Warrant and Proper Function*. New York: Oxford University Press, 1993.

Pojman, Louis P., ed. *The Theory of Knowledge*. Belmont, Calif.: Wadsworth, 1993.

CHAPTER 4: THE PROBLEM OF SKEPTICISM

DeRose, Keith, and Ted A. Warfield. *Skepticism: A Contemporary Reader*. New York: Oxford University Press, 1999.

Fumerton, Richard. *Metaepistemology and Skepticism*. Lanham, Md.: Rowman & Littlefield, 1995.

Greco, John. *Putting Skeptics in Their Place*. Cambridge: Cambridge University Press, 2000.

Johnson, Oliver A. *Skepticism and Cognitivism*. Berkeley: University of California Press, 1978.

Klein, Peter D. *Certainty: A Refutation of Skepticism*. Minneapolis: University of Minnesota Press, 1981.

Slote, Michael A. *Reason and Skepticism*. London: George Allen & Unwin, 1970.

Stroud, Barry. *The Significance of Philosophical Skepticism*. Oxford: Oxford University Press, 1984.

Unger, Peter. *Ignorance: A Case for Skepticism*. Oxford: Clarendon, 1975.

CHAPTER 5: THE STRUCTURE OF JUSTIFICATION

Audi, Robert. *Epistemology: A Contemporary Introduction to the Theory of Knowledge*. London: Routledge, 1998.

Baergen, Ralph. *Contemporary Epistemology*. Forth Worth, Tex.: Harcourt Brace, 1995.

BonJour, Laurence. *The Structure of Empirical Knowledge*. Cambridge, Mass.: Harvard University Press, 1985.

Chisholm, Roderick M. *The Theory of Knowledge*. 3d ed. Englewood Cliffs, N.J.: Prentice Hall, 1989.

Dancy, Jonathan. *An Introduction to Contemporary Epistemology*. Oxford: Blackwell, 1985.

CHAPTER 6: THEORIES OF TRUTH AND POSTMODERNISM

Cahoone, Lawrence, ed. *From Modernism to Postmodernism: An Anthology*. Oxford, Blackwell, 1996.

Eagleton, Terry. *The Illusions of Postmodernism*. Oxford: Blackwell, 1996.

Groothuis, Douglas. *Truth Decay*. Downers Grove, Ill.: InterVarsity Press, 2000.

Harris, James. *Against Relativism*. Chicago: Open Court, 1992.

Harré, Rom, and Michael Krausz. *Varieties of Relativism*. Cambridge, Mass.: Blackwell, 1996.

Kirkham, Richard L. *Theories of Truth*. Cambridge, Mass.: MIT Press, 1997.

Nagel, Thomas. *The Last Word*. New York: Oxford, 1997.

Natoli, Joseph. *A Primer to Postmodernism*. Oxford: Blackwell, 1997.

Norris, Christopher. *The Truth About Postmodernism*. Oxford: Blackwell, 1993.

Willard, Dallas. "How Concepts Relate the Mind to Its Objects: The 'God's Eye View' Vindicated?" *Philosophia Christi*, 2d ser., vol. 1, no. 2 (1999): 5-20.

CHAPTER 7: RELIGIOUS EPISTEMOLOGY

Alston, William P. *Perceiving God*. Ithaca, N.Y.: Cornell University Press, 1991.

Evans, C. Stephen, and Merold Westphal, eds. *Christian Perspectives on Religious Knowledge*. Grand Rapids, Mich.: Eerdmans, 1993.

Geivett, R. Douglas, and Brendan Sweetman, eds. *Contemporary Perspectives on Religious Epistemology*. Oxford: Oxford University Press, 1992.

Hasker, William. "The Foundations of Theism: Scoring the Quinn-Plantinga Debate." *Faith and Philosophy* 15 (1998): 52-67.

Howard-Snyder, Daniel, and Paul Moser, eds. *Divine Hiddenness: New Essays*. New York: Cambridge University Press, 2001.

Jordan, Jeff, ed. *Gambling on God*. Lanham, Md.: Rowman & Littlefield, 1994.

Kvanvig, Jonathan L., ed. *Warrant in Contemporary Epistemology*. Lanham, Md.: Rowman & Littlefield, 1996.

Plantinga, Alvin. "The Foundations of Theism: A Reply." *Faith and Philosophy* 3 (1986): 298-313.

——. "Is Belief in God Properly Basic?" *Noûs* (1981): 41-51.

——. *Warrant: The Current Debate*. Oxford: Oxford University Press, 1993.

——. *Warrant and Proper Function*. Oxford: Oxford University Press, 1993.

——. *Warranted Christian Belief*. Oxford: Oxford University Press, 2000.

Plantinga, Alvin, and Nicholas Wolterstorff. *Faith and Rationality*. Notre Dame, Ind.: University of Notre Dame Press, 1983.

Pojman, Louis, ed. *Philosophy of Religion*. Part 7. 3d ed. Belmont, Cal.: Wadsworth, 1998.

Quinn, Philip L. "The Foundations of Theism Again: A Rejoinder to Plantinga." In *Rational Faith*, pp. 14-47. Edited by Linda Zagzebski. Notre Dame, Ind.: University of Notre Dame Press, 1993.

Swinburne, Richard. *Faith and Reason*. Oxford: Clarendon, 1981.

CHAPTER 8: WHAT IS METAPHYSICS?

Chisholm, Roderick M. *On Metaphysics.* Minneapolis: University of Minnesota Press, 1989.

Grossmann, Reinhardt. *The Existence of the World.* London: Routledge, 1992.

Kripke, Saul A. *Naming and Necessity.* Cambridge, Mass.: Harvard University Press, 1972.

Loux, Michael. *Metaphysics.* London: Routledge, 1998.

Plantinga, Alvin. *The Nature of Necessity.* Oxford: Clarendon, 1974.

van Inwagen, Peter. *Metaphysics.* Boulder, Colo.: Westview, 1993.

van Inwagen, Peter, and Dean W. Zimmerman, eds. *Metaphysics: The Big Questions.* Oxford: Blackwell, 1998.

CHAPTER 9: GENERAL ONTOLOGY: EXISTENCE, IDENTITY AND REDUCTIONISM

Brody, Baruch A. *Identity and Essence.* Princeton, N.J.: Princeton University Press, 1980.

Butchvarov, Panayot. *Being Qua Being.* Bloomington, Ind.: Indiana University Press, 1979.

Charles, David, and Kathleen Lennon, eds. *Reduction, Explanation and Realism.* Oxford: Clarendon, 1992.

Chisholm, Roderick M. *A Realistic Theory of Categories.* Cambridge: Cambridge University Press, 1996.

Craig, William Lane, and J. P. Moreland, eds. *Naturalism: A Critical Analysis.* London: Routledge, 2000.

Grossmann, Reinhardt. *The Categorial Structure of the World.* Bloomington, Ind.: Indiana University Press, 1983.

Lowe, E. J. *The Possibility of Metaphysics.* Oxford: Clarendon, 1998.

Morris, Thomas V. *Understanding Identity Statements.* Great Britain: Aberdeen University Press, 1984.

Suárez, Francis. *On the Various Kinds of Distinctions.* Milwaukee, Wis.: Marquette University Press, 1947.

CHAPTER 10: GENERAL ONTOLOGY: TWO CATEGORIES— PROPERTY AND SUBSTANCE

Armstrong, D. M. *Nominalism and Realism.* Vol. 1 of *Universals and Scientific Realism.* Cambridge: Cambridge University Press, 1978.

———. *A Theory of Universals.* Vol. 2 of *Universals and Scientific Realism.* Cambridge: Cambridge University Press, 1978.

Campbell, Keith. *Abstract Particulars.* Oxford: Blackwell, 1990.

Connell, Richard. *Substance and Modern Science.* Notre Dame, Ind.: University of Notre Dame Press, 1988.

Gilson, Etienne. *From Aristotle to Darwin and Back Again.* Notre Dame, Ind.: University of Notre Dame Press, 1984.

Hoffman, Joshua, and Gary S. Rosenkrantz. *Substance: Its Existence and Nature.* London: Routledge, 1997.

Loux, Michael. *Substance and Attribute.* Dordrecht: D. Reidel, 1978.

Moreland, J. P. *Universals.* Montreal: McGill-Queen's University Press, 2001.

Rea, Michael, ed. *Material Constitution: A Reader.* Lanham, Md.: Rowman & Littlefield, 1997.

Wiggins, David. *Sameness and Substance Renewed.* New York: Cambridge University Press, 2001.

CHAPTERS 11 AND 12: THE MIND-BODY PROBLEM

Brown, Warren S., Nancey Murphy and H. Newton Malony. *Whatever Happened to the Soul?* Minneapolis: Fortress, 1998.

Churchland, Paul. *Matter and Consciousness.* Cambridge, Mass.: MIT Press, 1984.

Cooper, John W. *Body, Soul and Life Everlasting.* Rev. ed. Grand Rapids, Mich.: Eerdmans, 2000.

Corcoran, Kevin, ed. *Soul, Body and Survival.* Ithaca, N.Y.: Cornell University Press, 2001.

Foster, John. *The Immaterial Self.* London: Routledge, 1991.

Hasker, William. *The Emergent Self.* Ithaca, N.Y.: Cornell University Press, 1999.

Kim, Jaegwon. *Philosophy of Mind.* Boulder, Colo.: Westview, 1996.

———. *Mind in a Physical World.* Cambridge, Mass.: MIT Press, 1998.

Moreland, J. P., and Scott Rae. *Body and Soul: Human Nature and the Crisis in Ethics.* Downers Grove, Ill.: InterVarsity Press, 2000.

Moser, Paul K., and J. D. Trout. *Contemporary Materialism: A Reader.* London: Routledge, 1995.

Searle, John. *The Rediscovery of the Mind.* Cambridge, Mass.: MIT Press, 1992.

Smythies, John R., and John Beloff, eds. *The Case for Dualism.* Charlottesville: University Press of Virginia, 1989.

Swinburne, Richard. *The Evolution of the Soul.* Rev. ed. Oxford: Clarendon, 1997.

Taliaferro, Charles. *Consciousness and the Mind of God.* Cambridge: Cambridge University Press, 1994.

CHAPTER 13: FREE WILL AND DETERMINISM

Bishop, John. *Natural Agency.* Cambridge: Cambridge University Press, 1989.

Double, Richard. *The Non-Reality of Free Will.* New York: Oxford University Press, 1991.

Fischer, John Martin. *The Metaphysics of Free Will.* Oxford: Blackwell, 1994.

Kane, Robert. *The Significance of Free Will.* New York: Oxford University Press, 1996.

O'Connor, Timothy. *Persons and Causes.* New York: Oxford University Press, 2000.

O'Connor, Timothy, ed. *Agents, Causes and Events.* New York: Oxford University Press, 1995.

Rowe, William L. *Thomas Reid on Freedom and Morality.* Ithaca, N.Y.: Cornell University Press, 1991.

CHAPTER 14: PERSONAL IDENTITY AND LIFE AFTER DEATH

Davis, Steven T., ed. *Death and Afterlife.* New York: St. Martin's Press, 1989.

Hick, John H. *Death and Eternal Life.* San Francisco: Harper & Row, 1976.

Madell, Geoffrey. *The Identity of the Self.* Edinburgh: University of Edinburgh Press, 1981.

———. *Mind and Materialism.* Edinburgh: University of Edinburgh Press, 1988.

Nagel, Thomas. *The View from Nowhere.* New York: Oxford University Press, 1986.

Olson, Eric T. *The Human Animal.* New York: Oxford University Press, 1997.

Parfit, Derek. *Reasons and Persons.* Oxford: Oxford University Press, 1984.

Shoemaker, Sydney, and Richard Swinburne. *Personal Identity.* Oxford: Blackwell, 1984.

CHAPTER 15: SCIENTIFIC METHODOLOGY

Harré, Rom. *The Philosophies of Science: An Introductory Survey.* Oxford: Oxford University Press, 1972.

Kourany, Janet A., ed. *Scientific Knowledge: Basic Issues in the Philosophy of Science.* Belmont, Calif.: Wadsworth, 1987.

Montgomery, John Warwick. "The Theologian's Craft." In *Suicide of Christian Theology,* pp. 267-313. Minneapolis: Bethany, 1970.

Moreland, J. P. *Christianity and the Nature of Science.* Grand Rapids, Mich.: Baker, 1989.

Pearcey, Nancy, and Charles Thaxton. *The Soul of Science.* Wheaton, Ill.: Crossway, 1994.

Ratzsch, Del. *Science and Its Limits: The Natural Sciences in Christian Perspective.* Downers Grove, Ill.: InterVarsity Press, 2000.

CHAPTER 16: THE REALISM-ANTIREALISM DEBATE

French, Peter A., Theodore E. Uehling Jr. and Howard K. Wettstein, eds. *Realism and Antirealism.* Minneapolis: University of Minnesota Press, 1988.

Kuhn, Thomas. *The Structure of Scientific Revolutions.* 2d. ed., enlarged. Chicago: University of Chicago Press, 1970.

Lakatos, Imre, and Alan Musgrave, eds. *Criticism and the Growth of Knowledge.* Cambridge: Cambridge University Press, 1970.

Laudan, Larry. *Progress and Its Problems: Towards a Theory of Scientific Growth.* Berkeley: University of California Press, 1977.

————. *Science and Values: An Essay on the Aims of Science and Their Role in Scientific Debate.* Berkeley: University of California Press, 1984.

Leplin, Jarrett, ed. *Scientific Realism.* Berkeley: University of California Press, 1984.

Newton-Smith, W. H. *The Rationality of Science.* Boston: Routledge & Kegan Paul, 1981.

van Fraassen, Bas C. *The Scientific Image.* Oxford: Oxford University Press, 1980.

CHAPTER 17: PHILOSOPHY AND THE INTEGRATION OF SCIENCE AND THEOLOGY

Barbour, Ian. *Religion in an Age of Science.* San Francisco: Harper & Row, 1990.

Bube, Richard. *Putting It All Together.* Lanham, Md.: University Press of America, 1995.

Dembski, William A. *Intelligent Design.* Downers Grove, Ill.: InterVarsity Press, 1999.

Denton, Michael. *Evolution: A Theory in Crisis.* London: Burnett Books, 1985.

Ferngren, Gary B., ed. *The History of Science and Religion in the Western Tradition.* New York: Garland, 2000.

Johnson, Phillip. *Darwin on Trial.* Dowers Grove, Ill.: InterVarsity Press, 1991.

Moreland, J. P., ed. *The Creation Hypothesis.* Downers Grove, Ill: InterVarsity Press, 1993.

Morris, Henry. *Scientific Creationism.* El Cajon, Calif.: Master Books, 1985.

Peacocke, Arthur. *Theology for a Scientific Age.* Minneapolis: Fortress, 1993.

Ratzsch, Del. *The Battle of Beginnings.* Downers Grove, Ill.: InterVarsity Press, 1996.

————. *Nature, Design and Science.* Albany, N.Y.: State University of New York Press, 2001.

Ross, Hugh. *The Fingerprint of God.* 2d. ed. Orange, Calif.: Promise Publishing Co., 1991.

————. *Creation and Time.* Colorado Springs, Colo.: NavPress, 1994.

Thaxton, Charles, and Walter Bradley. *The Mystery of Life's Origin.* New York: Philosophical Library, 1984.

Van Till, Howard J., et al. *Portraits of Creation.* Grand Rapids, Mich.: Eerdmans, 1990.

Van Till, Howard J., Davis A. Young and Clarence Menninga. *Science Held Hostage.* Downers Grove, Ill.: InterVarsity Press, 1988.

Wells, Jonathan. *Icons of Evolution.* Washington, D.C.: Regnery, 2000.

CHAPTER 18: PHILOSOPHY OF TIME AND SPACE

Broad, C. D. *An Examination of McTaggart's Philosophy.* 2 vols. Cambridge: Cambridge University Press, 1938; New York: Octagon Books, 1976.

Craig, William Lane. *The Tensed Theory of Time: A Critical Examination.* Synthese Library 293. Dordrecht: Kluwer Academic, 2000.

———. *The Tenseless Theory of Time: A Critical Examination.* Synthese Library 294. Dordrecht: Kluwer Academic, 2000.

Einstein, Albert. *Relativity: The Special and General Theories.* London: Methuen, 1954.

Gale, Richard. *The Language of Time.* International Library of Philosophy and Scientific Method. London: Routledge & Kegan Paul, 1968.

Holton, Gerald. *Thematic Origins of Scientific Thought: Kepler to Einstein.* Cambridge, Mass.: Harvard University Press, 1973.

McTaggart, J. M. E. *The Nature of Existence.* 2 vols. Edited by C. D. Broad. 1927. Cambridge: Cambridge University Press, 1968.

Mellor, D. H. *Real Time.* Cambridge: Cambridge University Press, 1981.

Miller, Arthur I. *Albert Einstein's Special Theory of Relativity.* Reading, Mass.: Addison-Wesley, 1981.

Oaklander, L. Nathan, and Quentin Smith, eds. *The New Theory of Time.* Part 1. New Haven, Conn.: Yale University Press, 1994.

Prokhovnik, Simon J. *Light in Einstein's Universe.* Dordrecht: D. Reidel, 1985.

Schlesinger, George. *Aspects of Time.* Indianapolis: Hackett, 1980.

Smith, Quentin. *Language and Time.* New York: Oxford University Press, 1993.

Whitrow, G. J. *The Natural Philosophy of Time.* 2d ed. Oxford: Oxford University Press, 1980 (esp. chap. 4).

CHAPTERS 19-22: ISSUES IN ETHICS

Beauchamp, Tom L. *Philosophical Ethics.* 2d. ed. New York: McGraw-Hill, 1991.

Beckwith, Francis J. *Politically Correct Death.* Grand Rapids, Mich.: Baker, 1992.

———. *Do the Right Thing.* Boston: Jones & Bartlett, 1996.

Finnis, John. *Natural Law and Natural Rights.* Oxford: Clarendon, 1980.

Geisler, Norman L. *Christian Ethics: Options and Issues.* Grand Rapids, Mich.: Baker, 1989.

Hauerwas, Stanley. *Suffering Presence.* Notre Dame, Ind.: University of Notre Dame Press, 1986.

Johnson, Alan J. "Is There Biblical Warrant for Natural-Law Theories?" *Journal of the Evangelical Theological Society* 25 (June 1982): 185-99.

Kilner, John F., Nigel M. de S. Cameron and David Schiedermayer, eds. *Bioethics and the Future of Medicine: A Christian Appraisal.* Grand Rapids, Mich.: Eerdmans, 1995.

Montgomery, John Warwick. *Human Rights and Human Dignity.* Grand Rapids, Mich.: Zondervan, 1986.

Moreland, J. P., and Norman L. Geisler. *The Life and Death Debate.* Westport, Conn.: Praeger, 1990.

Pellegrino, Edmund D., and David C. Thomasma. *For the Patient's Good.* New York: Oxford University Press, 1988.

————. *A Philosophical Basis of Medical Practice.* New York: Oxford University Press, 1981.

Pojman, Louis P. *Ethics: Discovering Right and Wrong.* Belmont, Calif.: Wadsworth, 1995.

Rae, Scott. *Moral Choices: An Introduction to Ethics.* 2d ed. Grand Rapids, Mich.: Zondervan, 2000.

Rae, Scott, and Paul Cox. *Bioethics: A Christian Approach in a Pluralistic Age.* Grand Rapids, Mich.: Eerdmans, 1999.

Rae, Scott, and Kenman Wong. *Beyond Integrity: A Judeo-Christian Approach to Business Ethics.* Grand Rapids, Mich.: Zondervan, 1996.

CHAPTERS 23 AND 24: THE EXISTENCE OF GOD

Barrow, John D., and Frank J. Tipler. *The Anthropic Cosmological Principle.* Oxford: Clarendon, 1986.

Beck, W. David. "The Cosmological Argument: A Current Bibliographical Appraisal." *Philosophia Christi* 2 (2000): 283-304.

Burrill, Donald R. *The Cosmological Arguments.* Garden City, N.Y.: Doubleday, 1967.

Collins, Robin. "A Scientific Argument for the Existence of God: The Fine-Tuning Design Argument." In *Reason for the Hope Within,* pp. 47-75. Edited by Michael J. Murray. Grand Rapids, Mich.: Eerdmans, 1999.

————. *The Well-Tempered Universe: God, Fine-Tuning and the Laws of Nature.* 2 vols. (forthcoming).

Craig, William Lane. *The Cosmological Argument from Plato to Leibniz.* Reprint, Eugene, Ore: Wipf & Stock, 2001.

————. *The Kalam Cosmological Argument.* 1979. Reprint, Eugene, Ore.: Wipf & Stock, 2000.

————. "Naturalism and Cosmology." In *Naturalism: A Critical Analysis,* pp. 215-52. Edited by William L. Craig and J. P. Moreland. London: Routledge, 2000.

Craig, William Lane, and Quentin Smith. *Theism, Atheism and Big Bang Cosmology.* Oxford: Clarendon, 1993.

Davis, Stephen T. *God, Reason and Theistic Proofs.* Grand Rapids, Mich.: Eerdmans, 1997.

Dembski, William A. *The Design Inference: Eliminating Chance Through Small Probabilities.* Cambridge: Cambridge University Press, 1998.

Denton, Michael. *Evolution: A Theory in Crisis.* Bethesda, Md.: Adler & Adler, 1986.

————. *Nature's Destiny: How the Laws of Biology Reveal Purpose in the Universe.* New York: Free Press, 1998.

Gale, Richard M. *On the Existence and Nature of God.* New York: Cambridge University Press, 1991.

Ganssle, Gregory E. "Necessary Moral Truths and the Need for Explanation." *Philosophia Christi* 2 (2000): 105-12.

Hackett, Stuart C. *The Resurrection of Theism.* 2d ed. Grand Rapids, Mich.: Baker, 1982.

Hume, David. *Dialogues Concerning Natural Religion.* Edited with an introduction by Norman Kemp Smith. New York: Bobbs-Merrill, 1947.

Harrison, Jonathan. *God, Freedom and Immortality.* Avebury Series in Philosophy. Burlington, Vt.: Ashgate, 1999.

Hick, John. *Arguments for the Existence of God.* London: Macmillan, 1971.

Hick, John H., and Arthur C. McGill. *The Many-Faced Argument.* New York: Macmillan, 1967.

Leslie, John, ed. *Modern Cosmology and Philosophy.* 2d ed. Amherst, N.Y.: Prometheus, 1998.

————. *Universes*. London: Routledge, 1989.

Mackie, John L. *The Miracle of Theism*. Oxford: Clarendon, 1982.

Martin, Michael. *Atheism: A Philosophical Justification*. Philadelphia: Temple University Press, 1990.

Oppy, Graham. *Ontological Arguments and Belief in God*. Cambridge: Cambridge University Press, 1995.

Plantinga, Alvin. *The Nature of Necessity*. Oxford: Clarendon, 1974.

Plantinga, Alvin, ed. *The Ontological Argument*. Garden City, N.Y.: Doubleday, 1965.

Ratzsch, Del. *Nature, Design and Science*. Albany: State University of New York, 2001.

Rowe, William L. "Circular Explanations, Cosmological Arguments and Sufficient Reasons." *Midwest Studies in Philosophy* 21 (1997): 188-99.

Sorley, William R. *Moral Values and the Idea of God*. New York: Macmillan, 1930.

Swinburne, Richard. *The Existence of God*. Rev. ed. Oxford: Clarendon, 1991.

Taylor, A. E. *The Faith of a Moralist*. London: Macmillan, 1930.

Vallicella, William. "On an Insufficient Argument Against Sufficient Reason." *Ratio* 10 (1997): 76-81.

CHAPTERS 25 AND 26: THE COHERENCE OF THEISM

Adams, Robert. "Divine Necessity." *Journal of Philosophy* 80 (1983): 741-52.

————. *Finite and Infinite Goods*. Oxford: Oxford University Press, 2000.

————. "Has It Been Proved That All Real Existence Is Contingent?" *American Philosophical Quarterly* 8 (1971): 284-91.

Blount, Douglas Keith. "An Essay on Divine Presence." Ph.D. diss., University of Notre Dame, 1997.

Craig, William Lane. *Divine Foreknowledge and Human Freedom: The Coherence of Theism I: Omniscience*. Brill's Studies in Intellectual History 19. Leiden: E. J. Brill, 1990.

————. *God, Time and Eternity: The Coherence of Theism II: Eternity*. Dordrecht: Kluwer Academic, 2001.

Creel, Richard. *Divine Impassibility*. Cambridge: Cambridge University Press, 1986.

Davis, Richard Brian. *The Metaphysics of Theism and Modality*. American University Studies 189. New York: Peter Lang, 2001.

Fisher, John Martin, ed. *God, Foreknowledge and Freedom*. Stanford Series in Philosophy. Stanford, Calif.: Stanford University Press, 1989.

Flint, Thomas P., and Alfred J. Freddoso. "Maximal Power." In *The Existence and Nature of God*, pp. 81-113. Edited by Alfred J. Freddoso. Notre Dame, Ind.: University of Notre Dame Press, 1983.

Ganssle, Gregory E., and David M. Woodruff, eds. *God and Time*. New York: Oxford University Press, 2001.

Hasker, William. *The Emergent Self*. Ithaca, N.Y.: Cornell University Press, 1999.

Hasker, William, David Basinger and Eef Dekker, eds. *Middle Knowledge: Theory and Applications*. Contributions to Philosophical Theology 4. Frankfurt am Main, Germany: Peter Lang, 2000.

Helm, Paul, ed. *Divine Commands and Morality*. Oxford: Oxford University Press, 1981.

Hughes, Christopher. *On a Complex Theory of a Simple God: An Investigation in Aquinas' Philosophical Theology*. Cornell Studies in Philosophy of Religion. Ithaca, N.Y.: Cornell University Press, 1989.

Idziak, Janine M., ed. *Divine Command Morality: Historical and Contemporary Readings*. Lewiston, N.Y.: Edwin Mellen, 1980.

Kenny, Anthony. *The God of the Philosophers*. Oxford: Clarendon, 1979.

Kvanvig, Jonathan L. *The Possibility of an All-Knowing God.* New York: St. Martin's Press, 1986.

Leftow, Brian. "God and Abstract Entities." *Faith and Philosophy* 7 (1990): 193-217.

———. *Time and Eternity.* Cornell Studies in the Philosophy of Religion. Ithaca, N.Y.: Cornell, University Press, 1991.

Mann, William E. "Necessity." In *A Companion to Philosophy of Religion.* Edited by Philip L. Quinn and Charles Taliaferro. Oxford: Blackwell, 1997.

Molina, Luis de. *On Divine Foreknowledge: Part IV of the "Concordia."* Translated with an introduction and notes by Alfred J. Freddoso. Ithaca, N.Y.: Cornell University Press, 1988.

Morris, Thomas V., and Christopher Menzel. "Absolute Creation." In *Anselmian Explorations,* pp. 161-78. Notre Dame, Ind.: University of Notre Dame Press, 1987.

Nielsen, Kai. *Ethics Without God.* London: Pemberton, 1973.

Padgett, Alan G. *God, Eternity and the Nature of Time.* New York: St. Martin's Press, 1992.

Plantinga, Alvin. *Does God Have a Nature?* Milwaukee, Wis.: Marquette University Press, 1980.

———. "How to Be an Anti-Realist." *Proceedings of the American Philosophical Association* 56 (1982): 47-70.

———. *The Nature of Necessity.* Clarendon Library of Logic and Philosophy. Oxford: Clarendon, 1974.

Prior, A. N. "The Formalities of Omniscience." In *Papers on Time and Tense,* pp. 26-44. Oxford: Clarendon, 1968.

Quinn, Philip L. *Divine Commands and Moral Requirements.* Oxford: Clarendon, 1978.

Taliaferro, Charles. *Consciousness and the Mind of God.* Cambridge: Cambridge University Press, 1994.

Wierenga, Edward. *The Nature of God.* Cornell Studies in the Philosophy of Religion. New York: Cornell University Press, 1989.

Wolterstorff, Nicholas. "Divine Simplicity." In *Philosophy of Religion,* pp. 531-52. Edited by James E. Tomberlin. Philosophical Perspectives 5. Altascadero, Calif.: Ridgeview, 1991.

Yates, John C. *The Timelessness of God.* Lanham, Md.: University Press of America, 1990.

CHAPTER 27: THE PROBLEM OF EVIL

Adams, Marilyn McCord. *Horrendous Evils and the Goodness of God.* Ithaca, N.Y.: Cornell University Press, 1999.

Bergman, Michael. "Might-Counterfactuals, Transworld Untrustworthiness and Plantinga's Free Will Defense." *Faith and Philosophy* 16 (1999): 336-51.

Draper, Paul. "Pain and Pleasure: An Evidential Problem for Theists." *Noûs* 23 (1979): 331-50.

Harrison, Jonathan. *God, Freedom, and Immortality.* Avebury Series in Philosophy. Burlington, Vt.: Ashgate, 1999.

Hick, John. *Evil and the God of Love.* New York: Harper & Row, 1977.

Howard-Snyder, Daniel, ed. *The Evidential Argument from Evil.* Bloomington, Ind.: Indiana University Press, 1996.

Martin, Michael. *Atheism.* Philadelphia: Temple University Press, 1990.

Plantinga, Alvin. *God, Freedom and Evil.* New York: Harper & Row, 1974.

———. *The Nature of Necessity.* Clarendon Library of Logic and Philosophy. Oxford: Clarendon, 1974.

Rowe, William. "The Problem of Evil and Some Varieties of Atheism." *American Philosophical Quarterly* 16 (1979): 335-41.

Swinburne, Richard. *The Existence of God.* Oxford: Clarendon, 1978.

van Inwagen, Peter. *God, Knowledge and Mystery.* Ithaca, N.Y.: Cornell University Press, 1995.

CHAPTER 28: CREATION, PROVIDENCE AND MIRACLE

Bilinskyji, Stephen S. "God, Nature and the Concept of Miracle." Ph.D. diss., University of Notre Dame, 1982.

Craig, William Lane. "Creation and Conservation Once More." *Religious Studies* 34 (1998): 177-88.

Craig, William Lane, and Quentin Smith. *Theism, Atheism and Big Bang Cosmology.* Oxford: Clarendon, 1993.

Earman, John. *Hume's Abject Failure.* Oxford: Oxford University Press, 2000.

Flew, Antony. "Miracles." In *Encyclopedia of Philosophy.* Edited by Paul Edwards. New York: Macmillan, 1967.

Flint, Thomas. *Divine Providence.* Cornell Studies in the Philosophy of Religion. Ithaca, N.Y.: Cornell University Press, 1998.

Freddoso, Alfred J. "The Necessity of Nature." *Midwest Studies in Philosophy* 11 (1986): 215-42.

Geivett, R. Douglas, and Gary R. Habermas. *In Defense of Miracles.* Downers Grove, Ill.: InterVarsity Press, 1997.

Hebblethwaite, Brian, and Edward Henderson, eds. *Divine Action.* Edinburgh: T & T Clark, 1990.

Helm, Paul. *The Providence of God.* Downer's Grove, Ill.: InterVarsity Press, 1994.

Hume, David. "Of Miracles." In *Enquiries Concerning Human Understanding and Concerning the Principles of Morals,* sect. 10, pp. 109-31. Edited by L. A. Selby-Bigge. 3d ed. edited by P. H. Nidditch. Oxford: Clarendon, 1975.

Molina, Luis de. *On Divine Foreknowledge: Part IV of the "Concordia."* Translated with an introduction and notes by Alfred J. Freddoso. Ithaca, N.Y.: Cornell University Press, 1988.

Morris, Thomas V., ed. *Divine and Human Action.* Ithaca, N.Y.: Cornell University Press, 1988. See especially articles by Quinn, Kvanvig and McCann, Flint, and Freddoso.

Quinn, Philip L. "Creation, Conservation and the Big Bang." In *Philosophical Problems of the Internal and External Worlds,* pp. 589-612. Edited by John Earman et al. Pittsburgh, Penn.: University of Pittsburgh Press, 1993.

Sorabji, Richard. *Time, Creation and the Continuum.* Ithaca, N.Y.: Cornell University Press, 1983.

Suárez, Francisco. *On Creation, Conservation and Concurrence: Metaphysical Disputations 20, 21 and 22.* Translated with notes and an introduction by Alfred J. Freddoso. South Bend, Ind.: St. Augustine's Press, 2002.

Swinburne, Richard. *The Concept of Miracle.* New York: Macmillan, 1970.

Swinburne, Richard, ed. *Miracles.* Philosophical Topics. New York: Macmillan, 1989.

Thomas Aquinas. *Summa contra gentiles.* 4 vols. Vol. 2, *Creation.* Translated with an introduction and notes by James F. Anderson; Vol. 3.1-2, *Providence.* Translated with an introduction and notes by Vernon J. Bourke. Notre Dame, Ind.: University of Notre Dame Press, 1975.

Tomberlin, James E., ed. *Philosophical Perspectives.* Vol. 5, *Philosophy of Religion.* Atascadero, Calif.: Ridgeview, 1991. See especially articles by Flint, Kvanvig and McCann, and Freddoso.

Zabell, S. L. "The Probabilistic Analysis of Testimony." *Journal of Statistical Planning and Inference* 20 (1988): 327-57.

CHAPTER 29: CHRISTIAN DOCTRINES (I): THE TRINITY

Bracken, Joseph A. *What Are They Saying About the Trinity?* New York: Paulist, 1979.

Davis, Stephen T., Daniel Kendall and Gerald O'Collins, eds. *The Trinity.* Oxford: Oxford University Press, 1999.

Feenstra, Ronald J., and Cornelius Plantinga Jr., eds. *Trinity, Incarnation and Atonement.* Library of Religious Philosophy 1. Notre Dame, Ind.: University of Notre Dame Press, 1989.

Hughes, Christopher. *On a Complex Theory of a Simple God.* Cornell Studies in the Philosophy of Religion. Ithaca, N.Y.: Cornell University Press, 1989.

Lampe, G. W. H. "Christian Theology in the Patristic Period." In *A History of Christian Doctrine,* pp. 23-180. Edited by Hubert Cunliffe-Jones. Philadelphia: Fortress, 1980.

Rusch, William G., ed. *The Trinitarian Controversy.* Sources of Early Christian Thought. Philadelphia: Fortress, 1980.

Pelikan, Jaroslav. *The Christian Tradition: A History of the Development of Doctrine.* Vol. 1, *The Emergence of the Catholic Tradition (100-600).* Chicago: University of Chicago Press, 1971.

Prestige, G. L. *God in Patristic Thought.* London: SPCK, 1952.

Senor, Thomas. "The Incarnation and the Trinity." In *Reason for the Hope Within.* Edited by Michael J. Murray. Grand Rapids, Mich.: Eerdmans, 1999.

Swinburne, Richard. *The Christian God.* Oxford: Clarendon, 1994.

van Inwagen, Peter. "And Yet They Are Not Three Gods But One God." In *Philosophy and the Christian Faith,* pp. 241-78. Edited by Thomas V. Morris. University of Notre Dame Studies in the Philosophy of Religion 5. Notre Dame, Ind.: University of Notre Dame Press, 1988.

CHAPTER 30: CHRISTIAN DOCTRINES (II): THE INCARNATION

Baillie, D. M. *God Was in Christ.* New York: Charles Scribner's Sons, 1948.

Bayne, Tim. "The Inclusion Model of the Incarnation: Problems and Prospects." *Religious Studies* 37 (2001): 125-41.

Bruce, A. B. *The Humiliation of Christ.* New York: George H. Doran Company, n.d.

Feenstra, Ronald J., and Cornelius Plantinga Jr., eds. *Trinity, Incarnation and Atonement.* Library of Religious Philosophy 1. Notre Dame, Ind.: University of Notre Dame Press, 1989.

Freddoso, Alfred J. "Human Nature, Potency and the Incarnation." *Faith and Philosophy* 3 (1986): 27-53.

Grillmeier, Aloys. *Christ in Christian Tradition.* Vol. 1, *From the Apostolic Age to Chalcedon (451).* 2d rev. ed. Translated by John Bowden. Atlanta: John Knox Press, 1975.

Harris, Murray J. *Jesus As God.* Grand Rapids, Mich.: Baker, 1992.

Morris, Thomas V. *The Logic of God Incarnate.* Ithaca, N.Y.: Cornell University Press, 1986.

Relton, H. Maurice. *A Study in Christology.* London: Macmillan, 1929.

Sanday, William. *Christologies Ancient and Modern.* Oxford: Clarendon, 1910.

Swinburne, Richard. *The Christian God.* Oxford: Clarendon, 1994.

van Inwagen, Peter. "Not by Confusion of Substance, but by Unity of Person." In *God, Knowledge and Mystery,* pp. 260-79. Ithaca, N.Y.: Cornell University Press, 1995.

Witherington, Ben, III. *The Christology of Jesus.* Minneapolis: Fortress, 1990.

Zamoyta, Vincent, ed. *A Theology of Christ: Sources.* Milwaukee: Bruce Publishing Co., 1967.

CHAPTER 31: CHRISTIAN DOCTRINES (III): CHRISTIAN PARTICULARISM

Craig, William Lane. "Talbott's Universalism." *Religious Studies* 27 (1991): 297-308.

———. "Should Peter Go to the Mission Field?" *Faith and Philosophy* 10 (1993): 261-65.

Faith and Philosophy 14 (1997): 277-320. See articles by Hick, Alston, Mavrodes, Plantinga, van Inwagen and Clark.

Geivett, Douglas. "Some Misgivings About Evangelical Inclusivism." In *Who Will Be Saved?* Edited by Paul R. House and Gregory A. Thornbury. Wheaton, Ill.: Crossway, 2000.

Griffiths, Paul J. *Problems of Religious Diversity.* Oxford: Blackwell, 2001.

Hasker, William. "Middle Knowledge and the Damnation of the Heathen: A Response to William Craig." *Faith and Philosophy* 8 (1991): 380-89.

Hick, John H. *An Interpretation of Religion.* New Haven, Conn.: Yale University Press, 1989.

Kvanvig, Jonathan L. *The Problem of Hell.* Oxford: Oxford University Press, 1993.

Murray, Michael J. "Heaven and Hell." In *A Reason for the Hope Within*, pp. 287-317. Edited by Michael J. Murray. Grand Rapids, Mich.: Eerdmans, 1999.

Okholm, Dennis L., and Timothy R. Phillips, eds. *Four Views on Salvation in a Pluralistic World.* Grand Rapids, Mich.: Zondervan, 1996.

Quinn, Philip L., and Kevin Meeker, eds. *The Philosophical Challenge of Religious Diversity.* Oxford: Oxford University Press, 2000.

Talbott, Thomas. "Providence, Freedom and Human Destiny." *Religious Studies* 26 (1990): 227-45.

van Inwagen, Peter. "Non Est Hick." In *God, Knowledge and Mystery*, pp. 191-216. Ithaca, N.Y.: Cornell University Press, 1995.

Name Index

al-Farabi, 502
al-Ghazali, 465
Alexander, Peter, 310n
Alston, William, 526
Amico, Robert P., 99n
Anselm, 7, 18, 465, 496, 499, 502, 511, 517
Apollinarius, 598-600, 608-609
Arcesilaus, 92
Aristotle, 2, 11, 71, 85, 113, 130, 134, 173, 176-177, 185, 215, 216, 218, 261, 270, 275, 280, 365, 406, 454, 463, 465, 475, 502, 511, 517-518, 526, 579, 582, 598, 606
Arius, 580-581, 588
Arminius, Jacobus, 281
Armstrong, D. M., 206, 208, 264, 530
Athanasius, 581, 583, 589, 599
Athenagoras, 577-578
Audi, Robert, 112, 121
Augustine, 2, 12, 18, 26, 91, 92-93, 173, 228, 505, 511, 526, 575, 584-585, 593, 615
Ayer, A. J., 292
Babbage, Charles, 570
Bacon, Francis, 310
Baillie, D. M., 605
Baker, Lynne Rudder, 262
Barbour, Ian, 307
Barrow, John, 486, 489, 558
Basil, 155, 264, 582
Behe, Michael, 356
Bentham, Jeremy, 434
Berkeley, George, 24, 145, 190, 360
Bishop, John, 267
Blanshard, Brand, 110, 121
Boethius, Anicius Manlius Severinus, 173, 506, 511
Bohm, David, 469
Boltzmann, Ludwig, 488-489
BonJour, Laurence, 83
Boyd, Richard, 328

Bradley, F. H., 121
Bradley, Walter, 353
Bridgman, P. W., 337
Broad, C. D., 388
Brodie, Benjamin, 336
Bruce, A. B., 604, 610
Bube, Richard, 353
Butler, Joseph, 187, 290, 298, 427
Calvin, John, 18, 162, 168, 281
Campbell, Keith, 205
Cantor, Georg, 471, 473
Carnap, Rudolf, 321
Carneades, 92
Carson, D. A., 561
Chisholm, Roderick, 99, 110, 112-113, 121, 252
Churchland, Paul, 244, 259, 264
Clarke, Samuel, 4, 560
Clifford, W. K., 160, 339
Clinton, William Jefferson, 173
Collins, Robin, 484n
Copernicus, Nicolaus, 315, 365
Corcoran, Kevin, 301
Craig, William Lane, 138n, 513n, 518n, 558n
d'Abro, A., 385-386
Darwin, Charles, 103, 263-264, 354, 361, 482
Davies, Paul, 483, 485
de Vries, Paul, 358
Dembski, William, 356-358, 484
Dennett, Daniel, 263, 270
Derrida, Jacques, 145
Descartes, René, 84, 91, 92-93, 99, 113, 145, 148, 173, 190, 465, 496, 527-528
Dewey, John, 144
Dickerson, Richard, 364
Dostoyevsky, Fyodor, 493, 551
Draper, Paul, 549
Dunn, James D. G., 168n
Duns Scotus, John, 4, 465, 496, 511, 555-556
Ebrard, J. H. August, 604-605
Eddington, A. S., 336, 477
Edwards, Jonathan, 18, 517
Einstein, Albert, 20, 43, 333, 335, 368-369,

372-379, 385, 387, 476
Eusebius of Caesarea, 581
Evans, C. Stephen, 154
Feigl, Herbert, 252
Feinberg, John S., 594n
Findlay, J. M., 378
Fine, Arthur, 387
FitzGerald, George Francis, 372
Flew, Antony, 154-156
Flint, Thomas, 55-56, 138n, 528
Foucault, Michel, 145
Frankfurt, Harry, 273
Freddoso, Alfred J., 521n, 523, 528
Frege, Gottlob, 197-198
Fresnel, Augustin Jean, 334
Freud, Sigmund, 15
Friedman, Alexander, 476-477
Friedman, William, 379
Gager, John G., 16
Galileo Galilei, 323, 358
Ganssle, Gregory, 138n
Geisler, Norman L., 420n
Gess, Wolfgang Friedrich, 604
Gettier, Edmund, 74-76, 78-80, 82-83, 88-89, 96
Gish, Duane, 353
Goldman, Alvin, 80, 81
Gould, Stephen Jay, 361
Gregory of Nazianzus, 582, 608
Gregory of Nyssa, 583-584, 599
Grossman, Reinhardt, 184n, 206, 209
Gruber, Howard, 263
Hare, R. M., 155n
Harré, Rom, 312, 328
Harris, Charles, 611
Hartshorne, Charles, 496, 511
Hegel, Georg Wilhelm Friedrich, 142, 463
Heidegger, Martin, 145
Hempel, Carl, 313, 317, 321
Henry, Carl, 18
Herschel, J. F. W., 310
Hick, John, 616
Hilary, 583, 591
Hilbert, David, 471-473, 481
Hobbes, Thomas, 270

Holton, Gerald, 376
Hospers, John, 425, 426
Howard-Snyder, Daniel, 549
Hubble, Edwin, 476
Hume, David, 11, 24, 107, 145, 211, 269-270, 285, 293, 299, 349, 464, 467-468, 482, 502, 536, 538-539, 569-571, 573
Hummel, Charles, 358
Husserl, Edmund, 139
ibn Sina, 465
Irenaeus, 578
Jackson, Frank, 236-237
Jaki, Stanley, 319
James, William, 144, 160, 169, 265, 495, 610
Johnson, Phillip E., 62, 356
Johnstone, Patrick, 545
Jordan, Jeff, 158-159
Justin Martyr, 18, 577
Kant, Immanuel, 145, 176-177, 185, 190, 242, 446, 449-450, 452-454, 464, 502, 531
Kekes, John, 348
Kekule, F. A., 314
Kepler, Johannes, 323, 376
Kitcher, Philip, 360
Kretzmann, Norman, 512
Kripke, Saul, 253, 422
Kuhn, Thomas, 145, 314, 317, 326, 332, 335, 340-341, 345
Kurtz, Paul, 492
Kvanvig, Jonathan, 513
Laertius, Diogenes, 91
Larmor, Joseph, 372
Laudan, Larry, 338n
Lavoisier, A. L., 199
Leftow, Brian, 512-513, 587-590
Lehrer, Keith, 121
Leibniz, Gottfried Wilhelm, 145, 173, 194-195, 202, 203, 204, 287, 290, 315, 465-469, 480, 482, 496, 560
Lemaître, Georges, 476-477
Leontius of Byzantium, 609
Leslie, John, 483-484, 486
Leucippus, 267